PERSONAL AWARENESS

A PSYCHOLOGY
OF ADJUSTMENT

Second Edition

RICHARD G. WARGA
Bucks County Community College

HOUGHTON MIFFLIN COMPANY
Boston
Dallas   Geneva, Illinois
Hopewell, New Jersey   Palo Alto
London

UNIT–OPENER PHOTO CREDITS

Unit 1 Mike Goldberg/Stock, Boston   *Unit 2* David Seymour/Magnum Photos   *Unit 3* Charles Gatewood   *Unit 4* Mark Chester   *Unit 5* Constantine Manos/Magnum Photos *Unit 6* Donald Wright Patterson/Stock, Boston   *Unit 7* Photo by Charles D. Druss *Unit 8* Eric Hansen   *Unit 9* George W. Gardner   *Unit 10* Ginger Chih from Peter Arnold   *Unit 11* Charles Gatewood/Magnum Photos   *Unit 12* Charles Gatewood /Magnum Photos   *Unit 13* Donald Dietz/Stock, Boston   *Unit 14* Charles Harbutt/Magnum Photos   *Unit 15* George W. Gardner   *Unit 16* Ken Wittenberg   *Unit 17* Read D. Brugger/The Picture Cube   *Unit 18* The National Maritime Museum, London *Unit 19* Jeff Albertson/Stock, Boston

The word list on page 177 is from Richard Kammann, Instructor's Sourcebook for *General Psychology: Modeling Behavior and Experience* by William N. Dember and James J. Jenkins, copyright © 1971 by Prentice-Hall, Inc., Englewood Cliffs, N.J.

Printed in the U.S.A.

Library of Congress Catalog Card Number: 78-69531

ISBN: 0-395-26795-1

There is a limited amount of perseverance and attention to detail in my home. Fortunately, my spouse has the greater proportion of those attributes. If she did not—if they were evenly distributed—it is quite possible that this edition would never have been completed. It is fitting, therefore, that credit should be given where credit is due. Accordingly, this book is dedicated to my spouse, Mary Elizabeth, who kept the project alive.

CONTENTS

PREFACE

As the title suggests, this is a book about personal adjustment. I have written it in order to satisfy criteria that came to mind when I began to think of what my students look for when they enroll in introduction to psychology and personal adjustment courses. Their reactions helped me set certain standards for the text.

I wanted the book to seem personal, to make readers feel that it applies to them. Many students enroll in psychology courses in order to learn more about themselves. When they run into the impersonal and academic treatment of human behavior that so many introductory courses offer, they often feel cheated and become resentful. I believe that instructors "turn off" many persons who would continue studying human behavior if they could find any meaning in their first course or two. The same thing can be said about many personal adjustment courses, in which the words *I* and *me* are rarely heard. For this reason, I have written the text in the colloquial language that typically characterizes personal relationships.

Many educational psychologists insist that students learn best when they are actively involved in the learning process and if what they are studying is meaningful to them. Students using this book have to satisfy instructional goals, which are given in the form of action requirements. At the beginning of Units 1 through 15 the goals are listed. Then after text discussion of each goal, students are asked to try to satisfy the task that the goal sets for them. Writing their answers directly in the book makes them active participants in the learning process.

The book deals with some of the problems students must face in their own lives. The first seven units present general ideas about the fundamental topics of psychology: how people learn, what personality is, what motivates people to do what they do, and so on. These subjects are given rather broad treatment, to help students get a feeling of expertise as they look at specific problems, discussed in Units 8 through 15. Consideration of topics such as hassles in the family, drugs, death, and prejudice allows readers to analyze their own feelings and possibly to make some beneficial changes in their outlooks and lifestyles. Throughout, ideas are presented and readers are asked to answer the fundamental question "What does this mean to me?" The last four units offer some applications and exercises through which students can work to improve the aspects of their lives that they feel need improvement.

The French have a saying, *Plus ca change, plus c'est la même chose,* which means, "The more things change, the more they stay the same." Perhaps this is true in the long run, but in the short term it does not apply to the turbulent field of human behavior! One might think that the human personality and a person's reactions to his or her environment would remain the same from year to year, but this does not happen. We tend to drift with the tides of social ferment. When the first edition of *Personal Awareness: A Psychology of Adjustment* was written, the entire nation was involved in or affected by social protest, and at times it seemed that we were quite close to armed rebellion. Now, merely half a decade later, the militance is gone. Those who fought in the streets may still be dissatisfied, but, for the most part, they are no longer choosing the violent road.

One of the reasons for revising the text is that times have changed, and—despite the wisdom of the French—they are not the same as they were in 1974. To reflect this change the second edition has substituted a new chapter on love for a chapter that dealt with the alienation society was demonstrating. The first-edition unit on suicide has been expanded in this revision to include discussion of our changing attitudes toward death and dying. Also, in the second edition there has been a shift in approach from the abstract to the pragmatic that is represented by the condensation of a chapter on the theory of learning and its combination with one that emphasizes the practical application of the principles of learning. This should make the topic of learning more personal, meaningful, and useful as students learn to apply the theory to themselves.

Personal Awareness differs from conventional programmed textbooks in that the programmed books instantly indicate whether students' responses are right or wrong. Many of the goals in this book have no right or wrong answers. They ask readers to interpret or analyze information in their own terms. Their only feedback about the correctness of answers is in their own minds. The results are students' unique responses to the instructional goals.

It is certainly possible for readers to pick up *Personal Awareness* and learn a great deal about themselves strictly on their own. However, the richness you and they might get from group interaction should not be discounted. Through group discussions each member can get a sense of direction from the rest of the participants. Moreover, this method allows for study outside of a regularly scheduled and organized class.When the book is used outside the classroom— by a community group, for example—the group members should select a leader. The instructor or leader can conduct some of the activities described in the Instructor's Manual, a valuable souce of additional ideas and resources.

After each unit (with the exception of Unit 19), I have included some articles by other writers to give students a feeling of what others have to say about certain topics and to enhance interest by changing the reading style a little. The articles have interested me and are pertinent to the topics under discussion in the units. Do not get the idea that the articles say all there is to say. They do not. When students start to branch out on their own reading, they will find articles that contradict each other or supplement each other and authors who ignore completely what others have said. As a matter of fact, putting readings into *Personal Awareness* is a sneaky way to encourage students to read contemporary literature to find out what a turbulent area they are entering when they start to think and learn about personal adjustment, both their own and that of others.

This book is an effort to offer an exploratory course in personally applied psychology, from both preventive and corrective viewpoints. It gives guidelines by which readers can grow in a logical and meaningful way and places emphasis on the functional aspects of the psychology of daily living.

In addition to this substantive revision of first-edition material, the usual corrections, amplifications, and face lifting have been made to improve readability and usefulness of the text. I hope that you will enjoy the new material.

Many individuals took time to read the manuscript of this book and to offer valuable criticisms and suggestions. I am grateful to them all for their efforts and want to specially thank Doris Faissole, Jersey City State College; Edward G. Lamp, Terra Technical College; Kevin M. Ramirez, Sacramento City College; J. L. Slosser, Chemeketa Community College; Stuart Stiles, Jr., Orange County Community College; and Jerry Wesson, El Centro College, for their careful reviews. The text has benefited greatly from their work.

R.G.W.

PERSONAL AWARENESS

A PSYCHOLOGY
OF ADJUSTMENT

UNIT 1

DEFINING
ADJUSTMENT

☐ One of the biggest problems we run into when looking at mental adjustment is deciding who is acting normally and who is not. Often we see people who seem to be acting peculiarly, but when we investigate and find out the reasons for their behavior, we then understand and put them back in our personal classification of normal. Suppose you are downtown one day, and as you stop for a traffic light a seedy-looking man sidles up to you and offers you a five-dollar bill. What would you do? You might pull back, start looking for a police officer, and when you find one, report the man. Why? Because you think no normal person—especially a poor one—would give a perfect stranger a five-dollar bill. Suppose the police officer just laughs at you. You might become angry and press the issue, and the officer might then tell you that the man is a psychologist who is filming people's reactions when he approaches them and offers them money. Presumably this explanation would satisfy you, and you would go on about your business. You might even stay around and watch the fun for a little while. Once you had gotten a logical reason for the offbeat behavior, you would be willing to accept it and forget all about it.

As you read this account, you may have wondered what the point of it is. Here are a few questions for you to mull over: On what basis did you decide that the seedy-looking man was acting strangely? How unusual must behavior be for you to get aroused and classify it as abnormal? How reasonable must an explanation be before you'll forget about unusual acts? In this unit you will be looking at some of the most common ways in which we classify behavior as normal and abnormal, or adjusted and maladjusted. You will have a chance to think about the weak spots in the common definitions of normal and abnormal behavior, and you will take a quick look at your own adjustment. Then you will be asked to create your own definition of adjustment, so that you will have a personal base from which to learn about some of the factors that govern adjustment.

As you begin to study this material and try to answer the questions that are posed, you may feel frustrated because there are no set answers to be copied and memorized. If you search out the concept involved, however, and write it down in your own words, you will gain a greater understanding than if you merely copied a given statement.

When you have completed this unit, you should be able to:

1. *Describe how interpersonal relationships can be used to assess mental adjustment.*
2. *Give the pros and cons of describing mental adjustment in terms of interpersonal relationships.*
3. *Define in a general way the terms* normal, abnormal, neurotic, *and* psychotic.
4. *Explain why the concepts of normality and abnormality may be invalid for judging behavior.*
5. *Define the terms* sane *and* insane.
6. *Describe the problems involved in the use of the terms* sane *and* insane.

7. *Explain how knowledge of therapeutic treatment may be a basis for a measure of adjustment.*
8. *Describe adverse reactions that people who have had psychiatric care may have to endure.*
9. *Explain how self-evaluation can be used to measure adjustment.*
10. *Indicate whether you think individuals can accurately evaluate their own mental adjustment.*
11. *Explain how the ability to cope with the environment may be a measure of personal adjustment.*
12. *State the flaws of measuring personal adjustment in terms of coping with the environment.*
13. *Explain how specific behaviors can be used as evidence of maladjustment.*
14. *Summarize the results of your personal evaluation.*
15. *Define personal adjustment.*

INTERPERSONAL RELATIONSHIPS AND ADJUSTMENT

Some people seem to thrive on being with people. Others suffer from it. A.J. is a typical hail-fellow-well-met. He has all the marks of a big man on campus. He belongs to many clubs and is usually an officer or has a lot of responsibility in an organization. He rarely refuses a request to contribute his services to worthy causes. The word is out, "If you want a doer, get A.J." B.K., on the other hand, is almost completely unknown on her campus. When her classmates hear her name, they usually ask, "Who?" Her professors know her only by her written work because she never participates in class. Strangely enough, they seem to know her quite well. C.L. is well known in his neighborhood. His

Is he maladjusted? (Bohdan Hrynewych)

house is next to an empty lot where the neighborhood kids like to play. He is likely to call their parents or the police if the kids get noisy. From these descriptions, rate A.J., B.K., and C.L. as adjusted or maladjusted:

	Adjusted	Maladjusted
A.J.	_____	_____
B.K.	_____	_____
C.L.	_____	_____

No, he's a member of a pantomime group. (Bohdan Hrynewych)

What you have done is to estimate the mental health of these three individuals on the basis of their relationships with other people.

1. *Describe how interpersonal relationships can be used to assess mental adjustment.*

_____

_____

_____

_____

USING INTERPERSONAL RELATIONSHIPS
TO MEASURE ADJUSTMENT

Now add the following information to what you already know about B.K. and C.L. B.K. is very intelligent. She remains quiet in class because she has learned from bitter experience that when she makes comments she embarrasses her classmates and sometimes her professors. She is usually so far ahead of the class that they feel sheepish. Rather than risk complete ostracism, she has learned to hide her intelligence.

Do you now consider B.K. maladjusted? Have your feelings about her changed now that you have more information? Describe what you think of B.K.'s adjustment.

_____

_____

_____

_____

C.L. suffers from two problems. He works nights and needs to sleep during the daytime. He usually tries to sleep in the afternoon—just when the lot next door becomes the playground for the neighborhood. C.L. also frequently has such severe headaches that he becomes physically sick. Do you now think of him as the neighborhood crab? How have your feelings about him changed?

_____

_____

_____

_____

Clearly, the use of a person's interpersonal relations as a measure of adjustment has several weaknesses. Often our evaluations are based on incomplete information, or we judge another person's adjustment by using our own standards of what behavior should be.

2. *Give the pros and cons of describing mental adjustment in terms of interpersonal relationships.*

_____

_____

_____

_____

NORMALITY AND ABNORMALITY

"Loony as a pet coon," "skizzy as hell," "bats in the belfry," "flattened affective responses"—these are but a few of the picturesque descriptions we use for abnormal behavior. In the following blanks, write six more phrases that describe behavior. Try to write three that describe normal behavior and three that describe abnormal behavior.

1. _____   4. _____

2. _____   5. _____

3. _____   6. _____

How did you make out? If you are like many others, you found it wasn't as hard to describe abnormal actions as it was to describe normal ones. This is because we tend to take normal actions for granted and don't pay much attention to them, but we seem to zero in on unusual behavior and develop lots of terms to describe it. Take a look at your descriptions again. Which were the most forceful and the most picturesque? Again, if you are like most people, your descriptions of abnormal behavior are more imaginative. Probably most of your terms were slang, and you gave special interpretations to the words you used. Why? It may be that the words we use to describe behavior don't have enough substance. Or maybe we just don't understand what they mean.

Go back to your phrases describing normal behavior, and expand them into a paragraph that describes what you think of as a normal person.

_____

_____

_____

_____

If your description included each of these characteristics, you did a fine job of identifying a normal person:

1. Behaves according to accepted social standards
2. Controls his or her emotions
3. Fulfills his or her human potential
4. Conforms to social customs
5. Is able to recognize consequences and thus guide his or her behavior
6. Can postpone immediate gratification to achieve long-range goals
7. Learns from experience
8. Is usually happy

The opposite of normality is, of course, abnormality, which you have already described. When you listed phrases to describe abnormal behavior, you may have used the words *neurotic* and *psychotic.* These are technical terms describing certain kinds of abnormality. You have probably heard of people who have claustrophobia or who are hypochondriacs. Phobias and hypochondria are neuroses. There are several types of neurotic disorder, but all neurotics have some characteristics in common. Neurotic people suffer from great anxiety that makes them indulge in what is often called *nonproductive behavior.* Some people are afraid of high places; some must dress and undress in a fixed and rigid routine; some actually seem to enjoy bad health. Neurotics use these kinds of action to protect themselves from the anxiety they feel. These actions are called "nonproductive" because they usually do not eliminate the cause of the anxious feelings; they merely hide the reasons for these feelings behind a symbolic screen. For example, have you ever mislaid something you had to have in a hurry? Did you keep looking again and again in the same places for it? If so, you were acting in a neurotic, nonproductive way. What purpose was served by looking in places where you had already searched, other than making you feel you were doing something? These two characteristics, anxiety and nonproductive behavior, are the two major traits of a neurotic person.

Most neurotics are capable of coping with their environment and do not need to be protected from themselves. They are coherent and their thinking is logical. Many are aware that their behavior is peculiar and some admit it openly. Most of the time they do not know the underlying reasons for their anxiety. They are in touch with reality because they know what is going on around them and do not suffer from delusions and hallucinations. Neurotics generally behave in socially acceptable ways and usually are capable of managing themselves, though they may not be self-supporting. They can be helped by psychotherapy, and their condition usually does not worsen.

In the space that follows, list four characteristics of a neurotic person:

1. _____

2. _____

3. _____

4. _____

Another technical term used to describe abnormal behavior is *psychosis.* The psychotic person usually displays specific behaviors that are characteristic of the particular psychosis. He or she will, however, share certain common symptoms with other psychotic persons. A psychotic usually displays unusual and bizarre behavior patterns, such as laughing when others are sad or raging at things that cause other people to laugh. The psychotic has lost self-control. Often suffering from uncontrollable emotions, psychotics can be dangerous to others and to themselves. Thus many psychotics have to be put into mental institutions. They may hallucinate and have delusions; they often cannot distinguish what is real from what is unreal. They have lost touch with reality. The treatment of psychosis emphasizes control rather than therapy, because therapy cannot begin until the patient has re-established contact with reality.

In the space that follows, list four characteristics that differentiate psychotic from neurotic and normal individuals:

1. _____

2. _____

3. _____

4. _____

Thus you can see that mental adjustment can be defined in terms of normal and abnormal behavior and that we have two major categories of abnormal behavior—neurotic and psychotic—that refine the description of abnormal behavior.

3. *Define in a general way the terms* normal, abnormal, neurotic, *and* psychotic.

_____

_____
_____
_____

DEFINING NORMALITY AND ABNORMALITY

Behind the concept of normality is the assumption that there is a standard type of behavior. But some people are to the right of exact center and some to the left. Is anyone to the left or right normal? If you said that some individuals to either the right or the left can still be normal, you have described the concept of the average, because the average represents the middle group between the extremes. But how far to the left or the right can a person be? Is Joe Normal the person who says, ''Burn, baby, burn,'' or the fellow who believes in apple pie and motherhood? If you reject either one of these stances as being too far away from the center or average, then you have to define exactly what the outer limit of average is. In other words, you have to answer everyone's question, ''How far from the center can I be and still be accepted?''

The problem can be pictured statistically. Suppose we take a characteristic that everyone in our country and for that matter in the world has to some degree: intelligence. Intelligence has been measured by tests and described by a number called the intelligence quotient, or IQ. (Let's not get into an argument right now about whether the IQ is a good or bad measure; we can save that for later. Right now, just accept the fact that intelligence is considered measurable.) If you plotted the IQs of all people on a graph, you'd get a bell-shaped curve called the normal curve (see Figure 1.1). When you look at the curve carefully, you'll find that about 60 percent of the people fall under its highest

FIGURE 1.1 GENERAL DISTRIBUTION OF IQS

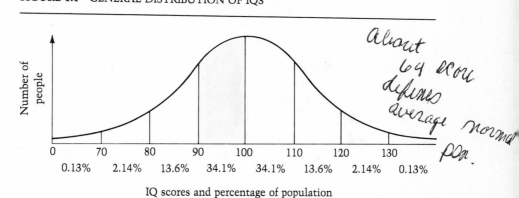

about 64 score defines average normal pn. (handwritten)

IQ scores and percentage of population

points. Those people are called the average group. You can see that their IQs cluster around the value of 100, which is thus called the average value of the IQ. As you move farther and farther away from the average, the proportion of people under the curve decreases, and the values of their IQs change considerably. For example, a person with an IQ over 130 is in the top 0.13 percent of the population. If you happen to know your IQ, you can place yourself on the curve and pretty well tell whether you are average, above average, or below average.

This procedure works well for things that can be measured, such as IQs and shoe sizes. But what do you do with less measurable things? For example, where do you mark the line called "average" when you are trying to classify dress standards? You could put the dude with the prayer beads and the patched leather pants on the average line, or you could use the man in the gray flannel suit. The problem is to decide what kind of behavior is average or normal and then decide how far from the average you will let people go before you brand them as abnormal. There are no nice neat numbers to help you do that.

What may be normal to one social group may be unacceptable to another. For example, Americans abroad are usually very easy to detect. All you have to do is watch them eat. They insist on cutting food with the knife in the right hand and then transferring the fork to the right hand in order to lift the food to the mouth. Most Europeans think this is silly. They are content to use their left hand to lift the food to their mouths. This, to an American, is bad manners.

The same problem arises if you reverse the process and try to delineate abnormal behavior. The notions of neurotic and psychotic behavior pose some problems for the untrained layperson. Descriptions of various neuroses and accompanying behaviors are specific; yet even highly trained psychologists and psychiatrists sometimes disagree on a diagnosis. Also, a situation may not be clearly understood, so the behavior caused by that situation is not clearly understood. In the paragraph describing A.J., B.K., and C.L., you were asked to judge whether these people were adjusted or maladjusted. Review A.J.'s case history and your decision about him. Now add the following information: A.J. suffers from terrible feelings of self-doubt. When he is alone for any length of time, he begins to get intense feelings of inadequacy and anxiety. His outgoing behavior is really based on a strong fear of being alone. From this viewpoint, A.J. is displaying neurotic behavior. But how many of us have the technical skill to discover this by observing A.J. in his social whirl?

Further difficulties result from the fact that, although only two categories of abnormal behavior have been discussed thus far, there are actually ten categories. This diversity obviously complicates the problem.

4. *Explain why the concepts of normality and abnormality may be invalid for judging behavior.*

_____

_____

SANITY AND INSANITY

Another way to try to categorize behavior is to use the legal words *sane* and *insane*. Whenever a person is tried for a particularly bizarre murder, a considerable amount of time usually is spent trying to determine the accused's sanity. Is the defendant responsible for his or her actions? Does he or she know right from wrong? These questions have been posed at many fascinating trials. Perhaps you know of some that have occurred in your own area. Another aspect of the definition of sanity is whether the individual is competent to contribute to his or her own defense.

An interesting side issue in this discussion of knowing right from wrong is that of temporary insanity. Many persons have been acquitted because the court ruled that they were suffering from an attack of emotion that temporarily deprived them of their sanity. Because of this temporary insanity, they were not responsible for their actions, even though they usually were able to distinguish between right and wrong. Obviously, the many nuances and interpretations of sanity make it a sophisticated concept.

5. *Define the terms* sane *and* insane.

_____

_____

_____

_____

DETERMINING SANITY

The use of the terms *sane* and *insane* has caused some insurmountable problems for psychologists and lawyers. Essentially, they are expected to get into an accused person's head and reconstruct how that person felt when the crime was committed. Since they cannot do this, they can only substitute a study of how the person acts and feels after the fact; such a study may not indicate accurately how the person felt at the time. What makes diagnosis even stickier is that behavioral scientists may disagree with each other. A judge and jury may hear several experts flatly contradict each other, not only about the diagnosis of sanity but even about how to get that diagnosis. Small wonder, then, that the people who sit in judgment are confused. The state of the diagnostic art is not good enough for us to be able to diagnose sanity with any high probability of being right.

6. Describe the problems involved in the use of the terms sane *and* insane.

_____

_____

_____

_____

THERAPY AND NORMALITY

Imagine the following scene: You are in the personnel office of a firm where you are anxious to be employed. You have been screened in an initial interview and apparently have made a good impression because you have been given an employee information blank to fill out. As you work your way down the form, you encounter this question: "Have you ever been under, or are you now undergoing, mental treatment?" You remember that your mother took you to a psychiatrist to help you conquer an overwhelming fear of dogs that you acquired when you were bitten by a stray, but you hesitate before noting this experience on the form.

Why do you hesitate? Do you think this information might be detrimental to your chances of being hired? Why do you think the company is asking the question? It seems fairly obvious that the company is defining mental adjustment in a context implying that those who have been under treatment are maladjusted and those who have not are normal. The personnel interviewers will obviously look twice before they hire an applicant who has any record of mental treatment. (Fortunately, this practice has been made illegal by civil-rights legislation. Nevertheless, it might still be encountered.)

7. Explain how knowledge of therapeutic treatment may be a basis for a measurement of adjustment.

_____

_____

_____

_____

USING THERAPY TO MEASURE NORMALITY

The imaginary scene in which you answered a question about mental treatment suggests another way of judging mental adjustment—by assuming that if you ever have been to a "shrink" you are maladjusted. But suppose you have been seeing a mental therapist and have been making progress? Are you a greater or worse risk than the person who may be tied up in knots inside but doesn't have the courage or the insight to admit it? Not too long ago, a mental hospital asked a township zoning board for permission to establish a residence to be used as a staging facility to prepare patients for returning to the community. The patients would live in a conventional house in a familylike arrangement, so that their adjustment to home life could be made easier. The howl of protest that went up from the community was deafening. Residents expressed fears of being murdered in their beds or having their children assaulted and abused. The uproar was so great that the hospital reluctantly had to cancel its request.

For some, the idea of having someone in the family who is mentally ill is disturbing because it suggests family weakness or "bad blood." Many people dismiss from the family a relative who is in a mental hospital and never speak of that person again. Guilt and shame bother these people because they feel that their family is tainted. The stigma attached to such an individual may be permanent. Even after the person has recovered and returned to society, he or she is pointed out and shunned. This is another reason for avoiding the labels *neurotic* and *psychotic*.

8. *Describe adverse reactions that people who have had psychiatric care may have to endure.*

_____

_____

_____

_____

SELF-EVALUATION OF NORMALITY

Check the appropriate response:

	Yes	No
1. Are you happy?	____	____
2. Are you satisfied with the way things are?	____	____
3. Do you like people?	____	____
4. Do you use your full potential?	____	____

If you answered any of these questions with no, don't lose any sleep over it. This is a sketchy example of a personal, subjective evaluation. It is not accurate, nor has it been statistically checked out. Some researchers use subjective evaluations to measure people's adjustment in terms of their own expressed feelings. The technique can be expanded to make adjustment more measurable and thus even more detailed. For example, check the appropriate response:

	Often	Usually	Rarely
1. Are you happy?	____	____	____
2. Are you satisfied with the way things are?	____	____	____
3. Do you like people?	____	____	____
4. Do you use your full potential?	____	____	____

This rating system sets up a quantity or degree rating for the statements you made earlier, so that you have a greater chance to see how happy you are, how much you like people, and so on. If you want to obtain a more specific rating value, you can continue to expand the scale.

This way of describing adjustment is based on the person's answers to certain questions. The main premise of this system is very simple: If you want to learn how well-adjusted a person is, ask some leading questions.

9. Explain how self-evaluation can be used to measure adjustment.

_____

_____

_____

_____

THE ACCURACY OF SELF-EVALUATION

The basic theme explored here is that you can find out about people's mental adjustment by asking them about it. Offhand, this seems to be a good, positive approach. However, many studies of self-evaluation show that this form of rating is often misleading. Most questions dealing with feelings or social values are so transparent that it is hard to hide their intent. Therefore, it is possible to slant the answers to give what are obviously the right ones.

If a questionnaire is designed so that the respondent cannot tell what the approved answer is, the questions form what is termed a *projective* test. However, just as the meaning of the question is hidden from the respondent, so is the meaning of the answer frequently hidden from the analyst. These kinds of tests are quite subjective, and even experts may disagree on the meanings of the results.

The evaluation of responses is also complicated by a semantic problem. The word *happy*, for example, means different things to different people. It may mean a temporary absence of anxiety; it may mean a special state of intense joy. Words carry so many shades of meaning that interpreting them is often difficult.

Another problem is that of accurately knowing oneself. We often lack the insight to judge ourselves objectively. A person who has an uncontrollable temper might consider terrifying rages normal.

10. *Indicate whether you think individuals can accurately evaluate their own mental adjustment.*

_____

_____

_____

_____

COPING AND ADJUSTMENT

How well people are able to cope with the demands of their environment and how well they can accept radical changes in it are often taken as measures of mental adjustment. Some people are said to be "strong"; that is, they can stand up to disasters and misfortunes without cracking. They seem to be able to face the "slings and arrows of outrageous fortune." On the other hand, to some individuals a broken can opener is a potential death sentence. Some of us are able to discuss complicated issues with our friends without feeling tension, yet quiver with terror if we are asked to do the same before an audience of strangers.

Have you ever seen a person come unglued because of a radical change in his or her environment? If you have, briefly describe the incident here.

_____

_____

_____

_____

Would you say the individual was basically maladjusted or just overreacting to the situation that existed at the time? In other words, was the person

Who is to say reactions are positive or negative or odd? (Ken Wittenberg)

chronically maladjusted, or was the abnormal behavior situational and temporary?

_____

_____

_____

_____

11. *Explain how the ability to cope with the environment may be a measure of personal adjustment.*

_____

_____

_____

_____

USING COPING TO MEASURE ADJUSTMENT

Suppose a person suddenly facing a threatening environment responds excessively to the threat, so that as a result society disapproves of what he or she does. Society's reaction may make that individual feel even more threatened; he or she may overreact more, causing society's disapproval to increase. . . . Implied in the idea of coping is a requirement that we react to a situation in a positive manner. We tend to feel that people should master their environment rather than give in to it. However, who is to determine what is a positive reaction and what is a negative one? In the Bible is the statement "Eye for eye, tooth for tooth." Individuals who guide their actions according to this philosophy will probably be aggressive and vengeful. The Bible also says to turn the other cheek. A positive way of coping with a situation under this rule would be to give in to frustrations. The two biblical statements are in direct opposition to each other. Who is to say which is preferable?

Not only do we have the problem of deciding which standards to follow, we also have the complication that stems from different groups in our society. Many standards arise from factors over which we have no control. Take the reactions to stress of lower-class and middle-class children. Lower-class children appear to be more defeatist when subjected to frustration, probably because of experience they have gained from interaction with their environment. But are these children less mentally healthy because they react in this way? Should they be "cured" of their defeatism? Should we go along with their defeatism? If you feel that we should go along, then you're talking about multiple standards. Who is to say which standards are the right ones? With multiple standards, who can decide who is successfully coping with the environment and who is failing to do so?

12. *State the flaws of measuring personal adjustment in terms of coping with the environment.*

_____

_____

_____

_____

SPECIFIC BEHAVIORS

We commonly judge people by their actions. Unusual behavior is often considered a sign of maladjustment. For example, if Johnny wets the bed, he will seem to many to be maladjusted, particularly if he is fifteen years old. Or consider the student who has problems concentrating. Sometimes she is so restless that she can't bear the thought of sitting still for a whole class period, so she cuts class. Although no specific pattern of behavior exists, she still can be thought to be showing maladjustment. Many neuroses and psychoses are manifested by specific acts. Some behavior, however, does not follow a pattern of a neurotic or a psychotic illness but does reveal a disturbance. Nail biting, knuckle cracking, hyperactivity, and high emotionality may be signs of maladjustment. In the space that follows, name five other behaviors that laypeople often consider to be indications of maladjustment.

1. _____   4. _____

2. _____   5. _____

3. _____

Did you think of chronic lying, stealing, overeating, drug addiction, alcoholism, and compulsive gambling? These are behaviors that may be symptomatic of deeper internal problems. In some classifications of mental disorder, they are often considered abnormal behavior.

13. *Explain how specific behaviors can be used as evidence of maladjustment.*

_____

_____

_____

_____

A PERSONAL EVALUATION

Having considered various ways of defining mental adjustment, you should now be ready for an exercise in self-evaluation. Before you begin, however, consider this: The definitions of mental adjustment you have been studying deal with adjustment on an either/or basis: Either you are adjusted or you are not. They do not take into account the idea that adjustment is a minute-by-minute, on-going process. Neither do they take into account the idea that adjustment can change as situations change. The ideas you have been considering also ignore the issues of how comfortable people feel about themselves and how much of their potential they think they are reaching. Keeping these limitations in mind, do the exercise that follows.

EXERCISE 1. ANALYZING PERSONAL ADJUSTMENT

Listed below are descriptions of behavior. Rate yourself according to the scale beside each statement. Check the appropriate response.

	Always		*Sometimes*		*Rarely*
	1	2	3	4	5
1. Treats others as individuals					
2. Works at full potential					
3. Is productive in society					
4. Can enjoy many things					
5. Can resolve external stress					
6. Can resolve internal stress					
7. Identifies with other people, accepts and understands them whether liking them or not					
8. Gets things done					
9. Is not emotionally disturbed by stress					
10. Has a native curiosity to find out and know about things					

Obviously, the closer you rated yourself to the ideal ("always," number 1), the more positively you apparently feel about yourself. Were you inclined to hesitate? Were you afraid of being thought conceited if you gave yourself good marks? On the other hand, were you unwilling to delve into some areas, and did you thus mark yourself in a noncommittal way?

The general interpretation of this exercise if fairly obvious. The statements are considered to be descriptive of an adjusted person. Answers under the higher numbers may indicate maladjustment. If the statements do not seem to describe you, then you apparently do not think you compare favorably to an adjusted person. However, you should not attach too much importance to this test. It is merely an indication of how you look at yourself. It was designed to have you think about yourself and to commit you in writing to a statement of your feelings about yourself.

14. *Summarize the results of your personal evaluation.*

_____

_____

_____

_____

A PERSONAL DEFINITION

You should now be able to write your own definition of personal adjustment.

15. *Define* personal adjustment.

_____

_____

_____

_____

□ A POINT OF VIEW

The central idea of Unit 1 is that the judgment of adjustment is an individual matter and greatly depends on where you stand when you evaluate another person. D. L. Rosenhan proved this beautifully when he showed that normal people who voluntarily committed themselves to a mental institution were judged by the staff to be behaving very strangely. The staff expected them to be peculiar and consequently read peculiar significance into otherwise normal actions. Read this article and see whether it doesn't support the idea that normality and abnormality lie in the eye of the beholder. As you read it, you should be aware that it is a very controversial article. Not everyone agrees with the conclusions it reaches. If you are interested in this topic and would like to go into it in a little more detail, you might enjoy these three articles:

Edward Shoben, "Toward a Concept of Normal Personality," *American Psychologist* 12 (1957): 183–189.

David Freides, "Toward the Elimination of the Concept of Normality," *Journal of Consulting Psychology* 24 (1960): 128–133.

Ray Jeffery, "The Psychologist as an Expert Witness on the Issue of Insanity," *American Psychologist* 19 (1964): 838–843.

D. L. ROSENHAN

ON BEING SANE IN INSANE PLACES

If sanity and insanity exist, how shall we know them?

The question is neither capricious nor itself insane. However much we may be personally convinced that we can tell the normal from the

Reprinted from *Science* 179 (January 19, 1973): 250–258, by permission of D. L. Rosenhan and the American Association for the Advancement of Science. Copyright © 1973 by the American Association for the Advancement of Science.

abnormal, the evidence is simply not compelling. It is commonplace, for example, to read about murder trials wherein eminent psychiatrists for the defense are contradicted by equally eminent psychiatrists for the prosecution on the matter of the defendant's sanity. More generally, there are a great deal of conflicting data on the reliability, utility, and meaning of such terms as "sanity," "insanity," "mental illness," and "schizophrenia" (1). Finally, as early as 1934, Benedict suggested that normality and abnormality are not universal (2). What is viewed as normal in one culture may be seen as quite aberrant in another. Thus, notions of normality and abnormality may not be quite as accurate as people believe they are.

To raise questions regarding normality and abnormality is in no way to question the fact that some behaviors are deviant or odd. Murder is deviant. So, too, are hallucinations. Nor does raising such questions deny the existence of the personal anguish that is often associated with "mental illness." Anxiety and depression exist. Psychological suffering exists. But normality and abnormality, sanity and insanity, and the diagnoses that flow from them may be less substantive than many believe them to be.

At its heart, the question of whether the sane can be distinguished from the insane (and whether degrees of insanity can be distinguished from each other) is a simple matter: do the salient characteristics that lead to diagnoses reside in the patients themselves or in the environments and contexts in which observers find them? From Bleuler, through Kretchmer, through the formulators of the recently revised *Diagnostic and Statistical Manual* of the American Psychiatric Association, the belief has been strong that patients present symptoms, that those symptoms can be categorized, and, implicitly, that the sane are distinguishable from the insane. More recently, however, this belief has been questioned. Based in part on theoretical and anthropological considerations, but also on philosophical, legal, and therapeutic ones, the view has grown that psychological categorization of mental illness is useless at best and downright harmful, misleading, and pejorative at worst. Psychiatric diagnoses, in this view, are in the minds of the observers and are not valid summaries of characteristics displayed by the observed (3–5).

Gains can be made in deciding which of these is more nearly accurate by getting normal people (that is, people who do not have, and have never suffered, symptoms of serious psychiatric disorders) admitted to psychiatric hospitals and then determining whether they were discovered to be sane and, if so, how. If the sanity of such pseudopatients were always detected, there would be prima facie evidence that a sane individual can be distinguished from the insane context in which he is found. Normality (and presumably abnormality) is distinct enough that it can be recognized wherever it occurs, for it is carried within the person. If, on the other hand, the sanity of the pseudopatients were never discovered, serious difficulties would arise for those who support traditional modes of psychiatric diagnosis. Given that the hospital staff was not incompetent, that the pseudopatient had been behaving as sanely as he had been outside of the hospital, and that it had never been previously suggested that he belonged in a psychiatric hospital, such an unlikely outcome would support the view that psychiatric diagnosis betrays little about the patient but much about the environment in which an observer finds him.

This article describes such an experiment. Eight sane people gained secret admission to 12 different hospitals (6). Their diagnostic experiences constitute the data of the first part of this article; the remainder is devoted to a description of their experiences in psychiatric institutions. Too few psychiatrists and psychologists, even those who have worked in such hospitals, know what the experience is like. They rarely talk about it with former patients, perhaps because they distrust information coming from the previously insane. Those who have worked in psychiatric hospitals are likely to have adapted so thoroughly to the settings that they are insensitive to the impact of that experience.

And while there have been occasional reports of researchers who submitted themselves to psychiatric hospitalization (7), these researchers have commonly remained in the hospitals for short periods of time, often with the knowledge of the hospital staff. It is difficult to know the extent to which they were treated like patients or like research colleagues. Nevertheless, their reports about the inside of the psychiatric hospital have been valuable. This article extends those efforts.

PSEUDOPATIENTS AND THEIR SETTINGS

The eight pseudopatients were a varied group. One was a psychology graduate student in his 20's. The remaining seven were older and "established." Among them were three psychologists, a pediatrician, a psychiatrist, a painter, and a housewife. Three pseudopatients were women, five were men. All of them employed pseudonyms, lest their alleged diagnoses embarrass them later. Those who were in mental health professions alleged another occupation in order to avoid the special attentions that might be accorded by staff, as a matter of courtesy or caution, to ailing colleagues (8). With the exception of myself (I was the first pseudopatient and my presence was known to the hospital administrator and chief psychologist and, so far as I can tell, to them alone), the presence of pseudopatients and the nature of the research program was not known to the hospital staffs (9).

The settings were similarly varied. In order to generalize the findings, admission into a variety of hospitals was sought. The 12 hospitals in the sample were located in five different states on the East and West coasts. Some were old and shabby, some were quite new. Some were research-oriented, others not. Some had good staff-patient ratios, others were quite understaffed. Only one was a strictly private hospital. All of the others were supported by state or federal funds or, in one instance, by university funds.

After calling the hospital for an appointment,

the pseudopatient arrived at the admissions office complaining that he had been hearing voices. Asked what the voices said, he replied that they were often unclear, but as far as he could tell they said "empty," "hollow," and "thud." The voices were unfamiliar and were of the same sex as the pseudopatient. The choice of these symptoms was occasioned by their apparent similarity to existential symptoms. Such symptoms are alleged to arise from painful concerns about the perceived meaninglessness of one's life. It is as if the hallucinating person were saying, "My life is empty and hollow." The choice of these symptoms was also determined by the *absence* of a single report of existential psychoses in the literature.

Beyond alleging the symptoms and falsifying name, vocation, and employment, no further alterations of person, history, or circumstances were made. The significant events of the pseudopatient's life history were presented as they had actually occurred. Relationships with parents and siblings, with spouse and children, with people at work and in school, consistent with the aforementioned exceptions, were described as they were or had been. Frustrations and upsets were described along with joys and satisfactions. These facts are important to remember. If anything, they strongly biased the subsequent results in favor of detecting sanity, since none of their histories or current behaviors were seriously pathological in any way.

Immediately upon admission to the psychiatric ward, the pseudopatient ceased simulating *any* symptoms of abnormality. In some cases, there was a brief period of mild nervousness and anxiety, since none of the pseudopatients really believed that they would be admitted so easily. Indeed, their shared fear was that they would be immediately exposed as frauds and greatly embarrassed. Moreover, many of them had never visited a psychiatric ward; even those who had, nevertheless had some genuine fears about what might happen to them. Their nervousness, then, was quite appropriate to the novelty of the hospital setting, and it abated rapidly.

Apart from that short-lived nervousness, the pseudopatient behaved on the ward as he "normally" behaved. The pseudopatient spoke to patients and staff as he might ordinarily. Because there is uncommonly little to do on a psychiatric ward, he attempted to engage others in conversation. When asked by staff how he was feeling, he indicated that he was fine, that he no longer experienced symptoms. He responded to instructions from attendants, to calls for medication (which was not swallowed), and to dining-hall instructions. Beyond such activities as were available to him on the admissions ward, he spent his time writing down his observations about the ward, its patients, and the staff. Initially these notes were written "secretly," but as it soon became clear that no one much cared, they were subsequently written on standard tablets of paper in such public places as the dayroom. No secret was made of these activities.

The pseudopatient, very much as a true psychiatric patient, entered a hospital with no foreknowledge of when he would be discharged. Each was told that he would have to get out by his own devices, essentially by convincing the staff that he was sane. The psychological stresses associated with hospitalization were considerable, and all but one of the pseudopatients desired to be discharged almost immediately after being admitted. They were, therefore, motivated not only to behave sanely, but to be paragons of cooperation. That their behavior was in no way disruptive is confirmed by nursing reports, which have been obtained on most of the patients. These reports uniformly indicate that the patients were "friendly," "cooperative," and "exhibited no abnormal indications."

THE NORMAL ARE NOT DETECTABLY SANE

Despite their public "show" of sanity, the pseudopatients were never detected. Admitted, except in one case, with a diagnosis of schizophrenia (*10*), each was discharged with a diagnosis of schizophrenia "in remission." The label "in remission" should in no way be dismissed as a formality, for at no time during any hospitalization had any question been raised about any pseudopatient's simulation. Nor are there any indications in the hospital records that the pseudopatient's status was suspect. Rather, the evidence is strong that, once labeled schizophrenic, the pseudopatient was stuck with that label. If the pseudopatient was to be discharged, he must naturally be "in remission"; but he was not sane, nor, in the institution's view, had he ever been sane.

The uniform failure to recognize sanity cannot be attributed to the quality of the hospitals, for, although there were considerable variations among them, several are considered excellent. Nor can it be alleged that there was simply not enough time to observe the pseudopatients. Length of hospitalization ranged from 7 to 52 days, with an average of 19 days. The pseudopatients were not, in fact, carefully observed, but this failure clearly speaks more to traditions within psychiatric hospitals than to lack of opportunity.

Finally, it cannot be said that the failure to recognize the pseudopatients' sanity was due to the fact that they were not behaving sanely. While there was clearly some tension present in all of them, their daily visitors could detect no serious behavioral consequences—nor, indeed, could other patients. It was quite common for the patients to "detect" the pseudopatients' sanity. During the first three hospitalizations, when accurate counts were kept, 35 of a total of 118 patients on the admissions ward voiced their suspicions, some vigorously. "You're not crazy. You're a journalist, or a professor [referring to the continual notetaking]. You're checking up on the hospital." While most of the patients were reassured by the pseudopatient's insistence that he had been sick before he came in but was fine now, some continued to believe that the pseudopatient was sane throughout his hospitalization [11]. The fact that the patients often recognized normality when staff did not raises important questions.

Failure to detect sanity during the course of hospitalization may be due to the fact that

physicians operate with a strong bias toward what statisticians call the type 2 error [5]. This is to say that physicians are more inclined to call a healthy person sick (a false positive, type 2) than a sick person healthy (a false negative, type 1). The reasons for this are not hard to find: it is clearly more dangerous to misdiagnose illness than health. Better to err on the side of caution, to suspect illness even among the healthy.

But what holds for medicine does not hold equally well for psychiatry. Medical illnesses, while unfortunate, are not commonly pejorative. Psychiatric diagnoses, on the contrary, carry with them personal, legal and social stigmas [12]. It was therefore important to see whether the tendency toward diagnosing the sane insane could be reversed. The following experiment was arranged at a research and teaching hospital whose staff had heard these findings but doubted that such an error could occur in their hospital. The staff was informed that at some time during the following 3 months, one or more pseudopatients would attempt to be admitted into the psychiatric hospital. Each staff member was asked to rate each patient who presented himself at admissions or on the ward according to the likelihood that the patient was a pseudopatient. A 10-point scale was used, with a 1 and 2 reflecting high confidence that the patient was a pseudopatient.

Judgments were obtained on 193 patients who were admitted for psychiatric treatment. All staff who had had sustained contact with or primary responsibility for the patient— attendants, nurses, psychiatrists, physicians, and psychologists—were asked to make judgments. Forty-one patients were alleged, with high confidence, to be pseudopatients by at least one member of the staff. Twenty-three were considered suspect by at least one psychiatrist. Nineteen were suspected by one psychiatrist *and* one other staff member. Actually, no genuine pseudopatient (at least from my group) presented himself during this period.

The experiment is instructive. It indicates

that the tendency to designate sane people as insane can be reversed when the stakes (in this case, prestige and diagnostic acumen) are high. But what can be said of the 19 people who were suspected of being "sane" by one psychiatrist and another staff member? Were these people truly "sane," or was it rather the case that in the course of avoiding the type 2 error the staff tended to make more errors of the first sort— calling the crazy "sane"? There is no way of knowing. But one thing is certain: any diagnostic process that lends itself so readily to massive errors of this sort cannot be a very reliable one.

THE STICKINESS OF PSYCHODIAGNOSTIC LABELS

Beyond the tendency to call the healthy sick—a tendency that accounts better for diagnostic behavior on admission than it does for such behavior after a lengthy period of exposure—the data speak to the massive role of labeling in psychiatric assessment. Having once been labeled schizophrenic, there is nothing the pseudopatient can do to overcome the tag. The tag profoundly colors others' perceptions of him and his behavior.

From one viewpoint, these data are hardly surprising, for it has long been known that elements are given meaning by the context in which they occur. Gestalt psychology made this point vigorously, and Asch (13) demonstrated that there are "central" personality traits (such as "warm" versus "cold") which are so powerful that they markedly color the meaning of other information in forming an impression of a given personality (14). "Insane," "schizophrenic," "manic-depressive," and "crazy" are probably among the most powerful of such central traits. Once a person is designated abnormal, all of his other behaviors and characteristics are colored by that label. Indeed, that label is so powerful that many of the pseudopatients' normal behaviors were overlooked entirely or profoundly misinterpreted. Some examples may clarify this issue.

Earlier I indicated that there were no changes in the pseudopatient's personal history and current status beyond those of name, employment, and, where necessary, vocation. Otherwise, a veridical description of personal history and circumstances was offered. Those circumstances were not psychotic. How were they made consonant with the diagnosis of psychosis? Or were those diagnoses modified in such a way as to bring them into accord with the circumstances of the pseudopatient's life, as described by him?

As far as I can determine, diagnoses were in no way affected by the relative health of the circumstances of a pseudopatient's life. Rather, the reverse occurred: the perception of his circumstances was shaped entirely by the diagnosis. A clear example of such translation is found in the case of a pseudopatient who had had a close relationship with his mother but was rather remote from his father during his early childhood. During adolescence and beyond, however, his father became a close friend, while his relationship with his mother cooled. His present relationship with his wife was characteristically close and warm. Apart from occasional angry exchanges, friction was minimal. The children had rarely been spanked. Surely there is nothing especially pathological about such a history. Indeed, many readers may see a similar pattern in their own experiences, with no markedly deleterious consequences. Observe, however, how such a history was translated in the psychopathological context, this from the case summary prepared after the patient was discharged.

> This white 39-year-old male . . . manifests a long history of considerable ambivalence in close relationships, which begins in early childhood. A warm relationship with his mother cools during his adolescence. A distant relationship to his father is described as becoming very intense. Affective stability is absent. His attempts to control emotionality with his wife and children are punctuated by angry outbursts and, in the case of the children,

spankings. And while he says that he has several good friends, one senses considerable ambivalence embedded in those relationships also.

The facts of the case were unintentionally distorted by the staff to achieve consistency with a popular theory of the dynamics of a schizophrenic reaction (15). Nothing of an ambivalent nature had been described in relations with parents, spouse, or friends. To the extent that ambivalence could be inferred, it was probably not greater than is found in all human relationships. It is true the pseudopatient's relationships with his parents changed over time, but in the ordinary context that would hardly be remarkable—indeed, it might very well be expected. Clearly, the meaning ascribed to his verbalizations (that is, ambivalence, affective instability) was determined by the diagnosis: schizophrenia. An entirely different meaning would have been ascribed if it were known that the man was "normal."

All pseudopatients took extensive notes publicly. Under ordinary circumstances, such behavior would have raised questions in the minds of observers, as, in fact, it did among patients. Indeed, it seemed so certain that the notes would elicit suspicion that elaborate precautions were taken to remove them from the ward each day. But the precautions proved needless. The closest any staff member came to questioning these notes occurred when one pseudopatient asked his physician what kind of medication he was receiving and began to write down the response. "You needn't write it," he was told gently. "If you have trouble remembering, just ask me again."

If no questions were asked of the pseudopatients, how was their writing interpreted? Nursing records for three patients indicate that the writing was seen as an aspect of their pathological behavior. "Patient engages in writing behavior" was the daily nursing comment on one of the pseudopatients who was never questioned about his writing. Given that the patient is in the hospital, he must be psychologically disturbed. And given that he is disturbed, continuous writing must be a behavioral manifestation of that disturbance, perhaps a subset of the compulsive behaviors that are sometimes correlated with schizophrenia.

One tacit characteristic of psychiatric diagnosis is that it locates the sources of aberration within the individual and only rarely within the complex of stimuli that surrounds him. Consequently, behaviors that are stimulated by the environment are commonly misattributed to the patient's disorder. For example, one kindly nurse found a pseudopatient pacing the long hospital corridors. "Nervous, Mr. X?" she asked. "No, bored," he said.

The notes kept by pseudopatients are full of patient behaviors that were misinterpreted by well-intentioned staff. Often enough, a patient would go "berserk" because he had, wittingly or unwittingly, been mistreated by, say, an attendant. A nurse coming upon the scene would rarely inquire even cursorily into the environmental stimuli of the patient's behavior. Rather, she assumed that his upset derived from his pathology, not from his present interactions with other staff members. Occasionally, the staff might assume that the patient's family (especially when they had recently visited) or other patients had stimulated the outburst. But never were the staff found to assume that one of themselves or the structure of the hospital had anything to do with a patient's behavior. One psychiatrist pointed to a group of patients who were sitting outside the cafeteria entrance half an hour before lunchtime. To a group of young residents he indicated that such behavior was characteristic of the oral-acquisitive nature of the syndrome. It seemed not to occur to him that there were very few things to anticipate in a psychiatric hospital besides eating.

A psychiatric label has a life and an influence of its own. Once the impression has been formed that the patient is schizophrenic, the expectation is that he will continue to be schizophrenic. When a sufficient amount of time has passed, during which the patient has done nothing bizarre, he is considered to be in remission and available for discharge. But the label endures beyond discharge, with the unconfirmed expectation that he will behave as a schizophrenic again. Such labels, conferred by mental health professionals, are as influential on the patient as they are on his relatives and friends, and it should not surprise anyone that the diagnosis acts on all of them as a self-fulfilling prophecy. Eventually, the patient himself accepts the diagnosis, with all of its surplus meanings and expectations, and behaves accordingly (5).

The inferences to be made from these matters are quite simple. Much as Zigler and Phillips have demonstrated that there is enormous overlap in the symptoms presented by patients who have been variously diagnosed (16), so there is enormous overlap in the behaviors of the sane and the insane. The sane are not "sane" all of the time. We lose our tempers "for no good reason." We are occasionally depressed or anxious, again for no good reason. And we may find it difficult to get along with one or another person—again for no reason that we can specify. Similarly, the insane are not always insane. Indeed, it was the impression of the pseudopatients while living with them that they were sane for long periods of time—that the bizarre behaviors upon which their diagnoses were allegedly predicated constituted only a small fraction of their total behavior. If it makes no sense to label ourselves permanently depressed on the basis of an occasional depression, then it takes better evidence than is presently available to label all patients insane or schizophrenic on the basis of bizarre behaviors or cognitions. It seems more useful, as Mischel (17) has pointed out, to limit our discussions to *behaviors*, the stimuli that provoke them, and their correlates.

It is not known why powerful impressions of personality traits, such as "crazy" or "insane," arise. Conceivably, when the origins of and stimuli that give rise to a behavior are remote or unknown, or when the behavior strikes us as immutable, trait labels regarding the *behaver* arise. When, on the other hand, the origins and stimuli are known and available, discourse is limited to the behavior itself. Thus, I may hallucinate because I am sleeping, or I may hallucinate because I have ingested a peculiar drug. These are termed sleep-induced hallucinations, or dreams, and drug-induced hallucinations, respectively. But when the stimuli to my hallucinations are unknown, that is called craziness, or schizophrenia—as if that inference were somehow as illuminating as the others.

THE EXPERIENCE OF PSYCHIATRIC HOSPITALIZATION

The term "mental illness" is of recent origin. It was coined by people who were humane in their inclinations and who wanted very much to raise the station of (and the public's sympathies toward) the psychologically disturbed from that of witches and "crazies" to one that was akin to the physically ill. And they were at least partially successful, for the treatment of the mentally ill *has* improved considerably over the years. But while treatment has improved, it is doubtful that people really regard the mentally ill in the same way that they view the physically ill. A broken leg is something one recovers from, but mental illness allegedly endures forever (18). A broken leg does not threaten the observer, but a crazy schizophrenic? There is by now a host of evidence that attitudes toward the mentally ill are characterized by fear, hostility, aloofness, suspicion, and dread (19). The mentally ill are society's lepers.

That such attitudes infect the general population is perhaps not surprising, only upsetting. But that they affect the professionals—attendants, nurses, physicians, psychologists, and social workers—who treat and deal with the mentally ill is more disconcerting, both because such attitudes are self-evidently pernicious and because they are unwitting. Most mental health professionals would insist that they are sympathetic toward the mentally ill, that they are neither avoidant nor hostile. But it is more likely that an exquisite ambivalence characterizes their relations with psychiatric patients, such that their avowed impulses are only part of their entire attitude. Negative attitudes are there too and can easily be detected. Such attitudes should not surprise us. They are the natural offspring of the labels patients wear and the places in which they are found.

Consider the structure of the typical psychiatric hospital. Staff and patients are strictly segregated. Staff have their own living space, including their dining facilities, bathrooms, and assembly places. The glassed quarters that contain the professional staff, which the pseudopatients came to call "the cage," sit out on every dayroom. The staff emerge primarily for caretaking purposes—to give medication, to conduct a therapy or group meeting, to instruct or reprimand a patient. Otherwise, staff keep to themselves, almost as if the disorder that afflicts their charges is somehow catching.

So much is patient-staff segregation the rule that, for four public hospitals in which an attempt was made to measure the degree to which staff and patients mingle, it was necessary to use "time out of the staff cage" as the operational measure. While it was not the case that all time spent out of the cage was spent mingling with patients (attendants, for example, would occasionally emerge to watch television in the dayroom), it was the only way in which one could gather reliable data on time for measuring.

The average amount of time spent by attendants outside of the cage was 11.3 percent (range, 3 to 52 percent). This figure does not represent only time spent mingling with patients, but also includes time spent on such chores as folding laundry, supervising patients while they shave, directing ward clean-up, and sending patients to off-ward activities. It was the relatively rare attendant who spent time talking with patients or playing games with them. It proved impossible to obtain a "percent mingling time" for nurses, since the amount of time they spent out of the cage was too brief. Rather, we counted instances of emergence from the cage. On the average, daytime nurses emerged from the cage 11.5 times per shift, including instances when they left the ward entirely (range, 4 to 39 times).

Late afternoon and night nurses were even less available, emerging on the average 9.4 times per shift (range, 4 to 41 times). Data on early morning nurses, who arrived usually after midnight and departed at 8 a.m., are not available because patients were asleep during most of this period.

Physicians, especially psychiatrists, were even less available. They were rarely seen on the wards. Quite commonly, they would be seen only when they arrived and departed, with the remaining time being spent in their offices or in the cage. On the average, physicians emerged on the ward 6.7 times per day (range, 1 to 17 times). It proved difficult to make an accurate estimate in this regard, since physicians often maintained hours that allowed them to come and go at different times.

The hierarchical organization of the psychiatric hospital has been commented on before (20), but the latent meaning of that kind of organization is worth noting again. Those with the most power have least to do with patients, and those with the least power are most involved with them. Recall, however, that the acquisition of role-appropriate behaviors occurs mainly through the observation of others, with the most powerful having the most influence. Consequently, it is understandable that attendants not only spend more time with patients than do any other members of the staff—that is required by their station in the hierarchy—but also, insofar as they learn from their superiors' behavior, spend as little time with patients as they can. Attendants are seen mainly in the cage, which is where the models, the action, and the power are.

I turn now to a different set of studies, these dealing with staff response to patient-initiated contact. It has long been known that the amount of time a person spends with you can be an index of your significance to him. If he initiates and maintains eye contact, there is reason to believe that he is considering your requests and needs. If he pauses to chat or actually stops and talks, there is added reason to infer that he is individuating you. In four hospitals, the pseudopatient approached the staff member with a request which took the following form: "Pardon me, Mr. [or Dr. or Mrs.] X, could you tell me when I will be eligible for grounds privileges?" (or " . . . when I will be presented at the staff meeting?" or " . . . when I am likely to be discharged?"). While the content of the question varied according to the appropriateness of the target and the pseudopatient's (apparent) current needs the form was always a courteous and relevant request for information. Care was taken never to approach a particular member of the staff more than once a day, lest the staff member become suspicious or irritated. In examing these data, remember that the behavior of the pseudopatients was neither bizarre nor disruptive. One could indeed engage in good conversation with them.

The data for these experiments are shown in Table 1, separately for physicians (column 1) and for nurses and attendants (column 2). Minor differences between these four institutions were overwhelmed by the degree to which staff avoided continuing contacts that patients had initiated. By far, their most common response consisted of either a brief response to the question, offered while they were "on the move" and with head averted, or no response at all.

The encounter frequently took the following bizarre form: (pseudopatient) "Pardon me, Dr. X. Could you tell me when I am eligible for grounds privileges?" (physician) "Good morning, Dave. How are you today?" (Moves off without waiting for a response.)

It is instructive to compare these data with data recently obtained at Stanford University. It has been alleged that large and eminent universities are characterized by faculty who are so busy that they have no time for students. For this comparison, a young lady approached individual faculty members who seemed to be walking purposefully to some meeting or teaching engagement and asked them the following six questions.

TABLE 1 SELF-INITIATED CONTACT BY PSEUDOPATIENTS WITH PSYCHIATRISTS AND NURSES AND ATTENDANTS, COMPARED TO CONTACT WITH OTHER GROUPS

| | Psychiatric hospitals | | | University campus (non-medical) | University medical center | |
| | | | | | Physicians | |
Contact	(1) Psychiatrists	(2) Nurses and attendants	(3) Faculty	(4) "Looking for a psychiatrist"	(5) "Looking for an internist"	(6) No additional comment
Responses						
Moves on, head averted (%)	71	88	0	0	0	0
Makes eye contact (%)	23	10	0	11	0	0
Pauses and chats (%)	2	2	0	11	0	10
Stops and talks (%)	4	0.5	100	78	100	90
Mean number of questions answered (out of 6)	[a]	[a]	6	3.8	4.8	4.5
Respondents (no.)	13	47	14	18	15	10
Attempts (no.)	185	1283	14	18	15	10

[a]Not applicable.

1. "Pardon me, could you direct me to Encina Hall?" (at the medical school: ". . . to the Clinical Research Center?").
2. "Do you know where Fish Annex is?" (there is no Fish Annex at Stanford).
3. "Do you teach here?"
4. "How does one apply for admission to the college?" (at the medical school: ". . . to the medical school?").
5. "Is it difficult to get in?"
6. "Is there financial aid?"

Without exception, as can be seen in Table 1 (column 3), all of the questions were answered. No matter how rushed they were, all respondents not only maintained eye contact, but stopped to talk. Indeed, many of the respondents went out of their way to direct or take the questioner to the office she was seeking, to try to locate "Fish Annex," or to discuss with her the possibilities of being admitted to the university.

Similar data, also shown in Table 1 (columns 4, 5, and 6), were obtained in the hospital. Here too, the young lady came prepared with six questions. After the first question, however, she remarked to 18 of her respondents (column 4), "I'm looking for a psychiatrist," and to 15 others (column 5), "I'm looking for an internist." Ten other respondents received no inserted comment (column 6). The general degree of cooperative responses is considerably higher for these university groups than it was for pseudopatients in psychiatric hospitals. Even so, differences are apparent within the medical school setting. Once having indicated that she was looking for a psychiatrist, the degree of cooperation elicited was less than when she sought an internist.

POWERLESSNESS AND DEPERSONALIZATION

Eye contact and verbal contact reflect concern and individuation; their absence, avoidance and depersonalization. The data I have presented do not do justice to the rich daily encounters that grew up around matters of depersonalization and avoidance. I have records of patients who were beaten by staff for the sin of having initiated verbal contact. During my own experience, for example, one patient was beaten in the presence of other patients for having approached an attendant and told him, "I like you." Occasionally, punishment meted out to patients for misdemeanors seemed so excessive that it could not be justified by the most radical interpretations of psychiatric canon. Nevertheless, they appeared to go unquestioned. Tempers were often short. A patient who had not heard a call for medication would be roundly excoriated, and the morning attendants would often wake patients with, "Come on, you m——f——s, out of bed!"

Neither anecdotal nor "hard" data can convey the overwhelming sense of powerlessness which invades the individual as he is continually exposed to the depersonalization of the psychiatric hospital. It hardly matters *which* psychiatric hospital—the excellent public ones and the very plush private hospital were better than the rural and shabby ones in this regard, but, again, the features that psychiatric hospitals had in common overwhelmed by far their apparent differences.

Powerlessness was evident everywhere. The patient is deprived of many of his legal rights by dint of his psychiatric commitment (*21*). He is shorn of credibility by virtue of his psychiatric label. His freedom of movement is restricted. He cannot initiate contact with the staff, but may only respond to such overtures as they make. Personal privacy is minimal. Patient quarters and possessions can be entered and examined by any staff member, for whatever reason. His personal history and anguish is available to any staff member (often including the "grey lady" and "candy striper" volunteer) who chooses to read his folder, regardless of their therapeutic relationship to him. His personal hygiene and waste evacuation are often monitored. The water closets may have no doors.

At times, depersonalization reached such proportions that pseudopatients had the sense that they were invisible, or at least unworthy of account. Upon being admitted, I and other pseudopatients took the initial physical examinations in a semipublic room, where staff members went about their own business as if we were not there.

On the ward, attendants delivered verbal and occasionally serious physical abuse to patients in the presence of other observing patients, some of whom (the pseudopatients) were writing it all down. Abusive behavior, on the other hand, terminated quite abruptly when other staff members were known to be coming. Staff are credible witnesses. Patients are not.

A nurse unbuttoned her uniform to adjust her brassiere in the presence of an entire ward of viewing men. One did not have the sense that she was being seductive. Rather, she didn't notice us. A group of staff persons might point to a patient in the dayroom and discuss him animatedly, as if he were not there.

One illuminating instance of depersonalization and invisibility occurred with regard to medications. All told, the pseudopatients were administered nearly 2100 pills, including Elavil, Stelazine, Compazine, and Thorazine, to name but a few. (That such a variety of medications should have been administered to patients presenting identical symptoms is itself worthy of note.) Only two were swallowed. The rest were either pocketed or deposited in the toilet. The pseudopatients were not alone in this. Although I have no precise records on how many patients rejected their medications, the pseudopatients frequently found the medications of other patients in the toilet before they deposited their own. As long as they were cooperative, their behavior and the pseudopatients' own in this matter, as in other important matters, went unnoticed throughout.

Reactions to such depersonalization among pseudopatients were intense. Although they had come to the hospital as participant observers and were fully aware that they did not "belong," they nevertheless found themselves caught up in and fighting the process of depersonalization. Some examples: a graduate student in psychology asked his wife to bring his textbooks to the hospital so he could "catch up on his homework"—this despite the elaborate precautions taken to conceal his professional association. The same student, who had trained for quite some time to get into the hospital, and who had looked forward to the experience, "remembered" some drag races that he had wanted to see on the weekend and insisted that he be discharged by that time. Another pseudopatient attempted a romance with a nurse. Subsequently, he informed the staff that he was applying for admission to graduate school in psychology and was very likely to be admitted, since a graduate professor was one of his regular hospital visitors. The same person began to engage in psychotherapy with other patients—all of this as a way of becoming a person in an impersonal environment.

THE SOURCES OF DEPERSONALIZATION

What are the origins of depersonalization? I have already mentioned two. First are attitudes held by all of us toward the mentally ill—including those who treat them—attitudes characterized by fear, distrust, and horrible expectations on the one hand, and benevolent intentions on the other. Our ambivalence leads, in this instance as in others, to avoidance.

Second, and not entirely separate, the hierarchical structure of the psychiatric hospital facilitates depersonalization. Those who are at the top have least to do with patients, and their behavior inspires the rest of the staff. Average daily contact with psychiatrists, psychologists, residents, and physicians combined ranged from 3.9 to 25.1 minutes, with an overall mean of 6.8 (six pseudopatients over a total of 129 days of hospitalization). Included in this average are time spent in the admissions interview, ward meetings in the presence of a senior staff member, group and individual psychotherapy contacts, case presentation conferences, and discharge meetings. Clearly, patients do not spend much time in interpersonal contact with doctoral staff. And doctoral staff serve as models for nurses and attendants.

There are probably other sources. Psychiatric installations are presently in serious financial straits. Staff shortages are pervasive, staff time at a premium. Something has to give, and that something is patient contact. Yet, while financial stresses are realities, too much can be made of them. I have the impression that the psychological forces that result in depersonalization are much stronger than the fiscal ones and that the addition of more staff would not correspondingly improve patient care in this regard. The incidence of staff meetings and the enormous amount of record-keeping on patients, for example, have not been as substantially reduced as has patient contact. Priorities exist, even during hard times. Patient contact is not a significant priority in the traditional psychiatric hospital, and fiscal pressures do not account for this. Avoidance and depersonalization may.

Heavy reliance upon psychotropic medication tacitly contributes to depersonalization by convincing staff that treatment is indeed being conducted and that further patient contact may not be necessary. Even here, however, caution needs to be exercised in understanding the role of psychotropic drugs. If patients were powerful rather than powerless, if they were viewed as interesting individuals rather than diagnostic entities, if they were socially significant rather than social lepers, if their anguish truly and wholly compelled our sympathies and concerns, would we not *seek* contact with them, despite the availability of medications? Perhaps for the pleasure of it all?

THE CONSEQUENCES OF LABELING AND DEPERSONALIZATION

Whenever the ratio of what is known to what needs to be known approaches zero, we tend to invent "knowledge" and assume that we understand more than we actually do. We seem unable to acknowledge that we simply don't know. The needs for diagnosis and remediation of behavioral and emotional problems are enormous. But rather than acknowledge that we are just embarking on understanding, we continue to label patients "schizophrenic," "manic-depressive," and "insane," as if in those words we had captured the essence of understanding. The facts of the matter are that we have known for a long time that diagnoses are often not useful or reliable, but we have nevertheless continued to use them. We now know that we cannot distinguish insanity from sanity. It is depressing to consider how that information will be used.

Not merely depressing, but frightening. How many people, one wonders, are sane but not recognized as such in our psychiatric institutions? How many have been needlessly stripped of their privileges of citizenship, from the right to vote and drive to that of handling their own accounts? How many have feigned insanity in order to avoid the criminal consequences of their behavior, and, conversely, how many would rather stand trial than live interminably in a psychiatric hospital—but are wrongly thought to be mentally ill? How many have been stigmatized by well-intentioned, but nevertheless erroneous, diagnoses? On the last point, recall again that a "type 2 error" in psychiatric diagnosis does not have the same consequences it does in medical diagnosis. A diagnosis of cancer that has been found to be in error is cause for celebration. But psychiatric diagnoses are rarely found to be in error. The label sticks, a mark of inadequacy forever.

Finally, how many patients might be "sane" outside the psychiatric hospital but seem insane in it—not because craziness resides in them, as it were, but because they are responding to a bizarre setting, one that may be unique to institutions which harbor nether people? Goffman (4) calls the process of socialization to such institutions "mortification"—an apt metaphor that includes the processes of depersonalization that have been described here. And while it is impossible to know whether the pseudopatients' responses to these processes are characteristic of all inmates—they were, after all, not real patients—it is difficult to believe that these processes of socialization to a psychiatric hospital provide useful attitudes or habits of response for living in the "real world."

SUMMARY AND CONCLUSIONS

It is clear that we cannot distinguish the sane from the insane in psychiatric hospitals. The hospital itself imposes a special environment in which the meanings of behavior can easily be misunderstood. The consequences to patients hospitalized in such an environment—the powerlessness, depersonalization, segregation, mortification, and self-labeling—seem undoubtedly countertherapeutic.

I do not, even now, understand this problem well enough to perceive solutions. But two matters seem to have some promise. The first concerns the proliferation of community mental health facilities, of crisis intervention centers, of the human potential movement, and of behavior therapies that, for all of their own problems, tend to avoid psychiatric labels, to focus on specific problems and behaviors, and to retain the individual in a relatively nonpejorative environment. Clearly, to the extent that we refrain from sending the distressed to insane places, our impressions of them are less likely to be distorted. (The risk of distorted perceptions, it seems to me, is always present, since we are much more sensitive to an individual's behaviors and verbalizations than we are to the subtle contextual stimuli that often promote them. At issue here is a matter of magnitude. And, as I have shown, the magnitude of distortion is exceedingly high in the extreme context that is a psychiatric hospital.)

The second matter that might prove promising speaks to the need to increase the sensitivity of mental health workers and researchers to the *Catch 22* position of psychiatric patients. Simply reading materials in this area will be of help to some such workers and researchers. For others, directly experiencing the impact of psychiatric hospitalization will be of enormous use. Clearly, further research into the social psychology of such total institutions will both facilitate treatment and deepen understanding.

I and the other pseudopatients in the psychiatric setting had distinctly negative reactions. We do not pretend to describe the subjective experiences of true patients. Theirs may be different from ours, particularly with the passage of time and the necessary process of adaptation to one's environment. But we can and do speak to the relatively more objective indices of treatment within the hospital. It could be a mistake, and a very unfortunate one, to consider that what happened to us derived from malice or stupidity on the part of the staff. Quite the contrary, our overwhelming impression of them was of people who really cared, who were committed and who were uncommonly intelligent. Where they failed, as they sometimes did painfully, it would be more accurate to attribute those failures to the environment in which they, too, found themselves than to personal callousness. Their perceptions and behavior were controlled by the situation, rather than being motivated by a malicious disposition. In a more benign environment, one that was less attached to global diagnosis, their behaviors and judgments might have been more benign and effective.

REFERENCES AND NOTES

1. P. Ash, *J. Abnorm. Soc. Psychol.* 44, 272 (1949); A. T. Beck, *Amer. J. Psychiat.* 119, 210 (1962); A. T. Boisen, *Psychiatry* 2, 233 (1938); N. Kreitman, *J. Ment. Sci.* 107, 876 (1961); N. Kreitman, P. Sainsbury, J. Morrisey, J. Towers, J. Scrivener, *ibid.*, p. 887; H. O. Schmitt and C. P. Fonda, *J. Abnorm. Soc. Psychol.* 52, 262 (1956); W. Seeman, *J. Nerv. Ment. Dis.* 118, 541 (1953). For an analysis of these artifacts and summaries of the disputes, see J. Zubin, *Annu. Rev. Psychol.* 18, 373 (1967); L. Phillips and J. G. Draguns, *ibid.* 22, 447 (1971).

2. R. Benedict, *J. Gen. Psychol.* 10, 59 (1934).

3. See in this regard H. Becker, *Outsiders: Studies in the Sociology of Deviance* (Free Press, New York, 1963); B. M. Braginsky, D. D. Braginsky, K. Ring, *Methods of Madness: The Mental Hospital as a Last Resort* (Holt, Rinehart and Winston, New York, 1969); G. M. Crocetti and P. V. Lemkau, *Amer. Sociol. Rev.* 30, 577 (1965); E. Goffman, *Behavior in Public Places* (Free Press, New York, 1964); R. D. Laing, *The Divided Self: A Study of Sanity and Madness* (Quadrangle,

Chicago, 1960); D. L. Phillips, *Amer. Sociol. Rev.* 28, 963 (1963); T. R. Sarbin, *Psychol. Today* 6, 18 (1972); E. Schur, *Amer. J. Sociol.* 75, 309 (1969); T. Szasz, *Law, Liberty and Psychiatry* (Macmillan, New York, 1963); *The Myth of Mental Illness: Foundations of a Theory of Mental Illness* (Hoeber Harper, New York, 1963). For a critique of some of these views, see W. R. Gove, *Amer. Sociol. Rev.* 35, 873 (1970).

4. E. Goffman, *Asylums* (Doubleday, Garden City, N.Y., 1961).

5. T. J. Scheff, *Being Mentally Ill: A Sociological Theory* (Aldine, Chicago, 1966).

6. Data from a ninth pseudopatient are not incorporated in this report because, although his sanity went undetected, he falsified aspects of his personal history, including his marital status and parental relationships. His experimental behaviors therefore were not identical to those of the other pseudopatients.

7. A. Barry, *Bellevue Is a State of Mind* (Harcourt Brace Jovanovich, New York, 1971); I. Belknap, *Human Problems of a State Mental Hospital* (McGraw-Hill, New York, 1956); W. Caudill, F. C. Redlich, H. R. Gilmore, E. B. Brody, *Amer. J. Orthopsychiat.* 22, 314 (1952); A. R. Goldman, R. H. Bohr, T. A. Steinberg, *Prof. Psychol.* 1, 427 (1970); unauthored, *Roche Report* (No. 13), 8 (1971).

8. Beyond the personal difficulties that the pseudopatient is likely to experience in the hospital, there are legal and social ones that, combined, require considerable attention before entry. For example, once admitted to a psychiatric institution, it is difficult, if not impossible, to be discharged on short notice, state law to the contrary notwithstanding. I was not sensitive to these difficulties at the outset of the project, nor to the personal and situational emergencies that can arise, but later a writ of habeas corpus was prepared for each of the entering pseudopatients and an attorney was kept "on call" during every hospitalization. I am grateful to John Kaplan and Robert Bartels for legal advice and assistance in these matters.

9. However distasteful such concealment is, it was a necessary first step to examining these questions. Without concealment, there would have been no way to know how valid these experiences were; nor was there any way of knowing whether whatever detections occurred were a tribute to the diagnostic acumen of the staff or to the hospital's rumor network. Obviously, since my concerns are general ones that cut across individual hospitals and staffs, I have respected their anonymity and have eliminated clues that might lead to their identification.

10. Interestingly, of the 12 admissions, 11 were diagnosed as schizophrenic and one, with the identical symptomatology, as manic-depressive psychosis. This diagnosis has a more favorable prognosis, and it was given by the only private hospital in our sample. On the relations between social class and psychiatric diagnosis, see A. deB. Hollingshead and F. C. Redlich, *Social Class and Mental Illness: A Community Study* (Wiley, New York, 1958).

11. It is possible, of course, that patients have quite broad latitudes in diagnosis and therefore are inclined to call many people sane, even those whose behavior is patently aberrant. However, although we have no hard data on this matter, it was our distinct impression that this was not the case. In many instances, patients not only singled us out for attention, but came to imitate our behaviors and styles.

12. J. Cumming and E. Cumming, *Community Ment. Health* 1, 135 (1965); A. Farina and K. Ring, *J. Abnorm. Psychol.* 70, 47 (1965); H. E. Freeman and O. G. Simmons, *The Mental Patient Comes Home* (Wiley, New York, 1963); W. J. Johannsen, *Ment. Hygiene* 53, 218 (1969); A. S. Linsky, *Soc. Psychiat.* 5, 166 (1970).

13. S. E. Asch, *J. Abnorm. Soc. Psychol.* 41, 258 (1946); *Social Psychology* (Prentice-Hall, New York, 1952).

14. See also I. N. Mensh and J. Wishner, *J. Personality* 16, 188 (1947); J. Wishner, *Psychol. Rev.* 67, 96 (1960); J. S. Bruner and R. Tagiuri, in *Handbook of Social Psychology*, G. Lindzey, ed. (Addison-Wesley, Cambridge, Mass., 1954), vol. 2, pp. 634–654; J. S. Bruner, D. Shapiro, R. Tagiuri, in *Person Perception and Interpersonal Behavior*, R. Tagiuri and L. Petrullo, eds. (Stanford Univ. Press, Stanford, Calif., 1958), pp. 277–288.

15. For an example of a similar self-fulfilling prophecy, in this instance dealing with the "central" trait of intelligence, see R. Rosenthal and L. Jacobson, *Pygmalion in the Classroom* (Holt, Rinehart and Winston, New York, 1968).

16. E. Zigler and L. Phillips, *J. Abnorm. Soc. Psychol.* 63, 69 (1961). See also R. K. Freudenberg and J. P. Robertson, *A.M.A. Arch. Neurol. Psychiatr.* 76, 14 (1956).

17. W. Mischel, *Personality and Assessment* (Wiley, New York, 1968).

18. The most recent and unfortunate instance of this tenet is that of Senator Thomas Eagleton.

19. T. R. Sarbin and J. C. Mancuso, *J. Clin. Consult. Psychol.* 35, 159 (1970); T. R. Sarbin, *ibid.* 31, 447 (1967); J. C. Nunnally, Jr., *Popular Conceptions of Mental Health* (Holt, Rinehart and Winston, New York, 1961).

20. A. H. Stanton and M. S. Schwartz, *The Mental Hospital: A Study of Institutional Participation in Psychiatric Illness and Treatment* (Basic, New York, 1954).

21. D. B. Wexler and S. E. Scoville, *Ariz. Law Rev.* 13, 1 (1971).

22. I thank W. Mischel, E. Orne, and M. S. Rosenhan for comments on an earlier draft of this manuscript.

UNIT 2

MOTIVATION

□ "Give me a place to place my lever, and I can move the world," said Archimedes. "Give me motivation in my students, and I can teach them anything," say educators. "Dedicated workers are what I need," says the plant manager. In science, education, and management, motivation is a key ingredient of progress. What motivates people? What makes them act? If we can get an understanding of the complexities of motivation, we might be able to learn not only how to manipulate others but, more important, how to motivate ourselves into greater personal realization.

When you have completed this unit, you should be able to:

1. *Explain Sigmund Freud's ideas about instinctive drives.*
2. *List the general principles of needs-drives theories of motivation.*
3. *Define* functional autonomy *and* homeostasis, *and give a personal example of them.*
4. *Summarize the biological theory of motivation that relates human beings to their animal origins.*
5. *State the philosophical implications of the psychophysiological theories of motivation.*
6. *Describe Alfred Adler's ideas about human motivation.*
7. *Summarize Carl Jung's ideas about human motivation.*
8. *Explain Erich Fromm's ideas about freedom and his distinction between productive and nonproductive people.*
9. *Describe Abraham Maslow's hierarchy of needs.*
10. *Discuss the general philosophical implications of the theories of Adler, Jung, Fromm, and Maslow.*
11. *Explain what is meant by a need for achievement and a fear of failure.*
12. *Describe attribution theory and locus of control.*
13. *Contrast the three schools of motivational theory.*
14. *Select the specific theory that is most appealing to you, and explain your reasons for selecting it.*
15. *Write your own theory of motivation.*

FREUD'S IDEAS ON MOTIVATION

Probably the most famous theory of motivation is that of Sigmund Freud, who was one of the first psychologists to set forth a coherent account of human behavior. His theory describes motivation, development, and the dynamics of personality. In this section we will consider only his ideas about human motivation.

Food and drink provide the human body with energy to operate and to do work. Part of this energy is transformed into psychic energy, which is used for thinking and perceiving. Psychic energy is derived from the instincts, which according to Freud are the organizers of the thought process. The instincts have a source, an aim, an object, and an impetus. They stem from bodily needs. Their aim is to eliminate the bodily need and return the body to the quiet state it felt before the need excited it. Because of this, an instinct may be called regressive. Because it stresses return to an earlier state, an instinct may be considered a conservative force. Bodily needs keep returning, so the surging of instincts also occurs in cycles or repeated patterns. The object of an instinct is the means of extinguishing a need, as food is an object of the hunger instinct. An instinct's impetus is its strength. The hungrier a person is, the stronger is the impetus of the hunger instinct.

In the space that follows, name and describe four characteristics of an instinct.

1. _____

2. _____

3. _____

4. _____

There are as many instincts as there are bodily needs, but Freud divided instincts into two main types—those serving the life wish and those serving the death wish. These are a person's two basic wishes. The death wish is a desire to achieve what Freud considered the most pleasurable state of being—complete freedom from tensions. The aim of the death wish is to restore oneself to the inorganic state from which one came. According to Freud, the goal of all life is death and the satisfactions of the grave—rest and repose. Because people are torn between the desire to die and the wish to live, they turn their self-destructive urges outward and behave aggressively and destructively toward others. The life wish shows itself in many ways, but the main indication of it is the urge for reproduction—the sex urge. Sometimes the two wishes neutralize conflict; sometimes one takes supremacy. Often, the two oppose each other. Many times, a person's actions are based on a fusion of instincts—a combining of various bodily needs or driving forces and resisting forces. Essentially, human behavior is a system of compromises between the two wishes.

1. Explain Freud's ideas about instinctive drives.

_____

_____

_____

_____

A NEEDS-DRIVES THEORY OF MOTIVATION

Freud's theory is a specialized version of the general biological theory of motivation. The general theory does not go so far as Freud in dividing the drives into opposing forces. However, its basic idea is that physiological needs produce psychological drives, and these drives cause an organism to act. This idea is just about the same in the two theories. When the body acts to reduce the drive and the need, tension within the body is reduced. The reduction of tension is pleasurable; thus the next time a person feels the need that was extinguished, he or she will try to repeat whatever action reduced it. In this way a repertoire of actions is built up in response to needs-drives. As learning goes on, the interaction of needs-drives and consequent actions becomes complex—sometimes so complex that identifying the needs that are the basis of the action is almost impossible. Why, for instance, are you studying this book? Can you trace this action back to a specific physiological need?

Some motivational theorists distinguish between primary and secondary drives. Primary drives are unlearned. They tend to arouse the organism before it has undergone any special training or experiences. These are the basic biological conditions of pain, hunger, thirst, and sex, the need for air, and the need to eliminate wastes. These drives interact, so that one has a tendency to override another. For instance, hunger may overcome sexual urgings, and fear of suffocation may serve to reduce awareness of pain. Sometimes our efforts to reduce these drives are successful, and the lessening of their intensity acts as a sort of reward, increasing the odds that, when we feel the need again, we will repeat the act that first reduced it. Often, however, our reasons for doing things cannot necessarily be traced back to the primary drives but may result from other motives.

The other motivations are secondary drives. They are learned responses and do not come from biological needs. Secondary drives include all the conditioning and training a person has experienced. Many theorists argue that most of a person's actions are attempts to gain pleasure or to avoid pain and frustration. Others maintain that positive events such as social approval and reward are also powerful determiners of behavior. The reverse could also be argued: that adverse conditions control our actions.

Consider your own reasons for doing things. When you strip away all the high-sounding phrases, are you really doing things to avoid punishment or frustration? List everything you have done today, and then judge whether you acted to stave off something unpleasant. Do you agree with those who say we act to avoid pain and punishment? Or do you consider yourself to be a hedonist, a pleasure seeker?

_____

_____

_____

_____

2. List the general principles of needs-drives theories of motivation.

_____

_____

_____

_____

FUNCTIONAL AUTONOMY AND HOMEOSTASIS

Equal balance between 2 things

The problem of tracing our actions back to primary drives has interested the experts for a long time. One solution was proposed by Gordon Allport, who coined the phrase *functional autonomy.* Allport observed that people's habits sometimes become independent of the motivations that originally prompted them. We start to do something that we feel must be done and then continue to carry on that action long after the need for it is gone. In some way, we change the action into a satisfier for a new need or purpose that we have developed. The satisfier then becomes independent of the original motive. A miser, for example, originally starts to collect money for the advantages it can bring. However, the acts of accumulating money and counting it soon replace the original purpose for seeking it, and the hoarding of money becomes a functionally autonomous action. A whole new set of reasons supports the miser's behavior. A fisherman who finds more enjoyment in the physical activity of rowing to a distant part of a lake than in fishing near shore is also displaying a functionally autonomous habit. By using the idea of changing motivation, Allport attempted to explain how basic motivations become complicated and unrelated to the original pressure that caused us to act.

Allport identified two kinds of functional autonomy: perseverative and propriate. *Perseverative* motives come from our biology. They are habits that once allowed us to adapt to our environment but are no longer needed. Homesickness and eating every day are examples. *Propriate* autonomy deals with social values and a person's interests and attitudes. For example, a student may take a course because his or her parents wish it or because it is a required part of the curriculum. If that student becomes fascinated by the subject and continues to study it, he or she is developing a propriate autonomous habit.

Biological theories of motivation, such as Freud's and the needs-drives theories, may be better understood by examining the concept of *homeostasis.* What do you do when you are too warm? When you are thirsty? When you are out of breath? You take some action to cool off, slake your thirst, or catch your breath. What you are doing is restoring your system to a more tolerable state. This process is called homeostasis. The body takes all sorts of actions to protect itself and to stay in the best possible balance with the environment. When you are hot, you perspire. You normally have little control over this homeostatic reaction of the body. The biological theories of needs-drives and Freud's ideas are essentially homeostatic. They emphasize the attempt to restore the status quo of the body or to make the best compromise with the environment.

3. *Define* functional autonomy *and* homeostasis, *and give a personal example of these concepts.*

_____

_____

_____

_____

THE BIOLOGICAL THEORY

Several writers have recently tried to relate human beings to their animal past. They have attempted to explain people's actions and problems by interpreting human social interactions. To do so, these writers look through the window at humanity's evolutionary past. In *The African Genesis* and *The Social Contract*, Robert Ardrey says that much human behavior can and should be so interpreted. By stressing our animal origins, he maintains, we will understand that our behavior is an indication of our animal nature. Aggression, according to Ardrey, is a manifestation of the instinct of territoriality. Just as many animals display the urge to seize and defend a specific piece of ground, so do human beings, although in a disguised way. Realizing that the urge is an innate feeling may allow us to deal with it effectively. Ardrey believes that many of our social actions and basic motivations can best be understood by referring to our animal origins and relating our actions to these sources.

This, of course, is a very controversial stand. Richard F. Leakey and Roger Levin, both noted anthropologists, argue from the opposite viewpoint. In their book *Origins: What New Discoveries Reveal About the Emergence of Our Species and Its Possible Future*, they state that animal nature is cooperative but that it can be modified by the environment. Thus we should blame violence on a socially conditioned desire to possess land rather than on our genetic makeup.

4. *Summarize the biological theory of motivation that relates human beings to their animal origins.*

_____

_____

IMPLICATIONS OF THE BIOLOGICAL THEORIES

If you accept the ideas of Freud, the needs-drives theorists, or Robert Ardrey, what sort of future do you think humanity has? Can people rise above their animal nature or overcome their bodies' demands? These theories are rather pessimistic. According to them, a person is constantly engaged in an internal struggle, sensing needs and working to satisfy them. Life is nothing more than a struggle between needs and their satisfaction, and our complicated sets of moral values and ideals rest on a false premise. Human beings, in this view, are

Is an instinctive desire for territory the cause of this behavior? (Bob Adelman/Magnum Photos)

ruled by their physiology, not by spiritual goodness. They are basically animals, and ideas of spirit and soul are thus irrelevant.

5. *State the philosophical implications of the psychophysiological theories of motivation.*

_____

_____

_____

_____

ADLER'S CONCEPTS

Other motivational theorists examine human behavior from different viewpoints. One approach is that of Alfred Adler, who coined the phrase *inferiority complex*. Adler disagreed with Freud about the importance of sex in a person's life. Adler's studies led him to believe that people are more socially motivated and less pushed by the desires of the body than Freud was willing to concede. According to Adler, everyone is born with feelings of inferiority that may be increased by experiences such as parental rejection or overprotection. Thus everyone struggles constantly to overcome real or imagined deficiencies. By means of a will to power, a person may overcome feelings of inferiority and develop a creative self, a unique lifestyle, and sound personal adjustment. The will to power also induces a person to strive for superiority over other individuals. Adler seems to look ahead toward an individual's betterment, instead of considering everyone a prisoner of his or her past or biology.

What do you think of Adler's ideas? Did you ever act to overcome feelings of inferiority? Briefly describe the occasion.

_____

_____

_____

_____

6. *Describe Alfred Adler's ideas about human motivation.*

_____

_____

JUNG'S THEORY

Another theory about motivation was put forth by Carl Jung, who believed that people are occupied by a struggle within themselves. Like Adler, Jung broke with Freud over his emphasis on the biological nature of human beings. In Jung's view, people are controlled by an inborn desire for balance and harmony. Each person is divided into two parts: persona and shadow. The persona is the mask a person shows to the world; it is that individual's face as seen by others. Within each person, however, is another spirit that may be the exact opposite of the persona; this is the shadow. Another expression of this twofold division is found in Jung's famous terms *extrovert* and *introvert*. Usually one style is dominant within a person. If you are an extrovert, you are outgoing and interested in other people and in the external world. If you are an introvert, you are more concerned with your thoughts and are withdrawn and reflective. Both forces coexist within us, and our experiences and learning determine which we display.

Within us there is always a struggle to maintain a balanced or an *integrated self*. The struggle is carried out in four ways: by thinking, feeling, intuiting, and sensing. Each way provides a method of relating to the world. All four are active, but one tends to dominate. A person governed by sensation is regulated by the sensory organs. Someone governed by feeling is led by the emotions. If intuition is dominant, an individual operates on a mystical, spiritual level. If thinking is pre-eminent, a person uses analytical procedures to determine his or her actions. Each way of relating to the world and to all the internal opposing divisions causes a person to try to realize selfhood, which is a dynamic middle point of balance integrating the divisions of the personality into a whole.

One of Jung's most controversial ideas was his notion of the *collective unconscious*. By this he meant the "deposit of ancestral experiences from untold millions of years . . . to which each century adds an infinitesimally small amount of variation." In other words, we inherit not only our physical forms from our ancestors but also social and cultural factors that influence us. Jung believed, for example, that the taboo against incest, which is nearly universal, derived from a collective inheritance from our ancestors and was not a specific prohibition that came into being independently in many cultures. Ardrey supports this idea to some extent when he suggests that many of our actions are based on customs inherited from our ancestors. He uses as an example the natural tendency of human beings to limit the size of their social groups to a dozen or so individuals. He suggests that this tendency is a result of our history as hunters, in that this number of people proved to be the largest that a hunting coalition could optimally support.

Can you identify opposing forces within yourself? For example, are you outwardly an introvert and internally an extrovert, or vice versa? Which of the four ways of relating to the world dominates your activities?

_____

_____

_____

_____

7. Summarize Carl Jung's ideas about human motivation.

_____

_____

_____

_____

FROMM'S IDEAS

Erich Fromm has a somewhat different view of human motivation. He believes that humanity has alienated itself from nature, and that as a result individuals feel isolated and independent of others. This freedom produces feelings of insecurity: The freer people are, the lonelier and more anxious they become. To overcome their insecurity, people want to suppress their individuality and avoid freedom. In doing this, an individual can choose to be a nonproductive person or a productive person.

According to Fromm, there are four kinds of nonproductive people: hoarding, exploitative, receptive, and marketing. (You might remember these categories by using the mnemonic HERM.) Hoarders are misers; they jealously guard what they have and give nothing. Exploitative individuals use others; they are aggressive and will lie, cheat, steal, or trick to get what they want. Receptive people are dependent; seeing nothing of value in themselves, they depend on others. Marketing individuals are for sale: What you want them to be, they will be; their success is measured by your acceptance.

An individual who is able to reject these styles may become productive. Before this goal can be reached, however, a person must experience self-love, though not in a narcissistic way. Fromm refers to self-respect and self-esteem. Before you can offer love to others and be loved, you must have enough respect for yourself so you will not be defensive, as nonproductive people are. A productive person can view the world openly and realistically without fear and defensiveness. Life is not a threat to a productive individual; it is something to be cherished.

Do you know any hoarding, exploitative, receptive, or marketing people? Describe them in the space that follows.

Hoarding_____

_____

Exploitative_____

_____

Receptive_____

_____

Marketing_____

_____

8. *Explain Erich Fromm's ideas about freedom and his distinction between productive and nonproductive people.*

_____

_____

_____

_____

MASLOW'S HIERARCHY OF NEEDS

Psychosocial theorists such as Adler, Jung, and Fromm emphasize humanity's inborn desire to improve itself, to raise itself above its animal nature. Abraham Maslow, another member of this group, has defined the needs a person must satisfy and has arranged them in an order of increasing importance (see Figure 2.1). At the first (lowest) level of Maslow's hierarchy are physiological needs. When these have been satisfied, safety needs—the desire for security and protection—emerge. At the next level are love and belonging—the need for friendship and acceptance. As this need is met, self-esteem becomes an important motive. At the top of Maslow's hierarchy is self-actualization—the desire to function at one's highest level, to learn for the sake of learning.

From studying eminent historical figures such as Abraham Lincoln, Ludwig van Beethoven, Albert Einstein, and Eleanor Roosevelt, Maslow was able to draw up a description of self-actualized people. Such people are able to perceive reality effectively, judging others accurately and tolerating uncertainty. They

FIGURE 2.1   MASLOW'S HIERARCHY OF NEEDS

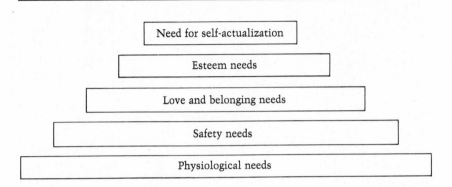

Adapted from A. H. Maslow, "A Theory of Human Motivation," *Psychological Review* 50(1943): 370–396. Copyright 1943 by the American Psychological Association and reproduced by permission.

accept themselves. They show spontaneity. They are problem centered, not ego centered. They need privacy and can look at life with detachment. They are relatively independent of their culture and society but are not nonconformists for the sake of being different. They appreciate the basic experiences of life. Many have had mystical experiences. They have a social interest and identify with humanity as a whole. They are capable of maintaining intense interpersonal relationships. They are democratic and respect all people. They are able to enjoy the means to ends and can differentiate between the two. They have a sense of humor that tends to be philosophical and not hostile. They are creative, being both original and productive. They do not comply blindly with the demands of their culture.

Try to remember what you did between the hours of seven and ten last night. In the space that follows, list your actions and after each action indicate which need in Maslow's hierarchy was being satisfied. For example, does taking a shower meet a physical need or a need for security (to avoid being condemned by others for smelling bad)? Remember that the desire to learn, if it is to be considered an aspect of self-actualization, must be completely voluntary. Studying because of pressure of any kind is not a search for knowledge. When you have finished your list, determine the average level on which you were operating.

Renowned cellist Pablo Casals, a self-actualized person. (Paul Conklin)

Look at Maslow's description of the self-actualized person. In the spaces that follow, list the characteristics of such a person. Then after each characteristic check the rating that best applies to yourself.

	Most like me		Somewhat like me		Least like me
	1	2	3	4	5
1. _____	_____				
2. _____	_____				

	Most like me		Somewhat like me		Least like me
	1	2	3	4	5

3. _____   _____

4. _____   _____

5. _____   _____

6. _____   _____

7. _____   _____

8. _____   _____

9. _____   _____

10. _____   _____

11. _____   _____

12. _____   _____

13. _____   _____

14. _____   _____

15. _____   _____

9. Describe Abraham Maslow's hierarchy of needs.

_____

_____

_____

_____

A COMPARISON OF ADLER, JUNG, FROMM, AND MASLOW

Although the theories of Adler, Jung, Fromm, and Maslow differ in important ways, parts of the theories seem to be alike. All stress that people must have a purpose and that they have an inborn urge to improve themselves. Each theorist uses a different term to describe the attainment of full potential but is expressing the same thought. Adler, Jung, Fromm, and Maslow emphasize the interaction of people in society. They acknowledge the existence of biological urges but discount their force. They have an optimistic view of humanity; they believe people can and do try to improve themselves. Jung differs a little from the others because he sees human effort at self-betterment as an internal struggle; Adler, Fromm, and Maslow consider the conflict to be between human beings and their environment. They all reject the Freudian belief in the overriding power of the sexual urge.

The theories of these four famous psychologists are interesting from a philosophical viewpoint. All reflect a belief in the purposeful nature of humanity. Each maintains that people have in themselves a need to do more than just satisfy their physiological urges. The fundamental goal of human beings, according to these theorists, is to improve. They tie in the idea of becoming a better person with society's definition of *better*. In other words, society is the force behind an individual's internal goal-driven behavior, pointing it in a direction that will bring improvement. Society thus has a big part in the improvement of a person because it defines good and bad. Adler, Jung, Fromm, and Maslow see people engaged in a struggle with their environment, both physical and social, and they see this environment as a bad influence as well as a good one. Although Jung considers the struggle to be primarily an internal one between opposing forces in human beings, he also takes into account social influences with his concept of the collective unconscious. Signs of the duality of human nature put forth by Jung and the opposing forces described by the other theorists can be seen in human religions. Most emphasize the goodness in people but recognize that powerful forces can act to prevent them from becoming good. Religion itself is a social force that tries to overcome evil, so that individuals can reach their goal of self-improvement.

Not only must we decide which forces to follow in order to satisfy our deeply rooted urge to become, in Maslow's words, self-actualized persons; we also must resolve the complication that comes from differing ideas about acceptable behavior held by various groups in our society. Many of the differences are the result of different forces acting on the groups. As we mingle with various groups, we find ourselves being pressured to act in ways that may or may not be agreeable. Knowing that we have urges deep within us makes the problem of whom to listen to as we strive to improve ourselves harder to solve.

10. *Discuss the general philosophical implications of the theories of Adler, Jung, Fromm, and Maslow.*

_____

_____

THE ACHIEVEMENT MOTIVE

The achievement motive has been extensively investigated and has far-reaching implications for other concepts of motivation. David C. McClelland, who has been studying the achievement motive for over twenty years, has defined a strong desire to do one's best as *need achievement*. The first problem he encountered in his research was the lack of a technique by which this need could be measured. Thus McClelland and his associates developed a system to analyze stories made up by individuals in response to stimulus pictures or situations. The stories were analyzed for need achievement, and the results were used to establish an objective scoring system for need achievement.

The results of this research are quite interesting. It was found that people with a high need for achievement are driven individuals. They are not artistically sensitive but are more likely to be concerned with being better, faster, and more efficient. They are competitive but are not gamblers. They like to be challenged.

There is a strong socioeconomic bias in need achievement. Individuals of middle-class backgrounds tend to have a higher level of need achievement than those of lower- and upper-class backgrounds. Executives in smaller industries have a high level of need achievement. However, in larger industries, those on the middle rung of management have the highest level of need achievement.

Need achievement is not automatically transmitted from parent to child. Parents who allow their children more opportunities for exploration and experimentation create a high level of need achievement in their children. Thus need achievement is learned and not innate. In teaching businesspeople all over the world how to acquire a higher level of need achievement, McClelland found that this motive can also be taught later in life.

Profit and wages are not good motivators for people who have a high level of need achievement. Rather, the challenge is what intrigues them. This finding can be extended to apply to cultures as well as individuals. McClelland's research showed that an analysis of the art and literature of a nation could be used to predict that nation's economic rise or fall. Usually a trend in the need-achievement index preceded a corresponding trend in the economic index by about fifty years. An analysis of second-, third-, and fourth-grade readers in the educational systems of various countries allowed a prediction about the economic future of each country. If readers had a high level of need achievement, then a country could be expected to improve its economic status in about twenty years.

Achievement motivation seems to be a reasonable, straightforward explanation of how one particular motive affects the behavior of individuals and their society. However, some follow-up research has shown that need achievement may be more complicated. Another factor involved in need achievement is the probability of failure. When the chances for failure are great, some individuals are adversely affected. This effect, the fear of failure, apparently modifies the strength of need achievement.

If you usually think of success as a probability, then your tendency toward success is a function of your motivation to succeed as acted on by the probability of success and the incentive value of the successful act. If you usually think of failure as a probability, then you will tend to avoid failure. This tendency is a function of your motivation to avoid failure interacting with the probability of failure and the incentive value of that failure. If you combine these two different ways of thinking, then the actual need for achievement is the sum of the tendency to succeed and the tendency to avoid failure. The former is always positive in value and the latter is negative. Thus if the motivation to avoid failure is greater than the motivation to succeed, you will be unlikely to act.

What does this mean? Here is a situation that exemplifies this concept. Listed below are four possible combinations of these two variables: need achievement (n-ach) and fear of failure (FF). Analyze these combinations by predicting where a person with each particular combination would be likely to stand in a game of ring toss; the choices are three, five, seven, nine, and eleven feet from the target. Place an *x* at the distance you believe each person would choose:

	3	*5*	*7*	*9*	*11*
1. High n-ach/high FF					
2. High n-ach/low FF					
3. Low n-ach/high FF					
4. Low n-ach/low FF					

Check your marks against these answers: (1) 7; (2) 11; (3) 3; (4) ?. Why might there be a question mark for combination 4? Think about it. This person really doesn't care. Most of the time he or she would not even be in the game unless forced to play, and even then he or she would probably only go through the motions. By the way, where do you predict you would stand? What does this tell you about the influences of these combinations on decisions such as career choices and other significant problems in life?

11. Explain what is meant by a need for achievement and a fear of failure.

_____

_____

ATTRIBUTION THEORY AND LOCUS OF CONTROL

It is sometimes amusing to follow fads in research. If you examine the topics being researched and reported on over a span of years, you will often find that many researchers have been moving down the same avenue. During the last decade, much research was done on a topic called the *locus of control.* Even today, some research reports revolve around this term. Locus of control refers to the manner in which people perceive responsibility for the results of their efforts. They can see themselves as the masters of their fate, or they can imagine that their fortunes are completely out of their own control.

Research on the locus of control has led to a new approach to motivation: *attribution theory.* Attribution theory considers the perceptions of people who are experiencing success or failure. Two elements are involved in these perceptions: the cognitive realization of what is happening and the emotional element that accompanies it. They affect individuals' need for achievement, their goal expectancies, and the values of those goals. If people are asked to explain what caused their successes or failures, they tend to describe their results along the dimension known as the locus of control. The differences among responses are significant. People with an internal locus of control tend to see their successes or failures as the consequences of their own actions and characteristics. People with an external locus of control tend to credit or blame outside forces. Four factors are usually cited in explaining success or failure: personal ability, task difficulty, personal effort, and luck. Ability and effort are personal in nature, but task difficulty and luck are external. Personal ability and task difficulty are stable factors, whereas effort and luck are variable. People who have a good self-image tend to attribute events to an internal locus of control, whereas those with less self-regard tend to credit or blame outside forces.

Success and failure bring on feelings of pride or shame in individuals with an internal locus of control. These people consider two variables: ability and effort. Since ability is considered to be fixed and unchangeable, the only variable they feel they can modify is effort. Thus when people with an internal locus of control fail, they blame themselves for a lack of effort. However, if faced with similar tasks in the future, these people will go on trying because they feel that by working harder they can succeed. In contrast, people with an external locus of control see success or failure as being the result of two fixed factors: task difficulty and ability. Thus if they fail, they will not see any hope of improvement in the future and probably will not persevere.

Attribution theory pays a great deal of attention to the past history of individuals as an explanation and a predictor of future actions. People who have a negative self-image and who blame outside forces for the results of their efforts are much less likely to want to enter into new tasks or to undertake tasks where there has been a history of failure. The key seems to be whether you feel that you have any say about your efforts.

12. Describe attribution theory and locus of control.

_____

_____

_____

_____

CONTRASTING THE THEORIES

You have now learned about three sets of ideas on motivation: the psycho-physiological, the psychosocial, and the cognitive theories. The three types of theory differ in many interesting and significant ways, and by now you should be able to identify those differences.

13. Contrast the three schools of motivational theory.

_____

_____

_____

_____

A PERSONAL CHOICE

Do you favor the psychophysiological theories of human motivation? Or do you find more merit in the psychosocial or the cognitive theories? Distinguish among the theories in your own mind and think about their implications. Then choose the one that appeals most to you.

14. Select the specific theory that is most appealing to you, and explain your reasons for selecting it.

_____

_____

_____

_____

A PERSONAL THEORY

Perhaps you feel that all the theories have good and bad points and that picking one over the others wasn't the right thing to do. Now you can resolve that problem and summarize what you learned in this unit by describing what makes you get up and go.

15. Write your own theory of motivation.

_____

_____

_____

_____

If this unit leaves you a little dissatisfied because you cannot apply what you have learned to yourself, don't worry about it. After you have studied how people learn, how personalities are formed, and some other general topics, we will reconsider motivation. Then you will be able to develop some ideas of how to motivate yourself in what you are doing so that you can do a better job and enjoy it more.

□ A POINT OF VIEW

Regardless of where you are in the study of human behavior, you invariably get back to dealing with motivation. Some psychologists argue that the whole idea of motivation should be done away with because people use it to explain unusual behavior that can't be explained by what they know. Much of the study of motivation has been carried out by industrial psychologists. Motivated workers mean profits for a company. Frederick Herzberg in "One More Time: How Do You Motivate Employees?" deals with a pressing problem in an easy-to-read but thoughtful way. He gives a short history of management's attempts to motivate workers. If motivation interests you, you might look up some of these books:

Albert Bandura and R. H. Waters, *Social Learning and Personality Development* (New York: Holt, Rinehart and Winston, 1963).

Charles N. Cofer and M. H. Appley, *Motivation: Theory and Research* (New York: Wiley, 1964).

Leon Festinger, *A Theory of Cognitive Dissonance* (Stanford, Calif.: Stanford University Press, 1957).

David C. McClelland et al., *The Achievement Motive* (New York: Appleton-Century-Crofts, 1953).

Edward J. Murray, *Motivation and Emotion* (Englewood Cliffs, N.J.: Prentice-Hall, 1964).

Carl R. Rogers, *On Becoming a Person* (Boston: Houghton Mifflin, 1961).

B. F. Skinner, *Science and Human Behavior* (New York: Macmillan, 1953).

Frederick Herzberg, "One More Time: How Do You Motivate Employees?" *Harvard Business Review*, January–February 1968, Copyright © 1967 by the President and Fellows of Harvard College; all rights reserved.

Author's note: I should like to acknowledge the contributions that Robert Ford of the American Telephone and Telegraph Company has made to the ideas expressed in this paper, and in particular to the successful application of these ideas in improving work performance and the job satisfaction of employees.

FREDERICK HERZBERG

ONE MORE TIME: HOW DO YOU MOTIVATE EMPLOYEES?

How many articles, books, speeches, and workshops have pleaded plaintively, "How do I get an employee to do what I want him to do?"

The psychology of motivation is tremendously complex, and what has been unraveled with any degree of assurance is small indeed. But the dismal ratio of knowledge to speculation has not dampened the enthusiasm for new forms of snake oil that are constantly coming on the market, many of them with academic testimonials. Doubtless this article will have no depressing impact on the market for snake oil, but since the ideas expressed in it have been tested in many corporations and other organizations, it will help—I hope—to redress the imbalance in the aforementioned ratio.

"MOTIVATING" WITH KITA

In lectures to industry on the problem, I have found that the audiences are anxious for quick and practical answers, so I will begin with a straightforward, practical formula for moving people.

What is the simplest, surest, and most direct way of getting someone to do something? Ask him? But if he responds that he does not want to do it, then that calls for a psychological consultation to determine the reason for his obstinacy. Tell him? His response shows that he does not understand you, and now an expert in communication methods has to be brought in to show you how to get through to him. Give him a monetary incentive? I do not need to remind the reader of the complexity and difficulty involved in setting up and administering an incentive system. Show him? This means a costly training program. We need a simple way.

Every audience contains the "direct action" manager who shouts, "Kick him!" And this type of manager is right. The surest and least circumlocuted way of getting someone to do something is to kick him in the pants—give him what might be called the KITA.

There are various forms of KITA, and here are some of them:

NEGATIVE PHYSICAL KITA

This is a literal application of the term and was frequently used in the past. It has, however, three major drawbacks: (1) it is inelegant: (2) it contradicts the precious image of benevolence that most organizations cherish; and (3) since it is a physical attack, it directly stimulates the autonomic nervous system, and this often results in negative feedback—the employee may just kick you in return. These factors give rise to certain taboos against negative physical KITA.

The psychologist has come to the rescue of those who are no longer permitted to use negative physical KITA. He has uncovered infinite sources of psychological vulnerabilities and the appropriate methods to play tunes on them. "He took my rug away"; "I wonder what he meant by that"; "The boss is always going around me"—these symptomatic expressions of ego sores that have been rubbed raw are the result of application of:

NEGATIVE PSYCHOLOGICAL KITA

This has several advantages over negative physical KITA. First, the cruelty is not visible; the bleeding is internal and comes much later. Second, since it affects the higher cortical centers of the brain with its inhibitory powers, it reduces the possibility of physical backlash. Third, since the number of psychological pains that a person can feel is almost infinite, the direction and site possibilities of the KITA are increased many times. Fourth, the person administering the kick can manage to be above it all and let the system accomplish the dirty work. Fifth, those who practice it receive some ego satisfaction (one-upmanship), whereas they would find drawing blood abhorrent. Finally, if the employee does complain, he can always be accused of being paranoid, since there is no tangible evidence of an actual attack.

Now, what does negative KITA accomplish? If I kick you in the rear (physically or psychologically), who is motivated? *I* am motivated; *you*

move! Negative KITA does not lead to motivation, but to movement.

So:

POSITIVE KITA

Let us consider motivation. If I say to you, "Do this for me or the company, and in return I will give you a reward, an incentive, more status, a promotion, all the quid pro quos that exist in the industrial organization," am I motivating you? The overwhelming opinion I receive from management people is, "Yes, this is motivation."

I have a year-old Schnauzer. When it was a small puppy and I wanted it to move, I kicked it in the rear and it moved. Now that I have finished its obedience training, I hold up a dog biscuit when I want the Schnauzer to move. In this instance, who is motivated—I or the dog? The dog wants the biscuit, but it is I who want it to move. Again, I am the one who is motivated, and the dog is the one who moves. In this instance all I did was apply KITA frontally; I exerted a pull instead of a push. When industry wishes to use such positive KITAs, it has available an incredible number and variety of dog biscuits (jelly beans for humans) to wave in front of the employee to get him to jump.

Why is it that managerial audiences are quick to see that negative KITA is *not* motivation, while they are almost unanimous in their judgment that positive KITA *is* motivation? It is because negative KITA is rape, and positive KITA is seduction. But it is infinitely worse to be seduced than to be raped; the latter is an unfortunate occurrence, while the former signifies that you were a party to your own downfall. This is why positive KITA is so popular: it is a tradition; it is in the American way. The organization does not have to kick you; you kick yourself.

MYTHS ABOUT MOTIVATION

Why is KITA not motivation? If I kick my dog (from the front or the back), he will move. And when I want him to move again, what must I do? I must kick him again. Similarly, I can charge a man's battery, and then recharge it, and recharge it again. But it is only when he has his own generator that we can talk about motivation. He then needs no outside stimulation. He *wants* to do it.

With this in mind, we can review some positive KITA personnel practices that were developed as attempts to instill "motivation":

1. *Reducing time spent at work.* This represents a marvelous way of motivating people to work—getting them off the job! We have reduced (formally and informally) the time spent on the job over the last 50 or 60 years until we are finally on the way to the "6½-day weekend." An interesting variant of this approach is the development of off-hour recreation programs. The philosophy here seems to be that those who play together, work together. The fact is that motivated people seek more hours of work, not fewer.

2. *Spiraling wages.* Have these motivated people? Yes, to seek the next wage increase. Some medievalists still can be heard to say that a good depression will get employees moving. They feel that if rising wages don't or won't do the job, perhaps reducing them will.

3. *Fringe benefits.* Industry has outdone the most welfare-minded of welfare states in dispensing cradle-to-the-grave succor. One company I know of had an informal "fringe benefit of the month club" going for a while. The cost of fringe benefits in this country has reached approximately 25% of the wage dollar, and we still cry for motivation.

People spend less time working for more money and more security than ever before, and the trend cannot be reversed. These benefits are no longer rewards; they are rights. A 6-day week is inhuman, a 10-hour day is exploitation, extended medical coverage is a basic decency, and stock options are the salvation of American initiative. Unless the ante is continuously raised, the psychological reaction of employees is that the company is turning back the clock.

When industry began to realize that both the economic nerve and the lazy nerve of their employees had insatiable appetites, it started to listen to the behavioral scientists who, more out of a humanist tradition than from scientific study, criticized management for not knowing how to deal with people. The next KITA easily followed.

4. *Human relations training.* Over 30 years of teaching and, in many instances, of practicing psychological approaches to handling people have resulted in costly human relations programs and, in the end, the same question: How do you motivate workers? Here, too, escalations have taken place. Thirty years ago it was necessary to request, "Please don't spit on the floor." Today the same admonition requires three "please"s before the employee feels that his superior has demonstrated the psychologically proper attitudes toward him.

The failure of human relations training to produce motivation led to the conclusion that the supervisor or manager himself was not psychologically true to himself in his practice of interpersonal decency. So an advanced form of human relations KITA, sensitivity training, was unfolded.

5. *Sensitivity training.* Do you really, really understand yourself? Do you really, really, really trust the other man? Do you really, really, really, really cooperate? The failure of sensitivity training is now being explained, by those who have become opportunistic exploiters of the technique, as a failure to really (five times) conduct proper sensitivity training courses.

With the realization that there are only temporary gains from comfort and economic and interpersonal KITA, personnel managers concluded that the fault lay not in what they were doing, but in the employee's failure to appreciate what they were doing. This opened up the field of communications, a whole new area of "scientifically" sanctioned KITA.

6. *Communications.* The professor of communications was invited to join the faculty of management training programs and help in making employees understand what management was doing for them. House organs, briefing sessions, supervisory instruction on the

importance of communication, and all sorts of propaganda have proliferated until today there is even an International Council of Industrial Editors. But no motivation resulted, and the obvious thought occurred that perhaps management was not hearing what the employees were saying. That led to the next KITA.

7. *Two-way communication*. Management ordered morale surveys, suggestion plans, and group participation programs. Then both employees and management were communicating and listening to each other more than ever, but without much improvement in motivation.

The behavioral scientists began to take another look at their conceptions and their data, and they took human relations one step further. A glimmer of truth was beginning to show through in the writings of the so-called higher-order-need psychologists. People, so they said, want to actualize themselves. Unfortunately, the "actualizing" psychologists got mixed up with the human relations psychologists, and a new KITA emerged.

8. *Job participation*. Though it may not have been the theoretical intention, job participation often became a "give them the big picture" approach. For example, if a man is tightening 10,000 nuts a day on an assembly line with a torque wrench, tell him he is building a Chevrolet. Another approach had the goal of giving the employee a *feeling* that he is determining, in some measure, what he does on his job. The goal was to provide a *sense* of achievement rather than a substantive achievement in his task. Real achievement, of course, requires a task that makes it possible.

But still there was no motivation. This led to the inevitable conclusion that the employees must be sick, and therefore to the next KITA.

9. *Employee counseling*. The initial use of this form of KITA in a systematic fashion can be credited to the Hawthorne experiment of the Western Electric Company during the early 1930's. At that time, it was found that the employees harbored irrational feelings that were interfering with the rational operation of the factory. Counseling in this instance was a means of letting the employees unburden themselves by talking to someone about their problems. Although the counseling techniques were primitive, the program was large indeed.

The counseling approach suffered as a result of experiences during World War II, when the programs themselves were found to be interfering with the operation of the organizations; the counselors had forgotten their role of benevolent listeners and were attempting to do something about the problems that they heard about. Psychological counseling, however, has managed to survive the negative impact of World War II experiences and today is beginning to flourish with renewed sophistication. But, alas, many of these programs, like all the others, do not seem to have lessened the pressure of demands to find out how to motivate workers.

Since KITA results only in short-term movement, it is safe to predict that the cost of these programs will increase steadily and new varieties will be developed as old positive KITAs reach their satiation points.

HYGIENE VS. MOTIVATORS

Let me rephrase the perennial question this way: How do you install a generator in an employee? A brief review of my motivation-hygiene theory of job attitudes is required before theoretical and practical suggestions can be offered. The theory was first drawn from an examination of events in the lives of engineers and accountants. At least 16 other investigations, using a wide variety of populations (including some in the Communist countries), have since been completed, making the original research one of the most replicated studies in the field of job attitudes.

The findings of these studies, along with corroboration from many other investigations using different procedures, suggest that the factors involved in producing job satisfaction (and motivation) are separate and distinct from the factors that lead to job dissatisfaction. Since separate factors need to be considered, depending on whether job satisfaction or job dissatisfaction is being examined, it follows that these two feelings are not opposites of each other. The opposite of job satisfaction is not job dissatisfaction but, rather, *no* job satisfaction; and, similarly, the opposite of job dissatisfaction is not job satisfaction, but *no* job dissatisfaction.

Stating the concept presents a problem in semantics, for we normally think of satisfaction and dissatisfaction as opposites—i.e., what is not satisfying must be dissatisfying, and vice versa. But when it comes to understanding the behavior of people in their jobs, more than a play on words is involved.

Two different needs of man are involved here. One set of needs can be thought of as stemming from his animal nature—the built-in drive to avoid pain from the environment, plus all the learned drives which become conditioned to the basic biological needs. For example, hunger, a basic biological drive, makes it necessary to earn money, and then money becomes a specific drive. The other set of needs relates to that unique human characteristic, the ability to achieve and, through achievement, to experience psychological growth. The stimuli for the growth needs are tasks that induce growth; in the industrial setting, they are the *job content*. Contrariwise, the stimuli inducing pain-avoidance behavior are found in the *job environment*.

The growth or *motivator* factors that are intrinsic to the job are: achievement, recognition for achievement, the work itself, responsibility, and growth or advancement. The dissatisfaction-avoidance or *hygiene* (KITA) factors that are extrinsic to the job include: company policy and administration, supervision, interpersonal relationships, working conditions, salary, status, and security.

A composite of the factors that are involved in causing job satisfaction and job dissatisfaction, drawn from samples of 1,685 employees, is shown in Exhibit 1. The results indicate that motivators were the primary cause of satisfaction, and hygiene factors the primary cause of unhappiness on the job. The employees, studied in 12 different investigations, included lower-level supervisors, professional women, agricultural administrators, men about to retire from management positions, hospital maintenance personnel, manufacturing supervisors, nurses, food handlers, military officers, engineers, scientists, housekeepers, teachers, technicians, female assemblers, accountants, Finnish foremen, and Hungarian engineers.

They were asked what job events had occurred in their work that had led to extreme satisfaction or extreme dissatisfaction on their part. Their responses are broken down in the exhibit into percentages of total "positive" job events and of total "negative" job events. (The figures total more than 100% on both the "hygiene" and "motivators" sides because often at least two factors can be attributed to a single event; advancement, for instance, often accompanies assumption of responsibility.)

To illustrate, a typical response involving achievement that had a negative effect for the employee was, "I was unhappy because I didn't do the job successfully." A typical response in the small number of positive job events in the Company Policy and Administration grouping was, "I was happy because the company reorganized the section so that I didn't report any longer to the guy I didn't get along with."

As the lower left-hand part of the exhibit shows, of all the factors contributing to job satisfaction, 81% were motivators. And of all the factors contributing to the employees' dissatisfaction over their work, 69% involved hygiene elements.

ETERNAL TRIANGLE

There are three general philosophies of personnel management. The first is based on organizational theory, the second on industrial engineering, and the third on behavioral science.

The organizational theorist believes that human needs are either so irrational or so varied and adjustable to specific situations that the

EXHIBIT 1   FACTORS AFFECTING JOB ATTITUDES, AS REPORTED IN 12 INVESTIGATIONS

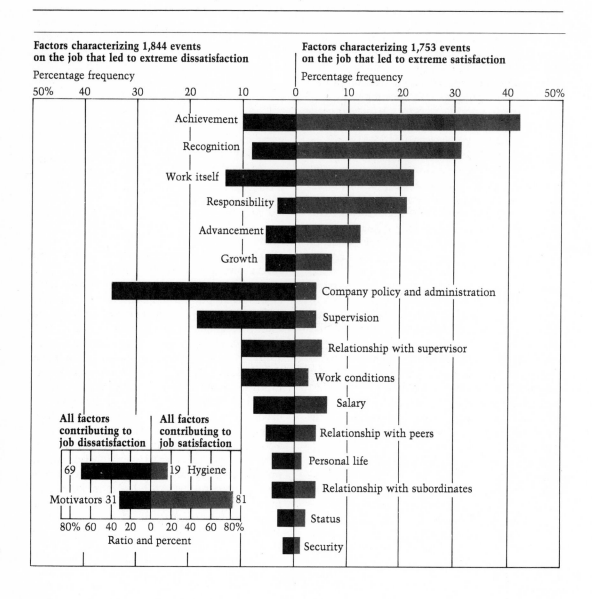

Factors characterizing 1,844 events on the job that led to extreme dissatisfaction

Percentage frequency

Factors characterizing 1,753 events on the job that led to extreme satisfaction

Percentage frequency

Achievement

Recognition

Work itself

Responsibility

Advancement

Growth

Company policy and administration

Supervision

Relationship with supervisor

Work conditions

Salary

Relationship with peers

Personal life

Relationship with subordinates

Status

Security

All factors contributing to job dissatisfaction

All factors contributing to job satisfaction

69   19 Hygiene

Motivators 31   81

Ratio and percent

major function of personnel management is to be as pragmatic as the occasion demands. If jobs are organized in a proper manner, he reasons, the result will be the most efficient job structure, and the most favorable job attitudes will follow as a matter of course.

The industrial engineer holds that man is mechanistically oriented and economically motivated and his needs are best met by attuning the individual to the most efficient work process. The goal of personnel management therefore should be to concoct the most appropriate incentive system and to design the specific working conditions in a way that facilitates the most efficient use of the human machine. By structuring jobs in a manner that leads to the most efficient operation, the engineer believes that he can obtain the optimal organization of work and the proper work attitudes.

The behavioral scientist focuses on group sentiments, attitudes of individual employees, and the organization's social and psychological climate. According to his persuasion, he emphasizes one or more of the various hygiene and motivator needs. His approach to personnel management generally emphasizes some form of human relations education, in the hope of instilling healthy employee attitudes and an organizational climate which he considers to be felicitous to human values. He believes that proper attitudes will lead to efficient job and organizational structure.

There is always a lively debate as to the overall effectiveness of the approaches of the organizational theorist and the industrial engineer. Manifestly they have achieved much. But the nagging question for the behavioral scientist has been: What is the cost in human problems that eventually cause more expense to the organization—for instance, turnover, absenteeism, errors, violation of safety rules, strikes, restriction of output, higher wages, and greater fringe benefits? On the other hand, the behavioral scientist is hard put to document much manifest improvement in personnel management, using his approach.

The three philosophies can be depicted as a

EXHIBIT 2 "TRIANGLE" OF PHILOSOPHIES OF PERSONNEL MANAGEMENT

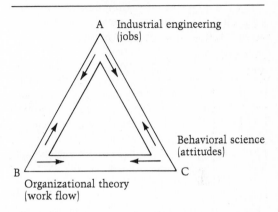

triangle, as is done in Exhibit 2, with each persuasion claiming the apex angle. The motivation-hygiene theory claims the same angle as industrial engineering, but for opposite goals. Rather than rationalizing the work to increase efficiency, the theory suggests that work be *enriched* to bring about effective utilization of personnel. Such a systematic attempt to motivate employees by manipulating the motivator factors is just beginning.

The term *job enrichment* describes this embryonic movement. An older term, job enlargement, should be avoided because it is associated with past failures stemming from a misunderstanding of the problem. Job enrichment provides the opportunity for the employee's psychological growth, while job enlargement merely makes a job structurally bigger. Since scientific job enrichment is very new, this article only suggests the principles and practical steps that have recently emerged from several successful experiments in industry.

JOB LOADING

In attempting to enrich an employee's job, management often succeeds in reducing the man's personal contribution, rather than giving him an opportunity for growth in his accustomed job. Such an endeavor, which I shall call horizontal job loading (as opposed to vertical loading, or providing motivator factors), has been the problem of earlier job enlargement programs. This activity merely enlarges the meaninglessness of the job. Some examples of this approach, and their effect, are:

Challenging the employee by increasing the amount of production expected of him. If he tightens 10,000 bolts a day, see if he can tighten 20,000 bolts a day. The arithmetic involved shows that multiplying zero by zero still equals zero.

Adding another meaningless task to the existing one, usually some routine clerical activity. The arithmetic here is adding zero to zero.

Rotating the assignments of a number of jobs that need to be enriched. This means washing dishes for a while, then washing silverware. The arithmetic is substituting one zero for another zero.

Removing the most difficult parts of the assignment in order to free the worker to accomplish more of the less challenging assignments. This traditional industrial engineering approach amounts to subtraction in the hope of accomplishing addition.

These are common forms of horizontal loading that frequently come up in preliminary brainstorming sessions on job enrichment. The principles of vertical loading have not all been worked out as yet, and they remain rather general, but I have furnished seven useful starting points for consideration in Exhibit 3.

EXHIBIT 3   PRINCIPLES OF VERTICAL JOB LOADING

Principle	Motivators involved
A. Removing some controls while retaining accountability	Responsibility and personal achievement
B. Increasing the accountability of individuals for own work	Responsibility and recognition
C. Giving a person a complete natural unit of work (module, division, area, and so on)	Responsibility, achievement, and recognition
D. Granting additional authority to an employee in his activity; job freedom	Responsibility, achievement, and recognition
E. Making periodic reports directly available to the worker himself rather than to the supervisor	Internal recognition
F. Introducing new and more difficult tasks not previously handled	Growth and learning
G. Assigning individuals specific or specialized tasks, enabling them to become experts	Responsibility, growth, and advancement

A SUCCESSFUL APPLICATION

An example from a highly successful job enrichment experiment can illustrate the distinction between horizontal and vertical loading of a job. The subjects of this study were the stockholder correspondents employed by a very large corporation. Seemingly, the task required of these carefully selected and highly trained correspon-dents was quite complex and challenging. But almost all indexes of performance and job attitudes were low, and exit interviewing confirmed that the challenge of the job existed merely as words.

A job enrichment project was initiated in the form of an experiment with one group, designated as an achieving unit, having its job enriched by the principles described in Exhibit 3. A control group continued to do its job in the traditional way. (There were also two "uncommitted" groups of correspondents formed to measure the so-called Hawthorne Effect—that is, to gauge whether productivity and attitudes toward the job changed artificially merely because employees sensed that the company was paying more attention to them in doing something different or novel. The results for these groups were substantially the same as for the control group, and for the sake of simplicity I do not deal with them in this summary.) No changes in hygiene were introduced for either group other than those that would have been made anyway, such as normal pay increases.

The changes for the achieving unit were introduced in the first two months, averaging one per week of the seven motivators listed in Exhibit 3. At the end of six months the members of the achieving unit were found to be outperforming their counterparts in the control group, and in addition indicated a marked increase in their liking for their jobs. Other results showed that the achieving group had lower absenteeism and, subsequently, a much higher rate of promotion.

Exhibit 4 illustrates the changes in performance, measured in February and March, before the study period began, and at the end of each month of the study period. The shareholder service index represents quality of letters, including accuracy of information, and speed of response to stockholders' letters of inquiry. The index of a current month was averaged into the average of the two prior months, which means that improvement was harder to obtain if the indexes of the previous months were low. The "achievers" were performing less well before the six-month period started, and their performance service index continued to decline after the introduction of the motivators, evidently because of uncertainty over their newly granted responsibilities. In the third month, however, performance improved, and soon the members of this group had reached a high level of accomplishment.

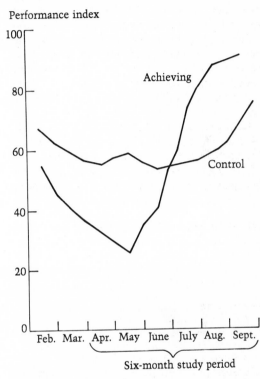

Exhibit 5 shows the two groups' attitudes toward their job, measured at the end of March, just before the first motivator was introduced, and again at the end of September. The correspondents were asked 16 questions, all involving motivation. A typical one was, "As you see it, how many opportunities do you feel that you have in your job for making worthwhile contributions?" The answers were scaled from 1 to 5, with 80 as the maximum possible score. The achievers became much more positive about their job, while the attitude of the control unit remained about the same (the drop is not statistically significant).

How was the job of these correspondents restructured? Exhibit 6 lists the suggestions made that were deemed to be horizontal loading, and the actual vertical loading changes that were incorporated in the job of the achieving unit. The capital letters under "Principle" after "Vertical loading" refer to the corresponding letters in Exhibit 3. The reader will note that the rejected forms of horizontal loading correspond closely to the list of common manifestations of the phenomenon on page 62.

STEPS TO JOB ENRICHMENT

Now that the motivator idea has been described in practice, here are the steps that managers should take in instituting the principle with their employees:

1. Select those jobs in which (a) the investment in industrial engineering does not make changes too costly, (b) attitudes are poor, (c) hygiene is becoming very costly, and (d) motivation will make a difference in performance.
2. Approach these jobs with the conviction that they can be changed. Years of tradition have led managers to believe that the content of the jobs is sacrosanct and the only scope of action that they have is in ways of stimulating people.
3. Brainstorm a list of changes that may enrich the jobs, without concern for their practicality.
4. Screen the list to eliminate suggestions that involve hygiene, rather than actual motivation.
5. Screen the list for generalities, such as "give them more responsibility," that are rarely followed in practice. This might seem obvious, but the motivator words have never left industry; the substance has just been rationalized and organized out. Words like "responsibility," "growth," "achievement," and "challenge," for example, have been elevated to the lyrics of the patriotic anthem for all organizations. It is the old problem typified by the pledge of allegiance to the flag being more important than

EXHIBIT 5   CHANGES IN ATTITUDES TOWARD TASKS IN COMPANY EXPERIMENT (CHANGES IN MEAN SCORES OVER 6-MONTH PERIOD)

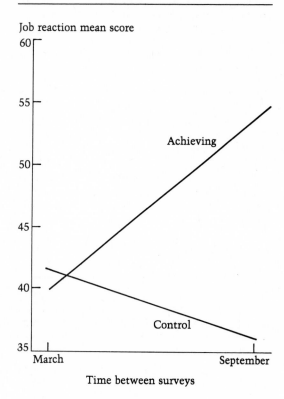

Job reaction mean score

contributions to the country—of following the form, rather than the substance.

6. Screen the list to eliminate any *horizontal* loading suggestions.
7. Avoid direct participation by the employees whose jobs are to be enriched. Ideas they have expressed previously certainly constitute a valuable source for recommended changes, but their direct involvement contaminates the process with human relations *hygiene* and, more specifically, gives them only a *sense* of making a contribution. The job is to be changed, and it is the content that will produce the motivation, not attitudes about being involved or the challenge

EXHIBIT 6 ENLARGEMENT VS. ENRICHMENT OF CORRESPONDENTS' TASKS IN COMPANY EXPERIMENT

Horizontal loading suggestions (rejected)	Vertical loading suggestions (adopted)	Principle
Firm quotas could be set for letters to be answered each day, using a rate which would be hard to reach.	Subject matter experts were appointed within each unit for other members of the unit to consult with before seeking supervisory help. (The supervisor had been answering all specialized and difficult questions.)	G
The women could type the letters themselves, as well as compose them, or take on any other clerical functions.	Correspondents signed their own names on letters. (The supervisor had been signing all letters.)	B
All difficult or complex inquiries could be channeled to a few women so that the remainder could achieve high rates of output. These jobs could be exchanged from time to time.	The work of the more experienced correspondents was proofread less frequently by supervisors and was done at the correspondents' desks, dropping verification from 100% to 10%. (Previously, all correspondents' letters had been checked by the supervisor.)	A
The women could be rotated through units handling different customers, and then sent back to their own units.	Production was discussed, but only in terms such as "a full day's work is expected." As time went on, this was no longer mentioned. (Before, the group had been constantly reminded of the number of letters that needed to be answered.)	D
	Outgoing mail went directly to the mailroom without going over supervisors' desks. (The letters had always been routed through the supervisors.)	A
	Correspondents were encouraged to answer letters in a more personalized way. (Reliance on the form-letter approach had been standard practice.)	C
	Each correspondent was held personally responsible for the quality and accuracy of letters. (This responsibility had been the province of the supervisor and the verifier.)	B, E

inherent in setting up a job. That process will be over shortly, and it is what the employees will be doing from then on that will determine their motivation. A sense of participation will result only in short-term movement.

8. In the initial attempts at job enrichment, set up a controlled experiment. At least two equivalent groups should be chosen, one an experimental unit in which the motivators are systematically introduced over a period of time, and the other one a control group in which no changes are made. For both groups, hygiene should be allowed to follow its natural course for the duration of the experiment. Pre- and post-installation tests of performance and job attitudes are necessary to evaluate the effectiveness of the job

enrichment program. The attitude test must be limited to motivator items in order to divorce the employee's view of the job he is given from all the surrounding hygiene feelings that he might have.

9. Be prepared for a drop in performance in the experimental group the first few weeks. The changeover to a new job may lead to a temporary reduction in efficiency.

10. Expect your first-line supervisors to experience some anxiety and hostility over the changes you are making. The anxiety comes from their fear that the changes will result in poorer performance for their unit. Hostility will arise when the employees start assuming what the supervisors regard as their own responsibility for performance. The supervisor without checking duties to perform may then be left with little to do.

After a successful experiment, however, the supervisor usually discovers the supervisory and managerial functions he has neglected, or which were never his because all his time was given over to checking the work of his subordinates. For example, in the R&D division of one large chemical company I know of, the supervisors of the laboratory assistants were theoretically responsible for their training and evaluation. These functions, however, had come to be performed in a routine, unsubstantial fashion. After the job enrichment program, during which the supervisors were not merely passive observers of the assistants' performance, the supervisors actually were devoting their time to reviewing performance and administering thorough training.

What has been called an employee-centered style of supervision will come about not through education of supervisors, but by changing the jobs that they do.

CONCLUDING NOTE

Job enrichment will not be a one-time proposition, but a continuous management function. The initial changes, however, should last for a very long period of time. There are a number of reasons for this:

The changes should bring the job up to the level of challenge commensurate with the skill that was hired.

Those who have still more ability eventually will be able to demonstrate it better and win promotion to higher-level jobs.

The very nature of motivators, as opposed to hygiene factors, is that they have a much longer-term effect on employees' attitudes. Perhaps the job will have to be enriched again, but this will not occur as frequently as the need for hygiene.

Not all jobs can be enriched, nor do all jobs need to be enriched. If only a small percentage of the time and money that is now devoted to hygiene, however, were given to job enrichment efforts, the return in human satisfaction and economic gain would be one of the largest dividends that industry and society have ever reaped through their efforts at better personnel management.

The argument for job enrichment can be summed up quite simply: If you have someone on a job, use him. If you can't use him on the job, get rid of him, either via automation or by selecting someone with lesser ability. If you can't use him and you can't get rid of him, you will have a motivation problem.

UNIT 3

PERSONALITY

□ You have no doubt heard someone say, "She has such a pleasant personality." If you were part of the conversation, you probably nodded your head and said something like, "Yes, she certainly has." What is infuriating to a psychologist is that both of you understood each other perfectly. Poor harassed psychologists, however, can't even agree on what the term *personality* means. As scientists, they have imposed on themselves a requirement to be able to measure their definitions. This no one has been able to do—at least to everyone's satisfaction—especially when defining personality.

This situation leads to a paradox. The word *personality* actually means something. It can mean the way you look at yourself. It can also mean how other people look at you or how you look at other people. Each of these definitions implies a different way of viewing and measuring personality. Not only is there a problem of measurement, there is a problem of approach. Some psychologists have interested themselves in how personality develops. Others consider how a personality acts, not worrying about where it comes from. Others examine the makeup of a personality. The paradox is that personality means so many things to so many different people that no single meaning can adequately define the word.

In this unit you will examine several theories about what personality is. You will learn about Sigmund Freud's ideas on the developmental and dynamic aspects of personality. You will also read about Erik H. Erikson's differences with Freud and about his own ideas on psychosocial development. Then you will have a chance to study a way of analyzing personality by breaking it down into parts. People's own impressions of themselves and the effects of these impressions on their behavior will be discussed. Finally, you will be given two exercises by which you can measure certain parts of your own personality.

When you have completed this unit, you should be able to:

1. *Summarize the theoretical basis that underlies Freud's ideas on the development of the personality.*
2. *List the stages of development that Freud described, and state the learning products that occur in each stage.*
3. *Explain Freud's Oedipus and Electra complexes.*
4. *Contrast Freud's and Erikson's ideas on the development of personality.*
5. *List the eight ages of man that Erikson described, and state the crisis that has to be resolved in each stage.*
6. *Explain what a trait theory of personality is.*
7. *State Gordon Allport's definition of personality and describe his traits theory.*
8. *Summarize Harry Stack Sullivan's theory of interpersonal relationships.*
9. *Explain what a self-concept is: how it originates, develops, changes, and functions.*
10. *Diagram a self and explain its parts.*
11. *Explain the relationships of the three selves.*
12. *Explain Freud's view of personality dynamics: how the id, ego, and superego develop and interrelate.*

13. *Contrast the major implications of the developmental theories, the trait theories, and the self theories of personality.*
14. *Decide which of the major schools of personality theory most appeals to you and defend your choice.*
15. *Describe your own personality, using the evidence you have gathered about yourself so far.*

PERSONALITY DEVELOPMENT ACCORDING TO FREUD

When Freud was mulling over his theory of human behavior, he had several problems to consider. First of all, he needed to explain what forces work on people, what makes them tick. Then he had to explain how people develop; what forces operate on individuals to shape them into socially functioning people. He also had to explain how people interact with others and with their environment. Thus his theory of personality dealt with three areas: motivation, development, and the dynamics of human behavior.

As Freud considered the nature of development, he had to include in his theorizing a conceptualization of what motivates people. Freud's ideas on motivating forces stressed basic physiological urges—in particular the sexual urge, which he thought overwhelms all others. If you think about it, you can see Freud's problem. How do you explain infant behavior in sexual terms? And how do you trace the development of a personality from birth to maturity in these terms?

Freud could have explained development in several ways. He could have agreed with a popular theory, the homunculus concept, which said that children are miniature adults. From birth on, all they need is the right nourishment, and their personalities will unfold into full-grown adult types, much as the rosebud unfolds. Or he could have compared the growth of personality to the growth of a pearl in an oyster. A solution of chemicals constantly washes the growing pearl, depositing thin layers on its outside. In this manner, the pearl grows in a continuous process from a tiny seed into full size, its development depending on the quality and quantity of its surrounding environment.

However, Freud discarded these ideas in favor of a theory that describes the growth of a personality as a series of steps or stages. Each stage is distinct, and the order of progression through each is fixed. In each, certain significant kinds of experience occur. The experiences are based in part on the environment in which the growing person lives and its effects on that person. The environment can be painful or pleasant. However, painful experiences can also come from inside the person as he or she reacts to the outside and interprets those reactions. Painful experiences may create feelings of inadequacy that, in turn, may create anxiety. In this analysis of the forces that bear on a person, Freud emphasized the effects of frustration, inadequacy, conflict, and anxiety. He felt that the way a person responds to these hostile forces shapes personality.

In order to describe sexual urges in children and to relate those drives to their reactions to their environments, Freud described the stages of personality development in terms of the growth of the sexual instinct. He believed that the way in which an adult responds to sexual instinct forms personality. He described what he called erogenous zones—parts of the body that give pleasure when stimulated. These zones shift as the person matures, creating new areas of sexual sensitivity to which the person responds. Thus, at different times in life, the person is responding to the search for pleasure and the avoidance of pain in different ways, depending on where his or her erogenous zone happens to be. The shifting gives each of us the ability to learn different ways of interacting with the world as we progress through the stages of growth. It also is a neat way of solving the problem of describing the operation of the sexual instinct in children. You'll see that Freud stressed the effect of early childhood experiences on the molding of the adult. He believed that early conflicts, frustrations, and painful experiences have a deep and lasting effect on the individual. In his treatments he made a great point of asking his patients to recall their developmental stages to uncover these incidents. Freud felt that the behavior of the adult could best be understood and changed by learning about the frustrations and the conflicts that the person had experienced as his or her personality was developing.

1. *Summarize the theoretical basis that underlies Freud's ideas on the development of the personality.*

_____

_____

_____

_____

FREUD'S STAGES OF GROWTH

Freud identified five psychosexual stages of growth: oral, anal, phallic, latent, and genital. In each stage a person has a chance to undergo significant experiences that will shape him or her into a certain kind of adult. The names of the stages identify the regions of the body that in turn become sexually sensitive.

In the *oral stage* infants derive sexual pleasure from sucking. Aggressive pleasure can also be obtained from biting or chewing. Oral satisfaction is gained when babies learn to avoid unpleasant-tasting substances by spitting them out. The mouth functions in five ways, or modes: taking in, holding on, biting, spitting out, and closing. Each mode may serve as a model for later adult behavior. Babies who are weaned suddenly may develop a holding-on charac-teristic behavior to overcome traumatic experiences. They may become greedy and insatiable adults. Babies whose mothers discipline them by giving or witholding food may become very dependent people. Babies who take pleasure in biting and chewing may develop many types of aggressive action. Spitting out may lead to a guarded, disdainful, contemptuous character.

In about the second year, the erogenous zone shifts from the mouth to the anus. Infants then obtain pleasure from the release of tension brought about by bowel evacuation. In the *anal stage* of development, infants first experience the process of socialization: toilet training. This period is critical because the parents' handling of toilet training will have a lifelong effect on their child. If they are strict and punitive, the child may be messy, irresponsible, disorderly, and wasteful. Because the child is rebelling against training, he or she will be impatient with order and neatness. If the training is pleasant, the child may grow up to be generous and outgoing. However, if too much emphasis is placed on the bowel movement and the child feels a sense of loss, he or she may become a hoarder and a collector.

The third stage of development is the *phallic stage.* It usually occurs when children are four or five years old. In this stage the erogenous zone shifts to the genitals. This is a crucial period because during it children become aware of sex and sexual differences. This stage marks the beginning of the difference in behavior of boys and girls. In Freudian theory the phallic is the most critical stage because it involves children's recognition of their own sex and guides them into the behaviors that are appropriate to it. It also sets the attitude of children toward sex. The natural practice of masturbation occurs during this stage, as does curiosity about sexual differences. If parents react violently to this exploration for pleasure through masturbation and childish curiosity, they may create feelings of guilt and shame that can seriously warp their children's adult personalities. If children don't learn the behavior that is proper for their sex, or if they are not able to identify themselves properly as belonging to a given sex, trouble can set in. Freud described this problem as the Oedipus-Electra conflict, which will be explained shortly.

From about the age of five until the age of twelve, there seem to be no outward signs of sexual activity. Freud called this the *latency stage.* During this time, children learn from other children of the same age as well as from their own parents. Normally their associations are with members of their own sex. In this period children begin to learn the rules of the game.

The *genital stage* begins at adolescence, when bodily changes bring about sexual maturity. Children's sexual activity begins to shift from a narcissistic interest in themselves to an interest in members of the opposite sex. The fifth and final stage covers courtship and adult life until old age, when there is a regression to the pregenital period.

Each of Freud's five stages of growth may be visualized as a floor in a house that is being constructed. If one of the floors is improperly built (if a person doesn't have the proper experience in a particular stage), the succeeding floors will rest on a distorted platform, and the house (personality) will be distorted. A person may be able to cope with daily affairs, but under severe stress his or her personality may collapse, resulting in regression to a form of behavior typical of the last stage in which that person was comfortable. This idea is probably the most important part of Freud's ideas on development. The other important part is that Freud believed that a person's personality was pretty well formed in the first five years of life.

2. *List the stages of development that Freud described, and state the learning products that occur in each stage.*

_____

_____

_____

_____

THE OEDIPUS-ELECTRA COMPLEX

The process by which children of five recognize their own sex and begin to act according to the social demands that set the proper behaviors for male and female was seen by Freud to be the resolution of a conflict. For both son and daughter, this conflict involves a sexual attraction to the parent of the opposite sex. It operates somewhat differently in male and female, and Freud gave the two conflicts different names to emphasize the difference.

The male conflict is called the *Oedipus complex.* During this conflict the boy develops incestuous desires for his mother. His feelings toward his father change, and he becomes jealous of him. He sees his father as a rival and becomes hostile to him. However, his father is so much bigger and more powerful that the boy fears him. He is afraid that his father will eliminate him as a rival by cutting off his penis. Freud called this fear *castration anxiety.* This anxiety prevents the boy from actively confronting his father. It causes him to give up his feelings for his mother. He adapts to the motto "If you can't beat them; join them." The boy represses his desires for his mother and models himself after his father. The strength of the forces competing within him—his feminine versus his masculine characteristics—is also critical in the process of achieving true sexual identity. If the boy's masculine characteristics are stronger, he will identify with his father. If his feminine feelings are stronger, he may identify with his mother, even though he has given up trying to possess her. The interaction of two forces—the Oedipus complex and castration anxiety on the one hand, and the relative strengths of masculinity and feminity on the other—determines how he will act in later life. In other words, his character and personality will be set by this conflict.

A girl experiences the *Electra complex.* She discovers that she doesn't have a penis. She blames her mother for this and withdraws from her. She is drawn toward her father who has what she wants. Freud called this *penis envy,* and it contrasts with the male's fear of losing his penis. Penis envy is also castration anxiety. The girl becomes attached to her father and is jealous of her mother.

The conflict is resolved through the interaction of the relative strength of the penis envy and the amounts of masculinity and femininity within the girl. The complex dies down in the girl as she gets older and as she realizes the impossibility of having her father as a lover. She normally begins to pattern herself after her mother as the desire for her father dies, although she never fully resolves the conflict. Freud explained the desire for motherhood as the symbolic shifting of the desire for a penis to having a baby, who replaces the lost penis.

One of the most important products of the Oedipus-Electra complex is the formation of the basis for the part of the personality that Freud called the *superego*, which will be described later. This part of the personality includes the conscience. Its development results in part from the resolution of the sexual conflict, because the modeling after the proper parent involves the adoption of the standards of behavior which that parent shows to the child.

3. Explain Freud's Oedipus and Electra complexes.

_____

_____

_____

_____

ERIKSON VERSUS FREUD

One of Freud's students was Erik H. Erikson. As Erikson began his own investigations, he came to disagree with Freud quite strongly. His main objection to Freud's ideas was to their emphasis on sex. Erikson believed that Freud overemphasized the power of the sexual drive and did not give society enough credit for shaping a person's personality. He felt that an individual's interaction with society was much more important than was the biology of sex. This disagreement led him to break with Freud and create his own description of personality development. In contrast to Freud's five psychosexual stages, Erikson defined eight psycho*social* stages. He felt that Freud had ignored an identifiable set of stages beyond adolescence. Erikson's stages of development are more extensive than Freud's and cover a person's life in more detail.

4. Contrast Freud's and Erikson's ideas on the development of personality.

_____

_____

ERIKSON'S EIGHT AGES OF MAN

Erikson identified certain learnings that have to take place in each psychosocial stage and that are thus critical to further development (see Figure 3.1). He
called these learnings *crises* and described the results if the learning crisis was
not overcome. His stages can be described as either/or propositions: Either you
learn what you must or your personality is distorted.

The first period generally runs from birth through the first year. The crisis to
be resolved is one of *trust versus mistrust.* By trust, Erikson means the growth
of confidence through infants' first relationships with the outside world. Their
ease of feeding, the depth of their sleep, and the relaxation of their bowels are
examples of their interactions with the world. The development of trust seems
to depend on the mother-child relationship. Children learn to put up with
frustration because of the feeling of purpose and meaning given to them by
their mothers. Should the crisis of trust not be resolved, children will have a
sense of being deprived or abandoned. In the first crisis, the socializing
influence is the mother.

The second crisis occurs between the ages of twelve and thirty-six months.
Erikson calls it *autonomy versus shame and doubt.* In this period of muscular
development, children need reassurance. They can move and do things on their
own. If they are encouraged, they will develop a sense of autonomy. If they are
shamed for their failures, they experience self-doubt. This stage is decisive in
developing the ratio of love to hate, compromise to willfulness, freedom of
self-expression to its suppression. Children's success in resolving the second
crisis determines whether they will be able to love or to hate, or to love *and*
hate; whether they can adjust to others' demands or stubbornly insist on
having their own way; whether they can give their own opinions to others or
are afraid to speak. Children must learn self-control without the loss of pride
and goodwill. The socializing influences are the parents, both mother and
father.

At the age of four or five, children face their next crisis, *initiative versus
guilt.* In this stage they seem to be full of energy. The doing that led to
autonomy is joined up with planning, undertaking, and attacking tasks, often
just for the sake of activity alone. Children begin to learn the traditional sex
roles. Boys take pleasure in attack and conquest. Girls, on the other hand, act
in the role of the "catcher." This stage involves rivalry with others, aggression,
manipulation, and coercion. The sex roles and genitality, if not properly
provided for, can lead to feelings of guilt over the acts that are thought about
and carried out. With proper guidance, however, this stage can be used to set
the direction toward the goals of active adult life.

Between the ages of six and twelve, children learn *industry versus inferiority.* This is the school age, be the school a classroom, field, or jungle. In this

FIGURE 3.1 ERIKSON'S EIGHT AGES OF MAN

VIII Maturity								Ego integrity vs. despair
VII Adulthood							Genera-tivity vs. stagnation	
VI Young adulthood						Intimacy vs. isolation		
V Puberty and adolescence					Identity vs. role confusion			
IV Latency				Industry vs. inferiority				
III Locomotor-genital			Initiative vs. guilt					
II Muscular-anal		Autonomy vs. shame, doubt						
I Oral sensory	Basic trust vs. mistrust							

Adapted from Erik H. Erikson, *Childhood and Society*, 2nd ed. rev. (New York, 1963), p. 273, by permission of W. W. Norton & Company, Inc. Copyright 1950 © 1963 by W. W. Norton & Company, Inc.

stage, the imagination is tamed and harnessed to the laws of impersonal things. Children become ready to apply themselves to skills and tasks. They develop a sense of industry by learning how to use utensils and tools and a sense of the technology of the world. If they do not succeed, there is the danger that they will feel inadequate and inferior. If they succeed too well, there is the danger that they will become a slave to work. The socializing influence is the school.

Industry versus inferiority is followed by a crisis at the age of adolescence involving the growth of a sense of identity, or, failing this, role confusion. Adolescents not only face the physiological changes of puberty but must fight the battle of personal identification. They become concerned with what they appear to be in the eyes of others as compared to what they feel they are. They have to connect their skills and learnings with occupational roles. They must develop a sense of their own identity, a summary of all they have experienced, and use it in the search for a career. The danger they face is role confusion; they don't know how to act as individuals in their own right or toward what career they should point themselves. If they are not sure of their sexual identity, mental disturbance may result. Their ego identity is built up by interaction with their peers. Ideals and values are tested. Erikson summarized the turbulence and critical nature of the crisis of *identity versus role confusion* by saying, "In order not to become cynically or apathetically lost, young people must somehow be able to convince themselves that those who succeed in their anticipated adult world thereby shoulder the obligation of being the best."

Having successfully established their identities, young adults face another crisis, *intimacy versus isolation.* Between the ages of eighteen and thirty-five, young adults seek to fuse their identities with those of others. In so doing, they must face up to the sacrifices and compromises that are called for in sharing. People demand sexual union in this stage. Sexual avoidance of fresh experiences because of a fear of ego loss may lead to a deep sense of isolation and self-absorption.

Mature individuals, having established themselves in a social group, face a new crisis. They must pass on the culture and institutions of their society to their offspring. Erikson believes that this is a basic necessity and that an older generation needs this relationship with a younger one. If it is not obtained, stagnation occurs and individuals become concerned primarily with their own physical well-being and begin to indulge themselves. This is the crisis of *generativity versus stagnation.*

The last conflict is *ego integrity versus despair.* In old age people are ready to defend the integrity of their lifestyles against all physical and economic threats. They accept their lives as part of an orderly pattern with some spiritual meaning. They accept the thought of death. If they fail to develop this ego integrity, a sharp fear of death occurs; there is a sense that life has been wasted, and despair sets in.

Erikson's final comment on his ages of man is rather revealing: "Trust (the first of our ego values) is here defined as 'the assured reliance on another's integrity, the last of our values.' . . . And it seems possible to further paraphrase the relation of adult integrity and infantile trust by saying that healthy children will not fear life if their elders have integrity enough not to fear death."

5. *List the eight ages of man that Erikson described, and state the crisis that has to be resolved in each stage.*

_____

_____

With old age can come an acceptance of life as part of an orderly pattern with some spiritual meaning. (Globe Photos)

THE TRAITS THEORY OF PERSONALITY

You have been considering how a personality grows. It is now time to shift gears a little and look at some ideas about what a personality is. When we say, "She has a pleasant personality," the word *pleasant* describes a dimension of a personality. Other words could just as easily have been used: *domineering, unpleasant, happy,* and so on. These words describe certain *traits*—ways that a person acts, or a characteristic way of acting. Personality can be described, as you have seen, in terms of a person's typical way of acting. Of course, an individual's behavior may change according to where he or she is. A person may be silent and thoughtful in church, happy and bubbly with friends, and serious and diligent at work. Most of us change to fit into a social situation, so that when we describe someone's behavior, we should also describe the social situation in which the individual is behaving.

Another problem that occurs when we describe a person according to traits is that we often go overboard and say that someone has only one trait, such as an outgoing manner. When we do this, we frequently disregard the possibility that the person is not always outgoing. At times he or she may be shy. Trait descriptions often lead to overgeneralizations about an individual's characteristics.

6. *Explain what a trait theory of personality is.*

_____

_____

_____

_____

ALLPORT'S TRAITS THEORY

Gordon Allport was a leading exponent of the traits theory. He described eight characteristics of traits:

1. They have more than a nominal existence.
2. They are more generalized than habits are.
3. They determine behavior.
4. Their existence may be established empirically.
5. They are only relatively independent of other traits.
6. They are not synonymous with moral or social judgments.
7. They may be viewed in the light of the personality that contains them or in the light of their distribution in the population.
8. Acts and even habits that are inconsistent with a trait are not proof of the nonexistence of the trait.

In his studies, Allport identified 18,000 words that describe traits of human behavior. He classified these traits as *cardinal dispositions* if they dominate a person's entire existence. He termed the small number of traits that happen to be highly characteristic of a person *central dispositions*. If the traits operate in limited situations, he called them *secondary dispositions*.

According to Allport, traits are distributed in a person in a measurable fashion. Therefore, it is possible to find out how much of a trait a person has. For example, how often a person tries to dominate others or how much he or she submits to others can be measured in such a way as to describe that person's tendencies. What makes Allport's theory interesting is that he argues that there is a normal distribution of all traits in a social population. Thus it is possible to measure a trait, such as dominance or submission, in a lot of people. The amounts measured can then be compared with the amounts in the general population. In this way, individuals can be measured against their peers and told where they stand in comparison.

Does this mean that everyone can be measured and typed—that is, is the computer-card approach valid? Not at all, says Allport. Although it is possible to measure certain common traits across the board, each person is an individual package of traits that cannot be measured accurately enough to be typed completely. Allport's definition of personality explains this very carefully: "The personality of an individual consists of the dynamic organization of those traits that determine how he adjusts uniquely to his environment." Because of the word *dynamic*, this definition implies a shifting or changing, which goes back to a previous point: that we change our patterns of behavior to fit our social situations. In his use of the word *uniquely*, Allport was emphasizing that each person has a bundle of traits that is not matched by any other person's. Allport spent much of his life measuring traits and defining personalities in terms of traits, but he was quick to deny that anyone could be totally described by such measurement.

7. *State Gordon Allport's definition of personality and describe his traits theory.*

SULLIVAN'S INTERPERSONAL RELATIONSHIPS THEORY

Gordon Allport's theory is not concerned with where an individual gets traits so much as it is with defining and measuring them. However, many theorists argue that you cannot measure personality in this way because you are ignoring what people think of themselves. Harry Stack Sullivan believed that the ways people acted were influenced by what they thought of themselves. If they believed they were basically good, they would react to situations as they thought a good person would. If they believed they were bad, they would act as they thought a bad person would.

The most important part of Sullivan's theory is his explanation of where our ideas about the self come from. Sullivan believed that they come from our own interpretations of our effects on other people, that interpersonal relationships are the basis for people's notions about themselves. From birth on, a person is constantly interacting with other people. During these interactions, that person is getting information—sometimes openly expressed, more often from subtle, unspoken cues—about how other people appraise him or her. These appraisals form the basis for an individual's self-evaluation.

People, said Sullivan, are motivated by two things: physical urges and personal security. Personal security is based on how comfortable individuals feel about themselves. A good sense of self, "good-me," provides a feeling of well-being, or euphoria. A "bad-me" concept leads to insecurity and may cause a person to be afraid of others. A good self-concept has to be present in order for healthy interpersonal relationships to happen. The most critical time for the establishment of a good self-concept is in early childhood, and the mother is the most important figure in this process.

8. Summarize Harry Stack Sullivan's theory of interpersonal relationships.

_____

_____

_____

_____

THE SELF-CONCEPT

The self-concept is a self-describing expression. It is what people think of themselves. It is an internal view. It is how people see themselves not as they say they are or as other people see them. The theorist Carl Rogers described the self-concept as an individual's whole version of *I* or *me* and how *I* and *me* relate to others and to other parts of life, as well as the values attached to the relationships. This is known as a phenomenological approach because it says that people's behavior is understandable only if we can understand their whole phenomenological field, their past experiences as well as their present interpretations of the situations they are in.

The self develops through experiences with other people, primarily through interpersonal relationships, Sullivan explained. As we develop, we have a very strong need for warmth, being liked, and being accepted. If we get these indications, we begin to fill a secondary need, that of positive self-regard. If your experiences are bad, your self-concept may be a negative one.

As your self-concept forms, you begin to act in ways that are consistent with it. We have an inner need to be consistent, and when we act inconsistently with our own internal versions of ourselves, we build up discomfort. This is perhaps the most important notion in the self-concept idea: Our versions of ourselves dictate how we act. If you see yourself as a "C" student, you will act as a "C" student. If you see yourself as an "A" student, you will act as an "A" student.

Suppose a man has developed a version of himself and has learned to live with it. For example, suppose he thinks he is a good planner, especially in taking care of minute details. Then suddenly he begins to get information (feedback) from his supervisors that his planning ability is not only unimportant but is poor. How can he resolve the conflict between what he thinks of himself and the new feedback? He can begin to change his ideas about himself and say, "Gee, I guess I'm not such a good planner after all." Or he can distort the feedback and make it fit into his established self-concept: "The plan was all right; they just did not do it right." Or: "They're jealous of my work." In other words, when the feedback is inconsistent with the self-concept, a person may change the feedback to fit his or her self-concept. Unfortunately, because the self-concept is not easy to change, this is an all too common way of absorbing inconsistent feedback. People who have spent their whole lives accumulating and filing evidence about themselves into some sort of logical pattern are usually not willing to make a drastic change in their personal evaluations very quickly, unless the feedback comes in massive doses. Even then, some people may crack under the stress of the inconsistent information rather than accept it.

9. *Explain what a self-concept is: how it originates, develops, changes, and functions.*

_____

_____

_____

_____

DIAGRAMMING A SELF

It may be helpful to you, as you grapple with the idea of what a self is, to visualize it. Let's consider the various kinds of information that exist about us. First of all, there is the knowledge that we have shared with others and that others have shared with us. This is what Sullivan was describing in his idea of reflected appraisals. Let's call this S, shared knowledge, known to us and to others. We also have a secret part that we have never shared with anyone. It is made up of our secret dreams, our hopes, our ambitions, our fears, our shame. These unexpressed feelings are known only to us. Let's call them H, hidden, known only to us. There are also all the past experiences and feelings that have been pushed down into our unconscious. These are the unrealized drives and desires of which we are not even aware. Let's label them B, blind, unknown to us. Finally, there is a part of the self also unknown to us. It is expressed in the feelings of others. It is how we rub off on other people, though we don't realize it. It is our social stimulus value to others, and our interpersonal relationships do not give us feedback on it. Let's call this O, for other knowledge. The four letters form the mnemonic BOSH.

Now if you draw a circle, you can fill in the parts to represent the self. Divide the circle into four sections. Label the two quarters on the left side B and O to stand for the unconscious and unknown parts of the self. The two quarters on the right half can be labeled S and H, to represent the self-concept:

This diagram shows the parts of the self as being of the same proportions. Actually this may not be. The B and O parts of the diagram will probably never be measurable, but this does not mean that they cannot be changed. The other parts are somewhat more readily measurable. Just as a matter of curiosity, what proportions would you assign to a diagram of your self? Would you fill it in like this:

or this:

or this?

Diagram your own self-concept here.

In this exercise, the unit formed by B and O was held constant. How do you think its proportions could be changed? What effects would you guess that this change would have on a person's personality?

_____

_____

_____

_____

Psychologists would leap into the air and click their heels with glee at that last question, because it leads into the heart of psychoanalytic treatment. According to Freud, who fathered this technique, we consistently repress matters that are very unpleasant for us. We shove these down into the unconscious, where they lie waiting for a chance to be expressed. Psychoanalysis involves bringing the repressed material into the conscious mind, examining it, and dealing with it. In this way the inner anxieties and the tensions a person feels as a result of his or her repressions are avoided. Does this mean that everyone needs to see a psychoanalyst? Not necessarily. There are other ways to deal with repression. We need to learn to avoid the use of repression in the present and the future. We need to teach ourselves and our children to face and understand conflicts. Understanding can lead to solutions, or at least to acceptance.

This would shrink B. But what about O? Here, those who believe in group therapy would clamor for attention, because the exchanges in group therapy do much to batter down the walls of a person's life space and get that person to learn and to accept how he or she comes across to other people. Again, the question is "Do I have to go into encounter and group-sensitivity sessions to learn how others react to me?" Again, the answer is, "Not necessarily." There are other ways to reach this goal. An exercise that comes along later in this unit turns to this problem, as well as to changing the proportions of the self-concept, the H and the S.

How do you think the diagram of a completely adjusted person would look? Take Fromm's productive person or Maslow's self-actualized person, or use any concept you might have about an adjusted person, and draw that person's diagram here.

Did your diagram fit Sidney Jourard's description of a healthy personality? Jourard was a noted professor of psychology, therapist, and author. He devoted much attention to the definition and description of healthy and unhealthy personalities. He said society calls on us to play certain roles. If we play them satisfactorily, we are considered sound, though not necessarily healthy. Healthy people play their roles satisfactorily and derive personal satisfaction from the role enactment; moreover, they keep growing and maintain a high level of physical well-being. Growth, according to Jourard, is a change toward becoming someone more desirable as a person defines desirable, not as others would define it for that person. Individuals become unhealthy when the roles they play do not do justice to their self-concepts. There may be no place where they can be themselves. Perhaps they do not know their self. They have become alienated from their real self. Self-alienation is a sickness. Jourard suggests that we must learn to disclose ourselves in order to learn about ourselves. We get to know another person's self when that person discloses it to us. By making ourselves known to someone else, we can get feedback and learn about the kind of people we are. Real-self disclosure is both a symptom of personal health and at the same time a means of ultimately achieving a healthy personality. Jourard said, "It is not until I am my real self and I act my real self that my real self is in a position to grow. . . . If I am struggling to avoid becoming known by others, then of course I must construct a false public self."

If you agree with Jourard, then the diagram of a healthy person's self would look like this:

This is because others will be able to show their knowledge of the person in response to his or her openness. In this way the size of both O and H will be drastically reduced. Look back at your diagram of your own self-concept and compare it to this one. How did you do? How do you compare to Jourard's healthy person? Is there room for improvement?

10. Diagram a self and explain its parts.

_____

_____

_____

_____

THE THREE SELVES

Jourard described an unhealthy person as one who is alienated from his or her real self. Such an individual may not even know what his or her real self is. This leads to an interesting play on words: If your self-concept is what you think of yourself, how can it be different from your real self? What did Jourard mean by "real self"?

As he discusses it in his book *Personal Adjustment*, he is using the expression in the sense brought out by Karen Horney and Erich Fromm. They view the self as "the basic inner reality, the actual feelings, wishes, thoughts, memories and fantasies of the person as these arise spontaneously." Jourard adds that the real self is a process, not an entity. He goes on to say that the real self can never be fully known because it is a process and not a thing. Hence it is continuously changing at faster or slower rates. However, he says, our likes, dislikes, attitudes, feelings, and beliefs do tend to become habitual and recurrent, so that it is possible to observe and describe them. The ego, according to Jourard, is the perceiver of the real self-process. As with external reality, the ego may perceive the real self objectively or subjectively. If the ego is strong, the individual's perceptions and beliefs about his or her real self will be accurate. When Jourard describes a self-structure created by the ego, he refers to the "beliefs, perceptions, ideals, expectations and demands which a person has come to formulate with respect to his own behavior and experience." A healthy personality has a real self that is closely congruent with the self-structure. A person whose real self and self-structure don't match closely is said to be self-alienated.

Apparently what Jourard means is that the real self is basically an internal truth or an unconscious statement of what an individual is. However, people can learn about themselves only through their own perceptions of their interactions with their environment and their successes and failures. Of course, there is another kind of self, that which is seen by others. This notion of a shadowy real self that defies description and analysis is not very useful. For example, if you see yourself as handsome, suave, and debonair, how can it be determined that this view actually differs from your real self? It may be that you have protected your self-concept by distorting feedback from your environment, and you are really boorish and socially inept. But the only way of finding this out is by seeing how others react to you. Jourard's idea of a shadowy kind of real self doesn't seem to do anything or help us understand ourselves. The so-called self-structure or self-concept has the greatest effect on our behavior, because it describes the way we feel about ourselves and practically forces us to act in a way that is consistent with this version of ourselves.

It is probably best to use a very narrow definition of the real self and say that this self is the version you hold of yourself. Right or wrong, realistic or distorted, the real self is what you think you are. A way of defining an unhealthy person that is better than Jourard's way is to use the concept of an

Real self/ideal self. (Frank Siteman)

ideal self. This kind of selfness might be defined as what you think you ought to be. This allows for a less muddy, less circular description of an unhealthy person. Unhealthy individuals are those whose version of themselves differs from what they think they would like to be or ought to be. If you picture your real self and your ideal self like this,

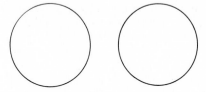

as separate and distinct, then you are totally dissatisfied with what your are. If, on the other hand, you accept your physical appearance and know enough about yourself to be reasonably satisfied with you as a person, the real and ideal selves might be like this.

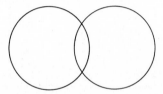

This arrangement would mean that you recognize that there are differences between what you are and what you would like to be or ought to be, but that these differences aren't so great that you see yourself as two persons. Ideally, the diagram of a completely healthy person's real self and ideal self would show concentric circles, like this,

and would indicate that such a person was totally comfortable as he or she is and that that person is what he or she would like to be. Of course, if people see themselves as ideal but others think they are far from ideal, then they may seem a bit loony. Adjusted people perceive and accept themselves as being what they are. Maladjusted people see themselves as something they are not; their real self is a distortion. The difference between the two cases can easily be determined by asking other people. Self-alienation involves other people and how they appraise you.

Notice that in this discussion a strong distinction has been made between two dimensions of the ideal self: what we would like to be and what we think we ought to be. Sometimes parents and society put moral values on us that we may not want to accept or that may be unattainable. Perhaps the self ought to have three dimensions—and three circles: (1) what I am, (2) what I would like to be, and (3) what I ought to be. The first two could easily be concentric circles, showing that we are fairly satisfied with ourselves, but the third circle might be a nagging reminder that we really should be something different. (To remember these three dimensions, use the mnemonic RIS: real, ideal, and the should be.) In effect, the *should* circle might be the moral values and spiritual ideals imposed on us by our parents and our society.

11. Explain the relationships of the three selves.

_____

_____

_____

_____

FREUD'S DYNAMICS OF PERSONALITY

Not surprisingly, Freud had ideas about the forces within us that make us act as we do. You might even decide that Freud had the best ideas. His divisions of the mind can be used quite effectively to describe the reasons for our behavior.

Freud believed we are full of animal-like needs and drives, many of which are unconscious. We are not aware of them; we merely feel an urge for satisfaction. The part of our personality that represents these needs and drives is called the *id* and is blind, unreasoning, and irrational. It doesn't care about anything or anybody. It just wants what it wants when it wants it. A newborn baby is pure id. So far as an infant is concerned, the world exists only to satisfy its needs. It will cry and scream until they are met.

For quite awhile in the lives of babies, everyone and everything seem to exist to serve them; babies are lord and master. Then they begin to realize that their cries and demands are not bringing immediate satisfaction. They sense a change in the emotional climate. They find that loud crying produces a new emotion, hostility, in others, and they learn to use other methods to get what they want. When babies learn this, we may say they have developed an ego. They have constructed a part of their personality, with which they will be dealing with the outside world. The ego deals with the realities of a situation. In effect it tells the id, "Yes, no, or accept this in place of what you really want."

Children go happily along developing their ego. They learn more ways to satisfy the id's demands, and they also learn to repress some of the demands by ignoring them or by substituting other satisfiers. Then a disturbing thing happens, usually when children are in their teens. The id may have demanded something, the ego may have said yes, but a third voice in the mind asks, "Should you?" This voice is the *superego*, which is the last part of the personality to develop. It is the keeper of parental and social values and acts as a person's conscience. It could be considered the ought-to-be part of the ideal self.

Freud believed that in mature, adjusted individuals the id, ego, and superego are in balance, though the ego is in command. In such individuals they form a shifting sort of relationship with each other so that the needs of the body, the demands of society, and the pressures of the conscience are all satisfied. If any conflict among the id, ego, and superego is not successfully repressed, tension and anxiety spring up, and people have to use what Freud called defense mechanisms to reduce them. The adjustment of individuals is judged by how often they use defense mechanisms and how this use affects their behavior. Though not completely accurate, a popular way of describing maladjustment is to say that adults who gratify all their desires have given in to their id. People who satisfy none of their desires because of an overconcern with the reactions of society are dominated by their ego. People driven by a superego over which they have lost control have an insatiable conscience. Their values and ideals govern them so much that they may not be dealing realistically with society.

The interactions of the id, ego, and superego are unconscious. People aren't aware of the checks and counterchecks that occur in the dynamic balance. They operate below the level of conscious thought.

Have you ever met someone who is driven by one of these parts instead of by a balance of all three? Have you ever met a person who is pure id? Pure ego? Pure superego? Describe how these people act.

Pure id _____

_____

Pure ego _____

_____

Pure superego _____

_____

12. *Explain Freud's view of personality dynamics: how the id, ego, and superego develop and interrelate.*

_____

_____

_____

_____

IMPLICATIONS OF THE THEORIES

Alexander Pope wrote, "'Tis education forms the common mind; Just as the twig is bent, so's the tree inclined." This might be the classical way of describing what the developmental theorists are saying. According to the two you have studied—Freud and Erikson—what you have learned will influence what you will learn. Erikson put it this way: "The strength acquired at any stage is tested by the necessity to transcend it in such a way that the individual can take chances in the next stage with what was vulnerably precious in the previous one." In other words, we build our personality house on what we have experienced in the past. In the developmental theories is the idea that a specific set of learnings must be dealt with at a certain stage of life. Again, the housebuilding anology fits. You can't construct the upper parts of your personality before you put up the lower framework. Should you blunder in any one stage, your subsequent learnings are almost sure to be weak and distorted.

If you believe in the developmental approach, which seems to be in agreement with the way we grow physically, then you have to accept certain things. First of all, you must agree that all people will go through the same stages, though at different paces. There is no magical or sacred schedule for development; each individual takes his or her own sweet time. You cannot look at a group of seemingly similar adults or children and assume they all are at the same stage of personality development. If you agree with the developmental ideas, then you must realize that we must create a society where everyone is given the best circumstances for learning what is to be learned when it is to be learned. As a parent, present or future, you have to recognize the stages and know the actions that are favorable and unfavorable for optimal growth. You need to know what stage your child is in and how to seek out and obtain experiences that will be beneficial.

The trait theories do not point to this kind of progression. The concern of Allport is not so much the origin of a trait as its identification and measurement. A trait theory is essentially a statistical frame in which measurements are balanced against each other to describe a person. Many people resent this approach. They feel as if they are numbers in a large group of numbers. To some it is dehumanizing. To many others the approach represents an invasion of privacy, because so much of a person can be revealed by measuring how he or she characteristically behaves in certain situations. On the other hand, comparing one person to others is basically the only way to identify healthy and unhealthy behavior. Much as we might rebel, we need to know what our society considers normal, so that we can tell on what basis we are being judged.

The self theories are much less concerned with what a person has been and how that stacks up with what others have been. They are interested in the viewpoints of individuals: what they think they are and what it makes them do. These theories do not lend themselves to measurement and comparative analysis. They stress individuals and their way of looking at things. The self theories are quite personal, because no one can really ever understand what and how another person is thinking. At least this doesn't seem possible as we deal with each other these days. What is striking about the self theories is the hope they hold out for people, should they choose to help themselves. I don't like what I am; I can change what I am: This is the message of these theories. In the words of a convicted murderer on death row, "But the Edgar Smith of today is no longer the restless, immature boy of 1957. Infinitely more patient and tolerant of others, better educated and with a greater insight into my own abilities and limitations, I have learned first to face myself as I am." This is the direction in which the self theories seem to point—toward self-understanding.

13. *Contrast the major implications of the developmental theories, the trait theories, and the self theories of personality.*

_____

_____

_____

_____

A PERSONAL CHOICE

You have now finished the information-acquiring portion of this unit. There are two goals left for you to deal with. One requires you to select the school of thought that most appeals to you and then defend your selection. The purpose of this goal is to get you to become personally involved in one of the theories. In order to satisfy this goal, you are going to have to think about each theory. It is hoped this will make the unit more meaningful to you.

14. *Decide which of the major schools of personality theory most appeals to you and defend your choice.*

_____

_____

_____

_____

DESCRIBING YOURSELF

Your last goal is to describe your own personality. Two exercises are provided for you here, in addition to the earlier one in which you diagrammed your own self. One of them is based on Jourard's notion that healthy people can disclose themselves. The two exercises should give you a basis for describing yourself.

EXERCISE 1. DISCLOSURE AND SHARING

This exercise needs a group of people, such as a class or a discussion group.

1. On a 3″ x 5″ card, write three secrets about yourself. Two of them may be false, but one must be a true secret that you have never told anyone. It may be a thought, act, wish, or feeling.
2. When you have written the secrets, you have a choice. You may offer the card to someone to share with you, or you may choose to keep the card to yourself. (Do *not* pick your best friend because you will lose some of the benefit of the exercise if you do.)
3. If you have been offered a card by someone else, you have a choice. You can refuse the card and thus refuse to share a secret with another person, or you can accept the card.

Go through this exercise and describe your feelings. How did you feel while you were writing your secrets? How did you feel about disclosing the secrets to someone else? Did you offer them or not? If not, why not? Did you accept someone else's card?

_____

_____

_____

_____

If someone else took your card, how did you feel about his or her reaction? What emotions did you have after the person had read your card? How do you feel about this person now? Do you have any different feelings about the person with whom you shared? What are they?

_____

_____

_____

_____

EXERCISE 2. A PERSONALITY ASSESSMENT

1. In the space that follows, describe as completely as you can two people you like very much.

_____

_____

_____

_____

2. Describe two people you dislike intensely.

_____

_____

_____

_____

3. Go back over the description of the people you like, and underline every word that names a characteristic or trait. Then do the same for those you dislike.

4. Now list all the adjectives and phrases you have used to describe the desirable people on the left side of a separate sheet of paper, and try to match them with the words and phrases you have used to describe the people you do not like. What you are doing is pairing opposite descriptions. If you can't find an opposite term, add one to complete the list.

5. Where do you put yourself in the list of characteristics? Do you favor the good side or the bad side, or are you somewhat in between? Take a good look at how you have rated yourself. Summarize the results in a paragraph.

_____

_____

_____

_____

15. *Describe your own personality, using the evidence you have gathered about yourself so far.*

_____

_____

_____

_____

☐ A POINT OF VIEW

Sidney Jourard's article on a healthy personality
and self-disclosure will give you the full flavor
of his ideas about what a healthy person is. If
you are interested in delving further into personality dynamics, perhaps the best way is to
read some of the writings of the theorist who
most interests you. Here are two books dealing
with a broad spectrum of personality theories:

Calvin S. Hall and Gardner Lindzey, *Theories of
Personality*, 2d ed. (New York: Wiley, 1970).

Robert M. Liebert and Michael D. Spiegler,
*Personality: An introduction to Theory and
Research* (Homewood, ILL.: Dorsey Press,
1970).

SIDNEY M. JOURARD

HEALTHY PERSONALITY AND
SELF-DISCLOSURE

For a long time, health and well-being have been
taken for granted as "givens," and disease has
been viewed as the problem for man to solve.
Today, however, increasing numbers of scientists have begun to adopt a reverse point of
view, regarding disease and trouble as the givens, with specification of positive health and its
conditions as the problem to solve. Physical,
mental and social health are values representing
restrictions on the total variance of being. The
scientific problem here consists in arriving at a
definition of health, determining its relevant
dimensions and then identifying the independent variables of which these are a function.

Scientists, however, are supposed to be hard-
boiled, and they insist that phenomena, to be
counted "real," must be public. Hence, many
behavioral scientists ignore man's self, or soul,
since it is essentially a private phenomenon.

Reprinted from *Mental Hygiene* 32 (1959): 499–507.
Courtesy of MH, the Mental Health Association, 1800 N.
Kent Street, Arlington, Virginia 22209.

Others, however, are not so quick to allocate
man's self to the limbo of the unimportant, and
they insist that we cannot understand man and
his lot until we take his self into account.

I probably fall into the camp of those investigators who want to explore health as a positive
problem in its own right, and who, further, take
man's self seriously—as a reality to be explained
and as a variable which produces consequences
for weal or woe. This paper gives me an opportunity to explore the connection between positive health and the disclosure of self. Let me
commence with some sociological truisms.

Social systems require their members to play
certain roles. Unless the roles are adequately
played, the social systems will not produce the
results for which they have been organized.
This flat statement applies to social systems as
simple as that provided by an engaged couple
and to those as complex as a total nation among
nations. Societies have socialization "factories"
and "mills"—families and schools—which
serve the function of training people to play the
age, sex and occupational roles which they shall
be obliged to play throughout their life in the
social system. Broadly speaking, if a person
plays his roles suitably, he can be regarded as a
more or less normal personality. Normal personalities, however, are not healthy personalities (Jourard 1958, 16–18).

Healthy personalities are people who play
their roles satisfactorily, and at the same time
derive personal satisfaction from role enactment; more, they keep growing and they maintain high-level physical wellness (Dunn 1958).
It is probably enough, speaking from the standpoint of a stable social system, for people to be
normal personalities. But it is possible to be a
normal personality and be absolutely miserable.
We would count such a normal personality
unhealthy. In fact, normality in some social
systems—successful acculturation to them—
reliably produces ulcers, paranoia, piles or com-
pulsiveness. We also have to regard as unhealthy personalities those people who have
never been able to enact the roles that legitimately can be expected from them.

Counselors, guidance workers and psychotherapists are obliged to treat with both patterns of unhealthy personality—those people who have been unable to learn their roles and those who play their roles quite well but suffer the agonies of boredom, frustration, anxiety or stultification. If our clients are to be helped they must change, and change in valued directions. A change in a valued direction may arbitrarily be called growth. We have yet to give explicit statement to these valued directions for growth, though a beginning has been made (Fromm 1947, Jahoda 1958, Jourard 1958, Maslow 1954, Rogers 1954). We who are professionally concerned with the happiness, growth and wellbeing of our clients may be regarded as professional lovers, not unlike the Cyprian sisterhood. It would be fascinating to pursue this parallel further, but let it suffice for us to be reminded that we do in fact share membership in the oldest profession in the world. Our branches of this oldest profession probably began at the same time that our sisters' branch began, and all branches will continue to flourish so long as they meet the needs of society. We are all concerned with promoting personality health in the people who consult us.

Now what has all this to do with selfdisclosure?

To answer this question, let's tune in on an imaginary interview between a client and his counselor. The client says, "I have never told this to a soul, doctor, but I can't stand my wife, my mother is a nag, my father is a bore, and my boss is an absolutely hateful and despicable tyrant. I have been carrying on an affair for the last ten years with the lady next door and at the same time I am a deacon in the church." The counselor says, showing great understanding and empathy, "Mm-humm!"

If we listened for a long enough period of time we would find that the client talks and talks about himself to this highly sympathetic and empathic listener. At some later time the client may eventually say, "Gosh, you have helped me a lot. I see what I must do and I will go ahead and do it."

Now this talking about oneself to another person is what I call self-disclosure. It would appear, without assuming anything, that selfdisclosure is a factor in the process of effective counseling or psychotherapy. Would it be too arbitrary an assumption to propose that people become clients because they have not disclosed themselves in some optimum degree to the people in their life?

An historical digression: Toward the end of the 19th century Joseph Breuer, a Viennese physician, discovered (probably accidentally) that when his hysterical patients talked about themselves, disclosing not only the verbal content of their memories but also the feelings that they had suppressed at the time of assorted "traumatic" experiences, their hysterical symptoms disappeared. Somewhere along the line Breuer withdrew from a situation which would have made his name identical with that of Freud in history's hall of fame. When Breuer permitted his patients "to be," it scared him, one gathers, because some of his female patients disclosed themselves to be quite sexy, and what was probably worse, they felt quite sexy toward him.

Freud, however, did not flinch. He made the momentous discovery that the neurotic people of his time were struggling like mad to avoid "being," to avoid being known, and in Allport's (1955) terms, to avoid "becoming." He learned that his patients, when they were given the opportunity to "be"—which free association on a couch is nicely designed to do—they would disclose that they had all manner of horrendous thoughts and feelings which they did not even dare disclose to themselves, much less express in the presence of another person. Freud learned to permit his patients to be, through permitting them to disclose themselves utterly to another human. He evidently didn't trust anyone enough to be willing to disclose *himself vis à vis*, so he disclosed himself to himself on paper (Freud 1955) and learned the extent to which he himself was self-alienated.

Roles for people in Victorian days were even more restrictive than they are today, and Freud discovered that when people struggled to avoid being and knowing themselves they got sick. They could only become well, and stay relatively well, when they came to know themselves through self-disclosure to another person. This makes me think of George Groddeck's magnificent *Book of the It (Id)* in which, in the guise of letters to a naive young woman, Groddeck shows the contrast between the public self—pretentious role-playing—and the warded off but highly dynamic id—which I here very loosely translate as "real self."

Let me at this point draw a distinction between role relationships and interpersonal relationships—a distinction which is often overlooked in the current spate of literature that has to do with human relations. Roles are inescapable. They must be played or else the social system will not work. A role by definition is a repertoire of behavior patterns which must be rattled off in appropriate contexts, and all behavior which is irrelevant to the role must be suppressed. But what we often forget is the fact that it is a person who is playing the role. This person has a self—or, I should say, he *is* a self. All too often the roles that a person plays do not do justice to all of his self. In fact, there may be nowhere that he may just *be* himself. Even more, the person may not *know* his self. He may, in Horney's (1950) terms, be self-alienated.

This fascinating term "self-alienation" means that an individual is estranged from his real self. His real self becomes a stranger, a feared and distrusted stranger. Estrangement—alienation from one's real self—is at the root of the "neurotic personality of our time" so eloquently described by Horney (1936). Fromm (1957) referred to the same phenomenon as a socially patterned defect.

Self-alienation is a sickness which is so widely shared that no one recognizes it. We may take it for granted that all the clients we encounter are self-alienated to a greater or lesser extent. If you ask anyone—a client, a patient, or one of the people here—to answer the question, "Who are you?" the answer will generally be, "I am a psychologist, a guidance worker, teacher or what have you." The respondent will probably tell you the name of the role with which he feels most closely identified. As a matter of fact, the respondent spends a greater part of his life trying to discover who he is, and once he has made some such discovery, he spends the rest of his life trying to play the part. Of course, some of the roles—age, sex, family or occupational roles—may be so restrictive that they fit a person in a manner not too different from the girdle of a 200-pound lady who is struggling to look like Brigitte Bardot. There is Faustian drama all about us in this world of role-playing. Everywhere we see people who have sold their souls—their real self, if you wish—in order to be a psychologist, a guidance worker, a nurse, a physician, a this or a that.

Now I have suggested that no social system can exist unless the members play their roles and play them with precision and elegance. But here is an odd observation, and yet one which you can all corroborate just by thinking back over your own experience. It's possible to be involved in a social group, such as a family or a work setting, for years and years, playing one's roles nicely with the other members—and never getting to know the *persons* who are playing the other roles. Roles can be played personally and impersonally, as we are beginning to discover in nursing. A husband can be married to his wife for fifteen years and never come to know her. He knows her as "the wife." This is the paradox of the "lonely crowd" (Riesman 1950). It is the loneliness which people try to counter with "togetherness." But much of today's "togetherness" is like the "parallel play" of 2-year-old children, or like the professors in Stringfellow Barr's novel (1958) who, when together socially, lecture past one another alternately and sometimes simultaneously. There is no real self-to-self or person-to-person meeting in such transactions.

Now what does it mean to know a person, or, more accurately, a person's self? I don't mean anything mysterious by "self." All I mean is the person's subjective side—what he thinks, feels, believes, wants, worries about, his past and so forth—the kind of thing one could never know unless one were told. We get to know the other person's self when he discloses it to us.

Self-disclosure, letting another person know what you think, feel or want, is the most direct means (though not the only means) by which an individual can make himself known to another person. Personality hygienists place great emphasis upon the importance for mental health of what they call "real self being," "self-realization," "discovering oneself" and so on. An operational analysis of what goes on in counseling and therapy shows that the patients and clients discover themselves through self-disclosure to the counselor. They talk, and to their shock and amazement the counselor listens.

I venture to say that there is probably no experience more horrifying and terrifying than that of self-disclosure to "significant others" whose probable reactions are assumed but not known. Hence the phenomenon of "resistance." This is what makes psychotherapy so difficult to take and so difficult to administer. If there is any skill to be learned in the art of counseling and psychotherapy, it is the art of coping with the terrors which attend self-disclosure, and the art of decoding the language—verbal and nonverbal—in which a person speaks about his inner experience.

Now, what is the connection between self-disclosure and healthy personality? Self-disclosure, or should I say "real" self-disclosure, is both a symptom of personality health (Jourard 1958, 218–21) and at the same time a means of ultimately achieving healthy personality. The discloser of self is an animated "real self be-er." This, of course, takes courage—the "courage to be" (Tillich 1954). I have known people who would rather die than become known, and in fact some did die when it appeared that the chances were great that they would become known. When I say that self-disclosure is a symptom of personality health, what I mean really is that a person who displays many of the other characteristics that betoken healthy personality (Jourard 1958, Maslow 1954) will also display the ability to make himself fully known to at least one other significant human being. When I say that self-disclosure is a means by which one achieves personality health, I mean something like the following: It is not until I *am* my real self and I *act* my real self that my real self is in a position to grow. One's self grows from the consequence of being. People's selves stop growing when they repress them. This growth—arrest in the self is what helps to account for the surprising paradox of finding an infant inside the skin of someone who is playing the role of an adult.

In a fascinating analysis of mental distress, Jurgen Ruesch (1957) describes assorted neurotics, psychotics and psychosomatic patients as persons with selective atrophy and overspecialization in the aspects of communication. I have come to believe that it is not communication *per se* which is fouled up in the mentally ill. Rather, it is a foul-up in the processes of knowing others and of becoming known to others. Neurotic and psychotic symptoms might be viewed as smokescreens interposed between the patient's real self and the gaze of the onlooker. We might call the symptoms devices to avoid becoming known. A new theory of schizophrenia has been proposed by an anonymous former patient (1958) who "was there" and he makes such a point.

Alienation from one's real self not only arrests one's growth as a person; it also tends to make a farce out of one's relationships with people. As the ex-patient mentioned above observed, the crucial break in schizophrenia is with sincerity, not reality (Anonymous, 1958). A self-alienated person—one who does not disclose himself truthfully and fully—can never love another person nor can he be loved by the other person. Effective loving calls for knowledge of the object (Fromm 1957, Jourard 1958). How can I love a person whom I do not know? How can the other person love me if he does not know me?

Hans Selye (1946) proposed and documented the hypothesis that illness as we know it arises in consequence of stress applied to the organism. Now I rather think that unhealthy personality has a similar root cause, and one which is related to Selye's concept of stress. It is this: Every maladjusted person is a person who has not made himself known to another human being, and in consequence does not know himself. Nor can he find himself. More than that, he struggles actively to avoid becoming known by another human being. He works at it ceaselessly, 24 hours daily, and it is work! The fact that resisting becoming known is work offers us a research opening, incidentally (Dittes 1958, Davis and Malmo 1951). I believe that in the effort to avoid becoming known a person provides for himself a cancerous kind of stress which is subtle and unrecognized but nonetheless effective in producing not only the assorted patterns of unhealthy personality that psychiatry talks about but also the wide array of physical ills that have come to be recognized as the stock in trade of psychosomatic medicine. Stated another way, I believe that other people come to be stressors to an individual in direct proportion to his degree of self-alienation.

If I am struggling to avoid becoming known by other persons then of course I must construct a false public self (Jourard 1958, 301–302). The greater the discrepancy between my unexpurgated real self and the version of myself that I present to others, the more dangerous will other people be for me. If becoming known by another person is a source of danger, then it follows that merely the presence of the other person can serve as a stimulus to evoke anxiety, heightened muscle tension and all the assorted visceral changes which occur when a person is under stress. A beginning already has been made in demonstrating the tension-evoking powers of the other person through the use of such instruments as are employed in the lie detector, the measurement of muscle tensions with electromyographic apparatus and so on (Davis and Malmo 1958, Dittes 1958).

Students of psychosomatic medicine have been intimating something of what I have just finished saying explicitly. They say (Alexander 1950) that ulcer patients, asthmatic patients, patients suffering from colitis, migraine and the like, are chronic repressors of certain needs and emotions, especially hostility and dependency. Now when you repress something, you are not only withholding awareness of this something from yourself; you are also withholding it from the scrutiny of the other person. In fact, the means by which repressions are overcome in the therapeutic situation is through relentless disclosure of self to the therapist. When a patient is finally able to follow the fundamental rule in psychoanalysis and disclose everything which passes through his mind, he is generally shocked and dismayed to observe the breadth, depth, range and diversity of thoughts, memories and emotions which pass out of his "unconscious" into overt disclosure. Incidentally, by the time a person is that free to disclose in the presence of another human being, he has doubtless completed much of his therapeutic sequence.

Self-disclosure, then, appears to be one of the means by which a person engages in that elegant activity that we call real-self-being. But is real-self-being synonymous with healthy personality? Not in and of itself. I would say that real-self-being is a necessary but not a sufficient condition for healthy personality. It is in fact possible for a person to be much "nicer" socially when he is not being his real self than when he is his real self. But an individual's obnoxious and immoral real self can never grow in the direction of greater maturity until the person has become acquainted with it and begins to be it. Real-self-being produces consequences, which in accordance with well-known principles of behavior (Skinner 1953) produce changes in the real self. Thus, there can be no real growth of the self without real-self-being. Full disclosure of the self to at least one other significant human being appears to be one means by which a person discovers not only the breadth and depth of his needs and feelings but also the nature of his own self-affirmed values.

There is no conflict between real-self-being and being an ethical or nice person, because for the average member of our society self-owned ethics are generally acquired during the process of growing up. All too often, however, the self-owned ethics are buried under authoritarian morals (Fromm 1947).

If self-disclosure is one of the means by which healthy personality is both achieved and maintained, we can also note that such activities as loving, psychotherapy, counseling, teaching and nursing all are impossible of achievement without the disclosure of the client. It is through self-disclosure that an individual reveals to himself and to the other party just exactly who, what and where he is. Just as thermometers, sphygmomanometers, etc. disclose information about the real state of the body, self-disclosure reveals the real nature of the soul or self. Such information is vital in order to conduct intelligent evaluations. All I mean by evaluation is comparing how a person is with some concept of optimum. You never really discover how truly sick your psychotherapy patient is until he discloses himself utterly to you. You cannot help your client in vocational guidance until he has disclosed to you something of the impasse in which he finds himself. You cannot love your spouse or your child or your friend unless he has permitted you to know him and to know what he needs to move toward greater health and well-being. Nurses cannot nurse patients in any meaningful way unless they have permitted the patients to disclose their needs, wants, worries, anxieties and doubts. Teachers cannot be very helpful to their students until they have permitted the students to disclose how utterly ignorant and misinformed they are. Teachers cannot even provide helpful information to the students until they have permitted the students to disclose exactly what they are interested in.

I believe we should reserve the term interpersonal relationships to refer to transactions between "I and thou" (Buber 1937), between person and person, not role and role. A truly personal relationship between two people involves disclosure of self, one to the other, in full and spontaneous honesty. The data that we have collected up to the present time (using very primitive data-collecting methods) have showed us some rather interesting phenomena. We found (Jourard and Lasakow 1958), for example, that women consistently are higher self-disclosers than men; they seem to have a greater capacity for establishing person-to-person relationships—interpersonal relationships—than men. This characteristic of women seems to be a socially-patterned phenomenon, which sociologists (Parsons and Bales 1955) refer to as the expressive role of women, in contradistinction to the instrumental role which men universally are obliged to adopt.

Men seem to be much more skilled at impersonal, instrumental role-playing. But public health officials, very concerned about the sex differential in mortality rates, have been wondering what it is about being a man, which makes males die younger than females. Here in Florida, Dr. Sowder, chief of the state health department, has been carrying on a long-term, multifaceted research program which he has termed "Project Fragile Male." Do you suppose that there is any connection whatsoever between the disclosure patterns of men and women and their differential death rates? I have already intimated that withholding self-disclosure seems to impose a certain stress on people. Maybe "being manly," whatever that means, is slow suicide!

I think there is a very general way of stating the relationship between self-disclosure and assorted values such as healthy personality, physical health, group effectiveness, successful marriage, effective teaching, effective nursing, etc. It is this: A person's self is known to be the immediate determiner of his overt behavior. This is a paraphrase of the phenomenological point of view in psychology (Snygg and Combs 1949). Now if we want to understand anything, explain it, control it or predict it, it is helpful if we have available as much pertinent information as we possibly can. Self-disclosure provides a source of information which is relevant. This information has often been overlooked. Where it has not been overlooked it has often been misinterpreted by observers and practitioners through such devices as projection or attribution. It seems to be difficult for people to accept the fact that they do not know the very person whom they are confronting at any given moment. We all seem to assume that we are expert psychologists and that we know the other person, when in fact we have only constructed a more or less autistic concept of him in our mind.

If we are to learn more about man's self, then we must learn more about self-disclosure—its conditions, dimensions and consequences. Beginning evidence (Rogers 1958) shows that actively accepting, empathic, loving, nonpunitive responses—in short, love—provides the optimum conditions under which man will disclose, or expose, his naked, quivering self to our gaze. It follows that if we would be helpful (or should I say human?) that we must grow to loving stature and learn, in Buber's terms, to confirm our fellow man in his very being. Probably this presumes that we must first confirm our own being.

REFERENCES

Alexander, Franz, *Psychosomatic Medicine*. New York, Norton, 1950.

Allport, Gordon, *Becoming: Basic Considerations for a Psychology of Personality*. New Haven, Yale University Press, 1955.

Anonymous, "A New Theory of Schizophrenia," *Journal of Abnormal Social Psychology*, 57 (1958), 226–36.

Barr, Stringfellow, *Purely Academic*, New York, Simon and Schuster, 1958.

Buber, Martin, *I and Thou*. New York, Scribners, 1937.

Davis, F. H., and R. B. Malmo, "Electromyographic Recording During Interview," *American Journal of Psychiatry*, 107 (1951), 908–16.

Dittes, J. E., "Extinction During Psychotherapy of GSR Accompanying 'Embarrassing' Sexual Statements," *Journal of Abnormal and Social Psychology*, 54 (1957), 187–91.

Dunn, H. L., "Higher-Level Wellness for Man and Society," *American Journal Public Health*, 1959.

Freud, Sigmund, *The Interpretation of Dreams*. New York, Basic Books, 1955.

Fromm, Erich, *Man for Himself*. New York, Rinehart, 1947.

Fromm, Erich, *The Sane Society*. New York, Rinehart, 1957.

Groddeck, G., *The Book of It*. New York and Washington, Nervous and Mental Diseases Publishing Co., 1928.

Horney, Karen, *Neurosis and Human Growth*. New York, Norton, 1950.

Horney, Karen, *The Neurotic Personality of Our Time*. New York, Norton, 1936.

Jahoda, Marie, *Current Concepts of Positive Mental Health*, New York, Basic Books, 1958.

Jourard, S. M., *Healthy Personality: An Approach through the Study of Healthy Personality*. New York, Harper and Brothers, 1958.

Jourard, S. M., and P. Lasakow, "Some Factors in Self-Disclosure," *Journal of Abnormal and Social Psychology*, 56 (1958), 91–98.

Maslow, A. H., *Motivation and Personality*. New York, Harper and Brothers, 1954.

Parsons, Talcott, and R. F. Bales, *Family, Socialization and Interaction Process*. Glencoe, Ill., Free Press, 1955.

Riesman, David, *The Lonely Crowd*. New Haven, Yale University Press, 1950.

Rogers, Carl R., *The Concept of the Fully-Functioning Person*. (Mimeographed manuscript, privately circulated, 1954.)

Rogers, Carl R., "The Characteristics of a Helping Relationship," *Personnel and Guidance Journal* (September 1958).

Ruesch, Jurgen, *Disturbed Communication*. New York, Norton, 1957.

Selye, Hans, "General Adaptation Syndrome and Diseases of Adaptation," *Journal of Clinical Endocrinology*, 6 (1946), 117–28.

Skinner, B. F., *Science and Human Behavior*. New York, Macmillan, 1953.

Snygg, D., and A. W. Combs, *Individual Behavior*. New York, Harper and Brothers, 1949.

UNIT 4

FRUSTRATION,
CONFLICT,
AND STRESS

☐ In this unit you are cast as the principal character in a story. The discussion that follows the story will help you to identify the terms and the points you should have learned. Two exercises will allow you to recognize some of the defensive techniques you use to avoid stress and will help you to figure out the level of stress you normally carry around with you.

When you have completed this unit, you should be able to:

1. *Describe two dimensions of frustration.*
2. *Describe Hans Selye's general adaptation syndrome.*
3. *Contrast the emotions of fear and anxiety.*
4. *Contrast stress and anxiety.*
5. *Describe two dimensions of conflict.*
6. *Explain three types of conflict and give some personal examples.*
7. *Comment on the idea that too little stress may be as harmful as too much.*
8. *Describe three ways by which you might have resolved your frustrations.*
9. *Explain how defense mechanisms function.*
10. *List and describe the defense mechanisms that are fight reactions.*
11. *List and describe the defense mechanisms that are flight reactions.*
12. *List and describe the defense mechanisms that are compromise reactions.*
13. *Explain why defense mechanisms may be useful.*
14. *Describe a personal conflict, and identify the defense mechanisms you used to resolve it.*
15. *Describe your own level of anxiety and tolerance to stress and the defense mechanisms you typically use.*

DIMENSIONS OF FRUSTRATION

The story begins five days ago. It started in the shopping mall where you had gone to buy a grammaloid for the kitchen. As you were walking back to the car, you just happened to look in the jeweler's window. That was the beginning of your downfall, for there in the window on a black velvet cloth in a spotlight of white light lay a golden toothpick.

Now other people might have shrugged and passed by, but not you. A gold toothpick has special significance to you. Your great-grandmother and great-grandfather both had their own gold toothpicks, and so did your grandfather and grandmother. They are a tradition in your family, and a gold toothpick has come to mean all the things you are looking for: respectability, maturity, success. If ever there was a status symbol, it is the golden toothpick so far as you are concerned.

Fascinated, you went into the jewelry store. "How much is that toothpick out there?" you asked.

"Well now," replied the salesperson, "that is a very special toothpick. It has been hand-carved from square stock. It's 22-carat gold. The point is tapered and curved. There are only fifty like it in the world, because the artist made a limited edition. . . ."

"Never mind that," you broke in. "How much?"

"Two hundred fifty dollars," was the answer, "and a tremendous bargain."

Your shoulders slumped and your stomach sank. Two hundred fifty dollars was impossible. There was no way you could pay that much. "Thank you very much," you said and walked out. As you went to the car, you avoided looking at the jeweler's window. It would have been too unsettling. All the way home your head was in a whirl. If I worked weekends. . . . If I sold the car. . . . I could borrow the dough. . . . Idea after idea came through, even the thought of stealing. You tried to put the toothpick out of your head, but you couldn't. The sight of it kept coming back. You were moody for the rest of the evening, until it became so apparent that your spouse asked you what was wrong. You described the toothpick and how you felt about it, but you didn't expect your spouse to understand, and you were right. You were sleepless all night, almost sick with longing. Then in the cold predawn gray you decided.

That afternoon, instead of coming home from work, you went over to your parents'. They were glad to see you but slightly mystified because you weren't in the habit of dropping in. Usually, you visited them on the weekends, and sometimes several months went by between visits. You were comfortable just knowing that they were there in case of need. You told them about the toothpick and how you had to have it. You asked them to lend you $250. Much to your chagrin, they refused. Angrily you slammed the door, climbed into your car, and roared off down the driveway. You were furious. "Stupid parents," you thought, "thinking only of themselves." In your rage you began to drive recklessly, bullying other drivers, cutting them off, playing chicken, speeding. Sure enough, the police siren sounded behind you. By the time you stopped your car, you were fit to be tied. The upshot of this was a $50 fine. This was the crowning blow. You broke down and cried with frustration. You were so upset that your spouse had to come and get you.

There was a good side to all this. When your spouse learned how much the toothpick meant to you, you both agreed that the two of you would go to the finance company and borrow the money. You arranged to meet the next day after work at the shopping mall, where there was a branch of the finance company. Unfortunately, you hit a snag, because the largest amount you were allowed to borrow was $200. No amount of wheedling helped. So you settled for what you could get and rushed over to the jeweler's shop.

Much to your horror, the toothpick was no longer on display in the window. When you asked about it, the clerk said that all of that model had been sold. He pulled out several cases of other styles, and you settled down to make a choice. The more you looked, the more confused you got. You really didn't want to buy any toothpick other than the one you had seen. On the other hand, you had the money, and it was probably the only time that you would have so much for a long, long time. Yet deep in your heart you were ashamed to put yourself in debt for a substitute for the real thing.

As these thoughts ran through your mind, you kept sorting out the types of toothpick. Some were too short and some were too long. Some were square and some were round. You more or less mechanically eliminated all except one, which was elegantly carved but lacked a carrying clip, and another, which was very serviceable but quite ordinary looking. Still undecided, you told the jeweler to hold those two and you would let him know.

That night, as your spouse slept, you found yourself wide awake. You slipped out of bed and went into the den, where you paced back and forth for the rest of the night. Half sick to your stomach, you paced, wondering what to do. Again the gray light of dawn crept in the windows as you wrestled with your problem. Your spouse tactfully avoided mentioning anything about the toothpick, a restraint you deeply appreciated.

When you backed out of the driveway on your way to work, something seemed to click in your brain. You drove directly to the mall. Without even a glance at the jewelry store, you returned the $200 to the finance company, paying for the loan charges from some money you had hidden away as a war fund. All the rest of the day you felt mysteriously happy. A great weight lifted from your shoulders. Your head no longer ached, your stomach lost its queasy feeling. You just felt good all over. You could hardly wait for quitting time so that you could rush home and tell your spouse about what you had done. Even as you settled down to sleep that night, there was a smile on your face, and your last waking thought was, "Who wants a stupid gold toothpick anyway?"

Now that you have been through a traumatic experience that has cost you something in both money and emotions, let's go back and look at it objectively. When you first saw the gold toothpick and craved it, you established a goal. Goals can be many things—objects, people, relationships, achievements—but they all are specific. You wanted something. Then when you went to price the toothpick, you were immediately thwarted. Somebody had placed a block between you and your goal. In this case it was a price tag. You were frustrated, but notice that your frustration had two parts. There was the actual fact that you could not get the toothpick, and there was something else. Because you were frustrated, you experienced some emotional disturbance. This emotional involvement was also part of frustration. How intense it was of course depended on how important your goal was to you.

1. Describe two dimensions of frustration.

_____

_____

_____

_____

SELYE'S GENERAL ADAPTATION SYNDROME

Your inability to sleep, restlessness, headaches, and upset stomach were all results of your frustration. They were your body's responses to stress. In technical terms, stress is anything that places a demand on the body. In your case, stress was specific and was psychological. In order to tie this idea down a little more firmly, psychologists have developed special meanings for *stress* and *stressor.*

An originator of a theory about stress is Hans Selye, who developed an idea that he has called the *general adaptation syndrome.* Selye's theory is an attempt to show that stress produces certain reactions in the human body. A *stressor*, according to Selye, is anything that creates tension. It may be a physical condition, such as injury or starvation, or some other physiological ailment. Or it may be a mental problem, such as intense fear or anxiety resulting from frustration and conflict. The body reacts to stress in three stages: (1) An alarm reaction causes the body to muster its forces to combat the problem. (2) A resistance stage occurs as long as the body maintains its defenses. (3) An exhaustion stage begins when the body can no longer defend itself. In the third stage of the syndrome, psychosomatic illnesses (illnesses caused by mental stress) may strike, and if the conflict is severe enough, death may result from them. Fortunately for you, your conflict was settled fairly quickly.

2. Describe Hans Selye's general adaptation syndrome.

_____

_____

_____

_____

FEAR AND ANXIETY

The word *anxiety* has a special meaning in psychology. When we are frightened, our bodies produce an alarm reaction. The adrenal glands are stimulated, blood pressure rises, heartbeat increases, and many other physiological reactions take place. Anxiety seems to create the same physiological reactions as does fear. However, though the reactions seem to be the same, anxiety lacks the specific object on which fear focuses. The verb *to fear* is transitive; that is, we fear something. On the other hand, we are anxious *about* something. Anxiety is a fearlike emotion about an ill-defined something.

3. Contrast the emotions of fear and anxiety.

_____

_____

_____

_____

STRESS AND ANXIETY

There is a subtle distinction between stress and anxiety. The cause of stress may be quite specific and may cause specific emotions. You may feel anger at being frustrated. You may feel sorrow at another stressful situation. Stressful events may thus cause you to have emotions, but the emotions may be quite different and specific. Anxiety, on the other hand, is an emotion called forth by conflict. It is similar to fear but lacks the specificity of fear. Many neurotics try to resolve their anxiety by developing specific symbolic fears called *phobias*, but the phobia is only a mask. Anxiety is really the dread of something nameless. It represents an internal conflict. Anxieties are also forward looking; that is, they are usually a dread of something that is going to happen.

To summarize, stress is an event or object that can call forth a specific emotion. Anxiety is caused by internal conflict. It is akin to fear. Other emotions can look forward or backward; anxiety looks forward.

4. Contrast stress and anxiety.

_____

_____

_____

_____

DIMENSIONS OF CONFLICT

You felt anxiety as well as anger at your frustration. The cause of your frustration was your inability to buy the toothpick, and the anxiety came from your conflicts about borrowing the money for something that you sensed might not be as important as you were making it. You felt anger as well as suffering from a sick stomach, headache, sleeplessness, and restlessness. But these discomforts were only part of your reaction. Notice how you reacted to frustration. You had other alternatives open to you. You could have withdrawn when you learned you couldn't afford the toothpick. You could have compromised as you started to do and bought a toothpick that you could have afforded. But you chose to fight the frustrations, and you did so by a series of actions that created a conflict situation for you.

A conflict is really a special sort of frustration. It isn't a straight blocking of a desire, as is frustration, because it involves making choices. In a conflict, you are always weighing alternatives. For example, on the way home you thought about stealing the toothpick and dismissed that idea. Instead, you went to your parents for money, even though you knew you weren't sure of getting it from them. Finally you borrowed the money, only to find that you still had some bad feelings about buying the toothpick. Conflict, like frustration, has two dimensions. A person with a conflict does not find the chosen goal directly blocked. However, he or she must choose between alternatives or goals. In our situation, the second dimension is the familiar sick stomach and the other body ailments that come from the problem of making choices.

5. Describe two dimensions of conflict.

_____

_____

_____

_____

TYPES OF CONFLICT

There are several kinds of conflict. In one you are torn between two desirable choices, as you were when you were finally down to selecting one of two toothpicks. This conflict is called *approach-approach* because it involves making a choice between two positive alternatives. The opposite of this is an *avoidance-avoidance* conflict, in which the alternatives are basically bad and you're damned if you choose one and doomed if you don't. You had to borrow money (an evil alternative) or do without the toothpick (also, at the time, a bad idea). Most conflicts do not involve choices between two goods and two evils that are as simple as these. You most often run into situations that have elements of good and evil on both sides. This combination is called *double-approach-avoidance*. Like frustration, conflicts can be resolved in three ways: fight, flight, or compromise.

6. Explain three types of conflict and give some personal examples.

_____

_____

_____

_____

STRESS, WHO NEEDS IT?

Let's digress from the story for a moment. How would you feel if there were no hassles, no frustrations, no conflicts? Do you think the world would be a wonderful place if you didn't have to face an emotion-packed fight with frustration and conflict day after day, year after year? Many people think such a world would be heaven. But would it, or would it be the opposite?

These questions are leading to the philosophical issue of the necessity of stress in our lives. John Dollard, who has studied this proposition, believes that frustration leads to aggression and that aggression is invariably a symptom of frustration. However, frustration can be overcome in nonaggressive ways. But can we do away with it? Probably not, says Dollard. Too little frustration would probably result in apathy and a lack of motivation. Without anything to inspire us, we probably would never move. Too much frustration, on the other hand, can lead to all sorts of action: anger, fear, anxiety, repression, and various other techniques to deal with the frustration. Somewhere in between is the happy medium—the situation with the exact amount of frustration necessary to keep us challenged and active. The problem is to find how much frustration is the right amount for each individual. Doing this is very difficult. Each one of us has a different level of tolerance to frustration. What is only a mild irritation to one person may send another away screaming. If you are now in charge of other people or become a supervisor, you will find that one of your trickiest problems is to determine how much pressure is effective and not ruinous for each of your subordinates.

7. Comment on the idea that too little stress may be as harmful as too much.

THREE REACTIONS TO FRUSTRATION

Back to your toothpick. Let's consider the courses of action you might have chosen to resolve your frustration. What fighting or aggressive actions did you take? You could have attacked the frustration directly, and you did think about doing so when the thought of stealing the toothpick crossed your mind. However, you decided not to steal it and experienced another frustration when your parents declined to lend you the money. You could have attacked them directly, but instead you expressed your frustration symbolically by taking out your aggressions on a door, on your automobile, and on other people whom you did not know. You could also have turned your anger inward and blamed

Cartoon by Ton Smits

yourself: "I guess I don't deserve the toothpick anyway." This type of aggression is common, and people use it in several situations. Many people who commit suicide, for example, take this form of aggression to the extreme of self-destruction.

Of course, you could have dropped the whole idea when you found out how much the toothpick cost. That decision would have been a withdrawal, or flight, from the frustration. We usually withdraw when we feel that the stakes are too high and the goal not worth the struggle. We are often struck with a strange contradiction in values, though. Our competitive society discourages the notion of being a quitter. A team that is hopelessly behind is expected to fight just as hard as if the score were tied. Chronic losers are not supposed to give up. Yet why play a silly game that you've no chance of winning? Critics of this viewpoint will be quick to point out that if quitters ever became dominant, no one would accomplish anything. But those of you who have experienced the corrosive effects of chronic failure might want to say something here.

Another alternative available to you was compromise. You could have made a deal with the situation. You almost did this when you started to buy a less desirable toothpick for a smaller amount of money. You also tried to compromise when you asked your parents for money because borrowing from them was not quite the same as borrowing from a finance company. Had you chosen to fulfill your goal, owning a golden toothpick, you would have had to compromise. Most of our frustrations and practically all our conflicts end in some sort of compromise.

8. Describe three ways by which you might have resolved your frustrations.

_____

_____

_____

_____

EGO DEFENSE MECHANISMS

So far we have been dealing in generalities, but certain specific actions do fall under the headings of fight, flight, and compromise. They are called *defense mechanisms* because Freud (who else?) originally described them as unconscious techniques used by the ego to defend itself from the anxiety it feels when the repressions and the unsatisfied demands of the id become too strong to be ignored. Freud's list of defense mechanisms has been amended and adapted, and the list that follows is an attempt to classify some of them in terms of the three alternatives given to you. Some experts would disagree with this list, and you also may choose to. If you do, rearrange it to your own satisfaction, but do remember the characteristics of each defense mechanism. As you study them you might be struck by the same idea that Freud had. Each mechanism distorts the truth, whatever it may be. Just as a self-concept may distort information that is inconsistent with it, so a defense mechanism may cause a distortion that makes the resolution of a conflict more palatable. You should remember, however, that the use of these mechanisms is not in itself abnormal or bad. To some extent we all use them. However, dealing with frustrations by using one mechanism until it almost becomes a lifestyle is a sign of bad adjustment.

9. Explain how defense mechanisms function.

_____

_____

_____

_____

FIGHT DEFENSE REACTIONS

Several fight reactions have already been touched upon. You used *projection* when you accused your parents of being selfish. Projection is the act of seeing your faults, feelings, or attitudes in other people.

Reaction formation is a fight reaction that involves behaving in a way that is exactly the opposite of the way you actually feel. If you had thanked your parents very much for listening to you and had told them that you appreciated their reasons for not lending you the money, you would have been using a reaction-formation technique.

Can you remember regressing in the incident? You did this when you broke down and cried. *Regression* is the act of going back to a less mature behavior that you once found effective in crises.

Of course, you could have ignored your desire for the gold toothpick. You could have decided that the *repression* of your feelings would most effectively end your frustration.

Another cunning device is *denial*. Had you used this technique, you might have replied, "Gold toothpick, what gold toothpick?" when someone asked you whether you'd been able to find one that suited you. Denial is not acknowledging even the existence of an event.

You finally resolved your conflict by saying, "Who needs a toothpick anyway?" Were you using a sour-grapes approach? Were you rationalizing away your desire? *Rationalization* is another fight defense.

Self-blame, too, is a fight defense. Afraid to use others as objects for the emotions caused by your frustration and unable to take out your emotions elsewhere, you turn your anger inward and blame yourself.

10. List and describe the defense mechanisms that are fight reactions.

_____

_____

_____

_____

FLIGHT DEFENSE REACTIONS

Flight defenses allow you to remove yourself from a conflict without seeming to forsake your goal. In your mind you remove the conflict. One way to do this is to talk about your problem calmly and in the third person. You *intellectualize* by talking about a problem until you remove emotion from it.

You could have spent a few happy hours daydreaming about your toothpick as if you already had it. In other words, you could have resorted to *fantasy*.

Another kind of flight is *avoidance*. By steadfastly staying away from the jeweler's window, you might have let the desire evaporate. Avoidance is a sort of "time heals all wounds" solution.

Of course, *withdrawal* is a flight technique. You could have decided that the gold toothpick was beyond your reach and immediately have given up the struggle to get it.

11. List and describe the defense mechanisms that are flight reactions.

_____

_____

_____

_____

COMPROMISE DEFENSE REACTIONS

By using compromise defense reactions, you change your actions to make them fit a situation. In effect, you make a deal with a situation. You have two basic alternatives: When circumstances denied you the gold toothpick, you could have bought an electric toothbrush so that you could feel that you have the cleanest teeth in town. Such *compensation* means counterbalancing a defect or lack by substituting something desirable. For example, a star football player who suffers a knee injury that bars him from football may turn to weightlifting.

You could also indulge in *sublimation*, which means expressing socially unacceptable motives in socially acceptable ways. Picking your teeth in public with a gold toothpick might be thought rude in parts of our society. You could probably have substituted another activity that could get you the status and recognition that caused you to want the toothpick. For example, you might have changed your goal to that of owning a one-carat diamond stickpin.

Both of these compromise reactions substitute something for your goal. Compensation and sublimation differ from each other in a subtle way, but they are important techniques for resolving frustrations.

12. List and describe the defense mechanisms that are compromise reactions.

_____

_____

_____

_____

USING DEFENSE MECHANISMS

Defense techniques are not in themselves harmful. In fact, some of them might be considered useful. Rationalization, for example, could lead you to examine a conflict in such a way that you would be able to solve it if you ever saw another gold toothpick. Through substitution, you might achieve good things for society. Defense mechanisms are harmful when you use them to distort, ignore, or deny the reality of a situation so that your reaction to a problem becomes irrational. When you come right down to it, we are seeking the ability to accept pain, discomfort, and frustration, not the ability to repress or avoid them.

13. Explain why defense mechanisms may be useful.

_____

_____

_____

_____

YOUR REACTION TO FRUSTRATION

To get from the abstract to the personal, recall the last time you felt a strong sense of frustration. Relive the occasion in your mind. What caused the feeling? How did you react to the frustration? How do you typically react to frustration?

14. *Describe a personal conflict, and identify the defense mechanisms you used to resolve it.*

_____

_____

_____

_____

EVALUATING YOUR ANXIETY LEVEL

Now you should be ready to describe your own level of anxiety and tolerance to stress and the defense mechanisms you typically use. Exercise 1 is designed to give you an idea of how anxious you are. Be sure to keep in mind that it, like all the exercises in this book, is not written on parchment in letters of gold. It is not an experiment that has been scientifically checked out. It is intended merely to give you an idea that you might follow up in your thinking about yourself. So don't get excited if you seem to show a chronic high level of anxiety. What you should do is then sit down and think about the results. Ask, "Does this fit what I know about myself? If so, what might I begin to do about it?"

EXERCISE 1.   EVALUATING YOUR LEVEL OF ANXIETY

Check the appropriate column.

How frequently do you:	*Often*	*Sometimes*	*Rarely*
1. Suffer from the blues	____	____	____
2. Have extreme swings of emotion	____	____	____
3. Have insomnia	____	____	____
4. Get excited under pressure	____	____	____
5. Blame yourself when things go wrong	____	____	____
6. Want to be left alone	____	____	____
7. Feel that others are out of step with you	____	____	____

EXERCISE 1. EVALUATING YOUR LEVEL OF ANXIETY (*cont.*)

Check the appropriate column.

How frequently do you:	*Often*	*Sometimes*	*Rarely*
8. Go back over your faux pas again and again	——	——	——
9. Feel tired	——	——	——
10. Have disturbing dreams	——	——	——
11. Wish you could live your life over again	——	——	——
12. Jump from one thing to another	——	——	——
13. Gloss over details	——	——	——
14. Worry about what others think	——	——	——
15. Feel nervous	——	——	——
16. Get angry at stupid people	——	——	——
17. Have an upset stomach, headaches, diarrhea	——	——	——
18. Want to get away from it all	——	——	——
19. Think people are no damn good	——	——	——
20. Feel a sense of impending disaster	——	——	——

Look at your answers. If your marks are predominantly in the left and middle columns, it is possible that your level of anxiety is fairly high. But remember that these items have not been statistically validated or analyzed. Think of the results as an indicator rather than as established fact.

15. *Describe your own level of anxiety and tolerance to stress and the defense mechanisms you typically use.*

_____

_____

_____

_____

PROBLEM ANALYSIS

One last point: If you do carry around a fairly high level of anxiety, you may not be aware of what is causing it. You may be helped by taking stock of your problems. When you have done this, you may be able to reduce your anxiety by becoming aware of its causes and doing something about them.

EXERCISE 2. PROBLEM INVENTORY

By asking yourself the following questions, you may be able to define the sources of your frustrations and identify the factors that produce them:

1. What is my conflict?
2. What are my long-range goals? What are my short-range goals?
3. What are my alternatives for each goal?
4. What are the advantages and disadvantages of each of my alternatives?
5. What course of action has the most advantages?

   This system may help you resolve current conflicts and future frustrations, but if you use it, you must be careful to avoid distorting reality.

EXERCISE 3. LIFE CHANGES RATING SCALE

Part 1: This questionnaire has been adapted from the research of Thomas Holmes. Place a check mark next to each of the life events listed that you have experienced in the past two years. Then total the number of life-change units associated with each of these events.

Life event	Unit values	Score
1. Death of spouse	100	_____
2. Divorce	73	_____
3. Marital separation	65	_____
4. Jail term	63	_____
5. Death of close family member	63	_____
6. Personal injury or illness	53	_____
7. Marriage	50	_____
8. Loss of job (fired or laid off)	47	_____

EXERCISE 3. LIFE CHANGES RATING SCALE *(cont.)*

Life event	Unit values	Score
9. Marital reconciliation	45	_____
10. Retirement	45	_____
11. Change in health of family member	44	_____
12. Pregnancy	40	_____
13. Sex difficulties	39	_____
14. Gain of new family member	39	_____
15. Change in financial state	38	_____
16. Death of close friend	37	_____
17. Change of job	36	_____
18. Change in number of arguments with spouse, girlfriend, or boyfriend	35	_____
19. Mortgage over $10,000	31	_____
20. Foreclosure of mortgage or loan	30	_____
21. Change in responsibilities at work (for example, promotion)	29	_____
22. Son or daughter leaving home	29	_____
23. Trouble with in-laws	29	_____
24. Outstanding personal achievement	28	_____
25. Spouse beginning or stopping work	26	_____
26. Beginning or ending school	26	_____
27. Revision of personal habits	24	_____
28. Trouble with employer	23	_____
29. Change in work hours or conditions	20	_____

EXERCISE 3. LIFE CHANGES RATING SCALE (*cont.*)

Life event	Unit values	Score
30. Change in residence	20	___
31. Change in schools	20	___
32. Change in recreation	19	___
33. Change in social activities	18	___
34. Mortgage or loan less than $10,000	17	___
35. Change in sleeping habits	16	___
36. Change in number of family gatherings	15	___
37. Change in eating habits	15	___
38. Vacation	13	___
39. Minor violation of the law (for example, traffic ticket)	11	___
Subtotal 1		___

Part 2: Holmes developed his scale to apply to all age groups, not just college students. There may have been events and changes in your life in the past two years that are not represented in the preceding list but that were nonetheless stressful. List those events and assign a life-change unit value to each of them. Use the values given in the preceding list as a guide for assigning values to these events.

Life event	Unit values	Score
1. _____	___	___
2. _____	___	___
3. _____	___	___
4. _____	___	___
Subtotal 2		___

Subtotal 1 _____

Subtotal 2 _____

Total _____

If your score is 300 or more, Holmes suggests that you may have approached a limit beyond which there is a strong possibility of a physiological breakdown. Of course, no specific score can guarantee either sickness or health in the future. (Adapted from April and Vincent O'Connel, *Workbook for Choosing and Changing* [Englewood Cliffs, N. J.: Prentice-Hall, 1978] 29–34.)

□ A POINT OF VIEW

Hans Selye, the originator of the general adaptation syndrome, has followed up his studies on stress with studies on how stress can be handled. In the following article he gives some warning signs of stress and then suggests what to do if you detect them. Perhaps these tricks, as he calls them, will be helpful to you.

There are so many books on the topic of stress and its results that stress seems to be the great American pastime. Therefore, I shall not suggest any specific titles. There are two directions in which you might go if you wish to read further. One is to follow the path of psychophysiological illnesses that has been discussed herein. The other is to learn how to cope with the stresses and strains in your own life. Selye's article gives you a little of both approaches.

HANS SELYE, M.D.

STRESS

What is stress? It's the spice of life or the kiss of death—depending on how we cope with it. Stress gives us the means to express our talents and energies, and pursue happiness; it can also cause exhaustion and illness, nervous breakdowns, heart attacks, accidents. Strictly speaking, stress is simply the body's non-specific response to any demand made on it, and is not necessarily synonymous with nervous tension or anxiety. Such conditions are not stress, but rather its effects on certain individuals—adults and children alike—under certain circumstances.

You should not and cannot avoid stress, because to eliminate it completely would mean to destroy life itself. Even while we sleep, the heart continues to beat, the muscles move that help the lungs to breathe, we continue to digest

Hans Selye, M.D., "How to Master Stress," *Parents' Magazine* 52 (November 1977). Reprinted by permission of *Parents' Magazine*, New York.

last night's meal, the brain functions as we dream. Whatever we do—run up a flight of stairs, play tennis, worry or fight starvation—demands for adjustments are made upon us. A lash of the whip and a passionate kiss can be equally stressful. Although one causes painful *distress* and the other delightful *eustress*, as I call it, both make certain common demands, requiring adaptation to a change in our normal resting equilibrium. The more we learn about mastering the ways to deal with the stress of life, the more we can enjoy eustress. It gives us the best outlet to express our talents and energies, to pursue a happy life.

Stress is often considered a particular hazard of modern society—for working people coping with fellow workers and bosses, for housewives and mothers meeting the countless demands of daily life, for children faced with competition in school, and so much that is frightening in contemporary life. Yet, such situations affect different people differently.

Quite a few misunderstandings about the nature of stress arise from the fact that everybody doesn't react in the same way under stress. This should not be surprising, since there are no two identical individuals; each of us is conditioned by internal and external factors: by inherited traits such as familial diseases, proneness to certain maladies or weaknesses of specific organs; and by various conditions in the environment.

Think, for instance, of a chain placed under physical tension—that is, stress. Just as in the chain, the weakest link snaps first, so with people there is always one organ or system which, either because of heredity or external influences, is most likely to break down under stress. In some people, it is the heart, in others the nervous system or the gastrointestinal tract. That is why people may develop different diseases under stress poorly handled.

Stress can result from tensions within a family, at work or from the restraining influence of social taboos or traditions. In fact, any situation in life that makes demands upon our adaptive mechanism creates stress. The most distressful experiences are frustration, failure and humiliation; the most eustressful experiences—however demanding they may have been—arise when we achieve victories and success.

Both pleasant and unpleasant experiences cause stress. The student caught cheating who has just learned he will be expelled from school, and the student who did excellently on an exam, and has just learned he will receive a desired medal, both experience a rapid heartbeat, rising blood pressure and other physical symptoms caused by stress. Though distress is much more likely than eustress to cause disease, there is evidence that, in excess, both can be harmful. However, eustress is less likely to be harmful probably because it rarely equals the intensity and duration of suffering.

There are a number of everyday manifestations of unhealthy response to stress, which we would be well advised to be aware of, so that if they appear in ourselves or our children, we can make an effort to divert ourselves from the stress-causing activity. The following conditions or behavior in children and adults are among the signs that the person needs to slow down, make a conscious effort to relax, and, if possible, avoid the particular situation. Not all such situations can be eliminated, but many can.

Without being aware of it, for example, parents sometimes expose their children to tremendous stresses whose results may be carried into adulthood. Children are often pressured to conform to their parents' aspirations and ambitions. If these are very different from the children's desires, or beyong their capacities, deep feelings of guilt, unworthiness and suppressed anger may develop in the children. Such anger may surface years later in the form of drug-taking, dropping out of school, running away and other destructive acts. Even before that, tension in children can silently reverberate across the family circle, disrupting harmonious relationships.

WARNING SIGNS

□ General irritability, associated with either unusual aggressiveness or passive indolence

□ Pounding of the heart, an indicator of high blood pressure (often due to stress)

□ Accident-proneness. Under great stress both children and adults are more likely to have accidents—children while playing, adults at work or while driving a car

□ "Floating anxiety," that is to say, we are afraid although we do not know exactly what we are afraid of

□ Trembling, nervous tics

□ Tendency to be easily startled

□ Stuttering and other speech difficulties which are frequently stress-induced

□ Grinding of the teeth

□ Insomnia, which is usually a consequence of being "keyed up"

□ The frequent need to urinate; in children, bed-wetting during sleep

□ Indigestion

□ Headaches

□ Premenstrual tension or missed menstrual cycles, both of which are frequently indicators of severe stress in women

□ Pain in the neck or lower back. Expressions such as "it turns my stomach," or "he gives me a pain in the neck," point to physical responses to feelings of stress

□ Either loss of appetite or excessive appetite

□ Increased alcohol and drug use

□ Nightmares

There are actually now various mechanical instruments—known as "stress meters" or "stress polygraphs"—that measure certain physical-chemical responses to stress which cannot be directly appraised. Yet even the best of these procedures fail to indicate the crucial difference between eustress and distress.

Fundamentally, it is not the quality or intensity of the events that counts. What matters is not what happens to us, but the way we take it. That is why I recommend that, in everyday life, you judge how you are taking the stress of your life at any particular moment; if there are too many signs of distress in your feelings and behavior, there are various little tricks to minimize these. Here are a few that could be useful in daily life:

□ Admit there is no such thing as perfection; be satisfied to strive for improvement, and praise your children for gains made. Don't give them the feeling that they must always prove themselves worthy.

□ Whatever your goals and your children's, consider whether they're worth fighting for; don't waste your efforts on unrealizable goals.

□ Try to keep your mind on the pleasant aspects of life. Without being a "Pollyanna," it's wise to teach your children we all have much to be thankful for and hopeful about.

□ Nothing paralyzes a person's efficiency more than frustration; nothing helps it more than success. After a defeat, the thought of being a failure is best combatted by taking stock of your past achievements. Such conscious stock-taking is most effective in reestablishing the confidence necessary for future success.

□ When faced with a task which is painful yet indispensable, don't procrastinate; get right to it, instead of prolonging the stress by delays.

Some of the unfortunate results of the distress encountered in daily life can be treated with medicines, others cannot. To counteract the effects of mental distress, people try out various techniques which claim to eradicate the ill effects, or at least help us to cope with them. Many people turn to psychotherapy, meditation, tranquilizers—the number of anti-stress medications and phychological techniques grows every day. When nothing seems to work, some find an outlet for their energy in violence, drugs or alcohol, thus creating still another

problem for themselves and for society. To my mind, the root of the problem lies in the lack of motivation and purpose.

"Love thy neighbor as thyself," one of the oldest guidelines for feeling and conduct, was propounded to please God and offer security to man. It is perhaps not surprising that, for centuries, throughout the world, so many of its elements have turned up again and again—in the most diverse religions and political doctrines.

If everyone loved his neighbor as himself, how could there be any war, crime, or even tension among people?

The trouble is that strict adherence to such behavior is incompatible with the laws of biology. Whether we like it or not, egoism is an essential feature of all living beings. When interests clash, I cannot expect others to take my interests as much to heart as their own.

However, I am convinced that we can adapt the principle "Love thy neighbor" to conform with biological laws, by rewording it to "Earn thy neighbor's love."

Thus expressed, we need not offer love on command to people who are unlovable; we need not love others as much as ourselves. The burden is instead on being neighborly ourselves. True enough, not every neighbor will respond positively, but fundamentally this should be seen as his or her problem, not our own. If we act so as to deserve another's respect and love that is about the best anyone can do. Naturally, not all of us will be equally good at it, but even so, the effort to follow the principle will give us a purpose. Humans are so constructed that, to maintain our physical and mental health, we must work for a purpose which we believe is well worth our efforts.

Viewed in the context of the eternal general laws governing nature, we are all surprisingly alike. Nature is the fountainhead of all our problems and solutions; the closer we keep to her the better we realize that, despite the divergencies in interpretation and explanation of nature's laws, these have always prevailed and can never become obsolete. To avoid the stress of conflict, frustration and hate, to achieve peace and happiness, we should devote more attention to a better understanding of the natural basis of motivation and behavior.

I don't think this is merely a pious or empty dictum, and I have, myself, tried to follow this philosophy as best I can. I frankly admit, in looking back, that I haven't always succeeded. But my failures have been due to my own shortcomings, not to those of the philosophy. And to the extent that trying to follow it has made me a happy person—and it has—if it can do the same for others, it will have proven its worth.

UNIT 5

SOCIAL
INTERACTION

☐ The interaction of human beings with one another is one of the major studies of psychology. A special branch of psychology concerns itself with how people affect and are affected by others. In this unit you will be learning about some of the processes of social psychology, including the factors that control human grouping; group dynamics; the functions of positions, role, and status; communications; and perceptions of people.

When you have completed this unit, you should be able to:

1. *Explain why human beings are called social animals, and describe the factors that induce them to form social affiliations.*
2. *Compare humans to other animals and explain how they differ from other animals.*
3. *Explain the implications of the concept of territoriality for human behavior.*
4. *Define a group, name its properties, and explain how they interact.*
5. *Explain how the terms position, role, and status are interrelated.*
6. *Explain why people join groups.*
7. *Describe how a group enforces conformity.*
8. *Compare the efficiency and morale produced by the various systems of group communication.*
9. *Discuss whether a group is better able to solve problems than an individual is.*
10. *Describe the effects of competition on an individual and among groups.*
11. *Describe the characteristics of attitudes—how they grow, interact, and change.*
12. *Name and briefly describe the techniques of persuasion.*
13. *Explain what body language is and give some examples of it.*
14. *Describe your own personal distance.*
15. *Describe your emotions, your feelings about others, and your learning as a result of a T-group exercise.*

HOMO SAPIENS, THE SOCIAL ANIMAL

"No man is an island entire of itself." John Donne's words may be the shortest but most accurate description of human beings and their relations to others. No one can live completely alone. People must mingle with others. Even hermits or recluses who seem to have withdrawn from the world probably use some of the goods and services their societies provide and have not ended all their social contacts. They may have severely limited their social interaction, but the odds are that they have not given up all communication with other people. If they had done so, they might have harmed themselves. Being out of touch with other people plays strange tricks on you. One of the most fascinating descriptions of the effects of being alone was written by Admiral Richard Byrd, who for a time was isolated from all human contact in the Antarctic. His only means of communicating with other people was by radio.

Is competition innate or learned? (Chester Higgins, Jr./Rapho/Photo Researchers, Inc.)

The changes he began to see in his habits as he lived in solitude were
remarkable. He noticed a steady deterioration in social niceties such as table
manners. It is interesting that he also tended to swear less when tackling
trying jobs.

Have you ever been alone? Utterly, completely isolated? If so, describe your
feelings and what happened to you. If not, spend a few minutes thinking about
how you might feel if you ever were completely out of communication with
other humans. How long do you think you could last? How do you think you
would change? Would you, like Byrd, stop swearing? Would you eventually
stop talking, or would you talk to yourself to preserve your sanity, even though
only you were listening?

Why are people so unable to be alone? Surely some forces must induce them to search out other humans with whom they can interact. What are the factors that practically force us into group life? Erich Fromm says one factor is fear. We have alienated ourselves from nature to such a degree that when we seek freedom—freedom from the restraints of others, freedom from the demands of others—we become so lonely and afraid that we must huddle together with others. We no longer feel comfortable by ourselves. Some experimental evidence supports the idea that the more fearful we are, the more we tend to band together for common comfort.

However, fear is not the only reason. Even when we are not afraid, we tend to join with other people. Some theorists say that one cause of this behavior is our need to measure ourselves. We all need to find out how well we can do things, actually to measure our own accomplishments. We can do this only by comparing our feats to those of others. Is a four-minute mile a good performance? How could you tell unless you had some idea of how many other people have run a four-minute mile? The desire to make social comparisons, says one group of theorists, prompts people to band together. This raises an interesting side issue. If we interact with others for no other reason than to evaluate our own abilities, does this mean that human beings are inherently competitive? Is being best, biggest, bravest, loudest, the most, a basic human need? If it is, can people live with each other in the peace and harmony that some seek? Can the frustrations of competition be avoided? If they can't, then the fact of losing may bring on aggression—not always, but often enough to make the notion of coexistence a questionable one.

What do you think? Are we basically competitive, so that we can't function without competing? Or can we learn to cooperate and get along with each other in a sharing way? Do you think we can continue to have a competitive society as more and more people join in it with us?

_____

_____

_____

_____

Some social psychologists say that a desire to affiliate is an innate human characteristic. They believe that an urge toward affiliation is instincitve. Others are not willing to go so far. They think that human beings band together because their young depend on adults for so long. Indeed, humans are the slowest of all animals to become self-sufficient. Human children left untended in their formative years would almost surely die. Even as people band together to raise their offspring, their offspring are learning to live in groups; so there is a sort of circularity here. It does seem that people must operate in some sort of group if they wish to preserve the species. By doing so, they learn to live peaceably with others. Another human urge, sexual need, also helps maintain the species. It promotes dependence and the learning that goes with group life.

1. *Explain why human beings are called social animals and describe the factors that induce them to form social affiliations.*

_____

_____

_____

_____

HUMANS AND ANIMALS

As we humans congratulate ourselves about the social nature of man, a baboon is likely to look at us and ask, "What else is new?" Its species has been living in social colonies for thousands of generations. Studies of these colonies show many of the interactions that take place in a group of humans. "Ah, yes," you may say, "but humans can use tools and other animals cannot." This, however, is not true. The sea otter floats on its back with a rock on its stomach that it uses to smash sea urchins or clams. Chimpanzees have been seen poking a stick in a termite mound to get a meal of termites. Even though these animals don't show the technical versatility of humans, they do demonstrate that animals use tools. "Well, then," you say, "people can communicate in meaningful terms." Yes, and so can porpoises and whales. Human beings have tape-recorded communications between porpoises and found meaningful patterns in them. The communication seems to be limited, but it does exist.

Basically, human social interactions do not seem to differ from those of other animals. People do nothing the other species do not do. Any difference seems to be one of degree. People seem to be better at communicating and using tools. And in this lies a clue. What apparently makes the difference between humans and other animals is the ability of humans to think in abstractions and develop conceptual relationships and to communicate these abstractions to other humans. A higher level of thinking thus distinguishes humanity, along with its more sophisticated communication. In many other ways, human beings are inferior to their cousins. They certainly are not as strong as the gorilla, nor can they run as fast as the cheetah or as far as the horse. They can't adjust to bad weather by hibernating as can the bear. When you look at the overall picture, human beings are really not very impressive. They are puny and, from a zoological viewpoint, very highly specialized—so much so that they lack a great deal of equipment that would help them survive in a hostile environment.

2. *Compare humans to other animals and explain how they differ from other
   animals.*

_____

_____

_____

_____

TERRITORIALITY

Would you like to devil someone in a subtle and indirect way? You can very
easily disturb someone, and if you are clever, that person won't realize why he
or she is feeling uneasy. All you have to do is invade the individual's territory.
For example, if the two of you are sitting at a table having a cup of coffee, you
can create quite a bit of stress in your companion by slyly moving your dishes
and utensils onto his or her half of the table. If you do this slowly, so that your
companion is unaware of what is happening, you'll begin to see signs of
tension. He or she will begin to fiddle with things and try to rearrange the
space to restore the balance. (This may not always work, but it's fun to try on
different people.)

What you are doing is invading another person's life space or territory. Most
people don't know of this strong feeling within themselves. Comparative
psychologists say that it is an extension of behavior that is common in
animals. When you hear a male mockingbird singing in the early morning, he's
not really serenading you. He is warning other mockingbirds that he's staking
out territory for himself and his family. Male seals and sea lions come ashore
early and fight to grab their own portions of an island for breeding and living
space. Species after species of animal have been discovered to have a sense of
personal territory. For some species it is for the individual space; for others it is
space for the group.

Dominant behavior takes over when territoriality cannot function, as in
prisons. Dominance is thus an alternative to territoriality. If a group of
individuals must share a space, dominance must be established.

The purpose of setting up a territory seems to involve survival needs.
Apparently the regulatory force that tells an animal how large a space it needs
to stake out is based on the amount of food available. Studies of birds have
shown that in good times territories are smaller than the spaces staked out
when times are hard. Many theorists insist that people's need for space is no
different from that of other animals. In *African Genesis*, Robert Ardrey
describes the importance of territory for a human:

> That the maintenance of and defense of territory is the chief characteris-
> tic of primate society was an observation unknown in Freud's day. That

territorial proprietors, whether group or individual, live in universal hostility towards their neighbours was a scientific conclusion unavailable to Freud in his puzzlement over human misbehaviour. That no successful primate, with the exception of the gibbon, maintains a society limited to the family unit; that every primate society so far observed maintains within its ranks a system of dominance; and that both territory and status may be compulsions more powerful than sex: none of this information was available to Freud, or is for that matter much more available to the doctor who today must tinker with the subtler compulsions of one's oedipus complex.

You can test this theory in a personal way. It should be pointed out again that this is a controversial issue. Some theorists maintain that territoriality is a learned behavior in humans.

3. *Explain the implications of the concept of territoriality for human behavior.*

_____

_____

_____

_____

THE NATURE OF GROUPS

People are never so alone as when they are in a crowd. One of the most disturbing experiences many people report is being alone in a big city with time on their hands. Even in the midst of a crowd, a person may have an uncomfortable sense of loneliness and rootlessness. Not so when a person is part of a group, because crowds and groups are very different. Nevertheless, our feelings of belonging are greater in some groups than in others. What factors help produce belonging?

A group is an assembly of people who come together because of some common motive or problem. As they gather to work on this problem or accomplish their common goal, they develop a set of rules that control their relationships. The members of the group begin to sort themselves out and assume positions as leaders or followers, and they make rules to describe how each member should act. Interpersonal rules become specialized for a particular group. In this way a group sets up standards of conduct. How thoroughly they are enforced depends to a great extent on how unified the group is about its goal or problem and how much each member is devoted to its solution. All groups have some common characteristics and problems, rules for interaction, and a disciplinary system.

Think of all the groups you belong to. How different or alike are they? In all probability no two are exactly alike; yet all are basically the same. Groups, you see, have certain common characteristics, regardless of the kinds of group they may be. One common property is size, which has some important effects on some other group characteristics.

Another group property is structure—how formally a group is organized, whether with bylaws, a constitution, and written rules about how members interact, or with no written rules at all. As you realize, the organization of groups can vary widely. As the size of a group grows, however, the group increasingly needs definite rules and regulations to govern itself. Thus to a certain extent size dictates the amount of formality or informality in the group's organization. The group has to avoid a structure so rigid and elaborate that interpersonal relationships are cut down. At the same time it must balance looseness in organization with loss in efficiency. A successful group has found that delicate balance point.

Group size also has a reverse effect on another group property—attitudinal uniformity. Usually when a group is small, there is a lot of interaction and communication among the members. This allows for close checking of personal ideas and feelings. As the size of the group increases, opportunities for personal interaction decrease. As a result, the close checking and interchange of opinions decrease, and the solidarity of attitudes begins to weaken. A general rule is that the larger the group, the less uniform will be the attitudes held by its members.

Groups have a sort of intangible property called cohesiveness, which is a combination of all the other properties. Cohesiveness is the closeness of the relationships of the members, the uniformity of their attitudes, how they communicate and interact. Cohesiveness is an overall sign of how effective and viable a group is. The greater the cohesiveness, the stronger is the group.

As you can see, size has a great deal to do with the nature of a group. Generally, large groups are less cohesive and more formally structured than smaller ones are and encourage less interaction among their members. This is not to say that the enlargement of a group is bad. Increased size does increase the versatility of a group. The more members there are, the greater will be the amount of talent available to attack the problems that the group faces, and the greater will be the opportunity for exposure to a variety of views and a wide basis for group decision making.

4. Define a group, *name its properties, and explain how they interact.*

_____

_____

_____

_____

POSITION, ROLE, AND STATUS

Think of any group to which you belong. Identify all the jobs that different members of your group perform. If your group is a reasonably formal one, someone acts as a leader. In effect, that individual is the group president. There might even be a group treasurer and secretary. These position names describe formal types of jobs. Certain responsibilities and duties go with each job title. Along with each position is an intangible set of standards of conduct that governs the behavior of all members in the positions. You expect people in certain positions to carry out their work in a certain way. These expectations are usually not written down, nor will many people be able to talk about them very easily. But they are there, and they are used for evaluation. People are judged by the way they carry out their work. Roles include all sorts of tangibles, such as the way a person dresses and speaks. For example, a Philadelphia taxi driver once remarked of the city's mayor, "He ain't got no class." What he was condemning was the mayor's thick Philadelphia accent, which put him in the same class as the taxi driver. In other words, the mayor's speech did not fit the taxi driver's notion of how a mayor should talk. Roles are both a group and an individual prescription, because not all people in a group will necessarily have the same role prescriptions. For example, there will rarely be complete unanimity about a teacher; some will like him or her, others will not. You might think of position as the content of a job and role as the style in which it is done.

Position and the evaluation of how well a person does a job combine to give a person *status*, or a position in the pecking order. The leader of a group will normally have a high status. Should the leader play the assigned role in an unpopular way, his or her status will probably suffer, even to the extent of causing his or her removal from the leadership position. Each person in a group has a certain status. It is the intangible that is used to rank members of a group and place them in a power structure.

5. *Explain how the terms* position, role, *and* status *are interrelated.*

_____

_____

_____

_____

JOINING GROUPS

Probably no other social structure is as tyrannical as an adolescent peer group. The peer group prescribes how members will dress, how they will speak, what they will like, and what they will dislike. If you look at any high school, you will see a tremendous similarity in the clothing worn by either boys or girls. Designs may be different, colors may be an individual's choice, but the style of the students' clothing is almost identical. Students would probably be shocked to be told that the amount of variation in their style of dress (not individual color or design) is probably less than that allowed on a military post. Just as clothing is prescribed, so also are speech, mannerisms, interests, and attitudes. There are usually quite a few peer groups in a high school's social structure. Each of them has different interests and attitudes. Within each, however, the conformity of interests and attitudes expressed is tight.

A fascinating question comes out of these observations. How does a group force people into an almost slavish dedication to its demands? Why, at the time adolescents are heavily interested in finding out who they are, do they knuckle under to such intensive personal regulation? This question can be expanded to any group for anyone. Why do we let ourselves be bullied and shackled by groups? One answer might lie in Abraham Maslow's hierarchy of needs. We have a need for belonging, for accepting and being accepted. We need the feeling of membership. Another answer might be that the group gives us guidance. It prescribes roles for us. We are not left without direction in social situations because standards of behavior have been set up.

Have you ever, as a complete stranger, had to join an already established group and interact with its members? How did you feel about doing this? How did you act? What were your position and status in relation to the others in the group? Describe the incident here.

If you felt inferior, you probably did little and said nothing for quite awhile. You probably watched carefully to see how the group members interacted and how they spoke to each other, and you probably also tried to determine the relative status of each person. In other words, you tried to find out what the rules were for the operation of that particular group. As you discovered the rules, you were able to move in and interact with the other members. You had learned the rules. This is how a group gives direction by example. But why do we voluntarily put ourselves under such control?

We often become members of groups as a matter of course. The groups are already there, and we join them because we are expected to do so or because we must. We are made to go to school, where there is a ready-made peer group waiting for us. We join a church congregation because our parents belong to that group and we more or less drift into it. As has already been suggested, we band together for security. There is safety in numbers.

People also join groups to satisfy different needs. We must belong to some groupings in our society—students, workers, consumers. We join them because of cultural and economic pressures. We really do not have much choice. Other groups, however, give us status or allow us to serve special needs and interests. A lapidary club, golf club, sewing circle, weight-watchers club—these are special-interest groups. Status groups are honorary fraternities and sororities, highly prestigious professional associations, and social circles whose members collectively have a certain amount of prestige.

Thus we join groups out of necessity, because our society demands that we do, or to satisfy a special interest or a need for status. For example, Charlie, Jack, Rod, and Bob are seniors in high school. They are not good students and will be lucky to get through. Their academic status is poor, and they are getting very little satisfaction from belonging to the formal school organization. As a substitute they have informally joined together into a motorcycle club. They wear black leather jackets as a sign of membership. Membership in this group gives them something they are not getting from school—a sense of belonging and mutual approval. Their status comes from their motorcycle club rather than from academic performance. Their interests revolve around their machines rather than around their books.

6. *Explain why people join groups.*

GROUP CONTROLS

One of the most horrible things that can happen to a teenager, or to anyone else for that matter, is to have to wear something that makes him or her stand out from the crowd. If all the clashes between parents and children that revolved around this problem were counted, the number would surely approach infinity. Fear of standing out from the group causes these arguments, but what causes the fear? The main cause of our dislike to be set apart (in technical terms, to be a deviate) is the strength of the group's reaction. Members of a group will turn on a deviate very quickly in order to get that person to return to the approved model of behavior. The first sign of a group's displeasure is usually aggressive ridicule. This is followed by a cutting of communications between the members and the offender. The last step is rejection of the diviating member by withholding privileges and participation in the group's activities. In other words, the person is ostracized. The Catholic Church excommunicates heretics. By so doing, it denies the excommunicated member the rights and privileges of membership in the church. Ostracism from other groups may not be so formal, but the result is the same. If the member does not conform to the group's expectations, he or she can no longer be a member.

The effectiveness of such punishment depends on the strength of a person's need to belong to a group. If he or she can join another social organization as a replacement, the penalty is not so severe. When a group begins to fail to satisfy a member's needs, the member usually begins to fail to conform to the group's standards and eventually withdraws. In such a case the group has not been able to enforce its demands on the person. At one time excommunication was a very severe penalty because in the Western world the Catholic Church was the only religious organization, and the punished one was barred from all sorts of benefits. Then, as Protestantism grew, dissident Catholics had a refuge and were able to join a competing group. So it is with any group that has a strong hold over a person. If a member has alternatives, the threat of dismissal is less potent, although social disapproval is a very strong force in any case.

Suppose you belong to a group that has a special cause, such as the preservation of leather buggy whips as symbols of our culture. People just don't recognize the importance of buggy whips in the growth of culture. When you first joined the group, you were all on fire about the buggy whip problem. Then your interests changed and you could not care less about buggy whips now. The group realizes this and begins to treat you as a deviate. It is beginning to cut down its communications with you and to withhold its privileges. But, since you no longer care about the whole issue, the privileges don't mean anything to you. As you and the group drift farther and and farther apart, the only way that the group can try to get you back is to punish you even more by withholding more and more of its privileges. To this you react with more and more indifference and thus infuriate the members of the group.

Do you see this happening in our society today? Are there people who no longer respond to the rewards that are given to members? How is the group acting toward them? How are they responding? What do you see as the final outcome of this problem?

_____

_____

_____

_____

Consider your own position in a group. Are you beginning to withdraw from it? Describe your original feelings toward the group, how they are changing, and what you think they will eventually be. Also describe how your relationships with the group are changing. Are your communications with other members shifting? Are other members withdrawing their support from you? What sanctions might be put into effect against you?

_____

_____

_____

_____

7. *Describe how a group enforces conformity.*

_____

_____

_____

_____

SYSTEMS OF COMMUNICATION

One characteristic of a group is the manner in which it communicates. There are four ways of communicating, depending on factors such as the group's organization and structure, formality, and size. One possibility is the committee structure, in which everyone has an equal voice and can talk freely to everyone else. Diagrammatically it can be shown thus:

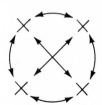

The group members feel that their power is equal. Morale in this type of group is usually high. Oddly enough, however, this structure, called the circle, is not always the most effective. In theory each member can contribute his or her own expertise to the solution of a group problem, so that the group's solution will have the benefit of all points of view. More often than not, however, each member goes on an ego trip and insists that some part of his or her ideas be included in the group solution. Whenever everyone has a voice in the decision making, decisions can be a long time coming. Therefore, the best solution may not be produced in the best possible time. Have you ever heard the saying that a camel is a horse that has been put together by a committee?

Another alternative is one in which the group is rigidly structured in a hierarchy. In order to communicate with the president, a member has to go through a succession of officers, such as the secretary, the first executive, the second executive, and the third executive, who can speak directly to the president. Schematically it goes like this:

Member $\rightarrow$ Secretary $\rightarrow$ Executive 1 $\rightarrow$ Executive 2 $\rightarrow$ Executive 3 $\rightarrow$ President

This chainlike system is quite poor. First of all, there is a possibility that messages will be distorted. Have you ever played the game in which a group of people lines up and the person at one end of the line whispers a message to the next person, who whispers it to the next, and so on? By the time the last person has gotten the message, it is nothing like what the first person said. Let's assume that you are a worker complaining about the decision of the first executive, and you have to go through the secretary to make your complaint heard. What are the chances that your message will reach the president? The reverse is also true. By the time a change the president wants gets passed down to the member, it may have been garbled beyond recognition. Another problem with this arrangement is that the secretary and the three executives may be competing for power and may deliberately mishandle messages. The chain system is thus low both in group satisfaction and in efficiency. It's surprising, however, how often you will encounter it.

A third way of communicating exists when some members can talk freely among themselves but still have to go through an intermediary (X1) to get to the top (X2):

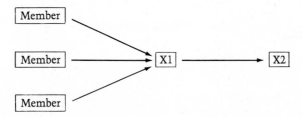

In this situation the danger of garbled messages is decreased, and you have a certain amount of equality. However, consider the position of X1. X1 acts as a shield between the members and X2. A tremendous amount of power is vested in X1. This person can stop or change messages going through his or her office. This system is very common in business. X1 is often the office secretary. Is it any wonder, then, that this structure is often called petticoat government? It is also known as the fork system of communications. It is reasonably efficient, more so than the chain and circle systems, but still likely to create dissatisfaction among those who feel insulated from X2. It produces higher efficiency than the circle system does.

In the fourth way of communicating, members are insulated from each other and must speak through an intermediary (1):

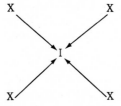

Because I is at the hub of this system, the system is often called a wheel. Because the intermediary processes all messages and decides who should act on each one, the system is efficient. No wasted effort and spinning wheels occur from too much talk. However, unless you are in the I position, you will probably feel left out of things. You will have a sense of dissatisfaction because you don't get to see the whole picture. For example, you may be a member of a group that composes hymns, but your job is to write the verses. You never get to hear the music or to see and hear the finished composition. Only the intermediary sees the whole picture. The wheel is the most efficient of the four ways of communicating but leads to low morale.

Some people disagree about the relative values of the different systems. A researcher named Harold J. Leavitt investigated the effectiveness of these models in 1951, using five-member groups. He found the wheel to be the most efficient in solving problems in the least amount of time and with the least error. The fork was second, the chain third, and the circle last. But efficiency was paid for in the loss of morale. The wheel produced lowest morale; the circle, highest. The circle was also the model in which the greatest amount of equality was experienced. Other, similar studies have come up with slightly different results. In them the all-channel net or circle was found to be fastest and had fewer errors. The moral of this story is that the greatest amount of free communications on an equal-membership basis, with no one screening or filtering the messages, will result in the highest morale, but some studies show that you pay for morale with a loss of efficiency. A leader, then, must trade off effectiveness against the satisfaction of the members of his or her group.

8. *Compare the efficiency and morale produced by the various systems of group communication.*

_____

_____

_____

_____

GROUP VERSUS INDIVIDUAL SOLUTIONS

If we want to run a tight ship and get the most for our money, should we use groups to attack problems or should we rely on individuals? There is a tremendous emphasis today on groups. There are committees that organize committees that create committees ad nauseam. This seems to be the age of the committee. Is this good or bad?

So far as effectiveness in problem solving goes, the evidence seems to point to a verdict of bad. There has been a considerable amount of research comparing individual problem solving to group efforts. So-called brainstorming or spitballing group sessions, where a group is given a problem and encouraged to create as many solutions as it can without criticizing or evaluating the suggestions from the members, have been carefully examined. In theory the different talents, backgrounds, and knowledge of the group members should produce more solutions than a person working alone could. Research shows that this does not happen. The group seems to inhibit production from its members; individuals working alone do not seem to feel this pressure and produce more.

However, a peculiar phenomenon occurs in groups. It is called *social facilitation.* For example, two people working in a room seem to work harder and are more productive than two people working alone, even though they may not know each other, do not talk to each other, and do not know what the other is doing. Researchers are not sure what causes this. Anxiety caused by another's presence may raise the work level. There may be some sort of implied competition. Several variables govern this effect, however. The type of work has to be reasonably simple. With difficult work you get a reverse effect: the level of production drops when others are present. If a person is too highly pressured by other people, the quality of the work seems to drop, and errors creep in. The more people there are, the more chances there are for distraction. Concentration drops and performance falls accordingly.

You are probably getting the impression that individual effort seems to be better than group work. To a certain extent this is true. Group solutions are essentially compromises. But if group work is so much less effective, why is there so much emphasis on the group or committee approach? There seem to be two reasons. One is the diversity of talent and ability a group can focus on a problem. An individual may not have the background in all areas needed to attack a problem. The second reason lies in the findings about communications. If a person is able to communicate and feels involved in solving a problem, he or she will probably be much more willing to help in carrying out the solution.

There is another peculiarity about group efforts. Many times an individual's solutions will be quite conservative. When a group presents a solution, its members together may often be much more willing to take risks than any one member of the group would be if the decision were his or hers alone. Apparently a dilution of responsibility in the group tends to encourage a little daring. This is called the *risky shift.*

However, the group can be hampered in making its decisions by what is known as *groupthink.* Groupthink occurs when the group closes itself off from outside communications and sources in its decision making. By so doing and by repressing internal dissent, the group can come to poorly thought-out decisions, such as the Bay of Pigs fiasco during John F. Kennedy's administration.

9. Discuss whether a group is better able to solve problems than an individual is.

_____

_____

_____

THE EFFECTS OF COMPETITION

You will remember that a question came up at the beginning of this unit about whether humans are inherently competitive. Some say they are and some say they are not. Is competition good or bad? You are probably familiar with the phenomena of in-groups and out-groups. The group to which you belong is the in-group; all others are out-groups. Quite naturally you will consider your group to be the best. If you did not, you wouldn't belong to it. Thus there is a certain amount of rivalry among groups. If the rivalry is pushed and competition sets in at extreme levels, strong currents are set up within the groups. Tremendous pressure is placed on the individual to maintain the group's position. When the group falters, scapegoating begins. The weak members lose status and may be ejected for failing to uphold the group's position. Internal tension and dissension begin to crop up. The individual must suppress his or her feelings and promote the group's survival.

As an aside, does the in-group/out-group phenomenon have a message for us? If this phenomenon exists, will it ever be possible to end discrimination and prejudice among groups? Think about this question. There may be facts of life that are not easily changed.

When it comes to individual competition, the results are mixed. Almost all of us are stimulated by mild competition, be it team or personal. When the stakes begin to get high, however, the enjoyment fades and we become grimmer and grimmer. If the pressures get too high, we may quit and refuse to compete. Each of us apparently has a different level of competitive spirit. Of course, the biggest factor in maintaining this spirit is how much success we have enjoyed. If we constantly win, we look for additional chances to compete. If we are chronic losers, we try to get away from any silly game as soon as we can. The amount of risk we are willing to take in any competitive game is based on our past experience. If we are familiar with the task and have done it well, we'll set a fairly high level of achievement as our goal. If we aren't familiar with the task, but have been reasonably successful at tasks that resemble it in some way, we'll still be confident and set a high goal. If we have been losers, we will do the reverse, because competition has blunted our estimate of what we can do or are willing to do.

Competition, then, can have a corrosive effect on the self-concept if failure is chronic or catastrophic. Although we seem to need competition and as individuals join into society in order to obtain it, we are extremely sensitive to failure, in whatever terms it is measured. How about you? Do you like to compete, or do you do better when left alone?

10. Describe the effects of competition on an individual and among groups.

_____

_____

_____

_____

CHARACTERISTICS OF ATTITUDES

One area of social psychology—the study of attitudes—holds a special fascination for all its researchers because it is the cornerstone of the field. You have learned that one of the characteristics of a group is attitudinal uniformity. You have also learned that the group puts a lot of pressure on each member to

Peer-group pressure is an important factor in the formation and maintenance of attitudes. (Charles Gatewood/Stock, Boston)

maintain this uniformity. Because of the importance of attitudes, investigators have done considerable research into where attitudes come from, what they do, and how they can be changed. On the basis of these investigations, it is safe to say that attitudes are learned. We learn them through socialization processes: through our parents, relatives, peers, schools, models, and experiences. However, attitudes do not have to be the results of experience. For example, how do you react to the idea of handling a snake? Most people recoil with horror. Of those who do, how many have ever touched a snake? The horror was learned, taught without benefit of personal experience.

Another characteristic of an attitude is that it has an emotional element. You can't have an attitude without some sort of positive or negative feeling. Emotions are part of an attitude. A third characteristic of an attitude is that it is an incitement to action. Our attitudes help us by telling us to move, either toward an object or away from it. A fourth characteristic is that attitudes are amazingly persistent. Once we have learned an attitude about something, we tend to stick with it come hell or high water. This area of prejudgment has intrigued many investigators. How do you change an attitude? The answer seems to be, not easily. There seems to be a need for consistency in our attitudes, just as there is in the self-concept. Whenever we run into an experience that challenges one of our attitudes, we tend to resist the new information. We also have the same problem when we have inconsistent attitudes. Within us there is a desire for harmony and balance. Anything that upsets the balance upsets us, and we have to restore both the balance and our peace of mind.

Consider various situations involving yourself and your parents. You and your parents may have genuinely positive feelings for each other. Your mother and your father may be positive toward each other, each of them may be positive toward you, and you may love them equally. This can be shown in a diagram like this:

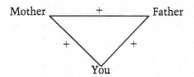

Another alternative is for your mother and father to be positive toward each other but for you to be closer to one than to the other. You might even be hostile to one. Two diagrams fit this possibility, one closer to your mother and the other showing you closer to your father:

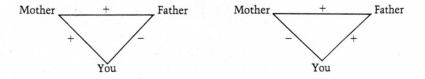

A fourth possibility is for each of you to be negative toward the other two:

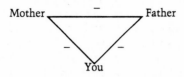

Three other possible relationships in this particular set of attitudes are possible. Can you diagram each of them?

Mother   Father   Mother   Father

                  You   You

Mother   Father

                  You

Now go back and look at the situations. Which of them are balanced? In which is there a strain in the relationship? If you are fond of your mother and dislike your father, for example, there is a strained set of attitudes:

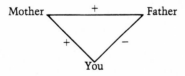

Analyze the rest of the relationships for balance or strain. When you have finished, use this rule to see whether you are correct: If the number of negative signs in the diagrams is one or three, the situations are unbalanced and the relationships are strained.

What can happen when relatonships are strained and unbalanced? There are three possibilities: (1) You could change your positive attitude toward your favored parent to a negative one. (2) You could change your negative feeling about your parent to a positive one, producing three plus signs that would signify a balance. (3) The positive relationship between your parents could change, so that they see each other differently. This would put two of the principals in harmony with each other and would team them against the third, a balanced though not a pleasant situation. The odds are that the least strongly held attitude will be changed to provide balance and that you will tend to do the least amount of changing required. In other words, you will tend not to change two attitudes if changing one will restore the balance.

This, of course, is a very simple examination of attitudes. Rarely are they as clear-cut and nicely laid out as the diagrams show. Most of the time other variables tend to muddy the waters. However, if you can strip your likes and dislikes down to the bare bones, you will often find this kind of three-way diagram. When you see it laid out for you this clearly, it may help you to bring your attitudes into balance and relieve the source of a good deal of tension—that is, conflicting attitudes.

Of course the million-dollar question is, "How do you change an attitude?" Can you talk a person into giving up an attitude? Can you punish an attitude to extinction? Can you con a person into changing? Can you confront a person with evidence to show the errors in his or her attitudes? Can you confuse an individual with the facts? These approaches have been and are being used with mixed results. For example, direct experience does not always change an attitude. Being required to handle a snake may cause such feelings of loathing that the aversion to snakes is reinforced rather than eliminated. Being required to work with minority groups may reinforce negative attitudes toward them. Punishing a person for a "bad" attitude may cause a person to agree with your version in your presence, but it will rarely change his or her basic feeling. Propaganda, persuasion, and gimmickry have limited effects on established attitudes. Apparently attitudes have to be unlearned in the same way that they are learned. When the individual feels that there is a payoff, either in material benefits or in social approval of some kind, that is enough to counterbalance the basic attitude, then an attitude change will occur. Of course, to change any established attitude, some sort of imbalance must be created.

11. *Describe the characteristics of attitudes—how they grow, interact, and change.*

_____

_____

_____

_____

TECHNIQUES OF PERSUASION

An imbalance must be created among your attitudes in order that change may take place. Every day in your life, you are being bombarded by efforts to create such an imbalance. The persuasive techniques or propaganda devices used on radio and television and by salespeople, teachers, and others generally fall into seven categories:

1. *Transfer and testimony* involves having a famous person give a sales pitch for a product. The idea behind this technique is that if a person of a high status uses the product, you should also.
2. *Bandwagon* is an effort to get you to join the group: "Ninety-nine homemakers out of one hundred use Brand Y." Obviously, you are a creature to be pitied unless you too use Brand Y.
3. *Plain folks* is an attempt to establish a common bond between salesperson and customer. "Look, I am one of you, just an ordinary person. What's good for me should be good for you."
4. *Glittering generalities* is an effort to impress the client with high-sounding phrases: "Buy Brand Y because the makers of Brand Y stand four-square behind antipollution."
5. *Appeals to prejudice* try to get you to go for a product because people like you are using it. Not long ago Rheingold beer had a series of commercials that ran, "Ninety percent of the Italians in New York like Rheingold. We must be doing something right."
6. *Card stacking* involves rigging the facts so that the evidence points in favor of the product. "Nine out of ten doctors use Brand A." What this approach doesn't tell you is that the doctors who were selected were specifically chosen so that the results were sure to come out in the company's favor.
7. *Name calling* associates the product with something pleasant. "Drink Slurp! It's cool and refreshing." This sounds better when you are hot and thirsty than "Slurp—a soft drink."

If you want to have some fun, sit down with this list of techniques and watch TV commercials or listen to the radio. Check off the technique that is being used on you. But be careful, because some sales pitches are pretty sophisticated and hard to identify.

There are some variables in the use of propaganda and the techniques of persuasion. One is the credibility of the source. Obviously the more expert you consider the seller to be, the more willing you will be to listen. So if you want to convince somebody of something, you should first convince that person that you know what you are talking about. Then, as a speaker, you need to decide whether to use a one-sided message or a two-sided argument. In general, a two-sided argument is more effective in changing people's minds; a one-sided argument reinforces the opinions people already hold. Don't ask people to change their ideas just a little. If you shoot for a major change, you will be more effective. If you get people to participate actively in the argument as devil's advocates, you will tend to change their views toward the side they are pretending to uphold. Most studies have shown that fear used as a persuasive device is not effective (this is the way your lungs will look if you smoke). If you want to scare people into changing, you must also give them some suggestions about ways to reduce their fear. Of course the higher the amount of fear you can arouse, the greater will be the change in their attitudes, unless you overplay your hand to the point where people ask, "What's the use?"

12. Name and briefly describe the techniques of persuasion.

_____

_____

_____

_____

BODY LANGUAGE

One of the most interesting areas now being explored in social psychology is body language. When we interact with other people, we are in a sense always playing games with them. Through these games we try to convince them of our point of view even while we are receiving other (perhaps opposing) messages from them. We have become increasingly adept at being able to figure out what other people are really saying or thinking, even though they may appear to be saying something completely different. We have learned to read their body language.

Recently a college president was being interviewed on television. The questions and answers were informal and cordial. They revolved around the tradition, size, curriculum, philosophy, and general excellence of the school. Then the interviewer asked, "Doctor, what is your attitude toward student violence on campus?" The president's physical response was much more revealing than his verbal answer. He immediately shifted from a relaxed posture. He brought his feet together and tucked them under the chair. He leaned forward and folded his arms across his chest. Although his words were conciliatory, it was obvious to observers that the question had touched on a subject about which the president had great anxiety. Unconsciously he revealed a great deal more about his attitudes than he intended to. This is body language. By the way that we manipulate our body, by the way it unconsciously responds to our unexpressed feelings, we often tell a great deal more about ourselves than we want to. On the other hand, we also have become experts at reading another person's body language. Have you ever caught a person with his or her back to you who was eavesdropping on your conversation? A certain rigidity of the head and neck is a dead giveaway.

People who study body language are kinesicists. Many fascinating studies deal with body language. The next time you see a group in which all the members are arranged in basically the same way, you'll know they agree on something. If you watch carefully, you might be able to identify the group leader, because when the leader changes posture, the others do the same. In groups of three people, quite often one person will arrange his or her body so that the upper part resembles the posture of one person and the lower part resembles that of someone else in the group. Here are some more signs: When a man preens by adjusting his tie, pulls at his coat sleeves, smooths his hair, or does things similar to these, you know he is courting. Similarly, when a woman "palms"—that is, turns her palm toward a man—she is unconsciously showing that she is courting him. A woman who stands and converses with her arms crossed or sits with her arms and legs crossed may be signifying that she is not interested. There are so many clues to our inner thoughts that it is almost impossible to conceal them all. To an expert in kinesics these cues make our thoughts an open book. However, signals must be considered in the social context in which they occur, because the state of the art is so new that it has no solid bank of supporting data at the present time. So far, the signals can only suggest possible meanings and should not be taken as fact.

13. Explain what body language is and give some examples of it.

_____

_____

_____

_____

YOUR PERSONAL SPACE

Two experimenters, Stuart Albert and James Dobbs, were interested in discovering at what distance most effective persuasion would occur. They assumed that it would be about six feet and were surprised to find that it was more like fourteen or fifteen feet. It seems that people being persuaded at this distance were most comfortable. Personal distance is a very important factor in communication. You should be aware of it so that you can take care not to invade another's personal distance, and you need to be aware of your own personal distance so that you can recognize why you occasionally feel uneasy in social interactions.

EXERCISE 1. PERSONAL SPACE

1. In a group of three or more, form a semicircle around one person, facing that person. Start at a distance of from six to eight feet. The person in the middle, who is having his or her distance tested, should signal each person individually to move forward a foot at a time. The person stops the circle when he or she feels uneasy. The space between that individual and the others is his or her personal distance. Measure this distance.
2. Repeat the procedure with the person in the center turning his or her back to the group.
3. Repeat the exercise with the person in the center blindfolded.

4. Repeat the procedure with just two people, one staying still while the other changes position.
5. Fill in the distances in the spaces provided:

	Distance from group		Distance from one person	
	Eyes open	Blindfolded	Eyes open	Blindfolded
Facing front	_____	_____	_____	_____
Facing back	_____	_____	_____	_____

14. *Describe your own personal distance.*

_____

_____

_____

_____

A GROUP EXPERIENCE

Now you will go through the experience of participating in a task group (T-group).

EXERCISE 2. A T-GROUP EXERCISE

1. All the group members form a circle so that they are all equally spaced.
2. All the members introduce themselves.
3. Each member makes a list of names of the group members, including his or her own.
4. Each member, in turn, defines the task of the group as he or she interprets it.
5. The group then agrees by consensus on the task before it.
6. Each member outlines the steps by which the task should be performed.
7. The group then agrees on the steps needed to accomplish the group task.
8. Each member volunteers to perform part of the task.
9. The group then divides the tasks among the members.
10. Depending on the nature of the task and the time available, the group may proceed to perform the task, or it may skip to step 11.
11. Each member ranks in order each member in the group, including himself or herself, on the value of his or her contribution to the task solution. The best rating is 1. There can be no ties.
12. The group appoints a leader.
13. The leader compiles all the ratings into a group rating for each member.

14. Each member then tells the group how he or she rated each member, including himself or herself, and tells why.
15. Each member tells the group something he or she has learned about each member, including himself or herself.

15. Describe your emotions, your feelings about others, and your learning as a result of a T-group exercise.

_____

_____

_____

_____

☐ A POINT OF VIEW

We all like to think of ourselves as being independent, the captains of our own ships, the managers of our own fates. We also like to think we are humane, kind people who would not deliberately hurt anyone. Read Stanley Milgram's "Behavioral Study of Obedience" to see how many of our ideas are illusions and how responsive we are to social pressures.

An outstanding book on group dynamics is Irving L. Janis's *Victims of Groupthink* (Boston: Houghton Mifflin, 1972). The author gives a fine description of groups engaged in decision making. His book is both frightening and informative.

Other aspects of social interaction are described by Jonathan L. Freedman et al. in *Social Psychology* (Englewood Cliffs, N.J.: Prentice-Hall, 1970).

STANLEY MILGRAM

BEHAVIORAL STUDY OF OBEDIENCE

Obedience is as basic an element in the structure of social life as one can point to. Some system of authority is a requirement of all communal living, and it is only the man dwelling in isolation who is not forced to respond, through defiance or submission, to the commands of others. Obediehce, as a determinant of behavior, is of particular relevance to our time. It has been reliably established that from 1933–45 millions of innocent persons were systematically slaughtered on command. Gas chambers

Reprinted from *Journal of Abnormal and Social Psychology* 67 (1963): 371–378, by permission of Stanley Milgram and the American Psychological Association. Copyright © 1963 by the American Psychological Association.

This research was supported by a grant (NSF G-17916) from the National Science Foundation. Exploratory studies conducted in 1960 were supported by a grant from the Higgins Fund at Yale University. The research assistance of Alan C. Elms and Jon Wayland is gratefully acknowledged.

were built, death camps were guarded, daily quotas of corpses were produced with the same efficiency as the manufacture of appliances. These inhumane policies may have originated in the mind of a single person, but they could only be carried out on a massive scale if a very large number of persons obeyed orders.

Obedience is the psychological mechanism that links individual action to political purpose. It is the dispositional cement that binds men to systems of authority. Facts of recent history and observation in daily life suggest that for many persons obedience may be a deeply ingrained behavior tendency, indeed, a prepotent impulse overriding training in ethics, sympathy, and moral conduct. C. P. Snow (1961) points to its importance when he writes:

> When you think of the long and gloomy history of man, you will find more hideous crimes have been committed in the name of obedience than have ever been committed in the name of rebellion. If you doubt that, read William Shirer's "Rise and Fall of the Third Reich." The German Officer Corps were brought up in the most rigorous code of obedience . . . in the name of obedience they were party to, and assisted in, the most wicked large scale actions in the history of the world [p. 24].

While the particular form of obedience dealt with in the present study has its antecedents in these episodes, it must not be thought all obedience entails acts of aggression against others. Obedience serves numerous productive functions. Indeed, the very life of society is predicated on its existence. Obedience may be ennobling and educative and refer to acts of charity and kindness, as well as to destruction.

GENERAL PROCEDURE

A procedure was devised which seems useful as a tool for studying obedience (Milgram, 1961). It consists of ordering a naive subject to administer electric shock to a victim. A simulated shock generator is used, with 30 clearly marked voltage levels that range from 15 to 450 volts. The instrument bears verbal designations that range from Slight Shock to Danger: Severe Shock. The responses of the victim, who is a trained confederate of the experimenter, are standarized. The orders to administer shocks are given to the naive subject in the context of a "learning experiment" ostensibly set up to study the effects of punishment on memory. As the experiment proceeds the naive subject is commanded to administer increasingly more intense shocks to the victim, even to the point of reaching the level marked Danger: Severe Shock. Internal resistances become stronger, and at a certain point the subject refuses to go on with the experiment. Behavior prior to this rupture is considered "obedience," in that the subject complies with the commands of the experimenter. The point of rupture is the act of disobedience. A quantitative value is assigned to the subject's performance based on the maximum intensity shock he is willing to administer before he refuses to participate further. Thus for any particular subject and for any for any particular experimental condition the degree of obedience may be specified with a numerical value. The crux of the study is to systematically vary the factors believed to alter the degree of obedience to the experimental commands.

The technique allows important variables to be manipulated at several points in the experiment. One may vary aspects of the source of command, content and form of command, instrumentalities for its execution, target object, general social setting, etc. The problem, therefore, is not of designing increasingly more numerous experimental conditions, but of selecting those that best illuminate the *process* of obedience from the socio-psychological standpoint.

RELATED STUDIES

The inquiry bears an important relation to philosophic analyses of obedience and authority (Arendt, 1958; Friedrich, 1958; Weber, 1947), an early experimental study of obedience by Frank (1944), studies in "authoritariansim" (Adorno,

Frenkel-Brunswik, Levinson, & Sanford, 1950; Rokeach, 1961), and a recent series of analytic and empirical studies in social power (Cartwright, 1959). It owes much to the long concern with *suggestion* in social psychology, both in its normal forms (e.g., Binet, 1900) and in its clinical manifestations (Charcot, 1881). But it derives, in the first instance, from direct observation of a social fact; the individual who is commanded by a legitimate authority ordinarily obeys. Obedience comes easily and often. It is a ubiquitous and indispensable feature of social life.

METHOD

SUBJECTS

The subjects were 40 males between the ages of 20 and 50, drawn from New Haven and the surrounding communities. Subjects were obtained by a newspaper advertisement and direct mail solicitation. Those who responded to the appeal believed they were to participate in a study of memory and learning at Yale University. A wide range of occupations is represented in the sample. Typical subjects were postal clerks, high school teachers, salesmen, engineers, and laborers. Subjects ranged in educational level from one who had not finished elementary school, to those who had doctorate and other professional degrees. They were paid $4.50 for their participation in the experiment. However, subjects were told that payment was simply for coming to the laboratory, and that the money was theirs no matter what happened after they arrived. Table 1 shows the proportion of age and occupational types assigned to the experimental condition.

PERSONNEL AND LOCALE

The experiment was conducted on the grounds of Yale University in the elegant interaction laboratory. (This detail is relevant to the perceived legitimacy of the experiment. In further variations, the experiment was dissociated from the university, with consequences for performance.) The role of experimenter was played by a

TABLE 1 DISTRIBUTION OF AGE AND
OCCUPATIONAL TYPES IN THE EXPERIMENT

Occupations	20–29 years N	30–39 years N	40–50 years N	Percentage of total (occupations)
Workers, skilled and unskilled	4	5	6	37.5
Sales, business, and white-collar	3	6	7	40.0
Professional	1	5	3	22.5
Percentage of total (age)	20	40	40	

Note: Total N = 40.

31-year-old high school teacher of biology. His manner was impassive, and his appearance somewhat stern throughout the experiment. He was dressed in a gray technician's coat. The victim was played by a 47-year-old accountant, trained for the role; he was of Irish-American stock, whom most observers found mild-mannered and likable.

PROCEDURE

One naive subject and one victim (an accomplice) performed in each experiment. A pretext had to be devised that would justify the administration of electric shock by the naive subject. This was effectively accomplished by the cover story. After a general introduction on the presumed relation between punishment and learning, subjects were told:

> But actually, we know *very little* about the effect of punishment on learning, because almost no truly scientific studies have been made of it in human beings.
>
> For instance, we don't know how *much* punishment is best for learning—and we don't know how much difference it makes as to who is giving the punishment, whether an adult learns best from a

younger or an older person than himself—or many things of that sort.

So in this study we are bringing together a number of adults of different occupations and ages. And we're asking some of them to be teachers and some of them to be learners.

We want to find out just what effect different people have on each other as teachers and learners, and also what effect *punishment* will have on learning in this situation.

Therefore, I'm going to ask one of you to be the teacher here tonight and the other one to be the learner.

Does either of you have a preference?

Subjects then drew slips of paper from a hat to determine who would be the teacher and who would be the learner in the experiment. The drawing was rigged so that the naive subject was always the teacher and the accomplice always the learner. (Both slips contained the word "Teacher.") Immediately after the drawing, the teacher and learner were taken to an adjacent room and the learner was strapped into an "electric chair" apparatus.

The experimenter explained that the straps were to prevent excessive movement while the learner was being shocked. The effect was to make it impossible for him to escape from the situation. An electrode was attached to the learner's wrist, and electrode paste was applied "to avoid blisters and burns." Subjects were told that the electrode was attached to the shock generator in the adjoining room.

In order to improve credibility the experimenter declared, in response to a question by the learner: "Although the shocks can be extremely painful, they cause no permanent tissue damage."

Learning task The lesson administered by the subject was a paired-associate learning task. The subject read a series of word pairs to the learner, and then read the first word of the pair along with four terms. The learner was to indicate which of the four terms had originally been paired with the first word. He communicated his answer by pressing one of four switches in front of him, which in turn lit up one of four numbered quadrants in an answer-box located atop the shock generator.

Shock generator The instrument panel consists of 30 lever switches set in a horizontal line. Each switch is clearly labeled with a voltage designation that ranges from 15 to 450 volts. There is a 15-volt increment from one switch to the next going from left to right. In addition, the following verbal designations are clearly indicated for groups of four switches going from left to right: Slight Shock, Moderate Shock, Strong Shock, Very Strong Shock, Intense Shock, Extreme Intensity Shock, Danger: Severe Shock. (Two switches after this last designation are simply marked XXX.)

Upon depressing a switch: a pilot light corresponding to each switch is illuminated in bright red; an electric buzzing is heard; an electric blue light, labeled "voltage energizer," flashes; the dial on the voltage meter swings to the right; various relay clicks are sounded.

The upper left-hand corner of the generator is labeled Shock Generator, Type ZLB, Dyson Instrument Company, Waltham, Mass. Output 15 Volts-450 Volts.

Details of the instrument were carefully handled to insure an appearance of authenticity. The panel was engraved by precision industrial engravers, and all components were of high quality. No subject in the experiment suspected that the instrument was merely a simulated shock generator.[1]

---

[1] A related technique, making use of a shock generator, was reported by Buss (1961) for the study of aggression in the laboratory. Despite the considerable similarity of technical detail in the experimental procedures, both investigators proceeded in ignorance of the other's work. Milgram provided plans and photographs of his shock generator, experimental procedure, and first results in a report to the National Science Foundation in January 1961. This report received only limited circulation. Buss reported his procedure 6 months later, but to a wider audience. Subsequently, technical information and reports were exchanged. The present article was first received in the Editor's office on December 27, 1961; it was resubmitted with deletions on July 27, 1962.

Sample shock Each naive subject is given a sample shock on the shock generator, prior to beginning his run as teacher. This shock is always 45 volts, and is applied by pressing the third switch of the generator. The shock is applied to the wrist of the naive subject, and has its source in a 45-volt battery wired into the generator. This further convinces the subject of the authenticity of the generator.

Shock instructions The subject is told to administer a shock to the learner each time he gives a wrong response. Moreover—and this is the key command—the subject is instructed to "move one level higher on the shock generator each time the learner flashes a wrong answer." He is also instructed to announce the voltage level before administering a shock. This serves to continually remind subjects of the increasing intensity of shocks administered to the learner.

Preliminary and regular run Pretests revealed that the procedure of reading words and administering shocks requires some practice before it can be handled smoothly. Therefore, immediately preceding the regular run, the teacher is given a preliminary series of 10 words to read to the learner. There are 3 neutral words in the practice series (i.e., words that the learner answers correctly), so that shocks are administered for 7 of the words, with the maximum shock at 105 volts (moderate shock). Almost all subjects master the procedure by the time the preliminary run is over.

Subjects are then presented with a second list, and are told that the procedure is the same as for the first list; the experimenter adds, however:

> When you get to the bottom of the list, repeat it over again, and continue giving shocks, until the learner has learned all the pairs correctly.

The experimenter instructs the subject to

> start from 15 volts and increase the shock level one step each time the learner gives a wrong answer.

Feedback from the victim In all conditions the learner gives a predetermined set of responses to the word pair test, based on a schedule of approximately three wrong answers to one correct answer. In the present experimental condition no vocal response or other sign of protest is heard from the learner until Shock Level 300 is reached. When the 300-volt shock is administered, the learner pounds on the wall of the room in which he is bound to the electric chair. The pounding can be heard by the subject. From this point on, the learner's answers no longer appear on the four-way panel.

At this juncture, subjects ordinarily turn to the experimenter for guidance. The experimenter instructs the subject to treat the absence of a response as a wrong answer, and to shock the subject according to the usual schedule. He advises the subjects to allow 5–10 seconds before considering no response as a wrong answer, and to increase the shock level one step each time the learner fails to respond correctly. The learner's pounding is repeated after the 315-volt shock is administered; afterwards he is not heard from, nor do his answers reappear on the four-way signal box.

Experimenter feedback At various points in the experiment the subject may turn to the experimenter for advice on whether he should continue to administer shocks. Or he may indicate that he does not wish to go on. It was important to standardize the experimenter's responses to these inquiries and reactions.

If the subject indicated his unwillingness to go on, the experimenter responded with a sequence of "prods," using as many as necessary to bring the subject into line.

Prod 1: Please continue, *or* Please go on.

Prod 2: The experiment requires that you continue.

Prod 3: It is absolutely essential that you continue.

Prod 4: You have no other choice, you *must* go on.

The prods were always made in sequence: Only if Prod 1 had been unsuccessful, could Prod 2 be used. If the subject refused to obey the experimenter after Prod 4, the experiment was terminated. The experimenter's tone of voice was at all times firm, but not impolite. The sequence was begun anew on each occasion that the subject balked or showed reluctance to follow orders.

Special prods If the subject asked if the learner was liable to suffer permanent physical injury, the experimenter said:

> Although the shocks may be painful, there is no permanent tissue damage, so please go on. [Followed by Prods 2, 3, and 4 if necessary.]

If the subject said that the learner did not want to go on, the experimenter replied:

> Whether the learner likes it or not, you must go on until he has learned all the word pairs correctly. So please go on. [Followed by Prods 2, 3, and 4 if necessary.]

DEPENDENT MEASURES

The primary dependent measure for any subject is the maximum shock he administers before he refuses to go any further. In principle this may vary from 0 (for a subject who refuses to administer even the first shock) to 30 (for a subject who administers the highest shock on the generator). A subject who breaks off the experiment at any point prior to administering the thirtieth shock level is termed a *defiant* subject. One who complies with experimental commands fully, and proceeds to administer all shock levels commanded, is termed an *obedient* subject.

Further records With few exceptions, experimental sessions were recorded on magnetic tape. Occasional photographs were taken through one-way mirrors. Notes were kept on any unusual behavior occurring during the course of the experiments. On occasion, additional observers were directed to write objective descriptions of the subjects' behavior. The latency and duration of shocks were measured by accurate timing devices.

Interview and dehoax Following the experiment, subjects were interviewed; open-ended questions, projective measures, and attitude scales were employed. After the interview, procedures were undertaken to assure that the subject would leave the laboratory in a state of well being. A friendly reconciliation was arranged between the subject and the victim, and an effort was made to reduce any tensions that arose as a result of the experiment.

RESULTS

PRELIMINARY NOTIONS

Before giving an account of the experimental results, it is instructive to consider how persons predict others will perform when commanded to administer powerful shocks to another person. Fourteen Yale seniors, all psychology majors, were provided with a detailed description of the experimental situation. They were asked to reflect carefully on it, and to predict the behavior of 100 hypothetical subjects. More specifically, they were instructed to plot the distribution of obedience of "100 Americans of diverse occupations, and ranging in age from 20 to 50 years," who were placed in the experimental situation.

There was considerable agreement among the respondents on the expected behavior of hypothetical subjects. All respondents predicted that only an insignificant minority would go through to the end of the shock series. (The estimates ranged from 0 to 3%; i.e., the most "pessimistic" member of the class predicted that of 100 persons, 3 would continue through to the most potent shock available on the shock generator—450 volts.) The class mean was 1.2%. The question was also posed informally

to colleagues of the author, and the most general feeling was that few if any subjects would go beyond the designation Very Strong Shock.

RESULT OF EXPERIMENT 1

Subjects accept situation With few exceptions subjects were convinced of the reality of the experimental situation, that they were administering shocks to another person, and the most potent shocks were extremely painful. In the post-experimental interview subjects were asked: "How painful to the learner were the last few shocks that you administered to him?" Subjects were instructed to indicate their answers on a printed 14-point scale ranging from "Not at all painful" to "Extremely painful." The modal response was 14 (Extremely painful) with the mean at 13.42.

Signs of extreme tension Many subjects showed signs of nervousness in the experimental situation, and especially upon administering the more powerful shocks. In a large number of cases the degree of tension reached extremes that are rarely seen in sociopsychological laboratory studies. Subjects were observed to sweat, tremble, stutter, bite their lips, groan, and dig their fingernails into their flesh. These were characteristic rather than exceptional responses to the experiment.

One sign of tension was the regular occurrence of nervous laughing fits. Fourteen of the 40 subjects showed definite signs of nervous laughter and smiling. The laughter seemed entirely out of place, even bizarre. Full-blown, uncontrollable seizures were observed for 3 subjects. On one occasion we observed a seizure so violently convulsive that it was necessary to call a halt to the experiment. The subject, a 46-year-old encyclopedia salesman, was seriously embarrassed by his untoward and uncontrollable behavior. In the post-experimental interviews subjects took pains to point out that they were not sadistic types, and that the laughter did not mean they enjoyed shocking the victim.

Distribution of scores It had been conjectured that persons would not, in general, agree to administer shocks beyond the level designated as Very Strong Shock. The distribution of maximum shocks for this experiment is shown in Table 2. The obtained distribution of scores deviates radically from the prediction.

Upon command of the experimenter, each of the 40 subjects went beyond the expected breakoff point. No subject stopped prior to administering Shock Level 20. (At this level—300 volts—the victim kicks on the wall and no longer provides answers to the teacher's multiple-choice questions.)

Of the 40 subjects, 5 refused to obey the experimental commands beyond the 300-volt level. Four more subjects administered one further shock, and then refused to go on. Two broke off at the 330-volt level, and 1 each at 345, 360, and 375 volts. Thus a total of 14 subjects defied the experimenter. It is instructive to reprint their remarks at the point of defiance, as transcribed from the tape recordings:

[0124] I think he's trying to communicate, he's knocking. . . . Well it's not fair to shock the guy . . . these are terrific volts. I don't think this is very humane. . . . Oh, I can't go on with this; no, this isn't right. It's a hell of an experiment. The guy is suffering in there. No, I don't want to go on. This is crazy. [Subject refused to administer more shocks.]

[0123] He's banging in there. I'm gonna chicken out. I'd like to continue, but I can't do that to a man. . . . I'm sorry I can't do that to a man. I'll hurt his heart. You take your check. . . . No really, I couldn't do it.

These subjects were frequently in a highly agitated and even angered state. Sometimes, verbal protest was at a minimum, and the subject simply got up from his chair in front of the shock generator, and indicated that he wished to leave the laboratory.

Of the 40 subjects, 26 obeyed the orders of the

TABLE 2 DISTRIBUTION OF BREAKOFF POINTS

Verbal designation and voltage indication	Number of subjects for whom this was maximum shock
Slight shock	
15	0
30	0
45	0
60	0
Moderate shock	
75	0
90	0
105	0
120	0
Strong shock	
135	0
150	0
165	0
180	0
Very strong shock	
195	0
210	0
225	0
240	0
Intense shock	
255	0
270	0
285	0
300	5
Extreme intensity shock	
315	4
330	2
345	1
360	1
Danger: severe shock	
375	1
390	0
405	0
420	0
XXX	
435	0
450	26

experimenter to the end, proceeding to punish the victim until they reached the most potent shock available on the shock generator. At that point, the experimenter called a halt to the session. (The maximum shock is labeled 450 volts, and is two steps beyond the designation: Danger: Severe Shock.) Although obedient subjects continued to administer shocks, they often did so under extreme stress. Some expressed reluctance to administer shocks beyond the 300-volt level, and displayed fears similar to those who defied the experimenter; yet they obeyed.

After the maximum shocks had been delivered, and the experimenter called a halt to the proceedings, many obedient subjects heaved sighs of relief, mopped their brows, rubbed their fingers over their eyes, or nervously fumbled cigarettes. Some shook their heads, apparently in regret. Some subjects had remained calm throughout the experiment, and displayed only minimal signs of tension from beginning to end.

DISCUSSION

The experiment yielded two findings that were surprising. The first finding concerns the sheer strength of obedient tendencies manifested in this situation. Subjects have learned from childhood that it is a fundamental breach of moral conduct to hurt another person against his will. Yet, 26 subjects abandon this tenet in following the instructions of an authority who has no special powers to enforce his commands. To disobey would bring no material loss to the subject; no punishment would ensue. It is clear from the remarks and outward behavior of many participants that in punishing the victim they are often acting against their own values. Subjects often expressed deep disapproval of shocking a man in the face of his objections, and others denounced it as stupid and senseless. Yet the majority complied with the experimental commands. This outcome was surprising from two perspectives: first, from the standpoint of predictions made in the questionnaire described earlier. (Here, however, it is possible that the

remoteness of the respondents from the actual situation, and the difficulty of conveying to them the concrete details of the experiment, could account for the serious underestimation of obedience.)

But the results were also unexpected to persons who observed the experiment in progress, through one-way mirrors. Observers often uttered expressions of disbelief upon seeing a subject administer more powerful shocks to the victim. These persons had a full acquaintance with the details of the situation, and yet systematically underestimated the amount of obedience that subjects would display.

The second unanticipated effect was the extraordinary tension generated by the procedures. One might suppose that a subject would simply break off or continue as his conscience dictated. Yet, this is very far from what happened. There were striking reactions of tension and emotional strain. One observer related:

> I observed a mature and initially poised businessman enter the laboratory smiling and confident. Within 20 minutes he was reduced to a twitching, stuttering wreck, who was rapidly approaching a point of nervous collapse. He constantly pulled on his earlobe, and twisted his hands. At one point he pushed his fist into his forehead and muttered: "Oh God, let's stop it." And yet he continued to respond to every word of the experimenter, and obeyed to the end.

Any understanding of the phenomenon of obedience must rest on an analysis of the particular conditions in which it occurs. The following features of the experiment go some distance in explaining the high amount of obedience observed in the situation.

1. The experiment is sponsored by and takes place on the grounds of an institution of unimpeachable reputation, Yale University. It may be reasonably presumed that the personnel are competent and reputable. The importance of this background authority is now being studied by conducting a series of experiments outside of

New Haven, and without any visible ties to the university.

2. The experiment is, on the face of it, designed to attain a worthy purpose—advancement of knowledge about learning and memory. Obedience occurs not as an end itself, but as an instrumental element in a situation that the subject construes as significant, and meaningful. He may not be able to see its full significance, but he may properly assume that the experimenter does.

3. The subject perceives that the victim has voluntarily submitted to the authority system of the experimenter. He is not (at first) an unwilling captive impressed for involuntary service. He has taken the trouble to come to the laboratory presumably to aid the experimental research. That he later becomes an involuntary subject does not alter the fact that, initially, he consented to participate without qualification. Thus he has in some degree incurred an obligation toward the experimenter.

4. The subject, too, has entered the experiment voluntarily, and perceives himself under obligation to aid the experimenter. He has made a commitment, and to disrupt the experiment is a repudiation of this initial promise of aid.

5. Certain features of the procedure strengthen the subject's sense of obligation to the experimenter. For one, he has been paid for coming to the laboratory. In part this is canceled out by the experimenter's statement that:

> Of course, as in all experiments, the money is yours simply for coming to the laboratory. From this point on, no matter what happens, the money is yours.[2]

6. From the subject's standpoint, the fact that he is the teacher and the other man the learner is purely a chance consequence (it is determined by drawing lots) and he, the subject, ran the same risk as the other man in being assigned the role of learner. Since the assignment of posi-

tions in the experiment was achieved by fair means, the learner is deprived of any basis or complaint on this count. (A similar situation obtains in Army units, in which—in the absence of volunteers—a particularly dangerous mission may be assigned by drawing lots, and the unlucky soldier is expected to bear his misfortune with sportsmanship.)

7. There is, at best, ambiguity with regard to the prerogatives of a psychologist and the corresponding rights of his subject. There is a vagueness of expectation concerning what a psychologist may require of his subject, and when he is overstepping acceptable limits. Moreover, the experiment occurs in a closed setting, and thus provides no opportunity for the subject to remove these ambiguities by discussion with others. There are few standards that seem directly applicable to the situation, which is a novel one for most subjects.

8. The subjects are assured that the shocks administered to the subject are "painful but not dangerous." Thus they assume that the discomfort caused the victim is momentary, while the scientific gains resulting from the experiment are enduring.

9. Through Shock Level 20 the victim continues to provide answers on the signal box. The subject may construe this as a sign that the victim is still willing to "play the game." It is only after Shock Level 20 that the victim repudiates the rules completely, refusing to answer further.

These features help to explain the high amount of obedience obtained in this experiment. Many of the arguments raised need not remain matters of speculation, but can be reduced to testable propositions to be confirmed or disproved by further experiments.[3]

The following features of the experiment concern the nature of the conflict which the subject faces.

10. The subject is placed in a position in which he must respond to the competing

---

[2]Forty-three subjects, undergraduates at Yale University, were run in the experiment without payment. The results are very similar to those obtained with paid subjects.

[3]A series of recently completed experiments employing the obedience paradigm is reported in Milgram (1964).

demands of two persons: the experimenter and the victim. The conflict must be resolved by meeting the demands of one or the other; satisfaction of the victim and the experimenter are mutually exclusive. Moreover, the resolution must take the form of a highly visible action, that of continuing to shock the victim or breaking off the experiment. Thus the subject is forced into a public conflict that does not permit any completely satisfactory solution.

11. While the demands of the experimenter carry the weight of scientific authority, the demands of the victim spring from his personal experience of pain and suffering. The two claims need not be regarded as equally pressing and legitimate. The experimenter seeks an abstract scientific datum; the victim cries out for relief from physical suffering caused by the subject's actions.

12. The experiment gives the subject little time for reflection. The conflict comes on rapidly. It is only minutes after the subject has been seated before the shock generator that the victim begins his protests. Moreover, the subject perceives that he has gone through but two-thirds of the shock levels at the time the victim's first protests are heard. Thus he understands that the conflict will have a persistent aspect to it, and may well become more intense as increasingly more powerful shocks are required. The rapidity with which the conflict descends on the subject, and his realization that

it is predictably recurrent may well be sources of tension to him.

13. At a more general level, the conflict stems from the opposition of two deeply ingrained behavior dispositions: first, the disposition not to harm other people, and second, the tendency to obey those whom we perceive to be legitimate authorities.

REFERENCES

Adorno, T., Frenkel-Brunswik, Else, Levinson, D. J., and Sanford, R. N. *The Authoritarian Personality*, New York: Harper, 1950.

Arendt, H. "What Was Authority?" In C. J. Friedrich (ed.), *Authority*. Cambridge: Harvard Univ. Press, 1958. Pp. 81–112.

Binet, A. *La suggestibilité*. Paris: Schleicher, 1900.

Buss, A. H. *The Psychology of Aggression*, New York: Wiley, 1961.

Cartwright, S. (ed.) *Studies in Social Power*. Ann Arbor: University of Michigan Institute for Social Research, 1959.

Charcot, J. M. *Oeuvres complètes*. Paris: Bureaux du Progrès Médical, 1881.

Frank, J. D. "Experimental Studies of Personal Pressure and Resistance." *J. Gen. Psychol.*, 1944, *30*, 23–64.

Friedrich, C. J. (ed.) *Authority*. Cambridge: Harvard Univ. Press, 1958.

Milgram, S. "Dynamics of Obedience." Washington: National Science Foundation, 25 January 1961. (Mimeo)

Milgram, S. "Some Conditions of Obedience and Disobedience to Authority." *Hum. Relat.*, 1964, *18*, 57–76.

Rokeach, M. "Authority, Authoritarianism, and Conformity." In I. A. Berg and B. M. Bass (eds.), *Conformity and Deviation*. New York: Harper, 1961. Pp. 230–257.

Snow, C. P. "Either-Or," *Progressive*, 1961 (Feb.), 24.

Weber, M. *The Theory of Social and Economic Organization*. Oxford: Oxford Univ. Press, 1947.

UNIT 6

LEARNING MANAGEMENT

□ The Pennsylvania Dutch say, "We are too soon old and too late smart." They know what they are talking about, because one of the things you find in your progression through life is that you never stop learning. Whether in formal school or in the school of hard knocks, you are always filing things in your mind as future guidelines on how to behave. This unit will help you to become a better learner by showing you how to apply to the project of learning the lessons you have learned in the other units. Some tricks will help you if you choose to apply them. Some require that you change your present habits and thus will not be easy for you. However, if you can cut the time you take to learn something in half and learn twice as much, isn't it foolish of you to crawl when you can be walking?

When you have completed this unit, you should be able to:

1. *Describe the learning theory of the associationists.*
2. *Explain cognitive learning theory.*
3. *Summarize the learning concepts of the humanists.*
4. *Explain the concept of relevance in learning.*
5. *Define the word* teleology, *and explain how teleology can be used to increase learning effectiveness.*
6. *Describe how feedback in learning operates, and give some personal examples.*
7. *Describe how remembering and forgetting operate in the human mind.*
8. *State how the serial-position effect, overlearning, and distributed practice are related to the learning process.*
9. *Explain what a learning curve does.*
10. *Define* mediation *and explain its effect on learning.*
11. *Relate time management to learning management.*
12. *Describe the influence of expertise and the group process on learning, and explain how you can make these factors work for you.*
13. *Explain what is meant by SQ3R.*
14. *Give a summary of study skills, covering note taking and preparing for tests.*
15. *Describe different learning styles and identify those that are typical of you.*

ASSOCIATIONIST LEARNING THEORY

As a preliminary step toward improving our learning effectiveness, we need to look at some ideas on how we learn. As you might expect from psychologists, there is strong disagreement. There are many theories about learning, many of which can be grouped according to certain common ideas. One of the most powerful groups is that of the associationists. These theorists say that we learn by association. We encounter a stimulus (S). The stimulus arouses us to action, and we respond (R). The results of the response either satisfy the situation in some way or fail. If they fail, we try another response until we succeed. Then the next time we are confronted with that stimulus, we remember the right response and we repeat it. In other words, we have created an association between the stimulus and the responses: S↔R.

Associationists believe that certain conditions are attached to the learning process. They feel that it requires an action by the learner. Most believe that the learner must perceive the consequences of the action in some sort of pleasure-pain–punishment-reward framework. They believe that practice or repetition must occur so that the bond between S and R is strengthened. They also believe that a learning organism learns to associate the stimulus with other responses (generalization) and that the organism must learn specifically what response to make to a specific stimulus (discrimination). The associationists have some trouble fitting motivation into their scheme of learning. Most of them feel that motivation exists on the physiological drive-reduction level—that is, that a person's bodily needs are involved. Personal and social motives are harder for them to account for. Most associationists feel that these two types of motive are based on internal drives like the bodily needs, but they are vague about this.

There are two schools of associationist thought. One describes classical conditioning; the other describes operant or instrumental conditioning. The conventional explanation of classical conditioning uses the study of the Russian physiologist Ivan Pavlov and his dogs. Pavlov's work led to the classical conditioning theory. It is probably described so often because it not only gives the history of the theory but is a beautiful example of how it works (see Figure 6.1).

Pavlov was studying basic digestive processes. One of his studies involved the relationship of saliva to digestion. Pavlov cut the salivary ducts of dogs so that their saliva dripped into containers and could be measured. He would then feed his dogs meat powder to see how the loss of saliva affected their digestion. Almost by accident he noticed that at mealtime the dogs began to salivate before they were fed when they heard the attendant's footsteps. Pavlov found that he could train the dogs to salivate when a specific stimulus such as a bell was presented. The training had four stages:

```
Bell ─────────────────────────→No reaction
Meat powder ─────────────────→Salivation
Bell and meat powder ────────→Salivation
Bell ─────────────────────────→Salivation
```

The bell alone was the neutral stimulus (NS). It was ineffective when first presented, and there was no response (NR). The meat powder was an unconditioning stimulus (US). At first, the salivation was an unconditioned response (UR). However, when the dog finally salivated at the sound of the bell, the sound became a conditioned stimulus (CS), and the salivation then was a conditioned response (CR). The four stages could be represented in this way:

$$
\begin{array}{l}
\text{NS} \longrightarrow \text{NR} \\
\text{US} \longrightarrow \text{UR} \\
\text{NS + US} \longrightarrow \text{UR} \\
\text{CS} \longrightarrow \text{CR}
\end{array}
$$

Pavlov and other experimenters found that it is possible to pyramid this kind of learning by taking one conditioning stimulus, CS1, and making it the unconditioning stimulus (US) or another conditioning stimulus. Thus the bell could be used to train the dog to salivate when it hears a buzzer (CS2) without using meat powder at all:

$$
\begin{array}{l}
\text{NS (buzzer)} \longrightarrow \text{NR} \\
\text{CS1 (bell)} \longrightarrow \text{CR1 (salivation)} \\
\text{CS1 + NS} \longrightarrow \text{CR1} \\
\text{CS2 (buzzer)} \longrightarrow \text{CR2}
\end{array}
$$

FIGURE 6.1 PAVLOV'S DOG

The dog was held in place by a harness. Saliva entered a calibrated test tube through a tube inserted in the dog's cheek. The arrival of each drop of saliva in the test tube activated a lever and stylus, recording the amount of secretion on a revolving drum.

Adapted from R. M. Yerkes and S. Morgulis, "The Method of Pavlov in Animal Psychology," *Psychological Bulletin* 6 (1909): 257-263. Copyright 1909 by the American Psychological Association. Reprinted by permission.

This procedure is known as high-order conditioning. It helps to explain how we can become sophisticated in our learning and develop multiple responses to different situations involving the same stimulus. Much of what we learn can be traced back to this form of learning. Most of our involuntary responses can be explained by it. Can you think of some CS-CR links you have learned?

_____

_____

_____

_____

Here is one example of a CS-CR link. Think of a lemon, a nice juicy lemon. Imagine that you have just cut it and both halves are dripping. Now imagine that you are squeezing the lemon into a glass and the juice is spurting out. You raise the glass to your lips and you start to drink. Are you salivating more than usual? If you have ever sucked a lemon, you probably did start to salivate heavily when you thought about this one.

You need to learn some technical terms that deal with the establishment of the S-R bond.

Reinforcement is the process of pairing a neutral stimulus with an unconditioning stimulus to establish the bond between the neutral stimulus and the response.

Extinction of the response occurs if the pairing of the two stimuli is stopped or if the reinforcement is halted; the response will eventually fade away and become extinct.

Spontaneous recovery is the reappearance without reinforcement, after a period of rest, of the association between the conditioned stimulus and the conditioned response.

Generalization is the ability of the organism to learn multiple conditioned stimuli for any response.

Discrimination is the ability of an organism to limit the response to a specific stimulus—for example, a bell of a certain volume or tone.

There is another way to establish a bond between S and R. This method is called *operant conditioning*. It differs considerably from the classical model. An experimenter who wishes to train an organism to do a specific thing uses a system of consequent reinforcement. Whenever the animal makes the right response, it is rewarded. Usually some sort of signal or cue is used to start the action. The animal responds to the cue and is reinforced, either positively or negatively. The cue is given again, the organism responds, and the organism is reinforced.

There are two basic ways to reinforce. One is by patiently waiting for the trainee to make the right response, or anything that looks like the right response, when the signal (stimulus) is given, and then offering the reward. A reward can be food or a pat on the head or anything that is pleasant to the trainee. If you wish, however, you can do the opposite and punish every time the signal is given and the right action isn't taken. By doing this, you hope to inhibit all possible wrong responses. Reinforcement by punishment is tricky. It is powerful, but you have to make sure the trainee knows the right response before you try to inhibit the wrong acts. A variation of this use of a negative feeling is called avoidance learning. When using this system, you give a stimulus and then make the trainee uncomfortable by administering shocks or doing something else unpleasant. The unpleasant feeling is stopped when the trainee carries out the right action, which thus becomes associated with relief or avoidance of some unpleasant feeling.

In all these cases, the cue is given, and the organism responds. The organism's action is reinforced. The more this pattern is repeated, the stronger becomes the response to the cue. For example, suppose you want to train your dog to sit up. Here is a sequence you can follow, using positive reinforcement.

First get your dog's attention by holding a piece of food in your hand above its head. Give the command, "Sit up." Whenever the dog makes any motion that leads to sitting up, reinforce this action by giving it a piece of food. Keep doing this but get more and more demanding about the act; that is, reinforce only the responses that will progressively lead to the dog's sitting up properly. Always associate the command with the right response and the reward. Then, as the dog gets better and better at it, gradually withdraw the food from sight until it responds to your words. Then gradually stop giving the reinforcement until the dog is sitting up every time without a reward. When your dog can do this, it has been conditioned to sit up on command. As described here, such conditioning seems quite simple. Actually it takes a very long time and needs to be repeated and repeated until it is mastered.

The conditioning just described has four elements. The dog has to be hungry (*drive*), or else you must use some other reinforcer. The *cue* you use is your voice. The *reinforcer* is the food, which in this case is a positive reinforcer. The *response* is, of course, the sitting up.

When you started to train your dog, you had a choice of signals or cues. You could have used a bell, a buzzer, a snap of your fingers, or even a hand movement that might be almost imperceptible to an observer. As you vary the strength and complexity of your signal, you of course vary its clarity. The more obscure it is, the harder it is for the learner to detect it and to pair it with the response. If you want to teach a response to a very slight stimulus, it is probably better either to start with a fairly obvious level and slowly reduce the intensity of the cue or to use an obvious cue first, create the response to it, and then use high-order conditioning to pair one cue with another. You also have to avoid using a stimulus that is too powerful. For example, if you scream at the dog, the volume of your voice may distract it from the response you want. Too intense a stimulus can be as troublesome as too low a cue level.

Not only do you have a choice in the kind of cue and its intensity; you also have to decide whether you will use a positive or a negative reinforcer. A positive reinforcer rewards a performance. It can be food or just a word of approval, such as "good." A negative reinforcer is used to eliminate unwanted responses or to create a specific response to a negative sensation. For example, if you wish to train a dog to avoid stepping on a brass plate in a cage, you have two choices. You can reward the dog when it avoids the plate, or you can punish it when it steps on the plate. You could connect the plate to an electrical source so that the dog is shocked every time it touches the plate. The aversive, negative reinforcement is quick and effective in this case, but it can be dangerous if it is overused or misused. For example, suppose a child repeatedly goes into the bathroom and turns on the faucets in the tub because he or she likes the sight and sound of running water. You can eliminate this behavior by paddling the child soundly or even by dunking the child into cold water when he or she does this. The child will probably quickly learn not to turn on the water *when you are around*, though he or she may still do it when you are not around. Then, too, you may have taught the child so well that you have to drag him or her kicking and screaming into the bathroom to take a bath.

To see the differences between these types of reinforcement, try this exercise:

EXERCISE 1. HOT AND COLD

1. Send one member of your group out of the room, and decide on a simple job for that person to do. Then call the individual back and explain that you want him or her to do something. The person must figure out what to do; you will reinforce him or her by saying "no" every time the actions are inappropriate. Record how many trials this person makes before doing the right thing. Ask the person how he or she felt while working through the problem.
2. Once again, send someone out of the room, and decide on a simple task. Call the person back and explain that you want him or her to do something, but that he or she must figure out what to do. Explain that you will reinforce him or her by saying "yes" only when the actions are appropriate. Record how many trials this person makes before doing the right thing. Ask the person to describe how he or she felt while working through the problem.
3. Repeat the exercise with a third person, but use both negative and positive reinforcers. Record the number of trials, and ask the person to describe his or her feelings.

Which system was most efficient? Which produced the best emotional climate for the learner?

Not only do you have a choice in the kind of cue, its intensity, and the type of reinforcer you use; you have a choice in the degree or amount by which you apply the reinforcer. When you trained your dog, you were told to reinforce whenever it made a move that would lead to sitting up. This is a good rule for a fairly complicated skill. Suppose you are working on a fairly simple skill, such as getting your dog to bark when you command, "Speak." In a situation like this, you can reward the dog every time it barks, or every fifth time, or at random. Can you predict what the different results will be? Number these from 1 to 3, with 1 being best:

Reward schedule	Quickest acquisition of learning	Easiest extinction of learning
Every time	_____	_____
Every fifth time	_____	_____
At random	_____	_____

Reinforcement every time will result in the quickest acquisition of learning, and random reinforcement will be the slowest. The reverse is true for retention: Reinforcement every time will result in easiest extinction, and random reinforcement will produce learning that is very difficult to extinguish.

How would you plan a reinforcement schedule for a fairly complicated skill, such as teaching a dog to roll over?

_____

_____

_____

_____

If you started with continuous reinforcement, switched to a schedule, and then ended with reinforcement at random, you have been conditioned to think correctly about operant conditioning.

You have now been exposed to two different teaching programs. How do they differ? In classical conditioning, you are generally trying to use an established response, mostly of an involuntary nature, and to devise several stimuli that evoke it. Diagrammatically it looks like this:

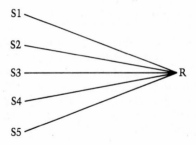

In operant conditioning, you are selecting one response out of a range of responses and connecting that response to a stimulus:

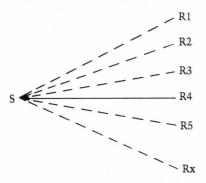

Another way of saying this is that in classical conditioning the organism responds to a change in the environment; in operant conditioning the organism responds to a stimulus by changing its environment.

1. Describe the learning theory of the associationists.

_____

_____

_____

_____

COGNITIVE LEARNING THEORY

Some learning specialists react violently to this set of principles. "That isn't the way at all," they say. "You are completely disregarding the person in your system. How can you explain the fact that it takes one person only three times to learn something, while another may need fifty? You are ignoring individual differences in your theory. You are not accounting for the influence of the person's interests, experience, desires, or emotional set. What you are doing might have worked with rats, but it doesn't apply to humans." These cognitive learning theory advocates argue that the S-R diagram is too simple and incomplete, that it must include the variable of the organism (O) itself to make the explanation of how learning occurs a meaningful one. When you include this variable, you then include a consideration of the person: his or her perceptions, past experiences, abilities, and desires. S-O-R is more appropriate.

The principles under which the cognitive theorists operate emphasize perceptual features; they analyze the connections between bits and pieces of information. From these bits and pieces a person creates a whole pattern into which the pieces fall in some sort of order. Thus, the cognitive theorists say, a person who has undergone cognitive education understands what is learned more than a person who has learned under operant conditioning. The motivation of the learner is of great importance in cognitive learning, as is the process of evaluation and feedback. According to the cognitive theorists, there is a regular problem-solving procedure that a person learns in cognitive learning.

The first step is *awareness.* The person becomes aware of a problem or incident that is puzzling and moves him or her to act. The second step is *fact finding.* The learner tries to accumulate as many facts as possible about the incident. The third step is *processing.* Within the learner's brain, the

Cognitive learning. (Charles Gatewood)

information is fed to the memory: Have I ever seen anything like this before? What was it? What did I do? What happened? This is the type of organization that goes on. The data are organized into a logical pattern. The fourth step, quite important in cognitive learning, is *incubation* and then *acquiring insight*. The learner may seem to forget complex problems. He or she may become occupied with other things. However, the problem is incubating. Suddenly, the pieces come together into a pattern, and the solution suggests itself in a flash of insight or understanding. A fifth step then takes place, *testing*. Does the solution work? Does it fit the data? If it does, the problem is solved. If it does not, the problem is analyzed all over again, with the input of the new information that the apparent solution does not work.

One of the most famous examples of this kind of problem solving was devised by Wolfgang Köhler, using an ape named Sultan. Outside of Sultan's cage, well out of reach of the ape, Köhler placed a banana. Closer to Sultan, but still outside the cage, two sticks were placed. The shorter stick was closer to the cage. It was just long enough to enable the ape to rake in the second stick, which was just long enough to reach the banana. When the ape first saw the banana, it went through all the gyrations you might expect. Finally, in frustration, it grabbed the short stick and tried to get the banana. When this

Köhler's ape. (Yerkes Regional Primate Research Center)

attempt failed, all activity stopped and the ape sat brooding. Suddenly, as if a light had gone on, Sultan used the short stick to pull in the long stick and used that to pull in the banana. This demonstration beautifully describes the procedures that, in the view of cognitive theorists, go on in problem solving.

2. Explain cognitive learning theory.

_____

_____

_____

_____

HUMANISTS AND LEARNING

Another group, known as humanists, has taken a position on learning. Strictly speaking, this group's ideas do not really state a theory of learning. The humanists are more concerned with the conditions of learning than with the specific mechanics involved. They concentrate heavily on the role of the individual learner in the learning process. They contend that the needs and interests of the individual must be considered; otherwise, learning can become an inefficient and dreary experience. The specific abilities and background of the learner should also be taken into account in order to avoid forcing the learner into a procedure that is too difficult to handle. Teaching and learning cannot ignore the cultural and environmental factors that surround the person: rather, these factors are terribly important when setting learning tasks. Most of all, however, the humanists are concerned with the emotional climate in which learning occurs. They maintain that if learning takes place in a negative climate, it will be poor in quality and will not be enduring in nature. For example, competition and constant comparison with other learners can be harmful to the individual in the long run, especially if the comparisons are usually negative.

Essentially, the humanists argue that there are two parts to every learning experience. One is the *cognitive*, the fact or the action, which is the intellectual component. The other, which is more important to the humanists is the *emotional* or *affective* part. If learning takes place under negative emotional conditions, then the result will be poor. Either the learning experience will be quickly lost in a form of motivated forgetting, or it will result in the individual's reluctance to use what has been learned because of the painful memory associated with it. This concept implies that the humanists are as concerned equally with how something is taught and with what is taught. They believe that the learning process should yield a healthy person rather than a neurotic, fact-filled wreck.

3. *Summarize the learning concepts of the humanists.*

_____

_____

_____

_____

RELEVANCE

In the last few years, the word *relevance* has been tiresomely overused in the educational field; yet it embodies such an important concept that no one who is trying to improve learning efficiency can afford to ignore it. When we speak of relevance, we are trying to answer the question, "Why am I trying to learn this stupid subject anyway?" If you have asked yourself this question and have come up with the answer, "Because someone is making me," then there is something wrong. In effect, what you are saying is that the topic is of no interest to you. Whenever we are forced to learn something, strange things happen. Learning becomes work, slavery, drudgery—you name it. We have to apply tremendous pressure to ourselves to learn. This pressure often backfires, and we start to use the ego-protective devices we normally use to avoid conflict. Have you personally felt or have you known someone who developed a school phobia? Did you ever get sick to your stomach just before schooltime? This is but one of many symptoms pointing to maladjustment in learning. When you pass a school with half the windowpanes knocked out by stones, would you say that the school is teaching relevant subjects?

Learning can be fun. You have experienced this, too. Everyone has sweat blood to learn something he or she wanted to learn—Morse code, the score or words of a popular song, or whatever. When a person wants to learn, learning isn't drudgery, although it is work. No learning is easy. How can learning be fun? You must relate what you are learning to your own interests: How can this topic help me to get where I want to go? You must sit down and figure out some answers to this question.

Suppose you are in college and are majoring in anthropology. One of the requirements for graduation is two years of Spanish. You hate studying languages because you have never learned one successfully. Bearing in mind your long-range and short-term objectives, list as many reasons as you can for studying languages.

_____

_____

_____

_____

You might have listed some of these reasons:

1. I want to be an anthropologist, and I need Spanish for special areas of anthropology.
2. General language proficiency is a must for anthropologists.
3. Spanish is a Romance language; knowing it will help me to learn other Romance languages.
4. Spanish may help me to refine my use of English.
5. If I can discipline myself to study Spanish, I will have improved my overall self-control.
6. I will impress my friends by speaking Spanish.

Having listed such reasons, you should have a sense of purpose. You should be able to justify why you need to suffer through two years of Spanish, because you have taken the trouble to relate the subject to yourself. Granted, you may never become wildly enthusiastic about Spanish, but at least you will see some value in learning it.

Relevance means that something is significant to you. If it isn't, then you, being logical, will tend to say, "It's spinach and to hell with it." If this happens, you have ten times as much trouble as you should. To overcome irrelevance, you need to sit down with yourself and make the topic fit into your personal scheme of things. You need to put it into a master plan so that you can see how it helps you get where you want to go.

4. Explain the concept of relevance in learning.

_____

_____

_____

_____

TELEOLOGY

Very closely allied to relevance, yet different from it, is the notion of *teleology*. The word itself means the study of final causes. It means being directed to a final goal or having an ultimate purpose. Philosophically, it can mean, "What purpose does humanity serve?" In Unit 3, "Personality," you were exposed to some theories that used the concept of the desire of human beings to find a meaning or purpose in life as their cornerstone. In an abstract way, every cause has an effect, and every effect has a cause. Therefore, everything we do has some sort of purpose. We may not be aware of it, but nevertheless it is there. Many philosophers believe that the purposefulness of human beings is a potent force. The application of teleology in this unit will show you how to harness this force. Here, *teleology* will be given a specialized meaning to describe a technique that can be valuable to you in learning management.

When you conned yourself into thinking that a two-year study of Spanish could be meaningful to you, what you actually were doing was relating Spanish to your goals, both long-range and short-term. Teleology will now take you one step farther. You have convinced yourself that the study of Spanish will be valuable to you in several ways. Your next step is to break down the study into a set of specific subgoals. For example, in order to complete your first year of Spanish successfully, you might decide that you have to (1) learn 1,500 Spanish words, (2) conjugate 100 Spanish verbs, (3) write simple paragraphs in Spanish on assigned subjects, and (4) sight-read (translate) selected passages from Spanish into English.

Listing specific objectives gives you specific targets to shoot at. You know what you need to do, and you can get down to doing it. The list gives you a sense of purpose, of things to do, of where to go. You have created specific steps that will lead you to your destination. The practice of creating specific goals for yourself so that you can see some purpose in what you are doing is teleology.

5. *Define the word* teleology, *and explain how teleology can be used to increase learning effectiveness.*

FEEDBACK

Feedback means knowledge of results. It is basic to the learning process. Nothing succeeds like success. When we get good feedback, usually we are encouraged to go on. When we get bad feedback, we often may quit. Knowledge of results, then, is an extremely powerful force. In our formal education experiences, it can make the difference between success and failure.

How can we manipulate this force so that it serves us? We must make our feedback personal. Most of the time, feedback is handed to us by someone else. A teacher, boss, or some other party tells us that we did well or poorly. When this happens, our future is at the disposal of others. They are exerting their power on us. However, there is no reason that we cannot learn to make our own feedback and manipulate it for ourselves.

Back to the Spanish-learning example: One of our specific subgoals was to learn 1,500 words. This involves straight memorization—sitting down and learning a list of words and what they mean. This kind of learning is one of the most familiar to us all. How can feedback help? Quite simply. Start memorizing and keep memorizing until you can identify each word and its meaning on sight, at random. Naturally, you can't accomplish this task at one sitting. Some of the material that follows will give you techniques to accomplish it. At some point in your first year of study, you'll be able to say to yourself, "Hey, I did it. I know 1,500 Spanish words." You'll be able to put a big check mark by the first goal and turn to the next one, conjugating 100 verbs. After considerable sweat and tears, you'll announce to yourself, "I can do that, too." Another big check mark will go on the list of goals.

Your check marks will give you a big lift. You will have a new feeling of confidence. You'll know you are making it; you're getting there. This feeling is feedback. It is one of the most exciting and powerful forces you can ever hope to master. The beauty of the technique is that it need not depend on any other person. You can use it yourself, by yourself, on yourself, and for yourself. All you have to do is set a goal to be accomplished and have that goal lead logically to the next one. These goals can cover one lesson, one whole day, or any period of time. Just set up a list of things to do, do them, and then check them off when you have finished them. Simple, yet powerful.

6. *Describe how feedback in learning operates, and give some personal examples.*

_____

_____

_____

_____

REMEMBERING AND FORGETTING

In the discussion of feedback, you were asked to memorize something. As a matter of fact, all learning involves memory, the ability to retain the results of our learning in our minds. It is a strange thing, but even after years of research, no one knows exactly how memorization takes place. It seems to be a complicated process. Apparently, when we receive a stimulus resulting in a sensation, we attend to it. If the stimulus is unimportant, we consider it briefly in what is called our short-term memory and then discard it. If it is important, we encode it into our long-term memory. It used to be thought that we encoded by creating certain neural pathways in our mind and that we strengthened these pathways by repeating the encoding again and again. In this way, the theory said, we burned a circuit into our brain. If we didn't use the circuit, it slowly degenerated. More recent evidence shows that memorization is much more complicated than this and involves chemical activity as well as electrical action within the brain. Specific learned information has been transmitted from one group of animals to another by chemical injection. Long-term memory encoding has also been inhibited. These processes hold fascinating possibilities for future generations. Think of learning a whole year's course of mathematics by injection! But at this time that is fantasy. Back to reality.

Memorization and repetition seem to be inseparable. Drill, drill, drill is the fundamental way to memorize. We learn something, check ourselves to see whether we know it, and then go back over it again until we are satisfied. This is the routine for committing things to memory. So far, no one has been able to come up with a better one. There is a way in which we often learn something after one or two trials, but its use is a bit impractical: When a situation causes a sufficiently high level of emotional intensity, the episode is encoded into our memory for life. Fear and pain will result in this type of learning. As creepers, some of us learned the hard way about poking something into an electrical socket. It usually takes one flash and one burn for us to realize that this is not the thing to do. Although the learning technique is much more effective than a parent's no-no, it is not very pleasant and sometimes may cause strange by-products that in themselves constitute bad learning. Effective learning can be accomplished in other ways.

Memorization, then, is connected in the human mind with repetition and drill. Emotions do enter into the learning process and can help in memorization. The more frequently we use an item stored in our memory, the more readily available it seems to be. While the processes inside our minds are still pretty much unknown to us, the ground rules by which they operate are clear. The problem for most of us is knowing how to use the power of our minds to encode effectively what we want to memorize.

One of the best ways for you to develop a good memory is to learn how to use a device called a *mnemonic*. You have been using mnemonic devices for years, but you probably haven't been using them efficiently. A mnemonic is nothing more than a way of hooking up something you want to learn with something you already know. "One is a bun, two is a shoe, three is a tree . . ." is a mnemonic.

The correct way to use a mnemonic device is to couple what you want to learn with a systematic list of what you already know, using visual imagery to make the connection ("One is a bun"). If you have a list of things you want to learn, such as names of people in a group, visually connect the first person, Joe Anderson, with a mental image of a bun on a plate. Connect the next person, Shirley Baker, with a picture of Shirley peering out over the top of an old shoe, and so. Then when you want to resurrect Shirley's name from your memory, think of the second person you met, connect her with a shoe, and dredge up the name of Shirley Baker. In this way you remember not only who every person is but the order in which you met them. In order to do this successfully, your images must become almost instinctive. You have to know the order of the list, be able to say it forward and backward, and be able to pick out any one item and know exactly where it fits in the list.

Here is a fifty-item list adapted from one made by Richard Kammann, a well-known psychologist. It has a format that makes the alphabet work for you. The first nine words begin with letters of the alphabet taken in their proper order. The tenth word and every succeeding tenth word ends in *N*. The words running from 11 through 19 begin with *A* and end in the proper letter to show their distance from 11. The *B's, C's,* and *D's* follow in a similar manner. When you have learned this scheme, you should be able to take any word and put it in its proper sequence.

1. altar	11. abscissa	21. boa	31. camera	41. diploma
2. beggar	12. A-bomb	22. bulb	32. club	42. daub
3. chandelier	13. alcoholic	23. bric-a-brac	33. cleric	43. doric
4. dagger	14. almond	24. bald	34. cupboard	44. diamond
5. ear	15. ape	25. bee	35. cake	45. dice
6. fakir	16. aloof	26. bluff	36. calf	46. dwarf
7. gator	17. angling	27. bug	37. cog	47. dog
8. hanger	18. arch	28. beach	38. coach	48. ditch
9. iron	19. anti	29. brevi	39. cacti	49. dei
10. acorn	20. balloon	30. cannon	40. dolphin	50. ensign

It is possible, of course, to extend this list so that you could manage 100, 150, or even 200 items.

Learn the list and practice it until you know it well. Then try it out with your friends. You'll be amazed at the results. Be sure to form a mental image of the item you are trying to learn by connecting it with a key word. The more outrageous the picture you form in your mind, the more readily it will stick in your memory.

7. Describe how remembering and forgetting operate in the human mind.

_____

_____

_____

_____

SERIAL POSITION EFFECT, OVERLEARNING, AND DISTRIBUTED PRACTICE

One of the strange things that always occurs when students are exposed to learning-management techniques is that they almost invariably say, "There's nothing new about this. I've been doing it for years." This statement is quite true. There is no magic key to learning, nor are there any secret methods that can make us geniuses overnight. Most of us are familiar with the techniques involved in committing things to memory. What we are not familiar with is how to use these techniques effectively and how to reduce interference with our learning efforts.

A statement of the *serial-position effect* tells us that we retain the ends of a list while forgetting its middle. Apparently, we code in such a way that we can usually memorize up to seven items at once. After that, we must break the items down into memorizable units or we will forget them.

What does this mean for learning management? If you need to learn any complicated or long items, you are better off breaking them into segments and learning the segments. When you do this, you must either be careful to change the break points every so often or take special precautions to make sure the breaks are hooked together. Otherwise, as you rattle merrily along, reciting whatever you have learned, you will suddenly come to a screeching halt. You will have forgotten the connection between subunits.

How do you know when you have finally memorized something? You can counter this question by asking, "How well do I have to know that particular item? Do I have to be letter-perfect, or can I give just the gist of the idea?" The degree to which you learn depends on the standards that have been set either by you or by someone else. For instance, in learning the list of Spanish words, you could be satisfied with 90 percent recognition of any sublist given to you, either in Spanish or in English.

In order to meet standards, we must practice. The degree and amount of practice necessary depend on how complicated the job is. Usually, we learn and relearn until we are satisfied that we can meet our standards. To be completely satisfied, we usually overlearn, guarding against the decay of our memory by performing at a standard higher than is called for. *Overlearning* is helpful in avoiding the effects of both retroactive and proactive interference. The former is caused by things we learn later; the latter is interference from something we learned earlier. By thoroughly learning at the start, you can prevent these two forces from crippling your efforts.

If you want or need to retain items—for instance, the 1,500 words—in your memory for a short period of time, you probably could sit down in one or two marathon sessions and learn them, though a week or two later you would probably remember only a few items at the beginning and end of the list. It would be far better if you broke the list down and learned ten items a day. If you practiced the old ones and learned the new ones, you would be studying in a cumulative manner, and your learning technique would be called *distributed practice.* The odds are that anything learned in that way will stay with you for a long time.

8. *State how the serial-position effect, overlearning, and distributed practice are related to the learning process.*

LEARNING CURVES

Some people use a learning curve to help themselves learn.

EXERCISE 1. PLOTTING A LEARNING CURVE

1. Place a mirror in front of yourself in such a way that you can see what you are writing on a piece of paper.
2. Looking only at the mirror, print your name on the paper, timing yourself as you do so.
3. Print your name twenty-five times, and write down how long you take each time.
4. Plot on Figure 6.2 the times for each trial.

FIGURE 6.2 LEARNING CURVE

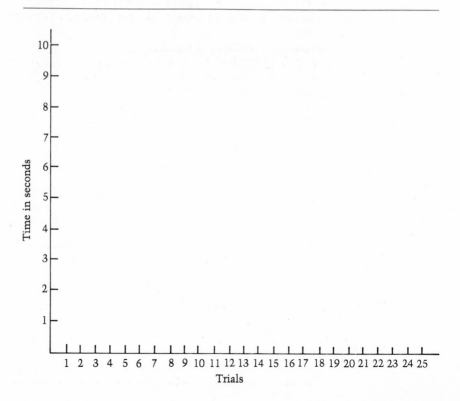

What kind of a curve did you get? Twenty-five trials isn't much of a base on which to operate, but the time it took you to write your name should have decreased steadily from your first effort to your twenty-fifth. A declining curve shows that you were learning; you were taking less time at the end of the exercise than at the beginning. The more you practice, the less time you should take, until you reach your physiological limit, at which you are writing as fast as you can.

Plotting a learning curve is useful when you are learning skills, because it records your progress. However, you must be prepared for one thing. Every so often you will hit a plateau; the curve will stay level and you won't seem to be making any improvement. Apparently, this is normal. In order to beat the plateau effect, you must either devote more time and energy to your task or change your learning procedures to match your new skill. You must be careful to guard against the negative feeling you will get when you see no progress. A typical learning curve is shown in Figure 6.3. In it the number of items learned or performed increases over a number of trials. The curve you made on Figure 6.2 will look different from this one because the time you needed for each trial decreased, whereas in Figure 6.3 the number of items learned in each trial increases. Your own curve should be declining, not rising.

When you start off, your learning techniques are usually imperfect and your learning slow. As you begin to get the hang of the system, your learning picks up. When it hits the plateau, you know you need to redirect your efforts and

FIGURE 6.3 TYPICAL LEARNING CURVE

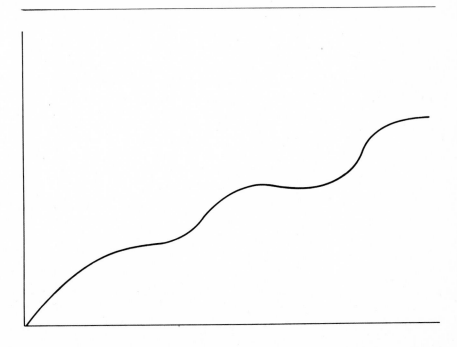

guard against a drop in enthusiasm. Next, you will start to learn quickly again until you reach another plateau. Having overcome such plateaus, you will finally reach a limit beyond which you cannot go.

9. Explain what a learning curve does.

_____

_____

_____

_____

MEDIATION

When learning something, have you ever put the items together, using extra words? For example, suppose you were given this list of paired terms to learn:

apple   pond
bear   tree
canoe   hill
bark   pail

You could painfully memorize the word pairs, but if you put them into sentences (The apple floated in the pond. The bear climbed the tree.), learning would be much easier. You would then be combining two words and linking them together with some meaning. Assigning a meaning—a process called *mediation*—makes all the difference in the world.

We will consider two types of mediation: verbal and pictorial. In verbal mediation, you put things together to form a meaning expressed in words; in pictorial mediation, you associate things by forming a mental image of them. A great many of us mediate and don't even know that we are doing so. It's a good technique and should be used consciously. What you are really doing when you mediate is creating a type of mnemonic. You can use mediation successfully for any form of learning.

10. Define mediation *and explain its effect on learning.*

_____

_____

_____

_____

TIME MANAGEMENT

The tips you have been given about feedback, learning curves, distributed practice, teleology, and memorization have all pointed to a variable that has not been mentioned but that is usually all-important. It is time. Many different things can vary in a formal educational system—teaching techniques, classroom climate, teaching aids, curriculum, and so on. However, one factor is almost invariably fixed. It is the amount of time that we are given to master a topic. Think it over. Hasn't the time factor been fixed for you in every course you have taken?

One educational psychologist says there are really no A, B, or C students. Rather, anyone can make an A in any course in any curriculum if properly motivated and able to climb out from under the time factor. Unfortunately, the system doesn't often let us do this, so we must make the most of the time available. In other words, we must learn time management.

A college course is usually set up so that two hours of preparation are required for every hour you spend in class. Most students have fifteen or sixteen hours of classes a week. Thus you might expect to devote forty-five or forty-eight hours a week to classroom and out-of-class study time. This is a pretty hefty load. Obviously, some students will need less time, and others should take more. In any case, most students are haphazard procrastinators and don't do as much work as they should.

One of the secrets of efficient time management is to combine it with teleology and feedback. Let's go back to the 1,500 Spanish words. Obviously, you wouldn't want to learn them in one or two big study binges. So why not adopt a schedule like this: There are fifteen weeks to a semester. You have two semesters in which to learn the words. Therefore you must learn fifty words a week. Fifty at one time is too much. So learn ten every weekday. On weekends either rest or review the fifty just learned. Divide the list into groups of ten words each and make up a schedule, listing the words to be learned on Monday, Tuesday, and so on. Each time you learn the day's words, put a check on your calendar.

This seems like a lot of trouble, doesn't it? And trouble is something that most of us like to avoid. The schedule pins us down. We have a lot of little subtasks to handle, and we have broken them down into a routine. Very few people like to commit themselves to this extent. But the technique is effective. By using a learning curve with this schedule and marking the total number of words learned and the time taken to learn each subgroup, you can keep tabs on your learning efficiency. As you begin your work and begin to check off the days, a strange thing happens. Positive feedback starts; you are doing your job. Time management has suddenly become an effective tool in your bag of learning tricks.

11. Relate time management to learning management.

EXPERTISE AND THE GROUP PROCESS

A revealing story about improving learning effectiveness has come from a researcher at a Southern university. He taught the students in his class who were doing poorly one simple act that raised their grades by at least one level. He taught them to raise their eyes and look at him when he asked a question. Simple and silly? Yes, but it worked.

Think of how you act in a classroom or in a group when a question is asked. If you are like 90 percent of all students, you immediately drop your eyes, simulating deep thought. What you are actually signaling through your body language is, "Don't call on me." If you do this consistently, and most students do, you begin to convince the instructor that you either don't know the answers or don't want to participate in class. Either impression is a negative one, and if any subjective element enters into that teacher's grading, you will be penalized. How much better it would be if you took a chance and dared the teacher to call on you. The odds still favor you, because only one person can be called on at a time. Even if you are called on and you fall flat on your face, you probably will still have made a better impression.

You can learn a small lesson here that can pay off: Take advantage of your expertise. There is bound to be some facet of any subject about which you know something. If you want to build up your reputation, bone up on that part until you are an expert. Then, when you walk into class, you'll be ready for anyone and begging for a chance to show off.

You can receive a peculiar personal benefit from this approach. The confidence you feel when you don't have to be defensive and hide in class is really a positive emotion. You may like it so much that you become more and more of an expert on other topics too. If you can tie in your own interests and abilities with a subject, and if you don't have to play hide-and-seek with the instructor, learning will become fun.

Why are you afraid that someone will call on you? Many times you may know the answer but still hate to be called on. Even when it's to your advantage to participate, you sit silent. Why? You fear the group. The group is so powerful that many people will go to great lengths to avoid its displeasure. If a student belongs to a peer group that scorns study, he or she can be dismissed from it for acting too smart. As a result, many students, particularly college freshmen, are virtually frozen with fear in the classroom. This shouldn't be!

Group pressure can be used productively, especially by those of us who are weak willed. Many of us start a new course with good intentions but slowly drift back into our delaying, last-minute study techniques. We seem to be unable to operate unless under pressure.

One way to get that pressure in a beneficial way is to commit yourself publicly to certain goals. If you announce to your group, "I'm going to be prepared for my classes and systematic about my study habits. I'm going to get a B in this course," you can be sure that your group will check on you. Their pressure will be a great motivating force. It's a little masochistic, perhaps, but it will keep you on your toes when your secret resolutions will not.

12. *Describe the influence of expertise and the group process on learning, and explain how you can make these factors work for you.*

_____

_____

_____

_____

SQ3R

The following explanation of SQ3R has been developed for students who are having academic trouble. SQ3R is a mnemonic for certain action words or steps used in one study method. These steps are survey, question, read, recite, review.

SURVEY

Look over the material to get a feel for it. Look at the titles and the headings of major chapter divisions. If there is a summary at the end of the chapter, read it through quickly. The point is to get a quick, one-minute idea of what the major themes of a unit are. This will help you to cluster your ideas around the organization of the topic. It will also help you to start questioning.

QUESTION

Having read the summary or gotten a quick idea of the topic and its coverage, go back to the beginning of the unit. Your job now is to turn all the major headings into questions. Go through the entire unit again, writing each question down. This questioning does two things: It makes you respond actively to each heading. It also arouses your curiosity by raising questions in your mind.

READ

Start at the beginning again and read with a purpose. You are now looking for answers to the questions you have written in your study notes. Pay attention only to the material that will help you to organize your answers. Don't mess around with tables, charts, or diagrams unless they refer directly to your question. Use a pencil or a marking pen to outline main ideas. Underlining the main thought in each paragraph and bracketing the supporting material might help you. Many students use a light-colored marking pencil to highlight an idea on the page without blotting it out. Put a star in the margin to mark an important point.

RECITE

As soon as you have finished reading the material concerning your first question, turn away from the book and try to answer it. As you recite, write down what you say. Leave space in your notes so you can add any material you may have missed. You'll find that you'll need space when you go back and compare what the book says with your own answer. Fill in the space. In this way, you will express the whole idea in your own words. Don't go overboard on this outline; keep it short and stick to the main point.

REVIEW

After you have finished reading the lesson, look over your notes. Check your recollection of each point by going over it until you are satisfied that you know it.

The beauty of this method is that you will wind up with a set of notes and a list of questions similar to those the instructor will use in tests, with answers in your own words. The amount of memory loss you will have will depend on how often and how thoroughly you review.

You might look out for a few things when practicing this technique. When you make your first survey, don't get too involved. It should take only a minute or two. Some people immediately plunge into deep study. The survey is not supposed to involve this. Don't neglect to rephrase headings into questions. It is easy to forget this step, but if you do, you will lose some of the effectiveness of this method. Don't forget to stop at the end of each topic and answer your question. Don't count on storing the answer in your memory until you reach the end of the unit. This causes confusion. Deal with each question separately. Use your own words and be sure to say those words to yourself. This recitation is important for getting the material into your memory.

13. *Explain what is meant by SQ3R.*

_____

_____

_____

_____

TAKING NOTES AND PREPARING FOR TESTS

The art of taking notes is valuable not only in the classroom. You can use this skill many times in other places—while listening to speeches, in group sessions, in seminar discussions, and so on. It is an easy technique to master if you get started in the right way. Here are a few suggestions about note taking that may help you to develop this skill.

LEARNING
MANAGEMENT

BASIC
ASSUMPTIONS
FOR NOTE
TAKING

1. The lecturer has something definite to say on a given subject.
2. The lecturer will probably present the material in a fairly well-organized fashion.
3. In most cases, the lecturer will present what he or she considers to be the highlights of the topic, placing major emphasis on the basic points.
4. In talking about a subject, the lecturer will make a series of basic statements and then will elaborate on each of these in turn, using devices such as repetition, restatement, illustration, contrast, and analysis.
5. An individual talks more rapidly than you can write.
6. You can do efficiently only one thing at a time—listening or writing.
7. Take notes that can be used later to help you recall certain information.
8. Well-organized written material is easy to read and promotes effective learning.

SUGGESTIONS
FOR NOTE
TAKING

1. Come prepared.
   a. Read over your notes from the previous lecture.
   b. Read the assignment on which the lecturer intends to talk.
   c. Come early enough to get a good seat near the front of the room.
   d. Have paper, pencils, and erasers handy.
2. Listen attentively.
   a. Identify immediately the general topic to be discussed.
   b. Determine as soon as possible the probable breakdown of that topic—chronological order (periods, stages, and so on), a series of isolated topics such as authors or elements, analysis.
   c. Develop skill in separating essential from nonessential statements.
3. Write efficiently.
   a. Write down only the general topic, main headings, and essential statements. Be brief but clear.
   b. Write neatly.
   c. Use abbreviations freely, but select only those you'll be able to identify readily later.
   d. If you miss a point, leave a few lines and get it from someone after class. Don't risk missing six other points by trying to get it immediately.
4. Organize carefully.
   a. Record your notes in outline form.
   b. Make your indentations stand out clearly.
   c. Don't crowd your work on a page; leave wide margins.
   d. Write on only one side of the page.
   e. Star the points that have been emphasized by the lecturer.
5. Use notes effectively.
   a. Review them briefly before reading your next assignment.
   b. Glance over them before the next lecture.
   c. Study them carefully before an examination. It often helps considerably to glance at the various headings, one at a time; then look away and try to recite the major points made under each heading. If this procedure is used, underline the major headings in one color and the minor ones in another.

d. Some students recopy the general topic and main subdivisions on three-by-five cards and use them for reviewing during odd moments.

Many students operate under the false impression that the closer their notes are to the words used by the lecturer, the better they are. They believe that quantity and exact wording are all-important. In order to get the teacher's exact words, they will write like mad, study shorthand or speedwriting, or even use recording machines.

Actually, good notes depend on selection and organization. The student's first task is to select critically the statements that are essential for understanding the topic the lecturer is presenting. The second task is to organize the statements in some meaningful fashion. Both tasks require understanding and reasoning that cannot be attained by any mechanical process. In brief, learning requires thought. Making—rather than taking—notes is one means of learning.

Your preparation for an examination should be spread out over a long period of time. Ideally, you should use a system of study throughout the course that allows for short periods of review at frequent intervals. Attempting to cram at the last minute results only in confusion and insecurity.

SUGGESTIONS FOR EXAM PREPARATION

1. Spaced review periods are more effective than one concentrated review. The time intervals allow for the assimilation and organization of material and assure better retention.
2. Any plan for review should be scheduled fairly rigidly. A schedule made out in advance will usually be pretty complete. It will allow you to see what progress you have made toward your goal and will help to prevent you from putting off your work.
3. During your review, maintain your usual habits of eating, sleeping, and exercise. Disturbing these patterns will result in confusion and fatigue.
4. Cut recreational activities to a reasonable minimum. They cannot be eliminated safely, but they can be reduced appreciably for this period of time. The activities that remain should be carefully scheduled.
5. Generally, it is better to study alone during the major portion of your review. The presence of another person may lead to situations that are not constructive. Once in awhile, however, certain types of material lend themselves well to joint study. On a few selected and difficult points, the help of another student may be advantageous. Remember, though, that someone else cannot learn your work for you.

TERMS IN EXAM QUESTIONS

Knowing what these words mean may be helpful to you when you answer test questions.

1. *Compare:* When you are asked to compare, you should examine qualities or characteristics in order to discover resemblances. The term implies that you emphasize similarities, although differences may be mentioned.
2. *Contrast:* When you are instructed to contrast associated things, events, or problems, their dissimilarities or differences should be stressed.
3. *Criticize:* Here you are expected to judge the correctness or merit of the

factors under consideration. You are expected to give the results of your own analysis and to discuss the limitations and advantages of the plan or work in question.

4. *Define:* Definitions call for concise, clear, authoritative meanings. In such statements, details are not required but the boundaries or limitations of the definition should be briefly cited. You must keep in mind the class to which a thing belongs and the characteristics that differentiate it from others in its class.

5. *Describe:* In a descriptive answer you should recount, characterize, sketch, or relate in narrative form.

6. *Diagram:* For a question that specifies a diagram, you should present a drawing, chart, plan, or other graphic representation. Usually you are also expected to label your diagram and, in some cases, to add a brief explanation or description.

7. *Discuss:* The term *discuss* directs you to examine, analyze carefully, and present considerations pro and con regarding the problems or items involved. This type of question calls for a complete and detailed answer.

8. *Enumerate or list:* These words specify a list of outline form of reply. In such questions you should recount, one by one, in concise form, the points required.

9. *Explain:* In an explanatory answer it is imperative that you clarify, elucidate, and interpret the material you present. In such an answer it is best to state the "how" or "why," reconcile differences in opinion or experimental results, and where possible, state causes. The aim is to make plain the conditions that give rise to whatever you are examining.

10. *Illustrate:* A question that asks for an illustration usually requires you to explain or clarify your answer by presenting a figure, picture, diagram, or concrete example.

11. *Interpret:* An interpretive question is similar to one requiring explanation. You are expected to translate, exemplify, solve, or comment upon the subject and usually to give your judgment or reaction to it.

12. *Outline:* An outlined answer is organized description. Give main points and essential supplementary materials, omitting minor details, and present the information in a systematic arrangement or classification.

13. *Relate:* In a question that asks you to show relationships or to relate, your answer should emphasize connections and associations in a descriptive way.

14. *Review:* A review specifies a critical examination. You should analyze and comment briefly in an organized sequence on the major points of the problem.

15. *Summarize:* When you are asked to summarize something or present a summary, you should give in condensed form the main points or facts about it. All details, illustrations, and elaborations are to be omitted.

16. *Trace:* When a question asks you to trace a course of events, you should give a description of progress, historical sequence, or development from the point of origin. Such narratives may call for probing or for deduction.

14. *Give a summary of study skills, covering note taking and preparing for tests.*

_____

_____

_____

_____

LEARNING STYLES

Different people use different techniques when they learn. A learning style is an individual's personal technique. There are three basic styles.

When someone gives you some information and then pops a question at you, do you answer quickly? Do you wait and ruminate for awhile before you answer? Already, we have identified two facets of one learning style. People seem to use one or the other. Either they solve a problem with little or no delay, or they answer in a slow and careful manner. Studies have shown that the learning styles of fast and slow answers remain relatively stable over fairly long periods of time. The style shows up in many different kinds of tasks and seems to be a part of the personality of the person. We have a tendency to think that the quick answerer is brighter and smarter than the slow answerer. This is not always so; it has been shown that the slower answer is usually more accurate.

Another learning style is based on the way in which information is processed when a new concept is being developed. In this case, we may use one of several processes. For example, if we are learning to recognize a horse, we first look at one horse carefully. Then we look at another animal to see whether it is identical to the first one; we find that it is, except that it's much heavier and bigger. We surmise that it too is a horse. We then look at another animal and see that it is gray, whereas our reference animal is black. We learn that this also is a horse. What we are doing is checking out one variable at a time—weight, size, color, and so on. This method is called *conservation selection.*

Some of us are not so methodical. We tend to be more impulsive. Given a reference (focus) horse, we look at another animal that differs in size, weight, color, and shape, take a chance, and say that it too is a horse. This surmise is that of an impulsive person using a technique called *focus gambling.*

Another way to describe this learning style is to use the terms *simultaneous scanning* and *successive scanning.* In simultaneous scanning, a person makes a guess. If the person knows that a horse is black and has two ears, four legs, a tail, and a certain shape, he or she checks other animals against this list, discarding those that do not have the appropriate characteristics. This technique calls for good concentration and a willingness to take chances. The successive scanner, on the other hand, takes each attribute and checks it through separately. This individual takes fewer risks and is slower in coming to a conclusion.

Are you a focus gambler, a guesser, or a successive scanner? Here are some other learning characteristics that you can use to gain information about your learning style. Once you have identified some of the strengths and weaknesses in your style, you can use your strengths to better advantage and work on your weaknesses.

Do you learn better through listening and speaking or through reading and writing?

Do you start studying easily and quickly, or does it take you awhile to get started?

Can you learn things more quickly early in the morning, in the middle of the day, late in the afternoon, or in the evening?

Which is the easiest way for you to learn: by hearing information, reading it, seeing it in pictures, writing it in your own words, explaining it to someone else, saying it to yourself, drawing it, or applying it to some situation?

Of the following learning situations, identify those that are least comfortable for you and those that you like most: large group sessions, small group sessions, competitive games, working by yourself, working with a partner, working in a quiet place, working in a noisy place, being interrupted in your work, having to quit before you have finished, finishing before other people and then sitting with nothing to do.

Do you communicate better in unstructured, informal situations or in structured, more formal circumstances?

When you can use movements of your body in studying (for example, drawing symbols in the air), do you learn more easily?

Now put all of this information about yourself into a paragraph that describes what kind of learner you are.

15. *Describe different learning styles and identify those that are typical of you.*

_____

_____

_____

_____

□ A POINT OF VIEW

The incredible complexity of the learning process leaves us in confusion. We don't know
enough even to define learning satisfactorily.
We do know, however, that different people
learn in different ways, as you probably gathered
from the last section. Of the following three
reading selections, the first two are condensa-
tions of research reports that show just how
complex the nature of learning is, even in
newborn infants. The third selection amplifies
the concept of meaningfulness in learning and
suggests that you may be able to evaluate the
meaningfulness of your own learning.

BRAIN/MIND BULLETIN

LEARNING AND SENSITIVITY IN NEWBORNS CONFIRMED BY TWO DECADES OF RESEARCH

In terms of infant learning, there's good news
and bad news.

The good news: human infants display an
astonishing range of sensory sophistication and
learning. The bad news is that they are highly
vulnerable to conditioning.

Lewis Lipsitt, director of the Child Study
Center, Brown University, has completed a
comprehensive survey of two decades of worldwide research on the sensory capabilities and
learning proficiencies of the newborn.

Color discrimination Very young babies track
a colored spotlight, and they show subtle hue
discrimination from about two months. Color
perception has also been shown by evoked
potentials in the EEG.

Detail discrimination Babies can distinguish
relatively fine patterns, and infants as young as

Reprinted from *Brain/Mind Bulletin* 22 (October 3, 1977),
published twice monthly, $15 per year, $19 first class U.S. and
Canada, $22 all other. Send stamped, self-addressed business-
size envelope for free sample to Box 42211, Los Angeles, Calif.
90042.

two months select curved over straight contours. Eye movements hover around contrast
borders and the vertices of triangles.

Depth perception In addition to fear of the
famous "visual cliff," infants exhibit depth
perception in their loud disappointment when
an apparently solid object—actually a three-D
illusion—fails to materialize in their grasp.

Hearing Newborns are sensitive to subtle auditory stimulation and can detect the direction
from which a sound comes. One-month-old
infants react differently to different phonemes
(see B/MB, vol. 1 #3).

The cry of another newborn causes more
restlessness and crying in experimental babies
than does a computer simulation of an infant
cry, suggesting that "the response is not driven
by the intensity of the stimulus, but rather that
there is something special about the human
voice and cry that results in a kind of early
imitation or 'empathetic' response."

Cardiac deceleration has been found to corre-
late with attention in infants. Babies' hearts
decelerate more in response to a female voice
than a male voice.

Taste Minimal changes in the chemical con-
stituency of fluids on the tongue cause sharp
responses in newborns. Infants suck less enthusiastically for plain water after sweet fluids.

Smell When infants were presented used
breast pads from two nursing mothers, they
oriented to that of their own mothers. "Such a
finding has implications for the capacity of the
newborn to detect its own mother, particularly
after a few days of experience with her, and to
become 'attached' to her," Lipsitt said. The
effect was not present within the first few days
but seemed to accrue.

Touch Newborns respond very precisely to
touch in certain areas—the corners of the
mouth, the palms, the chin, Lipsitt believes that
the so-called "rage" behavior of babies under

restraint is an important defense. Babies who can't free their respiratory passages when threatened may be at special risk for Sudden Infant Death Syndrome, Lipsitt believes.

Habituation Newborn males habituate more quickly to a four-square checkerboard target, females more quickly to a 144-square pattern. Newborns whose mothers had received high dosages of obstetric anesthesia required as many as four times more trials to habituate than those whose mothers had received little medication. And the difference was still there a month later.

Classical conditioning Newborns are classically conditionable—whether by stimulus or by timing, such as a fixed feeding schedule. Soviet researchers have obtained conditioned responses within the first three weeks.

Lipsitt suggests that painful neonatal experiences may alter the organism. He advocates the close observation of the effects of such routinely painful procedures as circumcision, venipuncture or the surgical removal of an extra digit.

Operant conditioning This is a well-established phenomenon—the pairing of positive reinforcement and specific behavior. Successful reinforcers include pictures, patterns and dextrose.

Lipsitt points out that the mother and other early factors have "visible and potentially critical effects upon the behavioral capabilities of the young child." Maternal anxiety is related to a child's adjustment as judged by tests at eight months.

"The newborn comes into the world with all sensory systems functional," Lipsitt said. It may learn to respond in specific ways, based on sensory preferences and intentional or unintentional conditioning. "All of this has enormous implications for the condition of behavioral reciprocity that characterizes the early interactions of mother and infant."

He believes that the current interest in the sensitivity and capacity of young children, which has encouraged parents and professionals

to provide a stimulating milieu, will "increase the range of human behavioral and cognitive potential." He compared it to the phenomenon in athletics in which "technology, human aspirations, competitiveness and increased professionalism all conspire to promote record-breaking performances, year after year."

(See *Clinics in Perinatology* 4,1: 163–186 and *Neuropadiatrie* 8: 107–133.)

BRAIN/MIND BULLETIN

LEFT, RIGHT BRAIN DIFFERENCES ARE MORE FUNDAMENTAL THAN VERBAL, NONVERBAL

New findings of specialization in infants' brains suggest that the so-called 'verbal' and 'non-verbal' processes reflect deeper, more fundamental differences between the left and right hemispheres.

Juhn Wada and Alan Davis of the Health Science Center Hospital, University of British Columbia, demonstrated that babies process a click stimulus in the left hemisphere, a visual flash in the right. This study, one of a series begun in 1973, confirms that asymmetry is innate and does not depend on language development.

Wada and Davis studied a group of 16 infants (mean age of five weeks) and 50 neonates ranging in age from one day to five weeks. They considered the click "highly structured auditory information," the flash "unstructured visual information." Localized coherent activity shifted to the left hemisphere for clicks, to the right for flash.

Earlier experiments had shown similar lateralization of response in adults.

The researchers had speculated in 1974 that

Reprinted from *Brain/Mind Bulletin* 22 (October 3, 1977), published twice monthly, $15 per year, $19 first class U.S. and Canada, $22 all other. Send stamped, self-addressed business-size envelope for free sample to Box 42211, Los Angeles, Calif. 90042.

hemisphere asymmetries are related to more fundamental processes than language. Other investigators have proposed that the fundamental process underlying lateralization is "meaningfulness."

If the specialization does not relate primarily to language, 'meaningfulness' is not a useful description. Wada and Davis believe that the left hemisphere deals with the "recognition of relationship" or "association with previous experience." Even on a pre-verbal level, one can recognize a resemblance between a meaningless shape and a real object, which leads to labeling—which leads in turn to language. Language, they suggest, is an epiphenomenon of a basic human neurological process of creating referents.

Wada and Davis emphasize the left-hemisphere process—the recognition of a relationship between a stimulus and past experience—rather than the stimulus itself.

"As examples of this type of referential processing," they said, "the left hemisphere would be more involved than the right in the processing of speech by a human [listener], in the processing of melodies by an experienced musician and printed words by a literate person."

For example, the right hemisphere has been associated with perception of music. Piano chords, for instance, produced more activation in infants' right hemispheres, human speech in the left. Wada and Davis say that these babies, a mean of six months old, were more accustomed to the sound of speech than piano chords.

Trained musicians listen to music with the left hemisphere as well as the right, and a 1974 study showed that individuals *recognized melody* more readily with the left than the right.

Wada and Davis add to the traditional definition of left-brain processes: not only analytic and sequential, but also *comparative, relational* and *referential*. And the right brain, with its handling of material for which there has been no previous reference, is not only holistic but *non-referential* and *integrative*.

Their report: *The Canadian Journal of Neurological Sciences* 4 (3): 203–207.

ROBERT GRIFFIN

PERSONAL MEANING AND PERSONAL LEARNING AS EDUCATIONAL CONCEPTS

Many teachers and others in education want to know answers to questions that relate to a student more personally than is usually obtained: Is the student involved in school learning with an understanding of its meaning to his or her life? Are the student's learning achievements personally satisfactory to him? Will he be able to continue learning on his own when the formal experience ends? Has the student incorporated his learnings into his behavior outside the class? Educators often talk of students being "into" a class, or "self-consciously participating," or being "self-directed," but usually they are not able to speak of these ideas precisely or measure them well. Typical achievement tests do not provide answers to these questions and concerns.

I have worked to define two interrelated educational concepts, "personal meaning" and "personal learning." The concepts are defined in terms of what a student says when asked to discuss his participation in a class. These concepts may provide educators and students with more precise ways of describing and dealing with certain dimensions of a student's experience, giving them a better conceptual "handle" to use as they analyze and work to create productive learning environments. They can go beyond concerns for the achievement of curriculum goals, regardless of their personal significance to the student or the student's manner of personal involvement in learning activities, or vague discussions of whether the class was "interesting" or "valuable." These concepts

Reprinted by permission of Heldref Publications from *Clearing House* 50 (January 1977): 227-230.

may also provide bases for measuring levels/
stages of personal meaning and personal learning among students.

PERSONAL LEARNING AND
PERSONAL MEANING DEFINED

My efforts have been influenced by the work of
Eugene Gendlin and his associates, who have
made effective use of an instrument, The Experiencing Scale, as a research tool in counseling
and psychotherapy (Klein; Mathieu; Gendlin;
Keisler, 1969). The Experiencing Scale is an
operationally defined instrument used to assess
whether a client verbally communicates his
personal perspective and uses these data to
enhance self-understanding and to achieve resolutions to personal problems. The Experiencing
Scale is based upon Gendlin's theory of personality and behavior change, which emphasizes
the importance of an individual's attention to
an on-going, immediate, bodily felt, sense or
feel of personal issues (Gendlin, 1962, 1968). My
work also stresses expression of subjective
reactions to events and personal meanings.
However, levels and stages of the personal
meaning and learning concepts refer directly to
thoughts and activities in educational rather
than counseling or therapeutic contexts. Too,
there is greater allowance of the kind of talk
that might be called "intellectualized" in therapy. And the emphasis of the Experiencing Scale
on the resolution of personal difficulties has
been replaced here by a concern for a student's
critical awareness and personal satisfaction
regarding the achievement of tasks likely to be
undertaken in schools.

In developing these concepts I interviewed
some twenty secondary level students. After
deciding upon a particular class as a frame of
reference, I asked them, "Tell me about your
experience in class." Following each student's
initial response, I continued probing, asking
them "Why" and "Can you say more about
that." The interviews ended when the students
said, in effect, "That is all I have to say."

From notes and tape recordings of these
interviews, I identified four levels of personal
meaning and five stages of personal learning.
The levels of personal meaning refer to four
ways a student may speak of a learning setting,
moving from the impersonal to the personal and
culminating in the learner's clear and elaborat-
ed description of the personal meaning of the
learning situation to himself or herself. The
highest level, level four, is incorporated into the
first of the five stages of the personal learning
concept. Thus, a student must be able to articu-
late a detailed sense of the personal significance
of the learning context as a necessary condition
to personal learning involvement. The five
stages define the dimensions of personal learning. If the student's talk is characteristic of stage
five, the top stage, he may be said to be
personally involved in learning. However, I do
not view personal learning as an "all or nothing," "yes-no" matter. A student, who is at
stage three of personal learning for example is
"higher" and more personally involved than a
student at stage one.

What follows are summaries of the levels/
stages of the two concepts. It would appear from
the stress on the verbal and the abstract in this
way of defining the two concepts that these
concepts most apply to secondary age students
and those older. There are several reasons for
the emphasis on verbal expression in these
concepts: It is assumed that learning behavior
itself, i.e., actions in class, scores on tests, does
not satisfactorily indicate the personal participation of a student. In my interviews I spoke
often with students who had "done well" in a
course—having high grades, received Teachers'
praise—who nevertheless appeared to be going
through the course experience only in a mechanical fashion and with little self-
consciousness. Also, there is the assumption
that students should be encouraged to make
their manner of involvement explicit through
language. Increased self-awareness, critical understanding of the relationship of the learning
activities to themselves, and personal autonomy result when they can verbalize on their
participation in a class. These are important

matters in terms of justice for students in schools and in furthering their personal and social development.

PERSONAL MEANING

LEVEL ONE: WHAT WE DID

A student at this level of personal meaning speaks impersonally about the learning situation, i.e., the class is described in terms of its assignments of activities.

The student may discuss "what the course was about," "why we (or I) have to take it," "what the teacher expects of us (or me)," or "what we learned (or ought to have learned)." He may describe activities in the class without referring to himself specifically. The student may, without elaboration, give some brief indication of his evaluation of the learning situation. Or, he may present a more extended evaluation of the learning circumstance in a fashion such as this: "We had this good discussion on Wednesday, but nothing much happened when we had the panel on Friday. The course was well planned, but it would have been better if the teacher had not talked so much . . ."

LEVEL TWO: WHAT I DID

In this level the involvement of the student in the class is explicit. However, while his comments describe what he did or learned, they do not define his reactions to his involvement in the class; nor do they discuss the significance of the situation to himself.

The student may talk of the learning problems he confronted. He may describe the books he read and the learning he gained from them. He may describe the position he took in a class discussion. He may speak of the learning he accomplished in the class. He may describe his interactions with teachers or other students. He may present a behavioral description of himself in the class and present briefly the implications of this behavior. However, there is no reaction to his quietness, and he does not detail or

explore how he is in this regard. These are decisions about himself that could have been derived from what others said to him. The consequences may have been chosen by others as well.

LEVEL THREE: BRIEF REACTIONS

The student makes unelaborated self-references which present some aspects of his inner perspective. However, the student's self-descriptions are tied to the immediate learning situation. They are not used as a basis for the exploration of the personal significance of the class to the student's life.

The student may present feelings or reactions regarding his behavior in class. However, there is no elaboration of this feeling or clarification of the cause, significance, or implications of this behavior. He may present his motives in the class. He may describe his feelings in a specific situation. He may describe his perceptions related to particular aspects of the course: "The book, _____, was really useful to me." The student may add a "because"—" . . . because it'll help me know more about our government"—but he does not elaborate on the response. He may describe how he is seen by others in the class. He may present unelaborated reactions to his work or judgments of himself in the class. He may describe external circumstances which caused his behavior.

LEVEL FOUR: MEANING EXPLORATION

In this level, the self-references go beyond the class situation in some way either to show what the student is like more generally in relation to the learning material or to explore his reactions to class. In exploring or elaborating on his feelings, reactions, assumptions, and goals in detail, he makes clear the personal meaning or significance of the learning situation to him.

The student may begin with any reaction listed in level three. He then may talk in detail about these feelings, assumptions, motives, perceptions, etc. By talking in detail, it is meant that he takes a global statement—"It is inappropriate for me to be in this class"—and specifies or elaborates on the meaning of the sense of inappropriateness. He "carves up" the notion of "inappropriate," finding more words and more precise, self-referring ways of expressing this thought. He then may discuss how this reaction is characteristic of him: "This is the way I am when I have to read something I don't consider relevant. For example, in that other course they made me read _____ and I didn't want to read it for the same reason." He then may discuss how this response is realistic in terms of his interests, needs, assumptions about himself, values, etc: "Why should I want to read that book, because I need to learn _____ and that book has nothing to do with helping me learn that." He then may explore the ramifications or implications of all this to himself: "So if all that is true, I'm going to have to do _____, which in turn will change the way I am in that other situation."

This is the key level in the concept of personal meaning. Here, the student has worked through to a detailed sense of the meaning, implications, or significance that this class has to him rather than speaking only of what "we did" (stage 1) or what "I learned" (stage 2) or presenting brief reactions (stage 3).

PERSONAL LEARNING

The concept of personal meaning deals with whether the learner demonstrates that he had thought through the significance or usefulness of the learning circumstances to himself. The concept of *personal learning* considers whether the student has integrated this level of self-understanding regarding the class into learning activities and outcomes which are self-consciously chosen, undertaken and achieved to attain his individual purposes. The concept of personal learning logically falls into stages, each presuming the accomplishment of those stages which precede it.

STAGE ONE: PERSONALIZED
LEARNING GOALS

The personal meaning and personal learning concepts interconnect, as this stage includes personal meaning level four. In addition to level four personal meaning responses, the student identifies in specific, clear terms his goals in the class. He links these objectives to his life generally; he demonstrates how the accomplishment of these aims can lead to development or behavior in ways significant to him as an individual.

Purposes in this sense contrast with those justified in terms of a curriculum designer's views of what is appropriate, or established student roles, or a vague notion of "future effectiveness." Rather, purposes are defined in terms of how the student views himself currently and how he envisions himself in the future. There is, of course, no necessary incongruity between course objectives as typically stated ("The student will analyze race relations in the United States") and these more personalized statements of purpose.

STAGE TWO: PERSONALIZED
LEARNING ACTIVITIES

In this stage the student describes the activities he is undertaking to achieve the learning objectives stated in stage one. He spells out why he is pursuing particular activities and completing assignments, i.e., demonstrating an understanding of their usefulness, given his objectives. The student is able to describe learning activities he might otherwise undertake and show how these options are of less value than those he is presently employing.

This stage emphasizes the distinction between uncritically engaging in certain learning activities and a student's understanding of these activities. From a test of a student's ability to engage in a particular inquiry skill, for example, it is not usually certain whether the student in fact understands that that is what he is doing; whether the student knows why he is doing it or what it implies for him; whether this activity is linked to his own well-considered set of purposes; or whether he is engaging in this activity with any knowledge of other options available to him which he might have selected if he had not spent his time involved in this effort.

STAGE THREE: PERSONALLY SATISFACTORY LEARNING ACHIEVEMENT

In this stage, the student reports how he has achieved a *personally satisfactory* (as the student judges it) conceptual or intellectual accomplishment of the learning objectives identified in stage one. He reports that he has "made a decision about," "cleared up," "analyzed," "understands," "taken a position on," or "developed the skill."

Here, there is the concern that the student can do more than perform certain intellectual operations, announce certain preferences, etc. Can he describe his achievement? Is he satisfied with his own accomplishment? Can the student link the learning to his personal aims?

STAGE FOUR: NEXT STEP FORWARD

The student describes what he would next learn if he were to continue and the way in which he would go ahead to learn—the particular book he would read, the activity he would undertake to develop a needed skill, and the particular relationship he would establish, among other things. It is not enough to say, "I would read a book on the subject." He must be able to name a specific book or name the specific place or person he would go to in order to find the book. He is able to justify this "way forward" as a means of further learning.

This stage underscores a concern for a student's learning *autonomy*. One criterion from which to judge a program is whether or not a student comes away from the experience with an understanding—in specific terms—of the "next step forward" for him. It should be a concern to measure what a student may accomplish while he is in class; it should also, however, be a concern to gain an indication of his ability to continue to grow when he is no longer in the particular class.

STAGE FIVE: PERSONAL GOAL IMPLEMENTATION

The student reports how he has gone forward to implement *personally satisfactory behavioral change* in himself *outside the class context,*

consistent with his analysis, position, or understanding as described in stage three. This stage adds to the educator's concern that certain changes take place, a concern for whether the *learner* values the behavioral outcomes. This stage also calls attention to the difference between *knowing* and *doing* and the difference between doing inside the class and action outside of the school. Schooling is undertaken not only to be good at school work and thus to know more about this or that. One test of any curriculum is the instrumental value it has in facilitating one's ability to behave in different, more satisfying, more productive ways in the world for which the school prepares students.

THE USES OF THE CONCEPTS

The two concepts, personal meaning and personal learning, give educators a more precise way of discussing and judging informally the involvement of students in a learning circumstance. From students who reveal a level four sense of the significance of the class to them, for example, educators may be able to talk about the distinction between students at level two of personal meaning ("what I did" or "what I learned"). Or, they may be able to distinguish between learning which is successfully achieved from the teacher's or the school's perspective which *is* personally satisfactory to the learner, and that which *is not*. Teachers and others can keep these concepts in mind as they develop, implement, and evaluate their efforts. The perspectives provided by the two concepts may also increase the effectiveness of students' participation in learning situations as well, giving them a way to talk about relevance, a way to judge their classes, and, perhaps, some goals to work toward with their teachers.

The two concepts can also be seen as a beginning for developing more formal measurements of student involvement. A student's responses to interview questions or perhaps his written responses to a questionniare could be categorized with the use of these definitions. A similar approach has been used with The Experiencing Scale. (Klein; Mathieu; Gendlin; and Keisler, 1969). One attempt has been made to measure the personal meaning concept, with an alpha correlation of .75 as a measure of interrater reliability (Griffin, 1974).

If reliable ways are found to measure personal meaning and/or personal learning, their relationship to conventional achievement, classroom climate, or motivation? Are students in a free or open school more meaningfully or personally involved than those in a traditional setting? Are levels of these concepts related to social class membership? What is their relationship to cognitive or moral development level? Are certain teacher behaviors, content areas, or learning activities associated with high levels of these concepts?

Whatever, I hope that the concepts of personal meaning and personal learning will increase our ability to help students define themselves in the world. Perhaps this will encourage teachers to ask students for their personal reactions to the learning context—and continue the invitations and probings until both teachers and students know how what is being studied relates to the lives of students.

UNIT 7

PERCEPTION
AND EMOTIONS

□ What you see is what you get. Or is it? Do you really see things as they are, or are they tinted by something else? Close your eyes for a moment and think of a tree. The tree is on the top of a little hill in the center of a field. It is lovely, branched, and full grown. Describe the tree in more detail. What kind is it? Does it have leaves or bare branches? What color are the leaves?

_____

_____

_____

_____

Compare your response with those of others doing this simple exercise. You will be surprised at the variety of trees that are mentioned. The point is that the stimulus word *tree* brings a vision to each person's mind, and the visions are quite different for different people. Even a common word like *tree* brings out a variety of mental images.

In this unit you will be introduced to the meanings of the word *perception*, and you will learn why people see different things even when they are exposed to the same stimulus. The individuality of perception will be emphasized, and you will see how your emotions color your perceptions. Finally, you'll have some opportunities to play with your emotional control.

When you have completed this unit, you should be able to:

1. *Define* stimulus, sensation, *and* perception, *and give examples of each concept.*
2. *Explain the importance of sensory adaptation in humans.*
3. *Name the factors that govern stimulus selection in humans, and give examples of these factors.*
4. *Explain how needs and values influence attention and thus perception.*
5. *Describe how emotions interact with the factors that govern stimulus selection and thus influence perception.*
6. *Describe the behaviorists' theory of sensation and perception by humans.*
7. *Summarize the gestalt theory of perception.*
8. *Compare the implications of the behaviorist and the gestalt theories of perception.*
9. *Name the five basic emotions, and explain how they can be related on a continuum.*
10. *Explain the relationship between maturity and emotional control.*
11. *Describe some cultural restrictions on the display of emotion.*
12. *Describe some effects of improper (inadequate or excessive) emotional control.*
13. *Analyze your own emotionalism.*
14. *Describe the results of giving vent to your feelings for an entire day.*
15. *Explain how listening helps you to be effective in discussions.*

DEFINING STIMULUS, SENSATION, AND PERCEPTION

We are constantly surrounded by physical energy. Light, heat, pressure, chemical energy are permanent parts of the world outside our bodies. The process of *perception* begins with stimulation by a stimulus. A *stimulus* is a form of physical energy that strikes our sensory receptors. This hitting triggers the receptors to send a message to the brain, which interprets the message as a sensation or feeling. *Sensations* are thus the translation of external energy. Theoretically, the brain could stop there, but it goes further. It translates combinations of sensations into meanings. For example, when you hold something that feels soft and furry, your brain could translate the sensation into any number of things. If the furry thing is warm, the sensation of warmth gives additional meaning to the experience of holding it. If the furry, warm thing moves and purrs, your sensations are translated into the perception of a kitten. Sensations are more or less the raw materials of sensory input. Perceptions are their meaningful translations. Perceptions are based on our past experiences, although we may also have a certain innate ability to interpret sensations meaningfully.

1. *Define* stimulus, sensation, *and* perception, *and give examples of each concept.*

_____

_____

_____

_____

SENSORY ADAPTATION

An interesting skill of human beings is their ability to adapt. When you put your hand in a bowl of hot water, you at first feel a great deal of pain. If you grit your teeth and hang in there, the pain will disappear in a relatively short period of time. You'll be able to pull your hand out of the water and put it right back in without feeling pain, even though the temperature of the water has not changed. If you keep your hand out of the water too long, however, you will again feel pain when you put it back in. The response of your hand to the heat of the water is a kind of adaptation. If people were unable to adapt, life would be very difficult. We would be able to tolerate only very limited intensities of stimuli. We would constantly have to guard against pain from overly intense stimuli. We would not be able to dismiss some sensations from our minds in order to be able to pay attention to others.

The ability to shift our attention is very significant, because we could not possibly function effectively if we did not screen and dismiss unimportant sensations. If they kept demanding equal time for our attention, we would rarely be able to concentrate and be effective mentally. Stop right now and listen. What noises do you suddenly notice? Let them come into your awareness. Were they going on before you became conscious of them? Had you been receiving but not paying attention to them? Actually, this selective screening is not adaptation in the strict sense of the word. A better example of adaptation is night vision. If we stay in a completely dark place for twenty or thirty minutes, our eyes adapt so that we are able to see fairly effectively, particularly if there is some illumination such as starlight. Our eyes' response to darkness, letting us see in it, is adaptation. It is a physiological process. Selective screening is a psychological counterpart to it.

2. *Explain the importance of sensory adaptation in humans.*

FACTORS GOVERNING STIMULUS SELECTION

The selection of certain stimuli for our consideration and the elimination of others is not a haphazard process. It is rather a finely organized operation that depends on the interplay of certain cues or factors: size, change, repetition, intensity, movement, and set. To remember these factors, use the mnemonic SCRIMS.

SIZE

One of our leading cues is size. We use it to judge importance. This is why the message the advertiser wants us to see is always in large, bold letters that stand out, while details about the weight, size, and content of the package are usually in fine print.

CHANGE

Consider an orator. One of the tricks of the trade is to keep changing the volume of the voice. One moment the orator is whispering, and you are straining to hear. The next minute he or she has you holding your hands over your ears. By changing the loudness of his or her voice, the orator keeps you off base so that you can't drop into inattention.

REPETITION

One way to command a person's attention is to repeat the same stimulus again and again. Such chronic bombardment eventually forces a person to pay attention. Why do you suppose advertisers insist that the name of their product be repeated over and over in commercials? Is the constant use of the phrase *you know* in conversations an example of such purposeful repetition?

INTENSITY

Up to a point, the louder you shout, the better you will be heard. The intensity of the stimulus—your voice—makes it stand out above other stimuli, so that others are forced to pay attention to you.

MOVEMENT

If you have ever looked for a female pheasant in the fall when the grass is brown and dead, you should be aware of the effect of movement. Usually you will step on the bird before you see her, unless she moves. Only when she starts and disturbs the pattern so that she becomes different from the background can you identify her.

SET

One of the most curious factors in stimulus selection is set. *Set* is sensations interpreted into a meaning that is based on what we expect to perceive. In effect, we have already decided what we are to feel. Such preorganization sometimes has a powerful effect on our interpretations. One day, a wise old colonel known for his eccentricity was inspecting a marine corps base. He seemed to be particularly interested in the fire-fighting skill of the troops and asked many questions about it. He wanted to know whether the field music (bugler) knew fire call, what every person was supposed to do when the call was sounded, and so on. The base commander assured the colonel that the fire-fighting skill of the base was superb. The colonel went on to other matters and did not finish his inspection that day. The next morning, when he reappeared, he turned to the field music and said, "Music, sound church call," whereupon the doors to the firehouse burst open and the engine roared off down the street. Did the troops perceive what they were expecting to perceive? Was their set accurate?

3. *Name the factors that govern stimulus selection in humans, and give examples of these factors.*

_____

_____

_____

_____

THE EFFECTS OF NEEDS AND VALUES

Through adaptation, training, and conscious effort, we are able to close out certain messages from both outside and inside our bodies. We need to do this in order to be able to concentrate better on the matter at hand. Without the ability to attend to one particular set of stimuli, our minds would be hopelessly confused by competing signals. Take the business of hearing. Most of us spend our lives surrounded by a veritable babel of sound. If we couldn't block some of these sounds out, wouldn't life be a hopelessly confusing state?

Our senses constantly receive information but select and discard much of it. We also have learned to reprogram the information that reaches our brain. We modify it to make it fit what we expect it to be. The result of this fitting process is set. Set is based partly on our past experiences and partly on our expectations. Set may say, "You have seen this stimulus before, and it has always meant this." Or: "You have seen this stimulus before, and it has always meant this, but you are expecting something different now; so this stimulus means something different at this time."

Of course, our needs and values affect this selectivity. Ancel Keys showed their effect in an experiment on the effects of hunger. Thirty-six men were systematically starved over a forty-eight-week period. The volunteers developed neuroses. They were apathetic; their sexual urges decreased markedly. They spent much of their time reading cookbooks. Their need for food affected their whole social structure, and they gave value only to material that dealt with hunger.

Some who practice the art of meditation say that by restricting awareness and being able to control it we can refresh our relationship with the world. When we return to it after meditating, all things seem fresh and new. Because the human body quickly adapts to new stimuli, we need to refresh ourselves by controlling our awareness fairly frequently so that we don't become habituated to our world. Suppose you come into a room where there is a noisy clock. In very short order you'll probably tune it out. You simply won't hear it. But if you were in complete control of your awareness, you would be able to continue hearing the clock. Yogis have been tested and have shown no habituation. Kasumatsu and Hiria used a clicking sound with ordinary people and with Zen masters. The subjects sat in a soundproof room and listened to a click repeated every fifteen seconds. During this time their brain activity was recorded. The brain activity of the ordinary people decreased after about four or five clicks. The sound had been habituated. The brain activity of the Zen masters, on the other hand, showed no decrease. They kept control of their awareness.

Some religions, primarily Eastern ones, say that set has caused human beings to close themselves off from awareness, to the point that they are no longer one with their own bodies and with the rest of the world. By practicing openness to all stimuli, proponents of these religions say, people can find themselves again. We can achieve this goal by controlling our attention and mastering it so that we do not shut off our awareness. We can also achieve it by taking time out to listen to all the messages we are getting, both from inside ourselves and from outside.

One who advocates this type of endeavor is Sidney Jourard. In his book *Disclosing Man to Himself*, he makes the point that because people's idea of themselves is a set, it tends to shut them off from incoming messages. If people do not take the time to check this self-concept and listen to incoming messages while not under its influence, they may become sterile and will not grow. Every so often, without any screening or editing, we must listen to what others are telling us about ourselves. We also need to listen to what our own bodies tell us about ourselves and translate these messages without the preordained definitions of a tyrannical self-concept. (In Unit 17 you will learn

Can you concentrate until you are aware of all the elements in this picture at once? (Stephen
Halpern)

how to practice listening to your body to find out what you are feeling.) By learning to recognize how our needs and values turn off and turn on incoming messages and by learning to control these factors, we can learn to reorganize our perceptual world significantly and to regain control over much of what we have given up to mastery by our self-concept.

4. Explain how needs and values influence attention and thus perception.

_____

_____

_____

_____

THE EFFECTS OF EMOTIONS ON PERCEPTION

As you can see, the factors that influence stimulus selection exert a powerful force on our perceptions. However, even more powerful factors weigh heavily on what we allow ourselves to feel. These factors are our emotions. They can affect our perceptions in a strange way. To show how, let's return to the idea of set. Set has just been explained as a sort of preconceived notion of what is going to happen. It can also be defined as the emotional press under which we operate at a given time. Set regulates the attention we pay to incoming stimulation. Most of the time the emotional press is the dominant factor. Emotions have a significant effect on our perceptions. Strong emotions tend to block stimuli. When we are under the influence of a strong emotion such as anger, we tend to screen out stimuli that are in opposition to the anger. We cannot feel two emotions at one time. If you are feeling angry and something funny happens, you will suppress your attention to the funny incident because it is interfering with your primary, dominant emotion. Thus a situation can create different perceptions, depending on your emotional state. What may seem hilarious at one time may be extremely irritating at some other time. You should understand the effects of emotion on perception. Perceptions are vulnerable to distortion or change because of your emotional status.

An excellent example that shows the inability to feel two competing emotions at one time is found in Joseph Wolpe's reciprocal inhibition system of therapy. Wolpe has put this system to good use in the treatment of many types of mental disturbance. He trains a person to feel relaxation and the good feeling that goes with it. He then leads the person into thinking about a problem while in the relaxed state. The relaxation prevents the surge of anxiety that usually occurs when the person is confronted with the problem, so he or she is able to do some constructive thinking about it without being blocked by emotion. In this way, a person can come up with some sort of solution much more readily than when feeling tense or anxious.

Wolpe's method works in this way: A boy is afraid of cats. He and the therapist together draw up a list of cat stimuli, ranging from least disturbing to most stressful. The list might go something like this: thinking of a cat, hearing a cat meow, thinking of holding a cat, actually holding a cat. The boy, after being put into a state of relaxation, progressively works through the list of stimuli until he has experienced them all, either actually or in his mind. He continues to work through them until the fear is conquered. (You will have a chance to test the effect of emotions in an exercise at the end of this unit.)

5. *Describe how emotions interact with the factors that govern stimulus selection and thus influence perception.*

_____

_____

_____

_____

BEHAVIORISTS AND PERCEPTION

As you have already learned, when any kind of psychological event occurs, there is usually a theory ready to cover it. We seem to be obsessed with a burning desire to explain why we act as we do. Therefore, it should be no surprise to you to learn that some theories have been thought up to explain the phenomenon of perception. One group that has concocted a theory is the behaviorists. They believe that we learn how to feel and how to perceive just as we learn everything else. According to a behaviorist, we must learn to use the sensory organs that we bring into the world with us. We must learn to translate sensations into meanings or perceptions. We do this through experience as we interact with our environment. We learn that certain things are painful and often dangerous. We learn that other things are pleasant and fun. We learn to anticipate certain unpleasant events and move to avoid them when signals tell us that they are about to happen. We learn to associate certain emotions with certain situations. We learn that certain things are amusing and certain things are sad. In other words, we learn to tie in our emotions with certain stimuli. This tying-in results from things that are taught to us indirectly as well as from our personal experiences. In both cases we learn to attach certain emotions to certain situations. Then we start refining. We learn to anticipate situations and to experience the emotions that will go with them before the actual events, or we learn to shut off emotions before we get to the situation. In this way, we translate incoming stimuli into perceptions.

Behaviorists maintain that everything is learned, that there are no inborn influences or tendencies that affect perception. Instead, our society teaches us to perceive just as it teaches us that certain events are funny and certain events are sad.

6. *Describe the behaviorists' theory of sensation and perception by humans.*

_____

_____

_____

_____

THE GESTALTISTS AND PERCEPTION

Almost completely opposed to the behaviorists is the gestalt school of perceptual psychology. (*Gestalt* is German for "configuration" or "pattern.") The gestaltists believe that the ability to perceive is innate. They feel that within us are inborn tendencies that affect our perceptions. In experiments, they have identified five of these tendencies: figure and ground, proximity, closure, good figure, and common movement.

FIGURE
AND GROUND

The objects we see are patterns that appear against a background. The background sets the boundaries of an object and establishes its contour (see Figure 7.1). This basic principle of perception applies to senses other than sight, but it is most frequently demonstrated in vision. We can hear a bird's song against a background of other forest noises or a violin against the musical background of a symphony orchestra.

FIGURE 7.1 FIGURE AND GROUND

PROXIMITY

Related to the principle of figure and ground is our tendency to make patterns out of stimuli that are close together. Pieces that are closely spaced have a characteristic called belongingness, particularly if they have something in common. If parts form a scheme within a larger pattern, they are perceived as being together—as a continuous part of a pattern; that is, they have continuity (see Figure 7.2). We automatically group elements according to proximity, similarity, and continuity.

FIGURE 7.2   PROXIMITY

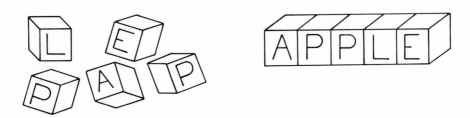

CLOSURE

We tend to see things as whole, continuous figures. This tendency is so strong that our minds often play tricks on us. If a pattern we are familiar with is incomplete, we tend to fill in the missing parts and perceive the pattern as complete. In other words, we have closed the contours of the figure (see Figure 7.3).

FIGURE 7.3   CLOSURE

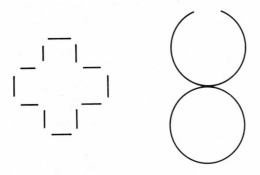

GOOD
FIGURE

Sometimes we can perceive a figure in two or more ways. When this happens, we tend to select the clearest and most easily definable figure and perceive it. The figure we choose is the "good" figure—the best of all the possibilities (see Figure 7.4).

COMMON
MOVEMENT

Usually a figure moves as a whole, and when it is in motion, we perceive it as a whole. If a part moves independently, we tend to perceive it as an independent figure. When you look at a unit of soldiers marching in step, it is hard to identify individuals. Yet if someone gets out of step, that person immediately stands out and becomes an independent figure.

FIGURE 7.4 GOOD FIGURE

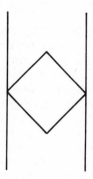

7. *Summarize the gestalt theory of perception.*

_____

_____

_____

_____

A COMPARISON OF BEHAVIORIST AND GESTALT THEORIES

One of the first things that you should remember about the behaviorists' position is their idea that all perceptions are learned. This means that people do not have within themselves a common store of preconceived perceptions. In other words, all humans have a common perceptual starting point: zero. Therefore, all our perceptions are individually learned and are unique to us. The same stimulus can evoke completely different perceptions from different people. However, we can have common experiences and find common meanings in certain situations. Our uniqueness can be tempered by our interactions with others as we discover their perceptions and compare theirs to ours. What we have learned, we can unlearn. In fact, we are constantly changing our perceptions of the world about us as we digest the results of our latest experiences.

How drastic this change can be is shown by some of the experiments of the social psychologists. They have demonstrated that social pressure can grossly distort our perceptions. Even though we may view a certain thing with aversion, we may ignore that aversion if there is enough social pressure to make us do so. We will change our perceptions to conform with a group. Our perceptions are thus heavily influenced not only by our individual learning experiences but also by social pressures. For these reasons, perceptions are dynamic and constantly changing.

What do we get from the gestalt point of view? First of all, we get the idea that people are created equal and all possess certain standard ways of processing perception. Gestaltists emphasize the inborn organization and processing of information to a much greater extent than do the behaviorists. Gestaltists are concerned with the form and structure of sensation and stimulation. To them, the act of perceiving involves organizing a situation into wholes and parts of wholes and determining the significance of one to the other. In other words, to them everything is relative. The integration of figure and ground becomes a basis for the gestalt theory of personality and therapeutic system. According to gestaltists, healthy people can control the ebb and flow of their figure-ground relationships. Unhealthy people fragment figure-ground relationships; therefore, they cannot see or understand whole patterns of their lives and place these patterns in a meaningful configuration. Thus, gestaltists maintain, if we wish to stay mentally healthy, we must be able to organize our perceptions so that relationships do not become distorted. Such perceptions will be influenced less by outside forces than by internal operations.

8. *Compare the implications of the behaviorist and the gestalt theories of perception.*

_____

_____

_____

_____

THE FIVE BASIC EMOTIONS

Throughout the study of psychology, a theme constantly reappears: the effect of emotions on our actions. Every psychological process is influenced in some way by the emotional set existing when the process occurs. Learning, stress, anything is influenced by how we feel—our emotions—at a particular time.

What are these emotions? There are only five of them, even though thousands of words in sophisticated languages describe their shades. They are fear, love, anger, sorrow, and joy. Notice the mnemonic FLASJ(H). There is an interesting relationship among four of the emotions; the first, fear, seems to be independent of the others. Love and anger seem to be opposites. You may feel love for a person, or you may feel anger. Purists might say that you can love a person even while you are angry with him or her, but certainly you do not feel any positive feelings for that person while you are angry. Thousands of words describe degrees of love or affection. Thousands of words also convey a greater or lesser degree of anger. It is possible to arrange these words on a line and to show the progression of feeling from one emotion to the other. We might use an example the progression love-affection-attraction-annoyance-irritation-anger. Joy and sorrow can be manipulated in the same way: sorrow-grief-despondency-happiness-ecstasy-joy. These lines can be combined into a sort of cross, like this:

We still have one emotion left: fear. It just does not fit in with the others in any way, except as an exclusionary emotion. That is, fear excludes all other emotions. This is not to say that fear does not have its own continuum. Can you construct this continuum, showing the degrees of fear from the weakest to the strongest?

_____

_____

_____

_____

9. Name the five basic emotions, and explain how they can be related on a continuum.

_____

_____

_____

_____

MATURITY AND EMOTIONAL CONTROL

When babies first come into the world, they don't seem to have any specific emotions; at least they don't show any. The only thing we can see in a baby that indicates any emotion at all is called a startle reflex. If strongly stimulated, a baby will show a generalized kind of excitement, arching the back and thrashing the arms and legs wildly. According to Katherine M. Bridges, observers can see distress and delight in an infant only after three months or so. After about six months the infant can break down its distress into fear, anger, and disgust. At twelve months the infant can show elation and affection. Joy does not appear until a child is two years old. According to Bridges, then, a person really doesn't have all the basic emotions until the age of two. But emotional development doesn't end then. People spend the rest of their lives learning what to do about their feelings.

In childhood, individuals have several emotional tasks to master. First they must learn which emotions are appropriate for which situations. This type of judgment involves a lot of learning. Children have to find out what is funny and what is not, what is sad and what is not. As they become more sophisticated, children begin to learn that the same event will provoke different emotional responses in different situations. A remark that seems uproarious to some people may shock and horrify others. Children pick up cues from their parents first. Then later, as they begin to mingle with peers and others, they get cues from them. You might say that emotion is refined through the process of socialization, as is most of our learning.

Attaching the right emotion to the right event at the right time in the right social group is only one of the tasks involved in growing up. There is also the development of emotional control—an aspect of emotions more important and potentially more deadly for each of us. Not only do we have to learn when to laugh and when to cry; we also have to learn how hard to laugh and how much to cry. Typically, children show the wrong feelings sometimes or show too much or too little of the right kind. As we grow up, more and more emphasis is put on the right degree of feeling. We also learn that some feelings must be suppressed or at least shown in very special ways. When are we allowed to show that we are angry at someone? Certainly not when the someone is bigger or older than we are. As a matter of fact, anger is one of the touchiest emotions. Because most of us learn to stifle our anger or to show it in limited ways, we sometimes turn our frustration inward and punish ourselves. Sometimes we pick a victim who is weaker than we are. Sometimes we pick a symbol as the object of our anger and try to get rid of it in a sort of displaced way. Whatever the means, we have to regulate our anger, both to society's standards and to our internal constitutions.

In our society, no mark distinguishes the adolescent from the adult. No physical stage of growth, no coming-of-age ceremony, divides girl from woman, boy from man. Any test we can think of—getting a driver's license, becoming self-supporting, graduating from school, voting—is artificial and has as many exceptions as instances. When you come right down to it, only one thing separates adolescents from adults. Adults are in full control of their emotions; adolescents are not. The appearance of wide swings of emotion forms one of the traits used to describe adolescence. The typical adolescent is not given credit for having complete emotional control; the adult, on the other hand, is. In the long run, we tend to associate maturity with the ability to keep the right kind of control over our emotions.

10. Explain the relationship between maturity and emotional control.

_____

_____

_____

_____

CULTURAL EFFECTS ON EMOTIONS

Although we place a great premium on an adult's ability to control his or her emotions, we do not insist that everyone show exactly the same kind and amount of emotion in every situation. Remember, our emotions depend on our learning, and our learning depends on our environment. No two people have or have had the same environment. Therefore, no two people have the same learning past to influence their perceptions and color their emotions.

By the same token, however, people are exposed to many common cultural values and ideas. These values and ideas shape them, because they're the things society passes on to individuals. They govern behavior tremendously, and one of the behaviors they closely control is how to deal with emotions. Of course, different cultures promote different systems of emotional control.

Western visitors to Japan, for instance, are often struck by the apparent Japanese insensitivity to another's suffering. When supervising the loading of a truck aboard a cargo ship, one such visitor observed the following accident. Just as the winch operator got the truck poised above the cargo hatch, one of the slings broke and the truck dropped down two decks. When it stopped bouncing, one of the Japanese stevedores could be seen lying under the truck. With considerable effort, he and his apparently broken leg were extricated, loaded into a sling, and delivered to a dockside ambulance. Although this accident was not uncommon, the Japanese stevedores' reaction to it seemed unusual to the Westerner. They didn't stop laughing until long after the injured man was gone. Were the Japanese insensitive? Of course not. Japanese usually disguise anger, annoyance, and fear with laughter. They hide their true negative emotions behind a mask of false gaiety. In this manner, culture influences emotions. Can you think of some other international examples? Write them here.

_____

_____

_____

If you were unable to think of any examples, try this. On the following line, rank these five nationalities from left to right, from most emotional to least emotional:

Danish, German, Japanese, Spanish, American

Most_____Least

Also consider these questions: Is it all right for a man to cry in public? How about a French man? An American man? Is there any time when it's all right for an American to cry in public? Is a man supposed to show fear? Is a man supposed to show pain? In our society, is a man supposed to give in to despair? If a football team is behind 72 to 0, are the players supposed to quit, or do we expect them to play as hard as if the score were 0 to 0?

Although some changes are now evident, it's interesting to consider the emotional differences that our culture has traditionally fostered between men and women. In our society, men have been expected to be much more stoical than women. Women may cry in public; they may show fear. Can you think of other examples of differences between the ways American men and women have been allowed to display emotion? If so, write them here.

_____

_____

_____

_____

By now you must realize that many culturally bound conventions control the ways we display our emotions. Although we may not even be aware of the restrictions, they are there at work. There seem to be more taboos on the display of negative emotions than on the display of positive ones, yet even positive emotions are fairly heavily inhibited. Consider, for instance, the restrictions imposed on displays of affection, especially between members of the same sex. If two men were to walk down the street holding hands, they would draw many censuring looks. If they walked arm in arm, they would be less censured but would still receive some criticism. Less would be said if two young girls did these things. However, what if two mature women walked down the street holding hands or arm in arm? Would that be considered

Are they likely to be English, American, French, German, or Russian? (United Press International)

unseemly? Probably. What seems strange is that the sight of a boy and a girl or a man and a woman holding hands would merely evoke tolerant amusement.

Also, think of this: If someone pays you a compliment, do you get embarrassed and try to put yourself down? If someone comes up to you and says, "You really look nice today," is your tendency to say something like, "I've had this for years"? Do you even get a little suspicious of a person who always is positive because you are much more used to an exchange like: "Hey, where did you get that old rag?" In this case, you could happily answer, "I got it out of your closet when you weren't looking." We are usually more comfortable with negative statements than with positive ones. In effect, we condone verbal aggression.

11. Describe some cultural restrictions on the display of emotion.

_____

_____

THE EFFECTS OF IMPROPER EMOTIONAL CONTROL

By this time you may have an idea that you are not expressing your emotions
as freely and easily as you thought you were. If you begin to get a picture of
yourself hemmed in by conventions and restrictions determining how you
show your feelings, you are absolutely right. We are pretty much inhibited in
our expression of feelings and, as was hinted at earlier, this inhibition
sometimes has deadly effects.

Have you ever burst into tears over some fairly minor event? Have you ever
had a temper tantrum or hit somebody in rage? Have you ever told someone
off? Have you ever jumped for joy? If so, you've done the unpardonable: You've
lost control. Of course, most of our transgressions are short-lived and
infrequent, because we sense an unspoken warning: This way lies madness.

It is much more common for us to suppress our feelings. Have you ever
watched a parade or exhibition that brought a lump to your throat and tears to
your eyes—tears that you didn't dare show and actually swallowed with a joke
to your friends to hide your feelings? In many ways, sitting on your emotions
can be deadlier than showing them too much. Emotions create energy in us.
The more powerful they are, the more energy we feel. When we try to bottle up
this energy within us, we create all kinds of problems. A strong jolt of emotion
provokes powerful physiological reactions. Adrenaline may flow; we may get
all charged up; and our bodies may ready themselves for action. If we suppress
all these emotional effects, we may tear ourselves apart. As you will see if you
study abnormal behavior, the suppression of strong emotion can cause
psychophysiological problems. A whole raft of ailments can be caused by this
process. No part of our bodies seems to be immune.

John Brady studied the effects of emotion on the gastrointestinal tract in an
interesting and now classic experiment involving two monkeys. Both animals
were given an electrical shock at several-second intervals. One of them (the
executive monkey) had access to a switch that would stop the shocks to both.
The other had access to a dummy switch and no control at all over what
happened. Only the executive monkey could control whether both monkeys
received a shock. During the course of the experiment, each monkey spent six
hours participating and then six hours not participating. Very soon the monkey
with the dummy switch seemed to adopt a "que sera, sera" attitude. The
executive monkey seemed to be conscious of the fact that it had something to
say about whether it would be shocked. The executive monkey had in effect
become emotionally involved in its situation. When it was in Brady's
apparatus, it felt great stress because of having to manipulate the switch. In the
six hours when this monkey was away from the experiment, its stress
decreased because it no longer had that switch to worry about.

After participating in the experiment for twenty-three days, the executive
monkey died, but the passive monkey with the dummy switch showed no

signs of ill health. The executive monkey wasn't killed by the shocks; it died as a result of the extreme variations in its emotions.

So what should we do? If we give vent to our feelings openly and uninhibitedly, we get into trouble with society. If we squelch our emotions, we get into trouble with ourselves as our bodies collapse under the strain. What is the answer? Apparently, we must learn to express our emotions in a socially approved way so that we don't do ourselves in. One or two suggestions will be given to you in this unit and a more extensive treatment will follow in Unit 17.

12. *Describe some effects of improper (inadequate or excessive) emotional control.*

_____

_____

_____

_____

AN EVALUATION OF YOUR EMOTIONALITY

Are you a very emotional person, or are you a calm, phlegmatic type? Here is an exercise that will help substantiate your answer. Remember, however, that it is not highly scientific and that the results may not be accurate.

EXERCISE 1. EMOTIONALITY SCALE

Check the column that most nearly describes you.

	Frequently	Sometimes	Rarely
1. I lose my cool.	_____	_____	_____
2. I have minor arguments with people but I get over them fast.	_____	_____	_____
3. Little things get under my skin.	_____	_____	_____
4. I can be irritable when things don't go right.	_____	_____	_____
5. Changes in temperature bother me.	_____	_____	_____

	Frequently	Sometimes	Rarely
6. I pop off and say things without thinking.	——	——	——
7. I feel strong emotions.	——	——	——
8. Minor injuries hurt me a lot.	——	——	——
9. I have trouble getting to sleep because my brain is going a mile a minute.	——	——	——
10. My life goes along on an even keel.	——	——	——
11. I squelch my feelings a lot.	——	——	——
12. I look at all the angles before I make my move.	——	——	——
13. I hold my opinions until I am asked.	——	——	——
14. I talk about my feelings with others.	——	——	——
15. When I like something, I really like it; when I dislike something, I hate it.	——	——	——
16. I get fits of the blues.	——	——	——
17. I can swing from anger to laughter in a very short period of time.	——	——	——
18. Sexual things bother me.	——	——	——
19. Competition bothers me.	——	——	——
20. Lots of things make me emotional.	——	——	——

If the majority of your check marks are in the "frequently" column, you may be an emotional person. Emotional people are easily stirred up. Their heartbeat speeds, their body tension increases, and they show other signs of bodily excitement quite often. They are sensitive to their physical environment and react strongly to it. They have a tendency to be more irritable and are usually open and expressive. Their emotions swing to extremes. Highly emotional people are greatly affected by pain.

If your check marks are primarily in the "rarely" column, your emotional characteristics are the opposite of those just mentioned. If the majority of your marks are in the middle, either you are playing this exercise very close or you are neither highly emotional nor very calm.

13. *Analyze your own emotionalism.*

_____

_____

_____

_____

LETTING GO OF YOUR EMOTIONS

So far, you have learned of the effects of your emotions, and you now know that bottling them up can be bad for you. You've also had a chance to decide whether you are an emotional person or a calm one. If you are calm, you tend to suppress your emotions; if you are emotional, you release them more easily. Whether calm or emotional, however, you are closely regulated by society, so that your emotional expression is considerably inhibited. So, again, you're in a box. If you don't get rid of your emotional energy and tension, they will build up and do strange things to your body. If you release your emotions uninhibitedly, you stand the chance of being called loony.

What can you do? The following exercises provide a couple of suggestions. Start with them and then develop your own techniques through experimentation. Both exercises release aggression, but any emotion can be vented in the same way. Because aggression is the emotion most difficult to express in a socially approved way, it is the one that usually gives us the most trouble. That is why most therapists concentrate on teaching people to express anger, although some people may find expressing affection even more difficult.

EXERCISE 2.   LET IT ALL GO

Clench your fists and bend your elbows so that your fists are close to your armpits. Pull your arms back until your shoulder muscles hurt. Then at the top of your voice, growl, "A-r-r-r-r," and let your arms go limp and fall to your sides.

Keep doing this until you've drained away all your anger. You can also do this to release joy, sorrow, and fear. Try the exercise, using the syllable *ah* but giving it an intonation appropriate to each emotion. You'll be surprised at how your pent-up emotions will pour out. For those people who are most inhibited, it's probably best to do this in private. Try the exercise on at least two days and analyze the results here.

_____

_____

_____

_____

Some of us are reluctant to verbalize our emotions. It's silly, though, to hold an emotion inside when verbalizing it might remove its cause. Verbalizing a good emotion might even make it more enjoyable.

The next time something is said or done that irritates you, speak up and say so. But do it in such a way that you don't threaten the person who caused your irritation or make that individual lose face. Don't attack the person. Don't say, "That's a stupid comment." Instead, coat the bitter pill. Say, "Hearing an intelligent person like you say that makes me angry."

If you are afraid, say so: "I am afraid to ride with you because you take chances beyond even your skill." Of course, you may also say positive things like, "I like what you are saying."

EXERCISE 3. SPEAKING OUT

Spend a whole day saying exactly what is on your mind, how you are feeling. Be careful not to attack someone personally. Attack actions or ideas, if you must, but do not put anyone down. Don't forget to say all your positive thoughts. If you do this for a day, you will at sometime during the day get a strange feeling of elation as you realize that you can talk about your feelings without having people laugh at you.

14. Describe the results of giving vent to your feelings for an entire day.

_____

_____

_____

_____

AN EXERCISE IN COMMUNICATIONS

Our communications with other people are significantly affected by how we perceive those people. If someone pays us a compliment, our emotions and response will depend on how we read that person. We are pleased if we perceive the person to be sincere and honest. We respond to this sincerity by believing the comment. If, however, we have any reason to doubt the person, the remark may make us hostile. If the individual is a salesperson, trying hard to pressure us into a sale, we may be annoyed. We are perceptive enough to pierce through the fakery and interpret the real purpose and meaning of the remark.

If we perceive someone to be threatening, we will deal with that person differently than we would if we pitied him or her. If you are talking and joking with your instructor, you will tend to be slightly on guard. If you are talking to a lifelong friend, you will be more relaxed, because your perceptions of the friend are far different from your perceptions of your teacher.

Communications with other people are also governed by the way they react to the messages we send. When we communicate with others, we are always looking to see whether we are getting our point across. We try to perceive clues that will answer this question. The feedback we receive lets us plot our next set of messages. If we are trying to sell something, we send out a series of messages to convince someone to buy. We watch closely to see whether the messages have any effect. If they do, then we keep up the attack. If they do not, we switch to another one. We keep doing this until we can tell that we are saying what the person wants to hear, and we then concentrate in that area.

Essentially, what we are trying to do when we communicate with others is to exchange information and to change existing attitudes. To accomplish these things, we must be able to recognize shifts in a person's emotional patterns, so that we can tell whether we have been effective. The ability to recognize emotional shifts is based on our perceptive ability to read other people. Without this finely tuned ability, we cannot really be good at interpersonal communications.

"Fine," you say. "But how do I tune up?" You listen; you strain to understand what the other person is really feeling and saying. Put aside your own emotions, sets, needs, and values, and try to understand the other person's feelings. You'll like the results.

The following exercise may seem strange. It calls for a sincere effort from you and your partner. You may encounter a certain amount of resistance on your part or your partner's, until both of you get the sense of what you are trying to achieve.

EXERCISE 4. LISTENING TO WIN

Select a partner and sit facing each other, fairly close but not touching. Try to come up with a topic on which you disagree so that you can get the most out of this exercise. Begin by letting your partner state how he or she feels about the chosen topic. (If you cannot agree to disagree on a topic, your partner may talk about what he or she feels about the situation or about you.) Give your partner enough time to develop his or her thoughts. Then it's your turn. However, before you start to express your feelings, you must paraphrase in your own words what your partner has just said. Your partner must accept your paraphrasing as what he or she really did say. Then you may express your feelings. When you have finished, your partner must paraphrase what you have said so that you agree with his or her interpretation. The discussion should continue in this way until you have finished.

Rule 1: You must not interrupt the speaker at any time. It is very hard not to interrupt, so you must practice.

Rule 2: Paraphrasing must be accurate and accepted by the original speaker. I once knew a person who had perfected the technique of waiting until you had finished and then saying, "Now, if I understood you correctly, you said. . . ." He would then proceed to distort your statements to fit in with his own argument. If you didn't object, he had you beaten even before you spoke.

The most difficult part of this exercise is to train yourself to listen. Most of us don't even hear what another person is saying; we are too busy thinking up our own argument. If you learn to listen, you have made a major step in learning to win arguments, at least in a discussion format.

15. *Explain how listening helps you to be effective in discussions.*

_____

_____

_____

_____

☐ A POINT OF VIEW

The first of the following two articles amplifies the idea of the exercise in which you gave vent to your emotions for a full day to see what would happen. This article is followed by another that gives a short but important admonition: Don't let out your emotions just for the sake of letting them out. Other people have the right not to be exposed to your feelings, regardless of how important they may be to you.

If you are interested in delving further into the subject of perception and emotions, the literature will point you in several directions. Much of it deals with the mechanics of how we perceive, how our sensory organs work. If you are interested in this area, you should read C. J. Herrick's *The Evolution of Human Nature* (Austin: University of Texas Press, 1956), or W.R. Hess's *The Biology of the Mind* (Chicago: University of Chicago Press, 1964).

If you are interested in the combination of emotion and motivation, read David C. McClelland's article "Toward a Theory of Motive Acquisition," *American Psychologist* 20 (1965): 321–333.

If you want to look at the relationship of emotions and abnormal behavior, you'll find many books on abnormal psychology that will give you information. Don't neglect the Lewises' book, *Psychosomatics: How Your Emotions Can Damage Your Health* (New York: Viking Press, 1972).

If you are interested in the mechanisms by which we hallucinate and have illusions, then you should read R. K. Siegel's scholarly dissertation in *The Scientific American* 237 (October 1977), 132–140.

JOHN KORD LAGEMANN

DON'T BE AFRAID TO LET YOUR FEELINGS SHOW

Looking at a series of Charlie Chaplin one-reelers the other night, I found myself laughing through tears. In just a few minutes of brilliant pantomime, Charlie expressed elation, tenderness, disappointment, joy, fear, resignation, pity, longing—and by enabling me to experience these feelings with him, he made me feel kin to the whole world. There was a healing magic about it. And that is something that is becoming harder and harder to find.

I grew up in a small Illinois city, before the present emotional ice age set in. It was perfectly natural to show emotion then. When you went to a movie with a sad ending, you could hear people all over the theater blowing their noses. There were times when my whole family would leave with tears in their eyes. We cared for things, and for each other, and we didn't hesitate to show it.

At home, my mother used to hug us when we got back from school, even in front of company; and the way she kissed my father good-by in the morning you would have thought he was off to the wars. We weren't very good at hiding our feelings—and we didn't try very hard. We could usually tell when someone had fallen in love, or done something he was proud or ashamed of, or was worried or puzzled, on top of the world or in the dumps. If it didn't show on his face, he'd *tell* you. Feelings were a living language that kept us in touch with each other, not as mere spectators but as participants in a never-ending drama.

The wisdom of feelings became clear to me only later. I joined a small-town weekly newspaper as junior partner to the publisher, who was getting on in years. He gave me carte blanche to reorganize the paper, and I pitched in with enthusiasm. But after a few weeks he

Reprinted from "Don't Be Afraid to Let Your Feelings Show," by John Kord Lagemann, *Reader's Digest*, May 1976.

began finding fault with everything I did. When I asked my father for advice, he said, "I don't know anything about the newspaper business, but I do know the old man. I think he feels left out."

That night I had a long talk with my partner. The paper was hardly mentioned. Instead, I listened to his life history, and I left with a better understanding of him, of the community and of myself. During the two years I remained with the paper, my partner gave me nothing but encouragement and support.

Since then, experience has taught me again and again that the secret of getting along with people is to *recognize how they feel*, and to let them know you know. When someone is rude or quarrelsome, it's often a way of saying, "Pay attention to my feelings." When we say of someone, "He understands me," we're really saying, "He knows how I feel."

Awareness of feelings in others comes naturally, if only you let it. I saw it happen one spring day just after a circus matinee as I walked by a crowd of small children waiting at a bus stop, each child holding a bright-colored balloon. As I watched, the string of a red balloon slipped through the fingers of a four-year-old, and his face curled up in grief at the loss. Instantly the child beside him caught his eye, extended his fist—and released his own balloon. Within seconds, a score of balloons were soaring skyward, and the four-year-old—tears still glistening on his cheeks—laughed with the others at the spectacle.

In difficult situations, the "right thing to do" is not hard to find if you let people's feelings come through to you and acknowledge your own. Not long ago, the minister of our church had to carry tragic news to the parents of a 12-year-old boy: their son had drowned on a school outing. Later, the parents told me, "Mr. Allen didn't preach or tell us to be brave. He broke into tears and wept with us. We will always love him for that."

Happiness, too, is the greater for being shared. "Isn't it a lovely day?" my wife remarked one day to a salesclerk who was humming softly under her breath and obviously pleased about something. "Is it ever!" said the girl—and then she blurted out the news that she had recently become engaged. "I just felt like telling someone," she said. "It makes it so much more real!"

"I felt like it"—that is the best reason in the world to laugh, or to be generous, or to applaud something. And that is what moods are— "feeling like it." Why fight them? Like the shifting of lights in the theater, moods enable you to see life in all its aspects. "I think creation comes initially out of mood," said Charlie Chaplin. In a melancholy mood you observe details that escape you in a mood of jubilation. Pensive, you filter out distractions and concentrate on deeper thoughts. Nostalgic, you capture the flavor of past events and see meanings that had escaped you before.

We mistrust moods because they change. Yet changing moods are perhaps the surest indication of a healthy personality. It is when a mood *doesn't* change that we should be concerned. To go through life in one mood, whether cheerful or glum, would be like trying to play a trombone with a stuck slide.

Happiness itself is just a mood, and there is very little logic to it. Wonderful moments of joy or sheer well-being come over us now and then without warning; elation appears out of nowhere. It happened in our house on a lazy Saturday morning while my wife and I sat in the living room reading the paper over our second cups of coffee. Sunlight streamed through the windows. On the radio the news program gave way to a concert, and the air was suddenly vibrant with the music of Mozart. Without a word my wife and I rose from our chairs, bowed to each other and started improvising the steps of a minuet. Our children, entering the room, regarded us questioningly—and then joined in the dance.

Such moments of spontaneously shared feelings are unpredictable and fleeting. But they linger on in the atmosphere of a place. Years ago, in Paris, a curator at the Louvre glanced at a young couple and said to me, "This is a wonderful place in which to fall in love." I had never thought of museums in quite that light, but I understood at once what he meant. The silent sharing of moods that occurs in looking at art, in watching a stirring play, or in listening to great music can bring people very close.

"My feelings got the better of me," we sometimes say when we are moved to act kindly or courageously. It's almost an apology. Yet feelings welling up from the depths of our personality, shaped by a lifetime of experience, provide a reliable and almost automatic self-guidance system. They may not help much in playing the stock market or in making out your income tax. But, as Sigmund Freud once observed, in all the really fundamental issues of life, the final decision is best left to feelings. How else is one to decide whom to marry, whom to trust as a friend or colleague, what to do when faced with a sudden life-or-death emergency?

More than 100 years ago, John Ruskin wrote: "The ennobling difference between one man and another is that one feels more than another." His words will always be true. I once heard Metropolitan Opera soprano Rose Bampton discussing two young singers who were rehearsing for a Met audition. Pointing to one of them, she said, "Her vocal range isn't exceptional, but her emotional range is tremendous. She gives more to her audience." Through feeling we gain self-insight, tap our creative powers, deepen and enrich our relationships with others.

Why, then, do we so often deny our feelings? Why do we cultivate a defensive, withdrawn quality, a deadpan emotional unresponsiveness? "It's the new untouchability," a college dean told me. "The idea is never to be shocked, surprised or deeply moved—or at least not to show it."

Feelings commit us one to another, and thus involve the risk of disappointment. They make us take sides, blurt out awkward truths, form personal preferences. "Playing it cool," on the other hand, means being "with it" until the going gets rough, then turning without regret to something else—another mate, another job, another cause. It may spare us a lot of heartache, self-searching and struggle. But when you sub-

tract feelings from marriage, friendship or work, what is left?

You can share money, food or sex with another and still remain complete strangers. In the end, the *only* way you can mean anything to another human being is to share his feelings.

WILLARD GAYLIN

UP FRONT: PUTTING IT BACK WHERE IT BELONGS

I have heard the cry, "Let it all hang out," and I have dogmatically decided it should not. Various insupportable habits are being insinuated into the social marketplace, displacing traditional and respectable modes of conduct under the guise of improvement. It is time to redress the balance by rediscovering old-fashioned virtues. I should like to start by making a case for containment.

Why should IT all hang out? I know that IT may seem so compelling as to have some claim to public recognition. Like the newborn infant, IT holds an idiosyncratic attractiveness to its parents that is rarely shared by others. But your personal insights, resentments, anguishes, judgments, and tempers—the home movies of your soul—are not as irresistible to the objective viewer as you so egocentrically assume. They should never be casually foisted, untested, on even your most constant and indulgent friends.

That "Out" in which you are choosing to let IT hang is ours as well as yours. Whether IT be the private parts of the exhibitionist or the

Reprinted by permission of Georges Borchardt, Inc., 136 East 57th St., New York, New York 10022. Copyright © 1977 by Willard Gaylin, M.D.

Willard Gaylin, M.D., is a practicing psychiatrist in New York City, clinical professor of psychiatry at Columbia University Medical School. He is also cofounder and President of the Institute of Society, Ethics and the Life Sciences, in Hastings, N.Y. This article is adapted from one that appeared originally in The Hastings Center Report.

private life of the narcissist, IT really ought not be hung out—uninvited—in the public marketplace. As British statesman Edmund Burke once said, "It has been the misfortune (not . . . the glory) of this age, that everything is to be discussed."

RAW SEWAGE OF UNREFINED EMOTION

Mind you, I am not talking about the elixir of conversation—distilled by discretion, consideration, tact, and courteous selectivity—with which we transmit our thoughts to others out of desire to communicate and share. I am referring to the raw sewage of unrefined emotion, discharged solely for purposes of expressing one's "true feelings" as a means of social exchange. In this form of intercourse, as in others, the unwilling or uninvited participant is unlikely to be comforted by your underlying purpose. For your intentions are no more relevant than your needs. In matters of this sort it is easier to deceive yourself than the other. One *knows* when one is being engaged as a person—or used as an emesis basin.

It is only somewhat less onerous when IT is printed, packaged, and purveyed to the unsuspecting consumer as a novel or entertainment. The exploitation here is more readily guarded against—one can more easily close a book than a mouth. But the inequity is compounded by the fact that in this form IT makes a demand on our purse as well as our patience.

This must not be construed as an attack on est and its ilk. Those generally harmless divertissements can be tolerated. Like red-light districts or nudist camps, they allow those in desperate need to encounter their own kind for the transaction of their particular pleasures. A compassionate, humane society can endure it's exposure among consenting adults in private enclaves. But the public at large must be protected from possible contamination.

A FORM OF PUBLIC LITTERING

My daughter once suggested to me that vile temper was a form of public littering, and protested that she would as soon have a casual acquaintance drop a dirty Kleenex on her, as his foul language and ill humor. Why is it that often the same individual who is so strident in his advocacy of ecological purity, so determined to protect the environment from material wastes, has an absolute compulsion to contaminate it with the spiritual droppings of his personal catharsis?

We have a responsibility not only to the social unit, which demands a certain amount of evasion, reserve, and dissembling (virtues badly in need of resurrection) but also to our personal dignity to keep IT in. There is a necessary distinction between the innermost and external you. Preserve it. It is to your advantage. Besides, there is pride in self-discipline. It feels good to keep IT in. Keep IT in!

So, please, tell IT to your spouse, tell IT to your lover; tell IT to your minister; tell IT to your analyst; tell IT to the Marines. Go tell IT on the mountain, but don't tell IT to me.

Unless, alas, you must. If for reasons of personal anguish you feel compelled to let IT all (must it really be *all*?) hang out—do so unwillingly, reluctantly, sheepishly, and with the recognition that I am doing you a favor in receiving IT, not you in giving IT to me.

UNIT 8

HASSLES IN THE FAMILY

☐ Every few years an article pops up—usually in the Sunday supplements— sounding the alarm for the decay of the family. The pressures of modern society, say the authors, are destroying family life. Parents no longer can control their children; family breakup is more and more noticeable. Readers nod their heads and agree. The only problem is this: Literature as far back as one cares to go is full of such dire forecasts. There is no doubt that the family, responding to changes in society, has been and is in a state of flux. However, there doesn't seem to be much evidence to show that the nuclear family— parents and their children—is doomed to extinction. The nuclear family has been identified in every known society, except for one tribe living in India, the Nayars. The family has existed and does exist. Thus the voices past and present that predict its end seem to be unduly pessimistic.

Of course, changes are going on, both in the ways families relate to their societies and in the ways they manage themselves. In this unit we will discuss some trends in the relationship of the family to society. You will learn about internal family relationships and about adjustment and causes of maladjustment in the family. You will conclude the unit by analyzing your own family. You will identify stress factors and will prepare a plan to reduce family conflict.

When you have completed this unit, you should be able to:

1. *Summarize the functions of a family.*
2. *Name and explain variations in family structure.*
3. *Describe shifts in family structure occurring in the last fifty years.*
4. *Speculate on the family structure of the future in the United States.*
5. *Define the term* generation gap *and give some examples of it.*
6. *Describe a well-adjusted family, and evaluate your own family's adjustment.*
7. *Give examples of typical family conflicts.*
8. *Describe some typical family reactions to conflict.*
9. *Give some examples of what happens to children raised by inadequate parents.*
10. *State Haim Ginott's views on child-parent relationships.*
11. *Describe the ideal version of discipline.*
12. *Describe recent developments in family therapy.*
13. *Describe the knowledge you have gained about your own extended family, and tell how your feelings have changed as a result of your investigation.*
14. *Identify stresses in your family life, and categorize them in terms of role conflicts, disciplinary structure, conflicting personal needs, inadequate functioning, and any other area you can define.*
15. *Prescribe a plan of action to relieve conflict situations in your own family.*

THE FUNCTIONS OF A FAMILY

What exactly does a family do? Because it is a universal social unit, it must have some reasons for existence. If not, it would soon disappear. The major function of the family is to promote the survival of the species. This is only part of the story, however. To see the rest we must put the family into a proper perspective and relate it to the overall society. The family—like any social unit—serves society, and society in turn serves it. Another way of saying this is that the family engages in transactions with other social units. In any transaction, there is give and take. Therefore, when imbalance occurs between social units, stresses appear and the units must readjust themselves.

Think about your own family for a minute or two. Think how it fits into society. What does it do for society, and what does society do for it? List a few of the things you can think of here.

_____

_____

_____

_____

You probably listed several ways in which the family interacts with society. The family has economic, political, community, and value-system—or external—functions. It also has some internal functions—task performance, family leadership, integration and solidarity, pattern maintenance.

The family exchanges labor for services in the economic sector of society. The family provides potential workers with the personality structure and the motivational attitudes that will make them productive. In the process of exchanging labor for goods and services, the family's routines must rotate around working conditions. This is a high-priced way of saying that a family, or at least someone within it, works. The worker produces something, buys what the family needs from society, and helps to consume the purchase. Thus the family both produces and consumes. Of course, the family also provides shelter and sustenance to its members so that they can survive.

Politically, the family submits itself to the regulation of a government in order to avoid chaos and anarchy. Families typically band together to form some sort of administrative structure that provides rules and some way of enforcing them. By doing this, the family pledges its loyalty to the leadership it selects. In return, the family gets the domestic tranquility and the law and order it needs to survive and carry out its other functions.

The family's community function differs slightly from its political one. By community function we mean the set of acts that a family performs in its relations with other families and people in its environment. By political function we mean something more rigid and formal. The community provides more of a social than a political environment, where families engage in community affairs and interact with each other. The community, for its part, acts as a force giving the family identity and recognizing its existence as a legitimate unit. It controls family social actions by its approval or disapproval. In this way it regulates family behavior. The community also serves as a reference for the family, giving it guidelines for approved behavior patterns, values, and politics.

When it comes to the value-system function, the family is very important. It is the smallest existing social unit preserving the values of society. A primary function of the family is to socialize children by teaching them approved social values.

It is through the transfer of social values that society maintains itself. Therefore, the family is an important agent of the preservation of the society in which it exists. To make this system work, society must set standards and the family must accept or conform to them. The pressure for this conformity is at times very strong and may place stress on the family structure.

All the functions we have talked about concern the family's interactions with the society surrounding it. Some other functions go on within the family. Take some time to think about how your family functions internally. What does your family do about its internal relationships? List your ideas here.

_____

_____

_____

_____

One of a family's functions is setting tasks for each of its members and setting standards for their performance. Someone must bring home the money; someone must buy and prepare food; someone must clean; and so on. It goes almost without saying that assigning the tasks, setting the standards, and evaluating those standards set the tone for relations within the family. If standards are strict and evaluation is impersonal, the interactions of the family members are also liable to be impersonal.

The process of assigning tasks, establishing standards for their performance, and evaluating them necessitates the establishment of a leadership position. Of course, families by their nature have certain established power relationships. Parents generally control their children. However, as in any power situation, all sorts of shifts in power occur; members manipulate to get power and to get their points across. Therefore, leadership shifts, in most families, depending on the kind of problem under consideration and the people involved in solving it. A chronic and trying power struggle comes between adolescent children and their parents. This struggle calls for a great deal of skill in family leadership and "followership."

Leadership within a family can be divisive and damaging if it does not allow for individual growth and personal satisfaction. Should there be a conflict in power seeking within the family, should some of the roles of parent and child be distorted or poorly played, the tensions that are aroused may tear the family apart. Obviously, the family as a unit has to pay attention to its own integration and solidarity. It must also keep itself together. However, as all interpersonal relationships call for give and take, those occurring within the family do, too. As a matter of fact, family relationships call for even more giving and taking.

One way to keep a person in the family is to promote his or her feelings of belonging and acceptance. Another way is to promote traditional family activities. The Thanksgiving turkey, for example, promotes solidarity. Community pressure also tends to keep a family together. Therefore, although the emotional forces unleashed by task assignment and leadership may seem disruptive, they may also operate to keep a family an integrated unit.

You already know that one of the family's primary jobs is to pass on the values of the society of which it is a part. But the family does more than this. It prescribes how its members should relate to one another and sets goals and rules for such relationships. It sets the behavior patterns for relationships with people outside the family. This socialization function is second in importance only to the family's function of keeping its young alive. Of course, family values are the values of the parents. Consequently, existing attitudes are conserved and change is resisted. This conservatism may cause stress in the family. Some values may be out of date. Also, because values are usually related to each other, if one is changed, then others must change. However, as you have already seen, attitudes are very hard to alter.

One product of the family's functions has not been mentioned because it is not, strictly speaking, a product but rather is a by-product of the manner in which the family operates. It is the personality development of children. Certain assigned tasks, for instance, can train boys in what society considers to be feminine jobs, such as washing dishes and making beds. The family's evaluation system and the organization of its relationships will also mold family members. A family where affectionate displays are unusual and repressed will certainly produce a different child than will a warm one. Personality, of course, will be affected by the leadership roles within the family, especially by the way solidarity is maintained.

1. Summarize the functions of a family.

_____

_____

_____

_____

VARIATIONS IN FAMILY STRUCTURE

So far we have been talking about the basic or nuclear family—parents and their offspring. Beyond it is a much larger family structure, the extended family, which consists of all the relatives—grandparents, cousins, uncles,

(Nina Leen *Life* Magazine © 1948 Time Inc.)

Whether extended or nuclear, the family has fundamental responsibility for
socializing children. (Alan Mercer/Stock, Boston)

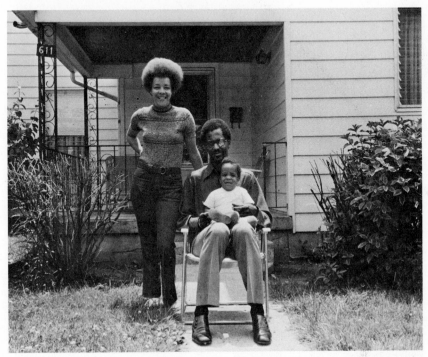

aunts, and the rest. The structure of the extended family can have some
variations that will affect family members and their relationships with society.
Three basic marriage systems can be found throughout the world: monogamy,
polygamy, and polyandry. In the United States, monogamy—marriage with
one person at a time—is now the legally enforced form. At one time the
Mormons practiced polygyny—one man with several wives. They were
persecuted and driven to the West, where they established their own
communities. Even there, however, dominant social values prevailed. Laws
were passed that forced them to be monogamous. Polyandry—one woman
with several husbands—has not been practiced by any large social group in this
country.

A second variation of family organization is in identity structure. Families
may be patrilineal, matrilineal, or bilateral. What these words describe is the
way that family governance is handled. In a patrilineal family, the male side
dominates, and identity is handed down from the oldest male of one generation
to the oldest male of the succeeding generation. In a matrilineal family,
identity descends through the female line. In a bilateral family, both parents
share identity and pass it on to their children regardless of their sex.

A third variation is in size. If children grow up in a family with a lot of cousins, uncles, and aunts, their relationships and experiences will be far different from those of an only child raised in a nuclear family.

A fourth variation in family structure arises from what might be called class type. There are significant differences in the operations of lower-, middle-, and upper-class families. These differences spill out into society, particularly when classes interact.

The final variation in family structure might be called idiosyncratic. It takes in individual family differences that come from the unique combinations of personalities that make up a family. No two families are alike; they will always differ somewhat in the way they handle their functions and in the way they are organized. Even though families throughout the world are strongly patterned by the cultures in which they exist, all are slightly different, even as individuals are different one from another.

2. Name and explain variations in family structure.

_____

_____

_____

_____

CHANGES IN FAMILY STRUCTURE

Important social developments have influenced the family in the last half-century. Some have created stresses that have modified family structure. There is enough space here to describe only some of the most significant developments.

TECHNOCRACY

In the past fifty years the technical achievements of our society have been spectacular. Our knowledge is increasing at a fantastic rate, and humans are performing technical feats that are beyond the imagination. Worldwide diseases have been wiped out; communications have become almost instantaneous. We have achieved space travel. Cross-country travel that took our ancestors six months or a year now takes three or four hours. However, technical achievements, particularly those in communication and transportation, have created a social paradox. As we have become more mobile, the extended family has become much less important. The nuclear family is becoming the dominant social unit. Moreover, in recent years the threat of overpopulation and the improvement of contraceptive methods have led to a revolution in thought. Large families were once considered desirable and inevitable. Now small families are preferred. This preference means that the nuclear family will be the basic social unit of years to come.

GOVERNMENT
PHILOSOPHY

Governments have increased their protection of the aged and infirm and of exceptional and handicapped children. By doing this, they have decreased the responsibilities of the extended family to care for its own members. This trend also reinforces the nuclear family as the dominant social unit.

SOCIAL
RESPONSIBILITY

The family formerly did a great many things for itself that it no longer is called upon to do. It does not have to grow its own food, make its own clothing, or care for its older members. Children in modern suburban and urban homes no longer have many meaningful household chores. There is no wood to chop, no ashes to take out, no animals to feed. Integrating children into the family by assigning them meaningful tasks is becoming difficult.

All this leads to the conclusion that the number of roles played by the family is decreasing. Changes in ways of life have forced changes within families. They have become increasingly specialized and have fewer and fewer functions. Moreover, the performance of the remaining functions has also changed.

WOMEN'S LIB
AND MARRIAGE

Attitudes about the family are changing. The women's liberation movement and new attitudes toward marriage have the potential of greatly affecting the family, but it is too early to say what their long-range effects will be. Women are becoming increasingly restive about the arbitrary assignment to them of family tasks and roles. Many resent their housewifely role and all that it implies. What they seem to want is to share their homemaking tasks equally with men. Some women also want to decide whether or not they should work. There is no doubt that more and more women are entering the work force, necessitating a revision of the usual role assignments within the family. The mother, traditionally the most important developer of a baby's earliest socialization processes, may be bowing out to an extent. It is not yet clear how or by whom the vacuum will be filled. For those who believe in the importance of early childhood experiences and the effects of these experiences on the adult person, this trend and the problems posed by it have tremendous significance.

The disdain with which some people have treated the legal sanctions of marriage is also becoming increasingly evident. The marriage certificate is only a piece of paper, they say, and has nothing to do with how two people manage to live with each other. Essentially, what they say is true. The ceremony of marriage merely places a legal sanction on a specific relationship. Yet it also does something else: It places pressure on the partners to stay together. Even though divorce has made it easier to dissolve unsuccessful attempts at partnership, there is still a strong social pressure to maintain the relationship.

A historical incident can give us some insight into the effects of the dissolution of the family. At one time the Russians attempted to eliminate the family as a social unit because they felt it was standing in the way of individuals' dedication to the philosophy of communism. They eliminated the marriage ceremony and allowed divorce by the request of one partner. Adultery, incest, and bigamy were eliminated as civil crimes. Children were taught that obedience to the state was more important than obedience to parents. The results of these policies, however, forced the Soviets to backtrack rather hurriedly. The birth rate dropped sharply. Because there was no family unit, community life with all its attendant pressures on values and conformity disappeared. Delinquency and hooliganism increased to epidemic proportions. Traditional morality declined, and thousands of women, loved and left, had to bear the brunt of childbirth and child rearing alone. Soon the government reinstated marriage and divorce laws, re-established inheritance procedures, made abortions illegal, and went all-out to re-establish the family as a social unit.

COMMUNAL
LIVING

The flare-up of communal living may also seriously affect family structure. Communes have been seen before in our society and in earlier ones. Usually they have had a shared-task structure, and the family unit has been preserved in them. The kibbutzim of Israel have worked in this way. There, the nuclear family has been recognized and permitted to exist. Yet the communal sharing of marriage partners and children, which we find in some modern social groups, is also not new. The Nayars of India did not recognize the father as a family member. Nayar mothers had many lovers, and male parentage was not identified. Even under this arrangement, however, there were some taboos on cohabitation with members of a lower caste, and there was a prohibition against incest. Although it could be said that the nuclear family did not exist in Nayar society, legal paternity was recognized; children did have a ritual father. The man in the tribe of the mother acted as the nuclear father in the upbringing of the children. Thus, even among these people, the functions of the family were acknowledged. Whether or not some current communes that do not identify partners in any way will develop their own customs in this respect cannot be predicted. However, if history gives us any clue at all, it is probable that a nuclear family structure will arise. It is interesting to note that those communes which have endured the longest have had an identifiable authority figure.

3. Describe shifts in family structure occurring in the last fifty years.

_____

_____

_____

_____

PROBABLE TRENDS IN FAMILY FUNCTIONS

Do these trends point to the complete dissolution of the American family? Will it disappear into oblivion, replaced by child-rearing institutions that take the child at birth and raise it according to scientifically created programs? In many respects this would be a good development, because the personality

disturbances that c
would such defect:
programs? Quite li

The importance
mobility increase
from home to fac
development nov
emphasis on birtl
Furthermore, it
government on
health programs
rather than by pa
and more instit
will have less to
that will integ
important soci
lessened, task
on—what will
development of interpe........

problem mo
revolutio
happeni
that :
cas

242

the family unit will become stronger and the childₓₑₙ
People will understand themselves and each other and will be able to pass o
their knowledge to their children. The family may not die. Although it will
have to make many adjustments, it may survive as the most powerful and
beneficial force in our society. What do you think?

4. Speculate on the family structure of the future in the United States.

_____

_____

_____

_____

THE GENERATION GAP

One of the favorite tricks of child psychologists is to quote a paragraph that
says that the children of today are rude, arrogant, spoiled, selfish, and so on.
Then, when parents agree, they gently point out that the paragraph they were
reading was written by Plato, Socrates, or some other ancient scholar. The
point being made is that every generation disagrees with the preceding one,
and every older generation views such disagreement with alarm, completely
forgetting its own rebellions.

We now call this disparity of views between young and old the *generation
gap*. It does seem to be more severe than preceding gaps, in ways that point to a

e serious than any that has ever before existed. The technical
in communications has enabled us not only to know what is
ng but to see it happening. Young people today know more—and know
hey know more—about things than their parents ever knew. In many
es this knowledge diminishes the parents' stature as authority figures. We
eldom award status to someone less informed than we are. Margaret Mead has
suggested that children should teach their parents. This is a very severe role
reversal that would produce a great deal of stress on traditional interpersonal
family relationships, especially those concerned with passing on society's
values and traditions. Parents who try to teach values are running into more
and more problems. One of the penalties of instant communication is that the
evils of the world are increasingly pushed upon us, and often news about good
things is sacrificed. When parents promote their values in the face of such
evils, the problem becomes intense. "Honesty is the best policy" is a hard
maxim to push when all around us people are benefiting from dishonesty.

One of the traditional functions of a family has been to provide shelter and
sustenance. However, as more and more material products have become
available to help the family do this, such provision takes on a lesser stature.
The government, through welfare programs, has also helped the less fortunate
to reduce their shelter and sustenance problems. These trends have created a
situation where the family is able to provide itself with many more material
possessions and creature comforts. In some families this has become the
primary reason for existence.

One of the current arguments of youth is that we are obsessed with material
things that we have neglected the spiritual. Young people also argue that our
values are so hopelessly out of date that they no longer are relevant. Youth is
increasingly disenchanted with materialism, hypocrisy, violence, corruption,
and pollution. They feel that the current generation has failed to handle its
social problems and is increasingly less willing to listen to the younger
generation. But 'twas ever thus and apparently ever will be. Social competence
always lags far behind technical ability, because people have an annoying habit
of being people: They resist manipulation.

Perhaps Alvin Toffler is right when he says in *Future Shock* that culture
shock is going to increase rather than lessen. If he is right and if we want our
society and our children to survive and maintain some form of rational sanity,
we need to teach people to anticipate change instead of relying on what has
been. To do this, we shall have to predict future values rather than rely on past
ones. "Honesty is the best policy" can remain, but the definition of honesty
must become a changing one designed to fit the times. We once defined
honesty as never telling a lie. Today we might define it as never lying unless
the truth will hurt someone terribly. Who knows? In the future we may say,
"Never tell the truth unless it will help you or someone else be a better
person."

The major point in this discussion of the generation gap is that every
generation tests the values of its society, discarding or revising those it finds
faulty. The process of revising and discarding becomes traumatic to both elders
and youth for two reasons: It involves negating what the elders have spent

their lives working for. (Remember Erikson's integrity versus despair?) The process also implies, "You have tried and made a mess of the world; now it's our turn." Somehow, better understanding of and correlation between changing times and changing values need to be established. Perhaps a more specialized nuclear family will have the knowledge and the ability to handle this transfer of values and power.

How about your family? What points at issue could you call generation-gap items? List them here.

_____

_____

_____

_____

5. *Define the term* generation gap *and give some examples of it.*

_____

_____

_____

_____

AN ADJUSTED FAMILY

So far we have been looking at how a family fits into society and at some of the processes that affect its fit. Now it is time to shift our attention slightly to look at the internal workings of the family and to see what makes it tick. To do so, we will examine a family that ticks smoothly—a well-adjusted family—and will stay with the nuclear unit rather than with the extended one. A well-adjusted family performs its tasks properly. Each member carries out tasks in such a way that the existence of the family group is enhanced and not threatened. A well-adjusted family operates as a team. Whatever it must accomplish, it delegates efficiently and smoothly. Not only are family task assignments satisfactorily made, but task roles—the ways in which the tasks are to be carried out—are spelled out. No doubt exists in a member's mind about how he or she should do his or her part. A well-adjusted family has clearly developed roles and few role conflicts. This situation fosters a feeling of solidarity, of being accepted and accepting. Similarly, well-adjusted families support their members and do not destroy them. Tasks, roles, and evaluations are carried out in such a way that a person is allowed to grow. This leads to strong positive emotional ties among family members. Of course, the family will have problems and personal disagreements. But disagreements are settled so that neither the family nor the individual is destroyed.

Notice that in this description we have carefully kept away from using such criteria as proper distribution of authority—shared or one-parent—and have ignored other variations in family operation. Adjustment is not really measured by whether the father or mother is dominant, or by whether parents reach a consensus in their decision making. It doesn't even depend on whether there are many wives or one, many husbands or one. The success or failure of a family depends on its effectiveness in doing its jobs and on the interpersonal relationships it develops as it does these jobs.

Write a one-paragraph evaluation of your family's adjustment, using the characteristics just discussed as a basis for your judgment.

_____

_____

_____

_____

6. *Describe a well-adjusted family, and evaluate your own family's adjustment.*

_____

_____

_____

_____

CONFLICTS IN THE FAMILY

Even in the most perfectly adjusted family, there are bound to be conflicts. Human nature makes them unavoidable. While parents are struggling to impose value systems on their children, the children are struggling to be individuals in their own right. The very nature of the nuclear family creates conflicts. It is usually small, consisting of two parents and several children. Because of its size and because of our way of life, intimacy is unavoidable. We mingle with other members of our family every day. Intimacy causes severe personal stress. Each of us has a need for privacy. In the hurly-burly of modern life, privacy is most difficult to obtain. We are forced to interact, whether we want to or not. Also, our family roles are so intertwined that we must depend on other members for our own need gratifications. Intimacy and small size create yet another area where conflict can occur. The family is in a state of constant change. It changes as children grow, as economic status varies, as locations shift. Without change, the family could not survive: yet the process of change strains interpersonal relationships and again leads to conflicts.

One process causing the strongest conflicts has already been mentioned: the organizing of the family and the assigning of roles. If a husband sees himself stereotyped as the head of the household who makes all decisions, but his wife sees herself as a partner with an equal voice, a role conflict ensues. If a wife goes to work and earns more than her husband, this reversal of traditional roles can lead to conflict.

As a family grows and the children clamor for a voice in family governance, patterns of interaction become more complicated. Soon, the network of relationships gets pretty complicated. A family without children might be diagrammed like this:

Husband_____Wife

The relationships in a family of three can be represented by a triangle:

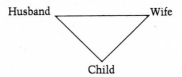

In a family with two children, the network becomes more intricate:

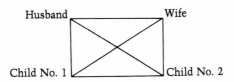

Three children in a family give rise to a complex system of interrelationships:

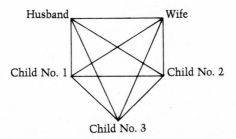

Do you want to go further, or has the point been proven? Naturally, complicated power structures and communications networks necessitate delicacy in the handling of task assignments and make the maintaining of roles critical. In families with complicated interrelationships, the chance that an individual will have all personal needs attended to is reduced because each individual is constantly required to submerge his or her own needs to satisfy those of the family. The inability of the family to satisfy personal needs becomes a second source of conflict.

A third source has also already been mentioned and is so well known that it hardly seems to need mentioning again. It is the conflict in values that occurs between parents and children and between individual members in the family. This conflict is especially critical and can frequently lead to a family's collapse.

Does your family have any role conflicts? Discuss them here.

_____

_____

_____

_____

7. Give examples of typical family conflicts.

_____

_____

_____

_____

FAMILY REACTIONS TO CONFLICTS

The typical family does have conflicts and, in order to survive, must resolve them. The well-adjusted family takes conflicts in its stride. The poorly adjusted family becomes increasingly disrupted as it tries to handle its problems. What methods do families use to eliminate conflict? How do they perpetuate it? What we will describe are the more or less typical ways in which group members can influence group action. In this respect, a family is no different from any other group.

A family may disguise conflict by sweeping it under the rug and denying its existence. A parent who denies that a child is mentally retarded or deviates in his or her behavior with peers is denying a conflict. Strangely enough, in some cases denial can be effective. If a problem is ignored, it may cure itself. True, the retarded child may not suddenly become normal, but the deviant may start to behave normally. However, the family cannot take credit for such a solution. Other social factors probably stepped in and did the work.

Another way to deal with conflicts is to intellectualize them. Here again, the family does not deal with the problem; it buries it under a barrage of words. Intellectualizing is an attempt to remove the conflict by talking it to death.

A family can also meet conflicts so emotionally that any constructive action is impossible. This too is not a positive way of dealing with the conflict. It is a non—problem-solving approach.

Another method used by many parents involves a sort of conditioned response called selective inattention. Parents tune in when they hear what they want to hear from their children; at other times they do not listen at all. Of course, children also master that art: "Sarah, why didn't you come in when I called you?" "Mommy, I didn't hear you the first two times you called."

There are other, more positive methods. One is compromise. In any conflict, everyone who is sincerely interested in a solution has to give up part of his or her position. This give and take is an essential part of family life. Although no one is completely satisfied in a compromise, balance is maintained. In a well-integrated family, the give and take is satisfying in itself.

Almost all families try to keep their problems to themselves. In families that retain an extended structure, many problems are solved by the family elders. But in situations where the extended family no longer exists, the family has no place to turn, and a great deal of internal pressure may build up. To relieve this pressure, counseling services have been created to help the family in its decision making. These agencies can be of great help to families that have no other place to turn.

Of course, the best approach to conflict is to air it openly through discussion. A democratic discussion, involving all family members, provides the best cure in conflict solutions. Recognition of each family member as an individual is a key part of this process.

How does your family typically resolve conflicts? Describe here the conflicts and how they are solved.

_____

_____

_____

_____

8. *Describe some typical family reactions to conflict.*

_____

_____

_____

_____

THE EFFECTS OF INADEQUATE PARENTS

Lewis J. Sherril in his book *The Struggle of the Soul* describes the effects that inadequate parents have on children. He says the basic problem the child faces is individuation—the process by which the child struggles to become a person. If a child is hampered by inadequate parents, this goal may never be reached. Inadequate parents, according to Sherril, are those who, because of their own personal problems, are unable to give their children love. Instead, they substitute material things for the love the child desperately needs, or they give up their parental responsibilities and let someone else raise their children. The primary cause of such parental behavior is emotional immaturity. It results in emotional immaturity in the child. In what Sherril terms the "drama of adolescence," weaning takes place. The adolescent of a well-adjusted family is well able to be weaned—to relate to others of the opposite sex. A disturbed family might produce an adolescent who can relate only to members of his or her own sex. If the family is inadequate, the adolescent who is starved for affection may go to any lengths to get it. Such an individual might also be a loner, with few, if any, friends. Should parental handling of the child be inadequate, weaning may result either in a child who will have nothing to do with its parents or one who never relinquishes the apron strings.

It is pretty well established that inadequate parents produce inadequate offspring. A recent study showed that children of retarded mothers often have signs of retardation themselves. However, if stimulated, these children can be mentally normal or even better than normal.

The news almost always carries a child-abuse story. Such abuse recurs so often within families that it is called the battered-child syndrome. Studies show that many abusive parents were themselves abused in their childhood. Their own experiences lead them to mistreat their children. Offhand, you would think that someone who was beaten would be a most tender and considerate parent. It doesn't seem to work that way, though.

Parents who are mentally unbalanced often have psychotic children. Likewise, families whose structure is based on rigid role definition that is contrary to the natures of the participants also contain disturbed young. In families of this type, no provision exists for role structures to change as the family changes. Each member is locked into a prescribed, fixed place. When an individual tries to break out of a mold, severe personality disturbances occur within the family. Studies show that some families structured in this manner have produced one, two, or even three generations of neurotic members.

Inadequate parents may also demonstrate one set of values and morals, yet verbally set forth a conflicting set. For parents to insist on strict sexual morality for their children and yet have extramarital affairs creates a conflict. Should the child do as the parents say or as the parents do? Childhood, particularly adolescence, is a time of idealism. Children are eager to accept values and moral behaviors, but they become badly disillusioned when they see one set of rules prescribed for grownups and another for them. Parental hypocrisy is often a troublesome problem for parents to overcome. If adults can drink alcohol, why can't children? Why can't American children drink when, say, Spanish children do so almost before they have been weaned, without disastrous effects?

What about this inadequate-parent idea? Does it give you some sobering thoughts about being a good parent to your children?

9. *Give some examples of what happens to children raised by inadequate parents.*

_____

_____

_____

_____

GINOTT'S IDEAS

Haim Ginott, who for a number of years wrote a syndicated newspaper column about child-rearing practices, doesn't feel that the problem of parenthood revolves around being too permissive or too demanding. He believes the problem lies in communications, in the ability to get to the child's level of understanding. He calls this ability "parent power" and says it is based on skill, not on intelligence. His point is that when we communicate with children we should respect them as people in their own right. All people have the right to maintain their own self-respect, and a parent should not take this right away from a child. When crises come up, a parent must attack the crisis and not the child. For example, a major problem in childhood is sibling rivalry. Children are constantly putting their parents on the spot by forcing them to take sides or act as referees. A skillful (and this does not mean indifferent) parent should refuse to do this and, by clever intervention, should require the squabblers to settle their own differences.

Both parents and children must be allowed to express their emotions freely. Parents must realize that the anger they feel against their children is not unnatural. Anger is not immoral, nor does it deny love. It should be permitted and expressed. The expression, however, should not be directed against the child's personality. The same may be said for negative or positive comments. Praise and criticism should always be directed to or against the act and not the person: "Your room looks good since you cleaned it," not: "You are a nice girl for cleaning your room."

10. *State Haim Ginott's views on child-parent relationships.*

_____

_____

THE IDEAL FORM OF DISCIPLINE

Parents face a constant problem: discipline. Opinions on how strong discipline should be and what form it should take vary incredibly. Discipline can range from savage beatings to mild punishment, scoldings, and logical discussion, to total permissiveness. No other subject unveils so much inexpertise in so many people. As a result, a young couple, sincerely trying to learn what is best, is confronted by a frightening cacophony of advice. The predictable result? The parents usually treat their children in the way they themselves were brought up. This perpetuates the inexpertise.

Discipline in the ideal sense is an act of love and is not punitive at all. Too many people associate it with punishment, and this should not be. Discipline should provide a learning situation: "You did this and the results were bad; consequently, you should not do it again." The parent should emphasize the tenets of the associationists, S↔R. These tenets apply to discipline, because ideal discipline is a teaching process. As Ginott says, do not criticize and punish the person; punish or praise the person's acts. Make the consequences of the act the thing to avoid, not you as a parent passing judgment.

Discipline should not be a confrontation. It should not cause parents to put their power and prestige on the line: "You are defying me." Or: "I told you no, and that's it." These responses will lead to personal challenges that parents cannot afford to ignore. A far better approach to discipline is to say, "These are the consequences. If you continue this behavior, which is bad because it leads to this result, you will be faced with this unpleasant consequence." In other words, present all the alternatives and let children save their self-respect by allowing them to make a choice. A rat when cornered will fight; a child when cornered will attack; a parent when cornered will attack. It is far better to give everyone a chance to avoid being cornered—to save face.

According to the Premack principle of behavior, behavior having a low probability of being adopted will occur more readily if it is coupled with behavior having a high probability of being adopted. This is a high-powered way of saying something that grandmothers and teachers have known for years: "Children, if we clean up this mess, we might be able to go and play for awhile." Some may call this bribery and object violently, but, to borrow from Patrick Henry, "If this be bribery, then give me bribery or give me confused and cowed children."

There are really two goals in discipline: to control an immediate situation and to prevent a future one. If a child goes out into the street—an immediate situation—how do you discipline the child without ruining future relations, and how do you make that child want to stay out of the street even when you are not watching? We often make the mistake of letting the two goals conflict.

In the immediate crisis, we ignore the self-control necessary to accomplish the long-range goal. When we take immediate forcible action, we may be unwittingly teaching that it's all right to do things as long as we don't find out about it. Therefore, the short-range goal should be subordinated to the long-range goal—self-control—for sooner or later Sherril's process of weaning must take place and, before it does, children have to learn to do things on their own and take the consequences.

A trap surrounds the concept of discipline; you can see it in this discussion. Notice the emphasis on the negative, on the prevention of behavior. There is an even better way to discipline than by inhibition, and it too is used by our friends in operant conditioning. The method is to praise desired behavior and systematically ignore, if possible, negative behavior. In the Skinner box, in the classroom, at work, we can show time after time that positive reinforcement for positive acts pays off in positive behavior. If we adopt this practice with our children, taking time to reinforce positive behavior, we are paving the way for the ideal situation, in which individuals do what is right not because they will be punished if they do wrong, but because they want to do right.

11. Describe the ideal version of discipline.

FAMILY THERAPY

One of the characteristics of a family that already has been briefly mentioned is the desire to handle problems behind closed doors. Problems, stresses, and dissension have traditionally been kept "in the family." This practice is upheld by our society. Too often, families feed, clothe, and shelter their children, yet systematically destroy them as people. You can probably think of a personal example to back up this general statement. Teachers, social workers, and neighbors may see this happening, yet they are legally powerless to intervene. The law sides with the family unless gross, deliberate, and harmful negligence can be proven. This, of course, is hard to do. Thus the family traditionally has muddled through with its problems and has not been required to get help in solving them.

To be perfectly fair, we must admit that there have not been many places to go for help. Few facilities have been equipped to handle the family as a unit and to solve problems of interpersonal relationships. Recently, however, some agencies have tried to fill this gap. In some communities, family-counseling centers deal not only with a problem person but with the family that created that person. These agencies have been helped by another recent development, group therapy. This combination extends hope to families that are having a hard time making personal adjustments.

There are three main approaches to family treatment. The first re-educates the family through guidance. This approach involves transmitting new values to the family and giving advice and assistance in reordering its priorities. The second approach deals with a reorganization of a family's methods of communication and techniques of speaking. Rational discussions replace shouting matches. Each person is respected as a person with the right to a point of view. This restructuring has done much to heal family rifts. The third approach treats emotional disorders in members of the family but deals with all members instead of concentrating exclusively on those who are disturbed. This type of therapy tries to relieve stresses and tensions and thus to improve the family's emotional climate. If successful, the family will be less vulnerable to conflicts and critical upsets and better able to carry out its functions constructively. This approach strengthens the solidarity of the family and reduces the individual's emotional problem.

As a technique and an approach, family therapy seems to be working. It does much to establish an understanding among family members, to reduce clashes between conflicting needs, and to promote understanding and better natural growth. The biggest problem in the future of family therapy is to provide enough trained therapists at a reasonable cost. Another problem is to convince families that it is no disgrace for a whole family to go see the "shrink." Perhaps in the not too distant future, as young people become more sophisticated in the art of living together, an encounter-group type of exchange will precede marriage. Then prospective parents will at least be able to communicate effectively with each other.

12. *Describe recent developments in family therapy.*

_____

_____

_____

_____

TRACING YOUR ROOTS

Who were your ancestors? Where did they come from? One of the marks of an integrated family is its ability to trace its roots back through preceding generations. How far back can you go? Use the following diagram to construct a family tree. Go back as far as you can, giving names, dates of birth, places of birth, occupations, and any other information you can dig up.

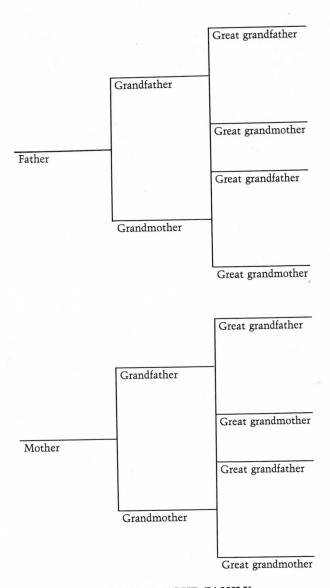

YOUR REACTIONS TO YOUR FAMILY

Now that you have found out more about your family and have had a chance to
put your knowledge is some sort of order, think about your feelings toward
your family. Have these feelings changed? Has learning more about your
ancestors affected your feelings about your roots? Think about these feelings,
and then summarize your reactions to your findings here.

_____

_____

_____

13. *Describe the knowledge you have gained about your own extended family, and tell how your feelings have changed as a result of your investigation.*

_____

_____

_____

_____

IDENTIFYING CONFLICTS IN YOUR FAMILY

Your next two tasks are purely expository. Do them as honestly and as candidly as you can. You may wish to look back at your comments in some of the preceding exercises before you do this one.

14. *Identify stresses in your family life, and categorize them in terms of role conflicts, disciplinary structure, conflicting personal needs, inadequate functioning, and any other area you can define.*

_____

_____

_____

_____

A PLAN OF ACTION

Now that you have listed your gripes, what can you do about them? Review this unit for suggestions. Remember that each person in your family, including yourself, has a right to be a person. Remember also the importance of communication in good child-parent relationships.

Here is an experiment you might try: When a problem comes up, do some reverse role playing. For example, if you are having an argument with your mother about being allowed to stay out late, ask her to switch roles with you and be the one who wants to stay out late, while you act the part of the one who has to grant the permission. If you both approach this experiment seriously, you might be surprised at the amount of flexibility both sides can develop.

Another experiment you could try is Exercise 4 in Unit 7. Again, you must each be careful to let the other person present his or her full story without interruption. This exercise can also work with more than two people and may be appropriate if several are arguing.

Do you reward behavior you want to establish in other members of the family? Do you socially punish undesired behavior? Unit 16, "Behavior Modification," gives you some guidelines in these techniques. Can you use the reward principle: "If you do this, I will do this"? Use all these techniques. They will do much to help improve your own family relationships. The important thing is that you use good techniques rather than force. Write an account of your efforts to relieve a particular stress situation here.

----

15. *Prescribe a plan of action to relieve conflict situations in your own family.*

☐ A POINT OF VIEW

Many articles and books deal with the family. The coverage ranges from sociological articles about the future of the family to therapy for families. Kahlil Gibran's *The Prophet*, however, says it all on how a family should be. If you are interested in delving further into various aspects of the family, you might want to look at these books:

Meyer Barash and Alice Scourby, eds., *Marriage and the Family: A Comparative Analysis of Contemporary Problems* (New York: Random House, 1970).

Norman W. Bell and Ezra F. Vogel, eds., *Modern Introduction to the Family*, rev. ed. (New York: Free Press, 1968).

Robert R. Bell, *Marriage and Family Interaction*, 3rd ed. (Homewood, Ill.: Dorsey Press, 1971).

Alan L. Grey, *Man, Woman and Marriage: Studies of Small Group Process in the Family* (Chicago: Aldine, 1969).

William F. Kenkel, *Family in Perspective*, 2nd ed. (New York: Appleton-Century-Crofts, 1960).

KAHLIL GIBRAN

ON MARRIAGE AND CHILDREN

Then Almitra spoke again and said, And what of Marriage, master?

And he answered saying:

You were born together, and together you shall be forevermore.

You shall be together when the white wings of death scatter your days.

Ay, you shall be together even in the silent memory of God.

But let there be spaces in your togetherness,

And let the winds of the heavens dance between you.

Love one another, but make not a bond of love:

Let it rather be a moving sea between the shores of your souls.

Fill each other's cup but drink not from one cup.

Give one another of your bread but eat not from the same loaf.

Sing and dance together and be joyous, but let each one of you be alone,

Even as the strings of a lute are alone though they quiver with the same music.

Give your hearts, but not into each other's keeping.

For only the hand of Life can contain your hearts.

And stand together yet not too near together:

For the pillars of the temple stand apart,

And the oak tree and the cypress grow not in each other's shadow.

And a woman who held a babe against her bosom said, Speak to us of Children.

And he said:

Your children are not your children.

They are the sons and daughters of Life's longing for itself.

They come through you but not from you,

And though they are with you yet they belong not to you.

You may give them your love but not your thoughts,

For they have their own thoughts.

You may house their bodies but not their souls,

For their souls dwell in the house of tomorrow, which you cannot visit, not even in your dreams.

You may strive to be like them, but seek not to make them like you.

For life goes not backward nor tarries with yesterday.

You are the bows from which your children as living arrows are sent forth.

The archer sees the mark upon the path of the infinite, and He bends you with His might that His arrows may go swift and far.

Let your bending in the Archer's hand be for gladness;

For even as He loves the arrow that flies, so He loves also the bow that is stable.

UNIT 9

THE PSYCHOLOGY
OF WORK

□ Mark Twain once said he wasn't afraid of hard work: He could lie down and go to sleep beside it. Most of us feel the same way. To us, the person who enjoys work and can't wait to go back to it is some kind of freak. Yet many of us also secretly envy that kind of person. Ideally, everyone should enjoy work; it should give great pleasure and be interesting. After all, most people spend almost one-third of their adult lives at work.

Almost everyone knows what work is, but very few understand its dynamics, its psychology, and the process of career development. In this unit we will consider the stages of occupational development, some aspects of the psychological motives for work, and approaches to work management. This unit will allow you to analyze yourself and to identify your stage of vocational development, and it will suggest how you can improve your work situation. It will also give you two views of work: that of a worker and that of a supervisor.

When you have completed this unit, you should be able to:

1. *Give three reasons why people work and explain what each reason involves.*
2. *Describe the relationship between life stages and work-development stages.*
3. *Describe various career patterns for both males and females.*
4. *Name and describe the factors involved in vocational development.*
5. *Explain the motivational aspects of work activity.*
6. *Describe the Hawthorne experience and explain its implications.*
7. *Describe the traditional philosophies of management.*
8. *Compare the assumptions of what Douglas McGregor calls management Theory X to McGregor's Theory Y.*
9. *Explain how McGregor's theory would change the traditional philosophies of management and compare it to Theory Z.*
10. *Describe the Scanlon Plan.*
11. *Evaluate the Scanlon Plan.*
12. *Describe some of the problems involved in performance appraisal.*
13. *Suggest methods for improving performance appraisals.*
14. *Explain how use of leisure is becoming an important part of vocational theory.*
15. *Analyze your world of work. Where do you stand in your career development? What satisfactions is your work providing? What needs is it filling—or not filling? How can you make your work situation more satisfactory?*

REASONS FOR WORKING

Why do people work? The obvious answer is so that they can eat and provide themselves with shelter. Hardly anyone will question this. But is it true for everyone? Do you know any women or men who work even though their spouses earn an acceptable income? How about wealthy individuals who already have all the money they need for their support? Why do they beat their brains out to earn a living? Surely there must be reasons other than personal needs for food and shelter that induce people to work. What do you think some of these reasons are?

_____

_____

_____

_____

Did you mention the search for personal identity? Today, people often feel alienated from society. They feel depersonalized—as if everyone takes them for granted. Many people work to avoid this feeling of anonymity. In Unit 2, "Motivation," you learned that several psychologist-philosophers made this point: People work to satisfy their needs, but their needs do not stop at the basic level of staying alive. People do not work exclusively to obtain material things. Even when their material wants are satisfied, they continue to work. Why? Because they have an inborn need to feel productive, to be active, to do something worthwhile.

Naturally, ideas of what is productive and what is worthwhile may look different to the worker and to society. For example, scientists who do "pure" research spend their time learning _about_ something, although there is no obvious potential application for their knowledge. In other words, their findings can't be converted into practical ideas to advance the state of humanity. Should scientists be paid to do this type of research? Many people will think they should not. "What a waste of time," they exclaim when they read of the researcher who spent a lifetime studying the life cycle of the oyster. However, that person was probably getting personal satisfaction out of that research.

Other people follow society's dictates; they prefer to work in a job with some prestige attached to it. They like the feeling of being respected for what they do, and, as a matter of fact, their status in the community often depends on their jobs. For example, how do you rank the following people in your community? First, in column 1, indicate their status by assigning them numbers, giving the highest 1 and the lowest 10.

1. Lawyer   _____   _____

2. Minister   _____   _____

3. Police officer   _____   _____

4. Schoolteacher   _____   _____

5. Doctor   _____   _____

6. Dentist   ____   ____

7. Bricklayer   ____   ____

8. Plumber   ____   ____

9. Truck driver   ____   ____

10. Auto mechanic   ____   ____

Then in column 2 rank these professions in the order of estimated income. Do the rankings stay the same? Do they show that a high salary necessarily implies a prestigious job?

We have discovered two reasons for working: personal satisfaction and prestige. But what of the third reason: the need for food, clothing, and shelter? Imagine that you are a person who has a great deal of technical knowledge in a very unstable area—electronics. Because of your specialized knowledge, you receive a fairly large salary from a firm where you have worked for seven years. One night at home you get a phone call from a rival company. They offer to double your salary if you will come to work for them. As you consider this

Working more for personal satisfaction than for prestige? (Patricia Hollander/Stock, Boston)

Working more for prestige than for personal satisfaction? (Ellis Herwig/Stock, Boston)

opportunity, you hesitate because the company has a reputation for ruthlessness. They will fire anyone almost overnight if their plans change or if the employee doesn't produce enough. You might be under a great deal of pressure if you worked for this company, but your income would probably double or triple. What would you do? Keep your present job? Change jobs?

Why did you make your choice? Was money everything, or did you consider things such as job security and working conditions? If you considered these factors and stayed put, you decided as a great many other people would have done. Money is not everything. Security and working conditions are important factors in providing the satisfaction necessary when working for essentials.

1. Give three reasons why people work and explain what each reason involves.

LIFE STAGES AND WORK STAGES

When factories were first established, working children ten years old or younger were not uncommon. Child-labor laws eventually prevented such exploitation. In the United States, more and more emphasis was placed on education as a way to protect children and give them opportunities to advance themselves. In the 1920s, it was fairly common for a person to go to work after grammar school. In the 1930s, the tendency was for adolescents to stay in school through high school. In the 1940s, many young people continued their education in college. At the end of World War II, the government tried to remove veterans from the labor market by subsidizing their higher education. The trend toward college education was dramatically emphasized in the 1950s and 1960s, when many young people completed at least two years of college. People now are not entering the world of work until they are 18, 19, 20, or older.

The development of Russia's Sputnik made Americans aware of the nation's educational shortcomings. As a result, an overwhelming stress was placed on unlimited education. (In contrast, some countries restrict the education of their children and direct some of them into careers on the basis of their schoolwork.) The American emphasis, plus the increasing sophistication of the work world, has created interesting problems for American young people. They must make their career decisions at an early age; yet they need a great deal of education and training before they can begin to work. Even worse, they not only must consider the rise and fall of job opportunities in the labor market but must face the fact that whole career patterns may become obsolete. (There is not much call for buggy-whip makers any more. In contrast, the need for farriers is increasing again.) If you think this situation is hard on the people, consider what it has done to the schools.

How do people enter the world of work? It is a scary process. To begin with, the average person enters the work world at a definite stage in life. There is a close relationship between development as a person and development as a worker. There have been many descriptions of a person's life stages. You have studied Freud's and Erikson's (see Unit 3). Freud's theory does not go beyond the onset of adolescence. Erikson describes psychosocial stages from birth to old age. The four stages and crises he identifies from adolescence on are:

1. puberty and adolescence (ages 12–16): identity versus role confusion
2. young adulthood (ages 17–35): intimacy versus isolation
3. adulthood (ages 36–60): generativity versus stagnation
4. maturity (after age 60): ego integrity versus despair

Erikson assigned to the adolescent period the problem of finding a meaning for life in terms of productivity:

> The sense of ego identity, then, is the accrued confidence that the inner sameness and continuity prepared in the past are matched by the sameness and continuity of one's meaning for others, as evidenced in the tangible promise of a "career." . . . In most instances, . . . it is the inability to settle on an occupational identity which disturbs individual young people.

In describing the next stage, young adulthood, Erikson goes on to say:

> In order to be of lasting social significance, the utopia of genitality should include:
> 1. mutuality of orgasm
> 2. with a loved partner
> 3. of the other sex
> 4. with whom one is able and willing to share a mutual trust
> 5. with whom one is able and willing to regulate the cycles of
>   a. *work* [emphasis added]
>   b. procreation
>   c. recreation
> 6. so as to secure to the offspring, too, all the stages of a satisfactory development

Erikson sees work as a major part of the development of the individual in adolescence and young adulthood.

Other investigators, adopting somewhat different viewpoints, have identified other stages. For example, Robert J. Havighurst describes stages of development in terms of developmental tasks. To him, each stage is distinguished by tasks that must be learned if a person is to become a functioning adult. In adolescence, an individual should master these developmental tasks:

1. Achieving new and more mature relations with age mates of both sexes
2. Achieving a masculine or feminine social role
3. Accepting one's physique and using the body effectively
4. Achieving emotional independence of parents and other adults
5. Achieving assurance of economic independence
6. Selecting and preparing for an occupation
7. Preparing for marriage and family life
8. Developing the intellectual skills and sufficiency necessary for civic competence
9. Desiring and achieving socially responsible behavior
10. Acquiring a set of values and an ethical system as a guide to behavior

In early adulthood, an individual must successfully learn these tasks:

1. Selecting a mate
2. Starting a family
3. Rearing children
4. Managing a home
5. Getting started in an occupation
6. Taking on civic responsibility
7. Finding a congenial social group

In middle age, a person should develop skill in these tasks:

1. Achieving adult, civic, and social responsibility
2. Establishing and maintaining an economic standard of living
3. Assisting teenagers to become responsible and happy adults
4. Developing adult leisure-time activities

5. Relating to one's spouse as a person
6. Accepting and adjusting to the physiological changes of middle age
7. Adjusting to aging parents

These tasks are similar to those devised by Charlotte Buehler. She analyzed life histories and came up with five stages:

1. Growth: from conception to age 14
2. Exploratory: from ages 15 through 25
3. Establishment: from ages 25 through 45
4. Maintenance: from ages 46 through 65
5. Decline: after age 65

Essentially, Erikson, Havighurst, and Buehler are saying the same thing but are using different words to say it. They all define adolescence as a time for exploration and the selection of a career and young adulthood as a time for the establishment of that career. Each of them defines adolescence as the period between ages 12 and 16 and young adulthood as the time between ages 17 and 35. They point out, however, that because every individual's rate of growth and development is unique, the span of years for each stage is an average. We have seen that people are not entering the world of work until their late teens and early twenties. What effect does this relatively late entry have on the other, later life stages?

_____

_____

_____

_____

Life-stage theories do not show the entire picture in the development of a career. Career development is part of the total problem of life development. Although distinct and separate, it is subject to an individual's progress through his or her life stages. Students of career development have found that work stages are just as definite as life stages. Delbert C. Miller and William H. Form identified five stages of career development:

1. Preparatory work period: An individual begins to be socialized to the world of work by family, friends, and community.
2. Initial work period: This stage begins when an individual is approximately 14 years old. At that time, the adolescent first experiences work, usually a part-time or summer job.
3. Trial work period: The age of a person in this period ranges from 16 to 25. During this time, an individual progresses from the first full-time job through a series of job changes until a stable position is reached. There is evidence, however, that this period is being shortened. More and more young people can hold good, responsible jobs.

4. Stable work period: This stage is just what the name implies. It is the period when an individual has decided on a career occupation and stays with it until retirement.
5. Retirement period: Between the ages of 60 and 65, most people withdraw from their careers and from the world of work.

2. *Describe the relationship between life stages and work-development stages.*

_____

_____

_____

_____

MALE AND FEMALE CAREER PATTERNS

It would be nice if human beings behaved exactly as theorists say they do and fit nicely into the pigeonholes prepared for them. They rarely do, however, as the proponents of career-development stages have found out. They discovered that they had to identify three career patterns to describe the ways that men progress through the stages they had outlined and seven patterns for women. The male stages were prepared by Miller and Form; the female stages were created by Donald Super. The male patterns are:

1. Stable career: In this pattern a person goes directly from education to his occupation. Such individuals have skipped the trial work period that Miller and Form described. Most professionals, many managers, and some skilled workers follow this pattern.
2. Conventional career: This pattern calls for a progression through each of the work stages. Most managers and clerical and skilled workers perform in this way.
3. Unstable career: A trial period, a stable period, and another trial period make up this pattern. A worker gives up a potential career to enter a different occupation. Most semiskilled and domestic workers follow this progression.

The female patterns are:

1. Stable homemaking career: Women following this pattern go from school to marriage with little or no work experience.
2. Conventional career: A woman moves from school to a short period of work and then marries and leaves the work force.
3. Stable working career: A woman goes from school to a money-making career.

4. Double-track career: In this pattern, a woman moves from education to work, marriage, and a double career. Both work and marriage continue.
5. Interrupted career: Here the sequence is work, marriage and exit from the work force, then return to work at a later date.
6. Unstable career: This pattern is like the male unstable career pattern.
7. Multiple careers: A woman following this pattern has a succession of unrelated jobs with stability in none.

This analysis was made in 1951. Today another male pattern may be emerging because of the emphasis on early retirement. This pattern might appear as trial, stable period, trial, stable period; it would reflect retired people's floundering through new jobs until they establish a second career. Female patterns may also be changing. More and more women in the job market now are not necessarily performing traditional "women's work." Women's career patterns may be increasingly shifting to follow the male model. We will probably see more of the unstable career pattern as our economic system becomes increasingly complex. The number of occupations open to an individual will grow and present problems. There will be a quicker phasing in and phasing out of jobs, so that a person might select a career and train for it, only to find that it is obsolescent and that therefore he or she must learn to do some other type of work.

3. Describe various career patterns for both males and females.

_____

_____

_____

_____

FACTORS IN VOCATIONAL DEVELOPMENT

Assuming that all people are alike (which they are not), what do you think might affect vocational development? You are already aware of one factor: sex. List a few other factors that you think have affected or will affect your vocational development.

_____

_____

_____

_____

Check the factors you noted against this list: availability, interest, ability, motivation, family, personality, luck.

Obviously, you can't enter a vocation unless jobs are available. Jobs and careers have fluctuated with the demands of the times. For example, from 1950 until 1970 there was a serious lack of qualified teachers. There are now signs that the shortage has been overcome and that there is an excess of prospective teachers. The supply of scientists is expected to exceed demands for them in the near future. There are indications that there will soon be a critical shortage of auto mechanics.

Career planning is a problem. Not only must you select a field; you must also look at it carefully to see whether it will be reasonably permanent. It is only common sense to avoid fields that have severe fluctuations in demand.

Vocational career patterns are definitely changing. Fewer manufacturing employees are needed, even though output is higher than ever. The number of farms is declining, but service industries—government, leisure time, repair, recreation, hotels, restaurants—are on the increase. This increase is a sign of need, and it reflects the changing lifestyle of an entire population with more leisure time and discretionary spending power.

Your interests, of course, are major factors affecting your career choice. Who wants to work at a dull job? As a matter of fact, interest is a key factor in vocational development. Several tests to measure interest are used extensively to counsel people about their vocational choices.

We are usually interested in what we are able to do reasonably well; interest tends to be related to ability. However, this is not always the case, especially in vocations where people do not get to practice in their field until they have spent a lot of time qualifying themselves. For example, doctors must spend at least six years in the traditional educational system before they can practice medicine. The cost of a medical education is tremendous, and people who invest time and money to become doctors and then find that they despise medicine suffer a terrific shock.

Families play important roles in vocational development. They instill values and attitudes and provide models for children to imitate. They determine much of the personality structure of the beginning worker. It is hardly questionable that the socioeconomic status of a family, as well as its ethnic and cultural background, has a tremendous effect on an individual's vocational development.

Your motivation and desires also affect your career choice. You have already studied motivation in general terms. In this unit you see a specific application of the ideas described in Unit 2.

Personality and lifestyle will help determine success or failure in a particular career. An introverted person will rarely enjoy or be a success at being a salesperson. Erich Fromm's classification of people—hoarding, exploitative, marketing, receptive—describes traits that would affect performance in a job.

We must not forget that immeasurable factor called luck. Being in the right place at the right time, or in the wrong place at the wrong time, can make the difference between success and failure. No one can plan for or guard against this factor. Some scientists insist that it is unscientific to mention luck. There is no such thing as luck, they claim. But don't you secretly believe in its importance?

4. Name and describe the factors involved in vocational development.

_____

_____

_____

_____

MOTIVATIONAL ASPECTS OF WORK

As you mentally review Unit 2 on motivation, you will remember two important motivational theories: the biological and the social. In order to discuss the interaction of motivation and work most clearly, we will use Abraham Maslow's hierarchy of needs.

Maslow suggested that our various needs have a sort of priority. We first must take care of our physiological needs and provide ourselves with food and shelter. Having accomplished this, we can turn our attention to security, which in the world of work is provided for by guaranteed terms of employment, protection against layoffs, and similar practices. Following security needs come those of belonging, of being accepted. Then comes a need for self-esteem or what Fromm calls self-love—a sense of respect and pride in oneself. Only when all these needs are met, says Maslow, can a person consider the highest need of all: self-actualization, a need satisfied by a sense of being productive and feeling useful.

Needs drive us in work as well as in other activities. If they are satisfied, we are happy in our work. If they are not, we may be in trouble.

Conduct the following survey among five of your relatives, friends, or neighbors. Explain each of the needs just discussed and then ask this question: "How well is your employer satisfying your need for (1) physiological satisfaction, (2) security, (3) belonging, (4) self-esteem, (5) self-actualization?" In a general statement, summarize the answers you obtained for each need. Then determine how well each of Maslow's needs is being met in these persons' work. Now answer the question for yourself. Does your answer resemble the others or differ from them?

_____

_____

———————————————————————————

———————————————————————————

The idea of needs has been translated into a motivation-hygiene description. One investigator found that only two kinds of factor—satisfiers and dissatisfiers—affect job satisfaction. These factors are not opposites of each other. For example, if we eliminate dissatisfiers, satisfaction on the job does not automatically occur. Similarly, job satisfiers, if taken away, do not automatically produce job dissatisfaction. Thus if either type of factor is missing or tampered with, the end product falls in an area between them, in what could be called *no* job satisfaction. What is interesting about this research and what makes it fall into Maslow's pattern fairly accurately is the nature of the two types of factor. Job dissatisfiers are things such as wages, working conditions, company policies, and supervision. They are termed hygienic factors. Even if they are managed to the complete satisfaction of the worker, something will still need to be furnished in order to raise the worker above the no-job-satisfaction condition. Job satisfiers are achievement, intrinsic interest, recognition of achievement, responsibility, advancement, and other personal feelings. Their absence, too, leads to no job satisfaction. Can you recognize the similarity between the motivation-hygiene theory and Maslow's hierarchy of needs?

5. *Explain the motivational aspects of work activity.*

———————————————————————————

———————————————————————————

———————————————————————————

———————————————————————————

THE HAWTHORNE EXPERIENCE

A classic account of how working conditions affect productivity is known as the Hawthorne Studies. In 1927, a group of scholars conducted experiments at Western Electric's Hawthorne plant in Cicero, Illinois, to investigate the effects of light, noise, rest periods, and so on on workers' output.

Workers were told about the experiment and divided into an experimental group and a control group. In the first part of the project, the level of illumination in certain work areas was gradually raised. As the light increased in the area of the experimental group, so did output. Although the lighting in the area of the control group remained constant, the output of the control group also increased. Later, the lighting in which the experimental group worked was reduced; yet the output of both groups still increased. Only when the lighting for the experimental group was reduced to the level of moonlight did that group's output decrease.

The experimenters then varied the number of rest periods to see how fatigue affected production. Rest periods were taken away, yet production went up. The output of the experimental group did not drop as the experimenters thought it would. Production increased even when the workers were deprived of some of their benefits. Why do you think this happened?

_____

_____

_____

_____

Are you an employer? What lesson does this experiment have for you? Are you an employee? Do you feel that your management is interested in you as a person? If you are neither, imagine that you are a boss. How do the results of the Hawthorne experiment strike you?

_____

_____

_____

_____

The key finding of the project was that the attention the workers were getting made them feel that they were special and that someone cared about them. They responded by increasing their level of production.

The Marine Corps frequently operates in the same way. Often marines are assigned to special duty that will keep them working hard for eighteen hours a day. They may be so far out in the weeds that daily liberty is a joke. Their quarters may be tents, the weather cold and wet. In spite of all this, their morale remains extremely high and their attitudes and performance outstanding. The marines see themselves as members of a special group and build up a team spirit.

6. *Describe the Hawthorne experience and explain its implications.*

_____

_____

_____

_____

PHILOSOPHIES OF MANAGEMENT

Douglas McGregor has defined what he considers to be traditional philosophies of management. He described some office supervisors considering the
problem of how to get people to work on time. Throughout their conference,
they discussed only gadgets or tricks. At no time did they think in terms of
motives or attitudes. McGregor regards such management by force as a basic
managerial philosophy: If people don't want to work, managers must compel
them to. If they do not perform satisfactorily, they can always be fired.
Management may use threat and fear to make workers docile and willing to
work harder. However, the aggression and hostility bred by this approach will
eventually burst out somewhere.

Another philosophy of management identified by McGregor is paternalistic:
You can make workers do what you want by being kind to them; people should
want to work harder when they are grateful. Unfortunately, however, gratitude
is not a good motivator. As a matter of fact, it backfires, especially when the
flow of kindness decreases or stops.

The third philosophy described by McGregor is a compromise between the
two just mentioned. In effect, it says, "Be firm but be fair." However, it is
essentially a combination of two unworkable principles.

If you are working, can you identify the philosophy your employers are
using? If your occupation is that of student, what philosophy has your school
adopted?

7. Describe the traditional philosophies of management.

_____

_____

_____

_____

THEORY X AND THEORY Y

McGregor has some feelings about the ways in which management looks at
workers. He describes two sets of attitudes about human nature and the nature
of work. At one extreme is the arrogant, paternalistic manager, whose

assumptions McGregor terms Theory X. According to Theory X, the average worker has an aversion to work and must be forced to work by bribery or threats of punishment. Most workers respond well to controls because of their apathy. The average person is lazy, lacks ambition, avoids decision making, cares little for others (especially for the organization), resists new ideas, is gullible, and is easily misled.

Comment on this philosophy. If you have no work experience, consider the classroom your work center. Can you tell whether management is making these assumptions about you? If so, how?

_____

_____

_____

_____

In opposition to Theory X, McGregor proposes some counterthoughts. He says that a satisfied need is not a motivator of behavior. If your security needs are being met, you have no reason to work harder to meet the need for security. What you need is to satisfy your higher needs: belonging, being accepted, giving and receiving friendship and love, self-esteem, and self-actualization. What needs do overtime pay, shift differentials, bonuses, health plans, and other fringe benefits satisfy? Would you predict that a pay raise would cause a worker to increase production or slow it down?

_____

_____

_____

_____

In contrast to Theory X, McGregor presents the democratic assumptions of Theory Y. A manager operating on these assumptions believes that it is as natural to use up energy in work as in play. The best way to get people to pay attention to their work is to give them some reason for doing so. This means that work objectives must be tied to personal objectives through a system of rewards. Thus management's goals and workers' objectives should be tied together. According to Theory Y, the average person will look for responsibility if conditions are right. Also, if conditions *are* right, an individual will show creativity and ingenuity on the job. These attributes are commonly found in the worker population, which is a rich, though little tapped, source of intellectual ability.

(Drawing by Alan Dunn © 1972. The New Yorker Magazine, Inc.)

"Leave it to good old G.M. to break the monotony of the assembly line!"

8. *Compare the assumptions of what Douglas McGregor calls management*
   Theory X to McGregor's Theory Y.

_____

_____

_____

_____

THEORY Y AND THEORY Z

From these ideas, Donald McGregor, in *The Human Side of Enterprise* (New York: McGraw-Hill, 1960), draws several conclusions about human motivation and human nature:

1. Management is responsible for organizing the elements of productive enterprise—money, materials, equipment, people—in the interest of economic ends.
2. People are *not* by nature passive or resistant to organizational needs. They have become so as a result of experience in organizations.
3. The motivation, the potential for development, the capacity for assuming responsibility, the readiness to direct behavior toward organizational goals are all present in people. Management does not put them there. It is a responsibility of management to make it possible for people to recognize and develop these human characteristics for themselves.
4. The essential task of management is to arrange organizational conditions and methods of operation so that people can achieve their own goals best by direction of their own efforts toward organizational objectives.

McGregor's approach has been criticized. The Theory X supervisor is in the chain of command, and decision making occurs at the top of the pyramid. The worker is just a cog. The Theory Y supervisor is a worker who participates with fellow workers in the decision making. Both schemes are too generalized. People do not behave in this either/or way. Research does not prove that either X or Y—each an extreme example—leads to better job satisfaction than does a managerial position in the middle of the road. Some people do not respond to increased personal responsibility.

Theory Z, which was created by a group of organizational psychologists, is a systems approach. It takes into account six aspects of organizations:

1. Organizational size
2. Degree of interaction
3. Employees' personalities
4. Congruence of employees' goals
5. The levels at which decision making takes place
6. The state of the system

Theory Z deals with the interplay of these factors. For example, as size increases, organizational structure becomes more formal and complex and tends to become authoritarian. To counteract this tendency, management should provide for a freer flow of information and ideas. Employees' personality needs should be recognized, and those who respond best to authority should feel it. The goals of the workers should be made congruent with those of management.

We can state Theory Z in terms of leadership styles. We can also state it in terms of styles of organizational structure. For example, should a firm be departmentalized or decentralized? A systems approach deals with the problems that McGregor dealt with, but in a more compromising way.

9. Explain how McGregor's theory would change the traditional philosophies of management, and compare it to Theory Z.

_____

_____

_____

_____

THE SCANLON PLAN

By now it should be obvious to you that there are some problems in management theory. The business of looking at workers as a commodity is not good. Employees have needs that are not being met. The division between labor and management is deep, and conflicts are sometimes bitter.

One of many possible ways to heal this rift is known as the Scanlon Plan, designed to produce both industrial peace and higher production. Its main thrust is to use democratic principles in the management process and to have both management and labor adopt the same goals.

The plan has two parts, a wage formula and a system for processing suggestions and putting them into effect. The wage-incentive portion ties wages to increased productivity. For example, if the Ace Buggy Whip Company increases its sales by 10 percent, everyone's—workers' and managers'—salary goes up 10 percent. This is sort of the old piecework idea, in which everyone participates. It permits valuable feedback to reach all departments about how improvements in the making of buggy whips are working out.

The second part of the plan involves the ways in which improvements are handled. Everyone who has an idea on how to improve production in any part of the plant can make a suggestion to a production committee. Every department has such a committee, composed of both workers and managers. The committee handles all suggestions involving its department, works out the details, and submits them to a screening committee working on a plantwide basis. This procedure formalizes a method by which workers can suggest technical improvements. It also gives workers a sense of participating in the welfare of the company and a chance to exercise their creativity. It therefore serves as a vehicle for satisfying some of the higher needs identified by Maslow.

The Scanlon Plan is quite revolutionary. It removes the traditional "them and us" postures of management and labor, substituting a common goal: increasing production for everyone's benefit.

10. Describe the Scanlon Plan.

_____

_____

_____

_____

AN EVALUATION OF THE SCANLON PLAN

What do you think of the Scanlon Plan? Do you think it could work in an organization of which you are a part? Work out some ideas that you think might be handled by this method.

_____

_____

_____

_____

As you might have guessed, the Scanlon Plan has had its ups and downs. Anything so revolutionary is bound to experience both success and failure. It has been tried in a number of places and found to be excellent. In others it has been a failure. It might pay to look at some of the reasons for failure, to see what factors caused it.

One of the things that the Scanlon Plan calls for is a tremendous increase in communication between workers and management. This places severe pressure on both management and the labor union. If, for example, the union reacts to the plan by carrying out all the suggestions made by management and by pressuring workers to work harder, the union soon begins to look like management, smell like management, and talk like management. If the union, on the other hand, uses the Scanlon Plan as one big grievance procedure, this puts tremendous pressure on management, because all management can do then is to respond to labor's gripes and demands.

Another problem is that the plant screening committee can get too far away from the workers, becoming a high-level management-union round table that ignores the worker in the shop. If this occurs, the worker, deprived of personal feedback, feels betrayed. If isolation is extreme, wildcat strikes and anti-union activity may take place as workers attempt to show their sense of loss and resentment.

The plan places a tremendous amount of stress on union officials and requires them to have a great deal of skill in handling interpersonal relationships. They must guard against sabotaging the plan, and they must guard against becoming management stooges.

Management may find the conflict to be even more devastating. Traditionally, authority has filtered from the top downward, and any measurement of effectiveness goes the same way. Under the Scanlon Plan it is possible for complaints about a superior's ineffectiveness to be brought up and aired in the screening committee. Unless the company management is composed of some very strong people, this can be a threatening experience. Can you imagine a teacher sitting happily in a conference with a principal while someone attacks his or her teaching ability? What if the person attacked is not a member of any of the committees and thus self-defense is impossible? Management, in order to make this plan work, must take steps to see that a worker's supervisors, as well as the worker, get a chance to participate. The company must also teach management how to live with personal criticism, a talent that for the most part is not taught now.

Because the Scanlon Plan involves an entire company, a worker in production is free to suggest how another department might improve its overall production. "If those knuckleheads in shipping would quit goofing off!" This approach can lead to interdepartmental competition and hostility, and situations such as these must be handled skillfully to prevent the whole suggestion scheme from becoming an interdepartmental donnybrook.

When all is said and done, however, the primary impact of the plan is on individual workers. It is their standards of production that must be raised, regardless of union rules. They must raise the upper limits of their output. Also, the lower limits must be raised. In fact, numerical limits need to be eliminated, and the principle "do the best job you can" needs to be acted on. It has been suggested that goals be set mutually by the entire department in a sort of group effort.

Some of this sounds quite a bit like the five-year plans of communist countries. There is one major difference, however. In the Scanlon Plan, decisions on goals, increased productivity, and effectiveness are formed by the company as a whole, not by an upper level of government.

Nonetheless, the Scanlon Plan is viewed by both unions and management as an incentive plan. Its use is declining. It is too hard to administer fairly. Although many managements are continuing some form of incentive plan, many companies are changing to a "better management" approach, which involves control through the use of an assembly line. This approach tends to discount employees' participation in management.

11. Evaluate the Scanlon Plan.

_____

_____

_____

_____

PROBLEMS IN PERFORMANCE APPRAISAL

The problem of performance appraisal is one of the stickiest of management theory. As long as a person is on an assembly line, producing one frammas after another, the problem is simple: You can measure how many frammases that person makes. But if an employee is promoted and is put in charge of the frammas department, how then do you check and evaluate his or her work?

This is not a stupid academic question; your whole career rides on the system by which your work is evaluated. Merit pay, bonuses, and promotions are all based on such evaluations. Many corporations evaluate their employees on a form or check list that the supervisor fills out every six months or so. Sometimes the worker gets to see the form; many times he or she does not. Some corporations require that a supervisor interview employees periodically to keep them informed of their progress. These systems have many snares and pitfalls. Some supervisors may not wish to hurt their subordinates' chances for promotion, or they may want to be popular. In either case, they will give everyone outstanding marks. Employee-supervisor interviews pose an even worse problem, especially if they are supposed to include constructive criticism. How do you tell people that you don't like the way they handle something without crushing them completely? After all, you are the one who will recommend a subordinate for promotion.

Let us take a particular career with which we are all familiar: teaching. Think back to the best teacher you ever had. List the things that you think made that teacher so good.

_____

_____

_____

_____

Now recall the worst teacher you ever had. List that person's characteristics.

_____

_____

_____

_____

You judged these teachers from a student's viewpoint. Now think of them from the viewpoint of your parents. Would they agree or disagree with your evaluation? Be honest!

How about the teachers' peers? Do they appear to agree with your appraisal?

Do they accept or reject the good teacher? The bad teacher? How about the administration? Do most of your fellow students share your appraisal of these teachers?

Now look at the characteristics that distinguished the good teacher from the bad one. Are they the sort of things that can be measured in any effective way? Can you *measure* honesty, friendliness, and whatever else you marked down? If you think you can, how would you begin?

_____

_____

_____

_____

The point of this exercise is to get you to understand that the two teachers could be judged from four different viewpoints: those of the student, parent, other teachers, and administration. Each of these groups could have different standards. Also, each person in each group could have a different idea of what makes a good teacher and what makes a bad one. With all these differences, is it any wonder that it is difficult to give teachers merit pay based on effective teaching? Which evaluating group should promote the teacher? Who should give a teacher tenure?

In order to be fair, the person being evaluated should know what the activities are on which the judgment will be based and what the criteria are for evaluation. Should teachers be judged on whether they return the window shades to the same level at the end of the day or on the amount of student-created material posted on the walls of the classroom? If not these criteria, then what? And how can you tell teachers face to face that they are good or bad?

Despite the drawbacks of performance appraisals, you should not adopt a completely negative view toward them. Performance appraisals do have many good points. For example, they require that all employees receive a periodic review of their work. From this can come counseling to improve performance, better communication, and an exchange of values and interests. These results in turn create a reservoir of employees within an organization who possess great potential.

12. Describe some of the problems involved in performance appraisal.

_____

_____

_____

_____

TECHNIQUES FOR PERFORMANCE APPRAISAL

Two approaches to the solution of the problems involved in performance appraisals will be suggested here. One is by Rensis Likert, the other by Douglas McGregor.

Likert approaches the problem from a measurement viewpoint. He feels that we should develop techniques by which we can measure the intangibles with which we have been wrestling. Common measurements would give management a sound basis for decision making. Managers could use these measurements to get feedback on a comparative basis so that adjustments could be made continously. Such a system would also put personnel policies on an objective basis rather than on the basis of "gut" reactions. Common measurements could also improve morale because employees would know on which variables they were being evaluated. The common language of universal data would help communication.

Of course, this is a great notion. But what are the things that should be measured? Likert suggests several:

1. Loyalty to the organization
2. Compatibility of organizational goals with the goals of employees at all levels
3. Levels of employees' motivation as shown by performance on the job
4. Suggestions for improving operations and products
5. The amount of trust and confidence among employees as well as the amount of teamwork among them
6. How much employees believe their ideas are used
7. Efficiency and direction of the channels of communication
8. The skills and attitudes of managers
9. Aptitude scores of employees

The instruments for doing the measuring need to be created, however.

Notice that Likert would use overall department records to judge management. Other than suggesting that aptitude scores be obtained, he does not really get into the problem of assessing individuals. The measurements he suggests would tell a supervisor a great deal about a department or a separate plant but little about individual workers.

Douglas McGregor proposes a completely different concept. He visualizes evaluation as a process initiated and carried out by the workers themselves. Workers establish a plan for their jobs for a specific period—six months, three months, one year, or what have you. They discuss the plan with their supervisors and revise it in accordance with the supervisors' suggestions. At the end of the period, they report their successes and failures to their supervisors and then create a new plan. In this way, the workers have something specific to act on, and the supervisors have something specific to measure. The supervisors also retain a measure of control, because they can make suggestions about items to be included in the plan.

This scheme relies heavily on what are known as behavior goals. In order to measure success or failure, workers are going to have to define their terms in such a way that they can tell whether they have reached their goal. For example, if one worker's goal is to improve personal relations with subordinates, that person will have to spell out what he or she means by improvement. The employee is going to have to say something like, "I will have no verbal arguments with any worker." Or: "I will speak to all workers and have them speak to me on a first-name basis." Or as a particular commanding general used to insist: "I will be able to give the name, number of years in the service, home town, marital status, name of spouse, and number of children for all the noncommissioned officers in my command." Specifying goals in measurable terms leaves no uncertainty in anyone's mind. It moves the appraisal technique from vague generalities to specific items.

There are, of course, other techniques for appraisal. Rating scales can be filled out by subordinates, by peers, and by superiors. Sometimes combinations of various techniques are used, such as interviews and rating scales.

Drawing on all the material you have been reading about job satisfactions, personal involvement, and evaluation, how do you think you could be better evaluated so that you could become more involved in what you are doing? Once you have developed some ideas on how to better your lot, do you think you might be able to suggest them to your school, your family, or the management of the place where you work? You might be surprised to see that teachers, family, and managers are interested in the ideas you come up with.

_____

_____

_____

_____

13. Suggest methods for improving performance appraisals.

_____

_____

_____

_____

THE IMPORTANCE OF LEISURE

In *Wheels*, Arthur Hailey describes the Detroit assembly lines of the automobile industry. He pictures in detail how the assembly line is so physically demanding and mentally stressful that many employees do not show up for work on Mondays and Fridays. The monotony of the never-ending line seems to drive some people into such a frenzy that they can't stand the pace. To compensate, they take time off and use leisure as a healing device.

We have recently started to take a good hard look at the whole topic of leisure. As the length of the work week decreases, people have more and more spare time. This may create problems. People who really like their work may become unhappy when deprived of it by a shortened work week. People who hate their work will be glad to be away from it, but having to come back to it will be unpleasant. Contrary to common opinion, leisure is not good for everyone. Think of the compulsive executive, for example. However, no leisure at all may be bad also. The problem is to find out how much leisure is good for us and then to manage to get the right amount.

Just what is the right amount? The Protestant work ethic keeps many people from enjoying leisure. They believe that idleness breeds mischief, that sitting back and thinking is sinful. Because of this belief, some of us spend our leisure time working harder than we do when we are officially working. The old Protestant ethic makes our idle moments uneasy. Tiring ourselves out in some frantic activity is certainly a form of leisure and does serve a good purpose by letting us get rid of our tensions and irritations. If you are angry, you can hit a baseball as hard as you can—instead of the person who made you angry. But hard play is not enough. We need to appreciate what the Italians call *dolce for niente*, sweet idleness. It's interesting that older civilizations didn't feel as we do about idleness. The Greeks used it to pursue culture. Leisure to them was not the device of the devil, as the Protestant ethic would have us feel.

It is not completely fair, however, to knock the Protestant work ethic. One of its effects originally was to transform every job into a potential service to the Creator. All workers considered their occupations to be in the service of the Lord. Thus workers were motivated to serve other people as they would serve God. Rest on the Sabbath was an essential part of the work ethic. Idleness, not leisure, was viewed as the defiant refusal of a person to accept the social and religious responsibility of being a productive member of the community. From this viewpoint, what kept people from enjoying leisure was their lack of commitment to any value system that gave purpose to life.

Leisure means different things to different people in our own times. Researchers have found different attitudes in various social classes and occupations. People at the bottom of the socioeconomic ladder depend on those higher up to give them opportunities for spare time. Leisure means different things to different kinds of workers. Industrial workers no longer seem to consider their jobs the center of their lives. Work to them is a means to buying their leisure. Their view of work prevents them from organizing their social and recreational life around their work associations. When the workday is over, they want to get far away from the job as soon as they can. This is why the efforts of some companies to form social and recreational groups among the workers are often unsuccessful. Asking workers to become more committed to their work through participating in management decisions seems to be shoveling sand against the tide. However, the technique may work for professional employees who have a greater personal commitment to their jobs.

A problem we face in this country is that our leisure time is increasing rapidly. Automation and new technology are reducing the number of hours of human labor needed for production. Workers are being phased out of the labor market at a relatively early age, while they still have vigor and energy left to burn. A minor reversal of this trend is occurring as social-security laws extend the age of retirement. However, some unions and companies continue to push for even earlier retirement ages. How should we siphon off this energy and talent into something more productive and satisfying than forced idleness? Just what to do and how to do it are still up for grabs. It does seem that one of our first moves should be to change our attitudes toward leisure. We need to teach people to be easy with leisure. Then we need to teach people how to use leisure for their own best interests without guilt.

How do you spend your spare time? Do you spend it actively? Do you feel any guilt when you sit and do nothing? Do you have an insane urge to work if your hands are idle? If so, you might think about this for a little bit: Just why are you frantically keeping busy? What is driving you? Think about changing your lifestyle a little. A philosopher has suggested that we have alienated ourselves from nature. Maybe what we need to do is to spend some time with it, not in a frantic swim of a thousand yards or a hike of a thousand miles, but in a day of watching a tidewater pond or a freshwater brook. Even if you live in a city, it isn't impossible for you to commune with nature. There are parks and open fields within your reach. What other ideas do you have? Think about this seriously, because there is nothing sadder than the person who doesn't know what to do with spare time. All you have to do to learn a good lesson is to look at a retired person who hasn't thought this out. Everyone needs a hobby or avocation for idle moments. Even doing absolutely nothing takes skill and practice.

14. *Explain how use of leisure is becoming an important part of vocational theory.*

_____

_____

_____

_____

A PERSONAL ANALYSIS

Now that this unit is almost complete, you should be ready to appraise where you stand in the world of work and what you need to do to get the maximal benefit from the unit's lessons. Exercise 1 should help you with this analysis.

EXERCISE 1.   ANALYSIS OF WORK

1. Do you consider your work a job, an occupation, or a position?
2. What life stage do you consider yourself to be in?
3. Have you established a career pattern yet? If you have, what is it?
4. Identify the factors that have operated in your vocational development, and arrange them in the order of their importance.
5. How well is your work satisfying these needs:

	Poorly	Well enough	Very well
Physiological needs	____	____	____
Security needs	____	____	____
Belonging needs	____	____	____
Self-esteem needs	____	____	____
Self-actualization needs	____	____	____

6. Does your work make you feel that you are a special person or that you are one of the mob?
7. Do you feel that you have a voice in setting work policies?
8. Do you understand and agree with the way you and your fellow workers are evaluated?
9. Summarize your answers in a short paragraph and look at the results.

Did you call your work a job? If you did, it may be that you are not particularly happy with what you are doing. If you said it is an occupation, you may have decided that you have found a suitable career. If you termed it a position, your feelings may include satisfaction with the prestige and status of your work. Consider your other answers in the same way, and try to see a general theme in them. Describe the theme in a brief paragraph.

15. *Analyze your world of work. Where do you stand in your career development? What satisfactions is your work providing? What needs is it filling—or not filling? How can you make your work situation more satisfactory?*

_____

_____

_____

_____

□ A POINT OF VIEW

The first chapter of *The Peter Principle*, by Laurence J. Peter and Raymond Hull, reads like a tongue-in-cheek treatment of work and promotion. But you will, if you ruminate enough, begin to see deep merit in what the authors say. It's fun reading with a message.

There are many books on work, leading in many different directions. Whether you are management or union oriented, a worker or a consumer, your position in the world of work will affect your selection of additional reading matter.

LAURENCE J. PETER AND RAYMOND HULL

THE PETER PRINCIPLE

"I begin to smell a rat."

M. de Cervantes

When I was a boy I was taught that the men upstairs knew what they were doing. I was told, "Peter, the more you know, the further you go." So I stayed in school until I graduated from college and then went forth into the world clutching firmly these ideas and my new teaching certificate. During the first year of teaching I was upset to find that a number of teachers, school principals, supervisors and superintendents appeared to be unaware of their professional responsibilities and incompetent in executing their duties. For example my principal's main concerns were that all window shades be at the same level, that classrooms should be quiet and that no one step on or near the rose beds. The superintendent's main concerns were that no minority group, no matter how fanatical, should ever be offended and that all official

forms be submitted on time. The children's education appeared farthest from the administrator mind.

At first I thought this was a special weakness of the school system in which I taught so I applied for certification in another province. I filled out the special forms, enclosed the required documents and complied willingly with all the red tape. Several weeks later, back came my application and all the documents!

No, there was nothing wrong with my credentials; the forms were correctly filled out; an official departmental stamp showed that they had been received in good order. But an accompanying letter said, "The new regulations require that such forms cannot be accepted by the Department of Education unless they have been registered at the Post Office to ensure safe delivery. Will you please remail the forms to the Department, making sure to register them this time?"

I began to suspect that the local school system did not have a monopoly on incompetence.

As I looked further afield, I saw that every organization contained a number of persons who could not do their jobs.

A UNIVERSAL PHENOMENON

Occupational incompetence is everywhere. Have you noticed it? Probably we all have noticed it.

We see indecisive politicians posing as resolute statesmen and the "authoritative source" who blames his misinformation on "situational imponderables." Limitless are the public servants who are indolent and insolent, military commanders whose behavioral timidity belies their dreadnaught rhetoric, and governors whose innate servility prevents their actually governing. In our sophistication, we virtually shrug aside the immoral cleric, corrupt judge, incoherent attorney, author who cannot write and English teacher who cannot spell. At universities we see proclamations authored by administrators whose own office communications are hopelessly muddled; and droning lectures from inaudible or incomprehensible instructors.

Seeing incompetence at all levels of every hierarchy—political, legal, educational and industrial—I hypothesized that the cause was some inherent feature of the rules governing the placement of employees. Thus began my serious study of the ways in which employees move upward through a hierarchy, and of what happens to them after promotion.

For my scientific data hundreds of case histories were collected. Here are three typical examples.

MUNICIPAL GOVERNMENT FILE, CASE NO. 17

J. S. Minion[1] was a maintenance foreman in the public works department of Excelsior City. He was a favorite of the senior officials at City Hall. They all praised his unfailing affability.

"I like Minion," said the superintendent of works. "He has good judgment and is always pleasant and agreeable."

This behavior was appropriate for Minion's position: he was not supposed to make policy, so he had no need to disagree with his superiors.

The superintendent of works retired and Minion succeeded him. Minion continued to agree with everyone. He passed to his foreman every suggestion that came from above. The resulting conflicts in policy, and the continual changing of plans, soon demoralized the department. Complaints poured in from the Mayor and other officials, from taxpayers and from the maintenance-workers' union.

Minion still says "yes" to everyone, and carries messages briskly back and forth between his superiors and his subordinates. Nominally a superintendent, he actually does the work of a messenger. The maintenance department regularly exceeds its budget, yet fails to fulfill its program of work. In short, Minion, a competent foreman, became an incompetent superintendent.

[1]Some names have been changed, in order to protect the guilty.

SERVICE INDUSTRIES FILE, CASE NO. 3

E. Tinker was exceptionally zealous and intelligent as an apprentice at G. Reece Auto Repair Inc., and soon rose to journeyman mechanic. In this job he showed outstanding ability in diagnosing obscure faults, and endless patience in correcting them. He was promoted to foreman of the repair shop.

But here his love of things mechanical and his perfectionism become liabilities. He will undertake any job that he thinks looks interesting, no matter how busy the shop may be. "We'll work it in somehow," he says.

He will not let a job go until he is fully satisfied with it.

He meddles constantly. He is seldom to be found at his desk. He is usually up to his elbows in a dismantled motor and while the man who should be doing the work stands watching, other workmen sit around waiting to be assigned new tasks. As a result the shop is always overcrowded with work, always in a muddle, and delivery times are often missed.

Tinker cannot understand that the average customer cares little about perfection—he wants his car back on time! He cannot understand that most of his men are less interested in motors than in their pay checks. So Tinker cannot get on with his customers or with his subordinates. He was a competent mechanic, but is now an incompetent foreman.

MILITARY FILE, CASE NO. 8

Consider the case of the late renowned General A. Goodwin. His hearty, informal manner, his racy style of speech, his scorn for petty regulations and his undoubted personal bravery made him the idol of his men. He led them to many well-deserved victories.

When Goodwin was promoted to field marshal he had to deal, not with ordinary soldiers, but with politicians and allied generalissimos.

He would not conform to the necessary protocol. He could not turn his tongue to the conventional courtesies and flatteries. He quarreled with all the dignitaries and took to lying for days at a time, drunk and sulking, in his trailer. The conduct of the war slipped out of his hands into those of his subordinates. He had been promoted to a position that he was incompetent to fill.

AN IMPORTANT CLUE!

In time I saw that all such cases had a common feature. The employee had been promoted from a position of competence to a position of incompetence. I saw that, sooner or later, this could happen to every employee in every hierarchy.

HYPOTHETICAL CASE FILE, CASE NO. 1

Suppose you own a pill-rolling factory, Perfect Pill Incorporated. Your foreman-pill roller dies of a perforated ulcer. You need a replacement. You naturally look among your rank-and-file pill rollers.

Miss Oval, Mrs. Cylinder, Mr. Ellipse and Mr. Cube all show various degrees of incompetence. They will naturally be ineligible for promotion. You will choose—other things being equal—your most competent pill roller, Mr. Sphere, and promote him to foreman.

Now suppose Mr. Sphere proves competent as foreman. Later, when your general foreman, Legree, moves up to Works Manager, Sphere will be eligible to take his place.

If, on the other hand, Sphere is an incompetent foreman, he will get no more promotion. He has reached what I call his "level of incompetence." He will stay there till the end of his career.

Some employees, like Ellipse and Cube, reach a level of incompetence in the lowest grade and are never promoted. Some, like Sphere (assuming he is not a satisfactory foreman), reach it after one promotion.

E. Tinker, the automobile repair-shop foreman, reached his level of incompetence on the third stage of the hierarchy. General Goodwin reached his level of incompetence at the very top of the hierarchy.

So my analysis of hundreds of cases of occupational incompetence led me on to formulate *The Peter Principle:*

In a Hierarchy Every Employee Tends to Rise to His Level of Incompetence.

A NEW SCIENCE!

Having formulated the Principle, I discovered that I had inadvertently founded a new science, hierarchiology, the study of hierarchies.

The term "hierarchy" was originally used to describe the system of church government by priests graded into ranks. The contemporary meaning includes any organization whose members or employees are arranged in order of rank, grade or class.

Hierarchiology, although a relatively recent discipline, appears to have great applicability to the fields of public and private administration.

THIS MEANS YOU!

My Principle is the key to an understanding of all hierarchical systems, and therefore to an understanding of the whole structure of civilization. A few eccentrics try to avoid getting involved with hierarchies, but everyone in business, industry, trade-unionism, politics, government, the armed forces, religion and education is so involved. All of them are controlled by the Peter Principle.

Many of them, to be sure, may win a promotion or two, moving from one level of competence to a higher level of competence. But competence in that new position qualifies them for still another promotion. For each individual, for *you*, for *me*, the final promotion is from a level of competence to a level of incompetence.[2]

So, given enough time—and assuming the

---

[2] The phenomena of "percussive sublimation" (commonly referred to as "being kicked upstairs") and of "the lateral arabesque" are not, as the casual observer might think, exceptions to the Principle. They are only pseudo-promotions, and will be dealt with in Chapter 3.

existence of enough ranks in the hierarchy—
each employee rises to, and remains at, his level
of incompetence. Peter's Corollary states:

*In time, every post tends to be occupied by an
employee who is incompetent to carry out its
duties.*

WHO TURNS THE WHEELS?

You will rarely find, of course, a system in
which *every* employee has reached his level of
incompetence. In most instances, something is
being done to further the ostensible purposes for
which the hierarchy exists.

*Work is accomplished by those employees who
have not yet reached their level of incompetence.*

UNIT 10

LOVE

☐ Along with sex, love is one of the most frequently met concepts in American society. Our literature abounds with discussions of love. We are constantly reminded that loving is all-important, that it is the primary source of happiness and contentment for the individual. We are told to love our country, our fellow human beings, our neighbors, our parents, our spouses, and our children. We are told to take heart in the love of God. We are supposed to love our work. We use the words *making love* as a euphemism for sexual intercourse. All this brings us to the perplexing question: If love is so all-fired important, why don't some languages even have a word for it?

This unit will explore the dimensions of love, its relationships to various aspects of our lives, its influence over us, and some of its misuses.

When you have completed this unit, you should be able to:

1. *Define* love.
2. *Explain Erich Fromm's concept of the nature of love.*
3. *Describe the various types of love.*
4. *Explain what functions love performs for us.*
5. *Give a short history of the rise and evolution of romantic or courtly love.*
6. *Describe the effects of culture on love.*
7. *Describe the type of love experienced in adolescence.*
8. *Describe adult love.*
9. *Relate love to sexuality.*
10. *Describe the effects of certain emotions on love.*
11. *Distinguish between infatuation and love.*
12. *Distinguish between liking and loving relationships.*
13. *Explain how love can be abused.*
14, *Describe the results of a loss of love.*
15. *Describe how love can be therapeutic.*

A DEFINITION OF LOVE

There was a popular ballad several years ago called "What Is This Thing Called Love?" It's still a good question. How can we define a word that simultaneously involves your feelings for your dog, your nextdoor neighbor, your country, your mother and father, your children, and your spouse? What kind of phenomenon are we talking about that is so widely dispersed and so generally applied? The dictionary defines *love* as follows:

> **love,** *n.* 1. An intense affectionate concern for another person. 2. An intense sexual desire for another person 3. A beloved person . . . 4. A strong fondness or enthusiasm for something. 5. *Capital* L. Eros or Cupid . . . 6. *Theology.* a. God's benevolence and mercy toward man. b. Man's devotion to or adoration of God. c. The benevolence, kindness, or brotherhood that man should rightfully feel toward others. 7. *Capital* L. *Christian Science.* God . . . **—fall in love.** To become enamored of or

sexually attracted to someone. **—for love.** As a favor; out of fondness; without payment . . . **—in love.** Feeling love for someone or something; enamored. **—make love.** 1. To copulate. 2. To embrace and caress . . . *v. tr.* 1. To feel love for. 2. To desire (another person) sexually. 3. To embrace or caress. 4. To like or desire enthusiastically; delight in. 5. To thrive on; need . . . Synonyms: *affection, devotion, fondness, infatuation.* These nouns refer to feelings of attraction and attachment experienced by persons. *Love* suggests a feeling more intense and less susceptible to control than that associated with its synonyms. *Affection* is a more unvarying feeling of warm regard for another person. *Devotion* is dedication and attachment to a person or thing; contrasted with *love,* it implies a more selfless and often a more settled feeling. *Fondness,* in its most common modern sense, is rather strong liking for a person or thing. *Infatuation* is extravagant attraction or attachment to a person or thing, usually short in duration and indicative of folly or faulty judgment. (Adapted from *The American Heritage Dictionary of the English Language,* ed. William Morris, Boston: American Heritage Co. and Houghton Mifflin, 1973.)

From all of this description, can you come up with a definition of love as applied to person-to-person relationships? Is it a feeling, positive or negative? Is it always directed toward another person? Does it involve putting the desires of another person above your own? Is it strictly an emotion, or are more factors involved, such as attitudes and behaviors? Try to write a definition of *love.*

Use the following as a check against your definition: Love is an intense feeling of positive regard toward another person in which the needs and desires of that person are put above those of the one who loves. Love is not just an emotion, although it is commonly defined as such. Love is much more. It includes attitudes, such as trust, positive approval, helpful criticism, positive acceptance, and a wish for the well-being of the loved one. It also includes the behaviors that accompany these attitudes. Love can run the gamut of many emotions: affection, joy, sexual desire, anger, respect, sympathy, and empathy.

1. Define love.

_____

_____

LOVE AS A RELATIONSHIP

Even though we have struggled with a definition of love and have perhaps acquired a concept of what love is, there are many ideas that we can explore to improve our understanding of the meaning of love. Erich Fromm has devoted a great deal of thought and study to love. Coming as he does from a background of prison and Nazi concentration camps, he has developed a deep sense of appreciation for the personal relationships of human beings. Fromm considers love a set of creative relationships. He includes four elements in these relationships: knowledge, care, respect, and responsibility.

By knowledge, Fromm means that people in love must know each other. He disparages the idea of love at first sight, because he considers this type of attraction to be a product of such factors as sexual arousal, fantasy, fascination, admiration, appreciation, attraction, identification, or good feelings. These are superficial attachments. For real love, people must experience each other, getting behind the facade of superficial attachments. For real knowing, one has to know the intimate, real self, stripped of the masks of polite society.

Caring involves concern about the loved one's health, growth, stability, and welfare. It is a sharing of the loved one's feelings, a joy in the loved one's joy, pain when the loved one feels hurt. Care implies a mutuality in a love relationship, in that both parties give as well as take.

By respect, Fromm means the mutual acceptance of loved ones as they are, as unique persons, as selves in their own right. Respect does not mean fear or deference. It does not involve a reshaping of the loved one to fit a certain image, but leaves his or her personality as it is and accepts it.

Responsibility, according to Fromm, really means responding to the loved person's needs, particularly emotional needs.

Thus love, as Fromm explains it, is a relationship of giving and taking, of mutual responding and reciprocal interaction. Love involves a sharing and a returning.

2. Explain Erich Fromm's concept of the nature of love.

_____

_____

_____

_____

TYPES OF LOVE

Obviously, there are different kinds of love. One school of thought divides love into sexual or erotic love and nonsexual love. Nonsexual love includes two major types of love: a love of humanity, called *agape,* and a familial kind of love. Fromm further divides familial love into motherly love and brotherly love. Motherly love is a regard for the weak and helpless. Brotherly love is the friendly love that exists among equals. Agape, love of humanity, is a religious or political type of love. It is really one's sexless love for one's fellow human beings. Agape can involve a sacrifice by the individual for the sake of other human beings.

Several types of erotic love can also be identified. John Olan Lee, in an article

Familial love is the friendly love that exists among equals. (Ginger Chih from Peter Arnold)

called "Styles of Loving" (*Psychology Today* 8, [1974], 43–51), identified six types of erotic love: eros, ludus, storge, pragma, mania, and agape.

Eros is the romantic love of fiction and fantasy. It is the love-at-first-sight phenomenon and quickly moves into sexual passion. Eros is an exclusive relationship in which the lovers do not like separation. However, they are not jealous, nor do they suffer from despair when they are separated.

Ludus is game-playing love. Here the lover likes to keep several partners on a string and avoids any intensely personal involvement. Ludus involves few deep emotional experiences. Those concerned seem to be playing at being in love.

Storge is the kind of love that begins as friendship, as with the person nextdoor, and then develops into love with a sexual attachment. Storge includes an element of seriousness and excludes game playing or love at first sight. It is a slow, steady, serious growth of love.

Pragma is the type of love wherein the partners sit down and draw up balance sheets on each other. A person develops a list of characteristics desirable in a mate and then goes hunting for the right mate. Compatibility of lifestyles and personality are the major considerations. Selection by computer is an extreme example of pragma.

Mania typifies the manic lover, one who is consumed by emotions; jealousy, joy, sorrow, despair, and ecstasy all flash by in rapid order. Manic lovers often destroy what they are seeking by the excess of their emotions. Often mania takes the form of love from afar of an unattainable person.

To Lee, *agape* does not mean a love for humanity. Rather, it signifies a selfless love for one person with no expectation of love in return. Lee admits that this may now be an imaginary concept. He found no examples of pure agape in his studies.

Outlines often help clarify a complicated concept such as love. Perhaps the following outline will help you:

Love

A. Asexual
  1. Agape: love of humanity
  2. Familial
     a. Motherly: love for the weak and helpless
     b. Brotherly: love for one's equals

B. Sexual
  1. Eros: romantic love
  2. Ludus: games of love
  3. Storge: serious, slow-growing love
  4. Pragma: score-keeping love
  5. Mania: emotional love
  6. Agape: selfless love

3. Describe the various types of love.

_____

_____

_____

FUNCTIONS OF LOVE

Do we need love? Is it some sort of psychological event that we must experience, something we cannot do without? Or is it purely an invention of civilized human beings to describe an artifact of their civilization? What do you think? Is it possible for a person to live a lifetime without love of any type and still have what might be called a reasonably satisfying life? Do you think you can do without love? Do you know of *anyone* who has?

_____

_____

_____

_____

Let's assume that you have decided that you cannot envision your life without love of some sort. The question then is: What does love do to you or for you?

Most of the humanists would agree that love is a very necessary ingredient in our lives. They point to the development of the human infant as partial proof of their position. Researchers such as Spitz and Skeels have shown that a stimulating environment, full of affection, is a virtual necessity for the infant. If the environment is one of hostility and cruelty, the infant begins to show signs of depression. Mental and physiological development may be slowed so that growth becomes stunted. Erikson points out that a hostile environment in the first year or so of life can result in a person who simply never learns to trust his or her environment. Most of the humanists also hold that these effects are virtually irreversible. Some disagree. Kagan, for example, has studied a tribe in Guatemala in which newborn infants and young children are practically ignored for several years; children are later accepted into the family. Kagan's studies showed no permanent ill effects, although there were some signs of poor development during the stage of neglect. The debate rages on, but it does seem that some bad and lasting consequences result from a lack of love in the early years of life.

Abraham Maslow made love and intimacy one of the prerequisites of achieving self-actualization, the realization of one's full potential. He felt that without a love experience, a person simply could not learn the self-esteem necessary for self-actualization. Obviously, Maslow felt that it is possible to live a life without love, but that such a life is on a rather low plane of existence. Erich Fromm agreed, but he reversed the sequence. He felt that before one person can love another, that person has to experience self-love in order to be able to risk the intimacy and self-disclosure required by a loving relationship. There does seem to be some merit to Fromm's argument. Some people seem to be unable to enter into a love relationship because they lack the self-confidence and the ability to disclose themselves to others. They grab at love, but true love seems to elude them because they cannot share.

Thus we seem to need the experience of some type of love, asexual or sexual, for our own personal development and for the fullest use of our own potential. Love serves a necessary function in that it aids in our search for self-actualization.

4. Explain what functions love performs for us.

_____

_____

_____

_____

ROMANTIC LOVE

The concept of chivalry is based on the rise of romantic or courtly love. Chivalry is peculiar because it seems so silly and illogical. Perhaps in the past it served a purpose that isn't clear to us now. The concept of romantic love, which arose during the Middle Ages, was the basis of this system of chivalry, in which men and women could relate to each other outside of marriage. The type of erotic love on which chivalry was based is Lee's agape: unrequited love from afar. The system called for a relationship in which a young man worshiped a lady, usually one of a higher social rank. It was a chaste relationship in which the man protected the woman. He might die for her but never have sexual relations with her. One strange aspect of this system was that a courtier could be completely under the influence of agape toward a woman of the court, yet he could be married and have children at home! One wonders what feelings his wife had while his service and adoration were being offered to another. At any rate, this type of love called for deprivation and suffering as a result of the lack of response. It involved an unfulfilled longing. When the barriers to fulfillment of the relationship were removed, agape tended to disappear.

Although romantic love still exists in our culture today, it has been modified as the barriers among cultures, nationalities, and races have eroded. *West Side Story* is still a reasonably plausible tale but is becoming steadily less believable. After all, a Hatfield recently married a McCoy! One could point out three processes that tended to destroy the barriers that resulted in romantic love. Social classes tended to even out as we left the feudal system. Youth gained more and more independence as the rural economy shifted to an industrial pattern in which children were not needed to continue the family enterprise. The gradual erosion of the extended family in favor of the nuclear family also caused a lessening of the power of kinship. Looking back at these changes, you might deduce that the era of romantic love wasn't so silly after all. It served a useful purpose in that it kept everyone in his or her place by making service to the nobility a desirable cultural convention.

An interesting stage in the evolution of romantic love was its importation to America. Here, the restraints of class, bloodlines, and kinship were materially reduced. Romantic love thus took on more of the flavor of eros than agape. It was theoretically possible in America for the beggar to marry the queen or for the maid to be wedded to the young master. To many Europeans, this adaptation to love at first sight and the relaxation of boundaries was extremely unsettling. In Europe it just wasn't done. However, a careful look at the underlying circumstances reveals that even in America a considerable influence was still exerted by family, religion, socioeconomic class, and race. Even today, as we lean more and more toward the relaxation of these boundaries, you must acknowledge that they still exist and still modify the concept of romantic love as the ideal.

5. *Give a short history of the rise and evolution of romantic or courtly love.*

_____

_____

_____

_____

LOVE AND CULTURE

In the introduction, we noted that some languages do not even have a word for love. If this is so, are there cultures in which love is not even considered? Is it possible that our notions about the necessity for love are pure rationalization? It seems that there are indeed cultures, particularly non-Western ones, that have no concept of love at all. In most of these cultures, the marriage relationship is one in which one spouse, usually the wife, is looked on as a possession that has been bought for a price, be it cattle, silver, or property. Naturally, this concept leads to a completely different relationship between men and women. Sexual love really does not exist between spouses. Relationships are formed on a purely economic basis, through consideration of the economic value of the wife. Infidelity or extramarital relationships with the opposite sex are looked on unfavorably only if they negatively affect the economic status of the household. This explains why the tribal chief can offer one of his wives to a visitor as a gesture of hospitality. There is no love involved as we know it.

In many societies of the past, marriages were arranged. The prospective bride and groom had little, if anything, to say about the arrangement. Major considerations were the social fit of the couple, the economic arrangements, and whether or not the marriage would improve the interfamily relationships or the socioeconomic status of the family. Love between the man and the woman was not a necessary ingredient in the formula. This is probably why the American notion that love should be part of the arrangement was considered silly and somewhat antisocial by non-Americans. It is easy to see how the system of arranged marriages could lead to the lack of any concept of love between husband and wife. The marital relationship was based mainly on duty, responsibility, and shared work. If love existed, it existed only in the form of asexual agape, or familial love. Any form of erotic love was almost inevitably of the unrequited type, involving suffering and despair because of the impossibility of establishing a meaningful relationship.

There are still some cultures in which the matchmaker, or arranger of marriages, is an important figure. However, these islands of conservatism seem to be disappearing under the wash of the American concept of romantic love, the idea of love at first sight, and the notion that the queen may marry the commoner. Because the trend is toward that attitude, less and less will be heard of barriers to love. The concept of love as a necessary ingredient in the establishment of a family seems to be the direction in which society is going.

One interesting variation on this theme is the group family or commune. Naturally, there are many variations in this lifestyle. However, in those where sexual relationships are involved, there seem to be two possible arrangements. In the first setup, although all other aspects of family life are shared, the relationship of husband and wife (or the mating portion) is still an exclusive one. Thus erotic love can still exist. In communes where sexual activity is also shared, however, it does not seem possible for erotic love to function. Nonsexual love, on the other hand, seems to be necessary in order to keep the community together.

Thus we see that cultural influences, particularly those that govern the creation and maintenance of the family, do control to a great extent the nature and function of whatever love exists. To go back to the question of whether love is necessary for human beings, it would seem that the humanists are not wrong, especially if love is considered in its broadest sense. Even if limited to its asexual forms, love is a strong factor in one's search for fulfillment.

6. Describe the effects of culture on love.

_____

_____

ADOLESCENT LOVE

Adolescence is a stage in life when sexual desires, ego identity, and love all seem to come together. This situation is explosive because each issue alone can be troublesome and produce stress. The love that a child experiences prior to adolescence may be considered internally oriented. That is, the child really is involved in self-gratification. His or her love relationships are one-way: The child takes but does not give. Neither does there seem to be any sexual drive in late childhood or preadolescence. With adolescence, the individual encounters a strong sexual urge. If this urge is gratified by sexual pleasure, even short of orgasm, it can serve to reward and thus to strengthen loving interactions and feelings.

In the adolescent stage, a person is searching for self-identity. To have someone share a relationship of intimacy, trust, caring, and all of the other manifestations of love is a tremendously exciting and stimulating experience, especially the first time. This willingness of another individual to share serves as proof that a person is indeed attractive to the opposite sex, thus fitting one more piece into the puzzle of self-discovery. Add the novelty of physical displays of affection—something the child and the preadolescent was warned against doing—and you have a truly exciting new experience.

There is a strong emphasis on the eros type of sexual love. Being together is highly rewarding to both individuals. One of the greatest rewards of eros is the sharing, the intimacy with a person who is outside the family and is also a fledgling adult. This intimacy drives a courting adolescent couple even closer together because they are in effect strangers to each other, at least in the beginning.

One of the phenomena of adolescent love is the experience of a series of infatuations or crushes. While these crushes seem infantile and silly to the adult observer, they do serve a useful purpose to the adolescent. They give the adolescent lover practice in establishing a love relationship and defining the type of person with whom he or she wishes to experience such a relationship. Joseph Stone and Joseph Church, in their book on childhood and adolescence, use a strange term in connection with this concept: love goat. Just as a person scapegoats, finding a powerless victim on which aggression and frustration can be vented, so the child and the adolescent look for a love goat, an individual on whom they can lavish their affection and love. In adolescence, the identity of the love goat changes from time to time, as the adolescent eagerly seeks new experiences and new thrills in the brand new game of loving and sharing.

One interesting characteristic of love in the adolescent is that it is usually an all-or-nothing experience; typical adolescent love does not hold anything back or keep any feelings in reserve. Adolescents seem to bear out the idea of zero-sum love. This concept views love as existing in a limited, finite quantity. If it is spent on one person, there is none left for another. Conversely, if the adolescent tries to spread love over more than one person, he or she is considered not to be in love at all. Rather, he or she is engaging in ludic love, or game playing, and is not considered sincere. In demanding all of his or her love, the adolescent's partner is using a zero-sum concept.

7. Describe the type of love experienced in adolescence.

_____

_____

_____

_____

ADULT LOVE

Very few except adolescents themselves take adolescent love affairs seriously. Adults know from experience the fickleness of infatuation, which is what adolescent love usually turns out to be. The implication is that adult love, as opposed to adolescent activity, is solid and permanent. Adult love is expected to last until death or even beyond. It is also expected to allow growth and maturation of both partners, even as they go through the stresses and strains of family life. I think that this is the point Erich Fromm was making. Adult love is supposed to transcend the starry-eyed period of courtship. In order to do so, it has to be based on firmer ground than the interactions of two persons putting their best foot forward in a whirlwind courtship.

Researchers have concluded that adult love is based on factors other than mere personal attractiveness of one partner to the other. While Americans may consider romantic involvement necessary in adult love, they will, when pressed, add other factors. The strongest of these factors are kinship, racial, and ethnic considerations. In a way, these factors seem more applicable to the pragma type of love, the balance sheet. However, both eros and pragma do seem to be needed to ensure an enduring adult love relationship. Some personality factors and interacting modes are also involved. Rapport, or feeling comfortable with someone, stimulates self-revelation, the disclosure of one's innermost thoughts. Self-revelation facilitates mutual dependence; each partner needs the other to share the feelings and satisfy the needs created by self-revelation.

8. Describe adult love.

_____

In adult love, each partner needs the other to share the feelings and satisfy the needs created by self-revelation. (Andy Mercado/Jeroboam, Inc.)

LOVE AND SEXUALITY

The word *sexuality*, as used here, means the behavior of a sex. It does not connote explicit sexual activity. In this discussion, it means the way in which love is expressed by men and by women. Zick Rubin, in his book *Liking and Loving* (New York: Holt, Rinehart and Winston, 1973, pp. 204–206), concludes from his studies that men are likely to be less picky and demanding than women. In other words, men seem to fall in love more readily than women. Both sexes agree on the American concept of romantic love, but men tend to be less choosy about the objects of their courtship. If you think about this for a moment, the reason may come to you. As Rubin says, in our society women usually take on the economic and social status of the men they marry. Therefore, a woman may tend to give more thought to the consequences of her decision. It is a more practical question for her. The result is that the woman is less likely to allow herself to be swept off her feet by just any man at any time. Willard Waller explained the difference in this way (*The Family: A Dynamic Interpretation*, New York: Dryden Press, 1938, p. 243): A man, when he marries, chooses a companion; a woman chooses a way of life as well as a companion. According to our stereotype, the female is more romantic than the male. She is supposed to be starry eyed and sentimental. In the light of Rubin's findings and Waller's comments, it would seem that the stereotype is wrong. It is the male who is more romantic, while the female is more pragmatic about her relationships. This theory is substantiated to some degree by the sexual behavior and attitudes of the two sexes. The male emphasizes sexual gratification through orgasm. His sexual focus is on getting the most sexual activity in exchange for the least evidence of love. Accordingly, most males seek body-centered sex, or sex just for fun. The female is taught that her most important role in life is to be a wife and mother. While the women's liberation movement has changed and is still changing some of these basic attitudes, the typical pattern of female socialization still gears her toward being a wife and mother. According to Ira L. Reiss (*Heterosexual Relationships Inside and Outside of Marriage*, Morristown, N.J.: General Learning Press, 1973), the female tends to consider courtship and marriage with an outlook toward person-centered sex, or sex with affection.

Willy, Vander, and Fisher make this point in their discussion of sexual hunger in women in *The Illustrated Encyclopedia of Sex* (New York: Cadillac Publishing Co., 1950, p. 251):

> The sexual hunger of women is by nature *quantitatively* the same as that of men but differs therefrom *qualitatively*. Women may be less sensual than men, but this is due to cultural, i.e., educational causes, no less than the frequent quantitative weakness and repression of the feminine libido. Undoubtedly, however, sexual life plays a far more important role in the life of a woman than in that of a man, and that is the ultimate reason for the qualitative difference between the feminine and masculine sexual instinct. The difference lies in the fact that the sexual instinct of a woman, unlike that of a man, is not concentrated exclusively on copulation, as the maternal instinct is a component part. The sexual instinct of women, as Marie Bonaparte so aptly remarked in her book, *The Sexuality of the Child*, is diluted, since it is divided between copulation and the processes of motherhood.

This doesn't mean that the female is purely a mercenary who will marry for status and not for love. According to Rubin, the research does not point this way at all. He finds that the female still believes strongly in romantic love as a necessary ingredient in marriage. Neither can it fairly be said that sexual activity is of little importance to a woman. A woman, just like a man, is a totally functioning person who can and does seek gratification through sexual activity. However, she is not so directly pushed toward orgasm as the ultimate result of sex; she tends to consider other things also, such as emotional relationships and the environment in which she finds herself.

It is interesting to speculate on how these aspects of sexuality and love would be different if men and women were social equals. What do you think? Would the behaviors and attitudes described differ? How?

_____

_____

_____

_____

9. Relate love to sexuality.

_____

_____

_____

_____

NEGATIVE EMOTIONS AND LOVE

Love, as it has been presented here, is a force that creates positive emotions in the person experiencing it. Generally, love is thought to be increased by positive experiences, such as rewarding responses from the loved one. This may not always be so or at least may not appear so on superficial examination. Some people report that their love is made stronger by rejection or by an emotion like jealousy. Sexual arousal can also appear to increase love. In these situations, the emotions underlying the apparent surge of love are acting on the body. Strong sexual arousal, for example, causes adrenalin to be pumped into the bloodstream. Since the physiological response to various emotions is the same, a person can misinterpret physiological arousal as an outburst of love when it is really the result of jealousy, anger, guilt, or sex drive.

Romantic love traditionally emphasized the enhancement of love by negative situations, such as despair, unreturned love, or rejection. "Absence makes the heart grow fonder." Jealousy over attentions paid to a rival were thought to increase one's love. Thus romantic love paid a great deal of attention to jealousy, an emotion closely tied to the love relationship. According to the concept of zero-sum love, where the amount of love is limited and therefore must be concentrated exclusively on one love object, jealousy is an almost inevitable emotion. Although jealousy is very powerful, little research on it has been done. However, some researchers have identified six types of jealousy: envy, possessiveness, exclusion, competition, egotism, and fear.

Envious jealousy is wishful thinking. It is the desire to own what belongs to another. Competitive jealousy is jealousy over another person's accomplishments. These two types of jealousy are not limited to love; they are found in other forms of social relationships. The possessive, exclusive, fearful, and egotistic types of jealousy are more directly related to love. Possessive jealousy regards the love object as a possession or projection of self. For example: "You are my wife; you belong to me." Possessive jealousy limits the autonomy and freedom of the loved one. Exclusive jealousy is the feeling that one is being left out of some part of the loved one's life. Fearful jealousy is the fear of losing the love object or of being rejected or deserted. This is the most common form of jealousy. Egotistic jealousy is the individual's wish to maintain his or her own life without interference from the demands of the partner. It can also take the form of an imposition on the partner of one's own ideas about proper role behavior.

Surprisingly, the emotion of guilt can also be activated by love. Freudian psychology attributes guilt to violations of taboos, whether in behavior, thoughts, or fantasy. These taboos or prohibitions are the products of our socialization. They can be parental, religious, or moral restrictions or merely group norms. Taboos may be many and diverse. For example, there may be a prohibition against a male's showing affection toward his partner because showing affection is considered a feminine act. Guilt can result from a conflict between love for parents and love for the partner. Unless guilt is dealt with, it can effectively destroy love.

Anger is often part of a love relationship. Anger has been defined in various ways, and its sources have been variously prescribed. I think that the best explanation for anger is that it arises when someone doesn't do what you want him or her to do. Anger is really a perfectly normal reaction. However, if it is used as a basis for attacking the partner, it can lead to the destruction of love. This situation will be dealt with later in the discussion of the abuses of love.

10. Describe the effects of certain emotions on love.

_____

_____

_____

_____

INFATUATION AND LOVE

The following exercise may point out to you some of the subtle differences between infatuation and love. Pretend that you are dating someone. You are in the middle stages of courtship; that is, you have progressed beyond mere acquaintance and are now fairly familiar with each other. You spend a great deal of your time with each other. Place a check mark at the point on the continuum to where you think your behaviors and feelings fit:

	Little or least			*Much or most*	
	1	2	3	4	5

1. You spend most of your time touching and caressing. _____

2. You cannot envision being with him/her without any physical contact. _____

3. You do not think that there are any bad points about him/her. _____

4. You usually wind up in sexual activity with him/her. _____

5. You understand that your dates with him/her will usually wind up in sexual activity, and you look forward to it. _____

6. You have some reservations about his/her background. _____

7. You have some reservations about being completely and irrevocably committed to him/her. _____

8. You cannot visualize a life of total commitment to him/her. _____

9. You would still like to date others. _____

While this is an artificial exercise, it may be informative if you fill out the answers based on your dating experiences. From the tenor of the items, you should be able to deduce the differences between love and infatuation. Generally speaking, infatuation is not a total commitment to someone. It does color your perceptions of a person so that you see no bad points. You usually engage in sexual activity on your dates. There is little exchange of other thoughts or feelings. You may share one particular interest, but there are gaps in your sharing. You may not have opened yourself up completely to your partner, and you may have the feeling that he or she has not completely opened up to you either. In short, the infatuation relationship is being used by you and/or your partner primarily to bolster ego. It is an inwardly oriented relationship based on what you are getting out of it—a somewhat selfish point of view.

11. Distinguish between infatuation and love.

_____

_____

_____

_____

LIKING AND LOVING

Let's say that you have decided that your relationship is not just an ego trip and that some good, solid ground shores it up. You now want to know whether you truly love your partner or just like him or her. The following exercise may help you to make the distinction. The items to which you will respond are adapted from Zick Rubin's work, which is directed toward establishing a measurable definition of love. Before you begin, you should be aware that these items are purely experimental. They have not been thoroughly checked out by research. Some studies are currently being conducted, but for now consider the items purely tentative and suggestive rather than truly indicative of liking or loving.

Place a check mark along the continuum from least to most where you think your behaviors and feelings lie.

	Least			*Most*	
	1	2	3	4	5

1. I feel completely free to reveal my innermost thoughts.

2. X is an extremely adjusted person.

3. I am willing to do almost anything for X.

4. I consider X to be a responsible person.

5. I feel miserable when I think of being separated from X.

6. I consider X to be exceptionally mature.

	Least			Most	
	1	2	3	4	5

7. I seek out X when I feel lonely. _____

8. I feel that X has good judgment. _____

9. I feel a concern for X's welfare. _____

10. I feel that most people react favorably to X even as a first impression. _____

11. I feel able to forgive X for almost anything. _____

12. I feel that X and I are very similar. _____

13. I feel responsible for X's well-being. _____

14. I would vote for X for an elected position. _____

15. I enjoy just looking at X. _____

16. I enjoy the confidences of X. _____

17. I consider X to be one of the most likable persons I know. _____

18. I feel that it would be hard to get along without X. _____

19. I would like to be like X. _____

When you have finished, add up your score on the odd-numbered items and average them. Do the same for the even-numbered items. The odd numbers reflect a scale of loving, while the even numbers are a scale of liking. If your score on the odd-numbered items is higher than your score on the even-numbered items, you may be involved in some sort of loving relationship. If your liking score is higher, you may like the person but may not be in a loving situation with him or her.

Again, this exercise may be artificial, in that you may not have been considering a real person. No matter, because the purpose of the exercise is to have you become aware of the differences between feelings of liking and feelings of loving. If you look at the even-numbered items and the odd-numbered items separately, you should be able to deduce the differences between liking and loving.

12. Distinguish between liking and loving relationships.

_____

_____

_____

_____

ABUSES OF LOVE

Many parents use a technique to reinforce a child's behavior that implies, "Mommy and Daddy won't love you if you behave like that." Essentially, this is saying to a child that love is earned by conforming behavior. The threat of the loss of love is enough to keep the child in line, and the parents thus have complete control. However, this technique is really an abuse of love. It uses love as a weapon, a commodity that can be given or taken away as the parents' will. Anyone who lives under this kind of threat is bound to experience anxiety. Even if the threat involves only material goods, the possibility of having someone arbitrarily take away your possessions because of an emotional decision is enough to cause anxiety. Suppose, for example, the dealership from which you bought your car insisted on the right to repossess it whenever they felt they needed it. Would you buy under such an arrangement?

"I won't love you unless . . ." is a form of blackmail. Its usual result is the creation of great anxiety in the person being blackmailed. Quite often the end result is a very strong feeling of aggression and hostility toward the blackmailer, even though this feeling may be kept hidden. It is also debatable whether genuine love is being offered by the blackmailer. The concepts of love we have discussed have implied an unqualified sort of relationship, an acceptance of another person without reservation, and a total, enduring commitment. Threats to withdraw love certainly aren't consistent with these characteristics.

Although in our example we pictured parents controlling a child, quite often children try to control their parents in this manner. Also, love can be abused in any type of relationship, not just that between parents and children.

The suggestion here is not that approval and disapproval of behavior or thoughts should not be voiced. The significant others in our lives need feedback and information on our responses. However, this responding should not be based on our approval or disapproval of the person involved. The point is to avoid inferring in any way that the regard you have for the other person has been changed by behavior of which you don't approve. As we have pointed out, a person can and quite frequently does feel emotions besides love toward a loved one, even such negative emotions as anger. However, if love is to prosper, negative feelings must be directed toward the behavior and not toward the loved one. The message should always be, "I still love you even though I disapprove of what you are doing or saying." To feel anger or sorrow or joy is perfectly natural, but to use such feelings as reasons for changing the status of the partner and thus to force the person into behaving the way you want is an abuse of the power of love.

Just as in person-to-person relationships, some cults and other groups also attempt deliberately to manipulate people by the use of love. These organizations often use the appeal of love and belonging to gain new members. Once a person has joined the group, a cult may prevent interaction between that person and anyone outside the cult, even members of the individual's immediate family.

13. Explain how love can be abused.

_____

_____

_____

_____

LOSS OF LOVE

The experience of love, according to Maslow, Fromm, and other humanists, is a virtual necessity if one is to reach self-actualization. Most humanists point to love as a positive experience in which growth occurs, from birth all the way through life. If this is so, what happens when a person experiences a loss of love? What happens to the adolescent who is dumped by a fickle lover? What happens to a person whose marriage inexplicably turns sour? What happens when one partner begins to show signs of disaffection? Has this ever happened to you? If so, what were the results? If not, have you observed the results in another person? What were they?

_____

_____

_____

_____

If you have ever had anything like the typical experience of losing love, you probably went through a period of depression, with all of its pain. Nothing seemed worthwhile. You looked at the world through ash-colored glasses. The more deeply you were committed to the love relationship, the more devastating the results of losing it. Considerable permanent damage may also have been incurred, especially if you have a tendency toward self-doubt or self-criticism—that is, a negative self-concept. For such a person, the loss of love can be quite devastating. Many people who have this experience become so badly scarred that they are never again able to offer themselves freely to another person. The pain of loss is so severe that they simply cannot take another chance. This is especially true of children who have lost a parent on whom they were very dependent.

Even if a person is not so deeply affected, loss of love is a blow to the ego. After all, there has been a sharing, a disclosure of the innermost thoughts and feelings. Then this sharing and intimacy are rejected. One cannot help wondering about the reasons. Most typically, a loss of love causes depression. However, even if a person does not become depressed, he or she is bound to experience anxiety and tension. How long these feelings last depends, of course, on the nature of the person. Some recover by the next day, while others may brood for months or even years. In Victorian times it was fashionable for the jilted woman to remain in semiseclusion for the rest of her life. Times have changed since then. We no longer ask for such long-term dedication. For most people, time heals all wounds, and the rejected person eventually gets over the hurt. However, this healing may be only superficial. Underneath, a person may be deeply scarred for life.

14. Describe the results of a loss of love.

_____

_____

_____

_____

LOVE AS THERAPY

Much of the misery in the world stems from a lack of love. Some people cannot really love others. Some cannot even love themselves. Some play games with love, using it to manipulate others and thus causing misery and unhappiness. Love could do much to alleviate such misery. Many violent, fearful, discontented, unhappy people have blossomed under the healing influence of love. Love as therapy can be inspiring, enabling, releasing, giving, and positive. Love gives many a person a reason for living.

Love means interacting with a person or with people. To those who are loved, the message is, "I find you to be a worthwhile person." Such a positive message and such interaction make people come out of their shells and move away from a sick form of egocentric thought. The ability to communicate with others is opened up. Love also acts as a positive force in people's other transactions with their world. The positive glow of being loved makes the rest of their world a more livable place. This is especially true for those people who already have some strikes against them. The handicapped need even more reassurance than those who are at least sound of mind and body.

Thus love is a way of making full human beings out of people who are merely existing. Those who are too timid, too shy, or too fearful of rejection can move out into the world, buoyed up by the knowledge that they have someone to help them if they falter. Loving and being loved can be a truly therapeutic force in life.

15. Describe how love can be therapeutic.

□ A POINT OF VIEW

In the following selection, a psychologist who deals with love defines it as he has experienced it and tells what meanings it has had for him. As you will see, the article is a very sensitive and personal account. As you read it, perhaps you will be able to identify and think about some of the various meanings that love has had for you.

Love is not a topic into which the scientific community has rushed pell-mell. There has been a dearth of solid scientific investigation in this area, probably due to the difficulty even of deciding what love is, let alone that of trying to observe and measure it. You might be interested in one person's struggles to arrive at an operational definition of love that could be used to quantify it and deal with it in experimental research. If so, read Zick Rubin's *Liking and Loving*. The other references suggested here are a random sampling of what is available on the topic of love.

Erich Fromm, *The Art of Loving* (New York: Harper, 1956).

John Alan Lee, "Styles of Loving," *Psychology Today* 8 (1974), 43–51.

Rollo May, *Love and Will* (New York: Norton, 1969).

Herbert H. Otto, *Love Today, A New Exploration* (New York: Association Press, 1972).

Zick Rubin, *Liking and Loving* (New York: Holt, Rinehart and Winston, 1973).

SIDNEY M. JOURARD

THE EXPERIENCE AND DISCLOSURE OF LOVE

Ol' mas' loves wine, and Miss loves silk, the piggies they love buttermilk,

From Sidney M. Jourard, *The Transparent Self*, New York, D. Van Nostrand Company, 1971, pp. 49–57. Reprinted by permission.

The kiddies love molasses,
  and the ladies love a ladies' man.
I love to shake a toe with the ladies,
I love to be a beau to the ladies,
Long as ever I know sweet sugar from sand,
I'm bound to be a ladies' man.
                    Folk song, Southeastern U.S.

Love, O love, O careless love. . . . . You see what careless love has done.
                    Folk song, U.S., 19th century

Plaisirs d'amour, ne durent qu'un moment. Chagrins d'amour durent toute la vie.
                    Folk song, French, very old

I sowed the seeds of love, and I sowed them in the springtime.
I gathered them up in the morning too soon, while the songbirds so sweetly sing.
                    Folk song, British, about 16th century

Amor patriae   *Motto*

For the love of God
                    Sometimes a prayer, sometimes not

Eros and *agape. Gemeinschaftsgefühl.* Love as an art. Love as behavior. The beloved as a "reinforcement magazine."* As sex object. As an object of worship and reverence. What does it mean to love? I will discuss love from the perspective of existential phenomenology.** From this vantage point, love is a state of being, it is an experience, it is a commitment and it is a relation.

Who is the lover, and who or what is the beloved? I will focus on love of persons by persons.

---

*When animals are being trained, the trainer often keeps pellets of food in a tube, or magazine. The pellets are released to the hungry animal whenever he behaves as he is supposed to. The food rewards are called "reinforcers."
**Existential phenomenology is the systematic study of a person's way of *experiencing* his world. It is concerned with determining how the world which is common to all is perceived, thought about, remembered, imagined, phantasied, and felt about. I study yours by asking you to disclose yourself to me. For a more systematic introduction to this discipline, see W. Luijpen's book, *Existential Phenomenology.*

What is a person?

To a biologist, a person is a mammalian organism, a system of organs. To a general, a person is cannon fodder, a warm body to carry a rifle, a means to storm a position. To an existential phenomenologist, a person is that which makes a specific view of the world, time, and space come into being. And a person is an origin for action which changes the world for himself and for others, for weal or woe. Further, a person is a situated being who embodies *projects*—plans, inventions, creations—that in time will be disclosed for the world to see. Projects are vows, commitments to transform self and world in some way that first exists as imagination, like a work of art. When consummated, they become *perceptible* to others and to the person who first invented them.

I experience another person in diverse modes. The other person can be likened to a source of disclosure about its being. A tree redundantly discloses its treeness twenty-four hours a day, 365 days a year, to all who would receive these "messages." A person discloses his personality to all who come within his range so long as he lives. To receive these transmissions is another way of saying "perception of the person." I can see, hear, feel, smell, and taste the other, as I can the tree.

But I don't spend all my time perceiving the other. I form a concept of the other, close off my perception, and perceive the disclosures of other beings that exist. Even if I stand before the other, I may not pay attention to his incessant disclosure, because I know enough to contend with him. My questions about him, for the time, are answered.

The other person exists for me perceptually and conceptually. If the other dies, or simply passes from my field of perceptual experience, I can "re-call" him in the recollective mode. And I can imagine him in all possible ways, so that he exists for me in the imaginative mode. I can dream about him. And I can limn him dimly in the phantasy mode, as one who "sucks me dry" or who "fills me." In any or all of these modes for experiencing the other, I can know an affective *quality*—of joy or sorrow, fear or anger, excitement or depression, eroticism or indifference.

The other is my experience of him in diverse modes. But if I touch him, especially if I touch him or if he touches me, he takes on a dimension of reality more real than if I just see or hear him. And he is more real if I smell and taste him. But perhaps he is most real if I touch him. "Touching is believing."

All I experience of the Other is his appearance before my several perceptual systems. But I infer that behind and beyond appearances there is a center, a source that is free. I may try to control and direct his behavior, his appearances, but his center always eludes me. If it does not, he ceases to be a person and becomes a machine or robot.

So to be a person, the other must have a source, a center that he is privy to and I am not.

I can will his freedom, or I can set up the project of trying to destroy this freedom. He will know which of these options is mine by his experience of me. I may be able to conceal or misrepresent my intent for a time, but in more time it will become known to him.

II

I love her. What does this mean? I want her to exist for me and to exist for herself. I want her alive. I want her to be and, moreover, to be in the way that she chooses to be. I want her free. As she discloses her being to me or before my gaze, my existence is enriched. I am more alive. I experience myself in dimensions that she evokes, such that my life is more meaningful and livable.

My beloved is a mystery that I want to make transparent. But the paradox is that I cannot make my beloved do anything. I can only invite and earn the disclosure that makes her transparent. I want to know my beloved. But for me to know, she must show. And for her to show her mysteries to me, she must be assured I will respect them, take delight in them. Whether the mysteries are the feel of her flesh against mine—something I cannot know until it happens—or what she is thinking, imagining, planning or feeling. Why should she disclose herself to me if I am indifferent or if I plan to use her for purposes I conceal from her? She would know me, the one who claims to love her.

If she would know me, then I must wish to be known. I must disclose my being to her, in dialogue, so that we know one another apace.

As soon as she discloses herself to me, I form a concept of her that is instantly out of date, for she has changed. As I reenter dialogue with her, my concept is shattered, and I must form it anew, again and again. If she is free and growing, then she will surprise me, upend my expectancies, "blow" my mind. Hopefully, in ways I like.

If I love her, I love her projects, since she is their source and origin. I may help her if she wants my help; or let her struggle with them unaided if this is meaningful to her. I respect her wishes in the matter.

If I love myself, I love my projects since they are my life. If she loves me, she confirms me in my projects, helps me with them, even if the help consists in leaving me alone. If she tries to control me, she doesn't love me. If I try to control her, I don't love her. I experience her as free and treasure her freedom. I experience myself as free and treasure my freedom.

I am a body. I am embodied. So is she. I like to be embodied, and I like her way of being embodied. If I do not like the way she appears, I tell her, for our love is truth.

I am a sexual being. So is she. Together, we produce an experience that is exquisite for us both. She invites me to know her sexually, and I invite her to know me sexually. We share our erotic possibilities in delight and ecstasy. If she wants me and I don't want her, I cannot lie. My body speaks only truth. And I cannot take her unless she gives herself. Her body cannot lie.

If I see and hear my beloved, I know her more than if I just see her. But if I touch, smell and taste her, I know her still more. But she will not allow me to come that close if she doesn't trust me or want me to know her.

III

I love my friend, and he loves me. He loves a woman, and so do I. He loves his children, I love mine, and I love his. He loves my children, though neither he nor I know the other's so well as we know our own. But I love my friend. I want to know him. We make life richer, more meaningful, more delightful for each other. My life is diminished without my friend being in it. I respect his projects, and he mine. I help him when he wants it, and stand by when he does not. I wish him well in his projects. I know he reciprocates, because he has shown that he does. When he and I talk, there is no semblance between us. He discloses his experience to me in truth—he wants me to know him. And I do likewise. When he wishes to close off conversation, he does so. I respect his privacy. He respects mine. I like the way he "refracts" the world. When he discloses his experience of his world to me, my experience is enriched, because he sees and does things I cannot do directly. Imaginatively, I live more through his experience.

IV

I love my children. They need me. They love in their way, which is not my way. I am essential to their existence, and they know it. I want to help them become less dependent, to be able to cope with problems and challenges without my protection and guidance. And so I watch them and watch over them. I make guesses about how ready they are to be set more free. But I welcome them back when they are hurt or afraid—unless I judge that for them to endure the hurt will help them grow. I want to help, not hinder, the growth of their possibilities. I am often wrong in my judgments, but I mean well. I set them too free too soon sometimes. And I deny them freedom sometimes when they are quite ready to handle it. But I try to get better at my judgments. And they know I intend their freedom and growth.

V

The people I love give meaning to my existence beyond simply filling my gut, feeding my vanity, or giving me pleasure. I treasure them. They help me remain inspirited, turned on to my life. And when they need help, I abandon the projects on which I was then engaged and use my time and resources to help them live more fully, joyously, and meaningfully. They give to me and, just as important, they accept from me. Their acceptance of my giving validates me, enhances my feeling of having worth. I know that I am a worthy being, but I feel more worthy when my existence enhances that of another.

There are billions of people in the world, but I don't love them in the concrete way I love my loved ones. I don't have time. Everybody in the world needs someone to love and to be loved by someone, and I hope it happens. But I am more sensitive to the needs and the disclosures of need uttered by my loved ones. I respond to their cries for help sooner, and in preference to the cries I hear coming from others. This is too bad, but I have to choose. There isn't enough time. I respond to others when I can, with what I can spare from what I have pledged to myself and my more immediate circle of loved ones. If I neglect them in favor of others whom they do not know, I do so because it is meaningful to me. If they love me, and they do—then I expect and receive their patience and confirmation. I have to do what is meaningful to me, and I am entitled to confirmation by my loved ones.

I "tune in" on my loved ones regularly to find out how it is with them. Since last we were in dialogue, a lot has happened to them. My concept of them and their condition is out of date, and I must renew it with fresh disclosures from them, fresh perception. I look, feel and listen.

VI

When I love—myself, family, friends—I see them in a special way. Not as the product of what they have been, of their heredity and schooling, though I notice that. I see them as the embodiment of incredible possibilities. I "see," imaginatively, what they might become if they choose. In fact, in loving them, I may invite them to activate possibilities that they may not have envisioned. I lend them my creative imagination, as it were. If they are weak, I invite them to invent themselves as stronger and to take the steps necessary to actualize their latent strength. If they have been shy or self-concealing, I invite them to try on boldness and self-disclosure for size, to be more creative artists-of-themselves. I too can be the artist-of-myself, if I love myself. And I do. In fact I am the artist of myself to the extent I am aware of my freedom and my responsibility. My situation my "facticity" and my freedom. The givens: my past upbringing and present habits, my body, my place, the people I am involved with, the relationships I now have with them and those they want to have with me. All these "givens" can be viewed as exact analogues of paint, canvas and brushes. They are what make me as I now am. As an artist in paint, I can produce pictures that I first imagine, limited only by my skill, imagination, and the plasticity of the medium. As the artist of myself and my world, I can reinvent myself again and again. That is what I usually do, day by day, but my inventions each day are well-nigh a carbon copy of yesterday's. Perhaps this perpetual "rebirth" of myself today in the same way I was yesterday is what the ancient Hindus meant by their concept of *samsara*, the Buddhists with their notion of the "wheel of rebirth," and, more generally, the ages old doctrine of reincarnation.

I can invent a new me in a new world, and strive to bring these into being. If my loved ones love me, they will help me fulfill this new possibility or tell me truly that they don't like it. In fact, they can serve as artistic consultants to help me bring the image into fruition.

I can serve in the same capacities for my loved ones. Inventing and reinventing ourselves, playing with our possibilities, and picking those that please.

VII

My relationship with those whom I love becomes stale and predictable. When it comes to pass that I have no more pleasant surprises and the predictability begins to bore and strangle me, I begin to reflect. What is happening? If the other is my peer, I let him or her know. She reveals that I am neglecting her, spending too much time at work or at play with others. I reveal that our ways of sharing time, satisfying up to last year or last week, are now boring. But she still likes these games. And I like my new ways of spending time, apart from her. We are at an impasse. What will we do? If she does not wish to come along with me, or if I do not want her along, one of us is going to be hurt, and the other guilty. If we love, we have to disclose this. We may have to start to reinvent our relationship. We may, for a time, spend less time with each other, more time with others, feeling somewhat sad and nostalgic for former good times that have passed and are no more.

We may have to reexamine our projects, to see which have lost meaning—our joint projects, and our singular projects. It may happen that, if we cannot invent or discover joint projects that infuse our life together with zest and meaning, we have to go separate ways. This becomes poignant if we are married, because we may decide—one, the other, or both—to become divorced. Or we may discover some new way to be married that looks like a "marriage of convenience"—no passion, not much delight, but some affection, trust and goodwill. She might take a lover; I might take a mistress. That might be hurtful to all concerned, or perhaps not. If we have loved each other, and still do, the most loving thing to do might be to part, to dissolve the legal connection, and live separate lives with the hope of finding someone new to love. It happens.

There is no end to this chapter, or to loving. Unless, afraid of possible hurt, we decide, not to love, but to control and use.

UNIT 11

SEX:
THE UNIVERSAL
STRESSOR

☐ If Venusians or Arcturians were to visit the United States, they would probably come to the conclusion that our principal preoccupation is sex. No matter what media you look at, wherever you turn, this interest is apparent— in fashion, entertainment, literature. Pornography is rampant, and in our society there is wild confusion about how to define it and great indecision about how to control it. In this unit, you will explore some of the reasons for this preoccupation, and you will analyze some of the current trends in sexuality in our culture.

When you have completed this unit, you should be able to:

1. *Explain how sex ranks as a basic motivating force in humans.*
2. *Give a short history of Victorian attitudes toward sex.*
3. *Describe Haim Ginott's stages of sexual development.*
4. *Explain how the social and environmental climates affect sexual activity.*
5. *Describe the changing emphasis on sex.*
6. *Describe some apparent trends in sexual behavior in this country.*
7. *Describe studies of two cultures in which social attitudes toward sex are diametrically opposed, and then derive some conclusions from these studies.*
8. *Explain the impact of contraception and world overpopulation on sexual practices.*
9. *Name six different current attitudes toward premarital sex in America.*
10. *Name some factors that affect adult sexual happiness.*
11. *Suggest some probable effects of the recent surge of books emphasizing sexual techniques.*
12. *Discuss the effects of the absence of norms on sexual behavior.*
13. *Identify major types of sexual maladjustment.*
14. *Describe the types of male and female sexual dysfunction.*
15. *Evaluate your own sexual adjustment.*

SEX AS A MOTIVATOR

In Unit 2 on motivation, you learned that sex is one of the strongest drives activating animals. It is a basic urge, yet a peculiar one. Often it seems to be terminal activity, for in many species death follows closely after mating. For these creatures, the act of reproduction ends the life cycle. In other species, particularly of mammals, the sex act is not so final. Most mammals undergo a number of reproductive cycles. It seems that nature has made a tradeoff in this respect. One-time breeders usually have thousands of offspring at once; species that are able to reproduce several times during their lives have fewer young at any one time.

At any rate, performance of the sex act apparently is an innate urge closely coupled with procreation and essential to the continued existence of the species. Demonstration after demonstration has shown that at specific times the sex urge transcends all others. Animals will stop eating and will even ignore danger while under the influence of the urge to mate. It seems that the more specific and limited the mating cycle is, the more urgent is the drive. Most animals, particularly females, show a pronounced reproductive cycle. Many are fertile and sexually active only during this period.

Not so the human. After adulthood is reached, the sexual urge is not restricted to a specific period of time. Both male and female are able to engage in the sexual act at will. It seems that the urge, not under periodic physiological control, is something like a conditioned process. Therein lies the whole story. Basic drives are essential to the survival of the organism. If we fail to satisfy them, we will die. If we stop breathing for a very short time, we will die. If we drink no liquids, death will come slowly, but it will come. If we don't eat, we will starve to death. Each of our basic urges is vital to our personal survival. If we tamper with them drastically, we do ourselves in. Except for some relatively inconsequential manipulations, we have not been able to change how we satisfy our basic needs. How many restrictions or customs are there that affect our breathing? Not many. We do have quite a few taboos and petty restrictions on eating and drinking, but we still eat and drink.

Now look at sex. It is the one basic urge that is not essential to life. People can engage in sexual acts or abstain without physical danger to themselves. In other words, you can thwart and manipulate the sexual urge without dying. Look at what we have done to ourselves. No other basic urge is so restricted by do's and don'ts. Every culture has imposed conditions on it. In many cases, the results have been catastrophic for individuals and for the culture. Recall Freud's insistence that sex is the primary urge in humans. He not only recognized it as basic, but also saw it as most important. Every mental aberration, according to Freud, is in some way the result of tampering with the sexual drive. He felt that the desire to continue the species is strong within us. When we tamper with it, we are playing with psychic dynamite.

1. *Explain how sex ranks as a basic motivating force in humans.*

_____

_____

_____

_____

VICTORIANS AND SEX

Freud's views need to be placed in historical perspective so that you can understand why he took his stand. Freud lived in the heart of the Victorian era, a cultural period that adopted some strange attitudes toward sex—attitudes that still affect society.

To Victorians, sex was dirty. It was never to be mentioned in public. A man would never discuss sex with a woman, and discussions of sex between men were not supposed to take place, though of course they did. The era was one of suppression, particularly for the female. Usually, she was completely innocent and, to a great extent, remained so throughout her whole life. Usually she was told about intercourse on the eve of her marriage; many times it was explained to her by her husband. A woman was supposed to be chaste until she married, and, if she never married, she was expected to carry her virginity to her grave.

For women, the era was fantastically repressive. Romanticism replaced the sexual urge. Love at first sight was the order of the day. A man and woman met; a blinding flash of empathy passed between them; they were in love. Such love was the answer to everything. It created a mystical, joyous relationship that made two people oblivious to the world around them. Mundane problems such as eating, sleeping, and going to the bathroom never pricked the bubble of a couple in love. Ideally, the euphoria lasted a lifetime.

Sex education for the young was virtually nonexistent, although children were taught that sex was bad. If children manipulated their genitalia for pleasure and were caught, they were quickly taught that masturbation was dreadful. Children were supposed to be innocent and unaware of sex. Teachers could be dismissed if they married. It was feared that the sexual experiences of male teachers might somehow influence the children.

However, during this period a strong double standard existed. Females were supposed to remain completely innocent. Any girl who had premarital intercourse was a fallen woman. A widow was suspect because of her sexual experience. A divorcée was considered a woman of the lowest morality, unacceptable to proper social groups. Males, on the other hand, were given much more latitude. The male also was supposed to remain chaste until marriage. However, the Victorians recognized that a man needed to "sow his wild oats" and allowed him to do so. Thus male premarital sex, although publicly frowned upon, was recognized and permitted.

The Victorian era was one of sexual repression. Sexual activity was supposed to take place in the marriage bed or not at all. You can imagine the problems that resulted from this repression. Two people who had been taught all their lives that sex was dirty suddenly at marriage were expected to perform that act as part of a relationship that had been previously described only in the most high-flying romantic phrases. Overnight they were supposed to adjust their entire education to encompass their new status. Is it any wonder that Freud saw sex as the basic problem in life? He was looking at the behavior of hundreds of patients who were the victims of the Victorian era.

Remember also that Victorian principles were prevalent until just recently. Even forty years ago, female teachers could be dismissed if they married. People born in the 1920s, 1930s, and 1940s are still influenced by Victorian morality.

2. Give a short history of Victorian attitudes toward sex.

1873

Edwin (to his Angelina): 'With you by my Side, my very Own, with *You*, I could wander among these *heavenly* Hills and Dales for *ever!*'

Angelina (to her Edwin): 'And so could *I* with *you*, my *veriest* own! for *ever*, and *ever*, and EVER!!!'

Angelina's Sister (to herself): 'O dear me! what a Trotting up and down it all is, to be Sure!'

_____

_____

_____

GINOTT'S STAGES OF SEXUAL DEVELOPMENT

By now, you should be familiar with Freud's stages of development, because you have been exposed to them fairly intensively. Their remarkable accuracy shows that Freud was a shrewd observer of life. However, many people are unwilling to develop the whole person around sexual stages. Other investigators have identified sexual stages of development but have separated them from the social development of the individual. Dr. Haim Ginott was one of these. He identified four stages in sexual growth: the infantile stage, the parent-identification stage, latency, and the adolescent stage. Note how closely they follow Freud's stages.

The infantile stage starts at birth and lasts until children are three years of age. It thus is comparable to Freud's oral and anal stages. Children in this stage get extreme pleasure out of oral stimulation. Everything goes into their mouths. Toward the end of this period, children shift their interest from oral to anal gratification. Usually, this occurs when children have imposed upon them their parents' standards of cleanliness. During this period, children actively explore their bodies to find out what they are and what they do. They enjoy stimulation of any kind—tickling, cuddling, petting. As part of their natural bodily exploration, children invariably explore their genitalia. The degree and kind of emotion with which parents greet this exploration and the approach they have toward toilet training can heavily influence their children's later approaches toward sex. If children are taught that manipulation of the sex organs is dirty, nasty, and brings punishment, later they may be inhibited in their attempts to learn normal sexual activity.

The parent-identification stage is usually evident at about four years of age. During it, children will masturbate rather than simply explore, because they have discovered that pleasure is associated with manipulating the genitals. At this time children become aware of the differences between the sexes. Also at this time different sex roles are identified and learned. Children usually pattern their behavior after that of the parent of the same sex.

In the latency stage, from the age of five to adolescence, sexual activity is negligible. As children begin to move out from the family and come under the influence of their peers, they begin to learn social values that may differ from those of their parents. In this stage children usually avoid the opposite sex. Instead, they emphasize learning behavior appropriate to their sex.

Then comes the bomb. In the adolescent stage, children's bodies suddenly start to play tricks on them. Their hormones change their chemistry, and their bodies change as they approach sexual maturity. They are subject to flashes of uncontrollable sexual excitation, sometimes for no apparent reason. Nature has played a cruel trick on human beings. Adolescence is the time during which they have the greatest sexual desire and are sexually most active. Yet human societies almost universally prohibit sexual activity at this stage. The taboo is more social than physical and acknowledges the fact that even though adolescents are physically capable of adult sexual activity and parenthood, they are socially too immature to carry out the corresponding responsibilities. Parenthood is the natural product of sexual activity except in cases of physical impairment or deliberate intervention by the participating couple.

The prohibition against sexual activity at this time results in tremendous conflicts. Masturbation is one tension-relieving technique. In the Victorian era, it was especially prohibited, and there were all sorts of dire warnings against it. It was said that people who masturbated went crazy. Such repression obviously did and still does have severe traumatic effects. Parents need to be careful about how they deal with masturbation. Probably the best approach is to recognize it for what it is—a natural tension-reducing device that replaces the forbidden sexual act.

Ginott went no further. However, it is possible to identify two more stages, one that is semisocial and one that is proving to be fictional. The semisocial stage is what might be called the adult period. In it, people settle down to regular sexual activity. Their relationships are planned and orderly. Frequency of intercourse is usually consonant with each individual's physiology. In the stable adult pattern, intercourse occurs with one steady partner, and this regular, routine type of sexual activity brings about deep pleasure and emotional satisfaction.

Old age is another stage. As many would have it, sexual activity slowly diminishes when people reach their forties and fifties and usually stops altogether when they are in their sixties. This is supposed to be the penalty of old age. However, as more and more data are compiled, it is becoming evident that sexual activity is not necessarily tied to age. Many couples have kept up satisfactory sexual activity when in their eighties. Therefore, doctors are now beginning to advise their patients that if they remain in good health they can maintain their sexual potency in their old age.

3. Describe Haim Ginott's stages of sexual development.

_____

_____

_____

_____

SOCIAL AND EMOTIONAL AFFECTS ON SEX

Whether or not you believe Freud, you must still acknowledge the influence of sex on the life of the individual, especially if you examine therapeutic diagnosis and rehabilitation. It seems that almost any change in a person's social environment will affect his or her sex life. That physiological changes brought about by accident or disease will do the same thing is so obvious that it needs no further comment. If you're feeling bad, your sex life is usually the first thing to go. But how does the social environment affect sex? The sexual urge is easily blocked by emotional overtones. Both men and women can become completely inhibited sexually by emotional discord. For some reason, emotional disturbances, especially those caused by negative emotions, may stop the enjoyment of the sexual act and block sexual excitation. Feelings of guilt, shame, fear, and anger may be inhibitors. In a stable adult relationship, the partners usually become extremely sensitive to each other's moods. Experience has taught them that lack of enjoyment by one partner may keep enjoyment from the other partner.

However, the emotional game works both ways. Myriad emotional disorders promote the use of sexual activity as a sort of defensive technique. Most so-called sexual aberrations are caused by emotional disturbances. Satyriasis, nymphomania, sadism, masochism, and others seem to represent an individual's unique sexual response to conflict. On the whole, however, deviant sexual behaviors seem to occur in people who are deeply maladjusted.

To summarize, sexual activity is vulnerable to being overridden by any of the emotions. It is extremely responsive to stress or anxiety.

4. *Explain how the social and environmental climates affect sexual activity.*

_____

_____

_____

_____

CHANGING EMPHASIS ON SEX

The Victorians cast a veil of secrecy around sex. In science and in literature it was mentioned indirectly and in the most romantic terms. Anything explicit was usually branded as pornography and banished from the library shelves and from proper bookstores. Because no one dared to talk about sex, most people assumed that there were no sexual problems—that children did not masturbate, that premarital intercourse rarely occurred, and that all was as it should be. Is it surprising that there was an abysmal ignorance of sex?

In 1948, a book was published that immediately became the center of a countrywide storm and shattered much of the remaining Victorian complacency about sex. The book, written by Alfred Kinsey and others, was *Sexual Behavior in the Human Male*. Five years later it was followed by *Sexual Behavior in the Human Female*. These two books did much to strip the veil from the subject of sex. Both were researched and written according to conventional scientific standards. This fact moved them out of the field of fiction and pornography.

It is hard to condemn or ignore something that has a scientific backing. Many researchers could and did quarrel with Kinsey's method of acquiring data—the interview. But the opponents were at a disadvantage. They had no data to fire back. Even today, researchers grumble about Kinsey's data, but they find it hard to refute his findings, which shot the air out of the Victorian balloon:

1. By the time of marriage, 41 percent of the females and 94 percent of the males had masturbated to orgasm.
2. Eighty-five percent of the males and 50 percent of the females had engaged in premarital intercourse.

3. Sexual excitement was the greatest at sixteen or seventeen years of age.
4. Men were much more preoccupied with sex than women were. Men were most susceptible to external stimuli, such as pictures of nude women, whereas women were most easily aroused by emotional interaction.

Although the findings were shocking, the impact of the book itself was most important. Authors had presented concrete sexual data for the first time in several generations. For the first time, men and women could see how their behavior compared to that of others in their society. Kinsey's pioneering work has led to a cautious and ever so slow further exploration of sex. Today the topic has become almost acceptable. There are several generations, however, that still struggle under the Victorian yoke. For them discussion of sex is painfully difficult. As a result, they are unable to be as forthright as the current generation. At this time, our society seems to be going through a transition stage. Freed from the numbing Victorian prohibitions, the topic of sex is getting an airing. In the last decade, hundreds of authors have rushed to fill in the blanks in our knowledge. Their efforts range from explicit how-to-do-it manuals to broad philosophical discussions of the meaning of love. The current preoccupation might make us feel that Freud was right and that sex truly is our greatest driving force. However, there is some evidence to show that interest in the subject may have reached its peak. At any rate, we have passed from one era to another—from one in which sex was dirty and the air was clean, to one where sex is clean and the air dirty. Not without some controversy, we are even beginning to teach about sex in the school systems.

5. Describe the changing emphasis on sex.

TRENDS IN SEXUAL BEHAVIORS

At the present, some strange sexual cross-currents exist in our culture. One of these concerns pornography. Pornography has been defined as anything that appeals to purient interests and is without any artistic merit. But how should we define these terms? What appeals to your prurient interest? The sight or picture of a nude person of the opposite sex? The sight or picture of a couple engaged in intercourse? A series of symbols representing intercourse? All these might appeal to your prurient interest. They might or might not affect someone else. Individualism again interferes with a nice, orderly concept. Objects, pictures, and acts that may be offensive to some are inoffensive to others. This makes wholesale regulation of pornography difficult, if not impossible. Defining a film, picture, or book as dirty and without artistic merit is even tougher than deciding whether it is unduly sexually stimulating. Some people might consider various statues of Venus artistic, whereas others would regard them as sexually suggestive and not artistic.

As the United States Supreme Court has recently indicated, there are some sticky problems in deciding what is pornography and what is art. A major limiting factor is the need to preserve the rights to free speech and artistic expression. When this text was being written, X-rated movies abounded in large cities, and "adult" bookstores could be found everywhere. This caused many people a great deal of concern. They saw blatant pornography as a symptom of the downfall of our society. They said that we are becoming increasingly depraved and immoral, that our moral disintegration will hasten the end of our society. And yet . . .

In some cities where pornographic movies sprang up like mushrooms and the prices of admission were fantastically high, there now seems to be a decrease in patronage. Many adult film houses have gone out of business, and others are having financial troubles. The same is occurring in the adult book market. After a brisk rush, the impetus seems to be slowing. Many stores are going out of business as quickly as they came into existence.

Denmark was one of the first nations to give up any effort to regulate pornography. The Danes permitted the open display and sale of pornographic material long before any other society was willing to do so. For a long while, Copenhagen was the Mecca of smut seekers. People flocked to Copenhagen from all over Europe and from America. But again satiation seems to have occurred. A roaring business had degenerated to a trickle, which for many entrepreneurs is no longer worth the effort.

What happened? One clue is found in research recently carried out under government auspices. In this investigation, male college students were systematically exposed to hard-core pornography under controlled conditions so that the level of their emotional excitation could be measured. Researchers found that what was initially exciting soon became boring and could even create aversion. The study seems to contradict a current theory: that constant exposure to pornography turns individuals into sex fiends.

Studies also show that most of the purchasers of pornographic material are middle-aged and old men. If we remember that Kinsey found the male to be more susceptible to pornography than the female is, we will not think portions of these findings unusual. What does seem strange, however, is that practically no young men of this generation seem to be at all interested. Could it be that current sexual frankness—being exposed to sex and knowing about sexual practices and particulars—is having an unpredicted effect? Traditionalists feel that the young will be corrupted if they are exposed to sexual material. Yet it would appear that older men, trying to catch up on something that was denied them, are the ones being corrupted.

It appears that sexual activity is increasing markedly and has become quite common among the young. There are many more teen-age pregnancies, and even preteen pregnancies are becoming common. The incidence of venereal diseases is increasing among the young, from preteens on. Cohabitation without marriage is no longer a rare phenomenon among young adults. Thus sexual activity seems no longer to be a forbidden act to the younger portion of the population. This group does not seem to regard sex with the same set of attitudes as did their parents.

6. Describe some apparent trends in sexual behavior in this country.

CULTURAL AFFECTS ON SEXUAL BEHAVIOR

In the March 1971 issue of *Psychology Today*, two articles reported on sociological studies of two very different cultures. One was called "The Lack of the Irish"; the other was called "Too Much of a Good Thing." The first dealt with a community living on a small island off the mainland of Ireland. A married couple investigating aspects of life on this isolated island found sexual customs similar to those of the Victorian era. Sex was mentioned only by husbands and wives. Indeed, some couples had never seen each other undressed. Sexual acts were carried out in the dark. As a result of this way of life, aggression and hostility were quite obvious, and sexual deviation seemed widespread, although it was difficult to confirm this fact because of the nature of the community and the taboo on sexual discussion.

The other article reported on a study of the social life of a Polynesian colony on the island of Mangaia, one of the lesser-known islands of the Samoan chain. There the sexual emphasis is completely different. Sex is not only permitted, it is encouraged. Adolescent girls are encouraged to have male suitors visit them at night in the family home while the family feigns sleep. Sexual emphasis is on creating pleasure for the partner, and both sexes practice this philosophy assiduously. Generally, couples remain faithful to each other, adhering to the form of marriage that the Samoans recognize. There is no stigma to being an unwed mother. The frequency of sexual activity is intense, and no inhibitions on time or place exist. In other words, sex is as freely satisfied among the Mangaians as any of the other basic drives.

The product of this situation is satiation and, in fact, almost an aversion. In middle age the male often becomes impotent and has to give up sexual activity for a period of time—six months to a year—before he can engage in it again. It is interesting to note that the researchers couldn't find any evidence of sexual deviation.

Some males seemed to prefer doing womanly tasks, but they seemed to be sexually normal. Apparently, a completely open sexual education from childhood on seemed to prevent deviation. The community was also found to be remarkably free of social tensions, aggression, and hostility.

7. *Describe studies of two cultures in which social attitudes toward sex are diametrically opposed, and then derive some conclusions from these studies.*

CONTRACEPTION AND SEXUAL BEHAVIOR

Two events have had a strong impact on our sexual customs. One is the realization that the world may become overpopulated. This realization is based on a very simple matter of mathematics. If two people produce four offspring, and each of these produces four offspring, and so on . . . You can see the problem. Left unchecked, the human race could actually breed itself out of standing room. It has suddenly become obvious that something has to be done, and the experts who talk about zero population growth (ZPG) or negative growth in families have begun to take on the stature of biblical prophets. (A ZPG family has two children and thus does not increase the world's popualtion. A negative-growth family has fewer than two children and, because the parents theoretically are not replaced by the children, decreases the world population.)

Now, all of a sudden, big families are unfashionable. In the days of farming's predominance, there used to be a reason for big families, particularly if they included many male children. The boys could help work the farm. Sons could support their parents in their old age, sharing ownership of the farm. Or if the oldest son took the farm, he took over the responsibility of caring for his parents as well. Younger sons often left the farm and struck out on their own.

As our technical ability has increased, the need for farm workers has decreased, and this pattern of family economics has died out. The need for a large family as insurance for the parents has disappeared in this country.

Another factor that has entered the population scene is the appearance of a successful method of birth control. Formerly, a healthy couple who had made a good sexual adjustment and were mutually interested in sexual activity had to face the consequences of that activity: large families. Because there was no reliable way to prevent conception, the alternative was abstinence. The birth-control pill has changed the situation. Now couples may engage in sexual activity without the fear of an unwanted pregnancy. So far, the contraceptive technique has involved tampering with the blood chemistry of the female by changing her hormone balance. Such alterations may be dangerous and tricky for women prone to certain diseases or women who suffer from severe side effects. There are, of course, other contraceptive devices, such as the intrauterine loop, the diaphragm, and foams and douches, but these are by no means completely effective or are inconvenient to use. The loop, for example, may slip or may cause ulceration and bleeding; the diaphragm requires conscious planning of the sexual act and may deaden the sensitivity of some women; foams and douches have the highest risk of pregnancy. The dangers of unwanted pregnancies from use of those devices cause many women to avoid them.

The other alternative for a female is sterilization by surgery to prevent the ovum from entering the uterus to be fertilized. This requires a fairly serious, dangerous, and irreversible operation. These problems, plus the expense, make sterilization an undesirable alternative for many women.

For males, the condom or sheath is the only practical technique that is readily available, except for coitus interruptus—the withdrawal of the penis just before ejaculation. The condom does not allow the ejaculate to enter the female's body. However, both techniques diminish sensation and thus enjoyment. Therefore they are rejected by many males.

Efforts to sterilize the male by vasectomy have been less well received than feminine contraceptive devices. Formerly, vasectomy was irreversible; when a male was sterilized, he remained sterile for life. However, recent experimentation indicates that it is possible to perform the operation in such a way that it can be reversed. If this technique becomes practical, the sterilization of the male by surgery may become the accepted contraceptive method of the future, because it is not particularly dangerous and has few physiological side effects. It can, however, occasionally create some psychological problems in men. Some men begin to doubt their virility and masculinity, which they feel have been diminished by the operation. Thus vasectomy is not a recommended alternative for all males.

At any rate, these two factors have strongly influenced our sexual customs. Knowledge of the threat of overpopulation encourages couples to control the number of children, and this desire leads them directly to a contraceptive technique of some kind. Our present ability to control fertility allows us to accomplish two goals that used to be contradictory: to have normal and frequent sexual relations and to have small families.

8. *Explain the impact of contraception and world overpopulation on sexual practices.*

_____

_____

_____

_____

CURRENT ATTITUDES TOWARD SEX

The adolescent is really caught in a crunch today. On the one hand, the body is demanding sexual activity; on the other, society is saying, "Thou shalt not, until you marry." The economic overtones of marriage are scary, and, indeed, early adolescent marriages are frowned upon. What is the adolescent to do?

The pure Victorian would say that sex is an urge that is beneath human dignity and should be ignored. Neither males nor females should ever have sexual relations until they are married. This is the doctrine of total abstinence.

The realistic Victorian would say: I know that you have some urges. The female, being pure, chaste, and innocent, is much more able to control her base impulses. Therefore, she may not indulge in premarital sex. However, the male, being made of coarser material, may not be able to withstand his urges. He may give in and have some premarital sexual experience. Although doing this won't make him a better person, it won't matter if he's discreet and doesn't tell the world about it. This attitude represents a double standard: one for the male and one for the female.

More liberal people in our society today would say that this view of women is nonsense. The female is no purer than the male. She, too, has healthy sexual urges that need satisfaction. However, she still needs to control herself. She can practice premarital sex with the man she loves and intends to marry. If she does any more than that, we'll call her a promiscuous, immoral woman. Naturally, the man is free to do whatever he likes before he gets married. Afterward, of course, both males and females are expected to restrict their sexual activity to that carried on with their spouses. As you can see, this view represents a transition from the orthodox double standard. However, a slightly more liberal attitude toward the male still exists.

An even more liberal group says that tying sexual activity to marriage is nonsense. The fact that a few words have been ritually mumbled has nothing to do with sexual intercourse. If two people love each other, let them engage in intercourse and forget about the marital restriction. In other words, sex is permissible if there is an emotional bond between the two partners.

The most liberal group removes any restrictions on sex. Its platform is that the sexual act is a physiological one, and that normal, healthy people need to be able to do it when they feel the urge. Our society has jazzed sex up with all sorts of romanticism and mysticism. If we tear away the trappings and recognize the act as a natural one occurring between a male and a female, we'll all be better off.

Another recurring question that is related to sexual activity is that of homosexuality. There is currently a great deal of unrest among homosexuals in this country. They are becoming more overt and aggressive in their search for social equality. Of course, there are many shades of opinion on sexual deviance, but a move toward greater tolerance can be detected. For example, the American Psychiatric Association has been seriously considering the elimination of sexual deviance in general, and homosexuality in particular, from the category of abnormal behavior. They would, in contrast, categorize as abnormal persons who are psychologically disturbed by their deviance. This redefinition, in effect, would assert that homosexuality is no longer to be considered abnormal behavior.

Thus, at least six different attitudes about sex exist in our society. There is some evidence that sex with love is becoming a more popular attitude. In any case, permissiveness is increasing and the double standard is being relaxed.

9. Name six different current attitudes toward premarital sex in America.

_____

_____

_____

_____

FACTORS OF SEXUAL HAPPINESS

It was pointed out earlier that physical and emotional well-being is necessary for good sexual adjustment. Ancel Keys showed that hunger could easily displace the sexual drive. Emotions can do the same thing.

Sex is most pleasurable when both partners experience pleasure. This, of course, is a truism only for sexually experienced adults. In sexual encounters between inexperienced partners, the instigator usually is interested only in discharging his or her own tensions and is not likely to consider the partner's feelings. In recognition of this empathetic pleasure, the Mangaians stress mutual satisfaction.

Emotional interaction is a strong factor in good sexual adjustment. Most women need a sense of emotional involvement. They seem to have a sense of receiving something, whereas the male is less emotionally bound. A strong emotional tie does seem to lead to increased sexual enjoyment for both persons. A sense of intimacy and the acceptance of the other person as a partner leads to a much greater enjoyment of the sexual act and deepens its significance.

To some of you, the wording of this discussion may seem cold and impersonal. Many people insist that love is an important part of the sexual act. This is true. Love can and does give sex a different emotional content. It intensifies the significance of sex, deepens the relationship between the partners, and makes the act a shared experience. Yet sex can be enjoyed by people who are not in love. It can be enjoyed even by persons who have established no intimacy or emotional involvement. However, the depth of sexual enjoyment that results and the kind of experience that occurs change drastically as the degree of emotional interaction changes. The deeper the interaction is, the deeper and more significant will be the enjoyment of the sexual act.

Of course, one major factor that affects adult sex and happiness is the recognition that sexual activity between men and women is completely normal and is a healthy manifestation. There is nothing shameful or depraved in participating in whatever sexual acts are appropriate to the social structures a person happens to accept.

In the past, many women's fear of consequences—pregnancy—was enough to decrease their enjoyment of intercourse. To some extent this fear has been alleviated by the new techniques of contraception. However, some moral and religious whiplash may occur among couples who have been taught that artificial contraception is a mortal sin. Strong conflicts can exist in these families and, if not resolved, may interfere with sexual adjustment.

10. Name some factors that affect adult sexual happiness.

_____

_____

_____

_____

SEX MANUALS

A recent phenomenon, closely associated with pornography and yet quite different from it, is the marked increase in sex-instruction books. *Everything You Always Wanted to Know About Sex but Were Afraid to Ask* is a typical title. Although many of these books could be labeled pornographic, others represent an author's serious efforts to explain how to perform the sexual act in a variety of ways. Obviously, there is more than one way to achieve coitus and an even greater number of ways to achieve orgasm. When sex was a forbidden topic of conversation, techniques were pretty much learned by self-discovery and self-experimentation. The degree to which a couple would and could experiment sexually depended on how inhibited they were.

Today, books offer suggestions on how to vary sex routines and promote great enjoyment. These books use the technique of reinforcement effectively. When a couple sees a procedure diagrammed in a technical manual, they will lose some of their fear of being deviates and will be less ashamed of their own acts. They will be more open to experimentation and to the idea of increased variations. However, there is a danger. An emphasis on technique may lead to an emphasis on performance. Instead of striving for mutual satisfaction, a couple may be misled into judging sexual performance by the number of variations built into the act. The male, for example, may be misled into equating virility with frequency. Performance becomes his guideline—not how well, but how often, with how many, in how many different ways.

The use of a standard based on performance can lead to a distortion of the sexual act.

Sex manuals have moved us another step toward complete and utter sexual frankness. They serve a useful purpose if they can prevent the negative experiences that can occur when two inept people know what they want to do but don't know how to go about doing it. From this standpoint and with this emphasis, these books can be valuable—if they don't distort the sexual act by emphasizing the wrong things.

11. *Suggest some probable effects of the recent surge of books emphasizing sexual techniques.*

_____

_____

_____

_____

NORMS FOR SEXUAL BEHAVIOR

When the Kinsey reports were published, a shock wave went out through the nation. For the first time, facts and figures, however suspect they might be, were published. There was a way by which people could compare themselves to the rest of society. Even now, you would probably learn a great deal about yourself by getting the reports out of the library and comparing yourself to the group that Kinsey described. The books are over twenty years old, yet their data have held reasonably firm.

When you can compare yourself against some standard, you have a chance to find out some things that we all want to know. Am I normal? Where do I differ from the group? How do I differ? Is my difference good or bad? In other words, the standard serves as a guide. We can judge our own behavior against it. This ability to compare has long been denied to people in our society, especially in the area of sexual behavior. There has been no solid bank of data on which judgments of normality and abnormality can be based. There is still a woeful lack of information.

This is why the how-to books can be dangerous. Because they emphasize variations in the sex act, they may create the impression that variations are normal and extensively practiced. Granted, intercourse is a private act between two persons who should not be swayed by what other people do or say they do. However, so much emotion and doubt have been focused on the act that couples need support and reassurance. Perhaps as later generations work their way through the complex act of love, such guidance and support will not be needed. It could and probably does provide comfort to couples in this time of ignorance. If data existed on what ordinary couples normally do in their sex life, perhaps distortions and deviations would be considerably reduced rather than emphasized.

12. Discuss the effects of the absence of norms on sexual behavior.

_____

_____

_____

_____

SEXUAL MALADJUSTMENT

There are many types of sexual deviation, some occurring fairly frequently and some rarely. Homosexuality in males and females are two deviations that have always stirred violent emotions in society. However, as was mentioned earlier, attitudes seem to be softening toward this form of behavior. There is considerable pressure to remove legal restraints on homosexuality and to allow homosexual acts between consenting adults. It may be that legal prosecution of homosexuals will change drastically; yet today, the homosexual is still looked down on as a deviate and a person of low moral character. Society as a whole has banded against homosexuals morally as well as legally.

No one is sure why homosexuality begins. In Freudian terms, it results from the unsatisfactory resolution of the Oedipus/Electra complex. A person, for some reason, doesn't learn the sexual behavior appropriate to his or her sex. A rejection of the opposite sex takes place, and sexually deviant behavior results. Not all homosexuals are completely incapable of having or unwilling to have sexual relations with the opposite sex. Some practicing homosexuals are married and have children. However, they do not prefer heterosexual relations, even though they are capable of having them. A "cure" for homosexuality has been elusive. Therapy has been largely ineffective except in cases where the individual is desperately unhappy and wants to change. Interestingly, it has been recommended that only in the latter case should homosexuality be considered a psychological problem. One note, on terminology: *Homosexuality* refers to either males or females who engage in sexual activity with members of the same sex. *Lesbianism* refers only to female homosexuals. An overall adjective commonly used to describe homosexuals of both sexes is *gay*.

Two other forms of sexual deviation are connected with aggression and hostility: sadism and masochism. A sadistic person gets sexual pleasure from inflicting physical pain on someone. This deviation seems to arise from extreme immaturity. Masochists turn their intense feelings of aggression and hostility inward and derive sexual satisfaction from pain someone inflicts on them. Sexual immaturity is also a root cause of this deviance.

Ten years ago, such a public stance would have been impossible. (Charles Gatewood)

In still another kind of deviation, people lose control over their sexual urge and constantly demand sexual relationships. In some cases, they may also demand many sexual partners. In males, this condition is known as satyriasis; in women, nymphomania. Those who explore this form of deviance emphasize that it is a kind of neurotic behavior in which sexual activity is used to cover a basic conflict and its resulting anxiety. As with most neuroses, successful therapy is possible but not inevitable. The longer the neurosis exists, the more difficult it may be to alleviate.

There are many other forms of sexual disorder. Over two hundred categories have been listed. However, most of these categories are quite rare. Those most frequently encountered are voyeurism, (peeping toms); exhibitionism, or exposure of the genitalia (flashing); pedophilia, or sex with young children; fetishism, or use of an object to obtain sexual gratification; and bestiality, or intercourse with animals.

13. Identify major types of sexual maladjustment.

_____

_____

_____

_____

SEXUAL DYSFUNCTIONS

Deep-seated psychosexual problems may manifest themselves in sexual behavior that is merely different from "normal"—that is, sexual maladjustment. The same psychosexual problems can also manifest themselves in an inability to carry out the sexual act—that is, sexual dysfunction. The word *psychosexual* is used here to emphasize that sexual dysfunctions are rarely the result of organic causes, at least in chronic cases. Every person will, if tired or ill, suffer a loss of sexual drive, but it is really not fair to call this type of loss a sexual dysfunction. The term *dysfunction* indicates a permanent or chronic problem.

Males and females differ in the types of sexual dysfunction from which they suffer. Males may display erectile dysfunction, premature ejaculation, or retarded ejaculation. Females may be affected by anorgasmia (frigidity) or vaginismus.

The inability of males to achieve an erection is, of course, a deterrent to sexual intercourse. Surprisingly, males can achieve orgasm in some cases even when the penis is flaccid. Erectile dysfunction is usually brought on by anxiety about sexual performance or by some other form of stress that overrides the sexual drive.

By far the most common complaint among males is premature ejaculation; that is, the male ejaculates before or just after penetration, thus leaving the female unsatisfied. It is difficult to define the term *premature* precisely. Should ejaculation take place after thirty seconds? Sixty seconds? To avoid this problem of definition, we might say that ejaculation is premature if the female partner does not reach orgasm before ejaculation at least 50 percent of the time. However, this definition assumes that the female is functioning normally and is herself capable of orgasm in each instance. Possibly a better definition is that ejaculation is premature if the male cannot control when it happens. At any rate, this condition seems to be caused by improper learning, as in masturbation, where one may try to reach a climax quickly.

Retarded ejaculation occurs when the male is able to achieve an erection but cannot achieve orgasm. Generally speaking, the reason for retarded ejaculation is stress that overrides the sexual drive. Keep in mind that the word *stress*, as used here, can encompass physiological factors, such as fatigue, illness, or drugs, and psychological states, such as anxiety or abnormal mental functioning.

Similarly, the female's frigidity is caused primarily by stress. It is quite rare for a chronic dysfunction to result from physical causes. Usually the causes are emotions such as shame, guilt, fear of letting go, or fear of abandonment. Vaginismus is a fear of penetration that causes the vaginal muscles to contract spasmodically, thus effectively preventing penetration. This reaction may be the direct result of a painful experience (and therefore a conditioned response), or it may stem from a psychological desire to avoid the sexual act.

Therapy for sexual dysfunctions is a very delicate procedure. There are many factors to combat. The individual's loss of self-esteem from what is perceived as inadequacy is one primary factor. Another is the delicate nature of the topic. Society is not yet ready to accept an open workshop that trains people in sexual techniques. Neither is the use of surrogate partners as instructors regarded highly by society at this time. Thus therapy is limited essentially to dysfunctioning couples. The findings of researchers in this area indicate that therapy needs to be directed not only at specific techniques but also at the psychological problems and emotions that are disturbing the person: shame, anger, guilt, hostility, fear, or even the loss of self-esteem as the result of perceived inadequacy. Sex therapy is in its infancy, but there are encouraging indications that it may become a productive, important therapeutic field.

14. Describe the types of male and female sexual dysfunction.

A PERSONAL EVALUATION

Significantly, because of the intimate nature of its subject, this unit has not involved you personally in experiments and has not delved into your experiences. In order to keep the censors at bay, the questions that follow are somewhat mild. They explore three areas—your knowledge and experience of sex and your attitudes toward it.

KNOWLEDGE

What do you know about the physiology of the sexual act? How is it connected to the reproductive process? What hormones are involved? Do you know the correct anatomical nomenclature for the male and female genitals? What are the methods of sexual intercourse? How frequently does a normal couple engage in sexual intercourse?

EXPERIENCE

Are you experienced in the sexual act? Do you achieve satisfaction regularly? Have you ever experienced difficulty in the sexual act? Have you displayed any of the sexual maladjustments that have been discussed? How do you compare with Kinsey's data or any other data you have found about sexual performance?

ATTITUDES

What are your feelings about the sexual act? Can you relate openly and freely with members of your own sex and show affection without sexual connotations? Do you feel guilt and shame when speaking about or experiencing sex? Are sexual thoughts always on your mind? Never on your mind? Are you excited or repelled by pornography? How do you think your attitudes toward sex compare with those of your peers?

Your answers to these questions are by no means definitive. If you are honest and candid, they may indicate problem areas for you, or they may indicate that you are making or have made a good adjustment. As a final guideline, remember that the more candid and open you are or can be with your sexual partner, the more pleasure you will get from intimacy and sharing, and the more adjusted you may consider yourself. Performance anad frequency are not the key; sharing is.

15. *Evaluate your own sexual adjustment.*

_____

_____

_____

_____

□ A POINT OF VIEW

The selections that follow are excerpts from two anthropological studies. The work of Donald S. Marshall and John C. Messenger will show you that there are indeed societies with attitudes toward sex and sexual customs very different from those of our culture. You will undoubtedly form your own opinion about the desirability of Mangaian and Irish views and practices.

DONALD S. MARSHALL

SEXUAL BEHAVIOR ON MANGAIA

SEXUAL ASPECTS OF THE LIFE CYCLE

The Mangaian is born, as he lives and loves and dies, in the midst of his clustered kinsmen. The woman in labor is surrounded by family members; assistance is given to her by the grandmother and the husband or father—and by the midwife. More powerful than the physical presence of these kinfolk is the social warmth and approval that envelop a newborn child. For the new member is additional insurance of the continued existence of the family. He is an added source of strength and power, an increment to their means of subsistence. In fact, he is the foundation of the marriage bond itself—which his conception may have caused to be formalized. Far from serving as a potential wedge between parents, as can occur in other societies—including our own—the birth of the child serves both to strengthen ties of sexual affection between mother and father and to extend the web of kinship; the child's conception has made more attractive, rather than less so, the sexual relations between the couple.

The Mangaian couple copulates regularly, up

Reprinted from Donald S. Marshall, "Sexual Behavior
on Mangaia," in *Human Sexual Behavior*, ed. Donald S.
Marshall and Robert C. Suggs (Blomington, Ind.: Institute for
Sex Research, 1971), by permission of Donald S. Marshall.

until the onset of labor pains. Some Mangaian men prefer intercourse with their wives during this period of pregnancy to that during any other time, for the woman's privates are believed to become "wetter, softer, fatter, and larger"; natural secretions provide the lubication that Managaian lovers prefer. Some slight adjustments in coital position are made, with the rear approach *(pāto'e)* being used more frequently than otherwise. There is a belief shared by some Mangaians that frequent copulation up until the time of delivery eases the path of the child (though some differ, and abstain from coitus with their wives—out of the jokingly expressed fear that "the baby will bite"). Copulation between the couple may be resumed within a few days after delivery, although the cultural ideal is to wait for three months or so.

Boys and girls may play together until they are three or four years of age. But between ages four and five, they separate into those sex-age groups that will distinguish them socially for the rest of their lives. Brothers and sisters, sweethearts and lovers, husband and wife, mother and father, old man and old woman—such pairs rarely mix together socially in public, despite their intense private relationships. A six-year-old Mangaian brother and his three-year-old sister would no more walk together hand in hand along the main street of the town than would the dignified Mangaian deacon think of walking down the same street with his wife on his way to church. Seeing such behavior by my children, my principal informant expressed this "don't" of the cultural system thus: No Māori brother and sister allowed to go together like that!"

The bare bottom and penis of the preschool Mangaian boy are only covered when going to church or on other formal occasions. Mothers attempt to justify this undress to the European visitor by saying that it's "hard to teach them to wear trousers." But there is no real shame associated with seeing a child's penis before he has been superincised, at about age twelve (or in seeing a little girl's genitals—up until she has reached age four or five). However, if the boy child has been circumcised in the European fashion at birth, he must then keep his organ covered. For it is the glans of the penis that must not be seen. Normally, this is covered up by the foreskin of the nonsuperincised male youth; but when this skin is cut, the penis then has "no hat," as the Mangaian expression goes, and must no longer be viewed by anyone.

Young children imitate the work and activities of their elders as a basis of play. In the course of this, according to some informants, they are thought to play at copulation. But this activity is never seen in public. In a somewhat different sense, the adult act itself is never socially acknowledged in public. For the Mangaian enjoys an extraordinary sense of "public privacy." He may copulate, at any age, in the single room of a hut that contains from five to fifteen family members of all ages—as have his ancestors before him. His daughter may receive and make love with each of her varied nightly suitors in that same room. Clothes are changed and accidents, such as public loss of a menstrual pad, may happen. But under most conditions, all of this takes place without social notice; everyone seems to be looking in another direction.

Despite varied sexual activities that occur continuously within the one-room houses, it is outside of the home that the child learns more intimate details of sex and their results—such as "where the babies come from." This knowledge is achieved at about age eight or nine. For just as brother and sister are not seen together in public, so they do not discuss sexual matters together, nor do they joke together. Brothers do not advise brothers, nor do closely related age-mates joke with one another. Mothers and daughters or fathers and sons do not discuss sexual matters with one another—or even with the older persons among whom they work.

These "dos" and "don'ts" of what is permissible at home and what must be discussed elsewhere produce odd contrasts. Offsetting the lack of discussion of sexual matters within the family are actual sexual acts that regularly take place in the home and the lingual manipulation of the penis of small children by women of the family. Just as anomalous is the cultural atmosphere in the Mangaian community itself. Despite lack of public social contact between sexes of all ages, there is a continual public evocation of sex. The slightest attention of an unrelated boy to a girl will raise the buzz of gossip, whether based upon a public compliment or a casual touch or smile. And a very common technique of active leadership is to introduce a sexual joking element into the public situation. The district chief, the territorial governor, the church elder, the proud storekeeper—each knows that a risqué remark, a suggestive comment, or a timeworn sexual proverb provides the element of public amusement that is required to keep things moving. As my pastor-friend and host noted, proverbs are *not* religious in this community, although local activities are geared to a religious calendar cycle. Such proverbs would, he explained, "only make the deacons and a pastor happy"—one needs a sexual story to "make all the people happy and work fast." The Mangaian proverb or story must have a biological, a scatological, or a sexual basis if it is to be used to get people in the mood for group work. The work leader must have a strong voice and a "good sense of humor"—that is, a good store of sexual proverbs and stories— or the work "never gets done." Hence, one may find oneself sitting in the village pastorate, listening to the local minister tell the anthropologist and visiting pastors a ribald story of how the island of Manihiki became renowned as a "finger work" island; while, from the next room, comes the sound of his daughter reading her Bible aloud. Or one may watch, over and over again, as the *Ekalesia* of the church increase their work efforts threefold in response to the ribald implication of a deacon's publicly told story.

Further compounding this apparent ambivalence in social attitudes is a typical Polynesian concern with the sexual genitalia and lack of concern with the rest of human anatomy. The Mangaian is completely flabbergasted at the American and European male's interest in the female breast, for the Polynesian considers this organ to be of interest only to a hungry baby. Yet, the Mangaian male is as fully concerned with the size, shape, and consistency of the mons Veneris as is the American male with the size, shape, and consistency of the female bust. Moreover, the Mangaian concern with sex is supplemented by considerable knowledge of the genital organs; the average Mangaian youth has fully as detailed a knowledge—perhaps more— of the gross anatomy of the penis and the vagina as does a European physician. In fact, the Mangaian vocabulary contains terms for features of the genitalia that users of English have not found necessary to specifically name or classify; for example, *tipipā*, the ridge of the glans of the penis; *ngutupakō*, the exposed area of the glans of the nonsuperincised penis; *keo* and *keokeo*, modifying terms for the shape of the clitoris. For the clitoris itself there are several synonyms (*kaka'i, nini'i, tore, teo,* etc.), as there are for the cunnus (*kāwawa, mete kōpapa, 'ika*). One indication of the significance attached to sexual organs is found in the fact that the clitoris, which is said to be some three-quarters of an inch long, is classified as either one or another degree of "sharpness" or is considered to be "blunt"; alternate terms describe it as "projecting," "erecting," or "protruding." (This fact may be functionally and physiologically related both to the deliberate manipulation of children's sexual organs by older people in an attempt to change their size and to the activity rate to which they are subjected.)

The principal sexual factor in the development of the Mangaian personality is, thus, the early and constant exposure to patterned ambivalence. There is an emphatic social division of the sexes, in an atmosphere redolent with cultural emphasis on sexual organs and sexual intercourse; unique modesty as to exposure of adult organs (Polynesian men are horrified at European casualness in exposing the penis in urination) is contrasted with extreme sensuousness in local dance and explicitly detailed accounts of sexual acts and organs in folktales; the utmost lack of interest in modern European-style clothing is offset by lavish use of perfumed scents and flowers; perhaps most importantly, intricate incest prohibitions are contrasted with the restriction of most social contacts to those that take place only between kinsmen.

A Mangaian boy supposedly first hears about masturbation (*tītoi, kurukuru,* or *pa'ore;* sometimes referred to in the village of Oneroa as "Ivirua poetry"—Ivirua being a neighboring village) sometime between the ages of seven and ten. He discusses it with his friends and, eventually, he experiments with himself while off feeding the pigs or fishing. Boys are often stimulated to do this by hearing the young men (*māpū*) talk about sex. Boys may masturbate themselves an average of two or three times a week; excessive masturbation is thought to expose the glans of the penis (*ngutupakō*) prior to superincision. Mangaians believe that boys with few friends tend to masturbate more than those who spend more time with other children. After erection, even without masturbation, the boy is said to notice the "pressure of fluid" on the penis. (This is different from the "morning erection," which goes down without trace after urination.) Boys also begin to experience nocturnal emissions ("wet dreams") at this age, although they tend to blame these upon the visits of variously described, but always sexually avaricious, "ghost women." The emission in wet dreams and the subsequent waking up always occur, however, before the penetration is made. Nocturnal emissions are much more frequent when the men are denied free access to women, as on the labor island of Makatea. Later, the Mangaian boy will frequently be brought to erection by sexual talk or even by sight of a girl.

Girls also masturbate (*tīrau*) by thigh pressure or by rocking on their heel. This female masturbation is known to have been practiced from life history data, and it has been witnessed in public by Europeans, in contrast to the privacy of the boy's behavior. But I have too few data available to discuss it more fully. And I have never seen, or known anyone who actually claims ever to have seen, boys masturbating publicly. Although parents may try to stop children from masturbating, once they know of it, their efforts are not very heavy nor their punishment severe. And, if without a girl, the older boy or traveling husband may masturbate. Only the hand is used, without elaborate devices. There is accompanying imagery of girls or thinking about the orgasm.

It is important to note that, up until recent years, very small children were taught who their kinsmen (*taeake*) were and learned their genealogy (*'akapapa'anga*) in great detail. This practice has now fallen away, leading to unfortunate results. . . .

SEXUAL ATTITUDES

Copulation is a principal concern of the Mangaian of either sex. This concern is evident in the number of words for coitus, for the sexual parts of the body, and for sexual activities and other intimate matters in the Mangaian insults. To tell a man *maumau 'ua te ure i āau'* is to tell him, insultingly, that he's lazy and that he's letting his penis go to waste, letting it "get rusty." For the act of coitus or copulation itself there is a formal specific word, *ai*, that is related only to the human act. *Oni* is the formal word for animal copulation, although this word may be used for human intercourse in a joking sense. There are innumerable synonyms including some that are similar to English usage. "To sleep" (*moe*) and "to lie down" (*takoto*) also mean "to copulate" and are often used as socially acceptable or "polite" terms. And the terms for "male" (*tāne*) and "female" (*wahine*), when used by a member of the opposite sex, may also infer copulation. The twenty-seventh night of the lunar month (also called *tāne*) is considered "an especially good night for searching out women," as well as for net fishing.

The Mangaians' approach to sex must be as indirect as the final proposition is direct. There is not dating whatsoever (in the American sense) between youths of the two sexes. In this day of public elementary school and general knowledge of writing, a note carried by an intermediary or left in a hidden location may ask the direct question; rarely would it be handed directly from writer to receiver. The slight pressure of a finger or arm in dancing, the raising of an eyebrow, the showing of a seed pod or flower cupped in the hand so as to provide a sexually suggestive sign are all that is required to raise the question in this society where boy is not seen with girl in public. Or (as will be seen later in the discussion of *motoro*) the boy (or girl) may simply go at night to the house and bed of the sought-after partner. Today the phrases "I love you" or "I want you" play a role in the note or the go-between's message, for "sweet talk" is recognized as a necessary social lubricant. But such phrases mean only "I want to copulate with you."

Whatever the indirect approach or whoever the social go-between, the proposition raised is direct and unmistakable. There is no contact between the sexes, no rendezvous, no equivalent of our "necking" that does not culminate directly and immediately in copulation. Coitus is the only imaginable end for any kind of sexual contact among Mangaians. Less than one out of a hundred girls, and even fewer boys—if, indeed, there are any exceptions in either sex—have *not* had substantial sexual experience prior to marriage. Although the sexual act is understood to be related to childbirth, Mangaians believe that if one spreads the relationship between varied partners and avoids continuous or regular intercourse with the same partner, pregnancy will not result. They also maintain that although sexual intercourse is one of the prerequisites between partners in formal marriage or in mating, it in itself bears no implication of love or connotation of marriage. . . .

PRINCIPAL FACTORS AND VARIANTS

Traditionally, there was a direct casual relationship between Mangaian religion and seemingly libertine sexual behavior. In the pre-Christian era, warriors and their women copulated on the temple grounds in order to conceive sons who would be warriors. (They would not, however, sleep with their women for three days before a battle, for fear it would lead to their death; the great warrior-heroes were continent for seven days before combat.) When the missionaries' wives first arrived, the heathen warriors assured themselves that they were "the same like us"—by manual investigation. But later, the downfall of the ancient gods (who did not die but were simply overwhelmed by the power of what is still referred to as "the new God"—Jehovah) eliminated the more obvious formal sexual aspects of Mangaian religion—though elderly women still dance the *'ura* in the meeting houses, when excited by hymn singing.

Today, the official position of the Cook Islands Christian Church reflects a European missionary view that sexual intercourse outside of Christian marriage is not to be tolerated. And, until recent years, on Mangaia—as in many other Polynesian islands—neither pleasure nor beauty was tolerated by the new Christians. Flowers could not be worn, boys could not be seen with unrelated girls, and deacons of the church had the equivalent of police powers to enforce an early curfew and to fine offenders against the church-inspired laws. There still is a rigid nine o'clock evening curfew, and all unmarried people must remain indoors or be taken to court; this curfew is used by the police to enforce a prohibition against wandering about or singing.

But today the church is losing its ethical hold, and local Polynesian pastors who now replace the European missionaries have a more relaxed viewpoint. A young man may temporarily be put out of the Boys' Brigade (a British church-connected version of the Boy Scouts) for fornication or the fathering of a child—when these acts are formally brought to public notice; alternatively, he may be let off with a mere "warning." Such aspects of sexual behavior as masturbation, the appropriateness of varied positions used in intercourse, and oral-genital contact are not brought up in church by church leaders. Althought the European missionary at his headquarters on Rarotonga says that the London Missionary Society *does* take a stand against premarital and extramarital fornication, "this is

up to the pastors to teach." And "officially"—as opposed to actual practice—the church encourages the concept of eliminating premarital and extramarital intercourse and making the initial sexual "coming together" a part of Christian marriage. But there is no prohibition against exotic coital positions ("What positions?") or other sexual activities, as the head missionary says that "the question doesn't arise."

Alcohol is consumed in the form of a locally brewed orange- or other fruit-based beer and is blamed for many sexual problems. Married or single Mangaians who drink beer often "do not go straight home," as "the beer makes you go find a woman" and gives a desire for sexual adventure which some men say is "irresistible." There is a legal prohibition in the Cook Islands despite large-scale consumption of liquor. For the most part, Mangaians cannot buy alcohol; hence most drinking is related to the surreptitious brewing of beer out in the bush. This beer drinking is formalized as either boy or girl "beer schools." As one informant said, in referring to his earlier days: "Things happen at beer schools and for young men only two things are important: women and beer. When we hear of a woman's beer school we go to it, no matter how far away it is. And this not just for the beer!"

Incest (*tātupu* or *tāneketupu*) is not infrequently practiced on Mangaia. It may include intercourse between a father and his biological daughter or his step- ("feeding") daughter, between first cousins, or brother and sister. Intercourse between father and step-daughter is the most usual. (None is known to occur between mother and son.) Discovery of such incest may lead to the suicide of a father who has copulated with his biological daughter or to (illegal) marriage with a step-daughter. Formerly, the couple were forced to confess—standing on a slit gong, they were given the equivalent of a third degree. After that, they were forced to walk around the entire island, shouting aloud their offense as people threw filth at them and publicly banished them from the villages. Today, despite grumblings from relatives of the guilty pair, there is no explicit social chastisement.

There is no bar sinister for illegitimate children on Mangaia, because the new lover, husband, or the understanding father treats offspring of a woman's previous lovers as he does his own children. Men may stay at home minding these children while their wife goes off to a local dance. And even the Mangaian pastors say, when someone reports that their Boys' Brigade officers are drinking and carrying on with girls: "Let them alone. This is their time. Our time has passed. They are young; we are old. Soon they will become like us. And besides, it will do no good to tell them not to, for they will do what they wish anyway!"

There are adverse factors to some of these apparently free and noble attitudes. Not infrequently a young mother, feuding with her lover, may allow their infant to die from her willful lack of care. And the Polynesian's "in-for-a-penny, in-for-a-pound" attitude leads to a distortion of behavior. A simple compliment to a woman means but one thing to her, or to anyone else—that the complimenter seeks her for a sexual partner. And even the local pastor, when accused of adultery because of inadvertent polite behavior or unintentional flattery, will rush to commit—in excess—the act of which he is accused, knowing that this transgression will lose him his pastorate and his social position. Since to laugh with a girl is to admit publicly that you are "doing things" with her, one must dance in silence and not even talk to one's partner, lest "tomorrow people will be saying things." Thus, in public, there is an almost complete social separation of the sexes—extending to husbands and wives.

Traditionally, a male goes from female to female—leaving one for another when he tires of the first or hears that she has gone with another man. People admire the boy who has had many girls, comparing him to "a strong man, like a bull, going from woman to woman." And people even admire the married New Zealand government official, with his wife and children with him on the island, who goes from Mangaian girl to Mangaian girl "like a bull." But they do not admire the girl who has many

boys, comparing her to a pig. And although "a man must chase a woman," it is considered a great shame for a woman to chase a man, for it shows she is a "silly pig."

Nevertheless, there is a fine but significant line between what one does "in private" (though with the full knowledge of everyone in the village) and those things that have become formal "public knowledge." Mangaians do not mind people fornicating under many and varied circumstances, as "this is only being as nature intended, and a man and a woman can't help it." But they "cannot stand things which bring shame on the family." Hence, the mother or father or brothers who procure a daughter or a sister for a European visitor or official, in anticipation of material gain, will insist that the girl return home before dawn—in order that the public not be offended. For what offends the Mangaian is not the copulation with a stranger at his whim or at a mother's or brother's avaricious insistence (other people consider the family and the girl to be "lucky," for the meat and cloth or the garments and presents that result from such a liaison); the social offense is to admit the action *publicly*, by shamelessly walking home from the liaison through the village in the daylight, instead of at night time under protective cover of darkness. "She thinks she owns the village!" is the indignant comment; *'Akanoanoa te 'orie o te atua-* "The village of God has been profaned!"

An outsider must not speak of sex or of genitalia in front of women, even though he is a doctor or a teacher. For the Mangaian assumes that to speak of sex or of the genitals in front of women is to indicate to them that one is seeking a new partner and that one of the women of the group has been "selected." But the concept of a celibate person is unknown on Mangaia. Of the Catholic priest, the Islanders ask in puzzlement, *Tuia i to nira?*—"Are his privates sewn up?" Even the term for "virgin" is not indigenous; it was adopted from the Bible and is a Greek derivative—*pārētenia*, from "parthogenesis." But there are no virgins in the biblical moral sense, and there are very few young girls with an intact hymen (*kuru*; also the term for "breadfruit" and for the closely cropped or bald head of a man"). In fact, there is considerable competition among men to be the one to introduce sexual activities to (*wā'ikuru*, "to deflorate") as many girls as possible. (*Na'a-te-kuru* is to lose the maidenhead, to have one's first sexual experience—said of a girl, but also [figuratively] of a boy; it is also used to describe being successful in fishing after a long run of poor luck.)

There are no professional prostitutes on Mangaia, although girls may be procured. And even young married women offer themselves to sailors, in return for cash or material gain, when a European vessel is visiting the island.

Apparently syphilis has not yet been brought to Mangaia, although gonorrhea is regularly brought in by sailors or by Mangaians returning home from other islands. Today this is cured by penicillin injections. Young men come to the dispensary voluntarily for treatment, but girls frequently have to be tracked down through men to whom they have transmitted the disease. No stigma is attached to either sex for having the disease, and the fact that a girl is diseased does not lower the Mangaian male's interest in her. Men do take the precaution of not ejaculating within the vagina of a girl known to be diseased, in conformance with the local belief that to practice coitus interruptus will preclude transmission of veneral disease. (Similarly, folk belief used to be that to copulate with a girl during her menses would induce venereal disease in a man.)

Technically, in the sense of sexually assaulting an unwilling girl, rape is frequently practiced on Mangaia. In fact, there are two terms for rape: *nane* and *kika*. Although young men and boys are occasionally convicted in court of such rape, the penalty may be less than that for stealing a pig. For rape does not carry the serious social connotation on Mangaia or in Polynesia that it does in European society. In the warlike past, a prerogative of the warrior was to rape wives of lesser men. And today, the gang rape (*tauati*) is a commonly used device to bring haughty young Mangaian women to terms with their male age mates. The girl may object, but she is too ashamed for having been taken by the group to go to the police. Moreover, the dividing line is hard to determine between actual gang rape and mutually agreeable sexual intercourse of a group of boys (of from two or three to ten or twelve) with a somewhat willing girl. Less attractive and otherwise poorly endowed girls may use this custom as a means of achieving attention, or they may be the not-too-unwilling butt of an idle decision on the part of village boys. Supposedly a girl can stop the act when she tires of it by putting her hair in her mouth, causing the boys to be unable to maintain an erection. And in this activity, as in other facets of sex, male participants are not related—"If you see a kinsman you go away."

Although Mangaians may use a cushion on which to prop up a woman's bottom for more satisfactory copulation, there is no indication of use of any artifice or device in association with sex. Apparently sexual fetishism is nonexistent on Mangaia; there are no paraphilias. There is also no circle intercourse, orgies, or copulation by one male with more than one female at a time. Copulation with animals is not entirely unknown, but the only recorded case (involving a pig) was obviously related to youthful experimentation.

Mangaian men do beat their wives occasionally, and supposedly some Mangaian women "like to be beaten." But there is no indication that this incipient masochism (explained by the female partner as, "How do I know that he loves me if he doesn't beat me?") is translated into self-induced whippings or any other sexually oriented, truly masochistic tendencies. It appears to be more of a device to demonstrate the continued closeness of ties of affection.

There are no aphrodisiacs. Traditionally there was a sort of love potion (*aratea*), obtained from a place called *Kikinātea*, "noontime erection"; reportedly there was no aphrodisiac effect. And no magic is used today.

Despite occasional self-masturbation (*pā'ore*) by young boys and women and by some old men, there is no trace whatsoever of homosexuality for either sex on Mangaia. However, Mangaians are aware of homosexuals on other islands, such as Tahiti, Rarotonga, and Samoa. (Rarotongan homosexuality, now said to be increasing among the young women, appears to have been imported from Tahiti.)

There are a very few individuals, perhaps two or three out of a population of 2,000, who—at least socially and perhaps biologically—are intersexual. These berdache are "men" who enjoy doing women's work, may have a feminine figure, and—to some degree—may dress like a woman. The possibility exists that there are also women who enjoy doing men's work (I have not seen them, but informants state they exist), although no specific cases were recorded. The males are well regarded socially, are liked by women and girls, and are frequently called upon to assist in cooking feasts, sewing pillowcases, and cutting out dresses and dress patterns. They sing in a female falsetto and are frequently considered to be the best dancers in the island. But they take no sexual interest in other men. And there is no admitted rectal intercourse with either sex. (Mangaian men who had not traveled had not even heard of sodomy; more worldly men had heard of it on some of the other Cook Islands but considered the idea ridiculous.)

SOME PRELIMINARY CONCLUSIONS

Having examined the sexual behavior in the Mangaian life cycle, from birth through marriage and death, let me now summarize the import of those data with regard to three principal areas: the *biological* (from the viewpoint of sterility and impotency), the *social* (from the viewpoint of homosexuality), and the *cultural* (with regard to the female orgasm). Each of these is obviously interrelated with many other facets.

BIOLOGICAL

There is little reason to doubt that the average Mangaian copulates more frequently and more vigorously than does the average European (also, the average American). But there is little doubt that many Mangaian males pay a biological penalty for this sociocultural fact; that is, the Mangaian male is probably far more subject to impotency and sterility in later years than is the American male. He is subject to *tira*, a condition in which the penis changes in its ability to rise and react, from an initial period of insatiable desire to a final stage in which the organ not only may be unable to be aroused but may actually retreat into the body and be "dead" and "lost"; according to local belief, this may bring about the death of the fear-stricken subject. The Mangaian treatment for this condition includes a mandate for absolute sexual abstinence for a period of six months or so. This treatment may be a clue to the cause of *tira*, attributed by local medical practitioners to overindulgence in coitus.

Concomitantly, there is a problem of sterility. Data on childbirth suggest that the well-known concept of adolescent sterility may be particularly applicable on Mangaia. For example, in a detailed sociocultural census that included specific data on this particular subject, of 474 individuals, fourteen years or older, no males of the 30 young men between fourteen and twenty years old and only 3 females of the 29 young women in the same age group had sired or given birth to children before reaching age twenty-one. More significant is the fact that of the sample of 179 females and 291 males over the age of fifteen, 29 percent of the females and 31 percent of the males had not had children. Of 51 females and 77 males over age fifty, 19.6 percent of the females and 15.6 percent of the males had never given birth to, or sired, children, even though most had been married. This may be substantially different than in non-Polynesian societies; these data should be carefully compared.

Obviously such factors as diet, venereal disease, and related biogeographic influences probably play their part in bringing about these conditions. But the continual use of the sexual organs may prove to play a major part.

SOCIAL

In such a permissive society as Mangaia, there would appear to be ample opportunity for innate homosexuality to flower unopposed. But, for this island—where there is little that goes on socially that is not a matter of almost immediate public knowledge—it can be flatly stated that there is no trace whatsoever of the active practice of homosexuality or of homosexual relationships. By homosexuality, I refer specifically to the deliberate effort of an individual to bring a member of the same sex to orgasm and/or an indication that an individual prefers a member of his same sex to a member of the opposite sex as a coital partner. I do not refer to the appearance of those stigmata of western society which are frequently mistaken for signs of homosexuality but may in fact reflect hermaphrodism (showing the biological characteristics of the two sexes) and/or transvestism (affecting the dress or activities of the opposite sex). In fact, there are several apparently incipient transvestites—*berdache*—on Mangaia. These are the boys and men who enjoy, and excel at, cooking and who like women's company, cutting out clothes for women to sew, sewing, and washing clothes. (Supposedly there are women who enjoy doing men's work or taking the lead with girl partners in ballroom dancing.) Some of the men bear such stigmata of the hermaphrodite as a high voice, dainty ways, a woman's walk, and a characteristically feminine carriage. But they are hard workers, incredibly cleanly, and show no apparent wish for male sexual partners.

Not only is there no indication whatsoever of any active homosexuality by members of either sex on Mangaia but there is no social disapproval of the indications of transvestism. On the contrary, both individually and collectively there is considerable social approval of the cleverness and diligence of such individuals. Their predilections are not condemned, and they play an active role in the social life of the island, both in religious and in secular activities.

Mangaian data lead to the supposition that the proportion of homosexuals need not be a fixed characteristic of human societies and that an explicit social or cultural acceptance of the stigmata of hermaphrodism and/or transvestism may eliminate some of those social pressures that make confirmed homosexuals of individuals who otherwise would not have moved in that direction.

CULTURAL

Lastly, Mangaian data indicate clearly that (1) the female must learn to achieve sexual orgasm; (2) all Mangaian women do, in fact, learn to achieve this climax; and (3) bringing a partner to orgasm and experiencing simultaneous culmination with her represent an important part of the Mangaian male's sexual pleasure. That the term for the orgasmic experience is the same as that for the achievement of perfection, pleasure, and comfort is evidence of the cultural significance of the last point. In developing techniques to please his partner, the Mangaian male employs those psychological, physiological, and sociocultural assets that are available to him. His responsibility in this matter is so ingrained into the Mangaian male that upon hearing that some American and European women cannot or do not achieve the climax, the Mangaian immediately asks (with real concern) whether this inability will not injure the married woman's health.

The fact that the orgasmic reaction can apparently be universally achieved in one society implies that such achievement could be learned in other societies by those individuals who now do without such an experience. Whether this general achievement of the climax would—in the long run—be socially cohesive or socially disruptive is a problem that must be left for another discussion.

REFERENCES

Marshall, D. S.:

1961. *Ra'ivavae: An Expedition to the Most Fascinating and Mysterious Island in Polynesia.* New York. Doubleday.

n.d. "Polynesian Sexual Behavior." Manuscript.

n.d. "The Village of God: An Ethnography of Mangaia." Manuscript.

JOHN C. MESSENGER

SEX AND REPRESSION IN AN IRISH FOLK COMMUNITY

Both lack of sexual knowledge and misconceptions about sex among adults combine to brand Inis Beag as one of the most sexually naive of the world's societies. Sex never is discussed in the home when children are about; only three mothers admitted giving advice, briefly and incompletely, to their daughters. We were told that boys are better advised than girls, but that the former learn about sex informally from older boys and men and from observing animals. Most respondents who were questioned about sexual instructions given to youths expressed the belief that "after marriage nature takes its course," thus negating the need for anxiety-creating and embarrassing personal confrontation of parents and offspring. We were unable to discover any cases of childlessness based on sexual ignorance of spouses, as reported from other regions of peasant Ireland. Also, we were unable to discover knowledge of the sexual categories utilized by researchers in sex: insertion of tongue while kissing, male mouth on female breast, female hand on penis, cunnilingus, fellatio, femoral coitus, anal coitus, extramarital coitus, manifest homosexuality, sexual contact with animals, fetishism, and sadomasochistic behavior. Some of these activities may be practiced by particular individuals and couples; however, without a doubt they are deviant forms in Inis Beag, about which information is difficult to come by.

Menstruation and menopause arouse profound misgivings among women of the island, because few of them comprehend their physiological significance. My wife was called on to explain these processes more than any other phenomena related to sex. When they reach puberty, most girls are unprepared for the first menstrual flow and find the experience a traumatic one—especially when their mothers are unable to provide a satisfactory explanation for it. And it is commonly believed that the menopause can induce "madness"; in order to ward off this condition, some women have retired from life in their mid-forties and, in a few cases, have confined themselves to bed until death, years later. Others have so retired as a result of depressive and masochistic states. Yet the harbingers of "insanity" are simply the physical symtoms announcing the onset of menopause. In Inis Beag, these include severe headaches, hot flashes, faintness in crowds and enclosed places, and severe anxiety. Mental illness is also held to be inherited or caused by inbreeding (or by the Devil, by God punishing a sinner, or by malignant pagan beings) and stigmatizes the family of the afflicted. One old man came close to revealing what is probably the major cause of neuroses and psychoses in Ireland, when he explained the incarceration of an Inis Beag curate in a mental institution for clerics as caused by his constant association with a pretty housekeeper, who "drove him mad from frustration." This elder advocated that only plain-appearing older women (who would not "gab" to "our man") be chosen for the task. Earlier, according to island opinion, the same priest had caused to be committed to the "madhouse" a local man who pubicly challenged certain of his actions. The unfortunate man was released six months later, as per law, since he was not mentally ill.

Sexual misconceptions are myriad in Inis Beag. The islanders share with most Western peoples the belief that men by nature are far more libidinous than women. The latter have been taught by some curates and in the home that sexual relations with their husbands are a "duty" which must be "endured," for to refuse coitus is a mortal sin. A frequently encountered assertion affixes the guilt for male sexual strivings on the enormous intake of potatoes of the Inis Beag male. (In Nigeria, among the people whom my wife and I studied, women are thought to be more sexually disposed than men

Reprinted from John C. Messenger, "Sex and Repression in an Irish Folk Community," in *Human Sexual Behavior*, ed. Donald S. Marshall and Robert C. Suggs (Bloomington, Ind.: Institute for Sex Research, 1971), by permission of John C. Messenger.

and are the repositories of sexual knowledge; it is they who initiate coitus and so pose a threat to their spouses. Nigerian men place the blame on clitoridectomy performed just prior to marriage.) Asked to compare the sexual proclivities of Inis Beag men and women, one mother of nine said, "Men can wait a long time before wanting 'it,' but we can wait a lot longer." There is much evidence to indicate that the female orgasm is unknown—or at least doubted, or considered a deviant response. One middle-aged bachelor, who considers himself wise in the ways of the outside world and has a reputation for making love to willing tourists, described one girl's violent bodily reactions to his fondling and asked for an explanation; when told the "facts of life" of what obviously was an orgasm, he admitted not realizing that women also could achieve a climax, although he was aware that some of them apparently enjoyed kissing and being handled.

Inis Beag men feel that sexual intercourse is debilitating, a common belief in primitive and folk societies. They will desist from sex the night before they are to perform a job which will require the expenditure of great energy. Women are not approached sexually during menstruation or for months after childbirth, since they are considered "dangerous" to the male at these times. Returned "Yanks" have been denounced from the pulpit for describing American sexual practices to island youths, and such "pornographic" magazines as *Time* and *Life,* mailed by kin from abroad, have aroused curates to spirited sermon and instruction.

The separation of the sexes, started within the family, is augmented by separation in almost all segments of adolescent and adult activity. Boys and girls are separated to some extent in classrooms, and completely in recess play and movement to and from school. During church services, there is a further separation of adult men and women, as well as boys and girls, and each of the four groups leaves the chapel in its turn. The pubs are frequented only by men or by women tourists and female teachers who have spent several years on the mainland while

training and thus are "set apart" (and, of course, by inquisitive female ethnographers). Women occasionally visit the shops to procure groceries, but it is more common for them to send their children to do so, since supplies and drinks are proffered across the same counter, and men are usually to be found on the premises. Even on the strand during summer months, male tourists tend to bathe at one end and women at the other. Some swimmers "daringly" change into bathing suits there, under towels and dresses—a custom practiced elsewhere in Ireland which has overtones of sexual catharsis.

It is often asserted that the major "escape valve" of sexual frustration among single persons in Ireland is masturbation; frustration-aggression theorists, however, would stress the ubiquity of drinking, alcoholism, disputes, and pugnacity as alternative outlets. Pugnacity can also be linked to the widespread problem of male identity. Our study revealed that male masturbation in Inis Beag seems to be common, premarital coitus unknown, and marital copulation limited as to foreplay and the manner of consummation. My wife and I never witnessed courting—"walking out"—in the island. Elders proudly insist that it does not occur, but male youths admit to it in rumor. The claims of young men focus on "petting" with tourists and a few local girls, whom the "bolder" of them kiss and fondle outside of their clothing. Island girls, it is held by their "lovers," do not confess these sins because they fail to experience pleasure from the contact. The male perpetrators also shun the confessional because of their fear of the priest.

We were unable to determine the frequency of marital coitus. A considerable amount of evidence indicates that privacy in the act is stressed and that foreplay is limited to kissing and rough fondling of the lower body, especially the buttocks. Sexual activity invariably is initiated by the husband. Only the male superior position is employed; intercourse takes place with underclothes not removed; and orgasm, for the man, is achieved quickly, almost immediately after which he falls asleep. (I must stress the provisional nature of these data, for they are based on a limited sample of respondents and relate to that area of sexual behavior least freely discussed.)

Many kinds of behavior disassociated from sex in other societies, such as nudity and physiological evacuation, are considered sexual in Inis Beag. Nudity is abhorred by the islanders, and the consequences of this attitude are numerous and significant for health and survival. Only infants have their entire bodies sponged once a week, on Saturday night; children, adolescents, and adults, on the same night, wash only their faces, necks, lower arms, hands, lower legs, and feet. Several times my wife and I created intense embarrassment by entering a room in which a man had just finished his weekly ablutions and was barefooted; once when this occurred, the man hurriedly pulled on his stockings and said with obvious relief, "Sure, it's good to get your clothes on again." Clothing always is changed in private, sometimes within the secrecy of the bedcovers, and it is usual for the islanders to sleep in their underclothes.

Despite the fact that Inis Beag men spend much of their time at sea in their canoes, as far as we could determine none of them can swim. Four rationales are given for this deficiency: the men are confident that nothing will happen to them, because they are excellent seamen and weather forecasters; a man who cannot swim will be more careful; it is best to drown immediately when a canoe capsizes far out in the ocean rather than swim futilely for minutes or even hours, thus prolonging the agony; and, finally, "When death is on a man, he can't be saved." The truth of the matter is that they have never dared to bare their bodies in order to learn the skill. Some women claim to have "bathed" at the back of the island during the heat of summer, but this means wading in small pools with skirts held knee-high, in complete privacy. Even the nudity of household pets can arouse anxiety, particularly when they are sexually aroused during time of heat. In some homes, dogs are whipped for licking their genitals and

soon learn to indulge in this practice outdoors. My wife, who can perform Irish step-dances and sing many of the popular folk songs, was once requested to sing a seldom-heard American Western ballad; she chose "The Lavendar Cowboy," who had only two hairs on his chest." The audience response was perfunctory and, needless to say, she never again was "called out" to sing that particular song.

The drowning of seamen, who might have saved themselves had they been able to swim, is not the only result of the sexual symbolism of nudity; men who were unwilling to face the nurse when ill, because it might have meant baring their bodies to her, were beyond help when finally treated. While my wife and I were on the island, a nurse was assaulted by the mother of a young man for diagnosing his illness and bathing his chest in the mother's absence. (In this case, Oedipal and sexual attitudes probably were at work in tandem.)

It must be pointed out that nudity is also shunned for "health" reasons, for another obtrusive Inis Beag character trait is hypochondria. In some cases, however, it is hard to determine whether concern with modesty or health is dominant in a particular behavioral response. Fear of colds and influenza is foremost among health concerns; rheumatism and related muscular joint ailments, migraine headaches and other psychosomatic disorders, tooth decay, indigestion ("nervous stomach"), and hypermetropia are other widespread pathologies which cause worry among the folk—not to mention those of supernatural origin.

Secrecy surrounds the acts of urination and defecation. The evacuation of infants before siblings and strangers is discouraged, and animals that discharge in the house are driven out. Chickens that habitually "dirty" their nests while setting are soon killed and eaten. Although some women drink spirits privately, they seldom do so at parties. In part this is because of the embarrassment involved in visiting the outside toilet with men in the "street" looking on. One of the most carefully guarded secrets of Inis Beag, unreported in the many works describing island culture, is the use of human manure mixed with sand as a fertilizer. We were on the island eight months before we discovered that compost is not "street drippings" and "scraw," but decomposed feces. With "turf" becoming more difficult to procure from the mainland, some islanders have taken to importing coal and processed peat and burning cattle dung. The dung is prepared for use in difficult-to-reach plots at the back of the island when tourists are few in number; it is burned covertly because of the overtones of sex and poverty. Another custom that my wife and I learned of late in our research, due to the secrecy surrounding it, concerns the thickening of wool; men are required to urinate in a container and tread the wool therein with their bare feet.

Other major manifestations of secual repression in Inis Beag are the lack of a "dirty joke" tradition (at least as the term is understood by ethnologists and folklorists) and the style of dancing, which allows little bodily contact among participants. I have heard men use various verbal devices—innuendoes, puns, and asides—that they believed bore sexual connota-tions; relatively speaking, they were pallid. In the song that I composed, one line of a verse refers to an island bachelor arising late in the day after "dreaming perhaps of a beautiful mate"; this is regarded as a highly suggestive phrase, and I have seen it redden cheeks and lower glances in a pub. Both step- and set-dancing are practiced in Inis Beag, although the former type is dying out. This rigid-body dancing, from which sex is removed by shifting attention below the hips, appears to have originated in Ireland during the early nineteenth century. The set patterns keep partners separated most of the time; but, even so, some girls refuse to dance, because it involves touching a boy. Inis Beag men, while watching a woman step-dance, stare fixedly at ther feet, and they take pains to appear indifferent when crowding at a party necessitates holding women on their laps and rubbing against them when moving from room to room. But they are extremely sensitive, nevertheless, to the entire body of the dancer and to these casual contacts, as are the women. Their covert emotional reactions (which become overt as much drink is taken) are a form of catharsis. . . .

UNIT 12

DRUGS

☐ In our kaleidoscopic, rapidly changing society, a strange and sinister event is casting a shadow over us. We have suddenly become aware of drugs. The medicinal use of drugs is as old as human culture, but their nonmedicinal use has never been so evident as at the present time. In this unit you will consider the reasons people take drugs, you will learn about three major drugs, and you will consider methods of drug control.

When you have completed this unit, you should be able to:

1. *Explain why our culture may well be called the drug culture.*
2. *Describe various classes of drugs on the basis of their effects.*
3. *Define* addiction, habituation, *and* dependence.
4. *Give a short history of drug abuse and identify some recent trends.*
5. *Give a short description of the development of alcoholism.*
6. *Identify sociopsychological factors in drug abuse.*
7. *Name some identifying behavioral symptoms of a drug user.*
8. *Describe the nature and effects of marihuana.*
9. *State the arguments in the alcohol-marihuana controversy.*
10. *Describe the nature of LSD and its effects.*
11. *Describe the nature of heroin and its effects.*
12. *Describe current programs for the control of drug abuse.*
13. *Evaluate current programs for the control of drug abuse.*
14. *Suggest alternative programs for the control of drug abuse.*
15. *Consider your own position on drugs.*

THE DRUG CULTURE

Although the technological advances of the last half-century have been impressive, nowhere have they been more spectacular than in chemistry, physics, and biochemistry. Today, we are on the threshold of manufacturing life itself. We are able to duplicate many complicated hormones and organic chemicals that our own bodies create and may soon have an almost unlimited capacity to control bodily functions. Birth-control pills are a good example of how far we have progressed.

Nowadays, there are drugs for virtually every purpose one might think of—to elevate blood pressure and to lower it, to increase kidney functioning and to suppress it. No part of our bodies is ignored. The use of drugs has skyrocketed. Many have been and still are available to anyone without prescription or control. Painkillers such as aspirin are readily available, as are a variety of other medicines. We have literally become a nation of pill poppers. We take drugs freely, with no restrictions or compunctions.

At this point, it might be wise to make a few distinctions. A *drug* may be defined as a chemical used in the treatment, diagnosis, or prevention of a disease. This definition emphasizes the use of drugs for beneficial purposes. Another definition of *drug* might include any chemical substance that affects. the functioning of the body. This definition is much broader and doesn't restrict the use of drugs to beneficent purposes. But it does lead us to the

We have become a nation of pill poppers, taking drugs freely with no restrictions or compunctions. (T. C. Fitzgerald/Picture Cube)

subject that many are worried about—the abuse of drugs and the consumption of drugs that may have latent or delayed harmful effects. This is the sinister part of the drug scene today.

1. Explain why our culture may well be called the drug culture.

———————————————————————————————————

———————————————————————————————————

TABLE 12.1 CLASSIFICATION OF DRUGS

Type	Nickname	How taken	Builds up tolerance
Sedatives			Yes
Narcotics			
Morphine	White stuff	Sniffed, injection	
Heroin	Smack, horse, H, junk, skag	Sniffed, injection	
Codeine	Schoolboy	Orally	
Restricted dangerous drugs			
Barbiturates	Barbs, downers	Pills, injection	
Nembutal	Nebbies, nemmies, yellow jackets		
Seconal	Red birds, reds, red devils		
Veronal			
Alcohol	Sauce, booze	Orally	
Stimulants			
Narcotic: Cocaine	Snow, coke, star dust	Sniffed	No
Restricted dangerous drugs			Yes
Amphetamines	Uppers, wake-ups, speed	Pills, injection	
Benzedrine	Bennies, benz		
Dexedrine	Dexies, brownies		
Methedrine	Meth		
Hallucinogens			No
LSD	Acid	Orally	
Hashish	Hash	Orally	
Marihuana	Grass, pot	Smoked	
Psilocybin		Orally	

CLASSES OF DRUGS

There are many ways to classify drugs: by source, physical properties, methods of ingestion. Some can be classified according to their effect on the human mind. There are two major categories of such drugs: stimulants and sedatives. Sedatives (also known as depressants) act to relieve pain, lessen nervousness, produce relaxation, induce sleep or stupor. They reduce physical ability and motor control. Stimulants work in the opposite way. They induce physical

Creates physiological dependence	Creates psychological dependence	Effects	Side effects
Yes	Yes	Euphoria, prevention of withdrawal	Addiction, constipation, loss of appetite
		Euphoria, reduced anxiety	Addiction, severe withdrawal, convulsions, psychosis
		Reduced tension, increased sociability	Addiction, toxic psychosis, physiological damage
No	Yes	Excitation	Depression convulsions, violent aggression
No	Yes	Alertness, wakefulness, loss of weight	Loss of appetite, delusions, hallucinations, psychosis
No	?	Sensory and cognitive distortion, alteration in temporal sense	Psychosis, loss of identity

activity. In large doses, they produce neuroses and tension and induce sleeplessness. (See Table 12.1)

Within these two major groupings it is possible to identify several subgroups: narcotics, restricted dangerous drugs, tranquilizers, hallucinogens, and others. *Narcotic* has both a medical and a legal definition. It can be defined medically as a drug that produces sleep or relieves pain. Legally, a narcotic is any drug that is regulated by federal laws. Narcotics can have sedative, stimulant, or hallucinogenic effects. Most sedatives are derivatives of opium and cause a pleasant trancelike state. The principal sedatives are morphine, methadone, heroin, codeine, dilaudic, paregoric, laudanum, pantopon, and percodan. The principal stimulant narcotic, cocaine, stimulates the central nervous system. It is probably the most dangerous of the narcotics because of its potential for abuse.

Interestingly, the use of cocaine was one subject on which Freud was mistaken. When it first became available and before its terrible addictive powers were known, Freud recommended it highly. As a matter of fact, he himself is supposed to have become addicted to it. He suffered from cancer of the face and took cocaine to relieve his pain.

Federal law restricts the use of many drugs, including stimulants and sedatives. Barbiturates are the major sedative drugs that are legally restricted. Because they act as depressants, they are usually prescribed as sleeping tablets. They are physically addicting, cause a loss of judgment, and impair mental functioning; they also slow physical reactions. Other major kinds of depressants are bromides, chloral hydrate, and alcohol. Taking more than one kind of depressant at a time—drinking and taking barbiturates, for example—may compound the effect of the individual drugs, with disastrous results for the taker.

Common stimulants are amphetamines such as Benzedrine, Dexedrine, and Methedrine. Originally, these drugs were used to treat mental disorders. They produce sleeplessness, nervous tension, and excitability. Although they are not addictive, they may cause tremendous, dangerous swings in emotion. When a person using stimulants is "down," he or she may take more of the drug to get rid of the depression, to get "high." Excessive doses cause confusion, loss of coordination, and hallucinations.

Tranquilizers are sedatives that lower blood pressure, control emotions, and release tensions. They may be addictive. The nonaddictive types—Serpasil, Serfin, Reserpex, Serpina—come from derivatives of *Rauwolfia serpertin.* Some addictive types are Equanil, Miltown, Librium, Valium, and Placidyl.

A hallucinogen evokes false sensations, leading to false perceptions and illusions. The drugs can affect any of the senses or a combination of them. Thus, one can see color flashes and hear accompanying music. The term *psychedelic drug* frequently crops up in the literature. Technically, a psychedelic drug is nonaddicting and alters perception and consciousness. The effects of psychedelic and hallucinogenic drugs are the same: They are "mind expanding" and alter the consciousness of the user. Several types of drugs control the workings of the mind, and others act both as hallucinogens and as stimulants. They are usually called hallucinogenic drugs, if this is their main characteristic.

A psychotogenic drug is one that generates mental activity similar to that of a psychotic person. Any of the mind-expanding drugs may be considered psychotogenic, because they divorce a person from reality. Thus, hallucinogenic drugs are psychedelic and psychotogenic all in one fell swoop. LSD, mescaline, hashish, peyote, marihuana, psilocybin, and DMT are the best-known hallucinogens.

The remaining category of drugs covers miscellaneous substances such as plastic glue, solvent, ether, paint thinner, and some gases. These substances can induce an intoxicated state that is stimulating, sedative, or hallucinogenic, depending on the substance and the dosage.

Ironically, any substance may be classified as a drug. For example, water, if misused, may cause hallucinations and mind expansion.

2. Describe various classes of drugs on the basis of their effects.

_____

_____

_____

_____

ADDICTION, HABITUATION, AND DEPENDENCE

There is quite a bit of confusion in the use of the terms *addiction, habituation,* and *dependence.* In the narrowest sense, an addictive drug is one that causes two effects in the human body. Initially, a very small dose may cause a reaction, but soon a tolerance develops and more and more of the drug is needed to produce the reaction. A steady drug user quite often can take what would be a lethal dose for a nonuser. The second effect of an addictive drug occurs when use of the drug is discontinued. As the body finds itself without the chemical to which it has adjusted, withdrawal effects become severe. In essence, the body has to have the drug, or the reaction to its absence becomes more distressing than the reaction to its presence. Addiction has two elements: tolerance and withdrawal.

Many drugs do not produce a physiological reaction of tolerance and withdrawal. However, they do create a strong mental reaction. This phenomenon is known as habituation, rather than addiction. People get so used to the way they feel when under the influence of the drug that they cannot do without it, even though they do not go through a withdrawal crisis. It might be said that addiction is a physiological event, whereas habituation is a psychological one. In withdrawal, the body reacts, showing symptoms such as a runny nose, cramps, and diarrhea; in the other case, the mind reacts, showing symptoms such as anxiety, stress, and depression.

It is sometimes quite impossible to categorize a drug as solely addictive or habituating, because some drugs apparently are both. Heroin is very addictive. The body rapidly builds up a large tolerance to it, and, although withdrawal symptoms vary with the individual, they can be quite severe. Yet heroin users who have undergone "cold turkey" treatment and have passed through the withdrawal reactions often return to the drug, even though they do not physically crave it. Their craving seems to be psychological rather than physiological. In other words, they have been habituated as well as addicted.

Early theorists thought the problem of addiction to be more evil than that of habituation. Lately, the dangers of habituation have been given equal weight. However, people, confused by the distinction between the two terms, have often followed a theory of treatment that dealt with one problem and not the other. In order to avoid this confusion, the term *dependence* has been widely adopted. The definition of dependence doesn't distinguish between physiological and psychological involvement; it merely describes a person who is involved with a drug. The World Health Organization defines dependence as a state arising from repeated administration of a drug on a periodic or continuous basis. Under this definition, the word *addict* can be abolished as misleading, and *dependent* should replace it.

3. *Define* addiction, habituation, *and* dependence.

_____

_____

_____

_____

A HISTORY OF DRUG ABUSE

Drugs have been known to humanity since antiquity. Marihuana, for instance, has been traced back to 2700 B.C. Opium was known to the Egyptians as long ago as 1500 B.C. Opium has been used consistently as a painkiller since the eighteenth century. To the medical profession, opium was almost a universal panacea and was at different times prescribed for pain of cancer, dysentery, gallstones, childbirth, and toothache.

The addictive properties of opium were not understood either by the ancients or by more recent doctors. Not until two refined products of opium—morphine and codeine—came into being in 1805 and 1832, respectively, were opium's addictive powers suspected. Strangely enough, it took a third advance, the invention of the hypodermic needle, to clarify the situation. During the Civil War, morphine and codeine were frequently injected. As a result, thousands of soldiers became addicted to these opiates, which were sold everywhere. The most devastating opium derivative, heroin, was synthesized in 1898. It too was available to everyone. Opium was not the only dependency-producing drug in common use. Until approximately 1902, Coca Cola contained a small dose of cocaine.

It might surprise you to learn that the levels of addiction today in no way equal those present in 1914, when the nation finally recognized the danger of opium and passed the Harrison Act to control it. At that time, it was estimated that one out of every four hundred people in our country was addicted. The estimate for 1965, in contrast, showed one in 3,300.

Several trends in drug use are quite disquieting. Before the 1940s, most drug-dependent people were middle-aged or older and usually were not from the lowest socioeconomic class. Most of them came to be dependent through medical channels, although some artists also used drugs. The picture changed after World War II, when a shift in use from middle class to lower class occurred. This change also involved a shift to use by ethnic and minority groups, particularly in large cities. For example, in the northeastern United States, 90 percent of the narcotics arrests have involved blacks living in slums. On the West Coast, arrests have involved whites, blacks, and Mexican Americans. Another disturbing trend is the shift in drug use from the middle-aged and older to the young. From 1940 to 1962, there was a steady increase in the under-eighteen group and a decrease in the over-forty group. Today, drug abuse is spreading from the cities to the suburbs and is involving younger and younger people of all social classes. It is no longer an affliction of the poor in the slums.

Another trend has been the tendency among drug users to get away from the use of a single drug, such as an opiate derivative. Speed, goofballs, glue sniffing, banana peels, and LSD—almost any substances that might create a reaction—have been used singly and in tandem.

A major social problem that did not exist earlier is the combining of criminality and drug dependence. Although most addicts must steal and rob in order to support their habit, which often costs sixty or seventy dollars a day, some evidence shows that the excitement of performing a criminal act may be a part of the psychological life of a drug user. In some mysterious way, the outlaw feeling becomes important, so that lawlessness may not necessarily be a result of drug dependency; it may be part of a whole way of life.

4. Give a short history of drug abuse and identify some recent trends.

_____

_____

_____

_____

ALCOHOLISM

The use and abuse of alcohol is a topic that has been studied widely, perhaps because of the special place that this powerful and dangerous drug has in our society. Alcohol is the only drug that is almost universally accepted in societies throughout the world. In our country, an extensive legislative framework surrounds the manufacture and sale of alcohol. Alcohol is heavily taxed and is an important source of revenue for the government. Establishments that sell alcohol must be licensed and are subject to many local regulations about the way that liquor is served. These regulations may vary widely, according to local laws, but one thing is universal: You can get alcohol anywhere you want to, legally or illegally. Efforts to prohibit its sale and consumption have been failures on both the local and the national level. Apparently the use of alcohol is considered to be an inviolable right by the citizenry. Efforts to tamper with that right meet stiff resistance.

Thus, while specific groups and individuals may campaign against it, alcohol is, by and large, legally sanctioned. It is virtually a way of life for the majority of Americans. Quite naturally, such freedom of access and constant exposure leads to problems, because some people fall victim to excessive consumption, or alcoholism. As a society, we recognize this possibility and take steps to prevent it. We prohibit the sale of alcohol to children and its consumption by them. We also punish people who become publicly drunk. Yet although public drunkenness is a legal offense almost everywhere in this country, we have an estimated population of 9 million alcoholics. Probably half as many more are borderline problem drinkers.

The stages by which one becomes an alcoholic are rather interesting. Initially, a person takes a drink or two to ease tension or stress. As a depressant, alcohol tends to act in this way. The person then begins to consume more alcohol to feel better. The rationale is, "If one drink makes me feel good, then two drinks will make me feel twice as good." The body develops a tolerance to the drug that reduces its effect; thus it actually does become necessary to take two drinks to feel the good effects that one drink initially produced. This is where the potential alcoholic slips. The first stage of alcoholism is called *prealcoholism*. It begins when a person has to take more of the drug to get the desired tension relief.

The second stage is the *prodromal* stage. As a prodromal alcoholic, the

This is fun, but it can be deadly. (Ginger Chih from Peter Arnold)

drinker begins to have blackouts and memory loss, even after only a few drinks. The individual recognizes that his or her drinking is now different from a mere release of tension and begins to hide it. Having enough to drink becomes an obsession, and the drinker plans ahead to make sure there will be enough. A party is not a party unless there is alcohol. To get set for the party, the drinker will need one or two doubles before the gang arrives. A prodromal alcoholic becomes sensitive to comments about his or her drinking and avoids talking about it. The time period for this stage is variable, ranging from months to years. In the prodromal stage, a person can still back away from becoming an alcoholic.

The *crucial* stage begins when the person can no longer control his or her drinking. Once the drinking has begun, the crucial drinker must continue until dead drunk. This loss of control is the key characteristic of this stage. Another is the rationalization, "I can take it or leave it alone." This reaction is usually in response to the social disapproval that the crucial drinker is beginning to feel. There is also a loss of self-esteem, as the individual realizes that he or she is in the grip of something uncontrollable. These feelings create even more tension and lead to more drinking. The drinker in the crucial stage may make some efforts to control his or her drinking (nothing before five o'clock or only on the weekends), but these efforts are usually feeble and doomed to failure. Self-pity sets in, and the person feels shut off from the world, which no longer understands. The sex drive lessens. The individual takes more and more to the bottle to bolster a now chronically disorganized personality.

In the last stage, the drinker fits the stereotype that we have of the town drunk. This is the *chronic* stage. The person now lives to drink and is usually in a state of chronic drunkenness. All social restraints are gone. Delusions and hallucinations set in. This stage marks the totally defeated alcoholic.

5. *Give a short description of the development of alcoholism.*

_____

_____

_____

_____

REASONS FOR USING DRUGS

Why do some people get hooked and destroy themselves? Why do we use drugs at all? Many say that human beings are basically hedonistic animals— pleasure seeking and pain avoiding. Although some people distort pain and abuse into pleasurable sensations, essentially we are all directed by the search for pleasure. Some drugs give feelings of pleasure. People take them for this reason. Their bodies build up an immunity to the drug, so that more and more of it becomes necessary to keep up the good feeling. Eventually, the good feeling departs, and what is left is an insatiable craving and, if that craving is not met, severe bodily reactions. Drug users can follow another path: If one dose makes me feel this good, what will two doses do? Addiction may not result, but habituation will.

Although the search for pleasure may be one explanation for drug abuse, it doesn't deal with the question completely. Why do some people turn to drugs even though they know of the dangers? Why do they insist on playing Russian roulette with themselves? There may be two answers to this question. One is that there is a certain social stature attached to drug use. It can be compared to smoking tobacco. For most people, the first cigarette can hardly be called pleasant. A person has to work to get the smoking habit. Smoking must give some satisfaction, however. What is it? Quite obviously, it is status. Younger people see smoking as a mark of maturity. Since we have legally restricted the use of tobacco to adults, youths who smoke will consider themselves adults.

The other reason for drug abuse is also a social one. Group pressure may lead someone into drug use. If a person is part of a group that smokes tobacco, that person too will probably begin to smoke. If a teenager becomes part of a group that smokes grass, it is quite likely that he or she will begin to smoke grass.

Social status and social pressure are thus two great forces inducing a person to use drugs. However, another factor exists. Many people drink alcohol and never lose their control over it. Many people have smoked marihuana and have never used other drugs. Others go right down the road to abuse. The difference lies in the personality of the user. The people who become hooked are the ones who feel inadequate. The drug fills their psychological need, and they become dependent on it. In a sense, this is paradoxical. The weak get a much deeper satisfaction from drug use than do the strong—at least for a short while. However, they are the ones who should never use drugs. The structure of their personalities is so inadequate that they cannot cope with the drug's effects.

It is probably safe to say that people are motivated as much by curiosity as by the desire to reach a certain social status and approval when they first try drugs. Many people report that they have tried LSD and marihuana just to see what would happen. Others are attracted to the mystic potential of the mind expanders; they are fascinated by the notion of mental exploration. Their curiosity is introspective. Fascination with the occult and the mysterious is probably one of the most dangerous reasons for drug use. Persons so motivated are likely to be susceptible to the intellectual confusions that drugs induce. Although mind-expanding drugs give a sense of discovery and provide visions of great and significant things that are beyond the understanding of the ordinary nonuser, you will find out in Unit 19 that you don't need drugs to achieve this sense. There are safer ways to do it.

In summary, then, we may say that several types of drug user can be identified. One seeks social status; another is socially pressured. A third is interested in the mysteries of the mind; a fourth is psychologically insecure.

TABLE 12.2 COLLEGE STUDENTS' REASONS
FOR USING HALLUCINOGENS

Reason	Number of students
Desire for a new experience	10
Curiosity about perceptual effects	10
Improve oneself	8
Religious-philosophical	7
Increase self-knowledge	7
Because friends took it	5
Rebellion against society and/or parents	4
Increase artistic creativity	4
Increase aesthetic appreciation	2
Learn more about people	2

Adapted from Herbert D. Kleber, "Student Use of Hallucinogens," *Journal of the American College Health Association* 14 (1965): 109–111.

Table 12.2 shows reasons mentioned by college students for their first use of
hallucinogens. Does the table say it all? Can you think of other reasons for
using drugs?

_____

_____

_____

_____

Did you list using drugs to get away from unpleasant thoughts and feelings,
such as anxiety and anger?

6. *Identify sociopsychological factors in drug abuse.*

_____

_____

_____

_____

SYMPTOMS OF A DRUG USER

How can I tell whether my child is using drugs? This is a question that thousands of concerned parents are asking. Many spouses, students, and youths are asking similar questions. What are the symptoms of the user? Here is a list of things to look for:

1. A change in social behavior: avoidance of friends, long hours spent in isolation, long periods in the bathroom, sudden absences from groups and then reappearance
2. A marked change in activity: slothfulness, lethargy, sleepiness, yawning
3. Inability to feel pain
4. Pupil size: either dilated or very small
5. Pupils unchanging when light intensity changes
6. Eyes red and watery
7. Speech thick and slurred
8. Nostrils irritated and running; frequent coughing
9. Marked body odor
10. Wearing clothing that covers the arms and legs (to hide the needle tracks)
11. Nervousness, restlessness, tension, irritability
12. Muscular tics and twitches, aches and pains, convulsions
13. Wide swings in mood from elation to depression; quarrelsomeness
14. Mental slowness, inability to cope with problems
15. Delusions and hallucinations, excitability, talkativeness
16. Loss of weight and emaciation
17. Rambling, incoherent talk, full of strange allusions to mystical thoughts
18. Introverted thoughts, little concern for others

Any one of these symptoms, or a combination of them, may indicate drug use. On the other hand, the symptoms may indicate other problems and may be the result of illness or mental disturbance. In other words, these descriptions are not proof; they are indicators. The most significant are unusual antisocial behavior, irritability, and emotional excitability.

7. Name some identifying behavioral symptoms of a drug user.

_____

_____

_____

_____

MARIHUANA

Marihuana is legally and medically classified as a narcotic. It has both sedative and stimulant characteristics and is also hallucinogenic. It is one of the oldest drugs known to humanity, having a record that dates back to 2700 B.C. Medically, marihuana has been abandoned because its effects are unpredictable, and some of its side effects sometimes become undesirable. Marihuana comes from a common weed, *Cannabis sativa*. The parts of the plant most frequently used to prepare the drug are the flowers and the tiny tender top leaves. Although *Cannabis* can be grown almost any place in the temperate zone, its potency is affected by the climate. Its quality varies according to where it has been grown. Usually, high-quality marihuana comes from plants grown under very dry conditions. Dryness causes the resin of the plant to be concentrated in the flowers and top leaves.

Marihuana is not considered addictive; it can cause dependency, however. It is a mood expander and has effects that are unpredictable and sometimes violent. It can cause distortion of one's sense of time and space. This quality has made it popular with musicians, who feel rightly or wrongly that it helps them keep rhythm. The perceptions of one using marihuana are altered, so that objects seem to change in size and relationship. Marihuana can also create delusions of strength and infallibility or power. Many times it enhances moods, making things seem tremendously funny or, at other times, depressing or frightening. It causes speech to become thick and disjointed and syllables to be slurred. Generally, marihuana alters perceptions and influences a person's judgment. Chronic users may show mental deterioration. They are usually full of grand plans that somehow never get done. Glorious ideas surge through their minds. They dismiss ordinary affairs as unworthy of consideration, compared to the mystical discoveries they are making.

8. *Describe the nature and effects of marihuana.*

_____

_____

_____

_____

THE MARIHUANA-ALCOHOL ARGUMENT

Nothing has been said about marihuana that does not apply to alcohol, and no hangover follows the use of marihuana. So why is alcohol legally sanctioned and marihuana not? Marihuana certainly is not treated like alcohol. Possession and use of marihuana are criminal offenses and can result in a significant prison sentence. In the United States, it is illegal to grow marihuana, buy it, sell it, or use it. Recently, some states have decriminalized its use. This means that these states will no longer prosecute individuals who, for example, are found to possess less than a certain amount of the drug. In essence, the states are not making the drug legal; they are merely saying that they will not punish the act of using it. In contrast, it is legal both to use and to own alcohol, provided you are of a specified age.

The arguments against marihuana are varied. A major one is that its use leads to the use of "hard" drugs. Those who argue this can point to data that show that an overwhelming majority of hard-drug users started with marihuana. To this, the proponents of marihuana reply, "Nonsense, you can make the same connection between milk and alcohol." Another argument is that the use of marihuana leads to criminality. Data can be produced to show that a high proportion of criminals are regular marihuana users. However, the data can also be analyzed to show that there is no connection between marihuana use and the crime rate.

Others argue that the person who gets the biggest charge out of marihuana is the one who should never use it. People who are psychologically inadequate are the easy prey of the weed. This argument is used to prevent drinking—or any other kind of moral temptation. Gambling, for example, is heavily controlled, partially to prevent the evil effects it may have on people. This approach, prohibiting something because it may lead to personal disaster, prompted Prohibition. Yet the country has never really recovered from the disastrous effects of that social experiment. Those favoring the legalization of marihuana therefore give the pragmatic argument that it is so widely used and so universally accepted that we are in fact repeating the Prohibition experience and will experience the same disastrous results.

It is interesting to note another similarity between alcohol and marihuana. The effect of either varies considerably with the dosage. We have actually defined a level of alcohol as intoxicating: 3.2 beer is not supposed to intoxicate; 100-proof alcohol is. The sale of the latter is restricted; that of the former is not. The same is true about grass: Some can be strong and some weak. The pure plant extract, tetrahydrocannabis, commonly known as hashish, is very powerful. As a matter of fact, the word *assassin* is derived from the word for hashish user and refers to this group's habit of becoming stoned and then going out to inflict ritual murder on the neighbors. Thus, in the case of both alcohol and grass, an argument about potency is meaningless unless the actual strength is known. To say that marihuana is harmless because it has so little effect is begging the question. The potency may have been slight.

So the argument rages. Alcohol to a large extent is legally sanctioned. It is a source of revenue for many segments of the government. It is culturally supported. Yet there are 9 million known chronic alcoholics in our society, and even more may be undiscovered.

Is marihuana dangerous to the body? This is a most intriguing question. So far, there is no evidence to show that it is, but there is no evidence to show that it is not. Its extract THC very definitely is dangerous. Alcohol, on the other hand, is very toxic when used in excess. Permanent tissue damage can occur quite early in the history of use.

Will the widespread use of marihuana ultimately result in its recognition on an "if you can't beat 'em, join 'em" basis? Will there be even more stringent efforts to eliminate its use? Will the inability to enforce laws against its use spell the doom of our legal structure and our system of government? The controversy rages; the answers are far from clear.

9. State the arguments in the alcohol-marihuana controversy.

_____

_____

_____

_____

LSD

Marihuana is an old, established drug. LSD can make no such claim. It is relatively new. It occurs naturally on rye plants and is easy to make synthetically. It was first created artificially in Switzerland by scientists searching for a cure for migraine headaches, and today it is usually produced by amateur chemists. Therefore, what is found on the market is of doubtful quality and purity. LSD is a very powerful drug; only a millionth of a gram produces remarkable effects on a user. Because of its tremendously unpredictable effects, it is not medically used except in a very limited number of research programs. LSD is a liquid with no taste, odor, or color. It is hard to identify in foods or drinks, so that they can easily be spiked without detection. It is not addictive.

LSD produces extravagant and magnificent illusions. Users feel that they have superperceptive knowledge, and their delusions seem real and mysteriously significant. All the effects of marihuana can be produced to a greater degree by LSD. It can induce satisfying perceptual distorions and frightening ones. Perceptions can be so unreal that psychosis results. LSD can also trigger latent psychosis into an active state. The effects of LSD can last for twelve or fifteen hours, weeks, or months. Sometimes flashbacks occur without warning. There is some evidence that protracted use causes chromosomal damage. There is also some disputed evidence showing that regular use causes a loss of mental effectiveness.

Like marihuana, LSD has its advocates and its critics. It has been touted as a drug that produces the most mystical and profound religious experiences. Some say that with experience users can control their delusions and avoid bad trips. Those against the drug point to the violence and unpredictability of its effects and to the deaths caused by LSD-induced psychoses. The verdict is not yet in. However, current evidence seems to indicate that you should be extremely wary about trying LSD. Mental soundness is a must in the user.

10. Describe the nature of LSD and its effects.

_____

_____

_____

_____

HEROIN

Heroin is a euphoria-producing synthetic derivative of morphine. It first appeared on the scene in 1898. It is a white powder and can be taken into the body in any number of ways. The most common way is by hypodermic. Heroin is the queen of the drugs. It is not the most powerful, but it is the most addictive. The body can build up a tolerance to heroin rather quickly. Withdrawal is not so severe as with cocaine, but it can be very unpleasant. There is no proof that heroin causes any bodily damage or brain disruption similar to that caused by alcohol.

To the drug user, heroin is the ultimate step. One evidence of its popularity is its number of nicknames. Boy, boss, caballo, doojee, H, Harry, horse, joy, powder, pack, scat, schmeck, and smack are some of the terms used to refer to it. Heroin users are the most sophisticated of the sophisticated. However, because of the body's ability to build a tolerance to the drug, users have a delicate problem of constantly balancing their state of euphoria by carefully regulating their dosage. They must try not to increase their tolerance but must also avoid withdrawal. This usually results in a treadmill situation, where the treadmill moves faster and faster until breakdown occurs.

Although some favor the legalization of LSD and marihuana, few, if any, favor the legalization of heroin in this country. In England, heroin has been made easily available through that country's program of socialized medicine. Doctors are able to prescribe it for addicts. This has seemed to lessen the amount of addiction. Also, by keeping addicts on maintenance doses, it has been possible to make them productive members of society.

Probably the most serious effect of heroin on users is helplessness. Because their habit is illegal, they can support it only at exorbitant rates. As their tolerance increases, they need more and more. Because costs grow daily, users need more and more money and must turn to theft or robbery. Thus hopelessly dependent people are driven to two crimes: the use of the drug itself and the acts they must perform to support their habit. It is estimated that heroin addicts steal about $2 billion worth of merchandise annually to support their habits.

11. Describe the nature of heroin and its effects.

_____

_____

_____

_____

DRUG-CONTROL PROGRAMS

Our society can attempt to control drug abuse in four ways: through legal channels, treatment and rehabilitation, research, and education and information.

LEGAL CONTROL

The common objective of any legal program is to control the production, distribution, and use of potentially harmful drugs. Essentially, the government attempts to protect society by restricting the availability of materials. It also monitors the purity of drugs used medically that are on the controlled list. A standardized program of testing and dosage makes possible the discovery of the effects of new chemicals before the drug is released for consumption.

Any part of a legal program must be backed by law enforcement. The illegal use or possession of drugs carries severe penalties. At this time, there is a fierce controversy raging over the legal status of users. Are they the victims of events over which they have little if any control, or are they an integral part of the drug scene? Is the pusher the real villain? Our society is ambivalent about this, and, as a result, there is ambivalence in our laws and their enforcement.

TREATMENT AND REHABILITATION

The earliest treatment received by addicts, including alcoholics, was punitive. A strong residual attitude in our society still supports this method. More recently, however, we have begun to regard the addict as a sick person and, as a consequence, we have increasingly emphasized rehabilitation. Increased knowledge of the uses of group therapy and its apparent effectiveness have led to the establishment of halfway houses, where drug dependents can interact socially in a limited way until they are ready to enter society again.

Another method of treatment is to replace one drug with another, less dangerous one. The methadone treatment of heroin dependence is a good example. It requires that the heroin user obtain methadone on a regular schedule. Methadone itself is addictive, but it causes the body to cease tolerating heroin. Methadone blocks the craving for heroin and also blocks any highs produced by it. It causes a less severe emotional reaction, so that a person who is on methadone can be a full-time member of society, but a heroin addict cannot. Some new drugs now under investigation may remove one of the main objections to methadone: its own addictive powers. Should these new drugs prove effective, some of the stigma of methadone treatment may be removed, or methadone may be completely replaced.

A third method of treatment is to classify drug users as a medical problem and to place them under medical supervision. This system gives addicts their supply under a medically controlled dosage. The beneficial effects are to remove the criminal element of the problem and to guarantee that addicts will always have a source of the drug that is pure enough to alleviate danger from overdose or impurities. The decriminalization of drugs does have certain attractive elements. However, it has not worked out that well in Great Britain. There, addicts have continued to buy additional supplies on the street, and rehabilitation has not been too effective. Generally speaking, this method of dealing with the problem has helped some people hold on to their social status and their ability to work. However, the whole program is currently under fire as being too expensive and ineffective.

RESEARCH

Accurate information on drugs is sadly lacking. Much more information is needed to blow away the emotional smoke. Are marihuana and LSD physiologically dangerous? Does the use of one drug lead to the use of others? What are the factors involved in drug use? In drug treatment? We, as a society, have been caught off base. Most people have a deep-seated fear and aversion to drug abuse, even though they themselves may be heavy drug users. Intuitively, most people think that the drug road leads to destruction. Consequently, they react emotionally against drugs. Proponents of drug use are just as adamant in their favor. The trouble at this time is that nobody really knows what it's all about. We need more facts. Unfortunately, research takes time.

EDUCATION AND INFORMATION

Society has undertaken a massive educational campaign to inform its members, particularly the young, about drugs. Speaker after speaker has appeared at schools, public forums, and meetings. Spot radio announcements, TV programs, and other techniques of propaganda have been focused on this subject. Reformed drug addicts appearing as expert speakers have played a major part in this effort. Newspapers have also participated freely in the campaign.

12. *Describe current programs for the control of drug abuse.*

_____

_____

_____

_____

AN EVALUATION OF DRUG-ABUSE PROGRAMS

Legal enforcement of existing drug-abuse laws appears to be ineffective. Drugs are small in volume and easy to hide. Their enormous value makes the gamble of detection worthwhile for many. Therefore, drugs are sold almost everywhere. The problem is aggravated by the ambivalence many people feel about the necessity of restricting the use of drugs such as marihuana. How easy would it be for you to buy drugs where you are? Would you be able to get what you wanted if price were not a factor? Probably so.

Since enforcement doesn't seem to be an effective way of controlling the illegal drug traffic, what about the treatment of the dependent person? If we can make it easier to rehabilitate the user, is this an answer to the drug problem? In many respects, this is a barn-door approach. The process should be preventive rather than curative.

It would seem that education and the giving of information are the programs that offer the most potential. However, some serious questions exist about the effectiveness of current programs. Most educational programs are based on a fear-arousal technique. Yet we know that this device is ineffective in changing people's attitudes; it hasn't persuaded people not to use alcohol, nor is it preventing the use of tobacco now. The same results may be predicted with other drugs.

There is little that can be said about research, because the facts are not in yet. However, we can point out that any facts discovered about drugs may merely be used to reinforce fear-arousal techniques and will consequently prove to be of little value.

Do you disagree with this appraisal of drug-abuse programs?

13. Evaluate current programs for the control of drug abuse.

_____

_____

_____

_____

ALTERNATIVE PROGRAMS

Obviously, a better system of rehabilitation for all drug-dependent people is needed. At the present time, the programs that are available are expensive, unwieldy, and largely untested. From England's experience of keeping heroin dependents on sustaining doses without increasing the number of addicts, we might think that the best program is one that provides supervised doses of good heroin as needed. Perhaps such a program would alleviate the compulsion to steal and the helplessness of the dependent. In any case, a heroin maintenance center should be established to see what does happen.

As was stated earlier, it is too early to tell whether effective replacements for methadone exist. If they do, then they should be explored as a way to counteract the effects of heroin. However, maintaining a habit ignores the problem and does not really solve it. A far better solution involves preventing a person from getting hooked at all.

By far the greatest change that needs to occur is a change in attitude. The social reinforcement presently offered by society to some aspects of drug use must stop. Emphasis should be placed on the strength of the person who doesn't need a pill to be a better person. If we can educate people to think of drug users as sick people, much of the social pressure for using drugs will be negated. Kids who smoke, thinking that this makes them adult, need to learn that they are even more juvenile than they think they are. How many people would smoke if others thought them weak minded because they had to rely on a weed for comfort? How many would drink if they were pitied for needing chemical support to interact with others? "Who needs drugs?" is a theme that should be taught to all, but especially to the younger generation. We should convince them that this behavior shows immaturity, not the maturity they are trying to grasp.

The treatment of dependents should also be based on the recognition that their dependency is an illness rather than a crime. Pity, not revenge, should be the reason for treatment. Today, no treatment has been proved best. However, one truism exists: Addicts will not be cured until they want to be. Society must convince them that they want to rid themselves of dependence. The easiest way to do this is to meet them with pity, not adulation.

The issue of drugs is a symptom of a deeper disease in society—the inability to interact with people. To counteract this disease, we need more intensive training in developing interpersonal relationships so that we have the knowledge and skills to interact in people-to-people activities. We need to be taught how to attend to our personal inadequacies and not hide them behind a screen of distortions and delusions. One alternative available to those looking for mind expansion and mystical significance is something that the Western world has ignored and the Eastern world has explored assiduously: the process of mind control and meditation. This process offers alternatives for those who seek mysticism but do not wish to blow their minds.

End of sermon.

14. Suggest alternative programs for the control of drug abuse.

_____

_____

_____

_____

A PERSONAL EVALUATION

Where do you stand on this whole drug business? It may help you to understand your reactions to the unit if you look at all your attitudes simultaneously. These questions are to help you do that. Check the appropriate answer.

1. How frequently do you use:	*Often*	*Sometimes*	*Never*
Coffee	____	____	____
Tobacco	____	____	____

	Often	Sometimes	Never
Marihuana	——	——	——
Tranquilizers	——	——	——
Aspirin	——	——	——
Amphetamines	——	——	——
Barbiturates	——	——	——
Alcohol	——	——	——
LSD	——	——	——
Heroin	——	——	——
Cocaine	——	——	——
Mescaline	——	——	——

2. What control should be applied to:

	Completely banned	Medically prescribed	Easily available
Coffee	——	——	——
Tobacco	——	——	——
Marihuana	——	——	——
Tranquilizers	——	——	——
Aspirin	——	——	——
Amphetamines	——	——	——
Barbiturates	——	——	——
Alcohol	——	——	——
LSD	——	——	——
Heroin	——	——	——
Cocaine	——	——	——
Mescaline	——	——	——

3. If the use of drugs is to be legally regulated, what should happen to people who violate the law?

_____ Punish users in accordance with current laws.

_____ Pass new laws with stricter penalties, and punish users in accordance with them.

_____ Give users medical assistance.

_____ Do nothing to users.

4. What should happen to people who sell drugs illegally?

_____ Punish pushers in accordance with current laws.

_____ Pass new laws with stricter penalties, and punish pushers in accordance with them.

_____ Pass new laws with milder penalties, and punish pushers in accordance with them.

_____ Do nothing to pushers.

On a separate sheet of paper, summarize what you have indicated in your answers to these four questions. Give reasons for your answers. In other words, justify yourself, giving some background on why you answered as you did.

15. *Consider your own position on drugs.*

_____

_____

_____

_____

□ A POINT OF VIEW

There is no lack of printed material on drugs. You'll find articles in popular magazines and technical reports in scientific journals of research efforts that have begun to bear fruit. A lot of information appears in publications of federal government agencies, such as the National Institute for Mental Health, and in state-issued resource guides. Oakley S. Ray's *Drugs, Society and Human Behavior*, (St. Louis: Mosby, 1972) is worthwhile reading. For more recent information on the marihuana issue, see the January 1978 issue of *Human Behavior*, which contains an article by Robert Carr entitled "Update: What Marihuana Does and Doesn't Do." The following article on alcohol by Rose De Wolf shows the dilemma we are in as we try to deal with an extremely potent drug that is both legally and socially sanctioned.

ROSE DE WOLF

SKOAL, PROSIT, DOWN THE HATCH, AND HERE'S MUD IN YOUR EYE

Americans have very mixed emotions about booze. You ask the average American what he (or she) thinks of it and he'll say: "terrible stuff" and proceed to drink it anyway.

Americans don't know what to do about booze. All the states, for example, have laws designed to promote "temperance." In some states, any place dispensing alcohol must have curtains in the windows. Presumably, that is so any right-thinking, non-drinking citizen walking by won't be exposed to the evil within and led to temptation. And, in some states, any place dispensing alcohol may not have curtains in the windows. Presumably, that is so those who have strayed from the path of righteousness will be exposed and shamed before their neighbors.

Similarly, some states require food to be served in bars and others prohibit food being served in bars. Which law better serves the cause of temperance?

In the opinion of Mark Keller, neither one.

Keller claims that most of our laws and beliefs about drinking are rooted in cultural and religious attitudes that are not necessarily related to known, scientific facts.

Actually, despite the fact that man has been drinking ever since some early caveman got a glow from some fermented berry juice he found, there has been amazingly little effort expended to get any scientific facts about the stuff.

"What we have," says Keller, "are just a series of compromises between the wets and the drys. Thirty percent of Americans are teetotalers and and that's not an insignificant influence. It isn't enough to bring about Prohibition but it brings about a little prohibition here and there. Liquor can't be sold on Sunday or to persons under a certain age or near a church or a school. We pass all kinds of rules and regulations about the way liquor is sold or the way liquor is advertised to give the impression that we are discouraging liquor consumption."

Most of these compromises, it seems, have little basis in any real scientific knowledge of alcohol and that's where the Rutgers Center of Alcohol Studies at New Brunswick, N.J. comes in. The center was founded at Yale University in the 1940s and moved to Rutgers, the State University of New Jersey, in 1962.

The center studies alcohol in many ways—its chemistry, its sociology, its physiological implications, public health implications. It has on its staff of 35, anthropologists as well as physiologists. It contains one of the world's largest libraries of alcohol research and it publishes the respected "Quarterly Journal of Studies on Alcohol." Mark Keller is the journal's editor.

The center is neither wet nor dry. It pushes no points of view, it merely investigates them. Its researches indicate that alcohol can at times be very beneficial, most of the time is not harmful,

Reprinted by permission of *The Evening and Sunday Bulletin*. From *Discover Magazine* of the *Philadelphia Evening and Sunday Bulletin*, October 28, 1973.

and yet sometimes is totally disastrous. How should society view alcohol, regulate alcohol, drink alcohol? The center's answer is that we'll know better if we first know more about alcohol.

"What little we know indicates that our advertising policies about liquor, for example, are ridiculous," says Keller. "The Joint Committee of the States to Study Alcoholic Beverage Laws found that a distiller developing a nationwide newspaper advertising campaign would have to make as many as 20 changes in copy and illustrations to comply with the different requirements of state agencies.

"After designing an ad which is generally acceptable, it may then become necessary to eliminate the portrayal of a woman . . . eliminate a picture of a large animal . . . eliminate a picture of a small animal . . . delete a reference to a holiday . . . eliminate a recipe . . . or delete a reference to a known personality . . . all in different states."

Why all the nit-picking? Says Keller: "It is all because of a widespread belief that advertising lures people to drink. There is plenty of evidence that advertising may convince drinkers to switch from one brand to another, but not that it convinces them to drink in the first place. There were, of course, plenty of hard drinkers long before the age of advertising, including Lot and Noah of Biblical fame. Russia has hordes of problem drinkers and yet there hasn't been an ad for vodka in Russia for 50 years."

One of the projects the center felt compelled to do was to find out just what were the habits of Americans when it came to drinking? And, as might be expected, it found that the facts did not necessarily coincide with popular belief.

For example . . . who would you suppose drinks more: the prosperous or the poor? Well, despite the generally bad press given the poor, their taprooms, their occasional skid-row representatives and the like, they don't hold a candle to the more affluent when it comes to drinking. According to the center's study, 80 percent of prosperous (more than $15,000 per annum)

citizens drink, 70 percent of average income, only 48 percent of the poor.

Here's some more "alcoholiana," courtesy of the center's researchers:

The percentage of drinkers in the U.S. adult population is 68 percent (77 percent men, 60 percent women). The percentage of drinkers is highest at ages 21 to 39 and then declines. The word drinkers can mean anybody who takes one drink a year to somebody who takes one drink an hour. About 12 percent of drinkers are considered heavy (a few a day) drinkers, 13 percent are moderate, 28 percent light, and 15 percent in the one or two drinks a year category.

The percentage of drinkers in the Middle Atlantic states—like Pennsylvania and New Jersey—far exceeds the national average (as you might guess from social experience.) Indeed, the Middle Atlantic states have the largest proportion of drinkers—83 percent. The New England states are second, the West Coast third. The non-drinkers dwell largely in the South and Southwest—that area known as the Bible Belt.

The young, the economically advantaged, the suburbanite, the more-educated, the religiously liberal are more frequently drinkers and these folks are likely to be found in these parts.

As the nation becomes increasingly suburban, better-educated, etc. it seems likely that drinking will increase. And it has increased in the past years.

There is little difference in the drinking habits between black and white men but black women tend to have larger percentages of both abstainers and heavy drinkers than white women. Cultural and ethnic backgrounds seem to have more bearing than race.

For example, researchers found that Italians in Italy and first generation Italians in America drink a lot but rarely become problem drinkers. That's because it is an Italian custom to drink wine with meals. However, second and third generation who have become Americanized are more likely to develop drinking problems. Why? Because, they retain the family custom of wine and also adopt the American custom of highballs. The result is that they drink more.

Among religions, Protestants drink least—mainly due to the conservative Protestant sects which frown on drinking completely.

Beer is easily the most popular booze. The consumption of beer among Americans aged 15 and over was 25.90 gallons per capita in 1971 (the most recent available figures). The per capita consumption of spirits was 2.62 gallons and wine, 2.08 gallons. Once again, contrary to popular belief, beer is an upper class drink as well as a working class drink.

Although alcoholics are a major health problem in the U.S., they are by far a minority of drinkers . . . even of heavy drinkers. There are 98 million drinkers in the U.S. and about 5.5 million of them are alcoholics. (Five men to one woman.)

"There is another widespread—but wrong—belief" says Keller, "that if you make liquor harder to get, you will decrease the number of alcoholics. You may decrease the number of drinks the moderate drinker gets—but not the alcoholic. The person who needs to drink will find a way to get one. Dry states have the same percentage of problem drinkers as wet ones. If 90 percent of liquor consumers in the U.S. cut their drinking to birthdays and holidays, it would reduce the amount of liquor consumed and probably bankrupt a lot of the liquor industry, but it wouldn't reduce a single alcohol problem.

"Another theory is that pricing policies should be used to influence consumers to buy weaker beverages—beer and wine. As if serious drinkers wouldn't still consume enough of whatever they could get to cause the same kind of problems.

"We have yet to learn," concedes Keller, "what does work with problem drinkers—we only know that much of what we do doesn't work."

With such statements, Keller sounds like a flack for the liquor industry. And one might be suspicious that the center is financed by same. It's not true. The center does not get a dime from the liquor giants—something Keller thinks is wrong.

"They should help finance studies into alcohol." he says. "But they are ostriches with their heads in the sand. They don't want to acknowledge that problems exist. They feel that donations will be looked upon as guilt money."

However, the fact that the liquor industry is not financing the studies does lend more credence to results that seem to favor alcohol. For example, in one study, 72 medical students were given complex problems to solve first without any alcohol and then with varying amounts. It turned out that the students did better after a couple of drinks (the equivalent of two ounces for a 150 pound man) than totally sober. However, after four ounces, they did only as well as they did sober and after six ounces, they did far worse.

Alcohol does relax people and that has its good points and its bad ones. Keller calls it the great facilitator . . . a little of it can help you be more the way you want to be . . . by releasing your inhibitions.

With a couple of drinks a shy fellow can be a bit bolder . . . an anxious man more content. On the other hand, alcohol also tends to release some of our nastier tendencies, too.

"We accept the idea that a man is not totally himself after imbibing," says Keller. "And therefore a man feels free to let loose a part of him that he normally keeps under wraps. A very nice person may have the wish to be aggressive, even nasty at times, and a few drinks permit him to be so. A withdrawn person may become the life of the party . . . at least in his own mind . . . if not to the rest of those at the party. Some people get violent. That seems to go against logic since alcohol is a depressant which makes most people quieter. Yet, if violent tendencies are what you've been holding back, a relaxing drink . . . or five . . . can open the gates."

It would be impossible to recite all the studies that the center has done . . . or hopes to do. Twenty years ago, it studied the drinking habits of 17,000 college students across the country. And some of the researchers then thought they had clues as to which of those students might become problem drinkers later on. They'd love to go back and find those students—now around 40 years of age—to see if those clues really did mean anything. All they need is a quarter of a million dollars and they'll do it.

They are now working on a study of the effect of alcohol combined with other drugs. People today take all kinds of things—tranquilizers and such—and continue to drink. The results are wildly varied.

A past study gives some idea of what it is in booze that leads to hang-over . . . and it isn't necessarily the alcohol. The popular brands of bourbon and vodka may not differ that much in alcohol, but bourbon gives a whale of a hang-over and vodka gives none at all. Why? One probability is that bourbon contains a lot of congeners—those are chemicals absorbed in the distilling process—and vodka contains none. Another study showed that bourbon drinkers take more risks than vodka drinkers—a trait also laid to congeners rather than alcohol.

The center also does historical studies such as one of drinking on the American frontier. Most people get their idea of that from movies and television which indicate that the saloons of the period were frequently the scenes of swinging, slinging, bottle-breaking, drunken brawls. The best research indicates that's exactly how it was.

You know that popular slogan: If you drink, don't drive. It's totally useless, says Dr. Leon Greenberg, director of laboratory research. That's because people do drink and drive and since very few ever get in trouble because of it, most people are bound to ignore the slogan.

What drinkers need to know, he adds, is not a simplistic slogan, but a realistic idea of when they've had too much. After all, of what use would speed limits be if cars had no speedometers? The law says you are drunk if you have .05 alcohol in your blood. Do you know when you'd reach that point?

Assume a couple goes to a party that lasts four hours. He weighs 190 pounds and drinks four martinis. She weighs 120 pounds and only drinks three martinis. Which one should drive the car home? Answer: he should. It isn't the number of drinks you have—but the relationship between that and the kind of drink, the hours of drinking, and your body weight. He'd have .04 alcohol in his blood—she'd have .06.

Dr. Greenberg developed a slide-rule device that figures everything out for you—he'd like to see them come as standard equipment in every motorist's glove compartment.

In the course of their researches, the scientists at Rutgers use humans more than animals . . . they throw a lot of parties . . . and they don't have trouble getting volunteers.

UNIT 13

THE DYNAMICS
OF PREJUDICE

☐ You have probably noticed that this unit's title mentions prejudice and not racism. This is because racism is but a narrow example of prejudice. We prejudge people on the basis of the way they dress, their gender, the way they speak, the part of the country they come from. We have prejudices about ideas and material objects as well as about human beings. Looking at the topic merely from a racial viewpoint would tend to give you tunnel vision. The aim of this unit is to let you understand the dynamics of prejudice, so that when you find yourself automatically assuming something you'll stop and think.

When you have completed this unit, you should be able to:

1. *State and analyze your feelings about minority and ethnic groups.*
2. *Define* ethnic prejudice.
3. *Explain why human beings tend to be prejudiced.*
4. *Differentiate between prejudice and discrimination, and give an example of each.*
5. *Describe the process by which discrimination is continued, and identify the factors that are responsible for its continuation.*
6. *Name and describe the operation of individual psychological processes that are involved in discrimination.*
7. *Describe some ways of showing prejudice.*
8. *Describe the prejudiced person.*
9. *State some of the effects of prejudice on the black victim group.*
10. *Compare the reactions of blacks to those of other ethnic victim groups.*
11. *Criticize the notion that contact among members of power groups and victim groups will reduce prejudice.*
12. *Evaluate educational approaches to reducing prejudice.*
13. *Evaluate legal approaches to reducing prejudice.*
14. *Describe the effects of the mass media on prejudice.*
15. *Prepare a program for reducing prejudice in your own environment.*

EXERCISE 1. EXPOSING YOUR PREJUDICE

In the list that follows are descriptions of human behavior and temperament. However, because of our tendency to use stereotypes, the listed characteristics may seem to apply more to one group than to another. After the descriptions is a list of groups who are the targets of stereotyping in America. You should note in passing that some stereotypes are favorable and others unfavorable, depending on the point of view of the observer. All, however, are equally in error because they always involve <u>false generalization.</u>

In the space following the name of each group, write the numbers of the characteristics that you automatically associate with it.

1. persistent	5. mercenary	9. ambitious
2. deceitful	6. industrious	10. devoted to family
3. flighty	7. intelligent	11. argumentative
4. shrewd	8. grasping	12. mechanically inclined

13. brave
14. efficient
15. snobbish
16. materialistic
17. calm
18. pleasure loving
19. cold
20. patriotic
21. impractical
22. talkative
23. pushy
24. clannish

25. covetous
26. underhanded
27. uncouth
28. tradition loving
29. loud
30. sensual
31. lazy
32. very religious
33. superstitious
34. ignorant
35. musical
36. ostentatious

37. unreliable
38. violent
39. artistic
40. passionate
41. not very strong
42. imaginative
43. affectionate
44. patient
45. physically dirty
46. methodical
47. good humored
48. courteous

Afro-Americans _____

_____

Chinese _____

_____

Italians _____

_____

Jews _____

_____

Mexican Americans _____

_____

Puerto Ricans _____

_____

WASPs _____

_____

Women _____

_____

On a separate piece of paper, write a paragraph describing the three groups to which you attributed the most characteristics. Then summarize your position. Would you say that you hold feelings of prejudice toward certain groups?

1. State and analyze your feelings about minority and ethnic groups.

_____

_____

_____

_____

DEFINING ETHNIC PREJUDICE

We all generalize about people. We think librarians tend to be prim and reserved, used-car dealers untrustworthy, upper-class Bostonians proper. Such generalizations are stereotypes—descriptions considered applicable to all members of a group. The unthinking, strict acceptance of stereotypes results in oversimplifications and unfair assumptions. Have all the librarians you've come into contact with really been prim? Rigid belief in stereotypes about people produces prejudice—preconceived (often negative) ideas, perhaps with no rational basis.

What you have done in Exercise 1 is to reveal your feelings about certain groups in our society. Look at your lists of numbers. Have you characterized some groups in mostly hostile and negative terms? Such descriptions are an important component of ethnic prejudice. Another important part is the reason for your characterizations. Are they based on fact? Have you ever had any dealings with individual members of the groups you described? If you have not, on what basis did you attribute characteristics to the group as a whole? Were you thoughtlessly applying stereotypes?

2. Define ethnic prejudice.

_____

_____

_____

_____

PSYCHOLOGICAL BASES FOR PREJUDICE

Where do your negative or hostile feelings come from? Is there some sort of evil chemistry within you that makes you prejudice and give in to prejudice? The answer is no. We all have a natural tendency to generalize, to sort and classify. Indeed, Jean Piaget has identified one stage of mental growth as the period during which we develop our minds in precisely this way. Nothing says that we must always be right when we generalize, nor must we be morally or socially in step. It is as possible for us to make up bad generalizations and categories as it is for us to form good ones.

The dynamics of how we arrive at generalizations, prejudgments, and prejudices are fairly straightforward. Having logical minds, we tend to sort impressions and experiences and file similar ones together. Labels and categories guide our cognitive processes. We solve many of the problems that face us by searching in our memory bank for just such similarities, labels, and categories. Without these aids, we would have to tackle each problem as a completely new incident. In effect, if we were not able to form general impressions, we would never learn. This is why we categorize.

Most of the time, the things we file in our minds tend to stay there. We usually resist changing concepts quickly and will admit exceptions rather than change our overall idea. (All Poles are quick tempered and dumb. Here is John, who is even tempered and smart. He is not a typical Pole). We can become so stubborn about changing our categories and attitudes that we distort information instead of changing our beliefs. This is especially true if our ideas are based on a small piece of truth.

One of our common tendencies is to blame our problems and ills on other people. We will blame groups of which we are not members—a typical "out-group" technique. In this way, we can focus on someone else our emotions resulting from frustration and conflict. Another tendency is to adopt an all-or-none approach. We think people and groups are all good or all bad. Rarely do we categorize people into groups with conflicting attributes. For example, we may think the English are sophisticated, tradition loving, and courteous; yet we may immediately block the favorable connotations of these traits by emphasizing British snobbishness, conservatism, and reserve.

We tend to assign people to "out-groups"—distinguishing between "us" and "them"—and then value them on the basis of this membership.

EXERCISE 2. VALUING OUT-GROUPS

1. In the first column of blanks, list some of the groups that you belong to.
2. In the second column, list groups that you feel are in some way opposed to those in the first. The opposing groups may differ from yours in belief, power, status, purpose, or in other ways.
3. Assign every group in the second column a positive or negative (plus or minus) rating, depending on how you feel about it.

1. _____   _____

2. _____   _____

3. _____   _____

4. _____   _____

5. _____   _____

Do your negatives outnumber the positives? They probably do. We naturally assign positive values to our own groups and negative ones to the opposition. If we did not, we would be forced to face a great deal of conflict within ourselves, because we would feel that we did not belong to the best groups.

To what extent can in-groups and out-groups get along? One major factor is relative power. Power will determine a group's status and its attitude toward another group. A second factor involves the nature of the interactions between groups. The attitudes of two groups that have common goals and are in fundamental agreement will be far different from those whose goals conflict. Another factor is centrality—the proximity of the out-groups and the depth of our feelings about whatever conflicts exist. We might feel mildly disturbed about a tribe that kills its physical misfits, but we would probably become highly antagonistic toward a group advocating that practice in our community. It all depends on whose ox is being gored. It does seem, however, that a natural state of competition exists among groups. If so, can the vision of a classless society with no competition among groups be realistic? Can struggles among groups ever be eliminated?

3. *Explain why human beings tend to be prejudiced.*

_____

_____

_____

_____

PREJUDICE AND DISCRIMINATION

Many pioneers had a deep and abiding hatred of all Indians. They were considered to be brutal murderers with no compassion or capacity for humane feeling; they seemed methodical, cruel, and unemotional and appeared to have no regard for the dignity of human (that is, white) life.

Obviously, those pioneers were prejudiced. Were they discriminatory? Is discrimination a fundamental part of prejudice? Not necessarily. It is possible to be deeply prejudiced and yet not discriminate in our treatment of others at all. Granted, the odds are against this, but it is possible.

Discrimination is different from prejudice because it is an act rather than just a feeling. Look back at the characteristics of ethnic groups that you listed. This list reveals how you feel about some groups. But have you ever knowingly done anything against a member of one of those groups? Discrimination involves actual differential treatment of someone because he or she is a member of a group. That person must be denied a privilege or a right that is granted to people who do not belong to that group.

Can you give some examples of discriminatory acts against yourself? If so, write them down here. Just as a starter, have you ever been denied something because it is not considered appropriate for your sex?

_____

_____

_____

_____

4. *Differentiate between prejudice and discrimination, and give an example of each.*

_____

_____

_____

_____

THE PERSISTENCE OF DISCRIMINATION

What is so disturbing about discrimination is its persistence. Once discriminatory practices begin, they seem to last forever. When ways of behaving get established in a group, they are hard to change. Often, groups are physically separated—segregated; environment may perpetuate group differences. Members of the in-group maintain their attitudes by the processes of group dynamics, which you have already studied. Group dynamics work to force members to discriminate, enforcing conformity to the group's attitudes and actions. The group rewards discriminatory acts and punishes those that are not. Also, the existence of prejudice and acts of discrimination serves as a basis for group interaction. Such behavior pulls the group together in a common cause. Of course, group leadership must actively support these attitudes. Usually, those most strongly dedicated to the group's attitudes are most likely to rise to leadership positions.

5. *Describe the process by which discrimination is continued, and identify the factors that are responsible for its continuation.*

_____

_____

_____

_____

PERSONAL PSYCHOLOGICAL BASES FOR DISCRIMINATION

It isn't fair to blame discrimination completely on the group, although it may be convenient for us to do so, because we can then say, "What can I do? I'm helpless." However, this reason is something of a copout. Personal factors also apply to the process of discrimination. One such factor has already been briefly mentioned: our tendency to turn on others aggressive feelings produced by our own frustration and conflict. Many times we cannot directly attack the things that are responsible for our frustration; they are simply too powerful. Instead, we find someone weaker than we are and turn our anger on that person. This behavior is called scapegoating. We scapegoat when we find someone with less power than we have and discriminate against that individual to relieve our own feelings. Of course, doing this does not solve our own problems; our frustration is not removed. The hostility we feel and act out continues.

Scapegoating is likely to occur when we feel threatened by a specific minority group. In many cases, the threat is economic. One working group feels it might be displaced by another. The typical "rednecks" who would use force to prevent desegregation are not members of the upper or middle classes. They themselves are low in the white class structure and stand in great danger of being replaced by another group.

People of a certain personality type are prone to have prejudices and to practice discrimination. Experiments have shown that individuals who are less able to tolerate confusing or ambiguous situations are most likely to be highly prejudiced. Apparently, prejudice removes ambiguity for them. It puts things either into a good or into a bad category.

Another personality need is the urge to satisfy an inferiority complex. If people feel inadequate and have the power to compensate for their feelings, they may resort to discrimination and scapegoating to relieve their feelings.

We all need consistency and balance. Regardless of where and how our attitudes originated, we go to great lengths to keep them intact. We need to keep our emotions, our conscious beliefs, and our actions toward specific people consistent.

6. *Name and describe the operation of individual psychological processes that are involved in discrimination.*

_____

_____

_____

_____

DISCRIMINATORY ACTIONS

We have already learned the causes of discrimination and factors involved in it, but we still haven't studied how discrimination is practiced. The United Nations has prepared a list of areas of life in which discrimination is practiced in various parts of the world:

1. Recognition before the law
2. Personal security (interference, arrest, disparagement because of group membership)
3. Freedom of movement and residence
4. Protection of freedom of thought, conscience, religion, enjoyment of free communication
5. Right to peaceful association
6. Treatment of those born out of wedlock
7. Right to marry and found a family
8. Free choice of employment
9. Regulation and treatment of ownership
10. Regulation and protection of authorship
11. Opportunity for education or the development of ability or talent
12. Opportunity for sharing the benefits of culture
13. Services rendered (health, protection, recreational facilities, housing)
14. Right to participate in government
15. Access to public office
16. Forced labor, slavery, special taxes, forced wearing of distinguishing insignia, and public libel of groups

These are public attitudes and actions. A similar list of private types of discrimination would be so long that it would be difficult to prepare. However, some principal forms of private discrimination occur in segregation, employment practices, membership regulations, promotions, treatment by the news media, enrollment practices, trade-union membership, housing, education . . . . The list could go on and on.

Another method of showing prejudice involves violence or actual physical attack. This method is the culmination of the two milder forms of prejudice: verbal hostility and discrimination. There is a progression from words to acts to violence. The Third Reich is a good example of this progression in action. First, Hitler spoke against the Jews. Then the nation discriminated against them by taking their property. Finally, it acted, exterminating millions.

If violence happens, you can be sure that the target group has been extensively prejudged. A long verbal campaign has occurred. Discriminatory acts have become normal and can be justified. Often the target group has been able to exert some sort of pressure that threatens the power group. As pressure builds, members of the power group experience a greater and greater sense of frustation, which makes them think in extremes. Discontent catalyzes words to action. If one person takes individual action, he or she reinforces the sentiments of the group, which in turn reinforces the person. Finally, some incident takes place that causes the power group to take action as a unit. Once action starts, if feeds upon itself.

A scene that can be found all over the world. (Struan Robertson/Magnum Photos)

Can you trace the troubles in Northern Ireland through this progression? It is a classic example of the progression from verbal attack, through discrimination, to violence.

7. *Describe some ways of showing prejudice.*

_____

_____

_____

_____

CHARACTERISTICS OF PREJUDICED PERSONS

You have seen that personality structure and personality needs are factors in the problem of prejudice. It should come as no surprise to you that some people are more prejudiced than others are. You may be surprised to learn, however, that people who display a considerable amount of prejudice have similar characteristics.

EXERCISE 3.   PERSONALITY INVENTORY

Fill in the blank with the letter of the response that best expresses your viewpoint.

_____   1. We need more discipline in this country.
          (a.) Yes
          b. No
_____   2. Our society should have a firm social structure, with people in command at various levels.
          (a.) Yes
          b. No
_____   3. Of these two groups, I empathize more with
          a. Napoleon and Patton
          (b.) Einstein and Lincoln
_____   4. The world is a dangerous place because people are basically evil and to be feared.
          (a.) Yes
          b. No
_____   5. Of these two types of criminal, the more fearsome is the
          (a.) Swindler
          b. Gangster
_____   6. What America needs is a strong leader.
          a. Yes
          (b.) No
_____   7. Teachers should tell students what to do and should not worry about what they want.
          (a.) Yes
          b. No
_____   8. I like to be told what to do.
          (a.) Yes
          b. No

_____   9. My parents were very strict with me.
             a. Yes
             b. No
_____   10. Law and order are what this country needs.
             a. Yes
             b. No
_____   11. Followers who disagree should
             a. Resign
             b. Rebel

If most of your answers are *a*'s, you have indicated that you have some of the feelings and beliefs of an authoritarian person. You dislike ambiguity and want things to be clearly one way or the other. You favor a hierarchy of power, with well-defined roles for people at each level. Authoritarian people are usually most intolerant of individuals whom they think are deviating from norms. Of course, the norms they use are those of the groups to which they themselves belong. In addition, they may be prejudiced against all ethnic groups (except the one they belong to), not just against one.

The beliefs and ideas of an authoritarian person are rigid. Once attitudes have been created, stereotypes drawn, and emotions raised, an authoritarian individual finds it extremely difficult to change them. Are you authoritarian? If so, you will probably have trouble admitting it, even to yourself. Remember, however, that your answers to the questions in Exercise 3 are not conclusive, but merely indicative.

8. Describe the prejudiced person.

_____

_____

_____

_____

REACTIONS TO PREJUDICE

Ethnic groups in America have experienced various kinds of prejudice and have reacted to it in different ways. Probably the most visible and most publicized reactions have been those of blacks. They have done what other minority groups failed to do—make Americans aware of their prejudice.

How has prejudice affected blacks? Some have disparaged or tried to ignore their blackness. Light-skinned individuals have had higher status than darker-skinned individuals, and some have adopted the standards of whites, the holders of power in American society. People who align themselves with a powerful group and in effect put themselves at odds with members of what ordinarily would be their own group are said to belong to an avoidance group. Today, the black avoidance group makes up a large portion of the black middle class. Most members are in business and the professions. They tend not to feel a common cause with the black community because in a sense they have moved away from it.

There is also an acceptance group, called Uncle Toms by black militants. These people believe that the domination of the power group is inevitable and to some extent right. They are subservient to the white world.

A third group of blacks is made up of the militants. They are proud of the black race and unwilling to accept white standards. These are the people who feel frustration and react to it aggressively. Some condone violence; others are nonviolent. Both groups, however, emphasize and develop the theme that black is beautiful.

9. State some of the effects of prejudice on the black victim group.

_____

_____

_____

_____

REACTIONS OF OTHER GROUPS TO PREJUDICE

Groups such as the Irish and the Italians arrived in America and were assimilated before civil rights and civil disobedience became rallying cries of prejudice fighters. The civil-rights movement developed around blacks but has had an impact on Americans' attitudes toward other minority groups. Early immigrant groups did not benefit from a well-organized civil-rights movement. Neither were they confronted by a labor market as restricted as the one facing minorities today.

Think of some of the other ethnic groups in this country—Irish, Italians, Mexican Americans, Puerto Ricans. Have their reactions to prejudice been similar to those of the blacks? In many ways they have been. However, other groups for the most part did not resort to violence. No aggressive subgroups evolved from their ranks. It is always dangerous to generalize, but it seems safe to say that nonblack minorities have had less trouble getting along with and being accepted by the white power group. They were not forcibly enslaved and brought to America; they did not have to struggle to define their cultural past and to develop ethnic pride and a sense of belonging to American life. It will be interesting to see how the most recently arrived groups—Puerto Ricans on the East Coast and Mexican Americans on the West Coast—become assimilated.

Like blacks, some members of these groups are identifiable by their physical appearance.

10. Compare the reactions of blacks to those of other ethnic victim groups.

_____

_____

_____

_____

THE EFFECTS OF DIRECT CONTACT

Will contact among members of the power group and the victim group reduce prejudice? If the members of diverse groups get a chance to know each other, will they become aware of the limitations of stereotypes and work to eliminate their prejudices? Not too long ago, a school board in a racially mixed school system where there had been much racial tension tried out this theory. A series of meetings with parents from both groups was scheduled in the hope that, when parents sat down and talked out their problems, tensions would dissolve. However, tensions were not reduced. The two groups became even more polarized.

The reasons for the failure are rather intricate. When two groups are brought together to interact but their status and roles are left unchanged, there will be little if any attitude change. In our example, each group saw the other as a threat before contact was made, and that view persisted at the meetings. Furthermore, the groups shared no perceived common goal. Each blamed the other for the problem. If the two groups had been placed on an equal footing, some blending might have occurred. However, in this case, the parents, though ostensibly equal, carried their social positions in the community into the meetings, and as a result the members of the discussion groups perceived an inequality.

Studies have shown that white workers whose jobs carry status equal to those of blacks have become less prejudiced in their work situations. However, these attitudes have not spread to such areas as housing and recreation.

If common contact will correct nothing except attitudes of equals in special situations, will a recognition of common fate and shared goals have any effect? In other words, if groups can be made to cooperate instead of compete, will prejudice decrease? Experimental evidence has shown that there is some hope for us here. When two groups in conflict have had to cooperate, their hostility has decreased. When they have seen themselves as teams, their prejudices have begun to dissipate. In our example, had subordinate groups been formed consisting of individuals from both racial groups who had a goal of attacking specific problems, some change might have occurred.

11. *Criticize the notion that contact among members of power groups and
victim groups will reduce prejudice.*

_____

_____

_____

_____

EDUCATIONAL APPROACHES

We have learned that we learn social attitudes from our parents, peer groups,
teachers, and friends. They are our first sources of prejudice. It would seem
logical that an organized and well-conducted educational program could help
us learn what has been learned somewhat haphazardly from these sources. But
is this so? Can we unlearn prejudice?

Several different educational approaches have been tried. Movies, books,
theater, and other media have been used to try to get prejudiced people to
identify with members of out-groups. Field projects and community surveys
and programs have pointed up the prejudice. Exhibits, pageants, and festivals
have been used to create a sympathetic attitude toward minority groups. For
example, a Catholic high school recently put on *Fiddler on the Roof*, a Jewish
play. Small-group interaction has been used to attack prejudice, and individual conferences have also been tried.

Evaluation of these programs is terribly difficult. Although we can determine that a student has learned the right answers to questions about prejudice,
can we say that the lesson has sunk in? Has the student merely learned to
parrot the expected thing? Has there been any gain at all? You might say that at
least the student has learned some attitudes that society feels are valuable.
Perhaps, in the long run, the lessons will sink in. This educational approach
doesn't seem to do any harm. However, if the truth were boldly stated, we
simply do not know whether it does or does not effectively relieve prejudice.
The use of films, plays, and fiction do decrease prejudice seems to have some
effect. However, the evidence is inconclusive.

12. *Evaluate educational approaches to reducing prejudice.*

_____

_____

_____

_____

THE EFFECTS OF LEGISLATION

Legislation against prejudice in this country is popularly known as civil-rights legislation. Its history is rather interesting. Our most important civil-rights documents are the Constitution and the Bill of Rights. One of their main themes is the equality of all citizens. Through the years, various constitutional amendments, designed to protect people against specific infringements by the state, have been passed. During the Civil War, a decree was issued freeing all slaves, and Congress later buttressed emancipation by passing a series of laws declaring the equality of former slaves. However, Southern states circumvented the civil-rights legislation and did their best to segregate blacks. As the South regained its political clout in Congress, it used that power to block civil-rights legislation. Thus the civil-rights initiative shifted from Congress to the Supreme Court. The court has forced a considerable amount of desegregation in the schools and has often become a champion of minority groups.

Three legal areas are of particular interest to minority groups—civil-rights, employment laws, and group libel laws. Civil-rights laws prohibit discrimination in entry or use of facilities because of race, creed, or color. Employment laws stress equal job opportunities. Group libel laws are meant to protect minorities against slanderous statements.

Legal attempts to dispel prejudice generally work, but they are extremely slow. As the black population moved northward, discrimination also moved so that the struggle for equality is now found in the North perhaps with an even greater intensity. Note the process of desegregating schools. Here, many side issues have been explored and are still being explored in an attempt to achieve a workable solution. Should a school that is 90 percent black bus in white students, even if they do not live in the community being served by that school? Problems of this type are still being fought out. Progress is slow, but it exists. The spirit of the laws is gradually being accepted; the details of compliance are being worked out.

Fair employment laws are in the same category. Progress is being made, but it is slow. Surprisingly, although initial resistance may have been high, when integration in work has been accomplished, the changeover has been remarkably free of violence.

Libel laws present a different sort of problem. Should speech be inhibited by law? Libel is extremely tricky to prove, and whether or not group libel laws serve any purpose is a difficult question.

In general, legal programs depend less on the laws themselves than on enforcement. It is difficult to force people to obey laws they do not believe in. Government after government has foundered when confronted by disobedience to unpopular programs. In this country, we face the problem of enforcing a program toward which many people give lip service but not wholehearted support.

To summarize, you can punish a person for discriminating against another because of race, creed, color, sex, or age, if you can prove some rather tricky legal points. However, are you just punishing a symptom and not achieving a cure? How do we rid ourselves of prejudice in the first place?

13. Evaluate legal approaches to reducing prejudice.

_____

_____

_____

_____

THE EFFECTS OF MASS MEDIA

There is no doubt that the news and entertainment media are powerful weapons to those who want to change or maintain attitudes. Today, these weapons are aimed at those who continue to discriminate. Because these weapons exist, people have become educated about prejudice and are very much aware of their attitudes. How much their basic prejudices have been altered is questionable. It seems that most of us will express a horror of discrimination, yet go blandly on practicing it as we did before.

The media carry out another less obvious but quite powerful role. They build stereotypes and thus perpetuate prejudice. The portrayal of German officers as fanatical, dedicated, supermilitary types used to be a common stereotype in movies. The tough cop, the humanitarian doctor, the self-sacrificing mother, the wise old man—probably these are all necessary in drama and fiction, but they are stereotypes.

The coverage of news events is often a barometer of prevailing opinion. Most news agencies publish not only the news that's fit to print, but also the news the public wants to hear. If you want proof of this, read of an incident involving ethnic prejudice in a paper sympathetic to the power group and in a paper sympathetic to the victim group. You'll wind up wondering whether the reporters were writing about the same incident.

Slanted news, stereotyped parts in drama and fiction, sensationalism—all indicate that the media are powerful but two-edged swords that preserve as much prejudice as they eliminate.

14. Describe the effects of the mass media on prejudice.

_____

_____

_____

_____

Popular ads can effectively break down prejudice. (Sepp Seitz/Magnum)

PREPARING A PROGRAM

Put your money where your mouth is: If you believe that prejudice and discrimination breed hatred and are divisive to our society, do something. Work out a program, no matter how modest, that will allow you to reduce prejudice in some way among people you know. On the basis of what you have learned in this unit, plus what you know about your school or community, propose a program to chip away at discrimination. One little action, even if it involves only yourself, should make this effort worthwhile. The easiest minds to change are those of children. Participatory actions requiring cooperation seem to be most effective in reducing prejudice. Stereotypes need to be knocked down rather than perpetuated.

15. *Prepare a program for reducing prejudice in your own environment.*

_____

_____

_____

_____

A POINT OF VIEW

Gordon Allport's "Prejudice and the Individual" is a very good overview of prejudice because it does not have the shrill overtones of emotional involvement. If you want to get deeper into this subject, there is no finer reference than Gordon Allport's book *The Nature of Prejudice* (New York: Doubleday, 1958). After reading it, you can take off in almost any direction. There is no dearth of books on prejudice against blacks, and there are many accounts of the racist treatment endured by American Indians. See, for example, Dee Brown's *Bury My Heart at Wounded Knee: An Indian History of the American West* (New York: Holt, Rinehart and Winston, 1971) for a good exposition of this subject from the Indians' viewpoint.

GORDON W. ALLPORT

PREJUDICE AND THE INDIVIDUAL

DEFINITION AND EXTENT OF PREJUDICE

There are two ingredients in any prejudiced state of mind: (a) a feeling of favorableness or unfavorableness which in turn is (b) based on unsupported judgment. While some prejudice can be *pro*, or "love prejudice" (as when we think too well of our own group), the ethnic attitudes that cause most social concern are *con*, or "hate prejudice."

A scholastic definition states that hate prejudice is "thinking ill of others without sufficient warrant." An equivalent slang definition says "prejudice is being down on something you are not up on." Whatever wording we prefer, there is always an element of inadequate knowledge or false judgment in prejudice; if not, then we

are dealing with a well-grounded dislike, not with prejudice. If a criminal gang threatens my safety, my fear and hatred of it are not prejudice; but if I say that no ex-convict can be trusted, I am overgeneralizing and am therefore prejudiced. Examples are legion. An Oxford student said, "I despise all Americans, but I have never met one I didn't like." "Every Jew will cheat you if he gets a chance." "Negroes are a violent lot; they carry razors." "Puerto Ricans are ignorant." "I couldn't trust any white man."

It should be added that overgeneralized prejudgments of this sort are prejudices only if they are not reversible when exposed to new knowledge. A person (*e.g.*, a child) can start with a misconception about Jews, Negroes, Puerto Ricans; but if he changes his mind when new evidence comes along he was not really prejudiced, only misinformed. Prejudices are inflexible, rigid and erroneous generalizations about groups of people.

DISCRIMINATION AND PREJUDICE

While discrimination ultimately rests on prejudice, the two processes are not identical. Discrimination denies people their natural or legal rights because of their membership in some unfavored group. Many people discriminate automatically (*e.g.*, in using a labeled waiting room) without being prejudiced; and others, the "gentle people of prejudice," feel irrational aversion, but are careful not to show it in discriminatory behavior. Yet in general, discrimination reinforces prejudices, and prejudices provide rationalizations for discrimination. The two concepts are most distinct when it comes to seeking remedies. The corrections for discrimination are legal, or lie in a direct change of social practices; whereas the remedy for prejudice lies in education and the conversion of attitudes. The best opinion today says that if we eliminate discrimination, then—as people become acquainted with one another on equal terms—attitudes are likely to change, perhaps more rapidly than through the continued preaching or teaching of tolerance.

"Prejudice and the Individual" by Gordon W. Allport from the book *The American Negro Reference Book* by John P. Davis, editor. Copyright © 1966 by Prentice-Hall, Inc. Published by Prentice-Hall, Inc., Englewood Cliffs, N.J.

GENERALITY OF PREJUDICE

While some people are prejudiced against one group only, it is more common to find that if a person is bigoted in regard to one nationality, race, or religion, he is likely to be bigoted regarding all "out-groups." He feels safe only within the narrow confines of his own familiar circle. It is this finding that argues most cogently for regarding prejudice as rooted in personal character structure.

HOW WIDESPREAD IS PREJUDICE?

Research suggests that perhaps 80 per cent of the American people harbor ethnic prejudice of some type and in some appreciable degree. Only 20 per cent of the people are, in Gandhi's terms, "equiminded" or completely democratic in all their attitudes.[1] Widespread though ethnic prejudice is, there is good reason to believe that in the United States it is declining year by year. One example may be given. A cross-section of the population responded to the question, "Do you think Negroes are as intelligent as white people—that is, can they learn things just as well if they are given the same education and training?" In 1946, 60 per cent of the Northern white population answered "yes," and the figure rose in 1956 to 82 per cent. The rise among Southern whites for the same decade was from 33 per cent to 59 per cent.[2]

ORIGINS OF PREJUDICE

While some animals have an instinctive aversion to others, this is not true among species that are cross-fertile. Human beings of all races can (and do) mate and procreate. There is therefore no reason to assume that instinctive aversion exists between ethnic and racial groups. A young child may be frightened by a person of unfamiliar color or appearance, but ordinarily this fear lasts only a few moments. It is well known that young children will play contentedly together whatever their race or national origin. Thus since prejudice is not inborn but acquired, the question is: what are

the chief factors in the complex process of learning?

Some prejudice is deliberately taught by parents. Children obediently learn the lesson, as in the case of the little girl who asked her mother, "What's the name of those children I am supposed to hate?" The parent may pass on prejudice by punishing a child for his friendliness to minority groups. A child thus punished may acquire a conditioned aversion to members of the out-group. Sometimes the teaching is subtler. Even to a four-year-old dark skin may suggest dirt; and since he is repeatedly warned to keep clean, he may develop an avoidance for dark-skinned people.

Tags are powerful factors in learning. Most children learn the emotional force of words long before they know the meanings of the words. An angry first grader once called his white teacher a "nigger." She asked him what "nigger" meant. He replied, "I don't know, but you're supposed to say it when you're mad." Before the child has knowledge of the meaning of Jap, Jew, nigger, Polack, and similar labels, he senses the potency of the negative feeling-tone behind these labels. Derogatory chatter in the home may thus dispose a child of six or eight to "think ill of others without sufficient warrant."

Much prejudice is *caught* rather than directly *taught*. The whole atmosphere of child training may be subtly decisive. Thus a child who is sometimes rejected, sometimes loved, who is punished harshly or capriciously, who does not know unconditional trust at home—such a child grows up "on guard." Unable to depend emotionally upon his parents, he enters school with a suspicious, fearful attitude toward people in general, and especially toward those who have an unfamiliar appearance, and (to him) odd and threatening ways of talking, or worshiping, or behaving. Although we cannot make the assertion with finality, it seems likely that the major factor in predisposing a child toward a lifetime of prejudice is this rejective, neglectful, harsh, or inconsistent style of preschool training.[3]

As the child grows older additional factors

may create or intensify prejudice. Around the age of 8 or 10 he goes through a period of fierce identification with his family. Whatever the family is, is "right" (whether it be Catholic, Jewish, white, Negro, Scotch Irish, or Hottentot). By comparison all other groups are of doubtful status and merit. At this point the church and the school have the opportunity of teaching the child the concept of reciprocity and basic equality among human groups. The lesson is difficult to learn, because as adolescence approaches the child seeks personal security and a new identity in his peer groups which usually are of his own color, class, and neighborhood. If adolescents are friendly with outgroups they risk a diffusion and loss of their own precarious identity.[4] To build up a sense of personal importance they often persecute outgroups. *The West Side Story* is an epic of this gang-age phenomenon.

Occasionally prejudice is formed on the basis of a single emotional trauma. A certain youngster who was chased by a Chinese laundryman felt ever after a terror of Orientals (a clear case of overgeneralizing from a single experience). Such traumatic origins are relatively rare. But we see that throughout childhood and youth there are many opportunities for irreversible and unfavorable belief systems to become set.

PSYCHODYNAMICS

However prejudice is learned it takes root in a personality because it meets certain basic needs or cravings. It works for the person, and may be a pivotal factor in the economy of his life.

NEED FOR CATEGORIZATION

All mortals require simplified rubrics to live by. We think of school teachers, of physicians, of blind people, of Russians, or of ex-convicts, as homogeneous groups. All Orientals, we perceive as mysterious (though many are not); we regard all weeds as inedible (though some are nutritious). Thus our thinking seems to be guided by a law of least effort. If I reject all foreigners (including the United Nations), I simplify my existence by ruling out the troublesome issues of international relations. If I say "all Negroes are ignorant," I dispose of 14 million more people. If I add "Catholics only know what the priest tells them," I eliminate 40 million more. With the conviction that Jews will skin me alive, I discard another 5 million. Labor unions I exclude by calling them "pirates." Intellectuals are simply "long-haired communists." And so it goes. My life is simplified when I invoke these stereotyped rejections. With the aid of aversive categories I avoid the painful task of dealing with individuals as individuals. Prejudice is thus an economical mode of thought, and is widely embraced for this very reason.

ANXIETY AND THE NEED FOR SECURITY

A major source of prejudice is the sense that one's security and status are threatened. One fears for one's job, for one's home, especially for one's prestige. American culture is enormously competitive, and so we find ourselves keenly fearful of our rivals. Downwardly mobile people on the whole are more prejudiced than people who hold a stable social position.[5] Now in cold logic it is very seldom that any minority group actually threatens the well being, safety, or equity or our lives, but we nonetheless perceive them as the cause of our distress. Racist agitators play upon this anxiety. The easiest idea to sell anyone is that he is better than someone else, and that this someone else must be kept "in his place" so that we may enjoy our own position of superiority.

SCAPEGOATING

When things go wrong we find it convenient to blame others. Since Biblical times it has been known that a scapegoat relieves our own sense of failure or guilt. We say it is the Jews who are keeping us from a promotion, or the migration of Negroes that takes away available jobs. Or we may vaguely blame our failures or discomforts upon "the politicians." Few people take blame upon themselves. They are quick to adopt an extrapunitive ego-defense.

SEXUAL CONFLICT

A peculiarly deep complex is found in accusations that out-groups (especially Negroes) are immoral. Simply because they are "forbidden fruit" many white people find Negroes sexually attractive; much miscegenation has been the result. Since looseness of morals is condemned, the white person may exonerate himself from his web of desire, fantasy, and guilt, by projecting it upon the Negro male, who, he says, is sexually aggressive—at heart a rapist. In Germany, Hitler accused the Jews of all manner of sexual irregularities; in the United States, it is the Negro who is the projection screen (the "living inkblot") for one's own frightening id-impulses.

THE AUTHORITARIAN PATTERN

To summarize these, and other similar emotional needs, trends, and twists that enter into the psychodynamics of prejudice, psychologists have formulated the concept of "authoritarianism."[6] It says that a person who is basically insecure, anxious, sexually repressed, suffering from unresolved Oedipal conflicts with his own parents, given to projection—such a person will develop a rigid, conventional, hostile style of life. Ethnic prejudice fits into this character syndrome. This formulation has been widely studied and debated. Just how to define it in detail is a matter of dispute, but most scholars believe that it contains an important truth. People having this syndrome are "functional bigots" whose whole style of life is hostile, fearful, rejective of out-groups. Such people need prejudice and are ready to follow a demagogue who focuses all this latent hate upon some ethnic target.

CONFORMITY

Although the authoritarian pattern clearly exists, we must not assume that it accounts for all prejudice. What we call "conformity prejudice" springs from the tendency of people to yield to local custom and to the legends and ideology of their own class.[7] If bigotry is in the air, they are bigots; if tolerance is customary, they are tolerant. Perhaps half of our population can be considered to be in this middle range. Since prejudice is to some degree prevalent, especially in the Southern regions of the United States, this half of the population can be expected to go along with the existing biases.

What we have called the authoritarian syndrome accounts for about the same amount of prejudice in both Northern and Southern states, but there is much more conformity prejudice in the South.[8]

VICTIMIZATION

Those who are victims of prejudice cannot be indifferent to their plight; they must constantly defend themselves from discomfort or insult. One study states that 50 per cent of Negroes say that when they are with a white person they expect him "to make a slip and say something wrong about Negroes."[9] Even when not expecting an insult, a minority group member must ordinarily plan his life within a racial or ethnic frame of reference.

Besides this chronic sensitization to the problem, additional psychological reactions to victimization may be noted; among them, withdrawal and apathy, slyness and cunning, clowning, rejection of one's own group—or quite the reverse, forming closer in-group ties—resignation, neuroticism, sympathy with other minorities, and enhanced striving and militancy.[10] Of course not all members of a minority group will show all of these types of response.

REDUCING PREJUDICE

Someone has said that it is easier to smash an atom than a prejudice. In the case of deep-dyed functional bigots this verdict may be true. And yet change in prejudice does occur, and has clearly occurred since World War II in America. Prejudiced attitudes change when it makes sociological, economic, and personal sense to change them. Not all people are incurably blind to their own illogical and harmful ways of

thinking. Education combats easy overgeneralizations, and as the educational level rises we
find reduction in stereotyped thinking.[11] Also
we know that increased self-knowledge and
personal insight reduce prejudice.[12] Education
for mental health works in this direction. Furthermore, militant protests call attention to
needed reforms and win the sympathy of potentially democratic citizens. Various measures of
prejudice have been invented to help follow
these trends, even the subtle factor of human-
heartedness within the population.[13]

All progress toward the reduction of prejudice
will be met by vociferous resistance from the
functional bigots. And yet, even when violence
flares up, the trend is unmistakable. Antidis-
crimination laws, revised school curricula and
effective desegregation, raising of educational
levels, open discussion and enlightenment,
nonviolent protests that focus attention and
win sympathy—all these, and other forces, are
working in a single direction. Let the reader also
keep in mind the fact that the problem we are
here discussing has had in the past 20 years
more attention and intelligent study among
people of goodwill than in all the millennia of
human history previously. Recent research on
ethnic prejudice has been remarkably rich and
informative,[14] and shows clearly that the forces
of social science are strongly arrayed in the
battle against bigotry.

NOTES

1. G. W. Allport, *The Nature of Prejudice*, New York: Doubleday Anchor Books, 1958, p. 77.

2. B. Bettelheim and M. Janowitz, *Social Change and Prejudice*, Glencoe, Ill.: Free Press, 1964, p. 11.

3. D. B. Harris, H. G. Gough, W. E. Martin, "Children's ethnic attitudes: II, Relationship to parental beliefs concerning child training," *Child Development*, 1950, *21*, 169–181. Also, D. P. Ausubel, *Ego Development and the Personality Disorders*, New York: Grune and Stratton, 1962.

4. B. Bettelheim and M. Janowitz, *op. cit.*, p. 57.

5. *Ibid.*, pp. 29–34.

6. T. W. Adorno, E. Frenkel-Brunswik, D. J. Levinson, and R. N. Sanford, *The Authoritarian Personality*, New York: Harper, 1950.

7. G. W. Allport, "Prejudice: Is it societal or personal?" *Journal of Social Issues*, 1961, *18*, 120–134.

8. T. F. Pettigrew, "Regional differences in anti–Negro prejudice," *Journal of Abnormal and Social Psychology*, 1959, *29*, 28–36.

9. R. M. Williams, Jr., *Strangers Next Door*, New York: Prentice-Hall, 1964, p. 47.

10. G. W. Allport, *The Nature of Prejudice*, New York: Doubleday Anchor Books, 1958, chapter 9.

11. C. H. Stember, *Education and Attitude Change*, New York: Institute of Human Relations Press, 1961. Also, H. G. Stetler, *Attitudes Toward Racial Integration in Connecticut*, Hartford: Commission on Civil Rights, 1961.

12. R. M. Jones, *An Application of Psychoanalysis to Education*, Springfield, Ill.: Charles C Thomas, 1960.

13. H. Schuman and J. Harding, "Sympathetic identification with the underdog," *Public Opinion Quarterly*, 1963, *27*, 230–241.

14. B. Berelson and G. A. Steiner, *Human Behavior: An Inventory of Scientific Findings*, New York: Harcourt Brace Jovanovich, 1964.

UNIT 14

ABNORMAL
BEHAVIOR

☐ In Unit 1 you explored what is normal behavior and what is abnormal behavior. That discussion left you with the impression that the identification and labeling of abnormal behavior is really a one-sided affair, based on the perceptions of the person doing the labeling. The process of defining behavior as abnormal is often prejudicial to the person under study. Nonetheless, certain kinds of unusual behavior have similarities and therefore can be lumped together under the same labels. Two characteristic types of abnormal behavior are described for you here. In addition, you will gain a broad understanding of some typical methods of therapy. An anecdotal method of self-analysis concludes this unit.

You should be aware that the two types of abnormal behavior discussed here are selected from ten recognized categories. The other categories are mental retardation, organic brain syndromes, personality disorders, psychophysiological disorders, special symptoms, transient situational disturbances, behavior disorders of childhood and adolescence, and nonspecific disorders.

Whenever you study abnormal behavior, you need to recognize several things. First of all, people are rarely as obliging as we would like them to be. They do not fit neatly into the categories we create for them. They mix their behaviors so that we cannot label them easily. Also, they have a habit of changing their patterns of behavior. What is one day labeled as an anxiety reaction could easily change into obsessive-compulsive behavior overnight. Then again, as we discussed in the first unit, it is very hard to make that fine distinction between abnormal and normal behavior. Before we judge, we need to know why. Only then can we really make any knowledgeable guess about the nature of the behavior. It is best to think of human behavior as very dynamic and shifting, involving a great deal more than surface appearances. You should always keep in mind that abnormal behavior, like beauty, is in the eye of the beholder.

There is one thing to guard against as you study this unit. While you read about the different kinds of mental abnormality, you'll probably think, "Hey, they're talking about me!" This is because the characteristics of abnormal behavior all appear in normal behavior. All of us occasionally have feelings of depression; we all daydream a little, back off from unpleasant situations, hallucinate mildly, and so on. However, abnormal people have specialized their behavior so much that they're stuck in a rut. Normal people are more flexible. So don't get upset if you think you recognize yourself; don't go gnawing your knuckles about being abnormal.

When you have completed this unit, you should be able to:

1. *Describe the typical neurotic.*
2. *Relate anxiety to neurosis.*
3. *Describe the nonproductive nature of neurotic behavior.*
4. *Identify different types of neurotic behavior.*
5. *Describe a typical psychotic.*
6. *Contrast the typical neurotic with the typical psychotic.*
7. *Identify the major types of psychotic behavior.*

8. *Classify the various methods of psychotherapy.*
9. *Describe the psychoanalytic technique.*
10. *Describe nondirective therapy.*
11. *Describe didactic therapy.*
12. *Describe behavioral therapy.*
13. *Describe the main idea of group therapy.*
14. *Describe experiential therapy.*
15. *Analyze your own behavior under stress, using anecdotal records.*

THE NEUROTIC PERSON

This material will essentially be a review for you; the basic information was given in Unit 1. It is repeated here to give structure to the specific descriptions of neurotic reactions that follow. You will recall that neurotic individuals can function in society. They can take care of themselves and do not need any kind of restraint or supervisory protection. However, they are hampered by their neurosis to some extent. All neurotics display certain typical characteristics. They operate at less than their full capacity. This in itself bothers them, as they indicate by their unhappiness. Neurotics are typically unhappy. Most of the time they are unconsciously motivated. Their patterns of behavior are usually rigid. Neurotics do not react well to changes, expecially if they are sudden. Neurotics always have feelings of tension and anxiety. They try to cover these feelings by engaging in behavior that helps to displace the feelings temporarily. However, this behavior does not go to the heart of the matter. Much of the behavior of neurotics is repetitive and unproductive, designed merely to mask the reasons for tension. Their responses to stress, regardless of its cause, might be called neurotic stupidity. The typical neurotic is extremely self-centered, preoccupied with his or her own thoughts and feelings. When with others, the neurotic is very sensitive to comment. The irritability caused by this sensitivity is part of his or her personality.

1. *Describe the typical neurotic.*

_____

_____

_____

_____

ANXIETY AND NEUROSIS

Anxiety is the most typical characteristic of neurotic individuals. It does not take much to send neurotics into a tailspin. Neurotic anxiety is caused by feelings of insecurity over what might seem to others to be fairly innocent or harmless events. The reason for this is that neurotics usually interpret the event as a threat to the defenses they have built to protect themselves against their feelings of inadequacy.

To review, anxiety is different from fear, because it is not focused on a specific object. We fear something but we are anxious *about* something. Much of the time the amount of anxiety a neurotic generates is out of proportion to the incident. Anxiety seems to dwell in the future rather than in the past. However, anxiety over past failures feeds present anxiety. It is this vague and indefinite fear that leads the neurotic into compulsive, irrational, and nonproductive behavior.

2. Relate anxiety to neurosis.

_____

_____

_____

_____

NONPRODUCTIVE NEUROTIC BEHAVIOR

Many neurotic actions are symbolic. For example, Lady Macbeth showed a form of neurotic behavior when she incessantly washed her hands. In her case, the symbolism is quite clear, because Shakespeare wanted it to be. But what of actions invented not by one who is creating characters but by the person who performs those actions? What of the secretary who suddenly develops cramps in her hands every time she sits down before her typewriter? What of the man whose left arm is suddenly paralyzed, yet doctors can find no medical reason for the paralysis? What of the compulsive eater? What of the child who gets violently sick just before going off to school? Most neurotics have developed these actions to defend their feelings. Because they are unable to cope with new situations, they resort to stereotyped activities in order to meet all problems. They give the same response time after time, even though it has clearly proved to be unsuccessful in other circumstances. Neurotics possess specialized responses that operate to their disadvantage. Whereas most of us are able to work out a proper answer to a challenge, the neurotics cannot. They have selected one way to meet all situations and use only that way.

3. Describe the nonproductive nature of neurotic behavior.

_____

_____

VARIETIES OF NEUROSES

Several types of behavior are usually considered neurotic: anxiety neurosis, conversion neurosis, dissociation neurosis, phobic neurosis, obsessive-compulsive neurosis, depressive neurosis, hypochondriacal neurosis, and neurasthenic neurosis. How do certain persons develop certain kinds of neurotic behavior? Some theorists feel that heredity and biological factors such as constitution and physique aren't related to neurosis and that you learn to be a neurotic. Thus, according to these theorists, parents and society determine whether or not a child will be neurotic. Not only can they create the neurosis; they can also help children to develop their individual specialized reactions.

ANXIETY
NEUROSIS

insecure

This form of neurosis usually occurs in individuals who have a history of immaturity or insecurity. Usually, their parents have overprotected them or rejected them. They relive childhood fears in their adult situation. They often have attacks of acute terror, during which they break out in a cold sweat, their bodies tremble, and they can hardly breathe. They never know when they might have one of these attacks. When they do have one, it practically incapacitates them.

CONVERSION
NEUROSIS

physical reaction

Those who display a conversion neurosis put their bodies between their conflict and themselves; they convert a psychological reaction into a physical one. Usually, they have a history of some illness that provided an excuse for not doing something. These individuals tend to be immature and like to be the center of attention. They enjoy dramatizing themselves and their problems. To do so, they develop a physical incapacity. They may have severe hand cramps, they may not be able to see; or they may become paralyzed in an arm or a leg.

DISSOCIATION
NEUROSIS

memories shutting mind off

In dissociation neurosis, neurotics isolate their difficulty by shutting off their minds, losing their memories in order to avoid their problems. These individuals are usually very immature and have a history of escaping into fantasy. Dissociatives are usually quite suggestible; their minds are easily influenced by suggestions either from themselves or from others.

PHOBIC NEUROSIS

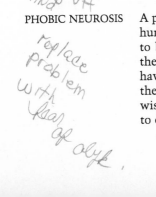
replace problem with fear of obj.

A phobia is an unnatural fear of some object, person, or situation. Nearly two hundred words describe different kinds of phobia. Phobic fears are considered to be symbols of deep conflict. Because phobic neurotics don't want to face their conflict, they replace it with a fear of something else. Phobic neurotics have a history of timidity and feelings of inadequacy. Sometimes they develop their phobias to protect themselves against what they see as unacceptable wishes or guilt feelings over past acts. Of course, someone who has been scared to death by a specific incident can develop a great nonneurotic fear of it.

OBSESSIVE-COMPULSIVE NEUROSIS

Psychoanalysts feel that obsessive-compulsive neuroses are caused by parental demands made during a child's period of toilet training. Other theorists aren't that specific, but many agree that parents may impose on their children standards that are too high. Most compulsive-obsessives are highly concerned over cleanliness. They may be very angry, but they mask their anger. It is possible for a person to have obsessions without compulsions and vice versa. However, the roots of both types of behavior are the same. Obsessives complain that they have the same thoughts running through their heads all the time. (Have you ever had a song in your mind that you couldn't get rid of?) Compulsives, on the other hand, feel a strong need to do certain things, such as putting on their clothes in a particular sequence. Often they feel that a terrible disaster may occur if they don't go through with their rituals.

DEPRESSIVE NEUROSIS

Depression is usually brought on by a precipitating event. Initially, a person feels low, but the feeling keeps going on and on. The individual thus stays in a slump. Depressive people typically feel inferior and fear a hostile society. Many have underlying hostile feelings. Often, for example, the conflict between grief and relief over a parent's death brings on the depression.

HYPOCHON-DRIACAL NEUROSIS

A hypochondriac is usually a middle-aged person who seems to enjoy poor health. This person is extremely self-centered, getting attention through illness. The typical hypochondriac is completely concerned with his or her bodily functions. Such individuals take refuge in their illnesses and hide their problems behind this physiological smoke screen.

NEURASTHENIC NEUROSIS

People who suffer from a neurasthenic neurosis complain of dizziness, headaches, and bodily discomforts. Usually, they are also tired and not able to function effectively. Much of their fatigue comes from their efforts to hold on to their internal anger. The major difference between neurasthenics and hypochondriacs is that neurasthenics are not really asking for attention; they are trying to escape an unhappy situation by focusing on bodily complaints.

You may get the idea that people consciously select their neuroses, deciding to be depressed or adopting a phobia. However, you should keep in mind that these reactions are almost completely worked out on the unconscious level. Neuroses are born in our unknowing reactions to conflict situations. Typical neurotics are usually aware that their behavior is odd but don't know why they act or feel the way they do.

Here are some case histories describing neurotic reactions. See whether you can correctly identify each neurosis.

Mrs. D. is a middle-aged homemaker. She has a good reputation among her neighbors because her house is absolutely spotless. In the early morning hours, when most people are having breakfast, she can be seen scrubbing her front sidewalk with soap and water and singing "Stormy Weather." When her neighbors tease her about her actions, she smiles shamefacedly and says, "I know I must look like a nut, but you can't be too careful about germs. They can cause all sorts of problems, you know. If we let them get the upper hand, we'll all be sick in bed."

Which neurosis is Mrs. D. suffering from? _____

Mr. A. is thin and looks worried all the time. He often is heard to say that the end of the world will come if we keep sending men to the moon. He trembles, breaks out in a sweat, and often seems immobilized by fear. He rarely shows himself in public. When he does, the slightest unusual event is enough to upset his emotional equilibrium and send him scurrying home. If the event is sudden, he may faint and experience heart tremors and difficulty in breathing.

What neurosis is Mr. A. suffering from? _____

Ms. I. L., a bookkeeper who has worked for the same company for years, has recently had some trouble on the job. Although she is very conscientious and works carefully, she recently made a large error in one of her accounts. Because of this, she was called into the front office and reprimanded. A week later, while she was sitting at her desk, she suddenly cried out, "I can't see." She was rushed to the hospital. After many tests, no reason for her affliction could be found.

What neurosis is Ms. I. L. suffering from? _____

A Marine private, first class, was put through a training course to become a tank driver. He performed very well and passed with a high endorsement. Shortly afterward, he was sent to a combat unit and was assigned to a tank. When his outfit went on maneuvers, he was ordered to drive "buttoned up," that is, with the tank cover closed. This was the first time he had ever been closed in like that. He panicked and lost control of his tank, crashing it into and completely demolishing a truck.

What neurosis was the Marine suffering from? _____

John Q. was walking down the street with his neighbor to catch a bus. Suddenly he stopped, looked bewildered, and asked, "Where am I?" He didn't recognize his neighbor, whom he had lived near for six years. He did not respond to his name and insisted that he was someone who lived in another city. His answers to questions showed that he was ten years behind the times in his orientation.

What neurosis was John Q. suffering from? _____

(There are really three varieties of John Q.'s neurosis. One is called *amnesia*—partial or total loss of memory. A person may block out a single unpleasant scene or incident from memory. Another variety is called *fugue*. Fugue is afflicting John Q. A fugue involves an event that the individual can't remember after recovering. A third, more dramatic, but fortunately very rare type is known as *multiple personality*. In this condition, a person actually becomes different people at various times. A person suffering from a conversion neurosis uses his or her body to block out a conflict; a person suffering from multiple personality uses the mind in a similar fashion.)

Jane C.'s sister recently died, and ever since the death Jane C. has been listless and dull. She has always been sensitive and shy. However, now she cries a lot and never smiles. Her sister was a very outgoing and hearty sort. Jane used to depend on her for invitations to events to which she would never have been invited otherwise. Secretly, Jane disliked her sister because she knew that her own social situation was really a reflection of her sister's. Now that her sister is gone, Jane feels guilty about her hidden dislike.

What neurosis is Jane C. suffering from? _____

(Jane's neurosis is found in psychotics, with some differences. A psychotic usually has developed some delusion to go along with his or her feelings. Moreover, for a psychotic the progression usually has not been precipitated by a particular event; it has been more of a steady downhill slide.)

Mrs. G. is a middle-aged homemaker who is hopelessly unhappy with her married life. She feels that her marriage has trapped her into a life of mediocrity. She is listless and chronically complains of headaches, heartburn, and dizziness. She is always tired; this is her major complaint. Because of her tiredness, she rarely gets things done.

What neurosis is Mrs. G. suffering from? _____

Al W. is the office pill popper. He spends more time in front of the mirror looking for telltale signs of physical collapse than he does at his desk. His conversations deal only with his own state of ill health. His fascination with sickness and his eagerness to pick up the latest ailment are the talk of the office. He has exhausted the patience of every doctor in town. He claims they can't understand his illnesses or diagnose his problems.

What neurosis is Al W. suffering from? _____

4. Identify different types of neurotic behavior.

_____

_____

_____

_____

A TYPICAL PSYCHOTIC

↑ can't deal

Neurotics are an unhappy people whose ability to cope with their environments is reduced but not absent. Psychotics are much more helpless. Most psychotics need help in order to survive. They have lost their ability to deal with the world in an effective way. They frequently have delusions and hallucinations that affect their reasoning powers. Psychotics have lost touch with reality and cannot tell whether their perceptions are true or false. They behave erratically and do not seem to be disturbed by what others might think of them. In other words, they have forgotten the requirements of social behavior. Their speech may be strange and irrational. They are capable of wild swings of emotion and also can shift from inaction to violent action, sometimes for no apparent reason.

5. Describe a typical psychotic.

_____

_____

_____

_____

NEUROSIS VERSUS PSYCHOSIS

Neurotics differ from psychotics in many ways, even though both have disturbed behavior patterns. Often, it is quite difficult to make an exact clinical diagnosis, but the differentiation between psychotics and neurotics should offer no problems, if the following guidelines are remembered.

Psychotics more than likely have a family history of psychotic behavior. Their psychoses may also be related to a physical imperfection that impairs their mental ability. Neurotics, on the other hand, do not suffer as the result of heredity or genetic accident. Their affliction is learned. The speech and thought of neurotics are usually coherent and logical, whereas psychotics may become irrational and suffer from hallucinations and delusions. Neurotics are all too conscious of the social consequences of their behavior. Psychotics couldn't care less. They have lost their ability to deal with the demands of society. Neurotics can make it in society, even though their adaptability may be limited. Because psychotics may cause harm to themselves or others, they usually need institutionalization for their own sake and that of society. Psychotics and neurotics do have one thing in common, however. Both may seriously contemplate suicide when they are suffering from depression.

Because neurotics can be talked to, they may respond to therapy. Psychotics often are so far out that no one can reach them. Because psychotherapy depends on being able to reach the person, it shows good promise for neurotics and little promise for psychotics. Likewise, neurotics can often be helped, or their neuroses level off eventually and then rarely get any worse. By throwing up defenses that work for them, neurotics have learned to live with their world. Psychotics, on the other hand, can continue to go downhill until their personality structure completely deteriorates.

6. Contrast the typical neurotic with the typical psychotic.

_____

_____

_____

_____

TYPES OF PSYCHOSIS

Psychotics can be divided into several main types: schizophrenics, affective psychotics, and paranoids. A fourth type of psychotic derives his or her illness from brain damage or organic dysfunctioning of some kind. This type will not be discussed here.

Schizophrenia was once called *dementia praecox* because it was most often seen in adolescents. However, as psychologists have become more sophisticated in identifying it, they have discarded the Latin term in favor of one that does not imply age limitations. There are several types of schizophrenia: simple schizophrenia, hebephrenia, catatonia, and paranoia.

Simple schizophrenics often have relatively good contact with reality, although they may drift off occasionally. They may be able to work outside of the mental institution that is treating them and even may be marginally self-supporting—if their routine is well established and no upsetting events occur. Typical simple schhizophrenics show little interest in the affairs of the world beyond their own little sphere. They care little for their personal appearance. They have few, if any, friends and are indifferent to people. They have made their own little world and do not leave it. Such individuals can work at a routine job that would be terribly boring to anyone else, eat lunch, and go home without having said five words to fellow workers during the day. They show few emotions, and it is almost impossible to establish emotional ties with them.

Hebephrenics on the other hand, are anything but quiet. They are always on the move. Although their actions may not make sense, they are never still. They may giggle, smirk childishly, and show strange mannerisms when talking. Their conversations are incoherent, because they cannot stick to any subject for any length of time. It seems that their thoughts are so far ahead of their words that they must hurry on to another topic before finishing the first. They hallucinate freely and may have strong delusions.

Phobic fears may be signs of neurosis. (Bohdan Hrynewych/Stock, Boston)

Catatonics are almost exactly the reverse of hebephrenics. Catatonics are withdrawn and usually are slow acting. If put into a strange posture, they will hold it for long periods of time. However, they can explode into violence without warning. They act as though they are afraid to make any movement because they fear that they may lose control of themselves. They too seem to suffer from hallucinations and delusions. When severely ill, they may require force feeding to stay alive.

Paranoid schizophrenics have all the symptoms of simple schizophrenia: the bizarre behavior, the garbled language, and the scrambled thought processes. However, they are even more socially withdrawn and are more likely to be moody and irritable. They usually have delusions of grandeur and very often suspect that others are after them. Because of this suspicion, paranoids are difficult to deal with.

Affective psychotics often show manic-depressive symptoms. Their moods swing from wild excitation to extreme depression, often without warning. These moods come on slowly, last indefinitely, and subside for a time, only to recur. In the manic stage, affective psychotics are highly elated, and overactive and have a tremendous amount of energy. Ideas bubble through their heads. If they have delusions, the delusions are grandiose. In the depressed state, they have difficulty thinking, and their physical reactions are slow. The degree of their depression may range from mild to stupor. It is, of course, possible for a person to be either manic or depressed and not alternate from one state of mind to the other.

A special form of depression is often called *involutional melancholia* to distinguish it from neurotic depression and the affective psychoses. It usually comes on in later life and is especially prevalent in middle-aged females. It seems to be connected with the chemistry of the change of life and with changes in the social environment. A common theme of many sufferers is that life is all over and there is no second chance. Involutional melancholia shows itself in worry, paranoid delusions, high anxiety, guilt feelings, and other complaints such as psychosomatic troubles. Periods of weeping may occur. Involutional melancholia often cures itself spontaneously after several months.

Paranoids are suspicious people. However, they are usually not too divorced from reality. Their mental ability does not deteriorate as it does in other psychoses. Nevertheless, paranoids are very sick and often dangerous. They usually create a world in which they are the heroes and all others are enemies. They usually have delusions of persecution and feel that others are ganging up to destroy them. Whereas the thought processes of a paranoid schizophrenic deteriorate, those of a true paranoid do not. The true paranoid merely suffers from feelings of persecution.

7. Identify the major types of psychotic behavior.

_____

_____

METHODS OF PSYCHOTHERAPY

Only a few basic methods for treating mentally ill patients—or clients, if you wish to get away from the notion of illness—exist. However, literally hundreds of different voices cry out, "Try my way, it's the best." In the medical method of treatment, something is done to the body to reduce the problem. Therapists may induce fever, administer chemical or electrical shock, or perform surgery. Each method emphasizes the need to change the body's functioning in order to reduce or control the mental dysfunctioning.

Psychotherapeutic methods of dealing with clients' problems also exist. There is a tremendous variety of techniques that can be classified into two main categories: emotionally oriented therapies and intellectual reconditioning. Although little evidence points to one method as better for a particular complaint than another, certain broad generalizations can be made and will be pointed out to you when each particular method is discussed. Psychoanalysis, client-centered therapy, gestalt treatment, hypnotherapy, and experiential therapy can all be classified as emotionally oriented therapies. Intellectual-reconditioning therapy includes techniques such as directive therapy, general semantics, learning theory, assertion-structured, and rational and group didactic therapy. Reciprocal inhibition and conditioned-reflex techniques may be considered two divisions of a special kind of intellectual-reconditioning therapy. Although a detailed explanation of each of these techniques would be impossible, the sections that follow will introduce you to the details of some representative techniques in order to give you a feeling for what is involved in therapy.

8. *Classify the various methods of psychotherapy.*

_____

_____

_____

_____

PSYCHOANALYSIS

Psychoanalysis might be called the granddaddy of all therapies because it was the first to be coherently described and widely practiced. Who do you suppose originated it? None other than our friend Freud. It has been, and still is, a highly touted method of treatment. It is the source of all the couch jokes, because therapists do use a couch or a chair for their patients so that they will relax completely and talk. In theory, as patients relax, ideas and thoughts that they have repressed will come into their minds and can be expressed.

As patients talk, they find it easier to bring the things that are bothering them into their conscious minds and to think about them. When they do so, they feel great relief. This process is called *catharsis*. An important part of psychoanalysis is dream interpretation, for, to a psychoanalyst, dreams represent repressed material struggling to come into the conscious mind.

The role of therapists is also important. They usually sit out of the direct sight of clients and make notes of recurring themes in order to detect the areas that seem to be troublesome to these individuals. They are the interpreters of words and dreams that help clients release their bottled-up feelings. In addition, therapists also serve as targets to which their clients can transfer their formerly repressed feelings) There are four major aspects of psychoanalysis: (1) free association—saying the first thing that comes into your head; (2) catharsis—the emotional result of releasing repressed material; (3) dream interpretation; and (4) transference—the use of the therapist as the symbol of repressed emotions toward others. The main idea of psychoanalysis is to let repressed material come out to be analyzed and faced.

9. Describe the psychoanalytic technique.

_____

_____

_____

_____

NONDIRECTIVE THERAPY

The psychoanalytic technique has many variations, stemming from each therapist's attempts to mold the style to fit his or her personality. Perhaps one of the major alterations was created by Carl Rogers in what he calls client-centered psychotherapy. Rogers rebelled against the idea of psychoanalysts' calling the shots in treatment. It seemed to him that analysts were imposing their standards and values on clients. Instead, clients should work through their own sets of values. Rogers feels that all people can work out their problems—if they can find someone who is willing to listen to them without interposing his or her own value systems. Rogers's system provides exactly that: a person who listens and helps clients when they have trouble expressing themselves but does no interpreting or analysis. This type of therapist is the empathetic listener. The system is based on the proposition that clients will work out their own solutions.

In this technique, there is no special seating arrangement or arrangement of furniture. The therapist and the client sit facing each other at an easy conversational distance. The emphasis is on an informal, relaxed meeting, rather than on fact-finding discussion. This technique calls for great skill on the part of the therapist. In effect, the therapist must provide the client with a friendly, supporting atmosphere in which to examine the client's troubles and must avoid criticism and censure. The therapist must make clear through actions that he or she accepts and has a warm positive regard for the client. This is not as easy as it sounds. Try it sometime, and you'll see.

10. Describe nondirective therapy.

_____

_____

_____

_____

DIDACTIC THERAPY

The didactic therapies are essentially teaching techniques. They stress a cognitive approach, using the intellect to correct mental misfunctioning. One technique is what Albert Ellis calls rational therapy. Ellis thinks that people make problems for themselves when they begin to think irrationally. For instance, if a woman goes to a cocktail party and meets one unpleasant guest who clearly shows that she does not like her, she may come home crushed and brood about the incident, thinking, "Isn't it terrible that so-and-so didn't like me? I must be a bad person." This is what Ellis calls irrational thinking. Not everyone in the world can and should like you. Most people, however, are considerate and sufficiently trained in social graces to hide their dislike. Why should you feel upset because someone does not like you and is crude enough to show it? Why don't you feel sorry for the boor and for his or her bad manners, rather than blame yourself? This is the Ellis approach. Here are some of the irrational thoughts Ellis has enumerated:

1. There is only one way a problem can be solved, and I am a goat for not being able to solve it in that way.
2. I must be successful in all respects.
3. I must be dependent on others and need someone on whom I can rely.
4. I should worry over someone else's problems.
5. I should be positively regarded by everyone I meet.
6. Certain people are evil and should be punished.
7. It is very bad when things do not go the way I want them to.
8. If something is dangerous, I should expect it to happen.

To combat irrationality, Ellis combines teaching with experience. For example, he may send the party goer to another party and another, until the person can face open dislike without being unduly disturbed.

You should remember that this is only one of many therapeutic teaching techniques. The Adlerians have their own elaborate system, and there are many others. Some are not quite so flamboyant as Ellis's, but they stress essentially the same idea: A person should reconstruct thinking that has gone into strange channels.

11. Describe didactic therapy.

_____

_____

_____

_____

BEHAVIORAL THERAPY

In Unit 16 you will be exposed to a system of behavioral therapy that is very close to the technique that Joseph Wolpe terms *reciprocal inhibition.* A person, says Wolpe, cannot feel two different emotions at one time. Thus, if a man is afraid of a cat and his emotions can be relaxed, he can think of a cat and not get upset. Through this technique, little by little, he can lose his fear.

Albert Bandura, on the other hand, says that behavioral advances occur through imitation. If a man is afraid of a cat and at a distance sees someone else playing with it, he can overcome his fear by moving in closer and closer, This technique emphasizes a social-facilitation approach, using the reinforcing effects of other people to overcome a problem.

Some purists will say that neither technique is true behavioral therapy. The trouble is that the term covers a multitude of techniques. However, since one technique will be shown to you in a later exercise and will be explained to you then, let the subject go for now and base your understanding of behavioral therapy on the two approaches just discussed.

12. Describe behavioral therapy.

_____

_____

_____

_____

GROUP THERAPY

No other system of therapy has stirred up so much interest and controversy as group therapy. This is probably so because of the publicity that some of the more flamboyant methods—nudity groups and sensitivity marathons—have generated. Some of these methods seem pretty drastic and questionable. However, since their results are not clear, a verdict cannot be given at this time.

Role playing, encounter groups, psychodrama, marathons—there are so many variations that they beggar description. Whatever the method, however, group therapy consists of clients dealing with their problems in concert. The essential part of this therapy seems to be that people in a group interact and get feedback from the group about themselves. A major emphasis is placed on opening up and expressing what is inside. Although the group may tear down, it can also support strongly when rebuilding takes place.

Group therapy has received much publicity lately as a treatment for drug users. If it is successful—and it seems to have had some success—it offers much hope, because the term of treatment is usually shorter than with other methods and the cost is less. Since there just are not enough qualified therapists around to handle today's potential case load, the group system offers some hope of treatment for all in need of it. As we get more sophisticated in the use of the group, perhaps therapy will come to be within the reach of everyone.

At the present time, group therapy is still in its infancy. Unfortunately, the publicity it has received has inspired many unqualified persons to practice the technique. "It's simple," they say. People sit around and tell the others what they think of them." However, the power of the group is so great that it can devastate someone if it is not wisely controlled. Group therapy is not a toy; it should not be permitted to suffer the demeaning fate of hypnosis, which got into the wrong hands.

13. Describe the main idea of group therapy.

_____

_____

_____

_____

EXPERIENTIAL THERAPY

By now you may be thinking that these systems of therapy are probably all right for people who have most of their marbles and are able to think rationally enough to communicate. But what about the poor soul who is almost

The group system of therapy offers some hope of treatment for all in need of it.
(Suzanne Arms/Jeroboam)

completely out of it? What about the person whose fears and perceptions are so
warped that intelligent communication is impossible? There are two methods
of dealing with these people. One is to drug or shock them in one way or
another so that they are brought back to reality for long enough to be treated.
This used to be the prevalent treatment for the severely afflicted patient, but it
is now fading out. Some therapists feel that the brutality involved in the
treatment is too great to justify the method. The other means of dealing with
severely ill patients is through experiential therapy. One of the more modern

proponents of this method is the Englishman Ronald Laing. He feels that psychotics, like neurotics, have developed a special technique to handle their situations. When we intervene with drugs and forceful methods, we are actually breaking down the patient's logical process. Laing believes that we should work with the patient's delusions and fancies, encouraging them when necessary. Laing claims that, if therapists take part in their patients' fantasies, they can encourage the patients to work through their defenses and become normal again. In other words, therapists should not attempt to discourage delusions, thereby making another conflict situation for patients when their delusions are denied. Instead, therapists should encourage patients to express their delusions, which can then be put to a useful purpose.

14. Describe experiential therapy.

_____

_____

_____

_____

A PERSONAL EVALUATION

How do you typically react under stress? Write two or three anecdotal records of incidents in your life that had great emotional content. Write them out as completely as you can. Then go back and analyze them. What were the stressors? What caused your emotions? What precisely were your emotions? This is important: How did you react under the stress? Did you react the same way in each case? Do you typically react in the same way when you feel tension? For example, every time you feel stress, do you beg off with a sick headache?

15. Analyze your own behavior under stress, using anecdotal records.

_____

_____

_____

_____

□ A POINT OF VIEW

Thomas Szasz's article "The Myth of Mental Illness" is nearly a classic in the arena of mental health and therapy. Szasz takes issue with the whole proposition of looking at maladjustment as mental illness. It is a hard-hitting article. Not so well known is a rebuttal by Frederick C. Thorne. Thorne attacks some of Szasz's statements. You can pay your money and make your choice about whom to believe.

For additional reading on this subject, start with a good textbook on abnormal psychology. Then, if you care to, get down to specifics by reading the notions of various authors in the therapy business. There are as many different ideas on how to treat people as there are therapists. A grain of salt is a good thing to keep by your side as you delve into each author's version of how to heal the mentally ill.

THOMAS S. SZASZ

THE MYTH OF MENTAL ILLNESS

MENTAL ILLNESS AS A SIGN OF BRAIN DISEASE

My aim in this essay is to raise the question "Is there such a thing as mental illness?" and to argue that there is not. Since the notion of mental illness is extremely widely used nowadays, inquiry into the ways in which this term is employed would seem to be especially indicated. Mental illness, of course, is not literally a "thing"—or physical object—and hence it can "exist" only in the same sort of way in which other theoretical concepts exist. Yet, familiar theories are in the habit of posing, sooner or later—at least to those who come to believe in

Reprinted from Thomas S. Szarz, "The Myth of Mental Illness," *American Psychologist* 15 (1960):113–118, by permission of the American Psychological Association and Thomas S. Szasz. Copyright @ 1960 by the American Psychological Association.

them—as "objective truths" (or "facts"). During certain historical periods, explanatory conceptions such as deities, witches, and microorganisms appeared not only as theories but as self-evident *causes* of a vast number of events. I submit that today mental illness is widely regarded in a somewhat similar fashion, that is, as the cause of innumerable diverse happenings. As an antidote to the complacent use of the notion of mental illness—whether as a self-evident phenomenon, theory, or cause—let us ask this question: What is meant when it is asserted that someone is mentally ill?

In what follows I shall describe briefly the main uses to which the concept of mental illness has been put. I shall argue that this notion has outlived whatever usefulness it might have had and that it now functions merely as a convenient myth.

The notion of mental illness derives its main support from such phenomena as syphilis of the brain or delirious conditions—intoxications, for instance—in which persons are known to manifest various peculiarities or disorders of thinking and behavior. Correctly speaking, however, these are diseases of the brain, not of the mind. According to one school of thought, *all* so-called mental illness is of this type. The assumption is made that some neurological defect, perhaps a very subtle one, will ultimately be found for all the disorders of thinking and behavior. Many contemporary psychiatrists, physicians, and other scientists hold this view. This position implies that people *cannot* have troubles—expressed in what are *now called* "mental illnesses"—because of differences in personal needs, opinions, social aspirations, values, and so on. *All problems* in living are attributed to physicochemical processes which in due time will be discovered by medical research.

"Mental illnesses" are thus regarded as basically no different than all other diseases (that is, of the body). The only difference, in this view, between mental and bodily diseases is that the former, affecting the brain, manifest themselves by means of mental symptoms; whereas the latter, affecting other organ systems (for example, the skin, liver, etc.), manifest themselves by means of symptoms referable to those parts of the body. This view rests on and expresses what are, in my opinion, fundamental errors.

In the first place, what central nervous system symptoms would correspond to a skin eruption or a fracture? It would *not* be some emotion or complex bit of behavior. Rather, it would be blindness or a paralysis of some part of the body. The crux of the matter is that a disease of the brain, analogous to a disease of the skin or bone, is a neurological defect, and not a problem in living. For example, a *defect* in a person's visual field may be satisfactorily explained by correlating it with certain definite lesions in the nervous system. On the other hand, a person's *belief*—whether this be a belief in Christianity, in Communism, or in the idea that his internal organs are "rotting" and that his body is, in fact, already "dead"—cannot be explained by a defect or disease of the nervous system. Explanations of this sort of occurrence—assuming that one is interested in the belief itself and does not regard it simply as a "sympton" or expression of something else that is *more interesting*—must be sought along different lines.

The second error in regarding complex psychosocial behavior, consisting of communications about ourselves and the world about us, as mere symptoms of neurological functioning is *epistemological*. In other words, it is an error pertaining not to any mistakes in observation or reasoning, as such, but rather to the way in which we organize and express our knowledge. In the present case, the error lies in making a symmetrical dualism between mental and physical (or bodily) symptoms, a dualism which is merely a habit of speech and to which no known observations can be found to correspond. Let us see if this is so. In medical practice, when we speak of physical disturbances, we mean either signs (for example, a fever) or symptoms (for example, pain). We speak of mental symptoms, on the other hand, when we refer to a patient's *communications about himself, others, and the world about him.* He might state

that he is Napoleon or that he is being persecuted by the Communists. These would be considered mental symptoms *only* if the observer believed that the patient was *not* Napoleon or that he was *not* being persecuted by the Communists. This makes it apparent that the statement that "*X* is a mental symptom" involves rendering a judgment. The judgment entails, moreover, a covert comparison or matching of the patient's ideas, concepts, or beliefs with those of the observer and the society in which they live. The notion of mental symptom is therefore inextricably tied to the *social* (including *ethical*) *context* in which it is made in much the same way as the notion of bodily symptom is tied to an *anatomical* and *genetic context* (Szasz, 1957a, 1957b).

To sum up what has been said thus far: I have tried to show that for those who regard mental symptoms as signs of brain disease, the concept of mental illness is unnecessary and misleading. For what they mean is that people so labeled suffer from diseases of the brain; and, if that is what they mean, it would seem better for the sake of clarity to say that and not something else.

MENTAL ILLNESS AS A NAME FOR PROBLEMS IN LIVING

The term "mental illness" is widely used to describe something which is very different than a disease of the brain. Many people today take it for granted that living is an arduous process. Its hardship for modern man, moreover, derives not so much from a struggle for biological survival as from the stresses and strains inherent in the social intercourse of complex human personalities. In this context, the notion of mental illness is used to identify or describe some feature of an individual's so-called personality. Mental illness—as a deformity of the personality, so to speak—is then regarded as the *cause* of the human disharmony. It is implicit in this view that social intercourse between people is regarded as something *inherently harmonious*, its disturbance being due solely to the presence of "mental illness" in many people. This is obviously fallacious reasoning, for it makes the abstraction "mental illness" into a *cause*, even though this abstraction was created in the first place to serve only as a shorthand expression for certain types of human behavior. It now becomes necessary to ask: "What kinds of behavior are regarded as indicative of mental illness, and by whom?"

The concept of illness, whether bodily or mental, implies *deviation from some clearly defined norm*. In the case of physical illness, the norm is the structural and functional integrity of the human body. Thus, although the desirability of physical health, as such, is an ethical value, what health *is* can be stated in anatomical and physiological terms. What is the norm deviation from which is regarded as mental illness? This question cannot be easily answered. But whatever this norm might be, we can be certain of only one thing: namely, that it is a norm that must be stated in terms of *psychosocial, ethical*, and *legal* concepts. For example, notions such as "excessive repression" or "acting out an unconscious impulse" illustrate the use of psychological concepts for judging (so-called) mental health and illness. The idea that chronic hostility, vengefulness, or divorce are indicative of mental illness would be illustrations of the use of ethical norms (that is, the desirability of love, kindness, and a stable marriage relationship). Finally, the widespread psychiatric opinion that only a mentally ill person would commit homicide illustrates the use of a legal concept as a norm of mental health. The norm from which deviation is measured whenever one speaks of a mental illness is a *psychosocial and ethical one*. Yet, the remedy is sought in terms of *medical measurers* which—it is hoped and assumed— are free from wide differences of ethical value. The definition of the disorder and the terms in which its remedy are sought are therefore at serious odds with one another. The practical significance of this covert conflict between the alleged nature of the defect and the remedy can hardly be exaggerated.

Having identified the norms used to measure deviations in cases of mental illness, we will now turn to the question: "Who defines the norms and hence the deviation?" Two basic answers may be offered: (*a*) It may be the person himself (that is, the patient) who decides that he deviates from a norm. For example, an artist may believe that he suffers from a work inhibition; and he may implement this conclusion by seeking help *for* himself from a psychotherapist. (*b*) It may be someone other than the patient who decides that the latter is deviant (for example, relatives, physicians, legal authorities, society generally, etc.). In such a case a psychiatrist may be hired by others to do something *to* the patient in order to correct the deviation.

These considerations underscore the importance of asking the question "Whose agent is the psychiatrist?" and of giving a candid answer to it (Szasz, 1956, 1958). The psychiatrist (psychologist or nonmedical psychotherapist), it now develops, may be the agent of the patient, of the relatives, of the school, of the military services, of a business organization, of a court of law, and so forth. In speaking of the psychiatrist as the agent of these persons or organizations, it is not implied that his values concerning norms, or his ideas and aims concerning the proper nature of remedial action, need to coincide exactly with those of his employer. For example, a patient in individual psychotherapy may believe that his salvation lies in a new marriage; his psychotherapist need not share this hypothesis. As the patient's agent, however, he must abstain from bringing social or legal force to bear on the patient which would prevent him from putting his beliefs into action. If his *contract* is with the patient, the psychiatrist (psychotherapist) may disagree with him or stop his treatment; but he cannot engage others to obstruct the patient's aspirations. Similarly, if a psychiatrist is engaged by a court to determine the sanity of a criminal, he need not fully share the legal authorities' values and intentions in regard to the criminal and the means available for dealing with him. But the psychiatrist is expressly barred from stating, for example, that it is not the criminal who is "insane" but the men who wrote the law on the basis of which the very actions that are being judged are regarded as "criminal." Such an opinion could be voiced, of course, but not in a courtroom, and not by a psychiatrist who makes it his practice to assist the court in performing its daily work.

To recapitulate: In actual contemporary social usage, the finding of a mental illness is made by establishing a deviance in behavior from certain psychosocial, ethical, or legal norms. The judgment may be made, as in medicine, by the patient, the physician (psychiatrist), or others. Remedial action, finally, tends to be sought in a therapeutic—or covertly medical—framework, thus creating a situation in which *psychosocial, ethical*, and/or *legal deviations* are claimed to be correctible by (so-called) *medical action*. Since medical action is designed to correct only medical deviations, it seems logically absurd to expect that it will help solve problems whose very existence has been defined and established on nonmedical grounds. I think that these considerations may be fruitfully applied to the present use of tranquilizers and, more generally, to what might be expected of drugs of whatever type in regard to the amelioration or solution of problems in human living.

THE ROLE OF ETHICS IN PSYCHIATRY

Anything that people *do*—in contrast to things that *happen* to them (Peters, 1958)—takes place in a context of value. In this broad sense, no human activity is devoid of ethical implications. When the values underlying certain activities are widely shared, those who participate in their pursuit may lose sight of them altogether. The discipline of medicine, both as a pure science (for example, research) and as a technology (for example, therapy), contains many ethical considerations and judgments. Unfortunately, these are often denied, minimized, or merely kept out of focus; for the ideal of the medical profession as well as of the people whom it serves seems to be having a system of medicine

(allegedly) free of ethical value. This sentimental notion is expressed by such things as the doctor's willingness to treat and help patients irrespective of their religious or political beliefs, whether they are rich or poor, etc. While there may be some grounds for this belief—albeit it is a view that is not impressively true even in these regards—the fact remains that ethical considerations encompass a vast range of human affairs. By making the practice of medicine neutral in regard to some specific issues of value need not, and cannot, mean that is can be kept free from all such values. The practice of medicine is intimately tied to ethics; and the first thing that we must do, it seems to me, is to try to make this clear and explicit. I shall let this matter rest here, for it does not concern us specifically in this essay. Lest there be any vagueness, however, about how or where ethics and medicine meet, let me remind the reader of such issues as birth control, abortion, suicide, and euthanasia as only a few of the major areas of current ethicomedical controversy.

Psychiatry, I submit, is very much more intimately tied to problems of ethics than is medicine. I use the word "psychiatry" here to refer to that contemporary discipline which is concerned with *problems in living* (and not with diseases of the brain, which are problems for neurology). Problems in human relations can be analyzed, interpreted, and given meaning only within given social and ethical contexts. Accordingly, it *does* make a difference— arguments to the contrary notwithstanding— what the psychiatrist's socioethical orientations happen to be; for these will influence his ideas on what is wrong with the patient, what deserves comment or interpretation, in what possible directions change might be desirable, and so forth. Even in medicine proper, these factors play a role, as for instance, in the divergent orientations which physicians, depending on their religious affiliations, have toward such things as birth control and therapeutic abortion. Can anyone really believe that a psychotherapist's ideas concerning religious belief, slavery, or other similar issues play no role in his practical work? If they do make a difference, what are we to infer from it? Does it not seem reasonable that we ought to have different psychiatric therapies—each expressly recognized for the ethical positions which they embody—for, say, Catholics and Jews, religious persons and agnostics, democrats and communists, white supremacists and Negroes, and so on? Indeed, if we look at how psychiatry is actually practiced today (especially in the United States), we find that people do seek psychiatric help in accordance with their social status and ethical beliefs (Hollingshead and Redlich, 1958). This should really not surprise us more than being told that practicing Catholics rarely frequent birth control clinics.

The foregoing position which holds that contemporary psychotherapists deal with problems in living, rather than with mental illnesses and their cures, stands in opposition to a currently prevalent claim, according to which mental illness is just as "real" and "objective" as bodily illness. This is a confusing claim since it is never known exactly what is meant by such words as "real" and "objective." I suspect, however, that what is intended by the proponents of this view is to create the idea in the popular mind that mental illness is some sort of disease entity, like an infection or a malignancy. If this were true, one could *catch* or *get* a "mental illness," one might *have* or *harbor* it, one might *transmit* it to others, and finally one could get *rid* of it. In my opinion, there is not a shred of evidence to support this idea. To the contrary, all the evidence is the other way and supports the view that what people now call mental illnesses are for the most part *communications* expressing unacceptable ideas, often framed, moreover, in an unusual idiom. The scope of this essay allows me to do no more than mention this alternative theoretical approach to this problem (Szasz, 1957c).

This is not the place to consider in detail the similarities and differences between bodily and mental illnesses. It shall suffice for us here to emphasize only one important difference between them: namely, that whereas bodily disease refers to public, physicochemical occurrences, the notion of mental illness is used to codify relatively more private, sociopsychological happenings of which the observer (diagnostician) forms a part. In other words, the psychiatrist does not stand *apart* from what he observes, but is, in Harry Stack Sullivan's apt words, a "participant observer." This means that he is *committed* to some picture of what he considers reality—and to what he thinks society considers reality—and he observes and judges the patient's behavior in the light of these considerations. This touches on our earlier observation that the notion of mental symptom itself implies a comparison between observer and observed, psychiatrist and patient. This is so obvious that I may be charged with belaboring trivialities. Let me therefore say once more that my aim in presenting this argument was expressly to criticize and counter a prevailing contemporary tendency to deny the moral aspects of psychiatry (and psychotherapy) and to substitute for them allegedly value-free medical considerations. Psychotherapy, for example, is being widely practiced as though it entailed nothing other than restoring the patient from a state of mental sickness to one of mental health. While it is generally accepted that mental illness has something to do with man's social (or interpersonal) relations, it is paradoxically maintained that problems of values (that is, of ethics) do not arise in this process.[1] Yet, in one sense, much of psychotherapy may revolve around nothing other than the elucidation and weighing of goals and values—many of which may be mutually contradictory—and the means whereby they might best be harmonized, realized, or relinquished.

---

[1]Freud went so far as to say that: "I consider ethics to be taken for granted. Actually I have never done a mean thing" (Jones, 1957, p. 247]. This surely is a strange thing to say for someone who has studied man as a social being as closely as did Freud. I mention it here to show how the notion of "illness" (in the case of psychoanalysis, "psychopathology," or "mental illness") was used by Freud—and by most of his followers—as a means for classifying certain forms of human behavior, as falling within the scope of medicine, and hence (by *fiat*) outside that of ethics!

The diversity of human values and the methods by means of which they may be realized is so vast, and many of them remain so unacknowledged, that they cannot fail but lead to conflicts in human relations. Indeed, to say that human relations at all levels—from mother to child, through husband and wife, to nation and nation—are fraught with stress, strain, and disharmony is, once again, making the obvious explicit. Yet, what may be obvious may be also poorly understood. This I think is the case here. For it seems to me that—at least in our scientific theories of behavior—we have failed to *accept* the simple fact that human relations are inherently fraught with difficulties and that to make them even relatively harmonious requires much patience and hard work. I submit that the idea of mental illness is now being put to work to obscure certain difficulties which at present may be inherent—not that they need be unmodifiable—in the social intercourse of persons. If this is true, the concept functions as a disguise; for instead of calling attention to conflicting human needs, aspirations, and values, the notion of mental illness provides an amoral and impersonal "thing" (an "illness") as an explanation for *problems in living* (Szasz, 1959). We may recall in this connection that not so long ago it was devils and witches who were held responsible for men's problems in social living. The belief in mental illness, as something other than man's trouble in getting along with his fellow man, is the proper heir to the belief in demonology and witchcraft. Mental illness exists or is "real" in exactly the same sense in which witches existed or were "real."

CHOICE, RESPONSIBILITY, AND PSYCHIATRY

While I have argued that mental illnesses do not exist, I obviously did not imply that the social and psychological occurrences to which this label is currently being attached also do not exist. Like the personal and social troubles which people had in the Middle Ages, they are real enough. It is the labels we give them that concerns us and, having labelled them, what we

do about them. While I cannot go into the ramified implications of this problem here, it is worth noting that a demonologic conception of problems in living gave rise to therapy along theological lines. Today, a belief in mental illness implies—nay, requires—therapy along medical or psychotherapeutic lines.

What is implied in the line of thought set forth here is something quite different. I do not intend to offer a new conception of "psychiatric illness" nor a new form of "therapy." My aim is more modest and yet also more ambitious. It is to suggest that the phemonema now called mental illnesses be looked at afresh and more simply, that they be removed from the category of illnesses, and that they be regarded as the expressions of man's struggle with the problem of *how* he should live. The last mentioned problem is obviously a vast one, its enormity reflecting not only man's inability to cope with his environment, but even more his increasing self-reflectiveness.

By problems in living, then, I refer to that truly explosive chain reaction which began with man's fall from divine grace by partaking of the fruit of the tree of knowledge. Man's awareness of himself and of the world about him seems to be a steadily expanding one, bringing in its wake an ever larger *burden of understanding* (an expression borrowed from Susanne Langer, 1953). *This burden*, then, *is to be expected and must not be misinterpreted.* Our only *rational* means for lightening it is *more understanding*, and appropriate *action* based on such understanding. The main alternative lies in acting as though the burden were not what in fact we perceive it to be and taking refuge in an outmoded theological view of man. In the latter view, man does not fashion his life and much of his world about him, but merely lives out his fate in a world created by superior beings. This may logically lead to pleading nonresponsibility in the face of seemingly unfathomable problems and difficulties. Yet, if man fails to take increasing responsibility for his actions, individually as well as collectively, it seems unlikely that some higher power or being would assume this task and carry this burden for him. Moreover, this seems hardly the proper time in human history for obscuring the issue of man's responsibility for his actions by hiding it behind the skirt of an all-explaining conception of mental illness.

CONCLUSIONS

I have tried to show that the notion of mental illness has outlived whatever usefulness it might have had and that it now functions merely as a convenient myth. As such, it is a true heir to religious myths in general, and to the belief in witchcraft in particular; the role of all these belief-systems was to act as *social tranquilizers*, thus encouraging the hope that mastery of certain specific problems may be achieved by means of substitutive (symbolic-magical) operations. The notion of mental illness thus serves mainly to obscure the everyday fact that life for most people is a continuous struggle, not for biological survival, but for a "place in the sun," "peace of mind," or some other human value. For man aware of himself and of the world about him, once the needs for preserving the body (and perhaps the race) are more or less satisfied, the problem arises as to what he should do with himself. Sustained adherence to the myth of mental illness allows people to avoid facing this problem, believing that mental health, conceived as the absence of mental illness, automatically insures the making of right and safe choices in one's conduct of life. But the facts are all the other way. It is the making of good choices in life that others regard, retrospectively, as good mental health!

The myth of mental illness encourages us, moreover, to believe in its logical corollary: that social intercourse would be harmonious, satisfying, and the secure basis of a "good life" were it not for the disrupting influences of mental illness or "psychopathology." The potentiality for universal human happiness, in this form at least, seems to me but another example of the I-wish-it-were-true type of fantasy. I do believe that human happiness or well-being on a hitherto unimaginably large scale, and not just for a

select few, is possible. This goal could be achieved, however, only at the cost of many men, and not just a few being willing and able to tackle their personal, social, and ethical conflicts. This means having the courage and integrity to forego waging battles on false fronts, finding solutions for substitute problems—for instance, fighting the battle of stomach acid and chronic fatigue instead of facing up to a marital conflict.

Our adversaries are not demons, witches, fate, or mental illness. We have no enemy whom we can fight, exorcise, or dispel by "cure." What we do have are *problems in living*—whether these be biologic, economic, political, or sociopsychological. In this essay I was concerned only with problems belonging in the last mentioned category, and within this group mainly with those pertaining to moral values. The field to which modern psychiatry addresses itself is vast, and I made no effort to encompass it all. My argument was limited to the proposition that mental illness is a myth, whose function it is to disguise and thus render more palatable the bitter pill of moral conflicts in human relations.

REFERENCES

Hollingshead, A. B., and Redlich, F. C. *Social class and mental illness.* New York: Wiley, 1958.

Jones, E. *The life and work of Sigmund Freud.* Vol. 3. New York: Basic Books, 1957.

Langer, S. K. *Philosophy in a new key.* New York: Mentor Books, 1953.

Peters, R. S. *The concept of motivation.* London: Routledge & Kegan Paul, 1958.

Szasz, T. S. Malingering: "Diagnosis" or social condemnation? *AMA Arch. Neurol. Psychiat.*, 1956, 76, 432–43.

Szasz, T. S. *Pain and pleasure: A study of bodily feelings.* New York: Basic Books, 1957. (a)

Szasz, T. S. The problem of psychiatric nosology: A contribution to a situational analysis of psychiatric operations, *Amer. J. Psychiat.*, 1957, 114, 405–13. (b)

Szasz, T. S. On the theory of psychoanalytic treatment, *Int. J. Psycho-Anal.*, 1957, 38, 166–82. (c)

Szasz, T. S. Psychiatry, ethics and the criminal law. *Columbia Law Rev.*, 1958, 58, 183–98.

Szasz, T. S. Moral conflict and psychiatry, *Yale Rev.*, 1959, in press.

FREDERICK C. THORNE

AN ANALYSIS OF SZASZ'S "MYTH OF MENTAL ILLNESS"

Thomas S. Szasz has recently created a great deal of public confusion concerning the concept of mental health by his contention that mental illness is a myth and, by implication, the claim that current psychiatric practices infringe on human rights by committing mental patients to hospitals against their will. Szasz has taken his arguments to the general public in popular articles and books, writing in a superficially convincing style which, however, involves serious untruths and distortions of facts.

Because Szasz's arguments might well set back the evolution of modern psychiatry and clinical psychology at a time when a huge national mental health program is just starting, it behooved the author to make an ideological analysis of his latest claims.

Following is an analysis of Szasz's claims in a *New York Times Magazine* article of June 12, 1966, entitled "The Myth of Mental Illness."

1. Mental illness is a myth because minds are not physical objects and consequently are not subject to physical disease in the medical sense.

Rebuttal: While mental disorder may have different causes than physical diseases, the functional effects are comparably disabling. "Illness" as a generic term refers to disablement rather than to any specific physical or psychological cause.

2. Insofar as men are human beings, they always have some choice in how they act—hence they are always responsible for their conduct.

Rebuttal: Not psychiatrically true. All mental disorder involves loss of self-control in some manner. The greater the impairment of self-control, the less a man is volitionally responsible for his conduct.

Reprinted from *American Journal of Psychiatry* 123 (1966): 652–656, by permission of the American Psychiatric Association and Frederick C. Thorne. Copyright © 1966 by the American Psychiatric Association.

3. There is method in madness . . .

Rebuttal: An overgeneralization implying that deliberate motives determine all symptomatology.

4. Social situations and human behavior in them are analogous to games. Confusion over changing rules for playing games results in conflict in trying to solve problems of living—some severe enough to be diagnosed as "mental illness" or "disease." This is invalid because we are dealing with disordered human relations.

Rebuttal: Not psychiatrically true. At best an oversimplification applicable only to limited cases. Mental disorder is more than just poor gamesmanship, as Szasz implies. There is a hen-egg problem here which Szasz does not realize. Are human relations disordered inevitably because of conflicting life or "game" styles? Or because either or all participants in a situation may be psychologically ill? Either may be true.

5. The historical model of mental hospitals is to serve as a place for institutionalizing many types of persons not adapting to society, including many others besides the overtly mentally ill.

Rebuttal: While it is true that the role of mental hospitals has been gradually extended to serve many clinical types other than the classically mentally disordered, the decision to admit other types of cases was made deliberately because better facilities were not available at the time and place.

6. Even though current laws authorize the involuntary commitment of psychotic persons to mental hospitals, such deprivations of human rights are not validly applicable to the aged, epileptics, alcoholics, etc., who do not have any mental disease. In fact, since there is no such thing as mental disease, the whole commitment system is unconstitutional and undemocratic.

Rebuttal: Practices regarding commitment of other groups besides the psychotic evolved as social expedients at a time when more specialized facilities were not economically feasible or professionally possible.

7. Intolerable abuses have occurred when persons have been committed against their will by psychiatrists who were reacting more to the demands of third persons or social authorities than to the needs of the patient, to whom he is first obligated.

Rebuttal: Abuses are possible in any situation involving humans. However, most civilized societies have recognized the physician as the one most able to diagnose and treat conduct disorders with an understanding, healing manner. Historically, greater abuses have occurred with nonpsychiatric case handling.

8. The social role of the psychiatrist is determined by the nature of the institutions in which he works. This role is determined by the "disease" concept and gives the psychiatrist directive, authoritative, controlling powers over unwilling patients, who actually have no "disease" but are only maladapted.

Rebuttal: A great step forward was taken when the old jungle-rule, "eye-for-an-eye" punitive system for discouraging conduct problems was replaced by the healing methods of the physician and hospital. In general, no widespread abuses have occurred under psychiatric management, which represents an evolutionary step forward until society develops something better.

9. Too often, "mental patients" are institutionalized for the convenience of others, with the psychiatrist representing the interests of third parties rather than the primary interest of the patient. Too often, commitment only protects the family or society at the expense of the civil rights of the patient.

Rebuttal: While such complaints occasionally are justified, this argument is an overstatement and overgeneralized. The ethical psychiatrist tries not to be unduly influenced by complaints of third parties against the patient. Moreover, too often third parties and society do need to be protected from the patient.

10. Szasz admits that in the organic psychoses there do occur lesions in the central nervous system such as those which underlie classical physical diseases. However, he claims that "functional" or "psychological" disorders involve conditions manifested chiefly by the person's behaving "differently" from usual social expectations. He contends that it is semantically invalid to categorize persons as "sick" just because they are different.

Rebuttal: Szasz minimizes the psychophysiological dysfunctions underlying all the psychoses, the severe psychoneuroses, epilepsy, alcoholism, addictions, and other conditions involving greater or lesser loss of self control. The important differentiation is not between being "different" but in being "disabled" and partially out of control.

11. It is invalid to classify a person as "ill" because of behavior expressing deviant social roles. Roles are social artifacts, and deviance has meaning only in terms of social customs or laws.

Rebuttal: An overgeneralization. Only when deviant behavior is dangerous or disabling does it command a psychiatric diagnosis or labeling.

12. Psychiatric opinion concerning the criteria of mental health determines the kinds of deviance regarded as "mental illness." Psychiatric opinion may be fallible, prejudiced by irrelevant factors, or even by ulterior motivations. Constitutional protection should be given against psychiatric invasion of the human rights of freedom and privacy.

Rebuttal: Theoretically true but practically unjustified. No type of clinical practice can be more perfect than what is scientifically known at the time and place. Well trained and competent psychiatric specialists are presumably wiser and more trustworthy in their decisions than are less qualified personnel.

13. Psychiatry creates new classes of mental illness every time it formulates new rules for mental health . . . (constantly expanding) the category of people who can be legitimately classified as psychologically sick. Labeling people as mentally ill is a special kind of name-calling . . . by a psychiatrist who makes a diagnosis (especially of an involuntary patient) and has more social power than the person he diagnoses.

Rebuttal: These arguments involve a cynical and perverse distortion of the whole process of diagnosis by a qualified specialist. Progress in all clinical sciences occurs by the progressive differentiation of previously unrecognized etiology and patterns of disorder. It is not name-calling to devise more refined diagnoses. Szasz provides no evidence of any widespread name-calling on the part of psychiatrists, the overwhelming majority of whom use diagnosis scientifically and not to discriminate against anybody.

14. Criminal insanity is a metaphorical and strategic concept, just as civil insanity is. . . . Insanity should (not) be an "excusing condition" for crime. Lawbreakers, irrespective of their "mental health," ought to be treated as offenders.

Rebuttal: This argument represents a regression to a prescientific failure to discriminate between the normal and the disabled. In general, hospitalization is more humane than penal incarceration. Penal systems do not provide adequate resources for disposing of many categories of psychiatric cases.

15. Many patients do not seek psychiatric treatment voluntarily and are coerced by relatives or authorities into a role not of their own choosing . . . like a prisoner sentenced to a term of servitude. Coercion has no place in psychiatric treatment, which requires a cooperative client.

Rebuttal: A classical symptom of many mental conditions is lack of insight, i.e., the person does not recognize the degree of his disability or impairment of judgment. In general, the greater the loss of insight and of self control, the more dangerous the person becomes.

16. The humanistic view of denying the existence of mental illness would remove the justification for involuntary hospitalization and treatment. We should empty out all our mental hospitals and provide more humane alternatives, including the use of nonmedical personnel such as clinical psychologists, social workers, ministers, educators, etc.

Rebuttal: This viewpoint does not give proper weight to the fact that psychiatry and our mental hospital and clinic resources represent the best that society has yet been able to devise. Szasz has no evidence that anything currently available would be any better.

17. Even the usual justification for committing persons on the grounds that they are dangerous to self or others is both illogical and unconstitutional.

Rebuttal: This argument seems to be leaning over backwards in protection of the disordered person at the expense of the rights of society, which also deserves protection.

18. Suicide should be recognized as a basic human right. The threat or attempt at suicide should not be made the basis for involuntary hospitalization.

Rebuttal: This view is contrary to established public mores based on Judeo-Christian morality. It disregards the fact that most suicides occur in depressive states which react well to therapy. It is logical that a completely normal person might be regarded as having the right to end his own life but not humane that a curable disordered person should be allowed to do so.

19. The social control of dangerous behavior is complicated by the fact that people disagree as to what is dangerous and also on how such control is to be established. Many persons now committed are dangerous only by "fiat" or in terms of some purely relative standard. This is dangerous to civil liberties and should be unconstitutional.

Rebuttal: Legal status in any era is always relative to the level of enlightenment of time and place. Legal codes and psychiatric standards are not whimsical judgments by irresponsible personnel but rather the best decisions which can be reached by the fairest and best qualified in society.

20. Szasz makes an impassioned appeal for a new humanistic psychiatry which will rethink its social obligations. The nominal aim of studying and treating mental disorders, implying the existence of a class of phenomena called "mental diseases" and embodying classical

coercive methods of institutionalization and treatment, should be replaced by inquiries into the conditions under which some persons may designate others as mentally ill and by a more free-thinking consideration of the games which people (including psychiatrists) play on each other.

Rebuttal: Szasz does not have a monopoly on humanistic wishes for the future. He portrays psychiatrists as a group as being nonperceptive of what they are actually doing, responsive to ulterior motivations secondary to the primary goal of satisfying the needs of the patient, heartless in their disregard of the need to be free and uncoerced, and slaves to an authoritarian tradition which gives them total control over the lives and destinies of other humans. While Szasz might gather instances of isolated abuses of clinical authority, he cannot marshal evidence of such an indictment of psychiatry in particular or society in general. He is simply jousting against straw men for the large part of his arguments.

21. The psychiatrist deals with moral and social problems rather than mental disease, hence he cannot keep from becoming embroiled in the moral conflicts of his patient and of society. The individual man can never escape the moral burden of his existence, and any (including psychiatrists) who attempt to take from him his moral burden must also take from him his liberty and hence his very humanity.

Rebuttal: Szasz is behind the times in not recognizing that many social psychiatrists have long been working in the humanistic direction which Szasz recommends. Carl R. Rogers recommended such ideals more than 25 years ago, as did many other pioneers in changing psychiatric practice and hospitals into genuinely humanistic ventures.

22. A humanistic psychiatry must repudiate its seemingly therapeutic mandate and goals of social control, and instead of trying to diminish man's moral burdens, should attempt to increase his powers and so make him equal to his task. Szasz endorses the statement of Camus that "The aim of life can only be to increase the sum of freedom and responsibility to be found in every man and in the world. It cannot, under any circumstances, be to reduce or suppress that freedom, even temporarily."

Rebuttal: This argument is very appealing and is valid as far as it goes. Certainly no responsible authority in society, much less psychiatrists, knowingly works to deprive anyone of civil liberties. The crucial question concerns persons who are too disabled or out of control to be able to utilize freedom responsibly. The uncontrolled, violently dangerous person requires external controls and institutionalization as long as he remains in such a state. The issue is not one of denying freedoms but of withholding them until the person is able to handle them responsibly.

DISCUSSION

Szasz's arguments contain a modicum of truth and of deserved criticism for psychiatric practices at their worst. Undoubtedly many abuses, injustices, and clinical errors have occurred during the growing up of a young clinical science whose personnel consist of fallible humans. However, it is unfair and irresponsible to criticize or categorize the entire profession of psychiatry as inhumane on the basis of isolated examples of malpractice. The profession of clinical psychology (and psychiatry to a lesser degree) has been its own worst critic in scientifically evaluating its clinical results to determine their validity and how they can be improved.

Many of the Szasz arguments are seen to be exaggerated, biased, alarmist, impractical, and even erroneous. This is the kind of harangue which would be expected from a demagogue rather than a responsible scientist. Does Szasz really believe that such immoderate attacks on his own profession will improve public confidence in the mental health movement? To the contrary, there already exist many intemperate groups who are actively lobbying against the mental health movement and whose misguided efforts are encouraged by such specious arguments as Szasz offers.

Szasz's role as an indealistic, liberal reformer would be considerably brighter if his efforts were more constructively directed. The issues he raises should be debated within scientific and professional councils rather than being broadcast to a public which does not have the background to judge the arguments. Szasz is grandiose in depicting himself as the savior of modern psychiatry at a time when a host of devoted colleagues are working with comparably high ideals.

One practical effect of Szasz's arguments has been to confuse the outlook of students, interns, residents, and young psychiatrists who do not have the experience to judge their validity. Perhaps the most important truth in the whole field of psychiatry relates to the refractoriness and difficulty in treating serious psychiatric conditions. In spite of recent progress with drugs, many psychiatric conditions do not respond to any known kind of therapy. Such cases do not respond even to the most humanitarian case handling, including a surfeit of love, every-thing that money can buy, kindness, warmth, acceptance, and nonjudgmental attitudes. In fact, some very experienced psychiatrists have stated that the most curative influence of the mental hospital was the unpleasantness of the situation, which stimulated the patient to mobilize all his forces to get out. And whether we wish to call severe psychiatric disorders "diseases," "illness," "disorders," "disturbed human relations," "disabilities," or "social deviances," the fact remains that we are dealing with something more malignant than a game.

While everyone wishes to do his utmost for all types of unfortunates, the fact remains that any one group cannot command more that its share of social resources, and the law of diminishing returns limits what can be invested in any single case, no matter how piteous. I suppose if nobody had anything with higher priority to do, one half of society could devote all its time to taking care of the less fortunate. Unfortunately, the work of the world must be done before such surplus resources as are available can be allocated to underprivileged groups, of which the psychiatrically disabled are only one.

UNIT 15

DEATH AND DYING

☐ It has been said that the topic of death and dying is as hard for parents to discuss with their children as is sex. These subjects do seem difficult for us. We have a tendency to try to sweep them under the rug and ignore them so that they won't bother us. When we are forced to talk about death, we use such euphemisms as: "passed away" or "is no longer with us." We don't say that people are dying; we say that they "are critically ill" or "have a guarded prognosis." Above all, as you probably already realize, we do not usually tell people that they are dying.

Only recently has death begun to be discussed more openly. Several factors seem to be responsible for this change. A major factor seems to be the research we have begun on the aging process in humans. Our inevitable march toward death is certainly a part of aging. As we study the psychology of aging, it is virtually impossible to ignore the impact of approaching death. Another, closely related factor is the trend toward an average older age of the world's population. Still another factor has been our technological progress in keeping people alive beyond the time when they would normally have died. This phenomenon has caused us to examine quite carefully just what death is from a legal standpoint and, more important, what our thoughts are on how and when a person should be allowed to die.

This unit will consider various aspects of death and dying. It will adopt a primarily personal viewpoint by asking you to analyze your feelings, attitudes, and beliefs. In this way it will perhaps make you more comfortable when the topics of death and dying are brought up. At least you will have had a chance to consider where you stand.

When you have completed this unit, you should be able to:

1. *Analyze your own attitudes toward death and dying.*
2. *Explain why the topics of death and dying are so difficult to discuss.*
3. *Define the different kinds of death.*
4. *Explain what is meant by physiological death, and cite some of the problems involved in defining it.*
5. *State your feelings about the death with dignity movement.*
6. *State your attitudes toward euthanasia.*
7. *Describe social death.*
8. *Present some thoughts about alleviating social death.*
9. *Explain what is meant by psychological death.*
10. *Give some reasons for suicide.*
11. *Describe some of society's attitudes toward suicide.*
12. *Describe a potentially suicidal person.*
13. *Suggest ways of helping a suicidal person.*
14. *Explain the stages of dying.*
15. *Suggest a program for dealing with a dying person.*
16. *Give some thoughts on the education of children about death and dying.*

A PERSONAL ANALYSIS

The following open-ended questions are designed to help you confront directly the topics of death and dying. You are asked to give your own feelings about each question. Be as open and candid as you can. If you really don't have an opinion or an attitude toward a particular concept, it may pay off if you stop and think about it.

1. Explain what death is.
2. Can you visualize your own death?
3. Do you think that death is good or bad—that is, would you like to be immortal or perhaps to live for one, two, or three thousand years?
4. Have you ever longed for death or thought of suicide?
5. Are you afraid of death? Explain your answer.
6. Should people have the right to kill themselves? Explain.
7. Do you believe in an afterlife? If so, describe it.
8. What effect do your religious beliefs have on your attitudes toward death, dying, and suicide?
9. Have you ever had, or seen someone else have, any mystic experiences such as astral levitation, out-of-body imagery, or clairvoyance? If so, how have these events affected your attitudes toward life and death?
10. Would you like to know the date of your own death?
11. Would you like to know how you are going to die?
12. Would you like to know how people close to you are going to die and when?
13. If you had a limited time to live, say two years, what would you do?
14. What do you think about funerals?
15. Have you ever given any thought to your funeral and how it should be conducted?
16. Would you dedicate your body to science?
17. What are your feelings about the death with dignity movement?
18. Explain how the decision to "pull the plug" and let a person die should be made.
19. Have you ever had contact with a person who was dying? How did you feel? How did you act?
20. What, when, where, and how should we teach children about the facts of death?

When you have answered these twenty questions, go back over your answers and summarize them in one paragraph that describes your feelings and attitudes toward death and dying.

1. Analyze your own attitudes toward death and dying.

_____

_____

THE DISCOMFORT OF TALKING ABOUT DEATH

It is remarkable that we have so much trouble talking about what is, after all, a very commonplace event. Death comes to all of us in one way or another. It is as natural as any of the rest of our life's processes. Yet we think about death reluctantly, if at all, and discuss it only when we are forced to. One can't help wondering why this aversion to the topics surrounding death is so strong.

Perhaps one reason is that we really do not know what is "out there." Human beings have been peculiarly reluctant to consider the proposition that death is the end of existence for a person. Naturally, the concept of life after death has been much debated, and many imaginative accounts of what life after death is have been put forward. Some accounts speak of a universal cosmic consciousness. Dante described with appalling clarity the depths of hell for sinners. Other thinkers have preferred to dwell on paradise. The whole point is that we do not *know*, and our tendency is to fear what we do not know or understand.

More complex is the influence of bereavement, the death of a person close to us. We have a sense of loss, abandonment, and separation from the person. We grieve. Since this experience is unpleasant, the whole topic of death thus becomes unpleasant, by association; we don't want to contemplate situations that are unpleasant.

From this experience and that of realizing that someone you know is dead comes these logical thoughts: *I* will die. I know that I am mortal like my fellow humans. I cannot prevent my death, although I can take some steps to delay it or avoid certain causes for it. From what I know about it, death is a final event for me. I will never again be able to walk on this earth, to enjoy my loved ones and my environment. I will probably cause grief and suffering to others when I die. My social upbringing has established within me various and sometimes confusing attitudes toward death. On the one hand, death may be looked on as a release from worldly boundaries to a life of perpetual ease and pleasure. On the other hand, death is threatening, because when I die my deeds will be evaluated, and I shall be required to pay the penalty for my misdeeds. Thus my death may lead to suffering and pain for me. This may be an eternal state, especially if I feel that I have sinned deeply. Because I know that I have not lived a perfect life as my society defines it, it is likely that I will experience punishment rather than pleasure. Thus my society may have instilled in me a fear of death.

Perhaps another unpleasant thought connected with death is our personal fear of suffering from a long and lingering disease. We have seen others go through such an experience and have watched them suffer and disintegrate before our eyes. Naturally, we translate this in terms of our own lives. We very definitely do not want to face that possibility. In this context, we tend to avoid any considerations of when we shall die or how. Most of us, when pressed, would express a preference for death to be unexpected and quick. We really do not want to know when we are going to die, and we especially don't want to go through pain and suffering before we die. Perhaps the inherent dread of this possibility leads to a form of anxiety or a dread of death. We don't want to think about it because it might be a horrible experience for us.

This outlook may be reinforced by our childhood experiences. We are often shielded from death but in a very inadequate way. When a member of the family dies, we are told that Aunt May has gone away. At the same time, we feel around us the negative emotions of sorrow and grief. We see the gathering of people, all of whom show signs that something serious or terrible has happened. We don't understand why. However, we do come to realize that such "going away" has some serious and unpleasant meaning to it. We respond to the emotional set of the group and begin to associate death with negative emotions. After all, that's what the adults around us have been doing, so apparently it's the right thing to do. From this base comes the very simple conclusion that death is something unpleasant and to be feared.

Suicide, the willful destruction of one's own life, is still another manifestation of an uncomfortable event. Many cultures regard suicide as an evil act. As you will see later, the reasons for some suicides are anger or hostility, and our feelings toward the deceased may involve the same emotions. Thus suicide may also have negative connotations for us. Curiously, however, we tend to honor those who have sacrificed themselves for others in battle or for love. Thus we can be ambivalent about the act of suicide. Ambivalence or uncertainty often leads to negative feelings because of confusion.

It seems, then, that unpleasant feelings about death and dying (including suicide) can be caused by three basic factors: the mystery of afterlife, the conditioning we have received in unpleasant episodes surrounding death, and our dislike of the unpredictable circumstances surrounding our own death. Thus fears of dying affect and color our fears of death.

2. *Explain why the topics of death and dying are so difficult to discuss.*

_____

_____

_____

_____

THE DIFFERENT FORMS OF DEATH

If you and I were talking about death and I asked you to name the different kinds of death, you would probably say, "Come on, Doc, when you're dead, you're dead!" If I pressed you further, you might bring up cases of people who were considered to be dead and were medically certified as such but then revived; we would probably agree that what these people experienced was not true death, but probably an erroneously diagnosed state. I might also mention the concept of a quick death, such as from an accident or a sudden heart attack, as opposed to a slow, lingering death from some debilitating disease, such as cancer. However, you could astutely point out that I was really discussing various conditions of dying rather than the phenomenon of death itself. We might then agree that death is death and that's all there is to it. However, we would be wrong.

The concept that there are various types of death has come from two sources. One is the study of what happens during the aging process. The other is medical technology. From studies of aging has come the realization that people can be socially dead—when they no longer have any meaningful interactions with society. Also from studies of aged people and those who are under strong stress for relatively long periods comes the realization that people can be psychologically dead—when they lose the will to live or reach a mental acceptance of imminent death and stop fighting it. Medical advances have resulted in an ability to keep our body organs functioning artificially, long after they would normally have stopped. This process might be considered an artificial prolongation of life, or at least of physiological functioning.

Thus it is possible to identify three different kinds of death: social, psychological, and physiological. Each kind has its own implications in the study of human behavior.

Parenthetically, another form of behavior has been labeled by Kastenbaum and Aisenberg *thanatomimetic* or *sham death*. (In Greek, *thanatos* means *death* and *mimos* means *imitation*; thus thanatomimetic death is imitation death.) They cite the behavior of various animals, especially the American opossum, that feign death when attacked. The question then comes up: Can a human feign death and is it ever done? This does not seem to be ordinary behavior for human beings. Yet might we not consider some miraculous revivals from death as evidence for this form of behavior in humans? A procedure was described in 1913 by which tonic immobility could be produced in humans. If you lean forward from the waist, place your hands over your abdomen, take a deep breath, and then are suddenly thrown on your back, you will go into a state of immobility that lasts for several seconds and seems to resemble the feigned death of the opossum. (I might add that I have not tried this procedure, so I am reporting strictly from hearsay.) Thus there might possibly be still another form of death: thanatomimetic or sham death in humans. This form of death definitely exists in the animal world.

3. Define the different kinds of death.

_____

_____

PHYSIOLOGICAL DEATH

In the good old days, the diagnosis of death was a relatively simple matter. If a person's heart was not beating and there was no pulse, it was permissible to label the state as death. If a person stopped breathing, this state could also be considered death. If a person no longer responded to stimulation, such as pain, he or she could be considered dead. If all three of these criteria coincided, there was little room for doubt.

Various criteria of this type have been developed to determine when death has occurred. The following list summarizes these criteria:

1. A lack of response to external stimulation (including pain), involving a deep unconsciousness
2. No reflex actions, such as responses of the pupils of the eye to light, or deep-tendon reflexes
3. No muscular movement at all
4. No breathing
5. A sudden fall in blood pressure to zero
6. No tracings on an electrocardiogram

In the last few decades, however, some new medical procedures have made definition on the basis of these criteria not only questionable but virtually unusable. Consider, for instance, a young man who is brought into a hospital suffering from massive brain damage. His skull has been so severely shattered that his brain has been almost totally destroyed. Yet his heart can be kept beating and his breathing can be maintained. The physician knows that this person will not, indeed cannot, live except by means of extraordinary measures. Even those measures will not undo the damage, and the individual will always need artificial support to remain alive. He will never again think or regain consciousness. Lying in another room is a person with a severely damaged heart. This heart patient can be saved from death by a heart transplant. Can the surgeon decide that the young man is dead and salvage his heart for the transplant? Or might he face a charge for murder?

It does no good to argue the predicament in terms of moral or social obligations, although the morality of the issue is certainly part of the problem. What is needed is a clear statement of the legal-medical definition of death that permits the use of living organs after the hope of reversal of the death of nonliving organs is gone. What makes this definition of death complicated is that our bodies do not die all at once. Organs and tissues remain alive. Even though the three cardinal organs—the heart, the lungs, and the brain—may have ceased to function, other organs continue to function. The muscles still respond to shock. The liver still manufactures glucose. The hair continues to grow. If only one of the three primary organs has failed, we can keep a person "alive." Thus, while there may be local death (whether a dead tooth or a dead brain) in a living body, so there may be local life in a dead body. Since we have an increasing ability to replace nonfunctioning organs with ones that are still functioning, how can we decide when a person is dead so that still-functioning organs can be used for other people?

The medical profession has established two different kinds of physiological death: clinical and biological. The distinction between the two types lies in their reversibility. Clinical death involves the criteria previously mentioned; however, it can be reversed, whereas biological death cannot. The question then becomes one of deciding when clinical death becomes biological death. Unfortunately, there is no fixed boundary between the two. For a young person, the change may take as long as nine minutes. For a person who has been ill, it may take only a minute. Ten minutes seems to be the longest possible time that clinical death can last before it turns into biological death. These measurements leave something to be desired because clinical death is still a vague construct that plagues all physicians. Unless they take all of the necessary technical actions to reverse clinical death, even though the situation appears hopeless, they must face the fact that they have broken their oath of service to humanity. This pressure leads physicians to decide that they must keep people on life-sustaining machines, preserving their clinical life indefinitely, even though there is no hope of reversing the destruction of the nonworking organ. Thus it is possible to keep a person alive by technology long after the hope of recovery, remission, or improvement is gone.

4. *Explain what is meant by physiological death, and cite some of the problems involved in defining it.*

_____

_____

_____

_____

DEATH WITH DIGNITY

Our technological advances have led us into several moral dilemmas. One of these is reflected in the death with dignity movement. The theme of this movement is that, if all hope is gone and death is inevitable, a person should be allowed to die. The doctor should not attempt to prolong life by artificial methods in such a case, especially if a person has come to an acceptance of death and is no longer emotionally disturbed by its imminence. In several instances, famous persons have been kept alive artificially; for example, former President Harry Truman was kept alive by machines and medication long after all hope was gone. This course of action aroused a national protest that made evident the fact that our technology and our sensibility were in direct conflict.

Those who advocate death with dignity argue that patients who have accepted death and are no longer emotionally disturbed by its imminence should be granted their wish to die. If, for example, they want to go home to die in familiar, pleasant surroundings, that wish should be granted. Many people feel so strongly about this issue that they have prepared directives that specifically prohibit their being kept alive by artificial means. They argue that such an extension of life is artificial and demeaning. They do not want to become mere extensions of a machine.

It seems that a reasonable compromise is to consider the desires of patients and their families. If patients who are capable of expressing their wishes seem to have accepted death and are no longer emotionally disturbed by it, and if their families agree, then such patients should be allowed to die as they wish.

However, this decision obviously dooms a patient. Who should be responsible for making it? It is unfair to put the burden on the patient's doctor. It is equally unfair to put the burden on the family, although logically they may be considered the ones who should make the decision. The problem is that, while the patient may have accepted death, the family may not have. They may still be emotionally upset to the point where they cannot handle the proposal. The burden of having a dying person in the home might seem unbearable to them. On top of this emotional turmoil is the nagging thought that while there's life, there's hope.

Thus death with dignity is indeed a threefold, complex problem with no easy solutions or glib answers in sight. It involves the doctor, the patient, and the family. What do you think about this issue?

5. *State your feelings about the death with dignity movement.*

_____

_____

_____

_____

EUTHANASIA

Closely allied to the death with dignity movement is the euthanasia or mercy-killing movement, which uses almost the same arguments with one significant difference. The death with dignity movement, as described above, restricts the problem to the cases of individuals who are capable of making a decision about ending their own lives. What about patients who are unconscious or unable to communicate for some other reason? These individuals cannot be a party to the decision. People who have signed directives saying that they do not wish their lives to be artificially prolonged are trying to prevent just this situation. They fear that they may not be able to communicate their wishes at the time of their illness. They are preparing for this possibility by stating their desires in advance.

In a sense, then, the death with dignity movement is only part of a larger problem. Now that we can maintain life long after it would normally have ceased, just when does the act of prolongation become a violation of our moral scruples? Several scenarios can serve to point up the problem.

Case A: A young girl fell into a deep coma after taking a mixture of drugs. Her organs remained functional but her conscious brain was lost. There was absolutely no evidence of any higher-level brain activity. After she had been kept alive for a year by a machine, her parents requested that the girl be allowed to die. The hospital refused to discontinue use of the machine to sustain the girl's life. After seeking religious counsel, the parents took the issue to court. The court ruled in their favor and the girl was taken off the machine.

Case B: A three-year-old girl was beaten so severely that her brain activity ceased. The child was kept alive by artificial means. Her parents requested that these efforts be terminated. The hospital refused. The parents sued but the case became moot when the girl died of heart failure.

Case C: A male, aged 35, was brought into the emergency ward horribly mangled from an industrial accident. His arms and legs were destroyed and his internal organs had been crushed. He was in extreme shock. It was obvious that he would die if left untended. However, with the use of machines, his damaged organs could be supplemented so that he would remain alive. He would never recover except as a quadriplegic with only his mind functioning. He would always need machine support.

Case D: A patient was suffering from a form of cancer that had progressed to the point where there was unbearable pain. It was a terminal case. In order to make the pain bearable, the patient had to be drugged into unconsciousness.

The dilemmas are obvious. We are torn between our technology and our concern for the suffering of others. Space does not allow for a review of all of the arguments concerning euthanasia, nor does it seem possible to present these arguments in such a way that the passions of those on both sides could be appeased. Thus I will not even attempt to summarize the pros and cons except to point out that most people seem to be extremely wary of any proposals for a decision-making process to permit euthanasia. Many have not forgotten that Hitler referred to the massacre of millions of Jews as euthanasia.

6. State your attitudes toward euthanasia.

_____

_____

SOCIAL DEATH

The term *social death* has already been described. Social death occurs when individuals have withdrawn from the world and no longer have a functional role in society. Their friends have left them; they have no attachments left; they have made a clean break with everyone. People are socially dead when they have settled their obligations, arranged for the care of their dependents, and no longer have any function or activity left. If they were to disappear in a split second, no one would miss them, need them, or need to adjust to their disappearance. This is social death.

7. Describe social death.

_____

_____

_____

_____

A PROGRAM FOR PREVENTING SOCIAL DEATH

Social death is generally thought to occur primarily among the aged. For example, there is one poignant story of a group of war veterans who gathered together in annual reunions. Then, as their ranks grew thinner through attrition by death, they made a rather touching arrangement. They bought a bottle of wine for the last survivor to use to drink a toast to his departed comrades. In effect, the group was anticipating the social death of the surviving comrade.

However, social death occurs in more insidious ways and is not necessarily limited to the elderly. Most people who are suffering from a terminal illness are socially dead. Once they are institutionalized, a wall of silence is built up around them. The doctors, the nurses, and the orderlies never mention death in their presence. Their families and friends maintain a bright, cheery fiction: "You'll be back on your feet in no time." While many people don't want to be told about their status, others do. Almost everyone in this situation does want to talk about it or needs to confide in someone.

Obviously, then, social death encompasses two different conditions. One involves people's loss of social contacts and their withdrawal from society, as well as society's withdrawal from them. In such cases, social programs need to take over. Our resources need to be mobilized so that people do not become lonely or isolated. Fortunately, there has been considerable progress along these lines. Senior citizens' groups have been created to provide social outlets for those who face the danger of becoming isolated. Such groups seem to be the right means by which to prevent the first kind of environmental, social death.

To combat the second kind, a strong educational training effort seems to be needed for those who deal with the dying. It does no good to rail at these professionals for having no feelings or for being cold and uncaring. Probably the reverse is true: These people care so much that they must protect their own mental health by avoiding any emotional involvement. They need to be educated on how to deal with a dying person. Individuals and families, including children, need to deal with death directly and fairly. Mysticism and fear need to be stripped away so that the topic can be thought about unemotionally and logically. Later sections in this unit will offer some suggestions along these lines. We need to do social work to prevent loneliness, and we need to do educational work to promote understanding and acceptance. The trick is to turn these two broad-brush approaches into action. The following questions may help you figure out how to do so:

1. What kinds of social programs are there in your community to combat loneliness among the elderly? To your knowledge, has anyone ever visited local nursing homes to do volunteer work for the elderly and the ill or to entertain them? Could you get together a group to visit and entertain the elderly in nursing homes?
2. Are there senior citizens' groups in your community? What facilities do they have available to them? What more could be given to them?
3. Have you ever discussed death and dying in any sort of discussion group or with members of your family?

8. *Present some thoughts about alleviating social death.*

_____

_____

_____

_____

PSYCHOLOGICAL DEATH

Psychological death follows social death; it happens when people have finally made their peace with the world and accept the fact that they are going to die. In other words, they have lost or put aside their will to live. People who are thus affected seem to wither away and die shortly after losing the will to live.

This phenomenon is well known to people who have seen inmates in prisons (especially in political prison camps and war camps) give up the struggle to live. The hopelessness of their situation overwhelms them so that they quit fighting. The will to live is apparently a very strong factor in keeping people alive. A good example of this will to live is the so-called anniversary death: the amazing correlation between the dates of significant events in a person's life, such as a wedding date or a birthdate, and the death of that person. It seems almost as if many people hang on until after a certain important date and then accept death and let go willingly. This letting go, this loss of the will to live, is psychological death.

9. Explain what is meant by psychological death.

_____

_____

_____

_____

REASONS FOR SUICIDE

In its most extreme form, psychological death, a state in which death is accepted and even welcomed, seems to overlap with suicide. For is not letting go and stopping the fight against death tantamount to willing oneself to die? And is not death by one's own will suicide?

This is a very gray area. Technically, we think of suicide as a self-inflicted death and an unnatural act. While we uneasily and intuitively recognize the strong possibility that people can actually will their own deaths, we prefer to say that they lose the will to live and then die through natural causes. In this way we rationalize the gray area between psychological death and suicide.

But what about the type of suicide in which individuals actually do such violence to their bodies that without doubt they cause their own deaths? Such an act is easier to explain. To destroy oneself goes so much against one's will to live that it must be the act of those who have lost their reason. Most of us cannot conceive of a logical train of thought that would end in a decision to kill oneself. However, there are theoretical models by which some people have tried to explain this apparently insane act.

Freud identified two major instincts in human beings: the instinct for life, which he called eros, and the wish for death, or thanatos. Both of these wishes show themselves in typical human behavior. The life wish is shown primarily through the sexual urge, and the death wish is shown through aggression and hostility toward others. However, we often repress our hatred and aggression, turning them inward on ourselves.

Freud believed that several things make a person vulnerable to suicide. The first is the death wish. Also, splitting the ego between the demands of the id and those of society causes feelings of guilt and shame. These feelings in turn cause in us a specific internal weakness—a weakness in the face of a shock, a significant event such as the loss of a loved one, a blow to the ego brought about by failure, an overwhelming surge of emotion such as rage, fear, guilt, or shame, or even exposure to another suicidal person. The occurrence of such an event may trigger a self-destructive attempt, especially in a person whose ego has a low tolerance to stress. Also vulnerable to suicide, according to Freud, are those who, because of early childhood training, are sadistically or masochistically inclined, those who have fantasized a great deal, those who have a tyrannical superego, or those who have shown a compulsive death wish through compulsive gambling or homosexuality.

Primarily, suicide represents an aggressive act toward others, a desire to kill that has been turned inward. The guilt, shame, doubt, and confusion brought about by some traumatic event brings out the death wish and causes people to destroy themselves instead of the object that they really want to destroy.

One of the most extensive and far-reaching studies of suicide was carried out by Emile Durkheim at the end of the nineteenth century. It is regarded as a classic and is still widely quoted. Durkheim suggested that there are three kinds of suicide. *Egoistic suicide* is caused by an individual's lack of group integration. The cry of "I'm just another computer card in with a lot of other cards" is a current example of the feeling. The stronger the forces that throw people on their own resources, the higher the suicide rate becomes. Egoistic suicide is prevalent in groups where a lack of social cohesion is marked. Durkheim found that in times of national crises suicide rates tended to drop, a fact which he thought proved that social integration helps to prevent suicide.

What Durkheim called *altruistic suicide* is almost the exact opposite of egoistic suicide. Here, the individual is closely bound to society or family and commits suicide in order to serve them better.

A third kind is what Durkheim called *anomic suicide*. It results from the breakdown of social norms. People's needs and satisfactions are intimately bound to a collective society. When something causes them to find themselves beyond the boundaries society has dictated, they become upset. For example, a poor man who suddenly inherits a large sum of money or a rich man who loses all his money finds himself in an unknown world. Likewise, divorced individuals who have lost a part of their way of life and do not know where they fit into society may be disoriented. People who do not see a clear set of roles for themselves do not know how to act. They are overwhelmed by their turn of fortune. This can lead them to self-destruction.

These patterns are not always clear, and mixtures of motives may occur, as in ego-altruist and altruist-anomic suicide. One last thought of Durkheim's: Suicide did not seem to him to indicate immorality. Instead, it was a breakdown of the collective conscience, a flaw in the social fabric.

Karl Menninger, in *Man Against Himself*, described a suicidal pattern similar to that set forth by Freud. He felt that a failure to develop leads to an incomplete turning outward of the self-directed destructiveness and constructiveness with which we are born. No one emerges completely free of

A person's job or idea of fun may be an expression of the death wish. (George Gardner)

self-destructive tendencies. Often, there is an overlap between constructiveness and destructiveness. Some people destroy themselves for what might be considered logical reasons, such as killing themselves to avoid a long painful death. Others seem to die by purposeless acts such as alcoholism. From these cases, Menninger drew three basic motives for suicide: the wish to kill, the internal wish to be killed, and the wish to die.

The wish to kill is characterized by aggression, blaming, eliminating, driving away, annihilating—all synonyms for *destroying*. Suicides with these characteristics are trying to avenge themselves on others. "You'll suffer because I killed myself" is their theme.

The wish to be killed is the extreme form of submission. Masochism, self-blame, and guilt are the basic themes of the wish to be killed. Again they represent the Freudian idea of aggression turned inward.

The wish to die is based on another form of submission: the desire to give up the struggle. Hopelessness, overwhelming fear, being tired of it all, and a sense of despair characterize this sort of motivation. One might call this the born-loser complex taken to the ultimate extreme.

Menninger said that these three basic motives are complicated by social attitudes, family customs, and incomplete personality development. Suicide cannot be explained by heredity, suggestion, or other symptoms of maladjustment. It is more a steady self-destructive progression conceived long before the consummation of the critical act.

Many other writers have speculated on this phenomenon. Victor Frankl tells of his experiences in concentration camps, where many inmates lost their sense of the meaning of life and simply allowed themselves to die. Many of those who attempted suicide and were not successful reported that they had experienced a feeling of helplessness and hopelessness about their situation. Accordingly, they either withdrew or tried to end it all by suicide.

Thus a wide variety of reasons are offered to explain why people commit suicide. It seems to boil down to a personal choice. Which theory do you think is most believable?

10. Give some reasons for suicide.

_____

_____

_____

_____

ATTITUDES TOWARD SUICIDE

As you might expect, philosophical positions on suicide range from total support to total condemnation. Historically, cultures that emphasized war often taught that there would be a special reward for death in combat. This philosophy was well known to the Crusaders and helped explain to them the ferocity of their opponents and to reconcile them to their own deaths. Among Nordic people, it was accepted that a warrior in combat might go berserk and, in that state, continue to move forward, attacking everything in front of him until he was victorious or was slain. Much of the same tradition still exists among tribes in the Philippines. This sort of action supports the kill-or-be-killed aspect of Freud's death wish.

A more subtle philosophy was and is still seen in Japan, another country with a tremendous tradition of the individual warrior, the samurai. In Japan, the loss of individual honor is a recognized and honored reason for self-destruction, and there is even a stylized way for killing oneself: hara-kiri. There are many examples in Japanese history of military officers or politicians who failed, "brought disgrace to the Emperor," and therefore committed suicide to absolve themselves of failure. This philosophy leads to what Durkheim called altruistic suicide.

The philosophies of the Judeo-Christian religions are well known to us. They condemn the act of suicide strongly. To them, the act is a violation of the laws of God. In Dante's *Inferno*, people who have committed suicide are placed in a low circle of hell along with those committing violent crimes against God or their neighbors.

For the most part, philosophers have reflected prevalent religious beliefs. William James, for example, in his essay "Is Life Worth Living?" called for vital existence rather than death. Immanuel Kant felt that self-destruction was a violation of moral law. However, the existentialists emphasize the freedom of human beings to make the choices by which they govern their lives. Rollo May belongs to this group. His thesis is that people can choose to accept themselves and their existence, or they can choose not to exist—to commit suicide. May believes that there is such a thing as psychological suicide. Certain people who have lived to carry out a certain task, such as finishing an important work, often die after they have succeeded. Also, the phenomenon known as anniversary death has already been described. In this case, people die after a meaningful date in their lives, such as a birthday or wedding anniversary. Having reached this date, they appear to let go and decide to die.

May seems to be emphasizing what Durkheim called egoistic suicide, or the decision of some people to divorce themselves from society. The existentialists emphasize that the choice of living or not living is purely the choice of the individual. They attach no moral judgment to this decision. Flatly stated, they say that people have a right to take their own lives.

Because philosophies can justify everything, from people's right to decide their own fate by killing themselves to personal subordination to a supreme moral law, it would seem that philosophers do not help us understand the phenomenon of suicide. They may muse about the morality or immorality of the act, but they certainly do not explain why the act happens when it happens. In other words, they do not help those of us who are trying to understand the roots of suicide so that we can prevent the act or eliminate its roots entirely.

By this time, you will have realized that people are considerably confused by suicide. Their confusion in attitude has led to confusion and contradictions in the treatment of those who attempt suicide. For example, in England suicide is regarded as a crime. Those who are successful will have their property confiscated. In this country, no such laws exist; yet the primary treatment for potential suicides remains old-fashioned and consists of prevention through force and persuasion. Authorities build nets and wire fences on bridges and high walls to thwart would-be jumpers. Cars are not allowed to stop on some bridges. People who threaten suicide and fail are often confined. Frequently, they are stripped of anything that might be used as a tool for self-destruction. Belts, shoelaces, knives, and forks are especially prohibited. People have also been brought into court and punished for attempting suicide. Reprisals are taken against successful suicides. They may be denied burial in church grounds. In the past, their bodies have been dragged through the streets, their families ridiculed and shamed.

Even today, potentially suicidal people may face perpetual torment in hell. In some cases, they can look forward to furtive burial in an unsanctified grave. They can foresee shame and ridicule for their families. If they fail, they might face a prison sentence or confinement. These consequences are designed to make people think twice about killing themselves.

Obviously, these measures have failed. So many means of suicide exist that no one can possibly prevent them all from being used. The threat of family shame may be exactly what some potentially suicidal people want, if they have a deep hatred for their kin. Of all the old-fashioned preventive techniques, only one has shown any effectiveness: keeping a person in a closely knit group. The stronger the group, the less chance exists that the person will resort to suicide.

Over the years, a set of beliefs about suicidal people has grown up and nearly become folklore. Check any of the following statements about suicidal people that you believe to be true. (See Edwin S. Shneidman and Norman L. Farberow, *Some Facts About Suicide*, Public Health Service Publication No. 852, Washington, D. C., 1961.)

_____ 1. People who talk about suicide don't commit suicide.

_____ 2. Suicide happens without warning.

_____ 3. Suicidal people are fully intent on dying.

_____ 4. Once a person is suicidal, he or she is suicidal forever.

_____ 5. Improvements following a suicidal crisis mean that the risk of suicide is over.

_____ 6. Suicide strikes more often among the rich, or, conversely, it occurs almost exclusively among the poor.

_____ 7. Suicidal tendencies are inherited or "run in the family."

_____ 8. All suicidal individuals are mentally ill, and suicide is always the act of a psychotic person.

If you think any of these statements is true, you are dead wrong. Each is a myth. Here are the facts:

1. Of any ten people who kill themselves, eight have given definite warnings about their suicidal intentions.
2. Studies reveal that suicidal people give many clues and warnings regarding their suicidal intentions.
3. Most suicidal people are undecided about living or dying, and they gamble with death, leaving it to others to save them. Almost no one commits suicide without letting others know how he or she is feeling.
4. Individuals who wish to kill themselves are suicidal for only a limited period of time.
5. Most suicides occur within about three months following the beginning of "improvement," when individuals have the energy to put their morbid thoughts and feelings into effect.

6. Suicide is neither the rich person's disease nor the poor person's curse. Suicide is very democratic and is represented proportionately among all levels of society.
7. Suicide does not run in families. It is an individual pattern.
8. Studies of hundreds of genuine suicide notes indicate that, although suicidal people are extremely unhappy, they are not necessarily mentally ill.

What all of this seems to point to is that there is great diversity in peoples attitudes toward suicide. What do you feel about it? Even more important, do you know the customs of your community concerning suicide? For example, what is the legal status of people who have committed suicide? What about their possessions and property? Do these things go untouched to the family of the suicide victim? How is the family looked on by the community?

11. Describe some of society's attitudes toward suicide.

_____

_____

_____

_____

CHARACTERISTICS OF A POTENTIAL SUICIDE

Imagine that you are standing watch over a hot line in a suicide-prevention center. The phone rings and you answer. A voice says, "Don't try to stop me. I've had it, and I'm going to get out of this lousy rat race." What should you do? Trained interviewers have been taught to get specific information from the suicidal person so that they can evaluate the seriousness of the threat and then take some sensible, helpful action.

AGE AND SEX

These are the first items to ask for, because they give a lot of information. For example, if the caller is male and his age is over fifty, the threat is probably a real one and may end in death. If the voice is female and her age is between fifteen and thirty-five, the threat is much less severe; this group typically has the largest number of attempts that end as failures.

ONSET OF SELF-DESTRUCTIVE BEHAVIOR

The trained interviewer then has to find out whether the person has ever tried to commit suicide before. If so, the threat is more severe than a first-time effort. Also, the more acute—that is, the more sudden—the desire to kill oneself, the greater the need for immediate action and the better the chance for a long-range cure. The chronically self-destructive person is less dangerous immediately, but long-range cure is less probable in such a case.

SUICIDE PLAN

The interviewer must next try to find out whether the person actually has worked out a suicide plan and what this plan is. If such a plan exists, and the date and time are specifically set, the situation is very serious. If the plan consists of just a vague statement, then the immediate problem is not so great.

LOSS OF A LOVED ONE OR A REJECTION

The next item of information to be asked is, "Have you just lost someone you loved? Have you just been divorced or separated? Has someone thrown you out?" Any information indicating some loss or rejection makes the threat more believable.

MEDICAL PROBLEMS

The interviewer must also ask about the caller's health. Has the person just found out that he or she has a disease or is suffering from some sort of chronic illness? Many illnesses, either real or imagined, can lead to mental depression and suicide. Depression is the key to look for here.

RESOURCES

The interviewer needs to find out what resources the person has. Is the caller's family supportive or not? Is the caller broke or wealthy? Does the caller feel that he or she has relied on family and friends as long as possible? Does the person have a feeling of aloneness and helplessness? All these are evidence of a serious suicide threat.

In addition to obtaining specific kinds of information, the interviewer must make some judgments or deductions from the conversation. Is the talker hostile or angry? Has he or she given any details about long-range planning for the event, such as writing a will or giving away possessions?

12. Describe a potentially suicidal person.

_____

_____

_____

_____

HOW TO HELP A SUICIDAL PERSON

Imagine that you are still on the telephone talking to a man who is threatening to kill himself. He is fifty years old. His wife died two weeks ago. You have decided that his threat is very serious and have asked that a police car go to his home. You tell him this, and he says that if the cops walk through the door, he will shoot himself immediately with the gun he has in his lap. What can you do?

_____

_____

_____

_____

If your ideas included the following points, you did very well in your trial as an interviewer:

1. Keep calm and interested, and *keep your caller talking.*
2. Tell him (and do this) that you have told the police not to enter until he asks them to come in.
3. Give him something to do. Ask him to make coffee for the police or to get a picture of his wife for them—anything to have him do something.
4. Try to develop some future action in which he might be interested that may keep him going. Suggest that someone might be able to help him get over his feelings if he will give you a chance to set up an interview.
5. Give him sympathetic support. Get him talking about how he feels. *Always keep him talking.*

13. Suggest ways of helping a suicidal person.

_____

_____

_____

_____

STAGES OF DYING

The behavior of people who are dying has recently been studied intensively. One of the foremost authorities on this behavior is Dr. Elisabeth Kübler-Ross. Her work with terminally ill people led her to write a description of the process. She describes the following stages through which dying people pass:

1. The first stage consists of denial and isolation. The person cannot accept the fact that it is happening to him or her but instead seeks out people who may deny the facts. The dying person disputes the reasoning that indicates that death is imminent.
2. The second stage is anger. The typical reaction is, "Why me? By what unjust fate am I the one selected to die?"
3. The third stage is bargaining. The person looks for any way to evade the imminent, bargaining with everyone: doctor, family, God. "Oh, Lord, if I am allowed to live . . ."
4. When it becomes apparent that no deal can be made, the person experiences deep depression and a sense of loss, thinks of all of the things that will no longer be, loses interest in people and the outside world and begins to grieve silently.

5. The last stage is acceptance. If the person is allowed to grieve, if life is not artificially prolonged, and if the family has learned to "let go," the dying individual will accept his or her fate with peace and resignation.

Dr. Kübler-Ross does not argue that these stages are fixed and irreversible. She acknowledges that some people do not progress through all of the stages. She also describes cases in which the patient reverses stages. In other cases, the patient seems to skip one or more stages completely. Nevertheless, these stages are states of mind that many people who have learned of imminent death pass through. Of course, Kübler-Ross's ideal is that dying individuals do progress until they have reached peace and acceptance. Kübler-Ross's humanism, warmth, and concern for people show through as she describes how she tries to help dying people reach acceptance.

It is interesting that another perceptive student of human behavior also described this phenomenon of the acceptance of death. Erik Erickson wrote of it when he described the last of his eight ages of man. Erikson conceived the last age as a struggle or a conflict to be resolved. He called the conflict ego integrity versus despair. In Erikson's mind, people must be able to look back at their lives with equanimity and approval, a feeling that "I fought the good fight. If I had it to do over again, I wouldn't do anything differently." If they cannot do that, they view oncoming death with despair because of a feeling of a wasted life.

It seems that both of these observers of human behavior are describing essentially the same thing but in different words, doesn't it? What do you think?

14. Explain the stages of dying.

_____

_____

_____

_____

A PROGRAM FOR THE DYING

Put yourself in this situation. You have gone to the hospital to visit a close relative who is dying of cancer. The end is quite close. The doctor has said that death can come any time, but will come within a week. Naturally, the patient looks ghastly, with deep-sunken eyes, drawn features, and a wasted body. You are shocked to see such physical deterioration. Yet the patient is alert and still very much "with it."

What should you do? Should you talk about the fact that death is near? Should you discuss the patient's condition with him or her frankly, or should

Hospices for the terminally ill embody Dr. Kübler-Ross's ideal of helping dying individuals attain peace and acceptance. (Cynthia Johnson)

you stay away from that topic completely? Should your conversation be matter of fact and unemotional, or should you allow your feelings to show? Just what do you talk about with a dying person? You can't talk about the future because there is none. Current events don't have the importance and the interest which they once had for the patient. If you think for a moment as you mentally place yourself beside the bed of a dying person, you will realize that there isn't a whole lot to talk about. How do you cheer your patient up? Try to jot down a few suggestions about what to do here.

_____

_____

_____

_____

Let's see whether any ground rules or suggestions can be created for this situation.

1. Should you try to insulate the patient from the knowledge of imminent death?
   Yes_____ No _____ Depends _____

If you marked *Depends*, you may be on the right track. Some people don't want to know, while others insist on knowing. It depends on the individual. Many wish to use the technique of denial for their own peace of mind.

2. Should you talk about death and dying to the patient, even in the most general terms?
   Yes _____ No _____ Depends _____

If you said *Depends*, you may again be on the right track. It depends on the person. Some may want to talk about death and dying, even in abstract religious or philosophical terms. Some may want to talk about their own specific situation in very intimate terms. You need to follow the lead of the person.

3. Should you show your grief and sorrow openly?
   Yes _____ No _____ Depends _____

In all probability, the best response would be not to show your emotions. We have been taught to be uncomfortable in the presence of extreme emotion. The dying person would probably be made more uncomfortable rather than being reassured. A quiet expression of your feelings would be best. Your self-control may be helpful to the patient in the control of his or her own feelings.

4. Should you talk about the future and the past?
   Yes _____ No _____ Depends _____

It all depends. It's extremely difficult to avoid any mention of the future. We tend to dwell on it a great deal. To mention things that will be happening, with the implied exclusion of the dying person, may create negative feelings. Here again, you must follow the lead of the dying person.

It would appear that the rules are simple. Keep calm and be matter of fact. Follow the lead of the person, allowing yourself to be guided into the topics he or she wants to talk about. Remember, to be a good conversationalist, you have to be a good listener.

15. Suggest a program for dealing with a dying person.

_____

_____

_____

_____

A PROGRAM FOR CHILDREN

One last point: We need to take a good look at our attitudes toward death and dying. We should see whether these attitudes can be changed. Children should be exposed to the concept of death so that as much mystery and negative feeling as possible can be stripped away. Certainly the negative outlook should be eliminated. Frank discussions and seminars should be held to make the topic less fearsome. Older people should be given the chance to join groups in which they can voice and explore their feelings about death and dying and can interact with others who are concerned with these topics. Although we should not become morbidly fascinated with the subject, we do need to remove many of our negative reactions to it. Certainly we should be able to discuss death—even our own deaths—without evasion or emotional upheaval.

Several years ago, I read a chronological log of the dreams of an individual who gave it to me to be analyzed. It struck me immediately that almost every dream involved the theme of death and dying. Yet when I asked that person about it, he was surprised. This fact had never occurred to him. As we talked, he remembered that he had lived across the street from a funeral home when he was very young. He could remember a constant stream of funerals and comments about them from his parents. Unfortunately, all of the comments were euphemisms that did nothing to explain to him what was actually happening across the street. As he remembers the situation now, his parents were acutely uncomfortable when discussing the funeral home's activities with him. As best he can tell, his preoccupation with the theme of death and dying started there.

While we may not realize it, we often condition our children to the notion that there is something bad and mysterious about death. If there is a death in the family, there is grief, crying, and excessive negative emotional feeling. Yet when the child tries to learn what is happening, he or she is put off with vague explanations, such as, "So-and-so has gone away." Went away where? Why is going away making everybody sad? If everybody else is crying, shouldn't I cry, too?

Even as we recognize the necessity for giving children the facts of life, so we should recognize the need to give them the facts of death. This may be hard because we ourselves have not learned what the facts are. Thus, in order to teach our children, we need to teach ourselves. It may be difficult for us to tackle this subject. One appraoach that has been suggested is the use of fiction to help a child grapple with the concept of death. A pamphlet has been published that provides a bibliography to assist in this approach (Rose M. Somerville, *Death Education as Part of Family Life Education: Using Imaginative Literature for Insights into Family Crises*, The Family Coordinator, July 1971). Incidentally, what do you think of the idea of having classes on death?

Think about these questions: Have you and your family and friends ever discussed dying and death? If your parents are alive, have they made their wills? Have they written out their funeral and burial wishes? If you are married, have you and your spouse talked over these matters? Have you written your wills? If you are single, do you have any idea where your property would go if you died? Do you have any specific desires about this? Do you need a will? Have you and your friends reached any conclusions about the nature of death in your discussions? In summary, are you accepting the idea that you *might* die? If or when you have children, what are you going to tell them?

16. *Give some thoughts on the education of children about death and dying.*

_____

_____

_____

_____

□ A POINT OF VIEW

If you want to explore the topic of dealing with dying people, the writings of Dr. Elisabeth Kübler-Ross will be of interest to you. If you are interested in how children can be taught about death, here is a partial list of books that might be suitable:

James Agee, *A Death in the Family* (New York: Avon, 1959).

William Blinn, *Brian's Song* (New York: Bantam Books, 1972).

John Gunther, *Death Be Not Proud* (New York: Harper and Row, 1965).

Elisabeth Kübler-Ross, *On Death and Dying* (New York: Macmillan, 1969).

Arthur Miller, *Death of a Salesman* (New York: Viking, 1949).

The selection that concludes this unit is a very poignant article. It was written by a sensitive man who learned that he was dying and had a chance to reflect on his situation. It tells its own story without any need for amplification or explanation.

ARCHIE J. HANLAN

NOTES OF A DYING PROFESSOR

There is a commercial on television (I've watched more television in recent months than I ever watched in my life), a stupid little commercial for Alka-Seltzer that shows this guy woefully sitting with people in a cafe or restaurant, and the waiter says, "Try it, you'll like it; try it, you'll like it." And the guy says: "I tried it—and I thought I'd die."

I listen to things like that differently now. It's a clever commercial; it's funny. But the punch

From "Notes of a Dying Professor" published in the *Pennsylvania Gazette*, March 1972, and written by Archie J. Hanlan, D.S.W., Associate Professor, School of Social Work, University of Pennsylvania, before his death in July 1973.

line is: I thought I would die. That, to me, is kind of symbolic of what it means to die, in our society. The actor didn't describe how he felt when he tried it and didn't like it—he thought he would die. That conveys what? "He thought he would die" means it was terrible—how worse could you feel than wanting to die? As though dying is something inherently painful; undesirable, stigmatized in our society.

Several months ago I was told that I am dying. I want to recount to you the process I went through in finding that out. I was hospitalized and told on the day that I was discharged, a week later, that I had a terminal illness and would have six months to three years to live.

So how did I get to that point?

I had been examined by my physician, an internist with all the equipment in his own office who does very thorough examinations, and I was given a thorough bill of health. Some weeks later, I returned to him because I had this peculiar symptom: I found that I could not trim the fingernails on my left hand by operating the fingernail clipper in my right hand. I thought: "Gee, that's stupid! Why can't I push those silly little tweezers together? I can do it with my left hand and clip the nails on my right hand, but I can't do it with my right hand."

I mentioned it to my wife. Here I had been to my doctor earlier and he said I was in good health , and this was beginning to bother me, I didn't have any strength in my right hand. And she said what I wanted to hear at that point, I guess: "Don't put it off." So I went back to the doctor. And he thought it was some kind of arthritis or whatever, some mild problem, but he said it ought to be checked out by an orthopedist, that he himself couldn't check out what it was.

On a Thursday afternoon I saw an orthopedist. He looked at my hand, and he ran some simple tests of my arm and concluded—well, let me see if I can recapture what happened with him.

A very nice man. My internist is a rather cold, impassive kind of guy. The orthopedist is a warmer, friendlier, outgoing middle-aged man. After his cursory examination I began to realize that he was becoming increasingly non-communicative. And that alarmed me. It frightened me a bit. *What is he not telling me?* And he became very grave and serious in his general demeanor. I asked him what he thought it was, but could get no reply.

He then let me know that this was something he could not diagnose and that I should see a neurologist immediately. Now, I was feeling fine, outside this stupid little complaint, so I thought whatever the worst was, it couldn't be all that complicated—until this non-verbal communication and tightening up of the orthopedist, letting me know, in his own way, that it was serious and I should go to a neurologist. He arranged for me to see a neurologist that evening.

I remember going back out into the waiting room, where my wife was, and feeling very frightened and confused. And she, of course, knowing me very well for 22 years, felt my own feelings coming through very quickly. We both figured out that something's up, that it's not just a simple matter of arthritis in my wrist. What it was, we didn't know. Some kind of neurological problem—but there are thousands of those. Whatever it was, it was serious.

So at seven o'clock that night I was at the neurologist's and he was more like my regular doctor: cold, aloof, highly efficient, a prominent researcher in the field of neurology. I tried to engage him in conversation but to no avail. He ran through the usual neurological examination, the whole routine, very standard procedure. It took maybe a half hour at the most. I tried to read his non-verbal responses, since I couldn't engage him in any verbal responses. And that was very difficult to do, because he's really a very masked kind of man, except that again there began to be a growing sense from him that this was something serious, that there was a gravity about what the examination was revealing.

I kept pressing him for a response, but there was absolutely no response at all. And the non-verbal response, the avoidance itself, generates considerable anxiety, fear, confusion, on the part of any patient in that kind of situation. While I may be hypersensitive to non-verbal clues because of my clinical training, I also think that most people, regarldless of how sophisticated or unsophisticated they are psychologically, pick up these non-verbal cues, so that this effort on the part of the physician or the neurologist to contain himself and mask whatever he was finding or whatever he felt about his findings really served the function of making me increasingly anxious.

As he concluded the examination, he told me that I would have to be hospitalized the following morning.

I said I wanted to know why I was going to the hospital. He said: To run a series of diagnostic tests. I did not want to go to the particular hospital he mentioned. I knew that hospital very well and I had a preference for another one. But he did not practice in that hospital, so I did not pursue it. The point I want to make clear is that I began to respond to his directive to be hospitalized. I didn't know what in the world I was being hospitalized for. I was not unwilling to be hospitalized, but I certainly had a particular choice of hospitals.

But suddenly I felt this fear and panic and kind of being put in a position of passivity, as though decisions were being made for me, that I didn't take part in those any more. What right did I have to make a big issue of what hospital I was being sent to?

Under ordinary circumstances, I would have made such a stink. What is significant is that I didn't. I did not feel able to fight even at that point. And this was only the first day of my discovering that something was radically wrong with me. I mention this because that process—feeling myself reduced in making decisions about my own fate—became increasingly reinforced and became very destructive psychologically.

The next day (Friday) I was supposed to go into the hospital, if a bed could be found. I had my bag packed and said goodbye to my wife and kids—and Saturday they finally found a bed. Saturday afternoon.

I had been in the hospital once before when I was 15 years old, for an appendectomy. So although I've seen the whole system of a hospital structure, both medical and psychiatric, I had never been very much on the patient end of it. I was greatly negatively impressed with how one gets processed as a patient. I went into the business office, the admissions room, and I was put in a wheelchair. And there wasn't a damn thing wrong with me. I could walk. The only limit to my physical activity had to do with my fingers, and other than that I had no physical impairment whatsoever. But I was put in a wheelchair.

Again, the sense was one of being passive, inactive; you immediately assume the role of the patient; this is the way you behave in a hospital. Also, I went through what seemed to me the incredible Alice-in-Wonderland business about my finances. I had to guarantee the hospital that I would pay the bill—and I didn't know what I was in the hospital for and how long I would be there—but I was supposed to sign a statement that I would pay whatever the cost was before I left the hospital.

That was just one more phase in that process of being identified as a patient. It struck me as: This isn't for real! But it was for real. And I refused to sign such a statement. It was ridiculous to commit myself to pay an amount I didn't know. I didn't know whether I had that much money. Anyway, they had to scurry around and ask the supervisor how they could go about admitting such a patient, who wouldn't sign this piece of paper.

But I got admitted as a patient. I got out of the admissions office and I was taken to a ward where post-operative neurosurgery patients were kept. I stress that because there were few patients like myself. The hospital was crowded; that's why I couldn't get in on Friday. And because there was no bed on the floor where my neurologist usually worked, I was put on the floor below that, where essentially the largest number of patients were failures of neurosurgery.

I had seen lobotomized patients in the back wards of psychiatric hospitals, but that doesn't sufficiently convey what I saw when I first came into that ward. Again, this was Saturday, I didn't know why I was in the hospital, I didn't know that I was in the wrong ward. My God, am I going to have some kind of brain surgery where I will wind up totally destroyed by some failure of the brain surgery, as these patients I saw being wheeled around the ward—totally speechless, grunting, staring, dishevelled men?

That was my first sight when I was put in that ward, and I was pretty shaken, to say the least. The time sequence from that time on becomes more clear to me. The neurologist was not on duty again till Monday. Why in the world was I put there Saturday and Sunday, when nothing could be done, no instructions could be left even in terms of beginning routine procedures? So I sat there through Saturday and Sunday.

Monday, things began to move a little bit. The neurologist showed up and introduced me to three resident interns—no, they were in their latter years of medical school. They were students of the neurologist, and they administered several of the examinations that I was to have. He ran through the neurological examination of me in bed. And again I got a reinforcement of the sense of not only am I a patient who is supposed to behave in a certain way, but I'm almost an object to demonstrate to people that I'm not really people any more, I'm something else. I'm a body that has some very interesting characteristics about it, which include twitching of the muscles, rather symptomatic of this particular disease.

And because it's a rare disease and not much is known about it, it was very instructive for these medical students to see these symptoms. But the point I want to make is that I felt treated as an object. Being a patient is one thing, but being an object is even less than being a patient. And I began to feel not only the fear of this unknown, dread thing that I have, that nobody knows anything about—and if they know, they're not going to tell me—but an anger and a resentment of "Goddamn it, I'm a human being and I want to be treated like one!"

And feeling that if I expressed that anger, I could be retaliated against, because I'm in a very vulnerable position. One, nobody is going to tell me what the hell is wrong with me, anyway. And two, if I do strike out, what's going to happen to me as a consequence? So there is a sense of anger, a sense of being terribly vulnerable—all of this setting in by Monday.

I might add that Sunday night was a bad night for me—this general malaise, this fear of being in the hospital. And I distinctly remember one of the few human beings I came in touch with during these first two nights, a black woman on duty during the night. It was nothing very dramatic that she did, but it stands out vividly in my mind that she was kind and gentle with me, concerned that I was fitful and disturbed. And she reassured me in a very spontaneous kind of way.

But she was one of the few people in that enormous institution who really dealt with me as a human being. That's why I recall it, because she treated me as a human being—and very few people did, the whole time I was there. So somehow I got through Sunday night and Monday night.

Monday started the routine. Take your temperature, check your blood pressure, urinalyses, etc.

Then we got down to the more basic stuff. On Tuesday, the two main examinations I had were both horribly painful—physically painful and psychologically devasting. I had no pain connected with the illness and still have virtually no pain connected with the illness, but I had excruciating pain in the examination.

It was on Tuesday that the team of young medical students were instructed to prepare me for a lumbar puncture, a spinal tap. I was frightened. Two of the medical students were a husband and wife. I found the wife more responsive, less uptight, I guess, than the two young men, and I got through to her that it was important for me to know what was going on: "I want to know about the lumbar puncture, everything about it, tell me what you're going to

do, explain it to me very carefully, it's important to me to know what's going on."

And she did. So I had the lumbar puncture. Part of the diagnostic value of that is not only to take fluid from the spinal column, but to test the pressure of the spinal fluid. The spinal tap in itself is painful, but my recollection is that was very minor compared to the other part of that examination, which was placing a collar around my neck and inflating it to exert pressure on the spinal column itself and take readings as the pressure is built up on the spinal column, to detect the extent of damage in the spinal column. This is an excruciatingly painful experience. It's the weirdest kind of pain, as though someone had inflated a balloon inside my spinal column and the pressure would almost explode inside my spine. It's a bizarre pain.

And this was administered in the ward where there were a few other patients. I screamed out and grunted with the pain. I remember thinking: This is nutty. The least they could have done is take me off into a room by myself. I asked for a towel to shove into my mouth, so I could grit my teeth and muffle my scream, so I wouldn't disturb the patients. I began to feel, even as I was having this horrible pain: My God, we're people; why should my going through this disturb the other patients; why should my screaming upset these other people?

Did anybody think about this? Somebody around this place ought to know that an examination this painful ought to be done in a place that at least provided privacy to the patient, and not put the burden on the patient like this.

The students did an efficient job. I was very exhausted and very frightened when it was over. They did not tell me anything at that time. I asked the physician the next day about any results and he was very evasive. In fact, there was very little I did know while I was in the hospital, until the last day.

The next exam was either on Wednesday or Thursday, but I want to tell a little about the time between the first and the second exam. I did a lot of reading. I read rapidly. My escape reading is fiction, which I do not ordinarily indulge in, so I had taken a couple of books, a very large novel of 800 pages, and I read about 400 pages the first 24 hours I was there. Then I declined in reading as an escape. I couldn't concentrate.

There was a little day room right off the ward, with windows, and it was sunny there, so I went in there on Wednesday, the day after the lumbar puncture. There was a man there in his early- or mid-fifties, with grayish-black hair, a stubble, just growing back after his surgery. He was strapped into this wheelchair, so that he could not get out or harm himself. He sat in the wheelchair grunting. At one time he seemed to want something. I asked him if he wanted something and he growled.

He had a pile of stuff in his lap and I was very curious as to what it was. As I looked at it more carefully, I saw that it was pieces of old canvas. As I sat there a few minutes more, he began to fix himself upon this pile of canvas and he began to rip apart—with this intense, livid, violent, expression on his face and his whole body—to shred this canvas. I had rarely seen a human being so violent, with such an intensity of focus—upon this canvas—and have it become the symbol of all his rage and fear. It seemed as though the surgery had excised everything but his soul. All he could do is give vent to his rage at this outrage that had occurred to him.

I felt pretty shaken after I watched that fellow and I had to get out of there. I wondered why I was so upset and finally had to accept that I was simply too vulnerable myself to deal with that kind of situation.

I guess there was some kind of learning in that. I throw that in because it was a point of looking at myself and maybe accepting that there were some things I couldn't deal with any longer. But along the way I had some excellent help from a social worker. It was the only real help I had, besides the terribly essential support of my family. I did have critical help from the social worker and I've had some help from another social worker since then, and I disagree with Elisabeth Kübler-Ross—the author of *On Death and Dying* (1969)—in some of the com-

ments about why social workers seem to deal better with dying people.

It was very critical in maintaining my own sanity in this situation. I needed a social worker after my experience with that man. I was beginning to confront myself with what this was all about.

But I want to get to the second examination. This was called an electromyogram—*myo* meaning muscle. (The symptoms of my disease are a continuing deterioration of the muscles, all the major muscles in my body.) The examination consists of long steel needles with an electric wire attached to them, so that an electric charge can be generated by the control of a technician through the needle into the muscle. A needle is stuck into every major and minor muscle in the body during a two-to-three hour examination.

The electric charge creates a response in the muscle, which is recorded on an oscilloscope and measures the response of the muscles. The oscilloscope makes a permanent TV tape of the test. I mention this because the process relates to the way in which this examination was conducted. There was relatively little pain involved in the insertion of the needle, but the way in which that examination was conducted was more physically exhausting and more psychologically upsetting than anything else that had happened in the hospital to me thus far.

The person who administered the electromyogram was a young girl who had been out of high school three or four years, a bright girl who had had special training.

She is an interesting person for me to attempt to describe to you, because in some ways she symbolizes, at least for me, treating the patient as an object, this dehumanizing of a person, particularly of a dying patient, more clearly than some of the professional staff in the hospital. Physicians, nurses, others, have a variety of ways of defending themselves against the impact of procedures in the hospital. She had her own ways, but they were not subtle at all.

So what I could see, as I thought back on that

exam, were some of the same psychological processes operating with her as well as with physicians and nurses, but not as subtly covered up. She was a little more direct and open about how she tried to handle her own feelings not only about the unpleasant examination, but— knowing that anybody who takes that exam is suspected of having a very serious neurological disease, if not terminal.

The way she dealt with this was to be very cheerful, bubbly, charming in some ways, purely superficial, using her charm and humor to maintain this mask of a cute little girl attending me, and so on. But it was very apparent to me, as we got into this interchange, that she was treating me as an object. It was my body, not me. Sticking needles into me and joking "Oh, I got the wrong muscle!" She did have a sense of humor, but I didn't appreciate it as such. She had this banter which on the one hand seemed like she was being very friendly, but really there was nothing friendly about it at all. I was being treated like an object.

The point I'm making in regard to that technician is that she was less sophisticated, her defenses were less well developed and complex, let's say, than the physician's, but essentially they were no different.

I remember at one point I was terribly anxious and sweating, and her nutty humor was finally getting to me, and the sense of being treated like a thing was making me angrier and angrier and I wondered how in the hell do I deal with her. I'm not just going to sit back and take this. Finally I decided to play her own game. I'll engage in this banter with her. She said something about the wrong muscle and I said: "If you make another mistake and I die, I'm going to sue the hospital." And she thought that was hilarious.

I figured I could communicate with her at that level, but it was purely premeditated and hostile; if she was going to keep her distance, I was going to keep mine, too.

Anyway, I got out of there thoroughly spent and psychologically exhausted, a mixture of physiological and psychological utter exhaus-

tion which became insufferable. It was a kind of exhaustion which had no comparison in my previous life.

I met with the social worker briefly Wednesday, Thursday, and Friday morning, before I saw the neurologist. I'm not sure how well I can convey the importance of having someone there, aside from my own immediate family and my own personal friends, in whom I could confide my own fears and concern about the gravity of the illness. There was no one in the hospital (around the clock) with whom I could engage in any real contact about the fact that I was there for something that was terribly serious. The only human being on that hospital staff I could talk to was the social worker.

And it was pretty important to have somebody who could acknowledge that I may be facing death, that it is a likely prospect, that I could cry about it, I could convey some of my rage, some expression of my own feelings, which were such a critical part of where I was at that point in my life. I can't underestimate the importance of that fact.

If I hadn't had that person in the hospital, I really don't know what psychological condition I would have been in. I could talk with my wife when she came to visit me and I could discuss with one of my friends that visited me, but I needed somebody on the spot to be able to communicate with, somebody who represented that hospital in all its treatment of me as an object, somebody who could confirm my doubts about whether I was a human being any more or just a thing.

By Friday the test results were all in. I knew that the major examinations had been completed. The main conference confrontation with the physician was about an hour before I was discharged. I had been in the hospital seven days. I was tired, irritable, angry—angry at the doctor who was still being evasive. I had told him from the start that I wanted him to be open with me, that I wanted to know the full implications of whatever it was that I had. And up until the last hour I was there it seemed to me that he could not face me with what he had to say.

He did then do essentially what I asked him to do, that is, to level with me regarding the diagnosis. It was a very hard thing for him to do. If he could have found any way of avoiding telling me, he would have. It was a terribly painful thing for him to have to lay it on the line. But he did. The way in which he did it was kind of staccato, impersonal, matter of fact. This is what the symptoms are, this is the progression of the symptoms. How long do I have to live? Six months to three years.

The only break in his facade was when I asked him to clarify. He had prepared a little speech. But any time I asked him for a little bit more information or a judgment on those facts, I could almost see his shell coming back.

Out of the hospital, there were other matters to consider. One was my dealings with my family. I don't think one ever deals with anything, with finality, in any one point in time, either with living or with death. I recall a Sunday *New York Times* review of a book by Robert Penn Warren. There was one quote from it: "The dream is a lie, the dreaming is true." Perhaps death is a lie and dying is true. The difference is between the nouns and the verbs. It's the "dealing" that is the truth, not the "deal."

That's a poor analogy, but at any rate, I haven't "dealt with" my feelings about my family. I am constantly dealing with them, as I always have, but in a new and different context since my illness.

Although there are relatively few physically painful aspects of the illness at this stage, the psychologically painful aspect has certainly been my feelings about my family.

I have a son at college and a daughter in college and a 10-year-old boy at home. And while I would like to see all my children well into adulthood, I find it particularly poignant and difficult that I may not see my youngest child into adulthood. I feel a personal responsibility, and always have, for seeing that my

children are on their own and psychologically and otherwise prepared to assume responsibility for themselves. And I certainly cannot expect a 10-year-old boy to be responsible for himself.

There are a variety of sources about why I feel very strongly in terms of my own family, which aren't terribly relevant here except that that was a strong part of my reaction, my depression, in the hospital. I never cry very much, but I certainly cried very profoundly, a depressive crying, in the hospital. And being self-analytical, I tried to ask myself what I was so depressed about.

At an intellectual level I could tell myself that I had some guilt feelings about my family, particularly about my children, and not deal with it very much beyond a kind of superficial recognition that it wasn't the illness or dying itself that was really bothering me, but something more related to my relationship with my family and my feelings of not really having been as good a father as I should have been.

I was able to discuss some of this with the social worker while in the hospital, but I did not really come to terms with it then. I might add that the social worker told me, the last day I was in the hospital, that she had never seen a patient with a terminal illness, who knew he was dying, to accept it so readily. I thought that was very interesting and complimentary, but I expect myself to be able to deal with whatever I have to deal with and I really didn't know what she meant until a colleague loaned me Kübler-Ross's book and I read about the "stage of acceptance."

I certainly have not come to terms with my conflicted feeling about my family—a sense of not having been as good a husband and father as I should have been, and which I never would be, anyway.

I guess there's one incident I want to relate to that. When I came out of the hospital, that Saturday and Sunday my wife and I made a point of having a few selected friends know about my illness and wanting to talk with them. I wanted some close friends with whom I could discuss this, and I needed some practical advice, particularly financial. My life seemed a total disaster economically at that point, and that concerned me, especially regarding my children. I figured that my wife, who is a trained professional, could fend for herself financially but certainly could not carry on the financial burden of getting three children through school.

I called a business friend, who came out on Sunday. He and his wife were among our close friends. We had had some other friends the day before and I was not feeling depressed. My friends were cheerful and I guess maybe I was, but not excessively so. But when my businessman friend came over and I told him about my feeling of desperation about the financial situation, I found myself getting increasingly depressed and somehow out of control emotionally, with the depression setting in a little bit like it had been in the hospital, a kind of overwhelming sea of depression.

I wondered why in the world just talking with him about finances—I had never been that uptight about money—why in the world was it upsetting me?

What he did was to refuse to accept what I stated as a problem—the money. And while he certainly is a whiz at finances and insurance problems and so on, and could give me the practical advice I needed, he refused to deal with me only at that level, and kept saying "Why is it so urgent; what is really making you so upset?"

I kept getting more annoyed with him. Why the hell doesn't he give me the advice I want and get over with it. Then I took the other track and wondered what *is* bugging me so much. And it suddenly hit me. I just feel horribly guilty about the children. I can't provide for them. And it's not just that I can't provide for them financially, but that I'm terribly guilty about my role with the kids.

At that point I burst out sobbing and my poor friend was sitting there with tears streaming down his face. I guess the point I'm trying to get at is that it took some while, and particularly that friend, to get me to the point—and that was a critical point—of my feelings about my family, of really acknowledging to myself the guilt and inadequacy that I felt about my role as a father. If I hadn't arrived at that point then, I would have had to reach it sometime or else be overwhelmed by the guilt and the depression that comes from it.

And I've not been depressed since then. A couple of months after I was discharged from the hospital I had a couple of periods of suddenly crying and saying to my wife, "It's not fair to David" (our younger son). I had to blurt that out and cry about it, but after that I didn't have to cry about it any more.

In terms of dealing directly with the children, when I got out of the hospital Friday, I think that very afternoon, we all gathered—my older boy was away at college at the time—I guess it was in my bedroom—and I told them the nature of my illness, the prognosis, and so on. And I remember crying as I told them that I wanted to be with them as long as possible, that I didn't have any fear of death or of dying, but I simply wasn't ready to die now, and I didn't want to leave them. And they cried.

I don't think we discussed at any great length the implications of my illness in terms of how long I had to live, although we have discussed as a whole family, when my son has been home from college, not only the implications for me of the illness, but for them in the plans for their future.

I suppose the most painful parts of the whole business—and it's still painful, but it's a reality and there isn't much I can do about that reality except to take what responsibility I can, particularly in terms of insuring their getting through college, however we can do that. I still don't know how we can do that, but we're trying.

I had a social worker for some two months after I got out of the hospital. (Not the same social worker I had in the hospital, but another one.) During that period of time I remember discussing with this social worker the guilt about my role as a father and what kind of father am I, becoming a cripple and so on, for a 10-year-old boy, and was it really better for me to think in terms of not being in the family, whatever that might mean. Perhaps I should make some other plans for myself, particularly in terms of this being a very hard time for my younger boy, and what can I really contribute to him by being in the home, what role as a father can I play.

Very quickly, with the social worker, I decided that that's a lot of baloney, and that I can play a role, an important role, for him and for me, regardless of what physical shape I'm in, and that it was important to him and important to me, as long as we can keep it that way, as long as I'm physically able to be around.

So I came to terms with that part of it. And that was very difficult, because I had some conflicting feelings about what this would mean psychologically for my young son. The other two children were old enough to psychologically take some greater responsibility for themselves. I didn't feel that a 10-year-old boy should have this kind of burden, but on the other hand there is nobody who's going to take the burden from him, either, so I may as well take some responsibility as his father. And we do have a very nice relationship.

My wife and I deal very honestly with one another. We did when I was in the hospital and we certainly have since. That was less of a direct conflict for me. My wife is a most unusual human being. The comment of the social worker at the hospital about coming to the acceptance of my illness was directed as much at her as it was at me.

It's not easy on a 10-year-old boy. He varies from week-to-week or day-to-day in how he deals with it. There was something that came up recently and I said, "I don't think this is something we should discuss with David." (The point is that there are very few things we think we shouldn't discuss with David.) I think it had something to do with planning or attempting to plan the terminal stages of my illness—to anticipate it—and we agreed that was not something he should be involved with. But short of that, he has been a part of everything. He has his own life. He has to help me in and out of the bathtub, whether he likes it or not. He's very

gentle and kind about doing it. Sometimes he'll gripe—like he would any time, like any pre-adolescent. My illness has not inhibited that.

An interesting question sometimes put to those in my predicament is whether personal values have changed as a result of knowing about such an illness. I myself wondered whether I would just want to go off on a wild binge or something. (All the hidden fantasies that I've never committed—now's the chance to do it, if ever.) But I've done my thing for a long, long while. I have very few regrets, if any, about what I've done.

In some ways I've lived a more liberated life than most people have. My wife and I, when we were first married, finishing up college, took off without any money and spent a year in Guatemala. There weren't many people of our generation who just took off into the wilds of Guatemala. But we did, and we had a fabulous year working with the United Nations, a UNESCO project.

And even before I was married, I had a variety of friends. I lived with a black family for a while in Watts, California, long before Watts became a terribly imprisoned ghetto. I've had a rich life with a variety of people. I have a great appreciation of black culture, of black music in particular. I don't ordinarily tell people this, but the point is that my life has been good enough for me, rich enough and varied enough, and it's been a great life. It's a cliché but both my wife and I have always done our own thing.

So knowing that I'm dying, knowing that I've only got a limited number of years to live, there is no sudden surge of "My God, I've got to start living!" I want to continue to live and enjoy the things I've enjoyed as long as I can, but there hasn't been any radical change. I get frustrated because there's some things I can't do. I wanted to hear a Ray Charles concert recently and I couldn't make it, or I was afraid to. I had a real fear of falling. That's a real fear, because I have fallen down, and I have to be very careful. So my world is getting restricted.

A lady once told me that death is a part of life,

which is a very pragmatic statement. This was after someone we knew committed suicide, maybe 20 years ago. It made sense to me, simple as it is. And I have had for some time a kind of existential approach to life, not with the full-blown philosophical and psychological paraphernalia of existentialism, but in a more pragmatic way. What is that little phrase we sometimes see printed up: "Today is the first day of the rest of your life." Which is an existential kind of statement.

I find that very nice. That's the way I live and have lived—in that sense, existentially, my wife and I—ever since we were married.

Immortality is rare, and I never thought of being immortal.

UNIT 16

BEHAVIOR MODIFICATION

☐ In this unit and those that follow, you will notice a significant shift in format. There are no instructional goals that direct your attention to specific topics and control the discussion. This change is deliberate because these units are experimental in nature. They are designed to encourage you to carry out the suggested programs. In other words, these units are oriented to a do-it-yourself approach rather than a cognitive-learning approach.

How would you like to be able to relate better to people? Would you like to be a leader of others rather than a follower? You have that power within you right now. This unit will show you how to use it to improve your personal relationships.

The scientific basis for this technique can be found in Units 2 and 6 on motivation and learning. Perhaps you should review these units, particularly the parts that deal with human social-motivational systems and operant conditioning. In learning how to modify behavior, you will be taking advantage of the human need to belong. You will also employ the processes of reinforcement, using positive and negative reinforcers and extinction. These elements form the heart of the technique.

Behavioral modification is not a new process; it is as old as humanity itself. It is used in teaching and in therapy, to mention two specialized fields. Behavioral modification has been explored extensively in business and work situations, but in many cases it has not yet been used wisely. Some individuals have learned to use it themselves by what seems to be an intuitive process of assimilation.

In the laboratory or in therapy, the application of behavioral-modification techniques is methodical. It consists of a series of steps that generally go something like this:

1. Identify the behavior you want to modify or create.
2. Set up a description of a terminal behavior so you will know when you have succeeded.
3. Establish a baseline of current behavior.
4. Find out whether your subject has the background or the ability necessary for the terminal behavior.
5. Determine what positive or negative reinforcers will be effective.
6. Decide on the type of reinforcer or combination of types that will be used.
7. Decide on criteria; that is, decide when you will apply the reinforcers.
8. Set up a series of steps that will lead to the desired terminal behavior, noting the reinforcers and criteria to be used in each step.
9. Set up a chart to keep track of your progress.
10. Keep revising steps 6, 7, and 8 until you have completed the training.

Suppose you want to help a person to stop smoking (1). You and A will settle for one cigarette a day as a successful effort (2). A smokes two packs of cigarettes a day (3). You know that A can stop and that making the effort to stop will not be harmful to A (4). You and A decide that A can have a piece of peppermint candy every time the desire to light a cigarette is consciously resisted. Every time A gives in, you will make A gargle with salted, soapy water (5). You plan to cut down on A's smoking gradually, allowing A one cigarette every two hours during the first week, one every four hours during the second week, and one a day during the third week (6, 7, 8). You keep a record of the number of cigarettes smoked each hour of each day (9).

This thumbnail case history illustrates how the scientific approach is worked out. You won't need such an elaborate plan to get the same results. For example, one student cured her boyfriend of the annoying habit of saying *you know* in every sentence. In three days of training she had achieved control and could turn the expression on or off at will. In five days she had eliminated it from his speech. In another age-old, classic tale, a class worked on its psychology professor, finally training him to lecture to them only from one corner of the classroom. How did they do this?

The technique is absurdly simple. All you must do is show some sort of approval when your subject says or does what you want. If the subject continues to do what you want, your approval worked. If not, then you will have to find some other way to reinforce the desired behavior. A smile, a nod, a word, or even the expression of an attitude is often all that is necessary to shape a person's behavior. Although positive reinforcers are usually best, if you wish you can use negative reinforcers—eliminating an unpleasant condition when a desired behavior is shown—or you can combine positive and negative reinforcers. Some people think that aversive social reactions to a person's behavior, including gestures of disapproval such as a frown or a shake of the head can be used as reinforcers. This is so when these reactions result in an increase in the behavior that led to them. Such social reactions usually work to eliminate the behavior that led you to make them. Here is how a negative reinforcer works. The psychology class mentioned previously did not pay attention to the professor when he did things that they did not want him to do. He felt uncomfortable when they ignored him. He could end his discomfort—that is, receive a negative reinforcement—only by doing what the students wanted him to do.

It is usually best not to tell your subject what you are doing, because we all resent being manipulated. The more subtle you are, the better will be your overall relationships. This statement leads to a philosophical digression. What has just been stated contains a message for you. People respond to you as you show yourself to them. If you are hostile, they will be hostile. If you are friendly, they will be friendly. If you show affection, they too will show affection. If you remember this lesson while you practice behavioral modification, you will find that you have modified your own behavior. You have changed it so that you are acting in a way that will get you want you want out of others. To paraphrase: As you act, so shall you reap.

There is one thing to be careful of, however. Be sure that the behavior you try to change is one that needs changing. Don't try to create a Pygmalion, an idealized person.

One last word: Behavioral modification works beautifully with children. They are particularly receptive to the positive reinforcers of warmth and affection, whereas adults sometimes tend to be a little wary of them, especially if they are laid on too heavily.

The following two reports are by people who tried behavior-modification techniques. The first writer is a college-age girl.

I worked to stop my boyfriend, Bill, from saying "man" with every sentence. For instance, he would say, "Hey, man, look at that car." His friends use the expression a lot, so evidently he must have picked it up from them. I decided to use a positive learning technique, because positive learning is more likely to be retained. Employing operant conditioning, I reinforced Bill every time he didn't say "man" by looking at him and really listening and showing interest in what he said. I must have done this constantly for over two weeks. It really became a game for me to see if I could make him modify his speech. If we were in the car and he'd say, "Hey, man, don't you think that house is really nice?" I'd just sit passively and say nothing. If he would then say, "Betty, did you like that house?" I'd answer yes or no.

In the beginning, he just assumed that I didn't hear his question. Then I think he noticed that when he didn't say "man" I answered him quickly and usually smiled. That was my only reinforcement, and he caught on. By the end of a couple of weeks, he had practically stopped saying "man." Now he usually says my name and, in return, he gets ready responses or answers. This keeps him happy, and not hearing "man" all the time makes me happy too.

The next report is much more sophisticated and exact. It was written by a married woman, Grace, who stopped her husband's frequent absences.

I think I want to change the following situation: Harry's frequent travel and late meetings. Instead, I want him home every night by 6 P.M. so that we can have supper together. I will try to restrict Harry to a monthly average of five nights away or late for dinner. If I can reach this average, I will consider my effort to be successful.

Harry likes demonstrations of affection. So meeting him at the door with a kiss will by my positive reinforcer. I'll also use another reinforcer. I'll plan a cocktail hour with time for talk without the kids each night that he gets home on time.

As a negative reinforcer, I will try to show no interest at all when he talks about his trips and late meetings. Also, I will not wait to eat with him when he is late. Instead, I'll prepare his meal and leave it in the oven. The later he is, the more dried out and tired his meal will be (I hope).

To keep track of her success, Grace devised the score sheet shown in Table 16.1. After four months, she exclaimed, "It worked! It really worked! Now, I'm looking for new worlds to conquer."

Behavior modification *will* work for you. To get a bit of personal practice, try this exercise. Select some person close to you and follow these steps:

1. Pick the behavior you want to modify. Be as specific as possible. Break down sets of behavior into separate actions.
2. Specify the goals or limits of behavior that you will consider acceptable.

TABLE 16.1   HARRY'S BEHAVIOR

Month	Number of work days	Number of days late or away	Number of times home on time
Before behavior modification			
April	22	13	9
May	21	16	5
June	12	15	7
After start of behavior modification			
July	19	9	10
August	23	6	17
September	20	4	16
October	20	2	19

3. Decide what reinforcers you will use and how you will apply them.
4. Remember to be discreet. People don't like to be manipulated.
5. Keep records of the behavior you want to change, to make sure you reach your goal.
6. Remember that if you are modifying behavior that may be an ego-protective device, the undesired behavior may increase at first. This reaction is normal. So if it occurs, don't think your work is a failure. The rate of bad behavior may shoot up temporarily until the person adjusts to the new game.

As you learn how to apply your techniques, it wouldn't hurt to use the scientific approach to be sure you are proceeding correctly. Make your project a planned one and be sure to write it up. No one can resist your efforts, providing you have chosen the right reinforcers and are skillful in applying them. The only problem you might face is the length of time behavioral modification may take.

☐ A POINT OF VIEW

The selections that follow make up a series dealing with the pros and cons of behavior modification in education. If you take a very broad viewpoint, every time you try to change someone's behavior, you are engaged in the process of education. Thus the pros and cons are applicable even though they may seem to deal with a very specialized area. At any rate, the articles provide a good discussion of the disagreements people have about behavior modification. Maybe reading them will help you to decide whether "behavior mod" is for you.

MURIEL PASKIN CARRISON

THE PERILS OF BEHAVIOR MOD

During the past few years there has been increasing use of a technique called "behavior modification" for improvement of classroom "discipline problems." This technique involves the use of Skinner's principles of operant conditioning to produce desired changes in the behavior of an individual without reference to the causes of this behavior. Behavior modification had its first experimental applications in mental hospitals.[1] Initially, these experiments were carefully limited to adult patients severely disabled by a type of psychosis known as catatonic schizophrenia for whom all other treatments had failed. Since the experiments showed initial dramatic improvement with these patients, the techniques were subsequently incorporated into experimental programs of institutions concerned with the treatment of autistic children. Here, too, behavior modification was "successful."

Today these methods, previously reserved only for severely disabled psychotics, are taught in the inservice programs of several school

Reprinted from *Phi Delta Kappan* 54 (May 1973): 593–595, by permission of Phi Delta Kappa and Muriel Paskin Carrison.

districts and have become a performance requirement in some colleges for the certification of student teachers. However, the rapid acceptance of behavior mod as a control system does not appear to have been accompanied by thoughtful consideration of overall effects. Growing numbers of educators are now concerned about possible unanticipated psychological and sociological effects resulting from its general application.

Operant conditioning is basically a system whereby the manipulator makes a "deal" with the subject so that the latter performs an act that pleases the master and in turn receives a reward from him. The efficacy of this system has been demonstrated beyond question in the training of animals, and there is little reason to doubt that it is similarly effective with humans. What is open for question is the total gestalt of results. Three possible questions which appear to need closer examination are the following: (1) What other conditionings may occur besides the simple one desired? (2) What type of personality modification is taking place along with the behavior modification? (3) What type of society will result when it consists of individuals trained in this manner?

In considering the first question, let us realize that the teacher's objective is usually quite direct and short-ranged. She simply wants the child to cease being a behavior problem. A child is labeled a "behavior problem" if he elects not to complete his math assignment and, instead, stares into space, raps his ruler on the desk, or bothers his neighbors. At this point the teacher who wishes to "modify" his behavior (i.e., make him stop staring and finish his math) is supposed to make a deal with him. Here's an example:

"Joe. I know you want to go out on the playground and stamp on the cans for the ecology drive. If you finish the math, you may stamp on the cans for 10 minutes."

Joe supposedly finishes his math, stamps on the cans for 10 minutes, and everybody is happy. This "new" psychology may be compared with the perennial mother-and-vegetable routine: "If you finish your vegetables, you can eat your dessert." The child may finish his vegetables. He may shape up and modify his behavior, if the proper enticer or reinforcer rewards his response at that moment. But what is *also* being inadvertently reinforced is a more permanent hierarchy of food likes and dislikes. Vegetables are *really* horrible, as the child has already suspected, and dessert is better. If the child did not like vegetables before, this technique may assure that he never will. One wonders what the long-term effect would be if mother had offered him some delicious vegetables for finishing the horrible dessert first.

Similarly, Joe's dislike for math—whatever its source—is further confirmed by his own teacher's kind understanding of his problem and recognition of the fact that it is much more satisfying to stamp on cans than to do math. In addition, we must face the fact that Joe has hereby been taught that adults find stamping on cans a more acceptable and desirable form of behavior than doing math. The negative effects of this training are incalculable. However, it should be plain that Joe has been taught to value trivial rewards and that there has been no effort to show a growing mind the intrinsic joy of intellectual achievement.

In consideration of our second question, just as the application of behavior modification techniques may inadvertently instill a hierarchy of values and likes and dislikes within the child, there is also the danger that the "con artist" type of personality may be encouraged. Children are less well informed, but just as intelligent, as adults. The child quickly catches on to this type of adult-instigated "if-you-do-this-I-will-give-you-that" deal. He will soon learn to ask, before he attempts to do anything, "What's in it for me? If I do this, what will you give me?" If a child is always given 25 cents for doing the dishes, he is in reality being denied the right of doing the dishes for the intrinsic joy of making some other person happy.

In addition, there appears to be considerable danger of the child's being so well trained in the performance/reward behavior set as to become fixated at this level of development. Two logical courses of action then follow: The child may either become unable to function without goals set and rewards offered by others, or he may learn to be a leader in the game as a successful shakedown artist. Proponents of behavior modification claim that the external concrete reinforcers may be gradually replaced by "social" rewards such as pats on the back, smiles, and verbal praise. However, these claims ignore the work of Harlow and his followers and their now-classic concepts embodied in the phrases "learning to learn" and "learning sets." The principle of learning sets was understood over 200 years ago when Alexander Pope wrote, "Just as the twig is bent, the tree's inclined." It becomes exceedingly difficult—and statistically impossible—to reverse the effects of early childhood experiences with interpersonal relations. This has been amply documented by those working with the "disadvantaged."[2] Oscar Lewis, in *The Culture of Poverty*, expresses his conviction that most of these effects are truly irreversible.[3]

While the unintentional outcomes of behavior modification may be to condition the child to permanent dislikes and to become the expert con artist, there is a far more important and deeper ethical point involved which must be considered. This brings us to our third question: What are the sociological effects of this sort of manipulation? Although Skinner feels that we are all being manipulated in one way or another, the mere fact that something exists—in whatever measurable quantity—does *not* necessarily make it acceptable or an ideal goal for which to strive.

The question of manipulation is the heart of the difference between honesty and hypocrisy in interpersonal relations. It was the crux of the youth rebellion in the sixties. It is the essential difference between education and propaganda. Education and propaganda differ in their ultimate goal. The goal of education is to help the child become independent; the goal of propaganda is to *keep* the child—or adult—dependent. While education basically should be a search for truth, propaganda too often necessitates the suppression of truth.

For optimum success, the manipulation advocated by the proponents of behavior modification necessitates that truth must be suppressed: The child (or pigeon) is only dimly aware, if at all, that he is being manipulated toward an objective or goal of the manipulator. Skinnerians hardly advocate that the child be told honestly that he is a disruptive "behavior problem," annoying his peers and setting his teacher's teeth on edge. Honest, heart-to-heart, after-3 p.m. dialogs between teacher and child concerning mutual problems do not appear in the currently popular behaviorist literature. Rather, the teacher is instructed to suppress her "affective domain" and figure out an enticing reward which will con the child into finishing a boring math ditto instead of "staring blankly into space."

Again, one must seriously question the previously noted defense of behavior modification: that a loving pat on the shoulder or a nodding smile are also acceptable as reinforcers. Is it ethical for professional teachers and student teachers to be instructed by their professors of education to smile dishonestly at students or pat them on the back when they really feel like exploding? Is it more honest to offer counterfeit affection than counterfeit money? While no professional today would seriously advocate physical violence, it does seem rational to suspect that there is some middle ground between the two extremes of an insincere love-pat and a heart-felt belting. Perhaps one alternative might be to suggest that the teacher observe the "problem" child for a period of time and silently think, "He's absolutely awful. Every teacher before me had trouble with him! No one likes him. The kids don't like him. His own mother doesn't even like him. That poor kid! No one likes him. No one is going to like him when he grows up. What a horrible thing to go through life with people hating you. Is there *anything* about this child that I could possibly like? Is there anything that I can do to make this child

happier?" Perhaps such an approach will sometimes lead to honest affection.

Since behavior modification is rapidly becoming basic methodology in many school districts and teacher education programs, it becomes imperative that professional educators address themselves to the question of the inherent differences between incentives, reinforcers, rewards, and bribes. It is also essential for educators involved in the inservice training of credentialed teachers and the preparation of student teachers to familiarize themselves with the origins of behavior modification. These origins were inaugurated in mental institutions with severely disturbed psychotic patients labeled as hopeless cases.[4] International psychiatric opinions claim that *qualitative* differences exist between the psychotic and the normal mind.[5] Ethically, this would seem to indicate that behavior modification should remain in the domain of professionally experienced and licensed psychologists and psychiatrists who work with referred cases of emotionally disturbed children in special hospitals and classrooms. Many responsible psychologists claim that "it would be extremely difficult for a classroom teacher to use these methods, since they require a one-to-one therapist-client relationship and elaborate and complete control of the environment."[6] Viewed in this light, behavior modification conducted by amateurs such as ordinary classroom teachers and student teachers appears to be a highly questionable educational procedure.

Finally, public school districts and college schools of education advocating and practicing behavior modification with children within the normal classroom place themselves in an exceedingly precarious legal position. This position essentially involves placing a child in therapy without parental consent, under the tutelage of a person unlicensed and unqualified according to the American Psychological Association code of professional ethics.[7] Current criticism of education focuses about public concern for subject matter competency. If educators blindly hop on the behavior mod bandwagon, they will open a Pandora's box of public outcry against the ethics of the entire profession. We must not let this happen.

NOTES

1. Leonard Ullmann and Leonard Krasner, *Case Studies in Behavior Modification* (New York: Holt, Rinehart and Winston, 1965).

2. Martin Deutsch et al., *The Disadvantaged Child* (New York: Basic Books, 1967).

3. Oscar Lewis, "The Culture of Poverty," *Scientific American*, October, 1966, pp. 19–28.

4. O. I. Lovass et al., "Experimental Studies in Childhood Schizophrenia: Building Social Behavior in Autistic Children by Use of Electric Shock," *Journal of Experimental Research in Personality*, January, 1965, pp. 99–109; Frank Hewett, *The Emotionally Disturbed Child in the Classroom* (Boston: Allyn and Bacon, 1968).

5. American Psychiatric Association, *Diagnostic and Statistical Manual of Mental Disorders* (Washington, D.C.: The Association, 1952).

6. Robert Biehler, *Psychology Applied to Teaching* (Boston: Houghton Mifflin, 1971), p. 519.

7. American Psychological Association, *Ethical Standards of Psychologists* (Washington, D.C.: The Association, 1963).

BRYAN L. LINDSEY AND
JAMES W. CUNNINGHAM

BEHAVIOR MODIFICATION: SOME DOUBTS AND DANGERS

For some time "the modification of behavior" has been the textbook definition of learning, but "behavior modification" has been redefined to focus more on discipline than on intellectual growth. It seeks to mold human behavior by arranging the events in a learner's environment so that he responds in a desirable and predictable direction. These contingencies are managed by offering rewards for acceptable behavior and by withholding rewards for unacceptable behavior.

There are a number of inconsistencies in logic

Reprinted from *Phi Delta Kappan* 54 (May 1973): 596–597, by permission of Phi Delta Kappa and Bryan L. Lindsey.

and some serious dangers involved in the use of behavior modification techniques in group and classroom situations. If behavior modification is used:

1. *It makes discipline a system of rewards,* which is no better than making it a system of punishments; good discipline is more than rewards and punishment; it is progress toward mutually established and worthwhile goals. A good disciplinarian is a leader who instigates and directs action toward these goals without great dependence on rewards or punishments but with an awareness of what to teach and how to teach it.

2. *It prepares students for a nonexistent world;* to ignore unacceptable behavior is to socialize for an unexisting society. An important aspect of most behavior modification is to disregard, as much as possible, inappropriate behavior. Society and nature do not ignore such behavior.

3. *It undermines existing internal control.* Behavior modification is a system to modify behavior in a classroom. But if students showing internal control in a class are learning, why should they be externally rewarded? Might they not then stop being self-directed and begin working only for external rewards?

4. *It is unfair.* To refrain from externally rewarding the behavior of some students for fear of weakening their internal control is to be faced with the alternative of providing rewards only for those without internal control. It will seem unfair to the students who have been doing what is expected of them without reward, while those having difficulty in doing what is expected of them are being rewarded. A point system or other reinforcement schedule shows a major weakness if allowance is made for individual differences, in that students already behaving in acceptable ways will remain unrewarded, while those exhibiting unacceptable behavior will be rewarded ("paid off") on occasions when they show modified behavior. But if no allowance is made for individual differences, students having a history of unacceptable

behavior will receive fewer total rewards than those who can easily conform and obtain maximum rewards.

5. *It could instruct children to be mercenary.* A system of rewards or punishments or both requires the teacher to decide how much conformity or nonconformity is enough. Since the student is exposed to many teachers with divergent standards of behavior, he could easily become confused about what acceptable behavior is and conclude that it is whatever is profitable in a material sense.

6. *It limits the expression of student discontent.* Unacceptable classroom behavior is often an indication that content and methods used in teaching are inappropriate for the needs of students. To this extent, such behavior is healthy; it is evidence that change is in order. A system of rewards or punishments which causes students to accept instruction they should reject might make it seem less necessary to modify that instruction, and thus limit student input into the curriculum.

7. *It denies human reasoning.* Many parents and teachers treat with ridicule the practice of reasoning with children about their behavior and academic performance. But despite the obvious imperfections of man, history and contemporary times are evidence of his overall good sense and practicality. A system of rewards which would "pay" for acceptable behavior and academic effort surrenders the appeal of the reasonableness of what the child is expected to do, substituting payoffs. The denial of reason, the opposite extreme from always reasoning with children, is no less ridiculous.

8. *It teaches action/reaction principles.* The complexity of human behavior is not adequately considered, since behavior modification uses action/reaction principles where there may be no logical action/reaction pattern for the learn-

er, but only for the teacher (manipulator). Such techniques deal with behavior in the cognitive domain when behavior should be dealt with in all domains. For behavior to be internalized, it is best that it be understood by the individual whose behavior is being changed.

9. *It encourages students to "act" as if they are learning, in order to obtain rewards.* Once the range of acceptable behaviors is established by the teacher, the student will be able to affect responses within that range, causing the teacher to assume that desired behavior patterns are being established, when in fact the student is merely "playing the game."

10. *It emphasizes short-range rather than long-range effects.* It emphasizes to a fault the conditions under which learning is to take place rather than appropriately emphasizing what the outcome should be. This limitation results in fragmented educational experiences, and may result in long-term ill effects.

11. *It would make the student assume a passive role in his own education.* Behavior modification focuses the student's attention on behavioral responses that are acceptable by the teacher, thus limiting the choice of behaviors for the student. This could result in frustration of personal goals toward creativity and self-actualization, weakening individual motives.

12. *It is a totalitarian concept in which the behavior shown by an individual is regarded as more important than the state of affairs in the individual's life leading to his behavior.* The use of behavior modification techniques is very often an attack upon symptoms of problems rather than an attack upon problems. Because it makes teachers the sole legitimizers of classroom behavior, it gives them an "out" from really confronting the problems met in teaching children.

CLIFFORD K. MADSEN

VALUES VERSUS TECHNIQUES: AN ANALYSIS OF BEHAVIOR MODIFICATION

A teacher stops by a child working on math and checks correct/incorrect responses. This teacher has observed that most students learn more efficiently when they are given academic feedback. She is using a principle of behavior modification to improve academic performance.

The same teacher sees another child engrossed in his work assignment. She moves quickly to his seat, gives him a smile, and whispers in his ear, "I'm so happy to see you working on your assignment." She has noticed that if she can praise him while he does his work, he works much more than when she recognizes him while he is not working. She is again using a principle of behavior modification.

The teacher goes back to her desk to correct more academic assignments. A little boy comes quickly to her desk and asks a question. She ignores him completely and calmly goes about correcting her papers. He stays about 15 seconds and then goes back to his work. The teacher smiles to herself as she checks a chart designed for this particular boy. She has almost extinguished his habit of running to her desk (only once this week; initially he did it 28 times a day and that was *after* she started recording it). The teacher sets her handkerchief on her desk as a reminder to go to this child after he has been in his seat for a few minutes. She hopes that his question was not a really important one, that it can wait two or three minutes.

She goes back to correcting assignments. It is important to her that she finish them by the end

Reprinted from *Phi Delta Kappan* 54 (May 1973): 598–601, by permission of Phi Delta Kappa and Clifford K. Madsen. Part of this article is condensed from two books dealing with behavior modification—one for teachers, *Teaching/Discipline: Behavioral Principles Toward a Positive Approach*; the other for parents, *Parents/Children/Discipline: A Positive Approach*. Both books are co-authored by Clifford K. Madsen and Charles H. Madsen, Jr., and published by Allyn and Bacon.

of the day. She has discovered that, by randomly picking out a different day of the week for children to take corrected papers home, she can dramatically increase their academic performance. Again, behavior modification.

She takes the time to check on the child who came to her desk—he wanted to know if he could get a book from the library—then returns to her seat. She hears Suzy starting to talk to her neighbor. The teacher immediately gets up, goes to Suzy, and firmly tells her that she should stop visiting until her work is done. The teacher notices that Suzy appears a little sad. She is a sensitive child, and the teacher has long since discovered that a bit of teacher disapproval will halt her inappropriate behavior. Behavior modification.

The teacher remembers that she used to yell nearly all day long (observers actually counted 146 times during one morning session). In those days she used disapproval about 80% of the time in efforts to modify social behavior, generally with little effect. Although she found that this percentage is about average for most teachers, she wanted to be more positive. At first it was difficult, not "natural." She had to learn behavior modification techniques: the reinforcement of certain academic and social behaviors. Now, when she hears a loud adult voice in an adjoining classroom, she thinks about a discussion of honesty she had with a colleague. Should a teacher be honestly disapproving most of the time because it is a "natural" response? She has learned better.

She stands in front of her class. "Children, I would like you to look at me. Suzy's looking at me. Sam is looking at me. Now David's looking at me. Now everyone is looking at me. That's nice." (Again, behavior modification.) "You may all stop your individual work and visit now until it's time for music." (When the youngsters helped make class rules earlier in the year, they expressed a desire for talk time. Establishing rules with student help has *nothing* to do with behavior modification.)

As the students visit, the teacher thinks

about the token system the school counselor is trying to establish in some of the rooms. She had read many reports about "token economy" systems and understands that they represent an effective application of behavioral principles, but she does not choose the technique for her class. She has never liked material rewards for learning (except for herself!) and prefers to use social reinforcers instead. Besides, she cannot imagine how her class could be much better than it is. She really likes it. She knows also that the counselor sometimes uses very strong disapproval as well as a special "timeout room" for some children. The effects of his procedures are also well documented and consistent with behavioral approaches, but she prefers not to use them.

WHAT IS BEHAVIOR MODIFICATION?

The above paragraphs describe procedures whose efficacy has been documented in behavioral research. In essence, this research shows that behavior is maintained and shaped by its consequences. (Strange, isn't it, that so obvious a truth should be so badly used in practice?) *Behavior* is a common word which is used quite casually in reference to many things. In the literature of behavior modification it refers to *anything* a person does, says, or thinks that can be observed directly or indirectly. Behavior modification theory deals with techniques of changing behavior as well as specific interaction effects. A "well-behaved student" is of course a person who behaves in ways that society (represented in school by the teacher) thinks are appropriate to a given situation.

Some people try to make a case against a behavioral approach by alluding to "attitudes" which are not a part of the process of behavior modification. Actually, these attitudes represent different value systems. *Principles* for teaching (shaping appropriate behaviors) should not be confused with value issues. Many teachers regard the questions of why, what, and who as considerably more important than how. But, after the teacher has decided what is

to be learned, why it should be learned, and who is going to learn it, then an effective approach to how it will be taught is vital, or the teacher's efforts as well as the student's will be wasted.

A very simple rationale explains the efficiency of behavioral approaches. *Behavioral change occurs for a reason:* Students work for things that bring them pleasure; they work for approval from people they admire; students change behaviors to satisfy the desires they have been taught to value; they generally avoid behaviors they associate with unpleasantness; and finally, students develop habitual behaviors when those behaviors are often repeated. The behavior modification approach derives from psychological experiments and represents nothing more than simple cause and effect relationships.

The current emphasis on behavior modification, or reinforcement theory (to use an older term), grew from the works of B. F. Skinner. Programmed instruction is the best-known result of his initial work. Other teaching systems, treatments of mental illness, and techniques in clinical psychology are based on Skinner's experiments. Many critics disagree with certain value choices and extensions proposed by Skinner, but this in no way invalidates the empirical relationships in learning established and stated by Skinnerian investigators. Indeed, the entire rationale of behavior modification is that most behavior is *learned*. Behavior thus defined includes emotional responses, attitudes, reading, listening, talking, looking into the mirror, liking a person, wanting to talk out a problem, hitting, being frustrated, sticking with a task, abandoning a task, responding appropriately to the desires of a teacher, not responding to the desires of a teacher, most "good" behavior, most "bad" behavior, disturbing one's neighbors, being "well-behaved," being excited about school work, hating to learn, and so on—and on—and on.

Exactly the same principles may be used to teach good social behavior as are used to teach appropriate academic skills (e.g., providing feedback about correct/incorrect responses). If a teacher wishes students to have a real desire to learn something, the teacher may find it necessary to structure the external environment so students will seek structured rewards for their work tasks. After initial manipulation, the rewards for proper behavior will often come from the reinforcement of the particular task itself, i.e., getting the right answer is often all the structure that is needed. Incidentally, this is precisely what most teachers do when they initially make a "game" out of learning. Students become enthusiastic concerning the game per se, not realizing that its purpose is to stimulate effective work. It is curious that some teachers who try desperately to make work fun also say they reject any "manipulation techniques." The teacher's job is to structure learning experiences. This structuring process involves manipulating the environment (i.e., setting up the correct situation, physical plant, materials, and so on) conducive to effective learning, whether the goal be simple obedience, complex problem solving, or self-discovery. The teacher must structure as wisely as possible, whether the school organization is open, free, pod, modular, or something else. One should know the subparts of any complex task and structure the situation so that each student can have a "rewarding learning experience." Irrespective of our cherished clichés, we actually do practice behavioral manipulation. It appears paradoxical for the teacher to reject manipulation when manipulation is the essence of her task.

BEHAVIOR RESULTS FROM ITS CONSEQUENCES

Behavioral research demonstrates that if work tasks can be (1) geared to the student's own level, (2) presented in logical sequence with (3) appropriate feedback concerning correct/incorrect responses, and (4) rewarded for successively better efforts to reach defined goals, then the student will certainly learn. Exactly the same principles apply to teaching proper social skills.

Critics say, "Yes, but isn't that a cold approach?" Certainly not. While behavior modification is the only branch of applied psychology based on scientific principles verified in the laboratory, it is the nature of the material to be learned that represents important value choices. Actually, because of its consistency and simplicity, behavioral modification effected through contingent reinforcement (approval /disapproval) usually represents a very kind and understandable system to students. The behavioral scientist who observes a school situation can classify almost everything that goes on behaviorally, regardless of how well the teachers involved understand principles of reinforcement. Cause and effect behaviors are always present. For example, some teachers do not realize when they are being sarcastic. "Why don't you just yell louder, Jimmy?" Problems are created when the student is not really sure of the teacher's meaning. Being taken literally is the price one sometimes pays for using sarcasm or irony.

The behavioral clinician can demonstrate how teachers might be more effective in the application of the child's or teacher's own values. Many teachers are surprised to learn how closely they approximate a strict behavioral approach. After being apprised of behavioral principles, many exclaim, "Why that's what I've been doing all the time!"

When learning is defined as a change or modification of behavior, then reinforcement principles constitute a method to promote or expedite this learning. In short, behavioral analysis asks, "How should we go about teaching in the best possible manner to ensure correct association?" Or, more specifically, "How should we go about teaching the student to concentrate, to read, to share, to clean his desk, to be honest, to develop his own values?" If a youngster responds favorably to our presentation, we assume that it functions as a reward for the student. But what if the student does not respond? Then we must restructure the external environment so that the student *does* receive proper motivation.

IF AT FIRST YOU DON'T SUCCEED?

If behaviors can be learned, they can also be unlearned or relearned. Sometimes, in our zeal to get through to our students, we make mistakes. Sometimes we make mistakes regardless of zeal. The efficacy of behavioral techniques with *severe* problem behaviors within mental hospitals and institutions for the retarded and handicapped perhaps should give us the encouragement to move forward. Behavioral techniques have demonstrated that even severely handicapped children can learn much faster and much more than we previously believed possible. And no, one does not need to be a medical or psychological specialist to provide academic and social approval. Teachers have been doing this for years.

What are the dynamics of changing social behavior? Since it is impossible for a person to maintain two contradictory responses, the skillful teacher will program to elicit responses *incompatible* with deviant behavior and thereby obviate the need for punishment. "Count to 10 before you get angry; think before you begin your work; take three big breaths before you cry." Punishment alone may stop deviant behavior, but it will not necessarily teach correct associations. The child who is hit with his spoon because he cannot use it properly will not necessarily learn proper etiquette. Similarly, the child who is punished for faulty reading will not necessarily learn to read efficiently. The one child might shun the spoon; the other child may stop reading. Setting up incompatible responses is perhaps the most effective behavioral technique of all, because it constitutes a double-edged approach. Not only is the inappropriate behavior eliminated but a correct response replaces it. Thus the child unlearns and relearns at the same time. The procedure eliminates the need for punishment and at the same time teaches correct associations.

Four principles for the teacher are:

1. *Pinpoint:* It is necessary to pinpoint explicitly the behavior that is to be eliminated or established. This takes place at many different levels relating to many differentiated academic as well as social behaviors. It leads to a hierarchical arrangement of skills and behaviors based upon expected specific behavioral objectives.

2. *Record:* This is a necessity in behavior modification and actually is what differentiates it from other techniques. Specified behaviors must be listed as they occur and thereby provide a precise record from which to proceed. The record must be accurate. If the behavior cannot in some way be measured, then one can never know if it has been established or unlearned. As maladaptive responses are eliminated, more time can then be devoted to more productive behaviors.

3. *Consequate:* This unique word, which you won't find in Webster's, means "setting up the external environmental contingencies (including primarily one's own personal responses) and proceeding with the teaching program." Contingencies include approval, disapproval, withdrawal of approval, threat of disapproval, or ignoring. Reinforcers may be words (spoken and written), expressions (facial and bodily), closeness (nearness and touching), activities (social and individual), and things (materials, food, playthings, and money). *Choice of reinforcers is an extremely important aspect of behavior modification* and constitutes an issue which should receive much discussion, debate, and criticism.

4. *Evaluate:* Evaluation should be continuous, but ultimate effects, which may be different from immediate effectiveness, must be ascertained. Hence a program must be allowed to operate for some time before final data analysis.

VALUES VERSUS TECHNIQUES

It should be apparent from the above that behavior modification represents the use of a series of scientifically verified techniques that may be used to promote more effective learning

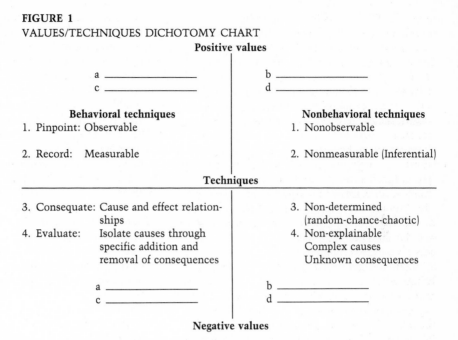

FIGURE 1
VALUES/TECHNIQUES DICHOTOMY CHART

Positive values

a _____   b _____
c _____   d _____

Behavioral techniques
1. Pinpoint: Observable

2. Record: Measurable

Nonbehavioral techniques
1. Nonobservable

2. Nonmeasurable (Inferential)

Techniques

3. Consequate: Cause and effect relation-
           ships
4. Evaluate: Isolate causes through
           specific addition and
           removal of consequences

3. Non-determined
   (random-chance-chaotic)
4. Non-explainable
   Complex causes
   Unknown consequences

a _____   b _____
c _____   d _____

Negative values

of both social and academic subject matter. A behavioral approach does not help the teacher decide why, what, and who is going to learn. These issues represent important value choices. However, after questions relating to these values have been answered, behavioral principles may be used to enhance learning of appropriate behavior. Of course, the choice of a particular technique as opposed to other approaches represents a value choice. Also, if a behavioral approach is implemented, then selection of specific behavioral procedures (e.g., approval rather than punishment), as well as choice of potential reinforcers, represents another value issue.

Opponents of behavior modification would do well to address themselves to the more important issues concerning learning rather than condemn a technique by alluding to many ancillary detriments that they feel might ensue from its application. (Generally, they make these pronouncements in the complete absence of data.)

Figure 1 illustrates this point. Fill in three or four of the most important values you think should be learned by students (academic, social, or both). For example, reading, writing, consideration for others, self-actualization—whatever *you* consider to be positive. It is obvious that behavioral techniques must be used to teach "negative" as well as "positive" values.

The purpose of this exercise is to indicate that behavioral methods, much like any product of man (atomic energy, jet propulsion, governments), may be used either to the benefit or detriment of other human beings. Behavioral techniques are characterized by definitions of behavior that can be observed (pinpointed) and then measured (recorded and counted). These techniques include the isolation of specific cause and effect relationships and thereby provide a scientific methodology for the evaluation of learning.

TEACHING—ART OR SCIENCE?

Through trial and error, it would seem that every teacher who cares can find effective ways to stimulate students to realize their full learning potential. With or without a full understanding of behavioral principles, this teacher will find better methods of behavioral control and character development.

The ability to recognize individual differences and structure the school environment with contingencies relevant to specific situations represents an outstanding accomplishment. Good sense and good taste are important, of course. I know of one seventh-grade teacher who controlled her class by having the problem children participate in a mock wedding ceremony if they were "very, very bad." When the children evidenced proper behavior, they were allowed to "get divorced." This disciplinary procedure was tremendously effective and used behavioral principles. However, the teacher's choice of activity raises serious questions regarding the acquisition of other behaviors and attitudes. Another teacher told me of a technique she used with 8- and 9-year-old boys: "When one of the boys misbehaves, I make him wear a girl's ribbon in his hair." Does it work? Very well; but again one must question the insensitivity of this teacher to other values. It is ironic that this same person thought it "terrible" to suggest to parents that occasionally they might send their problem children to school without breakfast, in order to promote proper behavior through *rewards* of cookies, cereal, and milk.

It seems apparent that no teaching technique can be effectively divorced from the person who uses it. This point, however, makes a case for more rigorous screening of prospective teachers, not for the abandonment of effective techniques. It is a curious argument that maintains that effective techniques must be kept from teachers because then teachers may actually teach more efficiently. Because of the effectiveness of behavioral techniques, perhaps the profession may now get down to the truly important issues:

What specifically should be learned? Or, more importantly, who will decide what is to be learned, both socially and academically? What values and accompanying behaviors evidencing selected values should be learned? When, where, and by whom?

Who should be given the responsibility to interact purposefully in the learning process, i.e., to teach?

Should society require any objective evidence for this learning, i.e., data from observation or other formal means?

If continued research demonstrates the efficacy of empirical cause and effect relationships (data based on observation), ought derived principles to be systematically implemented within the schools?

If so, then what should be the boundaries concerning choice and application of reinforcers, i.e., approval versus disapproval; punishment versus ignoring; the structuring of incompatible responses; the use of academic subject matter only as reward; social as opposed to material reinforcers. These issues represent the most important value issues within the technique of behavior modification.

Let us not waste time with such irrelevant arguments as "it's unfair." (Of course it's unfair, if unfair is defined as any individualization or discriminative assessment, e.g., differential grading.)

Then there is the charge: It's totalitarian. Nonsense! Who decides what values/behaviors should be taught to whom has nothing to do with behavior modification. Some schools are run mostly by teachers; others are controlled mostly by students. Another criticism goes something like this: Behavior mod teaches students to work for rewards. Right! Perhaps after awhile they may even find their subject matter rewarding.

Another criticism: It militates against internal control. Not so; actually, the process of partial reinforcement teaches youngsters to go for longer and longer periods of time without any external rewards. Incidentally, how long do adults maintain appropriate behavior without the occasional reinforcement from a loved one or perhaps a more tangible reward for professional behavior?

Then it is sometimes alleged that behavior modification denies human reasoning. If anything it *teaches* human reasoning—specifying in clear, consistent, and honest ways the cause and effect relationships of life.

Another charge: *It may teach other nonspecified behaviors.* Perhaps. But let's worry about those, if indeed they exist, when there is some evidence for them. And is anyone so naive as to believe that teachers are not already approving or disapproving certain student behaviors with or without a full understanding of behavior modification?

Finally, if we cannot agree on the above, at least we may begin to take data, i.e., make systematic observations concerning what is presently going on in schools, in order to build a sounder basis for the development of teaching techniques.

It is readily apparent that, regardless of how many "behavioral recipes" are available, the insensitive teacher will still be found wanting. The art of being a good teacher seems directly related to the behaviors of that teacher as a person. Modeling effects of an outstanding individual are still among the most powerful and far-reaching of teacher influences. The truly effective teacher will combine the science of behavior with the art of living to create that exceptionally rare atmosphere: an environment where children not only take excitement from discovery but learn to be nice people.

WILLIAM A. TRACY

PERIL OR PERIL-NOIA?

Ms. Carrison does not convince me by her examples that there is any significant difference between behavior modification and traditional methods of teaching (up to and including performance contracting), except that it involves admitting, finally, that the carrot-on-a-stick is

Reprinted from *Phi Delta Kappan* 54 (May 1973); 597, by permission of Phi Delta Kappa and William A. Tracy.

the only alternative to punitive, force-feeding education.[1] The examples of supposedly drastic behavior mod techniques based on Skinnerian principles quoted in the article are so ordinary that surely they have been used by parents and teachers for centuries; Skinner based his research on those very elemental teaching tactics.

Ms. Carrison's footnotes include works on therapy for schizophrenics and emotionally disturbed children, including one article on shock treatment. She opens and closes her article by mentioning that behavior mod techniques derive from methods used in treating severely disturbed patients in hospitals. I think this is putting the cart before the horse: These techniques were derived from traditional teaching techniques, intensified and concentrated— via B. F. Skinner. She never mentions in her somewhat anticlimactic article any use of these severe techniques in the classroom; indeed, her examples are quite tame. (In [his] article . . . Madsen suggests sending problem children to school without breakfast so they can be rewarded with cookies and milk. This illustrates a classic Skinnerian—or Pavlovian—principle; but I doubt that it is widely used.)

The two methods, positive and negative reinforcement, are actually one. Being deprived of a "right" like recess or getting a poor grade (provided the parents have complied with school practice by convincing the child that grades are indeed important—no guarantees against double jeopardy here!) are no more drastic punishments for a child than having a reward waved in front of him and then withdrawn because he did not fulfill his agreement with the teacher. Bringing the child to understand and accept a contract agreement is nine-

[1] I am avoiding the question of that minority of "gifted" children who take to reading and learning and questioning as to their natural element. These people *will* be educated, possibly with the help of the public schools. A great many American anti-elitist, knee-jerk liberal prejudices which have reared their heads since the overreaction to emphasis on schools for the gifted in the 1950s will have to be discarded. This is, however, a less pressing problem than that presented by the majority of first-graders who do not immediately see any practical use in reading or math.

tenths of the battle: Once he has recognized this basic element of all societal structures, Ms. Carrison's "peril" has already had its effect. Educators such as Ms. Carrison are overestimating their ability and opportunity to influence students who have had the behavior mod philosophy deeply ingrained in them long before they reach school. Otherwise, would it work? Educators of the world, relax!

The traditional grading system had the major weakness of an intangible, artificial value system imposed from above, having no real value to the student except insofar as he valued praise or feared punishment from parents and teachers. An immediate and preferably material reward is obviously more effective—and this is mirrored throughout all levels of our society today, for better or worse. For this reason, I question whether "honesty" in telling a child how and why he is a problem and to whom (usually the teacher) is a very effective method in today's child-centered schools. What fourth-grader cares more about what his teacher thinks than about what his peers think? And peers (at least from my not-so-recent experience) certainly do not judge him by what he does in school (except perhaps to censure him if he does too well).

Given that positive reinforcement in training is more effective than negative reinforcement, and that immediate gratification is (at least temporarily) more effective than delayed gratification, the so-called behavior modification techniques appear to me to be only natural—and it doesn't take B. F. Skinner to see that. Stripped down to the barest transaction, almost every process of civilization—between gods and men, governments and people, parents and children—turns out to be either carrot-on-a-stick or carry-a-big-stick. Skinner reduced these social processes to their lowest common denominator. I do not believe that the admitted

as opposed to the tacit use of these techniques poses any peril. As a matter of fact, I have decided that Behavior Modification (it now warrants capital letters) is probably the foundation of civilization. I imagine that behavior mod will turn out to be a tempest in a semantic teapot. Carrison's imperative to educators, to address themselves to the question of inherent differences between incentives, reinforcers, rewards and bribes, is perhaps the key. There is no inherent difference, but perhaps there is a tiny difference in the implications we give to words, "incentive" being good and "bribe" bad. If there is a difference, which one works best? What to you is an incentive may well seem a bribe to me. In any case they are both rewards and a reward is a reinforcement. I am not one, in this day and age, to cavil about *quality* of incentive or to make value judgments. Morals, ethics, religion are no longer universal standards for behavior, if they ever were. And it is harder to teach a child that being good, doing right, and learning math are their own rewards now that idealism and pragmatism are of like interest (i.e., none) to the vast majority of people. But when it comes to time/cost efficiency, pragmatism is where it's at. According to Carrison, this has created in Americans, and wherever education by these methods has been instituted, a con-man mentality. Admittedly the con-man view of life is not desirable; however, it is difficult to imagine America without it— perhaps again it's a matter of semantics. Is "con man" the correct term? Ambition, motivation, aspiration must all have goals. Getting our educational cards on the table instead of using increasingly valuable teacher time to convince students of the joys of learning for learning's sake could prove a great saving in both resources and in student frustration resulting from imperfect understanding of what is expected.

UNIT 17

KNOWING
YOURSELF

☐ In Unit 6 on learning, you found out that many people think that human behavior is learned. In contrast, in Unit 7 on perception and emotions, you found out that some people think that human beings are born with an innate capacity to blend and process in their awareness the information they are getting from their environment. So the dyed-in-the-wool behaviorist says we learn everything we know as the result of pleasure and pain, and the cognitive, humanistic, or existential theorist says we have certain built-in inner pushes that need only a proper environment to begin to act.

These arguments bring up an age-old discussion about the nature of the body and the mind. Are they two separate entities living in the same framework, or are they fused into one inseparable organism? This question has fascinated people for centuries. The behaviorists tend to discount the mind as a separate structure; the cognitive theorists, humanists, and existentialists believe the opposite. The disagreement provokes some very different approaches. This book is, to some extent, based on a behavioral approach to learning. In it, specific learning goals are established, information is presented concerning them, and then you are asked to integrate the two. However, the book is also dedicated to a humanistic purpose: to help you to understand yourself better and become a well-functioning person. Perhaps it could be said that the book's philosophy is humanistic and its methodology is behavioral. It is a compromise between the two points of view.

Recently, there has been an upsurge in interest and information—some old, some new—on matters directly related to the mind-body problem. People used to think that certain body functions were beyond our mental control. They felt that the autonomic nervous system, regulating nutritive, vascular, and reproductive activities, went serenely on its way, taking care of the physiology of the body without bothering with its mental state. People thought for years that the mind couldn't influence certain body functions at all and blandly ignored connections between the mind and bodily symptoms such as ulcers, high blood pressure, and headaches. They agreed that these ills were indeed caused by mental tension but said that we couldn't control their mental causes. However, more and more evidence is piling up that is too powerful for us to ignore. We can, for example, suggest illnesses to people (through hypnosis, if you wish) and have them clearly develop the appropriate symptoms. We can alter the state of our bodies by mental control: We can control heartbeat, blood pressure, rate of breathing, and the temperature of various parts of our bodies; we can produce pain or numbness whenever we wish. In short, it is becoming increasingly apparent that we can control our bodies to a degree never before suspected or admitted.

One of the most powerful tools for study in this area has been the recent use of biofeedback instruments. Biofeedback is nothing more than the process of measuring some body activity, such as pulse rate, muscle tension, blood pressure, sweating, or temperature, in such a way that the measurement is presented in a constant monitoring feedback system. For instance, muscle tension can be measured electrically by putting a sensor on a particular muscle—the muscle that controls the brow, for instance—and recording tension in terms of clicks or a changeable squeal. If people being tested then listen to the clicking or squealing and concentrate on changing it, they can usually reduce the amount of tension. In a short period of time, they become able to control tension at will through the use of feedback devices. This is a form of classical conditioning.

Quite recently, the control of alpha waves became a big thing. Alpha waves are certain rhythmic electrical patterns in the brain that seem to function when a person is conscious but not thinking. They are one of a set of four electrical wave patterns identified by the number of electrical cycles per second that they create. By using a biofeedback sensor with a signaling device, people can learn in a few hours to control the mind's activities so that they are in an alpha state. Those who have been able to do this report a very pleasant feeling of relaxation. As an additional help in attaining the alpha state, some people also use "alpha drivers," instruments that show a pulse—usually a strobe light or clicker—in a rhythmic frequency that is a harmonic of the alpha waves. (Have you ever driven for a long time with the windshield wipers clicking and moving back and forth in front of you?) However, these alpha drivers can be very dangerous because they can cause convulsions similar to epileptic seizures in some people. In any case, most people soon learn to control their alpha states easily without the use of alpha drivers. The biggest reason for failure to reach control is, paradoxically, trying too hard to relax. Oddly enough, the people who have learned how to reach control cannot tell others how they have done it.

At the present time, it is suspected that the state of alpha-wave generation is not connected to relaxation as directly as was previously supposed. The evidence shows that some people do not generate significant amounts of alpha waves and yet do relax; others who do generate significant amounts do not relax. Probably the mere process of relaxation is a more potent factor than the state of excitement of the brain. Currently, the preferred practice is to rely on muscle relaxation, using a specific muscle such as the frontalis, the brow muscle.

The evidence just presented, along with knowledge of the effectiveness of other techniques, such as acupuncture, the old practice of cupping and bleeding, and yoga-type meditation, lead us to some new thoughts about the relationship between the mind and the body. We are beginning to recognize that the mind does affect our body's functioning, to an extent greater than we ever thought possible. This knowledge leads to a closer examination of the gestalt ideas. Gestaltists believe that within us we have certain innate tendencies that influence the way that we perceive the world about us. If our mind becomes distorted through tension, we then distort our perceptions and begin to live in an unreal world. The best way for us to reorganize this distorted world is to pay attention to our bodies, which will signal to us when our minds are distorting the environment. In this way, the gestaltists tie in the body and the mind. A great deal of gestalt therapy involves developing means of sensitizing ourselves to the signs that the body gives to indicate tension and forces acting on the mind in a harmful way. The gestaltists say, "Pay attention to the signals the body is sending you so that you can reorganize what is happening in your mind."

In this unit, a set of exercises will be described for you to use to develop an increasing sensitivity to your body-mind messages. The exercises will be divided into those that you can do alone, those that you can do with a partner, and those that you can do in a group. Some might be called corrective exercises; others will merely be constructive. It's awfully hard to keep the two types separate, however, and there's really no good reason to do so.

The exercises that you can do alone to become more sensitive to your body's signals involve feeling and releasing tension, developing sensory awareness, and body energizing. There are many such exercises. The few that have been chosen here are easy to grasp, need no special equipment, and do not threaten your personality.

The key to these exercises, especially those involving tension and awareness, is the technique of introspection. You could call the technique meditation and not be too far off the track. Each exercise requires you to think about what is going on in your mind and in your body. Each calls for a certain amount of practice to develop your skill in carrying it out. If the way they are described, what you should look for, and what you are supposed to feel seem sketchy, remember that the techniques will be highly individual. No one can tell you specifically what to do and what you will experience. You will be reaching for an emotional experience without knowing the end result or the route you should take. Don't let this worry you. If you work on these exercises for awhile, you will begin to register pleasurable and worthwhile emotions and feelings, even though you don't know specifically what they will be ahead of time.

FEELING TENSION

Here are some things to do to acquaint yourself with the ways your muscles tell you how tense you are. Pick a quiet place where you can be undisturbed for a half-hour. Sit in a comfortable chair, picking a position comfortable enough so that you can stay motionless for quite awhile. Now wrinkle your brow. Tighten your whole scalp as much as you can. Wiggle your ears. Try to feel extreme tightness in your scalp and brow muscles. Next, deliberately try to relax your brow muscles and your scalp as much as you can. Tell yourself, "My brow and scalp muscles are relaxing. They are getting loose. There is no tension left in them. My whole head feels loose and warm." Practice this until you know what a relaxed muscle system feels like. Don't try too hard. If you do, you might be defeating yourself.

After you have gotten your scalp and facial muscles to relax and are familiar with the sensation, concentrate on your jaw muscles. They also often display tension. Tighten your jaw as much as you can. Make your jaw muscles bunch up as you clench your teeth. Now consciously loosen your jaws so that your mouth is almost open. Make sure that you can feel no tension in your jaws. Concentrate on becoming familiar with this tensionless feeling. While you are doing this, check frequently to make sure that you have not allowed your head and face to tighten up again. Progressively, you have now deliberately relaxed your head, face, and jaws.

Now turn your attention to your breathing. Try out different breathing rates—panting, the tight breathing you do when you are excited, and the slow, relaxed breathing you do when you are calm. Gradually work to be able to change your rate of breathing, so that it becomes calm and relaxed. Again, make sure that you have not allowed the other indicators—your head, face, and jaws—to tighten up on you.

You have now learned how it is to feel relaxed in three areas of your body that are commonly tense. Your next step is to discover how your indicators act when you are under tension. To do this, put yourself in the now-familiar state of relaxation that you have learned. Deliberately search your memory for some happening that was distasteful or bad for you. Think over all its details as clearly as you can. While you are thinking of them, pay attention to your body. Which part tenses up? Is it your breathing? Does it become fast and shallow? Is your body telling you that you are up tight by the way that you breathe or by the tension in your jaws or face or head? Practice alternating between periods of calm and tension until you can easily recognize each by your bodily sensations. Again, do not worry about the causes of your emotions; just recognize how your body feels when you are in a state of nervous tension. As you practice awareness, however, a sneaky thing will happen to you. You will find relaxation to be so much more pleasant than tension that you will find yourself deliberately relaxing your body. In other words, you will find yourself discounting unpleasant things in order to avoid feelings of tension.

There is no direct way to relax your skin receptors. You simply cannot say to yourself that your skin is relaxed and then try to consciously tighten it up to see what tension feels like. There is, however, a stimulation exercise that you can try that more or less tells you how you feel when your skin is vibrant and excited.

Stand up and let your hands and arms dangle in front of you as loosely as you can. Then let your body bend as low as it can without discomfort. Now start slapping your feet (if you can reach them), your ankles, and your legs. Slap lightly but firmly enough to make your skin tingle. Work your way up your body, slapping yourself lightly, finishing by slapping yourself on the top of your head. Then work your way down your body again. Your whole body should feel tingling and surprisingly refreshed by this exercise. It will make you more aware of the kind of input you can get from your skin. It will remind you of what you feel through its receptors. After all, you have been getting messages from your skin all your life; it can be easy to take them for granted.

DEVELOPING AWARENESS

An emotion tends to be one-way. Once established, it seems to want to rule the roost without interference. To do this, the emotion tends to screen the information that comes into the mind, letting the mind operate on and process only the information that will perpetuate the dominant emotion. For example, when you are angry at someone, you can't laugh at that person's jokes or think them funny. If you're ranting and raving at someone who is cracking jokes, you tend to be further infuriated. You simply don't recognize any humor in the situation. When you are under an emotional stress, such as anxiety, the same situation holds true. This is what the gestaltists mean when they say that the mind tends to distort reality.

One of the ways in which we can beat this distortion is to make ourselves more aware of the sensory inputs that enter our bodies. If we are able to do this, we can be more aware of what the mind is trying to screen out and can more easily avoid becoming dominated by any particular emotion. We can be more open to the world around us.

Developing awareness is a retraining operation. For most of our lives we have trained ourselves to ignore certain stimuli so that we are not distracted, tuning out certain things that are going on around us. When a teacher gives a boring lecture, you often retreat into yourself and daydream. Every so often, you send up an antenna to listen: Is the teacher still talking? Yep. Back to the daydream. In this way you learn to close out rather than to accept.

As was mentioned earlier, an experiment with some meditating Indian yogis checked their brain waves and found them to be in an alpha state. Then a ticking clock was introduced. From the yogis' brain-wave patterns, the experimenters could tell that they became aware of the clock and remained aware of it throughout their meditation. At the same time, the ticking did not affect their meditation. Another group of mediators who were not trained in yoga also became aware of the clock's ticking. However, it very quickly faded from their consciousness. The point is that the yogis were able to handle the extraneous input without disturbing their relaxation. The untrained people were not. Instead, they dismissed the unwanted stimulus from their attention when they found it was not relevant. In other words, they distorted their environment. In order to accomplish something that they wanted, they had to ignore something that was competing for their attention.

The exercises offered to you here will help you to train yourself to become more aware of stimulation and therefore more aware of what goes on around you. In a peculiar sort of way, they involve quite a bit of effort. Usually when you do any training, you can see some sort of progress. For example, when you are learning to throw a ball accurately, you can see whether you are beginning to throw longer and straighter. However, these exercises will not give you the same sort of feedback. There will be nothing tangible or measurable by which you can judge your progress. If you carry them out faithfully, however, and do learn to be able to include more stimulation in your perceptual field, you will suddenly, one day, recognize that you are much more aware of what is going on around you and that you control your emotions more thoroughly than they control you.

The first exercise involves, paradoxically enough, blocking out one way of receiving sensory stimulation. We ordinarily are very dependent on our eyes to give us information about our environment. Many times, this dependence causes us to block out what our ears and other sensory receptors are telling us.

So, for this exercise, try blocking out your visual input and listening to what goes on around you.

Find some private place where you won't be interrupted or where you will not feel uneasy or conspicuous. Relax yourself as you have learned to do. Then close your eyes or, better still, blindfold yourself so that you have to listen. Now verbalize everything you hear. "I hear the wind rustling the leaves. I hear my own breath. I hear the hum of insects. I hear the sound of an airplane. I hear an engine." Keep describing what you hear until you are satisfied that you have increased your awareness. Practice this several times. Try to keep aware of as many inputs as you can simultaneously. In other words, do not let perceptions fade from your mind once you have heard them and classified them: "I can hear an airplane, and I can hear it even while I am aware of the sound of an automobile engine and the sound of the wind." What you are doing is trying to expand the extent of your awareness of many events simultaneously. Again, this takes practice, and your progress will not be obvious until at some time you suddenly become aware of the fact that you are keeping track of the different events you are hearing without losing your train of thought.

Once you have developed hearing awareness, it is time for you to try to develop other sensory systems. Blindfold yourself, block your ears, and try to verbalize what you are receiving as sensory stimulation. What are your nose and tastebuds telling you? What is your skin telling you about what is going on around you? What are your muscles telling you about how you are positioned? Although you might not think it necessary, you also need to practice visual awareness. Plug your ears and make yourself as impervious to stimulation from the other senses as you can. Then practice verbalizing what you see. Practice maintaining awareness of as many inputs as you can simultaneously, until you are satisfied that you have become better at being able to hold several different stimuli together in your mind.

Once you have developed some skill in keeping track of what your different senses are telling you, it is time to try to combine them. First of all, try combining the skin, muscle, nose, and taste receptors. Work on verbalizing what each sense is telling you and keeping track of them simultaneously: "I can hear a clock ticking. I can smell cut grass. I can feel a warm wind. My muscles tell me that I am straining my left side." Eventually you will be able to handle quite a few inputs without losing track of them.

This sounds like a lot of work, but it really isn't. Once you have practiced a little with the blindfold, you can merely shut your eyes. You can also learn to block off your hearing without earplugs. You can practice anywhere you want to—sitting in a room, walking across a lawn, or anyplace you happen to be. You can take one or two minutes to work on these exercises, or you can take a half-hour. The times, places, and sites you choose are strictly up to you because, in the long run, they do not matter; it is the practice that makes the difference. If you are skeptical, try the exercises for one or two five-minute periods each day for a month, and see that they help to increase your awareness.

What do you gain from these efforts? You will gain the ability to be more fully aware of what is going on around you, the ability to be more fully aware of the state of your mind and what it processes in the way of sensory input. You will be less controlled or dominated by one particular emotion; you will exclude or distort your perceptions of your environment to a lesser degree. You will have a greater recognition of tension or anxiety and the ability to cope with it. These are your gains. If they seem worthwhile to you, work to achieve them.

One individual exercise that you can try is different from the exercises you have been given so far. It calls for action rather than introspection and meditation. It is also designed to serve a purpose different from the others in this section. Like those in the first group, it is designed to relieve tension. This exercise is not always practical because it must be done in a special place where you will not be too conspicuous and where you can sound off without attracting too much attention. It consists simply of jumping up and down for as long as you feel like it, while screaming at the top of your voice. Try it; you'll find it's great for getting rid of a full head of steam. However, just be sure that the people with the large white nets don't come to catch you.

DREAMS

What you have been given so far are exercises that enabled you consciously to assert the power of your mind in a direction leading to greater self-knowledge. However, there is another way of doing this, by looking at a process that to a great extent is involuntary and not under your control—dreaming. As you probably know, dreams have fascinated humans for centuries. They have been called visitations of the spirits. They have been credited to the Devil. They have been given mystical interpretations and practical meanings. Quite a few psychologists have said that dreams are the representation of our unconscious desires and needs expressed in a symbolic form that will not disturb the ego. As you will recall, Freud regarded dreams as realizations of unconscious or conscious wishes. He and his followers have created a very elaborate set of meanings and interpretations for dreams. When people dream and then remember what they have dreamed, they are recalling what is called the manifest content of their dreams. This is different from the latent content of the dreams. The latent content is much more direct and expresses much more clearly the repressed material that lurks in the dreamers' unconscious mind.

There are three states in a dream: anxiety, guilt, and longing. Anxiety indicates an outpouring of stress, frustration, and trauma. Guilt feelings reflect self-punishment, which is why our dreams are often so graphically concerned with death or suffering. Longing is also to some extent concerned with punishment, but it also indicates repressed desires. Each item that a person identifies in a dream is supposed to have a symbolic meaning that, when joined with other meanings, will give a picture of what is ordinarily hidden in the dreamers' unconscious mind. The Freudians, because they tie everything to sex, have developed a set of symbolic meanings that make quite earthy reading.

Some psychologists, however, do not believe that the things a person dreams about have standard meanings. For example, an open door does not need to mean a vagina. These psychologists feel that dream meanings are personal and cannot be interpreted in any uniform, overall, standardized way. This does not mean, however, that dreams cannot be useful to us. If we regard them as expressing thoughts, desires, or reactions that are more or less free of conscious censoring, they can help us to learn more about ourselves. Dreams can be considered projections of inner thoughts. If you look at all the people in your dreams as projections of your own personality, you may then have a basis for judging the meanings of your dreams. They are really you speaking out from the innermost depths of your mind.

Some people claim that they never dream, but this can be shown to be untrue. Every sleeping person goes through a period in which there are signs of changed breathing and emotional change. This stage can be identified by the movement of the eyes and is often called the rapid eye movement (REM) period. Studies have shown that if the REM period is prevented, the person will later show extreme swings of emotion and will frequently fly into a rage or show uncontrollable anger. Apparently, we use the REM period to throw off tension and emotion. If it doesn't occur, we have to release our emotions in other, less acceptable ways. If we agree with this interpretation, we may also agree that recalling the themes of our dreams may show us the roots of our tension-producing situations. But how can we remember what we have dreamed about? Here are some suggestions.

If you wish to remember a dream, make sure you are relaxed as you try to go to sleep. As you drift off, reminisce about the events of the day or the week so that you can set the stage for your dream. Suggest to yourself that you will dream tonight.

Keep a pad and pencil near your bed, so that you can write down the details of your dream while they are still fresh in your memory. If you wake during your dream, don't try to go back to sleep until you have recorded your dream as fully as you can. If you happen to have a tape recorder, so much the better. Use it to put down your impressions of your dream. Don't say to yourself that you will do it later, because dreams have a tendency to fade very quickly or become distorted by our conscious mind.

As soon as you can, sit down and reflect on the meaning of your dream. Give it all the interpretations you can, and then select from these the one that is most plausible, fits best, and makes most sense to you.

Keep a record of all your dreams in some sort of notebook, and study them in relation to each other. See whether a common theme keeps running through them. See whether the same dream reappears with different variations. If so, then try to find the underlying meaning. Quite often, after you have done this and have brought some basic conflict or theme into the open, that particular series of dreams will disappear. This can be particularly comforting if your dreams have been unpleasant, frightening, or disturbing.

A beneficial aspect of this dream exercise comes from sharing your dreams with other people. A Malay tribe, the Senoi, actually instructs its children through dream analysis and interpretation. It must work for them, because their history is remarkably free from any sort of criminal activity. Recently, in

Unusual groupings of things and people often appear in dreams—the gateway to the unconscious. (Jack Prelutsky)

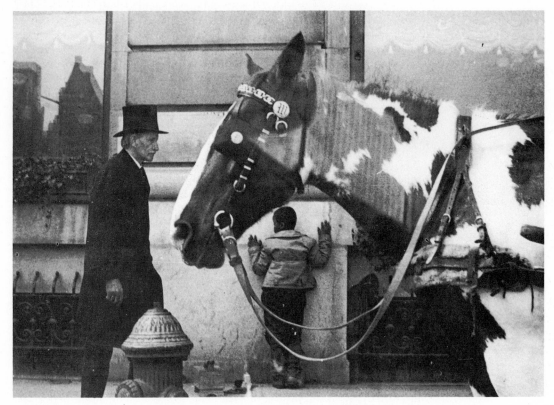

the United States, some groups have formed to achieve more self-understanding through the process of sharing each other's dreams and participating in their analysis. Those who have tried this report that a great deal of personal understanding seems to result. Perhaps you and some friends can get together regularly in such a group.

By using your dreams, you can become even better acquainted with yourself. Possibly, you can learn what is bugging you. You might learn more about your repressed feelings and the experiences that have been left incomplete. You may also be able to reduce some of your tensions and anxieties. Dream analysis is another tool in understanding yourself.

EXERCISES FOR PARTNERS

Exercises performed with a partner add a dimension to the idea of becoming aware of the messages that your body is sending you. They add the messages that your partner gives you, consciously or unconsciously. When you work out exercises with a partner, you should start becoming aware not only of yourself but of someone else. This is what sensitivity training is all about; it teaches you to be aware of the internal operations of your body and also to be aware of other people. It teaches you a little more about the way you affect others and about the way you are affected by them.

The exercises suggested to you here are very mild. They combine techniques of body awareness and communication. By this time, you are familiar with the intent of the awareness exercises. The communications exercises are designed to make you perceive others more clearly and learn indirect ways by which you and others can and do communicate.

You have already worked on one body-awareness exercise involving slapping yourself to get a feeling of how your skin communicates with you. The following exercise, which two people can do, is an extension of that exercise. One of you should assume the original position of the slapping exercise, bending forward with your arms dangling loosely. Your partner then should pummel you on the back, gently enough not to cause any damage but strongly enough to give you a remarkable sensation. Take turns doing this for several rounds. During this exercise, you will feel stimulation and relaxation at the same time.

An extension of this pummeling exercise—massage—is even more relaxing. One partner should stretch out face down on the floor while the other rubs his or her neck, shoulder, back, and leg muslces. You will find this to be most relaxing and great for getting rid of the body's tensions.

Massage exercises are closely related to lift exercises and can be done by partners or groups. In general, however, the lifts are usually better if they are done in a partnership. Let's start with leg lifts as an example. Most lift exercises are done in a similar manner. One partner should lie down on the floor face up, while the other kneels alongside and places his or her own hands even with the reclining partner's lower leg and ankles. The kneeler then puts his or her hands under the partner's calf and ankle, very slowly lifts the lower leg to an elevation that is high but not uncomfortable, and slowly lowers it until it is on the floor again. Then the kneeler shifts so that he or she is in position to lift and lower the other leg. The secret in doing this is to lift and lower as slowly as you can. When one partner has finished lifting and lowering both legs, the partners should change roles and repeat the exercise. The end result is hard to describe. The person whose leg is being lifted receives a definite feeling of relaxation and peace. The person who is doing the lifting receives a strange feeling of wanting to please and serve.

The same exercise can be done with the arms and with the head. As a matter of fact, the whole series can be done by partners. Remember that the slowness of the lifting and the lowering is important.

The other set of exercises for partners involves the use of nonverbal communications. Again, this set by no means represents all the different exercises that fit the design and purpose. However, the ones given here are mild enough to give you the idea and to get you to understand the processes of nonverbal communication without being too dramatic or too ego threatening.

The first exercise should tell you a little about how you feel about other people and how you can communicate without words. You and your partner should sit facing each other so that you are comfortable and able to look into each other's eyes without straining your posture. Now, both of you should attempt to communicate your most prevalent emotions to each other only through eye contact. Motions, facial movements, or head movements should be avoided. Only the message you can give to the other person by using your eyes and only the message you can receive from your partner by looking into his or her eyes are important here. Do you have the sensitivity to pick up any message at all from the other person? Can you satisfactorily transmit a message to the other person by using this method? Does this eyeball-to-eyeball contact make you uncomfortable? If so, try moving apart to see whether a certain distance will be more comfortable for you. This exercise should help you get used to the idea of communicating your ideas and feelings through a medium other than your voice.

You can also try to communicate nonverbally through body contact. Sit so that your back touches that of your partner. Now try to communicate what you are feeling by moving your back against your partner's back. Try to express friendship, concern, or anger. Try to have an argument with your partner, expressing your disagreement through your back movements. This exercise should help you to understand the nonverbal messages others are sending you. It should help you to be more aware of what others are feeling and telling you, even when they do not mean to tell you anything. At the same time, this kind of practice can help you to become aware of how you send messages to others through your body.

As was mentioned previously, lift exercises can be done by a group. If there are enough of you, you can practice lifting one person from the floor very slowly until he or she is overhead and then just as slowly lowering the person to the floor again. Although it is difficult to describe the sensation you will get from this, it can be characterized by calmness, togetherness, and trust.

Another nonverbal group exercise is called the mill. Here, the entire group moves around in a circle, trying to communicate with each other by touch or eye contact. Hugging, hand squeezing—any effort that will get your feelings across to others—is what is looked for. Again, you are seeking an increased awareness of the feelings of others as they express them without words. You will also get information on how you express yourself through your body without words.

To repeat, the essential goal of all these exercises—group and single—is to gain the ability to recognize what your body is telling you about its state of tension. If you can recognize that you are indeed feeling tension, you will know that you need to get rid of it. If you do not, then your body and mind will begin to close you off from the things that are making you tense. In order to avoid additional tension, they will begin to distort the input you are getting. This distortion cannot help but cause more discomfort and thus lead to more tension—a sort of self-defeating cycle. Once you have learned to recognize your body's signals, you can practice releasing tension. When you can do so effectively, you will be able to see things more clearly and thus will be able to deal more perceptively with the events that are making you feel tight. Awareness of your body and awareness of what other people are telling you in nonlanguage messages will help you to work your way through tense feelings.

LOOKING AHEAD—SETTING GOALS

Alvin Toffler, in *Future Shock*, suggests that we try to turn our thoughts from the past to the future. He says that people need to train themselves to think in terms of what's ahead rather than what's behind. It seems to be true that our past hangs heavily on us but our future does not. In an interesting experiment shown in an old film on hypnotism, the hypnotist takes away his subject's future. The subject then undergoes a pronounced personality change, becoming happy-go-lucky and carefree. When the past is taken away from him, however, he becomes afraid and has unpleasant feelings. This shows how the past tends to overshadow our feelings. However, looking back at what has been in the past can be unproductive; we need to look ahead if we want to progress.

Looking ahead constructively stimulates positive movement. As has been stated previously, most of us need goals for effective and planned progress. We need to have a clear idea of what we are doing and where it will lead. When we don't, we tend to drift, to be haphazard and indirect. It is much better for us if we can outline a set of goals that leads us progressively to the end point we wish to reach. With goals in mind, we can set up a series of tasks or accomplishments toward which we can dedicate ourselves in a meaningful, purposeful way.

The idea of setting up goals and stages of progress is particularly effective in getting us to make changes in ourselves. Having taken a good look at ourselves and having decided that we could benefit from some changes, we can then make those changes more profitably if we plan for them in a meaningful, constructive way. By planning rather than saying to ourselves, "I know I need to change, but I'll let time do it for me," we can increase the probability that we will make a motion toward change. Time has a habit of slipping up on us so that we never get around to some things unless we force ourselves into action.

When we talk about making changes in ourselves, just what do we mean? Are we thinking in terms of completely overhauling our personalities and becoming new people? Are we talking about making a new image from the wreck that exists? The answer is, not really. Remaking a whole person is a project that would require the skills and powers of a battery of experts—and even then it would probably be unsuccessful. What we are talking about here is the more gentle, more realizable goal of changing a few things about ourselves that we don't like or that we know are not good for us. Learning to control temper, learning to make independent decisions, learning to be more assured and confident in groups, learning how to get rid of tension—this is the scope of what is suggested here.

How should you go about this kind of personal restructuring? Obviously, some sort of sequence is needed. Just as the old saying goes, "In order to make a rabbit stew, first you catch a rabbit," so, in order to change yourself, you must first find out what you want to change. In substance, this is what this portion of the unit is all about. It is set up so that you will think about yourself and identify the things that you think you would like to change. It then asks you to plan ahead so that you can follow a reasonable course toward change. There are two critical parts ot the exercise: recognizing the things you wish to change and planning the way in which you intend to change them. Both steps are personal and need your own intuition and determination to make them work for you.

First things first: In order to plan for productive change, you need to recognize what should be changed. So follow this sequence: Sit down and meditate on the kind of person you are. Write a paragraph stating what things you like about yourself, being as complimentary and immodest as you please. After all, you have a right to like yourself, and you should.

_____

_____

_____

_____

Don't skip this exercise and go directly to the next one, writing down the things you don't like, because your results will probably be too negative. You will have a tendency to downgrade yourself too much if you don't buoy yourself up by analyzing yourself positively first. But, once you are floating high, change the picture around and write down the things you don't like about yourself. Here you need to be candid, open, and frank.

_____

_____

_____

_____

Now that you have engaged in both personal admiration and personal hatred, put the paragraphs away for at least two days. Put them out of your mind, too. In other words, don't dwell on them; just let them simmer along on the back burner of your mind for awhile. Then haul them out and look at them again. You may want to tear the paragraphs up and start over, or you may look at what you wrote and agree with it. In either case, take the description of what you don't like about yourself and rewrite it in positive terms, stating what you think you should be. For example, let's say that you wrote something like this: "One of my worst tendencies is to be a wise guy. I am always putting people down and trying to make them look ridiculous. I guess I do this so that I will feel superior to them, but I know it's irritating to others, and I really don't like myself when I do it. Besides, it costs me quite a few possible friends." Rewrite this comment positively, stating what you think you would rather be like: "When people around me say anything or do anything, I compliment them and support them positively, rather than tearing them down." Do this with your entire list. Some characteristics may be hard to rewrite because of their personal and internal nature, but for every shadow there has to be light, so go ahead and put some time into this. When you're done, you will have written below a set of positive statements describing how you would like to be.

_____

_____

_____

_____

These, then, are the things you want to accomplish in yourself. These are your goals for the future. If you have been able to go this far, you have come a long way. Recognizing faults and admitting them to yourself opening is a big step toward positive reform. However, there is still some work left before you get from here to there, from where you are to where you want to be.

In the next steps, you will combine purpose with meaningful action. Some of your goals look pretty simple and probably don't impress you as being all that tough to achieve. Probably some of them are not. Others, however, may not be so simple. Take, for example, a woman who has written, "I feel terribly anxious and tight whenever I am around other people, especially if there are strangers in the group." This description might be rewritten positively to read, "When I am in a group, I do not feel awkward or self-conscious, even though some of the group may be strangers to me." Trying to make this kind of shift is usually not an overnight procedure. It may take some rugged practice in trying situations to get out of your rut. Planning is necessary to help you escape the fear of being in groups and gain a freedom from anxiety is such situations.

Take each one of your positive statements and, if you can, break it up into steps. Put these steps down in a time frame if doing so will help you. For example, if you adopt a time frame of a year from now, how far do you think you can progress toward your ultimate goal? You will have to combine many things to make this estimate: what you will be doing a year from now, what opportunities will exist for you during this year, and what you will be able to do to change or manipulate your environment to make it work for you in achieving your goal. For example, the woman who is afraid of groups may still be in school. If so, then classes that include group discussions might be particularly painful. She might sweat and suffer in them; she might be really scared when she thinks she will be called on to speak in front of the class. By the end of the year, she will still be attending school, so her environment won't have changed. What can she do in this environment in the meantime? What can she hope to set up this year that will get her closer to her stated goal?

Here is the goal again: "When I am in a group, I do not feel awkward or self-conscious, even though some of the group may be strangers to me." This is really a lifetime goal, because the individual may take that long to achieve it. But she can work on it. Let's say that she looks at where she is and says, "Well, I don't think I can get from here to there in a year, but within the year I can get to the point where I will speak up in a group without hesitation, even though my heart will still hammer and I will get a sinking feeling in the pit of my stomach." So she writes as a goal for year one: "At the end of a year, I will speak up in groups and classes without hesitation, even though some of the group may be strangers to me."

Having gotten that far, her next step is to decide what else to shoot for. Suppose she takes a deep breath and writes down, "At the end of the second year, I will be able to speak up in a group of complete strangers without hesitation. By three years from now, I will be able to speak *to* a group of complete strangers without hesitation. By four years from now, when I am in a group, I will not feel awkward or self-conscious, even though some of the group may be strangers to me."

You can see that this person, in order to get to her final goal, has written an intermediate step that is even more stringent than her final goal. She does this because she knows herself pretty well and knows that she needs to overshoot before she can finally settle on her final goal.

Using this as an example, form a schedule for your own set of goals. For those that you think will take some time and strong effort, devise steps and an appropriate time span. A time frame of years might be helpful, but don't adopt it if some other time frame makes more sense to you. You might be in a very fast-moving part of your life where things are changing rapidly, so you might have a better chance to make changes than you would at another time. You might want to move fast, and you might be confident that you can do so. Therefore, set up your ultimate and intermediate goals according to whatever sequence and time schedule makes sense to you. But do it now and do it here.

_____

_____

_____

_____

Once again, set your ideas aside and let them simmer for awhile. Let at least two days pass before you haul them out and look at them again. Once more, you may feel an urge to rewrite completely, or you may be satisfied. Either way, you have still another step to go through. You now have to figure out how to accomplish your changes. Use the person who is afraid in groups as an example. Her first-year goal was to be able to speak up in groups without hesitation, even though some members of the group might be strangers to her. She knows pretty much what she has to do to get to that point. She has to start speaking up in class, regardless of how distasteful this may be to her. Therefore, her plan, simply stated, is to start speaking up in classes. For a person who is afraid to participate in groups, this is easier said than done. But this person is clever. She knows that she is pretty good in math and not so good in reading courses. Therefore, she plans to prepare extra well in math so that she thoroughly knows what she is talking about. Then she plans to ask a question or two about a familiar aspect of the subject, delving more deeply into it. In this way, she will make sure that she doesn't make a fool of herself when she practices speaking up. Then gradually, as she gets a little more confidence, she plans to extend this system into other courses, asking for deeper interpretations of thoughts and ideas on subjects that she knows well. By asking such questions, she is really not exposing herself to extreme danger. In addition, she also makes another plan. Whenever she sees somebody she knows talking to some person she does not know, she will try to enter the conversation. In this way, she will practice meeting strangers informally while under the protection of her friends. You might say that she is planning to get into the pool one inch at a time.

This individual has worked out a plan to make a significant and necessary change in herself. She has identified what she thinks is her primary weakness and has rewritten it in the form of a positive statement or long-range goal. She has then worked out a set of intermediate goals that she thinks will lead her to to her main goal. Furthermore, she has worked out a time schedule and a set of actions that she thinks will help her. From now on, her problem is really a fairly easy one. All she has to do is to execute her plan and monitor herself to make sure that she keeps to it.

With this as an example, establish your own intermediate goals, and set up your time frame for reaching them. Work out your ideas for reaching your goals by setting up a list of things to do. It may help if you quantify your intermediate goals as much as possible. Our fictitious friend could have said to herself, for example, "Each week for three months, I will make it a point to speak to at least three strangers." Doing this will provide you with material for a check-off sheet, which can be kept as a record of progress. The more steps you are able to check off, the more satisfaction you will get, and the more you will tend to stay on the ball. You will be using very powerful and sustaining motivating forces: the internal drive that makes you seek system, order, and the achievement of goals, and the power of feedback, or the knowledge of successful results. By identifying your personal problem, rewriting it in the form of a positive statement, breaking it down into increments, and then setting up actions that will lead to the achievement of the goals, you are using self-directional and motivational techniques that can't help leading you toward personal betterment.

In order to help you get on the right track in this project, here are two examples of what people have written down and worked out for themselves:

1. My good points are: I am orderly; I get on well with others; and I can be open with myself and think about my weak points in a constructive way. My faults are: I am a deep and constant worrier, and I find myself operating at a high level of tension all the time. This is probably because I have a very strong success drive. I find that the idea of coming out second best in any competitive situation is disturbing to me. Maybe my drive to be number one causes a high level of anxiety when I think I might not be.

I think I can restate my faults in a positive way by saying that I will not concern myself with how I compare with others in any competitive way. I will concentrate on knowing that I am doing my best.

Working this out in a time frame is very hard. I am still in college, and I'm not sure that I can fight the grading system to achieve my goal. But here is what I will try to do: First semester, my goal will be not to work for grades, because through them I try to make myself superior to others. I will figure out what I should learn or what I want to learn in my courses and concentrate on it. I will try to avoid the pressure to be number one in every class. As a matter of fact, in one course I will be deliberately try to make a grade lower than I know I can make just to get myself out of this grade business.

During my second semester, I will not try to be superior to others. To do this, I will try not to dominate groups as I do now. I will deliberately become a follower rather than a leader. Also, I will be more open with others and communicate my feelings to them. In this way, I might become less worried about what they think of me.

Next year, I will take a look at what I have done to see if it worked. Since I think it will, I will be much less driven by the need to be first. My tension will also go away because it is a symptom of striving rather than its cause. Right now, as I write this, I am full of fire and enthusiasm. I can hardly wait to try out my scheme.

2. The two positive terms that first come to my mind when describing myself are intelligent and perceptive. I feel myself to be both of these. These two attributes have brought a problem with them, though. It is one of anxiety. As I perceive and, hopefully, understand the implications of what is going on in society and the world, I have become quite anxious and have developed a somewhat negative outlook on the future of man. At the same time, I feel unable to bring about any large-scale change and can only hope to influence and change the people and environment in my own personal sphere of contact. I have an overwhelming need for constant change, am an exhibitionist, have a driving need to be independent, and have a high achievement need. Tests substantiate this analysis. What seems almost paradoxical is that I lack motivation and don't work hard enough to fulfill my needs. For the most part, I just lay back and see what life will bring. I guess this is my biggest fault. If I can

get off my back, maybe some of my other problems will solve themselves. Maybe then I will start to achieve more and get the social changes I want. I will also then start to feel that I am me.

My plan: My goal is to find a sense of purpose in life. I don't think a time schedule will help me in this. What I need to do is to sit down and think out what I would like to do for the rest of my life. Do I want to serve other people? Do I want to work for myself? What field am I interested in? What am I really good at? I know from my Vietnam experiences that I have a deep interest in the welfare of other people, but I also have a tendency to be impatient with them when they seem dependent. I don't think I would be good in social work—but I'm getting ahead of myself.

What I need to do is to find out what my real aptitudes and interests are. I know our counseling center does some of this kind of work. So my first step is to go over there and find out some things about myself. After that, I'll still need to figure out what field I can and should get into. This should take a month or two to work out, and that's as far as I can see myself going right now. Maybe after that I'll come back to this project and pick it up again.

So there you are. Two persons tried to work out their problems. One managed to establish a time frame and to do some things that looked productive. The other, suffering from a lack of motivation, fudged a little bit and did not commit himself to any kind of concrete program. However, he did decide to try to find an interest that would spur him on.

Now it's your turn. Work out your faults, turn them into positive goals, and then work out a program by which you can reach the goals. As you can see from the two examples, it is not an easy thing to do, especially when you must make a specific plan and program actual steps. This part of the exercise is hard because you can sense that it is a commitment to action. You might hesitate to commit yourself. But this is the way to make the changes you want in yourself. So slug your way through this project. It will definitely be helpful to you in the long run.

A worksheet might help you to organize your thoughts. Here is a format for you to use:

My problem _____

_____

Causes of my problem _____

_____

My main goal _____

_____

Subgoals to be achieved _____

_____

Steps to achieve subgoals _____

_____

Timetable _____

_____

□ A POINT OF VIEW

The following article on dreams is provocative because it suggests that we can control dream content if we wish to do so. Thus, not only can our dreams tell us more about our emotional control and preoccupations; they can be shaped deliberately to help us deal with our emotional problems.

For additional information about ways of getting to know yourself, you might want to hunt up these books:

Ann Faraday, *Dream Power* (New York: Coward, McCann and Geoghegan, 1972).

Thomas A. Harris, *I'm OK, You're OK: A Practical Guide to Transactional Analysis* (New York: Harper and Row, 1969).

Alexander Lowen, *Pleasure* (New York: Coward, McCann and Geoghegan, 1970).

Frederick Perls et al., *Gestalt Therapy: Excitement and Growth in the Human Personality* (New York: Julian Press, 1969).

William C. Schutz, *Joy: Expanding Human Awareness* (New York: Grove Press, 1967).

William C. Schutz, *Here Comes Everybody* (New York: Harper and Row, 1971).

Everett L. Shostrom, *Man the Manipulator: The Inner Journey from Manipulation to Actualization* (Marshall, Tenn.: Abington Press, 1967).

GURNEY WILLIAMS III

HOW TO CONTROL YOUR DREAMS

One of Dr. Arnold Mysior's patients at the Psychological Center of Georgetown University kept having nightmares about falling off a cliff. Dr. Mysior's prescription was simple. "Fly," he told her. After a few nights of suggesting to

From *Science Digest* 80 (July 1976): 50–57. Reprinted by permission of *Science Digest*. Copyright © 1976 The Hearst Corporation.

herself at bedtime that she could fly, she took off in her dreams. The nightmares ended.

A five-year-old boy from California dreamt nightly that a long-toothed tiger was jumping at him. His mother spent hours at bedtime rubbing his back and talking soothingly, but the extra care didn't do any good. One evening, she suggested that he remember in his dreams to call for help from friends in his imagination to save him. The boy's eyes widened. "Could I call for *Ultraman*?" he asked. She said he could. That night, a comic book character in the boy's unconscious killed the tiger.

The good dreams in both cases resulted from new and growing interest in this country in influencing your own dreams, as if they were movies and you were the director. Using simple techniques of autosuggestion and nightly record-keeping, an increasing number of sleepers are calling up dreams of love and happiness, conquering nightmare monsters and solving personal problems while they sleep.

Classes in such techniques at the University of California at Berkeley started a couple of years ago with a handful of students; now they draw up to 400 students per class. A book on planning and using dreams—*Creative Dreaming* by Patricia Garfield—was a recent bestseller in California, and its author estimates she's personally trained several thousand students in methods of dream control. Therapists like Mysior are using the techniques to treat neuroses. Thousands of normal people are finding that influencing their dreams is fun.

Attempts to control dreams aren't new. "There were experiments in the 1800s," said Dr. David Foulkes at the University of Arizona, one of the country's leading dream researchers. "People jabbed each other in the legs during sleep, that kind of thing, to see if it influenced dreams." (It did.) "But what's getting increased social emphasis today," Foulkes said, "is the idea that you can teach people certain techniques to control their *own* dreams."

The growth in interest has faced formidable odds in a society where dreams are often considered the ugly stepchild of the unconscious.

"Dreams tend to be immoral," said Dr. Charles Tart, professor of psychology at the University of California at Davis. "So there's an emphasis on repressing them. I mean if you're supposed to be exercising a certain sexual restraint and you dream of screwing around, you probably think it's a sin and forget it." And that repression, he said, cuts down the chances for healthy interaction between conscious thoughts and unconscious needs and drives.

If dreams aren't forgotton, they're sometimes elevated to a pedestal where only high priests— in our society, psychoanalysts—can approach them. "On the one hand, we relegate serious dream work to a specialized few," said Dr. Montague Ullman of Maimonides Medical Center in Brooklyn, "namely, psychoanalytically trained experts. Or people are left to go to the corner drugstore and buy a book on dream interpretation. The result is a mystique grows up either about the specialness of dream work or the ridiculousness of dream work.

"I don't think either approach is correct. People can get close to their own dreams. They can see the relation between their dreams and some of their emotional concerns and preoccupations."

Getting in touch with the unconscious is one major goal of dream experimentation. Mysior, for instance, encourages patients who have questions about themselves to try to find answers in their dreams.

"One of my patients in therapy kept asking, 'Am I making any progress?'" Mysior said. She had come to him complaining that she thought she was losing her mind. And that she had no love for herself or anyone.

"I suggested that she try to dream a dream that would tell her how she was doing in solving her problems," Mysior said.

Within a few nights, the girl dreamt she was on a pier jutting out into a body of water. There were two other figures with her, her younger brother and an aunt. Both fell into the water, she said, and she pulled both of them out, scolding them.

"When she told me the dream, I suggested we look at it closely," Mysior said. He asked her about her aunt and brother, the figures on the pier.

"She told me she just loved her brother; he was wonderful. And her aunt was the brain of the family. I suggested that the dream had some answers for us. In her dream, she had rescued her love. And she had done something to get her brain back."

The symbolic message was clear. In subsequent sessions, the girl made rapid progress away from her depression.

Another goal for some dream researchers is more—well—dreamy. A whole society of dreamers, some psychologists argue, would be a happier society. The evidence, they suggest, is in the mountainous jungles of Malaysia, where there is just such a society of dreamers. They're called Senoi, members of a tribe of about 12,000 primitive people who seem to know a lot more about dreaming and dream control than most modern Americans.

Breakfast among the Senoi is a time to discuss dreams, and the whole day is shaped by a crop of images and stories harvested from sleep. Parents question their children closely on dreams, and offer praise for having them. And—most surprisingly to Western observers—older family members make suggestions on how to control future dreams.

After breakfast, dream discussions continue in tribal councils. The day's activities are planned around the dreams of the night before. The Senoi perform songs and dances, paint pictures, work together on other projects that seem to have appeared in their dreams.

The Senoi are immune to the malaria which is likely to afflict the Western scientists who come to explore their dream life. Tribal members are apparently also immune to many of the psychological ills besieging Western society.

"There's practically no violent crime," Dr. Tart said. "Relationships are extremely harmonious. And apparently a major causative factor is the way they work through conflicts in lucid dreams [dreams in which the sleeper knows he's dreaming], and so cut them off at a low level."

The Senoi philosophy seems pretty weird to many Americans who picture the tribe as a bunch of sedentary hippies savoring dreams the way drug freaks drone on about the quality of their grass.

"But they don't sit around," Tart said. "They dream and then they take an hour at breakfast time to discuss their dreams. Is mental health worth the price of an hour a day?"

Tart added that transferring Senoi and other dream-control techniques into the mainstream of American life would be a "major problem." Techniques themselves, however, are simple.

There are two general approaches. Scientists have known for decades what religious leaders have realized for centuries: that dreams can be influenced by sounds, lights and setting—*external* cues ranging from the hardness of the bed to the noise of a stereo recording of a rooster. Other techniques growing in favor today involve *internal* cues, suggestions the sleeper makes to himself, orders to the unconscious that may take several days to be received.

Here's how dreams can be influenced, sometimes controlled:

EXTERNAL CUES

Pilgrims to the temples of certain gods in ancient Greece expected to be cured in their sleep by the appearance of the god. After fasting, they entered the god's temple, lay down on an animal skin that barely softened the hard ground. Frequently, they had vivid dreams in which godlike figures appeared and told them they would be cured. Priests in such temples did no interpretation; the dream was the medicine. Some Greeks still practice "temple sleep," a crude form of psychotherapy, today.

It's clear from descriptions of temple sleep that external cues—the smell of the animal skin, the hardness of the ground, sounds (sometimes pilgrims slept near pits of writhing,

hissing snakes)—had a strong effect on the content of the dreams.

Clear scientific evidence that dreams can be manipulated using the senses came after the discovery of REM sleep in the early 1950s. Researchers at the University of Chicago in 1953 noticed that sleepers often experienced periods of rapid eye movement (REM) during their sleep. Every sleeper, they discovered, had four to five REM periods per night in which eyes moved rapidly under closed lids, in unison. During other stages of sleep, they discovered no similar coordination of eye movement.

The discovery led to a major payoff in dream research. When the Chicago scientists woke up sleepers during REM periods, their subjects almost always reported a dream in progress. Further experimentation confirmed the finding: every normal sleeper has four or five dream periods a night, accompanied by rapid eye movements visible to anyone watching the sleeper.

REM signals make dream research easy; they've helped to prove that sounds and touches can work their way quickly into dreams.

Two of the best known dream researchers, William Dement and Edward Wolpert, ran an experiment years ago, for instance, to challenge the commonly held belief that dreams occur instantaneously—that no dream lasts more than a few seconds.

Dement and Wolpert squirted a fine spray of cold water from a hypodermic syringe onto the skin of subjects in REM sleep. Then they allowed the subject to dream on for a specific time, woke him and collected the dream. In ten instances, the experimenters found that water had suddenly appeared in the dream.

One man, for instance, was dreaming that he was an actor in a play when suddenly the leading lady collapsed with water dripping on her. He ran to her and felt water dripping on his back and head (the squirt had been directed at the sleeper's back). The roof of the theater was leaking, and he decided some plaster had fallen on her. He dragged her to the side of the stage and began pulling the curtains. Then he woke up.

Dement and Wolpert timed the dreamer's description of what had happened after the appearance of water and found that the action of the dream had taken place in roughly the same amount of time the experimenters had allowed sleep to continue. The conclusion: all dreams are not instantaneous.

Other experiments have subjected sleepers to recorded sounds ranging from traffic noises to the rumbling of a locomotive. Students at Stanford found that some sounds clearly influenced dreams more than others. Traffic noise had the least effect. Locomotives had the greatest. A crowing rooster was a strong contender.

"I was in the middle of a conversation with another student," said one subject in the study in his report of a dream, "when suddenly he jumped up on the table and started crowing"—a clear instance of stimulus incorporation.

Unfortunately, dream control by external cues requires assistance: someone to turn on the stereo while the partner's asleep. And the payoff in the experiments seems paltry: a bizarre collection of roosters, trains and irritating floods. There's no reason, however, why other stimuli couldn't be used during REM, such as perfume, soft words or gentle caresses.

"It might be an interesting experiment," Dr. Mysior said.

INTERNAL CUES

Want to fly in your dreams? Here's how Dr. Mysior taught himself to take off.

"I just said to myself one evening, 'Tonight in my dream I'm going to fly.'

"Nothing. I didn't dream at all that night. The second night I said the same thing. Nothing.

"The third night it worked. There is probably an incubation period between the time you give yourself the suggestion and the time it takes effect. The funny thing about this particular dream was that I really didn't fly but I sort of scooted over the ground about three feet in the air, but with amazing speed. It was a marvelous dream."

But it's more than just fun, he said; the technique can be used in therapy. One of his clients, a 14-year-old girl, reported that two people were chasing her in a dream and she wasn't able to escape. Dr. Mysior told the girl about his experience with flying and at her next session she told of another chase dream. This time, however, she had risen into the air during the chase, about five feet up, and managed to fly to a little house where she had hidden until her pursuers left.

The suggestion had been enough to change dream content. It had also given her a new and valuable sense of control over her life.

Self-suggestion is a kind of channel selector for dreams, calling up content you want to appear, sometimes several days after you request it. The technique is also useful in training yourself to use and control the dreams you may *not* want, according to Patricia Garfield.

An 11-year-old boy named Johnny had nightmares two or three times a week about a terrifying monster chasing him, driving him to panic. He would wake up and run to his parents for help. Dr. Leonard Handler, Johnny's therapist, took Johnny on his knee and asked him to close his eyes. Soothingly, he told the boy to imagine the monster. When Johnny indicated that the monster was at hand, Dr. Handler pounded on the desk in front of them, yelling: "Get out of here, you lousy monster; leave my friend John alone."

Then Johnny joined in the yelling. "Get away and leave me alone," he shouted.

As the session ended, he promised he would yell at the monster whenever he saw him. Johnny reported at the next session that he had seen the monster once, yelled at it and made it disappear. In the following half-year period, nightmares virtually stopped, because Johnny had learned to face the danger in his dreams. (The case was reported by Handler in *Psychotherapy: Theory, Research and Practice*, Vol. 9, No. 1, 1972.)

That, said Dr. Garfield, represents one of the most useful of the Senoi skills: facing and confronting danger in dreams. Tribal dreamers go a step further. From their earliest years they're taught to capture enemies in their dreams and force them to give something, a brief poem, a song, an artistic design. The booty from dream confrontations is presented to the whole family the next morning, amid congratulations on the victory.

Far out? Dr. Garfield said she's used the Senoi confrontation technique herself, and it's made her stronger in waking life.

In one dream, her husband and other men were chasing her and fighting with her. Because of training in Senoi technique, she was able to turn the dream around. The attackers suddenly became her friends and the battle turned into a banquet. A couple of days later, she said, she got into an argument with her husband.

"He was offended and angry," she reported. "I became angry too, but instead of dissolving into tears . . . I suddenly realized I didn't have to be upset because he was. Although I had been intellectually aware of this fact for a long time, I never felt it before. I stayed calm . . . It amazed me because I had a strong internal feeling of control under attack, just as I did in the dream."

The dream had been a kind of rehearsal, sharpening her response for the real thing.

Control improves, according to Dr. Garfield, when dreams are written down regularly. Keeping formal records stimulates greater recall, she said; the more feedback about nightly flights, bouts with monsters, psychic trips, the easier it becomes to dial the dreams you want.

For her own experiments, Dr. Garfield has taught herself to wake up after every dream (several nights in a laboratory wearing electric sensors near her eyes verified that she could do it). Several times a night she reaches for a pad and pen, jots down details of her dream in the dark. She's learned to sense when the pen runs out of ink, and uses her left hand as a marker at the beginning of each line to avoid overlapping her writing.

Over the years—since she was 14—she's amassed a collection of narratives and vignettes, vivid experiences with enough scenes of sex, love, adventure and fantasy to rival any modern novelist. Her writings in the dark now comprise well over 10,000 dreams in 17 volumes, more than filling a yard-wide bookcase, a unique record of an important part of her adult life that—increasingly, with practice—she controls.

UNIT 18

CONSTRUCTIVE
IMAGERY

☐ The term *constructive imagery* has been used for the exercise in this unit in order to avoid any negative connotations or fears. In essence, this exercise draws heavily from hypnosis and meditation, combining some aspects of both. Hypnosis, as practiced in the West, has traditionally involved two people: the one who induces the hypnotic state and the one hypnotized. Unfortunately, this technique has frequently fallen into the hands of charlatans, quacks, and showpeople, who exploit it by parading the spectacular abasement of people that it can induce. As a result, many people have an aversion to the idea of hypnosis and a fear of being hypnotized. Yet beneficial uses of hypnosis can be demonstrated all around us. Dentists are using hypnosis to teach their patients to suppress pain. Hospitals are using it to help patients recover quickly. It is even being used in group situations with good effect as a powerful therapeutic tool.

The process of meditation as practiced by those in Eastern cultures has emphasized the inward use of the mind. Through intensive training, individuals have been able to manipulate bodily functions once thought to be beyond human control. They have changed the alpha waves of the brain, stopped bleeding, and suppressed pain. Recently, Westerners too have recognized the terrific power of the mind and have begun to use it, particularly in medicine. Patients who are allergic to the chemicals used as anesthetics have been taught to suppress the pain of surgery. Women have been taught to go through childbirth with no anesthetic.

In this unit, you will learn a way to establish control over the power of your mind and to use that power in response to your day-to-day situations. It will not lead you into the path of meditation, although you can proceed from this unit down that path, if you wish. Neither will it attempt to teach you how to control your bodily functions, although this too is possible. Constructive imagery provides a way to cope with your daily frustrations, to interact with people less defensively, to achieve your life's goals, and to restructure yourself.

The technique you will learn is comparatively simple, and the routine that will be suggested is not demanding, requiring as a maximum no more than a half-hour a day. Your ability to use this technique will improve with practice. You may experience difficulty at first, although many people do not. Some people are not able to recognize relaxation when they have reached it. Consequently, they feel that they have failed, although they may actually have succeeded. When learning to use constructive imagery, as in many other activities, keep in mind that practice will make perfect. The technique is one that all people can learn if they are willing to trust themselves. Some may be wary, saying, "Suppose I do harm to myself? Suppose I put myself under and can't come out?" It will never happen. The most evil thing you can do is to put yourself to sleep. Your own mind will not allow you to harm yourself. So try the process, cautiously at first, then more boldly as you gain confidence.

RELAXATION

Although much has been written and passed down about the effectiveness of certain postures and conditions for including relaxation, no special posture, furniture, or equipment is needed. As a matter of fact, after you become proficient, you will be able to relax yourself when standing alone or in a crowd. At first, however, it will help to start out in a quiet place in complete privacy, so that your thought processes are not interrupted. Either sit in a soft chair or lie down on a bed or couch. All belts, straps, and tight-fitting clothing should be loosened. The idea is to make you body feel as relaxed as possible.

There are several ways of achieving the state of relaxation necessary for effective use of constructive imagery. Several alternative methods will be given to you here. Try them all and see which works best for you. As you become experienced, you will probably devise your own special system for relaxing. The object is to get your mind to force your body into the deepest state of relaxation possible. The deeper, the better. Regardless of the technique you use, let yourself go.

You should begin each method with a breathing exercise. Take in a deep breath and exhale as slowly as you can. Let the air just trickle out. Do this three times. Then let your breathing rhythm stabilize until it is slow and deep and regular. Keep saying, "My breathing is slow and deep and regular," until you feel that it is. Then go on with the remainder of the method.

1. *The candle or spot method:* If you like the added zest of gimmickry, buy a beeswax candle. Beeswax is suggested because its odor will contribute to your relaxed pleasure. Light it and place it so that it is several feet away from you and above your eye level. Stare at the candle flame fixedly and suggest to yourself, "My eyelids are getting heavy. I am getting sleepy. My eyelids are slowly closing, and, as they do, I am getting more and more comfortable and relaxed. My eyelids are getting heavier and heavier. I am getting more and more relaxed. My eyes are closed now, and I am completely relaxed." (If you don't want to use a candle, a spot on the wall above eye level will do as well.) Keep repeating this idea until your eyes do close and you are relaxed. As your eyes close, you will begin to feel comfortable and at ease. The peace that comes to you is one of the great dividends of the process. The more deeply you can relax, the more peaceful, euphoric, and contented you will feel.

2. *The step method:* Imagine yourself at the head of a long flight of circular stairs covered with carpeting so soft that your feet sink into it. Now imagine yourself going down the stairs, one at a time, counting as you go. One, two, three . . . With each descending step, consciously allow yourself to relax. By the time you have reached the fifteenth step, you should be completely relaxed. With practice, you will be able to relax after five or six steps. Descend as slowly as you wish, but make sure that you relax on each step.

3. *The differential relaxation method:* Turn your attention to your feet, making a conscious effort to relax their muscles. Next, relax your lower-leg muscles. Once they have relaxed, concentrate on your thigh muscles. It may help you to tighten your muscles deliberately first so that you can feel the difference between tightness and relaxation. Check your lower limbs to be sure that you have not allowed tension to filter into your feet or legs. Then turn your attention to your abdominal muscles, buttocks, chest, and

back. Keep rechecking to make sure that your muscles stay relaxed. Relax your neck, head, and face muscles. Now take three deep breaths, exhaling very slowly each time. As you exhale, imagine that, as your breath trickles out, all tension is leaving your body. Finally, relax your arms and hands. As you do this, imagine that any tension left in you is trickling out from the ends of your fingers. You should now be warm, comfortable, and relaxed. You can go back over your body again to deepen your state of relaxation.

When you first try these ways of relaxing, your mind may rebel, trying to escape by fluttering to all sorts of thoughts and ideas. Don't let this bother you. Just let the ideas pass through, and then bring your mind back to the business at hand—relaxing. Once you have caught the euphoria of deep relaxation, you'll find it easier to reach. Don't be discouraged if you don't succeed at first. You may need a month or two of patient effort.

Some people are discouraged because they don't feel any different when relaxed from the way they usually feel. Here are some techniques to check on your state of relaxation: Say to yourself, "My eyes are sealed shut. They are completely closed. I cannot open them." Then try to open them. If you are truly relaxed, a funny thing will happen to you. You will know perfectly well that you can open your eyes, and you will try to do so by fluttering your eyelids slightly, but you will also know intuitively that you'll break the spell if you do. As a result, you will voluntarily keep your eyes closed. You can also say to yourself, "My right hand is tingling. It feels just as if it is asleep, but the feeling is pleasant." Keep repeating this to yourself. Concentrate on staying relaxed and your hand will begin to tingle. Once you've convinced yourself that you are relaxed, all you have to do is say to yourself, "My right hand has stopped tingling now."

To deepen your relaxation, it may help you to create some further images in your mind. Imagine that you are in a shell, completely protected. No one can touch you or hurt you in any way. Now, knowing that you are safe, relax yourself even more. You may worry about what people will think if they see you in a relaxed state. Don't worry about looking ridiculous. You will usually appear to be asleep or dozing.

USE

Once you have achieved a state of relaxation in your shell, you can turn to a variety of things. You can, for example, imagine that your shell is bathed in a beautiful display of vibrant colors—and actually see the colors. You can imagine beautiful music to go along with the colors, and you will hear the music. Although this kind of play is amusing and entertaining, it *is* child's play. You can use the power of your mind for more constructive things. As you lie in your relaxed state, think in these terms: What do I want to happen to me today? What are all the good things that can and should happen? Savor these things by actually imagining that they are taking place. Visualize yourself as you enjoy these events.

Next, say, "How can I make these things happen? What steps do I need to take to make them occur?" Visualize each of these steps methodically and again imagine that you are going through them. Don't hurry this. Go through the sequence as carefully as you can.

Now think of some of the things you want to avoid. Be careful not to let negative thoughts affect your relaxation. If you sense yourself becoming tense, drop the idea and relax yourself again. Go through the same process again, saying, "How can I avoid these bad things? What steps should I take to prevent their happening?"

When using constructive imagery, look ahead, never behind. The whole purpose of this exercise is to progress without being held back by yesterday. Think of the future positively and make it happen. Work out as many details as you can.

COMING OUT

Once you have finished enjoying your relaxation and your imagery, bring yourself out of your state of relaxation. How you do this is most important. Of course, it is possible for you to say, "I am awake now," and cease relaxing. If you do this, however, you will miss out on a great deal. A better way is to start counting back from ten, making certain suggestions to yourself with each number. These suggestions can be specific. You can say, "Ten: Every time I want to smoke, I will imagine that I have just finished a cigarette and don't need one now." On the other hand, these suggestions can be general ones to help you enjoy the day. Here is a general list:

10. The next time I try to relax myself, it will be easier to do.
 9. My relaxation will be deeper and more pleasant next time.
 8. Today I will be more pleasant to people.
 7. Today people will be more pleasant to me.
 6. I will feel happy and contented today.
 5. Nothing will upset me today.
 4. My senses will be sharper today.
 3. I will hear and see things more clearly today.
 2. I will feel alert and refreshed.
 1. My eyes are open and I am awake.

These suggestions will work. You can create any mood you want for yourself. Most of us habitually work negatively, thinking, "I know I'll get a headache out of this," and then getting one. However, there is no reason that we should not and cannot accentuate the positive.

THE ROUTINE

When you practice constructive imagery is unimportant. You can relax yourself anytime it's convenient for you to do so. There is only one restriction: Do not try the technique in bed just before you plan to go to sleep, because you will indeed wind up asleep. One good routine is to relax just after you have awakened in the morning. Then, sometime in the early afternoon, take five or ten minutes to recharge your batteries and reorient yourself if you feel you need it. However, don't become too rigid in your timing. The trick is to use the technique when you need it. If you have just had an upsetting experience, take five to get control of yourself, whatever time of the day it may be.

The normal afternoon relaxation period should be in the late afternoon before dinner. Each normal relaxation period, morning and afternoon, should last approximately twenty minutes. As you get more skilled, you can relax yourself anywhere at any time. Don't worry about falling asleep in the morning or at any other time when you relax yourself. There is no such thing as putting yourself in a trance and not being able to get out of it. Of course, if you are having trouble sleeping, you can use your techniques to get a good night's rest.

CAUTION

Constructive imagery is a very powerful tool. Use it wisely. You can do yourself harm if you delude yourself or deny reality. For example, it is possible to deny the existence of a pain that is bothering you. When you do this, however, you may be denying the existence of a problem that should be checked by a doctor. Do not use imagery to hide from reality. Use it to face reality and to shape it into what you want it to be. Hallucinate all you want and have fun. You will actually be able to outperform any of the mind-expanding drugs if that's what you'd like to do. But don't delude yourself, for if you do, you are misusing the tremendous power of your mind.

Constructively used, the techniques you have learned can bring you freedom from tension and peaceful tranquillity. They can bring about interpersonal relationships conducted on a happy, affectionate level without defensiveness. They can bring happiness and peace of mind. But you must face your problems, not run away from them. Constructive imagery merely gives you a mechanism by which you can work out your problems in serenity.

Here are some students' statements about constructive imagery:

1. Constructive imagery, like behavior modification, has proven to be a very effective device in the day-to-day business of adjusting to and coping with our environment. I have found that constructive imagery can effectively release the fears and inhibitions I feel about certain things. As I mentioned in class, I have always feared flying. Even walking into an airport gives me clammy hands and an uncomfortable feeling. By using constructive imagery, I have completely examined an airplane from the nose to the tail and its flight from takeoff to landing. I have remembered every safety device I could and recalled all the stories I knew of unbelievable landings by highly qualified pilots. This coming spring, my wife and I plan to fly back to Kansas. Once a week, I "put myself under," so to speak, and review the flight. For my sake, and that of my ulcer, I hope my techniques prove effective.

2. Every time I use constructive imagery, it becomes easier and easier to do. I have been using the staircase method. When I first started, it took about a dozen steps to work myself into a deep state of relaxation. Now, it takes only three or four.
3. Working part-time at night, going to school full-time during the day, and undertaking the role of father and husband, all create a great deal of strain. By using constructive imagery, I can completely relax and come out feeling refreshed and ready to face another day. Constructive imagery has definitely gained another supporter.

□ A POINT OF VIEW

In "Svengali in the Mirror," Marilyn Elias describes uses of constructive imagery that go a little further than you will care to go. Nevertheless, you will profit by reading about some of the things that can be accomplished by constructive imagery, or hypnosis. The suppression of pain and various kinds of physiological control are relatively easy to learn. Constructive imagery is also very much used to relieve tension and anxiety. However, you should do more than reduce these stressors. It is important to get to the causes of these problem causers and eliminate them, instead of just sitting on them.

MARILYN ELIAS

SVENGALI IN THE MIRROR

Darlyne Mocklow settles back into a reclining leather chair, the kind of chair that easily evokes vivid, childlike dread in many of us who have been adults for years. Hanging fluorescent fixtures cast a harsh light on her face while sharp metal instruments, poised for use, wait nearby on white towels. Mocklow, an operating-room nurse, is about to undergo "restorative work," according, euphemistically, to her dentist. Dr. Robert Wallin is cheerful, but Mocklow looks like a prisoner who has just heard the cell door slam behind her. Though she witnesses gory surgical procedures as a matter of professional responsibility, Mocklow rarely musters up the courage to confront routine dental work. A mouthful of rotting teeth testifies to her success at dodging dentists.

Dr. Wallin slips out for a few minutes. Mocklow then promptly places her right hand on her face, counts to three, and her eyelids gently droop lower and lower until they stop at a closed position. The rigid facial tension so

From *Human Behavior* 2, no. 2 (May 1973): 56–61. Copyright © 1973 *Human Behavior* Magazine. Reprinted by permission.

prominent before softens and gradually dissipates, as a blissful sleep seems to overtake the 37-year-old patient. Her head bows. Dr. Wallin returns moments later and asks if she is ready to begin. Our apparently dead-to-the-world nurse does not wake up. But, nonetheless, she replies with perfect calm that she is ready!

The next 20 minutes are drowned in a buzz of deep drilling that would make the average person yelp with pain. But Macklow remains still and composed. From time to time, Dr. Wallin asks if she would please close her jaws a bit more or bite down on one tooth. She dutifully obeys, as though wide awake. But if awake, how can she stand the pain? If she's sleeping, how does this strange person manage to behave like an alert patient in every way, except for consciousness of pain?

Mocklow actually is neither asleep nor awake. She is in a dimly understood twilight consciousness available to practitioners of self-hypnosis. The face touching and counting form a conditioned hypnotic induction method which the nurse uses to attain this unusual mental state.

As electric drills burrowed deep into her teeth, the seemingly asleep patient was quite busy. "After I'm hypnotized," Mocklow explained later, "I concentrate on the teeth he's working on. I think over and over to myself, 'It's like a dead piece of wood, you will feel no pain.' I have to constantly tell myself that there is no pain." Dr. Wallin and Mocklow were delighted that self-hypnosis ushered in a painless experience, putting an end to a lifelong avoidance of dental care.

But one more problem sprang up. "She was a copious salivator," says the dentist, "and when the mouth is that wet, it really interferes with restorative work because you're always having to dry it out. After she succeeded with the pain removal, I asked her if there was something she could do about the copious salivation. She said, 'Maybe I can cause the salivary flow to slow down,' and then I left her alone for a while. It was dry before I started."

How did it happen? "I told myself, 'You're

going through a desert, it's so dry and you're thirsty. Your mouth feels like a piece of cotton, it's so dry, you're parched.' I began to alternate the dryness suggestion with no-pain sentences, and it worked," reports Mocklow.

Tales of such weird self-control feats may bounce off the typical observer like so much rhetoric. But despite the understandable skepticism it generates, autohypnosis is emerging as a major force in the burgeoning self-control movement. Along with bio-feedback, self-programming, meditation and extrasensory exploration, it has magnetized a growing cadre of devotees. People now learning and practicing have latched onto a science in its infancy, one whose historical roots sink down to the ancient world, but which also blossoms with modern, practical applications that are beyond present theoretical knowledge. An upsurge of interest in self-hypnosis is reflected in the crowded classes increasingly taught by lay hypnotists and in recent greater attention given to the phenomenon by psychotherapists.

Uses for the technique abound, embracing that bizarre but sadly real litany of foibles we all yearn to control at one time or another. Tension. Obesity. Stuttering. Pains. Smoking. Drug habit. Insomnia. And once a student has learned to do self-hypnosis effectively, the skill often can be applied to multiple areas. For example, nurse Mocklow learned from a gynecologist who prescribed autohypnotic sessions how to curb exceptionally painful mentrual cramps. After she attained success in easing these pains, Mocklow decided to attempt dentistry without anesthetics.

Steve Polivka, a young Los Angeles advertising worker, uses self-hypnosis to control anxieties that severely exacerbate his 23-year-old asthma condition. Since nervous tension often sets off asthma attacks, Polivka's job in a field mined with daggers and deadliness has led to painful explosions of his illness. The 25-year-old production assistant got help from Arthur Ellen, a private consultant who has garnered wide publicity for his successful work with sports and entertainment figures. Ellen teaches his clients a hand gesture while they are under hypnosis ($35 per session) which allows them to shift at will, on their own, into an hypnotic state.

"When I feel the symptoms coming on, the wheezing and breathing trouble, I just do it," relates Polivka, who hopes to become a producer in his ad agency's television department. "If there's an anxious situation at work, I use it to calm myself down. Like recently there was a situation where there was a deadline and I had to mail something very important. The instructions I was given were kind of garbled, so the package didn't get where it had to be on time. I was severely chastised for it, but I really didn't feel it was my fault. It irritated me so much, yet it wouldn't have done me any good to fight about it. By using the signal, I was able to calm down and control my behavior in a way that would benefit me.

"With self-hypnosis you feel a sort of gentle emotional subsiding, you find yourself getting very relaxed, not uptight anymore," Polivka says.

Physiological tension-ebbing benefits of the hypnotic state involve pulse and breathing changes. In a deep trance the EEG shows consciousness at an alpha rest rhythm, hallmark of serene alertness. Composure under stress, the ability to defuse your anxiety so you can control a situation, is a key goal for many autohypnosis buffs. And the technique is used to this end in a startling variety of ways.

Actor Fernando Lamas, another Ellen client, often found himself waking up at 4 a.m., his mind agitated by coming daytime events and his body unable to drift back into needed rest. "I started to learn self-hypnosis so I could put myself back to sleep, but I'm using it for emotional strain in the daytime now too. You do it and, boomp, you feel this sense of inner quieting, it's like a magic wand," says the film star.

At the other side of the country, all the policemen in one community are learning autohypnosis so they can keep cool amid heated law-enforcement skirmishes, improve quick judgments and sharpen memory. Police Chief Raymond E. Beary of Winter Park, Florida, is enthusiastic about the benefits of self-hypnosis for routine police work, in which a split-second action can spell the difference between life and death.

A narcotics detective on the Los Angeles Police Department, which is also getting involved in autohypnosis training, recently brought back to his instructor, George Klauss, a graphic, spine-chilling description of how the technique can work for cops. "He wanted to feel relaxed and mentally semi-removed," explains Klauss. "The suggestion I gave him in class was that when he put himself under, he would operate at a fast pace, have very sharp reflexes, while things around him would appear to be happening in slow motion. He told me about a case where they were called at about 2 a.m. for a drug bust at an East Los Angeles restaurant. The student used his self-hypnosis and as they burst into the room, he said the man inside actually appeared to be floating toward the other side of the room as he was very slowly reaching for an Army 45. The policeman said he's never felt so confident and relaxed, able to handle danger, because his lack of anxiety put him at a much faster pace than the others. It *would* appear like everyone was operating in slow motion."

People who undergo heterohypnosis (initiated by another person) sometimes report that the condition is nothing new to them, and certainly not as exotic as it's often portrayed. They liken a hypnotic trance to moments at dawn when one is conscious of drifting in a light sleep yet too drowsy to get up, or suggest that it's like traveling on a boring highway for long periods of time as the mind wanders, yet springs back into swift action when other motorists make unexpected lane changes imperative. These accounts describe lighter trances, the Walter Mitty-style daydreams which lift a person out of ordinary mental reality but leave open a quick passageway for return.

Self-hypnosis students differ from many of us only in that they use disciplined tools to manipulate their own behavior, exploiting the sug- gestible nature of the trance state rather than letting it come and go at random. But how do they induce autohypnosis at will? Can anybody do it?

Students learn either in classes or individually from therapists or from lay teachers who are technicians of the craft but often lack academic credentials in psychology. Typically, students are first put through body-relaxation exercises. These routines are not unique to hypnotism, but similar to preludes employed in other self-control techniques. After relaxation, the hypnotist insists, with arresting voice, that a student concentrate on a single object or the sound of the teacher's voice. As he concentrates deeply, a subject is told that his eyelids are growing heavier and heavier and soon will droop, and he won't be able to hold them open. At this point, one who wants to be hypnotized may experience a sensation of inevitability, a feeling that behavior seems to be slipping from his control into the hands of the hypnotist, that a chasm is widening between his will and the actions of his detached body. The release, the rest from having to be responsible for one's every step is refreshing and welcome, like a return to childhood.

Even when they are "under," students sometimes refuse to believe it. Teachers commonly tell subjects that they will be unable to lift their feet, or their eyes are glued shut, then invite them to try. Their surprise at their own rapid success springs from a popular myth that getting hypnotized is something like climbing Mount Everest. It's not supposed to be something you can do on your lunch hour. But at least seven out of 10 persons can reach the minimum of a light trance when working with a skilled hypnotist, and recent research suggests that improved induction methods could even raise this success rate.

Once hypnotized, what happens to a subject next depends upon whether he is learning from a mental health professional or from someone in lay classes. Therapists use hypnotism as a tool to ferret out destructive suggestions or habits which may be lodged in the subconscious mind. This can involve leading patients back to earlier years and inviting them to reel off impressions buried in childhood. The subconscious faithfully records even obscure events, while the conscious mind often remains unaware of these underlying perceptions and the powerful capacity they have for shaping behavior. A man's fear of flying may stem from conversations overheard as a child compounded by frightening storybook tales his parents read to him. The fear could show up as childhood nightmares and a growing phobia about air travel. The man who comes for help at 32, when his anxiety presents a career threat, may not consciously recall long-ago causes for his current anxiety. He just wants relief.

Therapists who uncover focal sources for rather clear-cut, uncomplicated problems teach self-hypnosis by informing patients while they are under how to put themselves through an hypnotic induction procedure on their own. But patients whose symptoms are entwined in a cluster of neuroses called for prolonged therapy frequently are generally not given self-hypnosis instructions by professionals, even if they want to learn. Or sometimes the hypnosis may be prescribed only in combination with other treatment.

This marks a major departure from the policies of many lay hypnosis instructors. Students attending classes generally are not coaxed backward in time or probed for causes. Some have been referred to teachers from physicians who already have made a diagnosis. But others are making a rudimentary stab at do-it-yourself when they need professional attention for serious problems. Lay teachers usually lack the background to identify these people rapidly, so a student's superficial reason for appearing in class is accepted at face value. Teachers plunge right into self-hypnosis instruction with few preliminaries. Students are expected to practice putting themselves under at home, using the hypnotic induction method taught. They give themselves positive suggestions while hypnotized, engraving new information on the subconscious which may replace old destructive

messages if the conditioning is repeated frequently and with strength.

Though hypnosis has been practiced for thousands of years, research on how and why it makes the subconscious so accessible is still at a fairly elementary stage. "In terms of clinical skill and practical application, we know a great deal about hypnosis, but the art of its application is far ahead of its scientific elucidation," note Drs. Erika Fromm and Ronald Shor, two of the most respected American researchers in the field, in their 1972 anthology, *Hypnosis: Research Developments and Perspectives* (Aldine-Atherton). It is believed that intense concentration on one aspect of reality fades the surrounding context (noises, pain, your child's nagging) which fills up the ordinary waking state. The singularity of this mental condition, free from competitive stimuli, seems to produce certain physical and brainwave states which also play an important role in other newly emerging routes to self-control, such as meditation and paranormal psychic powers. Experiments described by Sheila Ostrander and Lynn Schroeder in *Psychic Discoveries Behind the Iron Curtain* (Prentice-Hall, 1970) show how the hypnotic trance actually has been used to facilitate extrasensory experiences.

The departure from multiple distractions induced by hypnotic concentration, appears to signal a slipping away of the conscious mind's dominance. The potent subconscious is then no longer submerged, but readily available for direct suggestions.

Despite the scant scientific exploration of autohypnosis so far, a few important studies are emerging. One experiment, completed in 1972 by psychologist John C. Ruch at Stanford University, raised the startling possibility that experience with heterohypnosis actually inhibits a person's later ability to do self-hypnosis. Ruch found that naive subjects who weren't even given an induction, but who asked to self-hypnosis spontaneously instead, succeeded as well as more conventionally prepared people. He also discovered that those first hypnotized by others had a more difficult time doing it on their own, while students asked to start with self-hypnosis later turned out to be excellent heterohypnosis subjects. Ruch believes that if these findings are confirmed, therapists would be advised to reverse their methods—getting patients into autosuggestion first and following with conventional hypnotism. His work also poses questions about the necessity of induction procedures. The human capacity for inducing trance, with no prior cues, may be greater than yet imagined.

Many lay hypnotists are selling their craft at a high rate—as much as $35 per single half-hour session—and advertisements are even appearing now in some major metropolitan newspapers. More traditional therapists are disturbed by the hard sell and sketchy screening offered by teachers who are out to make a quick buck.

Dr. Herbert Spiegel, a psychiatrist and faculty member at Columbia University's College of Physicians and Surgeons, believes the lay hypnotists may be creating a lot of victims rather than improving lives. "When a patient comes in and says he wants to lose weight, sometimes it's a metaphorical statement of stress. They're really begging for help for something else," explains Dr. Spiegel. "They say they want to lose weight but actually they are depressed and only focusing on one facet of the depression.

"The odds are, such a person is going to fail with self-hypnosis because they're really not overcoming the depression that leads to overeating. If you recognize this depression, you can treat it properly. But if you let this person try self-hypnosis, you're setting him up for just another failure, another way of making his condition worse. It's like kicking them while they're down."

Another worry expressed by therapists is that undiagnosed prepsychotic students may be nudged toward psychosis by the body disorientation induced under a hypnotic trance. Dr. Spiegel believes the potential harm of lay hypnotists may justify a crackdown in licensing policies by state legislatures. This harm, balanced against the good done for others, furnish-

es a social dilemma which may have to be solved by future courts and lawmaking bodies, if the self-hypnosis movement continues to grow.

A barrier in the way of forming sensible conclusions about autohypnosis is the research vacuum in this fledgling field, points out Jean Holyroyd, a clinical psychologist and assistant professor of psychology at UCLA's Neuro-Psychiatric Institute. Holroyd, a Ph.D. from University of Minnesota, has been using hypnosis in her practice for about three years. She had had excellent success with pain cases, and also reports strong progress on anxiety problems when hypnotic techniques are used in conjunction with other methods.

"A prepsychotic person can get into difficulty with anything in life," Holroyd noted. "They can get into difficulty if they're crossing the street and a car comes screeching to a halt, they can get into difficulty from alcohol, they can get into difficuty from sexual intercourse. So all of life's experiences which involve emotional arousal and tapping into other parts of the mind than what one usually uses can get a prepsychotic person into difficulty. Saying self-hypnosis shouldn't be taught because prepsychotics will have problems is like saying I shouldn't learn how to drive a car because there are a certain number of accidents that occur on the highway. . . .

"We don't have research evidence to say that people like Pat Collins (a stage hypnotist who holds classes in her Sunset Strip nightclub) aren't doing more good than bad." Holroyd maintained. "I don't think we can predict that when people walk into Pat Collins's place because they smoke, that she can't help them, or that she will harm more people than she helps. . . . The likelihood is greater that if their anxiety is that severe, they won't be able to overcome whatever habit they have—overeating for example. The more disturbed the person, the more symptoms they have in their personality over a longer period of time, the less likelihood that they're going to be positively helped. The more focal the symptoms, such as flying phobia, the briefer the period of time, the more likelihood they'll be helped. But that's true for whatever treatment method is used."

Holroyd was reluctant to critcize one prestigious senior psychiatrist who flatly stated, "I don't think the lay public should do autohypnosis on themselves—you wouldn't allow surgery to be done on you by a janitor," but she did attribute some of the marked reservations about the technique to generational differences. The 36-year-old psychologist said that "younger clinicians and researchers probably are not as fearful about altered states of consciousness. . . . For many years," she added, "people were not helped with symptom removal through behavior modification techniques because organized psychiatry said there would be symptom substitution. But studies showed this usually was not the case. Now I'm concerned that because we know a few are hurt, self-hypnosis shouldn't be prevented from being developed in its tremendous positive use."

Perhaps the simplest yet most impressive use which practitioners report is toward attaining a condition in our frenetic world which no amount of money, status or conscious effort guarantees—relaxation, calm, beneficial escape from hassles. George Klauss, who holds self-hypnosis classes in Temple City, California, suggests a mobile cloud as vehicle while urging hypnotized pupils to take off on periodic hallucinatory trips "away from it all" to calm their nerves and restore energy for living. He has steered a number of young people off drugs and onto these perhaps safer trips.

But the current phenomenon of businessmen and homemakers puffing pot shows that temporary escape is not craved by youth alone. Some of the most enthusiastic autohypnotists using Klauss's "exercises" are straight folk who commute five days a week via clogged freeways to and from ordinary work. Kent Carlson, a 36-year-old office manager from the suburb of Gardena, California, says he was taking medication to curb a painful nervous stomach condi-

tion for a long time before beginning self-hypnosis instruction. The problem, not resulting from an ulcer, eased some when medicine was taken, "but it was nothing compared to the relief from pain after I learned self-hypnosis," Carlson says. He no longer has the condition, nor does he take medicine.

But he does take a "trip" in his den or backyard about once a week. "First I put myself under," reports the telephone company employee. "Then I just use my cloud as a transporting method, except it's evolved more toward an open-topped car with stubby little wings. Then it's a matter of going through careful autosuggestion. I go to a hidden place in the Colorado mountains. It's not a real place, but I used to live in Denver and saw vistas like it all the time. My place is cut out of the side of a cave, there are no roads, no cities visible. You're like a cave dweller, but it's furnished very comfortably and has one huge front window. I see all the details and colors very vividly; it's like you're really there. I sit and listen to music or sometimes I'm having good friends in and we're chatting. Nobody can reach you or bother you at all."

These mental trips seem to last for hours. "It's so relaxing, it's such a good experience, that you lose track of time and are just there forever." Carlson says at the beginning he was surprised to discover after waking himself up that he had only been under for five or ten minutes, but the time distortion gradually became easier to accept. Such trips were far more frequent when he started self-hypnosis last year. But Carlson says there seems to be less need for them because he's not so nervous during the day any more.

Students who enter self-hypnosis training often don't succeed, others like Kent Carlson succeed and use it for one specific problem, but some apply it heavily in numerous situations of their lives. To these people, it revolutionizes their approach to reality. One such true believer is Henry Santos, who shed 37 pounds within a few months of learning the technique and then branched out to develop radical memory recall, as well as soften tensions and anger common in everyday life. "There is no way that any given situation can cause me to become irrational or out of control, but I still have the full range of emotions," Santos declared. "I can give vent to my emotions and yet not become enraged or a blithering idiot. Usually the first thing that hits an enraged person is a feeling of helplessness. When I'm angry, I don't feel helpless. I just don't reach the point anymore of disabling myself of logic. Self-hypnosis," relates Santos, "allows you to look back at yourself as though you were looking at another person, and it's fascinating in that you have control over that person."

UNIT 19

PUTTING IT ALL
TOGETHER

☐ One of the most difficult ideas to grasp when studying about your own and others' behavior is how the different parts of psychology come together. For example, learning is influenced by our attitudes. If we are learning about blood sampling and we have a perception of blood (especially our own) as being a frightening thing to see, we are going to have trouble getting used to the sight of blood. As a matter of fact, there is a standing joke that a psychiatrist is a doctor who can't stand the sight of blood. The point is that our attitudes often get in the way of our learning. The same can be said about motivation. It is a lot harder to learn something in which we don't have the slightest interest than it is to learn something that seems fascinating. Yet our motivations depend very much on the way we percieve the instructor, the reasons for learning, and so on. Emotions can also affect learning. If we are sad, we tend to learn things that reinforce our sadness. When we are angry, what we learn will reflect that emotion. All these elements—learning, attitude, motivation, and emotion—interrelate.

When we study human behavior, we tend to compartmentalize things. We do this so that we can get a clear idea of the basics of a subject. When we are trying to write about learning, we cannot do a good job if we bring in all related topics and show how they interact. Not only will our writing become confusing, but the basic concepts we are trying to express will get lost in the muddle of interactions.

What you have been studying has been leading up to a basic theme: how you can improve your personal adjustment as you define it for yourself. You have taken part in a series of personal experiences designed to help you understand yourself, know yourself better, and make some changes in yourself in a systematic and productive way. The trouble is that the exercises you have performed may be filed in your mind in such a way that they seem to have no relationship to one another. You may not see how to get them all to work together. Therefore, the purpose of this unit is to get you to realize that many of your efforts can be combined to help you attain better adjustment. In this unit, you will find out how to consolidate your efforts and thus get the utmost from them. You will combine the techniques of motivation, learning, behavior modification, constructive imagery, and gaining self-knowledge, and you will see how you can concentrate your efforts to become a better person.

Let's take a fairly common example: the case of people who, when they have to take a test, freeze and, because of their terror, can't write down even the answers they know. If you are not this sort of person, change the example into something more meaningful. Perhaps you come close to collapse whenever you must face a group that periodically evaluates your work. In either case there is a loss of effectiveness because the extreme tension caused by the evaluation interferes with and diminishes productivity. What can you do to get over the whammies?

First of all, sit down and try to find out what is causing the tension. Meditate about the reasons for panic. In this case, there is no need to test for bodily signs of panic because they are already all too painfully evident. Instead, speculate about reasons. Perhaps you should get into a state of relaxation and ask, "What are the reasons for my terror? Am I afraid of ridicule? Am I reacting to an experience I once had that makes me afraid now? Is this test such a big thing in relation to my final goal? In other words, if I fail this test, will I have to change my plans and dreams? Did other tests I've taken have such a major effect on my long-range goals? Am I afraid of the reaction of others if I make a bad grade? Just why am I all choked up over a testing situation?"

The answers may not come easily. Indeed, they may not come at all. But it is entirely possible and probable that, by questioning yourself in this way, you may come up with the notion that you are really afraid of being made fun of by others in your class. Or you may feel that your whole future is threatened by your test performance. At any rate, as the result of meditation during periods of relaxation, let's say that you have come up with the idea that you panic because you fear that failure on a test will expose you to ridicule and pressure by others.

Your next step could be to set up a goal and a plan to reach it. You want to get over your terror. So you write out a positive statement: "By the end of a year, I will be confident and relaxed whenever I am in a testing situation." In order to get to this point, you reason that you must have confidence when you face a test. So you set a subgoal: "I will be in complete command of the subject on which I am to be tested whenever I take a test." This will do more to help you get over your panic than anything else.

Now, how should you go about getting complete command over the subject? This is where the ideas suggested in Unit 6 on learning management can help. If you apply those techniques to your studies and concentrate on the matter to be covered in the next test, you can make sure that you know your material well. This cannot help giving you the confidence you need when you walk into the classroom for the next test. Half of the battle is in knowing the stuff. If you have overlearned and can come forth with chapter and verse on demand, you should not have any trouble recalling the information as it is needed. But let's say that you have tried this and haven't been able to overcome your dread of being tested or evaluated. What else can you do?

Well, you can combine constructive imagery with a desensitization technique. You would follow a procedure something like this: Suppose you have figured out that the main cause of your fear is being laughed at by the rest of the group. This is what really bugs you. Here's how you can use the power of your mind to overcome that fear to a great extent. Relax yourself and then think progressively along the lines stated in the following paragraphs until you can handle each idea without tension. Each time you manage to reduce your anxiety to a manageable level, move to a more anxiety-provoking scene.

Imagine that you are in class and the teacher has just announced a test that will count for one-third of your final grade. While in a state of deep relaxation, visualize this scene until you no longer feel a sinking sensation in the pit of your stomach and all the other familiar signs of tension that your body gives you.

When you have taken the first step, visualize studying for the test. Work over the details of your study program, and imagine that you are not able to complete each portion of your work schedule successfully. Continue using constructive imagery until you feel no panic or tension because of this situation.

Then move on to the day of the test. Imagine getting up in the morning, shaky and scared, and going to class. Concentrate on this scene until you feel no fluttering of tension and no tightening of your body.

Now imagine sitting down and getting ready to take the test. Work this situation out in your mind until you feel no anxiety. As an added fillip to your imagination, work out a scene in which you look around the room at other students sitting relaxed and confident while you cram frantically.

Then visualize the teacher passing out the test. Look at the test and see that it is an essay test, whereas you prepared yourself for an objective one. Visualize this scene until you can control your anxiety.

Things are getting progressively worse: Visualize looking at the questions and finding absolutely none that seems to be remotely familiar. Again, control your anxiety.

Things are worse still. Imagine that you are sitting there with not one thought in your head. You look around and see that everyone else is writing industriously while you sit idle and miserable.

Now imagine that the teacher and others are beginning to stare and make comments about your inability to answer any questions. Imagine that you finally can't stand it any longer and get to your feet and hand in a blank paper. You stumble from the room to escape the giggling and remarks.

The next day, while discussing the test, the teacher pokes fun at you in front of the whole class. The class, in turn, joins in mocking you.

In this increasingly masochistic exercise, you will work yourself through a series of horror scenes while trying to keep calm. You may have to work on some of these scenes for quite awhile until you can teach yourself to control your panic. If you are able to work through these scenes and stay relaxed, what will the result be? In all probability, you will be able to walk into a test without feeling the unreasoning, blind panic that has been your Waterloo so many times. You have taught yourself to stay loose and hang in there, no matter what the situation turns out to be. However, if you have successfully trained yourself to stay relaxed, the test scene probably will be far better than the one you have created for yourself. The disastrous effects of panic won't immobilize you as they have before because you have worked yourself out of their control.

Another aspect of constructive imagery can be used in place of the desensitization technique, as a follow-up to it, or in conjunction with it. One of the problems that you may have discovered about yourself in our example is that the tension you feel during tests is the result of a very deep fear of failure. This fear immobilizes you; you are desperately afraid of losing the game. Again, the power of the mind can come to the rescue. During periods of relaxation, prepare a scenario that goes something like this:

1. Visualize yourself in the classroom as the test is handed out. You are relaxed and confident.

2. Check over the questions. Each one is familiar to you, and the answers start pouring out before you can get your pencil down. The test seems to be ridiculously easy.
3. Imagine that you work quickly and surely, answering the questions systematically and carefully. There are no hitches; your responses come as you need them.
4. You finish, check your paper, and get ready to turn it in. You look around and are quite surprised to see that you are the first one finished.
5. As you hand in your paper, you are conscious of the envious glances of your fellow students. There is a buzz of comment as you go out the door.
6. On the day that the papers are returned, the teacher announces the scores, and you are number one. You have made the highest score in the whole school on that particular test. The teacher compliments you and your schoolmates are highly impressed.

This kind of imagery accentuates the positive and emphasizes the social approval of others rather than the consequences of failure. It is in itself a strong motivator, helping you to aspire to bigger and better things. In the former case, you were working to reduce the effects of a fear of failure. In this case what you are working for is to stimulate your need for achievement. These two may sound the same but they are not. One produces slightly different effects from the other. For this reason anyone who has this kind of problem should try to reduce the fear of failure while also trying to increase the need for achievement.

This is not the only way that you can help yourself if you are in a bind. You can also take advantage of some of the tricks of behavioral modification. There is no reason that you can't deliberately train yourself through conditioning to do certain things, just as you may have trained others. For example, take Pavlov's classical conditioning experiment. However, instead of teaching yourself to salivate, you can teach yourself several other things. One is that when you sit down in a particular spot, it is the time and place for concentration. Train yourself by doing. That is, when you sit down in your study area, arrange yourself so that all you do is study. After a period of time, your mind will come to realize that no nonsense will be permitted. You must think and concentrate. One of the ways to ensure success in this effort is to make certain that you are thinking and concentrating all the time you are in your particular spot. If your mind begins to wander or if you need to rest, get away until you are ready to think once again. No daydreaming, no goofing off will be allowed while you are in your special studying place. Also, you can arrange your study spot in such a way that everything is organized. The familiarity of the scene will become a signal that you are at your place of work. This approach can be overdone, of course; you can actually overtrain yourself so that you aren't able to study in any other place than your special spot and then only if everything is set just so. However, this is a relatively minor problem. For you, the primary job is to get yourself into a program of effective study. You can learn to generalize this program later.

Incidentally, as a flashback to constructive imagery, one of the techniques you can teach yourself through the use of relaxation techniques and imagery is to make time go quickly or to have time stand still. For example, if you are concentrating fully on a sticky piece of work, it helps to make time stand still for you. In this way, the time spent concentrating can be stretched out while the concentration is deepened and made more effective.

Back to the conditioning techniques. You can also use operant conditioning on yourself. If you have broken down your studies into a series of increments, you can use a system of positive rewards to help yourself move through them. For example, you can reward yourself every time you have finished a piece of your project by taking a bite of candy, by allowing yourself to leave the study spot for a short period of time, by letting yourself watch a TV program, or by doing anything else that will act as a reward for you. This reward system is something that you can work out for yourself: Make a list of all the things you like that you can use to reward yourself when you have finished some piece of work. They may range from simple things such as a Coke and a stretch at the end of a part of a lesson, to a fancy meal or movie at the end of a project. By systematically using this system of rewards and also depriving yourself of rewards when you fail to reach your goal, you can effectively condition yourself toward better effort.

When I was writing this book, I was also quite involved in a series of other projects. The ideas for the book, however, began to be almost obsessive. I started to feel guilty whenever I wasn't at my typewriter cranking out words. This kind of obsessive guilt was starting to get to me. I could feel signs of tension, headaches, absent-mindedness, and strong feelings of pressure. I finally made a pact with myself to do a certain amount of writing each day and to reward myself during the increments. For example, when I finished one minor topic I would let myself go downstairs and have a Coke and some cookies. When I finished my allotted work for the day, I would let myself get into some big enjoyable activity, like playing a round of golf or letting myself watch a sports event on TV. By following this pattern, I found I was able to keep my compulsions under control, and I was able to work more systematically and calmly. I was also able to get rid of my tension and obsessive drive. If you find yourself in this situation, you might also try to work yourself out of it by using operant-conditioning techniques. Or, as is the case with our fictitious example, you can train yourself to be more productive by using a system of reward and punishment. This system does not need to be restricted to the problem of studying. You can apply it to almost any problem by doing what has already been suggested to you. First, break your positive goal down into subgoals and then work on each increment successively. Use the rewards and punishments to spur yourself on to the next goal.

The suggestions made in Unit 6 on learning management can be applied to activities other than straight studying, although they may seem to be applicable only to learning. However, the same system of managing your time and your interests in order to get the most out of your work can be applied to almost anything you try to do.

In short, what you can and should do is use any trick in your bag to help you get where you want to go. You should motivate yourself by creating a sense of purpose and setting up a series of steps or subgoals that help you chart your course. You should use the techniques of reward and reinforcement on yourself. You should use the ability you have learned to listen to your own body and to listen to what other people say to you, both directly and indirectly, in order to find out more about yourself. You should use the power of your mind to help you think constructively. By putting all these things together, you'll find that nothing can stand in the way of your becoming a better person.

GLOSSARY

Addiction: the creation of physiological dependence on a drug

Adolescent stage: the fourth stage in Ginott's stages of sexual development

Affective psychoses: types of psychosis in which emotional control is lost

Agape: a selfless brotherly or motherly love, one of Lee's six types of love

Alarm stage: a stage in the general adaptation syndrome where the body readies itself for fight or flight

Alpha waves: electrical waves generated by the brain during a particular type of brain functioning that approaches relaxation

Altruistic suicide: according to Durkheim, the killing of oneself to better one's society

Anal stage: Freud's second stage of personality development

Anomic suicide: according to Durkheim, the killing of oneself because one can no longer understand the society in which one lives

Anxiety: an emotion of dread anticipation that acts as a stressor

Anxiety neurosis: a neurosis characterized by an extremely high constant level of anxiety

Appeals to prejudice: a technique of persuasion that uses a desirable group as a model

Approach-approach: a type of conflict where all the alternatives are equally attractive

Associationist: one who believes in a stimulus-response model as an explanation of learning

Attitude: a cognitive belief combined with an emotional disposition toward an object or situation

Attitudinal uniformity: the holding in common of attitudes by individuals within a group

Attribution theory: a theory of motivation that considers to what or to whom one attributes responsibility for one's successes and failures

Avoidance-avoidance: a type of conflict where all the alternatives are equally unattractive

Bandwagon: a technique of persuasion that uses a join-the-group approach

Behaviorist: one who believes that the environment shapes a person

Behavior modification: a technique in which reinforcement is used to modify a person's behavior

Behavioral therapy: a form of psychotherapy in which principles of learning theory are used to change a person's behavior

Bilateral family: a family power structure in which the governance descends through both the male and the female sides

Biofeedback: the use of machines to provide information about the state of functioning of a body organ

Body language: the signals one gives about one's feelings through body movements

Card stacking: a technique of persuasion that arranges the data toward a favorable conclusion

Castration anxiety: the fear of the father as a rival in the Oedipus complex

Catatonia: a form of schizophrenic psychosis characterized by withdrawal from the environment

Catharsis: in psychoanalytic psychotherapy, the positive surge of emotion when repressed material is verbalized

Central dispositions: traits that are highly characteristic of a person

Chronic alcoholism: the final stage of alcoholism in which a person consistently stays drunk

Classical conditioning: a system of learning that uses an established stimulus to create another stimulus, which then evokes a response

Closure: the tendency of our minds to arrange sensory input into complete patterns

Cognitive learning theory: a theory of learning that emphasizes problem solving

Cohesiveness: the closeness of a group, its internal bonding together

Collective unconscious: according to Jung, the deposit of ancestral experiences that is the basis for our social behavior

Conditioned response: a response to a stimulus that has been introduced under specific circumstances but that would not normally evoke the response

Conditioned stimulus: a stimulus introduced to create a response that would not normally occur

Conflict: a requirement to choose among alternatives

Conservation selection: a learning style in which variables are considered one at a time in order to reach a decision

Constructive imagery: the use of a state of relaxation to achieve one's goals

Conversion neurosis: a neurosis in which the body is used to avoid a conflict

Compensation: counterbalancing a lack or a defect by substituting something desirable

Crucial stage: a stage of alcoholism in which drinkers lose control over their consumption of alcohol

Death wish: the desire to return to the tranquillity of the inorganic state

Denial: an ego defense technique that denies the existence of a conflict or a situation

Dependence: either a physiological or a psychological need for a drug

Depressive neurosis: a neurosis in which persistent feelings of sorrow and gloom affect one's behavior

Desired self: the type of person one would like to be

Developmental tasks: age-related social tasks necessary for proper socialization

Didactic therapy: a form of psychotherapy in which one is taught to change one's behavior

Discipline: a technique that ideally teaches self-control through reward, not punishment

Discrimination: 1. actions for or against those for whom we bear a prejudice; 2. the process of responding to a specific stimulus

Dissociation neurosis: a neurosis in which the mind is used to avoid a conflict by forgetting

Distributed practice: the spreading of learning over subsets of items and over a period of time

Double approach-avoidance: a type of conflict where the alternatives offer both attractive and unattractive situations

Drive: the action required to satisfy a need

Drug: a chemical substance that affects the functioning of the mind and/or the body

Ego: that portion of the personality which mediates between the physiological demands of the id and the restraints of society

Ego defense mechanisms: a form of reaction to anxiety that masks the anxiety but does not resolve the reason for it

Egoistic suicide: Durkheim's concept of suicide by one who lacks a sense of belonging, acceptance, and group integration

Electra complex: the conflict a female child encounters in achieving a normal sexual identity

Erectile dysfunction: a sexual dysfunction in which the male is unable to attain an erection of the penis

Erogenous zones: areas of the body that give pleasure when stimulated

Eros: 1. the life wish, according to Freud; 2. romantic love, one of Lee's six stages of love

Ethnic prejudice: stereotyped generalizations about classes of people

Exhaustion stage: a stage in the general adaptation syndrome where the body collapses after fighting a stressor

Exhibitionism: a sexual disorder involving showing the genitalia (flashing)

Experiential therapy: a form of psychotherapy in which one is encouraged to act out one's delusions and hallucinations in order to alleviate them

Extinction: the destruction of a connection between a stimulus and a response

Extrovert: a person who is outwardly oriented

Fantasy: an ego defense mechanism that combats anxiety by a withdrawal from reality

Feedback: knowledge of results

Fetishism: a sexual disorder involving the use of an object to attain sexual gratification

Focus gambling: an impulsive learning style that considers certain variables simultaneously in problem-solving learning and then risks an immediate answer

Frigidity: a sexual dysfunction in which the female is unable to reach orgasm (anorgasmia)

Frustration: the blocking of a goal

Functional autonomy: the displacement of motives while retaining the original behavior

Gay: an adjective describing homosexual or lesbian sexual behavior

General adaptation syndrome: Selye's theory dealing with the way that a body reacts to stress

Generalization: the association of a stimulus with other stimuli

Generation gap: the disparity between the views of the young and the old

Genital stage: Freud's fifth stage of personality development

Gestalt: a school of psychologists who studied the processes involved in perception; also a German word meaning *whole picture* or *configuration*

Glittering generalities: a technique of persuasion in which high-sounding phrases are used to bemuse a person

Group: an assembly of persons joined in a common purpose

Groupthink: an agreement reached by internal persuasive forces

Habituation: psychological dependence on a drug

Hallucinogenic: a drug that induces hallucinations

Hawthorne studies: a series of experiments that exposed the effects of motivation on workers' productivity

Hebephrenia: a form of schizophrenia characterized by childish, silly behavior

High-order conditioning: the use of a conditioned stimulus to create another conditioned stimulus

Homeostasis: the process of returning the body to a more tolerable state

Homosexuality: sexual preference for or activity with a member of one's own sex

Homunculus: the concept that children are miniature adults

Humanist: one who believes in the unique individuality of each human being

Hypochondriacal neurosis: a neurosis in which preoccupation with body functions is used to avoid a conflict

Id: the portion of the personality that represents the physiological needs of the body

Ideal self: the self one feels one ought to be

Infantile stage: the first stage of Ginott's stages of sexual development

Infatuation: a love relationship based on selfish motives

Inferiority complex: a chronic feeling of inferiority

In-group: a group to which one belongs

Instincts: the organizers of the thought process. Instincts having a source, an aim, an object and an impulse. They come from body needs. They are not learned.

Intellectualization: an ego defense technique that avoids the emotional impact of conflict

Introvert: a person who is inwardly oriented

Involutional melancholia: a form of affective psychosis that involves both depression and agitation

Kinesicists: those who study body language

KITA: a system of motivation based on force

Latency stage: the third stage of Ginott's stages of sexual development, which corresponds with Freud's fourth stage of personality development

Latent stage: Freud's fourth stage of personality development

Learning curve: a graphic device that indicates the progress of a learning effort

Lesbianism: female homosexuality

Life-change unit: a value of change in one's life that has an effect on physiological functioning; a potential stressor

Life wish: the desire to live expressed through the sexual urge (Eros)

Locus of control: the thing or person to which one assigns responsibility for one's success or failure; may be internal or external to oneself

Love: an intense feeling of positive regard for another, involving trust and acceptance

Love goating: selecting a person on whom to lavish affection

Ludus: game-playing love, one of Lee's six types of love

Mania: highly emotional, intensive love, one of Lee's six types of love

Masochism: a sexual disorder in which sexual pleasure is obtained from the inflicting of pain on oneself

Matrilineal: a family power structure in which the governance descends through the females

Mediation: the practice of assigning a meaning to items that are being learned in order to enhance their retention

Monogamy: marriage with one person

Mnemonic: a device to aid remembering

Name calling: a technique of persuasion that associates an object with something pleasant

Narcotic: a drug that induces sleep or reduces pain; legally, any drug that is restricted by law

Need: the physiological requirements of the body; tissue requirements

Need achievement: the strong desire for success (n-ach)

Negative population growth: a population trend in which the number of offspring is insufficient to maintain the population numerically

Neurasthenic neurosis: a neurosis in which body discomforts mask a dissatisfaction with one's situation

Neurotic: an anxious person who uses nonproductive behavior to mask problems

Nondirective therapy: a form of psychotherapy in which one is encouraged to seek one's own solutions to problems

Nymphomania: a sexual disorder involving excessive sexual drive in the female

Obsessive-compulsive neurosis: a neurosis in which persistent thoughts or mandatory actions control one's behavior

Oedipus complex: the incestuous desires of a male for his mother, which are resolved by his assumption of male behavior

Operant conditioning: the process of establishing an S↔R bond by applying consequences to responses to stimulation

Oral stage: Freud's initial stage of personality development

Out-group: a group to which one does not belong

Paranoia: a form of psychosis in which a person is unable to relate to others except with hostility and feelings of persecution

Paranoid schizophrenia: a form of schizophrenia in which delusions of grandeur and persecution accompany the deterioration of the thought processes

Parent-identification stage: the second stage in Ginott's stages of sexual development

Patrilineal: a family power structure in which family governance descends through the males

Pedophilia: a sexual disorder involving sexual relations with children

Penis envy: the female counterpart of castration anxiety; felt in the resolution of the Electra complex

Perserverative autonomy: motives that come from human biology

Persona: Jung's term for the mask a person shows to the world

Phallic stage: Freud's third stage of personality development

Phobic neurosis: a neurosis in which irrational fears are used to avoid a conflict

Plain folks: a technique of persuasion that establishes a common bond between the persuader and the audience

Polyandry: the marriage of one wife to several husbands

Polygyny: the marriage of one husband to several wives

Pornography: sexual material that appeals to the prurient interests without artistic merit

Position: the job title a person holds

Pragma: a calculated style of loving, one of Lee's six types of love

Prealcoholism: a stage in which alcohol is used to reduce tension

Premature ejaculation: a sexual dysfunction in which the male is unable to control the moment of orgasm

Primary drives: unlearned basic biological conditions of pain, hunger, thirst, and the needs for air, excretion, sex, and rest

Prodromal: a stage of alcoholism in which the drinker begins to experience blackouts

Projection: an ego defense mechanism that blames results on others

Propriate autonomy: motives that deal with social interests, values, and attitudes

Psychoanalysis: a form of psychotherapy involving the release of repressed material in order to resolve a conflict with the demands of society

Psychedelic: a drug that alters perception and consciousness

Psychotic: a person who displays bizarre behaviors, has lost self-control, suffers from delusions and hallucinations, and is no longer in touch with reality

Psychotogenic: a drug that induces psychoticlike reactions

Rationalization: an ego defense mechanism that combats anxiety by diminishing the importance of a conflict

Reaction formation: an ego defense mechanism in which one behaves opposite to the way one feels

Real self: the version of oneself which the one considers to be one's true self

Reinforcement: the establishment of a connection between a stimulus and a response

Reinforcer: any consequence that strengthens an S↔R bond

Regression: an ego defense mechanism in which a person reverts to childish behavior

Repression: an ego defense mechanism that blocks the expression of emotions

Resistance stage: a stage in the general adaptation syndrome where the body combats a persistent stressor

Retarded ejaculation: a sexual dysfunction in which the male is unable to reach orgasm

Role: the prescribed behavior for one's position

Romantic love (courtly love): a feudal custom of loving from afar; also the eros type of love at first sight

Sadism: a sexual disorder in which sexual pleasure is obtained by inflicting pain on others

Satyriasis: a sexual disorder involving an excessive sexual drive in the male

Scanlon plan: a system that attempts to integrate management and labor

Schizophrenia: a type of psychosis in which the thought processes are adversely affected

Sedative: a drug that reduces tension

Secondary dispositions: traits that operate in human behavior in limited situations

Secondary drives: learned responses that do not come from physiological needs but from socialization

Self-actualization: the desire to function at one's highest potential

Self-alienation: estrangement from oneself

Self-concept: the image one has of oneself

Self-contracting: a study technique in which one in effect specifies what one is to accomplish in one's study efforts

Semisocial stage: an additional stage of sexual development that might be added to Ginott's stages to cover the adult period of life

Sensory adaptation: the adjustment of our senses to external conditions

Serial-position effect: the effect on learning of the position of an item in a series of items

Set: an emotional predisposition that influences our perceptions

Sexuality: culturally defined behavior for the sex of an individual

Shadow: Jung's term for one's inner spirit, which opposes one's persona

Simultaneous scanning: a learning style that considers several variables at once in problem solving and gives an immediate, risk-taking solution

Social facilitation: the effect of individuals on each other in job performance

Spontaneous recovery: the reappearance of an S↔R association without training after this association has become extinguished

SQ3R: a systematic approach to study, involving the steps of survey, question, read, recite, and review

Status: the standing of an individual in a group

Stimulant: a drug that increases bodily and mental activity

Storge: a serious, slow-growing type of love, one of Lee's six types of love

Stressor: anything of a physical or psychological nature that creates tension in the body

Sublimation: the expression of socially unacceptable needs-drives in acceptable ways

Successive scanning: a learning style that considers variables in a problem one by one in order to arrive at a solution

Superego: the portion of the personality that represents the value system of the individual

Teleology: the study of final causes; goal setting as a means of motivation

Territoriality: a person's life space

Thanatos: the death wish

Theory X: a theory of management that considers it necessary to force workers to work

Theory Y: a theory of management that considers the worker as a self-motivated individual

Theory Z: a theory of management that utilizes a systems approach

Traits: characteristic ways in which a person behaves

Transfer and testimony: a technique of persuasion that uses a famous name as an influence

Transference: in psychoanalysis, the use of the therapist as a symbol on which one vents repressed emotions toward others

Vaginismus: a sexual dysfunction in which the female resists penetration into the vagina by muscle contraction

Vasectomy: a surgical technique for male sterilization

Voyeurism: a sexual disorder in which one spies on undressed persons (peeping tom)

Will to power: the drive to overcome feelings of inferiority and establish a productive lifestyle

Withdrawal: an ego defense mechanism that gives in to frustration

Zero population growth: a population trend in which the number of offspring does not increase the general population

INDEX